The Web of Conspiracy

BOOKS BY THEODORE ROSCOE

Novels

ONLY IN NEW ENGLAND

MURDER ON THE WAY

I'LL GRIND THEIR BONES

SEVEN MEN

THE WOMAN WHO TOOK A DARE

Histories

THIS IS YOUR NAVY

U.S. SUBMARINE OPERATIONS, WORLD WAR II

U.S. DESTROYER OPERATIONS, WORLD WAR II

PICTURE HISTORY OF THE U.S. NAVY (with Fred Freeman)

"The Conspirators," by General Lew Wallace. The scene is the grounds of the unfinished Capitol, Washington, D.C., during Lincoln's second inauguration. Testimony at the trial of the assassins of Lincoln indicated that the conspirators watched the ceremony in a group. General Wallace was a member of the commission that convicted the conspirators.

THE WEB
OF
CONSPIRACY

The Complete Story of the Men

Who Murdered Abraham Lincoln

THEODORE ROSCOE

Prentice-Hall, Inc., Englewood Cliffs, N.J.

To all good friends associated with Rochester
where the trail began with a briar pipe
at "Rattlesnake Pete's" . . .
And, of course, to Rosamond . . .

This effort is dedicated

Second Printing . . . . . February, 1960

© 1959 by THEODORE ROSCOE

Library of Congress Catalog Card Number 59–12430

Printed in the United States of America

94784

Preface

THIS is a murder mystery—one that may well be considered the darkest in American annals. Because the victim was President of the United States and the killer wore the cloak of an assassin, the slaying of Abraham Lincoln assumed an historic aura that has almost dissociated the homicide from the basic fact that it was a crime. Of the immense 19th century literature that exists on Lincoln's assassination, much of the writing treats the tragedy at Ford's Theater as though it were Grand Opera. Lincoln is a sort of awesome symbol. Booth is either Mephisto incarnate, or an insane Brutus gone berserk. The President's martyrdom serves as a catalyst which burns away the sordid truth that he was shot down in cold blood, that his murder culminated an ugly intrigue, that this heinous crime went unsolved, and that some of the guilty (and perhaps the killer himself) escaped punishment.

Applying perspective to the past, modern historians have brought the drama into somewhat more accurate focus. Yet only a few have seen the crime as a murder case: Lincoln dying by crass felony, Booth a stalking gunman leading a gang of primed henchmen, the murder plot containing ingredients as base as the profit motive. Seventy years after the crime, writers were garbing it with a dignity it did not deserve: Lincoln, the stereotyped martyr; Booth, the stereotyped villian; the assassination avenged by classic justice; conspiracy strangled; Virtue (in the robes of Government) emerging triumphant, and Lincoln "belonging to the Ages."

But the facts of the case are neither so satisfying nor so gratifying. For the facts indicate that the criminals responsible for Lincoln's death got away with murder.

If that truth has been lost, one cannot blame the historians. Historians know no more than the information made available to them, and for many years the United States War Department kept the records on Lincoln's assassination locked in files marked "secret." The War Department was in charge of the manhunt for Booth and his accomplices. It also assumed charge of the subsequent conspiracy trials. Although trial proceedings were published at the time, the Bureau of Military Justice sat on a great deal of conspiracy information, and the Army chiefs refused to release much data on the assassination and the pursuit of the conspirators. Not until the mid 1930's were pertinent War Department records placed in the public domain.

Accordingly, all previous accounts of the assassination were based on official Government statements and press releases angled, slanted and otherwise doctored to suit popular consumption, and on the sketchy (although voluminous) trial reports published by the official court reporters. Thus a towering edifice of so-called history was erected on sand. It made popular reading, but it lacked the exacting foundations of true historicity. How could the facts be known or assessed when the War Department withheld them from inquiring historians and even from such authorized investigators as senators and congressmen on contemporary Congressional Committees?

Many 19th century accounts of the manhunt for the assassination conspirators were based on a contemporary history published by General Lafayette C. Baker, Chief of the United States Secret Service—a most untrustworthy fountainhead. Even as Baker's distorted version was issued, critics assailed the General's alleged veracity and denounced his volume as trash. But errors tend to perpetuate themselves. Much of Baker's purple storytelling became ingrained in popular literature.

In 1901 Colonel Osborn H. Oldroyd compounded early errors with later ones in a volume on Lincoln's assassination which became a best-seller. Oldroyd's book had the blessing of General T. M. Harris, one of the more biased judges who sat on the Military Commission which tried the accused assassination conspirators. In the little volume's Introduction, General Harris states: "The facts recorded in this book have been gathered with the greatest care and will be found both new and interesting." A bland remark, considering the fact that General Harris must have known the War Department records were at that time buried under top "secrecy."

Contemporary historians and informed critics would scold Oldroyd for a number of errors. For instance, he credits Boston Corbett with shooting Booth in Garrett's barn, a detail long the subject of much controversy. But in the large picture, the matter of who fired the shot was not so important as who was shot. To bicker the lesser point was to strain at a gnat and swallow a camel, a feat seemingly common to many historians. For another instance, Oldroyd credits the conspiracy trial testimony of Sanford Conover and Dr. Merritt, two Government witnesses exposed for perjury soon after they left the witness stand. But Oldroyd did do some original research.

Shortly after Oldroyd's work went on the stands, David DeWitt endeavored to counter erroneous history with searching studies of the conspiracy trials and a work devoted to Mary Surratt. But DeWitt did not have the War Department records at his disposal. His discerning eye detected much fabrication and dissimulation in the 1865 Bureau of Military Justice. But he, too, was left to grope in the dark for information.

In the years between 1900 and 1930, dozens of historians and researchers continued to grope. Although suspicious of secondary sources, they could rely only on the official abridgments and the obviously semi-fictionalized accounts previously published. A great body of legend surrounded the Lincoln murder case. It had become almost impossible to separate fact from fancy and to write objectively of such facts as could be established.

So Booth's modern biographer, Francis Wilson, leaning almost entirely on secondary sources, contributed to the growing mythology a portrait of John Wilkes Booth that glosses the features of Lincoln's killer with much kindly sentiment. Wilson blurs the fact that Booth was a spy. But Confederate secret intelligence defies research, for most of the records were destroyed at the time Richmond fell. Some of the Civil War records of U.S. Army secret intelligence were in 1928 (and still are) under wraps. Painted in 1928, Wilson's portrait of Booth lacks background.

By that date, however, an enlightened public had begun to ask questions. Anyone interested in basic research could discover enormous incongruities and gaping holes in the popular accounts of the assassination conspiracy. A number of scholars launched major research efforts in an attempt to exhume the facts. Otto Eisenschiml and Philip Van Doren Stern, foremost authorities in recent years, led the field in this endeavor. In *The Man Who Killed Lincoln* (pub. 1939) Stern presented a new picture of John Wilkes Booth that brought the actor into focus as something less than a Satanic genius or a mad zealot. Eisenschiml's *Why Was Lincoln Murdered?** (1937) and *In The Shadow of Lincoln's Death* (1940) explored the whole vast scope of the assassination conspiracy. Both Eisenschiml and Stern possessed data previously denied American historians. In the mid 1930's, the War Department Records on the assassination conspiracy were put in the public domain. Eisenschiml was the first historian to research thoroughly the assassination data which had theretofore been buried in the files of the War Department. It was through his efforts that the Civil War records of Washington's Metropolitan Police were preserved. Eisenschiml and Stern followed literally hundreds of new trails. Unfortunately many of these trails were frozen at dead ends, or led into blind alleys. Time has contributed veils to the complexities of the Lincoln murder case.

The present volume was begun in Rochester, New York, in the early 1930's. On Front Street in Rochester, to be specific. In the backroom

---

* Eisenschiml's *Why Was Lincoln Murdered?* was first published by Little, Brown and Company, Boston, in 1937. Successive reprints were published by Halcyon House, New York, in 1939 and by Grosset and Dunlap Universal Library, Garden City, in 1957. All references to Dr. Eisenschiml's work in the present volume, either in text or footnoted as "Eisenschiml, *op. cit.,* etc." are from the Halcyon House (1939) edition of *Why Was Lincoln Murdered?*

museum of an old-time bar known as Rattlesnake Pete's. Among stuffed alligators, snake skulls and other curiosities on display was a small briar pipe. The item was captioned, "John Wilkes Booth's pipe."

Was it actually Booth's briar? Contemplating a news article on it, the writer went to the morgue of a local newspaper. The old Rochester *Advertiser* led him on, up a curious trail concerning a certain Dr. Tumblety, mysteriously involved as an alleged assassination conspirator from the banks of the Erie Canal. No connection with Booth's pipe, but Tumblety was an interesting man. Also interesting at that time was a mummy featured in a Western carnival as the last mortal remains of Lincoln's assassin. Upshot: a fictional story for a popular magazine—a tale concerning Booth's possible escape from Garrett's barn.

The fictional story evoked a fascinating fan letter from a lawyer in Rocky Mount, North Carolina. This correspondent stated that his uncles— according to family legend—had assisted Booth in an escape to Texas. The present writer was off on a research chase that has since gone through many files and over many miles. Perhaps the reader of this book will enjoy following the trail. A few of the paths are newly blazed. And a hypothetical solution to the mystery is suggested.

THEODORE ROSCOE
Washington, D.C.

Acknowledgments

O F THE MANY persons who offered generous assistance, welcome advice, background material, or kindly permissions to quote, the author wishes to express most grateful acknowledgments—

To Miss Rose Doonan, for a rare copy of Oldroyd.

To Rear Admiral Elmer E. Duvall, U.S.N. (Ret'd.) for a collector's-item copy of Buckingham's *Reminiscences and Souvenirs*, and for a photographic record of a memorable journey from Ford's Theater to Garrett's farm.

To the gracious lady of the household of Mr. Joseph Mudd, who permitted the author to see the parlor where Booth's leg was examined and to study the portrait over the mantel.

To the staff in charge of Old Army Records at the National Archives, for much helpful guidance.

To Miss Virginia Daiker, Prints and Photos Division, Library of Congress, for expert aid in picture selection.

To Mr. Jo Doan Thomas, Still Pictures Section, National Archives, for kindly assistance in locating unique pictures.

To Dr. Richard D. Mudd for helpful leads and for information concerning Dr. Samuel Mudd's portrait.

To Philip Van Doren Stern for a critical editorial reading of the manuscript, for many knowing leads and for kindly suggestions.

To Otto Eisenschiml for permission to quote liberally from his highly original text and to Grosset and Dunlap for publisher's permission.

To all the many other writers and publishers who have given me permission to quote from their works.

To the general at the Pentagon who advised the author that he might do better if he would write about the "Battle of Wounded Knee," but courteously arranged an introduction to the Judge Advocate's Office. And to the kindly colonel in that office who produced a file of old newspaper clippings reporting Booth's possible escape.

And finally—inevitably and with much gratitude—to Monroe Stearns, whose editorial insight and expert blue pencil endowed this text with whatever literary virtues it may possess, and who, one day, took time out to walk the author back to an afternoon in long ago at The Players.

Contents

IV
DEAD END

V
CONSPIRACY IS TRIED

*This assassination is not the act of one man;
but only one scene of a great drama.*

—Diary of Attorney-General Edward Bates

P A R T

I

Design for Murder

This shall make our purpose necessary and not envious; which so appearing to the common eyes, we shall be call'd purgers, not murderers.
—Julius Caesar

Good things of day begin to droop and drowse,
Whilse night's black agents to their prey do rouse.
—Macbeth

CHAPTER 1

Stage Set for Murder

*I am engaged to go to the theater with Mrs.
Lincoln. It is the kind of an engagement I
never break.*

—*Lincoln in a note to Senator
Wm. M. Stewart*

THE WAR DEPARTMENT's failure to protect President Lincoln on the
night he was murdered in the nation's capital remains one of the
best-kept secrets in American history. And one of the blackest.

On April 14, 1865, Abraham Lincoln was shot while he sat in a box at
Ford's Theater in Washington, D.C. That, of course, could not be kept
secret. No amount of official censorship, no Governmental juggling of
English, no propaganda treatment, no re-writing of history could conceal
the fact that the President of the United States had been shot down in
cold blood. Nor the fact that the celebrated actor, John Wilkes Booth, was
the slayer. But the designation of this murder as "assassination"—a word
associated with the dagger of Brutus, with the impassioned knife of
Charlotte Corday—served from the outset to obscure the motives behind
the crime. What censorship, phrase-juggling, propaganda, and the doctoring of history *did* conceal was the fact that Booth could not have murdered
Lincoln had not Lincoln been betrayed.

In effect, Americans were then (and have since been) induced to concentrate on Booth, the assassin, and on the act of assassination. The impression was created, and carefully fostered, that the fanatic Booth played a
lone hand. To be sure, somewhere in the background lurked a few petty
accomplices, prepared to aid Booth's getaway, but these henchmen were
seen as mere puppets. Booth's was the master hand.

This tidy oversimplification fell down almost as soon as it was publicized.
The fact came to light that Lincoln was not the only target marked for
assassination. Some of Booth's henchmen had been primed to kill two or
three other Northern leaders on the night of the assassination strike. Hence
a great conspiracy was detected in the wind, and Northern patriots could
readily believe this wind must have blown from the South.

Hold the South, then, the enemy Confederacy, responsible for Lincoln's
murder. Here was a "villain" every loyal Union man could prejudicially

indict. Indeed, evidence turned up which tended to prove the indictment. But by that date the Confederacy, as a State, no longer existed. The conspiracy had evaporated. Booth and his puppet band were more easily identified and symbolized than a ghostly enemy vaguely designated "Richmond." In the end the act of assassination would remain fixed in the public mind as the arch crime, with Booth in the role of arch criminal.

Lincoln was assassinated, and the assassin presumably was punished.

The betrayal which permitted a lone gunman to walk into a theater in the nation's capital and shoot down the President was securely hidden away.

The protection of the President of the United States during the Civil War was a War Department responsibility. As titular Commander-in-Chief of the United States Army, the Chief Executive depended on the U.S. Army for security. While in Washington he was under the specific protection of the military forces in charge of the nation's capital. The National Executive Police (Secret Service) were even more specifically charged with protecting the President. In common with the Army, the Secret Service was under War Department direction.

Neither the Army nor the Secret Service provided Lincoln with a theater guard on the night he was slain. That openly demonstrated and therefore undeniable fact is usually attributed to negligence, and somehow dismissed as such.

But could negligence (a term implying carelessness, but not necessarily intentional neglect) have been the case? Dereliction would seem the better term.

Yet, again, the term does not quite suit the case. Dereliction implies disobedience to orders, abandonment of duty. On the face of it, one cannot believe that Army Headquarters or Secret Service Headquarters would disobey or abandon orders to protect the nation's Chief Executive. Headquarters, in effect, are responsible for issuing orders rather than obeying them.

True, military orders of a kind had been issued months before to a cavalry guard assigned to White House detail. But this body of horse was more or less at the President's disposal, rather than under military direction. As often as not, Lincoln drove around town without the cavalry escort. In any event, these troopers would not have gone with him into a theater. Special guards were needed to protect President Lincoln that night. Special guards were not ordered.

A Headquarters blunder? Strategic blunders, military unpreparedness—these are incurred by vast complexities involving such unwieldy factors as mobilization, troop movements, logistics, fortifications. The protection of President Lincoln did not demand cannon, regiments, forts. Two or three soldiers or two or three Secret Service detectives might easily have sufficed.

It is not correct to say, as some historians have said, that Lincoln went unprotected because the war was over—Lee had surrendered the week before—and that with hostilities ended, the military had relaxed. Fighting was still going on. Confederate forces were resisting in the Carolinas, in Tennessee, in Alabama, and in Texas. Rebel raiders were on the loose less than thirty miles from Washington in Loudon County, Virginia.

Nor can it be held, in keeping with some apologists, that the attack on Lincoln was a bolt from the black—a stunning surprise. Lincoln's killing surprised few informed persons in the North. For many months exactly such a blow had been feared. Congressmen and Government officials predicted it. Editors and other spokesmen issued constant warnings. Lincoln's friends had long expressed the fear that his life was in jeopardy.

The War Department is said to have been disarmed by the cry of "wolf." But the Secretary of War, Stanton himself, continuously warned the President of possible assassination. So did Colonel (brevet General) Lafayette C. Baker, Chief of the Secret Service. Both had every reason to believe the threat to Lincoln's life was neither imaginary nor conjectural.

Abraham Lincoln was marked for murder the day he left Springfield for the White House. That was in February, 1861. He had been warned to stay away from the capital, and some of his friends feared he might never reach Washington alive.

Lincoln's friends had reason to be uneasy about the inaugural journey. The nation was close to anarchy.

From the Carolinas to Texas, Southern Secessionists were seizing Federal arsenals and forts. Shore batteries in Florida had opened fire on vessels flying the United States flag. At Mobile, Alabama, a mob had hanged a man sent ashore from the U.S.S. *Brooklyn* to purchase supplies. Crowds in Charleston, New Orleans, and elsewhere were beating up Yankees. Lincoln was savagely lampooned in the Southern press, wildly denounced at mass meetings. Soon after his election in November, 1860, ugly threats had begun to arrive in his mail.

Most of the vituperative scrawls were obviously crackpot. But some exuded a malevolence approaching the diabolical. An example is a malediction mailed to Lincoln from Fillmore, Louisiana, two weeks after his election. In this scream of hate and fury, the writer "god damned" Lincoln twenty-two times in a single paragraph.[1]

The wild threats of manifest maniacs might be ignored or shrugged off. A far more dangerous menace came from zealots and hothead chauvinists who wrapped their gangsterism in a flag.

---

[1] Carl Sandburg, *Abraham Lincoln: The War Years* (New York: Harcourt, Brace and Company, 1939), vol. IV, p. 322.

In February, 1861, the *Cincinnati Commercial* published a letter to Lincoln warning him of an assassination promise. The writer, who signed himself "a prominent citizen who resides in one of the Gulf States," said the vow had been uttered "by a man with a good name for veracity." Addressing a crowd, this man had sworn, "So help me God, I will kill him [Lincoln] if a thousand muskets are pointed at my head." He had exhibited a rifle jointed at the stock, a gun which could be folded under his coat. Lincoln's informant concluded: "My own life would be immediately taken if it were known I had divulged [these] plans. . . . Violent threats against your life are very common among street politicians and grocery rowdies, but these are beneath your notice. But it is far different with the person I have reference to."[2]

Federal detectives eventually traced the author of this letter to Montgomery, Alabama.[3] The firebrand who swore he would kill Lincoln was never identified.

By no means all of the threats directed at the President-elect emanated from febrile Southerners. While Lincoln was en route to Washington he learned that his journey through Maryland was menaced. The flash came from Allan Pinkerton. Killers were planning to ambush Lincoln in Baltimore.

The so-called "Baltimore Plot," exposed by Pinkerton, reads like a chapter out of blood-and-thunder melodrama. Pinkerton was accused of fictionalizing, but the little Scotchman's reports actually understated the menace.

Acting on alarming information volunteered by Miss Dorothea Lynde Dix, a lady philanthropist well informed on the South, railroad magnate Samuel Felton had hired the Pinkerton Agency to guard the right of way of the Philadelphia, Wilmington & Baltimore—the line Lincoln would take on his inaugural journey to Washington.[4] Advised that the Baltimore terminal of the P.W. & B. was the danger point, Pinkerton had gone with a team of ace detectives to the Maryland metropolis.

Pinkerton found Baltimore a hornets' nest buzzing with talk of sedition. Barroom braggarts told of a plot to waylay Lincoln's party as it passed through the city. Pinkerton ordered his people to track down the plotters. The detectives soon had the scent.[5]

The trail—or several trails—threaded through all levels of Baltimore society, from drawing rooms at top to slum hovels at bottom. Involved were members of the self-styled "National Volunteers," the "Baltimore

---

2 *Cincinnati Commercial,* February 26, 1861.

3 National Archives, War Department Records, File "A," JAO.

4 Dr. Francis Tiffany, *Life of Dorothea Lynde Dix* (Boston: Houghton Mifflin Company, 1890), pp. 333–334.

5 *Pinkerton Record Book,* quoted in *Lincoln and the Baltimore Plot,* ed. Norma B. Cuthbert (San Marino, Cal.: The Huntington Library, 1949).

Guards" and the "Palmetto Guards." Pinkerton soon suspected Police Chief George P. Kane of subversive leanings. But the arch mover of the local conspiracy to ambush and assassinate the President elect was one Cipriano Fernandina, known as "Captain" to his followers.[6]

This Fernandina (sometimes Ferrandina or Ferrandini) remains a mystery figure in American history. It seems he was an Italian immigrant who had lived in Charleston for a number of years. Migrating to Baltimore, he had brought with him a fierce black mustache, a stiletto, and the enthusiasms of a Latin anarchist heavily overlaid with Secessionism.

Fernandina was a barber whose shop in the basement of Barnum's Hotel was the rallying roost of the Baltimore assassination band. Most of the members were brainless young hotspurs of the cavalier set. A few were professional huggermuggers ready for any criminal enterprise.

Harry Davies, one of Pinkerton's best operatives, cultivated the acquaintance of Mr. O. K. Hillard (or Hillyard) sportsman, soldier-of-fortune, officer of the "National Volunteers." A few drams in the Fountain Hotel, and the acquaintance flowered into friendship, with Hillard ultimately confiding: "If our company would draw lots to see who would kill Lincoln, and the lot should fall on me, I would do it willingly."[7]

The company did draw lots. Detective Davies attended the drawing— an after-dark meeting in some secluded Baltimore grotto. Captain Fernandina presided as chairman.

The fiery Figaro delivered a gnashing oration that ranked high in the art of low gasconade. Then the company passed a resolution to slay Lincoln when he entered Baltimore. Then, to quote Pinkerton's account of the business:

> It was finally determined that ballots should be prepared and placed in a box . . . and that the person who drew a *red* ballot should perform the duty of assassination. . . . The room was rendered still darker, and everyone was pledged to secrecy as to the color of the ballot he drew. The leaders . . . doubting the courage of some of their number, instead of placing *one* red ballot in the box . . . placed eight of the designated color, and these eight ballots were drawn—each man who drew them believing that upon him, his courage, strength and devotion, depended the cause of the South—each supposing that he alone was charged with the execution of the deed.[8]

Davies' scalp must have prickled at this Baltimore camorra. But who had drawn the red ballots? The detective could not identify the eight sworn assassins, but he was able to report the time and place of the proposed ambush:

---

[6] *Ibid.*
[7] *Ibid.*, p. 47.
[8] Allan Pinkerton, *Spy of the Rebellion* (New York: G. W. Carleton & Co., 1883), pp. 78, 79.

The time when this was to be done was just as Mr. Lincoln would be passing through the narrow vestibule of the Depot at Calvert St. Station, to enter his carriage. A row or fight was to be got up by some outsiders to quell which the few policemen at the Depot would rush out, thus leaving Mr. Lincoln entirely unprotected. . . . A small steamer had been chartered and was lying in one of the Bays or little streams running into the Chesapeake, to which the murderers were to flee and it was immediately to put off for Virginia.[9]

Pinkerton shot into action. He had already stationed detectives at vulnerable railroad bridges and at the Susquehanna Ferry along the right of way, for word had come in that secret militia were threatening to attack Lincoln's train at these points. Of interest is the fact that one of Pinkerton's crack operatives, the famous Timothy Webster, reported such a partisan band was organizing in the Maryland backwoods at Bel Air. We shall hear of Bel Air again.

But the Baltimore menace was the emergency. Pinkerton had neither the force nor the authorization to round up and arrest the Fernandina gang. Suspicious of the local police, he had to act on his own. He raced to Philadelphia to meet the Lincoln party and confer with Lincoln.

Much against his personal inclination, Lincoln was prevailed upon to change the schedule of a side trip to Harrisburg, to return from Harrisburg on a special train, and to run south to Baltimore on a night express, traveling incognito, while Mrs. Lincoln and the rest of the party followed next day on the previously scheduled train. Telegraph lines were to be appropriately interrupted to prevent any disclosure of Lincoln's moves to the enemy.

The deceptive plan worked perfectly. At Philadelphia Lincoln entered the night train unnoticed, wearing a heavy shawl and an unfamiliar "Kossuth hat." The conductor was told that he was an invalid. With him traveled Mrs. Kate Warne (a Pinkerton agent), posing as his sister. Pinkerton, Ward Lamon, and several disguised guards boarded the sleeper. Throughout the southward run the detectives maintained vigilant nocturnal watch, with Mrs. Warne posted near the door to Lincoln's compartment, a seven-shooter under her cloak.[10]

The run to Baltimore proved uneventful. No one paid any attention to the anonymous passenger who crossed the sleeping city. And on to Washington on the B. & O., Lincoln's journey remained undisturbed. His train pulled into the capital terminal about six o'clock in the morning of February 23. Unannounced, Lincoln proceeded with his escorts to Willard's Hotel.

Pinkerton sent off a batch of wires to interested persons in Philadelphia and points north.

---

9 *Pinkerton Record Book,* quoted in Cuthbert, *op. cit.,* p. 7.
10 *Ibid.,* pp. 15–16. See also Pinkerton, *Spy of the Rebellion.*

To S. M. Felton, President of the P.W. & B. Railroad:

Arrived here all safe.

E. J. Allen.[11]

To Edward S. Sanford, President of the American Telegraph Company:

Plums arrived here with Nuts this morning—all right.

E. J. Allen.[12]

So Lincoln was smuggled into Washington. And when the story reached the news, the opposition press hooted. Cartoons showed a Lincoln masquerading in bonnet and gown as an old lady, and a terrified Lincoln peering from the door of a freight car at a bristling white cat.

Secure in their office chairs, Northern editors may not have believed the peril existed, but persons acquainted with the Secessionist element in Baltimore were not so skeptical. At some time during Lincoln's journey (or shortly thereafter), worried friends presented him with a dagger and a set of brass knuckles for self-protection. He was also presented with a queer pair of eye-shields resembling metal-hooded spectacles.[13] Had they heard of a threat to blind him with acid?

Ridicule of Pinkerton accompanied ridicule of Lincoln. Persistent doubters of the "Baltimore Plot" must have remained uninformed on ensuing events. Soon after the outbreak of the Civil War, a Baltimore mob attacked Federal troops passing through the city. Baltimore Police Chief Kane was apprehended as a Secession advocate; eventually he fled South to join the Confederate service.

Meanwhile, Detective Davies trailed the vicious O. K. Hillard to Washington. Then, the Pinkerton mission having been concluded by Lincoln's safe delivery to the capital, the detectives were called off the case. So Hillard disappeared with the other Baltimore plotters who scurried underground as soon as they read press reports of the plot's exposure. However, Hillard was not unknown to the Government. One finds his name in the records of a Congressional Committee which had been formed in January, 1861, to investigate subversion in Washington.[14]

Fernandina also mysteriously disappeared. If he ran true to type, he was first to vanish after the plot's disclosure. Congress seems to have made gestures to investigate the bloodthirsty barber, but by the time Federal authority clamped down on Baltimore, the bird had flown.

---

[11] Cuthbert, *op. cit.*, pp. 84–85.
[12] *Ibid.*
[13] Now on exhibit, Lincoln Museum, Washington, D.C.
[14] Library of Congress, *Reports of the Select Committee of Five*, 36th Cong., 2nd Session, Report No. 79, pp. 144–145.

Soon after escorting Lincoln to Washington, Allan Pinkerton returned to Chicago, satisfied he had served his country well. The security furnished Lincoln by the Pinkerton Agency stands as exemplary of what could be done by one small squad of trained (and loyal) detectives.

It was the last time Lincoln would be afforded such efficient protective service.

Washington, D.C., 1861: half Government seat, half swamp. A prospect of magnificent vistas—across seas of mud. A city where mansions rubbed elbows with rookeries, where public buildings gazed down on an avenue of sludge, where every other door was a boardinghouse, a livery stable, or a saloon. The capital entered by Lincoln bore little resemblance to today's postcard city of monuments and cherry blossoms.

Of the city's 264 miles of streets, only Pennsylvania Avenue was lighted for any appreciable distance. Here and there on side streets an occasional lamp flickered, and lonely lamps stood in the unkempt parks and public squares. Of the streets that were paved, most were potholed brick or lumpy cobblestone; however, most of the city's streets were unpaved. In winter Pennsylvania Avenue was a boulevard of slush; in summer it varied with the weather from dust to mire. That crime flourished in the dimly lit capital of that day is hardly surprising. The city, in February, 1861, was without an organized police force. There were no Federal police, no established constabulary. A few hired guards protected commercial properties. Civic protection depended on volunteers who were about as efficient as the farcical volunteer Fire Department.

When Lincoln entered Washington, the city's military defenses were almost on a par with its municipal police protection, which is to say they were virtually non-existent. Secession had all but paralyzed the United States Army and had nearly immobilized the Navy. So much for the security of the District of Columbia.

Security for the President of the United States was practically nil. There was no Federal Secret Service in 1861. No White House guard. No cavalry detail for Presidential escort. A few soldiers were posted to keep order at the inaugural ceremony when President James Buchanan bowed out of the worst situation faced by the nation before or since. Unguarded, President Lincoln took office in a capital as dangerous as a ticking time-bomb.

Outbreak of the war in April, 1861, did nothing to insure the President's security. Although Federal forces arrived to stiffen the capital's makeshift forts, the furies unleashed by military conflict put Lincoln's life, like the nation's, squarely at stake.

Four armies immediately invaded Washington City. First, the Union Army—Lincoln's 75,000 volunteers. Then an army of Government workers and construction workers—the administrative and logistical forces supporting the war effort. Then an army of camp followers—veritable regiments of prostitutes, pimps and blacklegs—the dirty skirt that trails every military force. And in step with these other armies came an army of underground invaders—Secession partisans, subversive agents, Confederate spies.

Breeding an epidemic of crime, the local underworld would in itself have constituted a serious problem for the authorities. Vice, acknowledging no loyalty, opened promiscuous arms to Federal servant and Rebel agent alike. By 1862 a glowing red-light section occupied the south side of Pennsylvania Avenue, midtown. Eventually the neighborhood came to be known as "Hooker's Division"—an obvious reference to its popularity with the soldiers of flamboyant General Joseph ("Fighting Joe") Hooker. Long after the Civil War colloquial Washington referred to streetwalkers as "Hookers."

More dangerous to the health of Union Army and commonweal than these girls were a number of socially prominent ladies who supported the Confederacy by spying on troop movements in Washington. Chief operator during the war's opening months was Mrs. Rose O. H. Greenhow, with mansion at 13th and "Eye" Street—a singularly apt name for the street. Information spirited by this social lioness to Beauregard's headquarters at Manassas probably wrought the Union defeat at Bull Run in July, 1861. Other female spies residing in the wartime capital were Mrs. Philip Phillips, Mrs. William Baxley, Mrs. William Hasler, Mrs. J. C. Levy, Miss Lilly A. Mackle and Miss E. M. Poole. A listing of these early espions shows the vulnerability of the nation's headquarters city.

It was soon apparent that United States Army moves were being betrayed right and left, and that something had to be done about espionage in Washington. Shortly after his appointment to Lincoln's Cabinet, Secretary of State Seward urged the formation of a detective corps to fumigate the national capital.[15] Allan Pinkerton was sent for.

Pinkerton soon rounded up Mrs. Greenhow and her keyhole sorority, but after this exploit he went to the battlefront to serve as McClellan's chief of military intelligence. When McClellan's star declined at Antietam and Stanton replaced him with a worse general (Pope), Pinkerton was also shelved. Meanwhile, Washington had again become a sieve. And the teaparty spies were supplanted by a far more dangerous type—the professional espion.

One may note parenthetically that throughout the Civil War both the North and the South pronounced "spying" an unethical abomination. Each side hotly accused the other of engaging in the nefarious deceits of espionage, and held up their hands in pious disavowal even as they dispatched their own secret agents on spy missions.

---

[15] Ben Perley Poore, *Perley's Reminiscences* (Philadelphia: Hubbard Brothers, 1886), p. 110.

Refusing to call their own espionage agents spies, the Confederates referred to them as "scouts"—a nice example of word-substitution. They were also called "blockade runners"—a term derived from the daring little vessels that ran the ironclad blockade which was eventually fastened by the U.S. Navy on the Confederacy's seaboard. The North, too, favored the euphemism of "scout" for "spy." The terms "operative" and "agent" were also in official usage. The spies, of course, were "heroes" to the side they were working for, and "wretches," "villains," "traitors" and "treacherous snakes" to the enemy.

Both sides employed women in the dangerous game of military spying. Heroines in Federal service were Elizabeth Van Lew, Pauline Cushman and Emma E. Edmonds. A Canadian, Miss Edmonds made several daring forays behind the Richmond lines in the disguise of a male Negro, a day laborer.[16] Her Confederate counterpart was Madam Loreta Velasquez, a lady of Cuban extraction who wanted to fight for the South, and to do so assumed the garb and whiskers of a Confederate Army officer. Posing as Lieutenant Harry Buford, C.S.A., this remarkable female strode in and out of frontline field headquarters seemingly at will.[17] Wearing male costume, she enlisted in the Confederate Secret Service. We will find her in crinoline and lace in Washington under circumstances equally extraordinary.

Closely linked with Confederate and Union espionage were the underground operations of saboteurs. Bribery, bombing, arson—it was war to the hilt. On both sides these secret forces were abetted by dissidents and irreconcilables—Union partisans in the South, pro-Secessionists in the North. But the point is that by the summer of Antietam the seething capital on the Potomac was a honeycomb of spy rings and subversive "cells." This enemy underground endangered Lincoln every day he held office.

In September, 1861, the Metropolitan Police Force was organized. This constabulary, the city's first, was under Major A. C. Richards, a capable officer. But Congress voted it an inadequate appropriation, patrolman jobs were political handouts, and many patrolmen who gained appointments were misfits. Even if every man had been upstanding, however, a force limited to some 150 men could hardly have policed the wartime capital.

Then, under Secretary of War Stanton's direction, a military regime was installed in 1862. Army provost marshals were given extensive police authority over the District of Columbia. The National Executive Police came into being—the nation's first Federal Secret Service. Headed by Colonel Lafayette C. Baker, these secret police were assigned the mission of counter-espionage and the repression of subversion.

At Stanton's insistence a squadron of Ohio light cavalry was assigned

---

[16] S. Emma E. Edmonds, *Nurse and Spy in the Union Army* (Hartford: W. S. Williams and Co., 1865).

[17] Loreta Janeta Velasquez, *The Woman in Battle* (Hartford: T. Belknap, 1876).

the duty of escorting the President's carriage. Lincoln seems to have thought this uniformed guard ostentatious. He did approve the formation of a plainclothes White House guard, its members selected from the Metropolitan Police Force; but he wanted no pretentious display of palace grenadiers, no glittering escort that smacked of king or dictator. Abraham Lincoln may have felt that in a capital now guarded by Army police and by a large corps of Federal secret agents his person was under sufficient protection.

Indeed, considering the forces available, it should have been. Baker's detectives were everywhere. Empowered with extraordinary authority, the Secret Service Chief flung a counter-espionage net that extended from the battlefronts to the far corners of the Union. Meshed into this net was another designed to snare subversives.

Rebel agents and Secession partisans might elude the secret police, but their activities seldom escaped detection. That the enemy underground posed a deadly menace to Lincoln was a fact well known to Lafayette C. Baker. Only War Secretary Stanton, possessed of military as well as Secret Service intelligence, could have had more information on the subject.

But by 1864 conspiracies to kidnap or murder Lincoln had become open secrets. It was the prime duty of War Secretary Stanton and Secret Service Chief Baker to protect the President of the United States from the conspirators.

Lincoln kept in his desk at the White House an envelope containing eighty or more letters theatening his life. Some of these savage epistles were maniacal frothings of the maledictory variety. Others were blunt, cold, ugly promises from gunmen and daggermen swearing to slay him.

There was the "Baltimore Plot" of 1861—a confirmed warning.

There were dire warnings that he would be murdered in 1862.

Operating in Richmond in the summer of 1863, Federal intelligence agents learned that a group of Virginia slave barons had formed a secret society which was raising a fund to be offered as a reward for Lincoln's assassination.

About the same time the Federal Secret Service obtained evidence that fanatic Knights of the Golden Circle and other "Copperhead" subversives in the North were signing blood-oaths to kill Lincoln.

One day (we are told) a woman spy disguised in widow's weeds, heavily veiled, walked into Lincoln's office and tried to poison him with a kiss. Smallpox.[18] The story may be apocryphal, but the President did, in fact, contract a mild case of varioloid.

In March, 1864, the New York *Tribune* published a letter, presumably from a pro-Union Southerner, exposing details of a plot to kidnap the

---

[18] Don Smith, *Peculiarities of the Presidents: Strange Facts Not Usually Found in History* (Van Wert, Ohio: Wilkinson Press, 1938), p. 144.

President. The letter said that original plans called for 150 picked men "to go secretly North and take quarters in Washington, Georgetown, Baltimore and Alexandria . . . and, upon a fixed day . . . assemble in Washington for the purpose of making the seizure." Lincoln was to be seized at the White House or while out driving in his carriage. The escaping kidnapers were to be joined "a few miles out of the city" by twenty-five or thirty armed horsemen.

The informant continued: "It was proposed to drive to Indian Point about twenty-five miles south of Washington on the Potomac—two or three relays of fleet horses being stationed on the way—where a boat was to be waiting to cross the river . . . [to] Occoquan. . . . To prevent pursuit, every bridge between Washington and Indian Point was to be mined. . . . Huge trees were also to be ready cut and thrown across the road. . . ."

The writer warned that this was not the only scheme devised for Lincoln's abduction. "Last summer a club or society of wealthy citizens of Richmond was formed for the purpose of raising a fund for this object. Circulars were sent to trustworthy citizens in every other city . . . in the Confederacy . . . and an immense sum of money was subscribed."

The informant concluded: "Whether these schemes have been abandoned, or whether the kidnapers are only awaiting a favorable opportunity to execute them, remains to be seen. . . ."[19]

Four weeks later, the *Tribune* published an item containing the alleged declaration of a conspirator who swore that he would "sell his soul to the devil" for an opportunity to participate in Lincoln's "destruction."[20]

The anonymous oath merely echoed the incantations of many Rebel firebrands and Lincoln-hating "Copperheads." But the kidnap plot, as outlined, was too plausibly detailed to be brushed aside as fabrication. The conspirators who were to stand by in Washington, Baltimore, Georgetown, the getaway to Indian Point on the lower Maryland peninsula (which meant the kidnapers intended to escape across Navy Yard Bridge and either take the main turnpike south through Piscataway, or use a backroad detour through a place called Surrattsville), the secret boat to carry the kidnapers across the misty Potomac—here was exceedingly vital information spelled out for the United States War Department and the Federal Secret Service.

And it seemed that enemy conspirators *were* awaiting a favorable opportunity either to abduct or to destroy President Lincoln.

In August, 1864, a shot was fired through Lincoln's hat by an unseen sniper hiding in roadside woods near the Soldiers' Home.

In October, 1864, the Confederates unleashed an all-out underground

---

[19] New York *Tribune*, March 19, 1864. Also quoted by Otto Eisenschiml, *Why Was Lincoln Murdered?* (New York: Grosset & Dunlap, Inc., 1939), p. 41.

[20] New York *Tribune*, April 17, 1864. See also Eisenschiml, *op. cit.*, p. 41.

campaign to sabotage the North with prison-breaks, bank-raids, train-wrecks, riots and arson.

In November, 1864, a Federal secret agent "scouting" in Canada reported an assassination plot brewing among Confederate leaders in Montreal and Rebel agents operating in Richmond and Washington (or so this Federal agent subsequently declared).

In December, 1864, a Southern newspaper ran the advertisement of a citizen offering to assassinate Lincoln, Seward, and newly elected Vice-President Johnson for a one-million-dollar reward.

Then the War Department was advised that Lincoln might be attacked by killers or kidnapers on or about March 4, 1865—the day of his second inaugural. Although the threatened attack did not take place on Inauguration Day, the Presidential carriage was ambushed on March 20 on the road to the Soldiers' Home. Only a fluke seems to have saved the President on this date.

True, some of the reports had come by anonymous letter, and others through the untrustworthy channels of rumor. But in respect to John Wilkes Booth and his co-conspirators the War Department had something more concrete to go on. Apparently the War Department received word as early as January, 1865, that Booth and company were operating.

The War Department had specific information that this gang frequently met in a boardinghouse in midtown Washington at 541 H Street, an establishment run by a widow named Mary Surratt. The Department was told that these plotters entertained a scheme to kidnap Lincoln and rush him out of the capital, by way of the Navy Yard Bridge, into southern Maryland. The Department had this word first-hand from an informer, Louis J. Wiechmann. This man was a Government employee, and a member of the "War Department Rifles." He was also an intimate of the Surratt family; he lodged at Mrs. Surratt's boardinghouse.

Official records on Wiechmann are confusing. One might well believe them deliberately confused. In them his name is spelled at least five different ways. Dates are curiously juggled. Wiechmann's testimony is garbled, vaguely worded, often contradictory. The vagueness, inconsistency and garbling may have been Wiechmann's fault or due to faulty transcriptions. But the serious fault—the War Department's failure to act on the tips delivered by Wiechmann—could not be laid to the informer.

According to historian Osborn H. Oldroyd, Wiechmann told a friend in the War Department that a conspiracy to abduct Lincoln was brewing in the boardinghouse where he lived. Basing the account on Wiechmann's testimony, Oldroyd dates this revelation as being made immediately after the Presidential carriage was ambushed near the Soldiers' Home on March 20.[21]

---

[21] Osborn H. Oldroyd, *The Assassination of Abraham Lincoln* (Washington, D.C.: Privately published, 1901), p. 172.

Wiechmann informed Captain D. H. L. Gleason, a fellow clerk in the office of the Commissary General of Prisoners, that he'd been "unnerved" by hectic doings in the house on H Street. He told of Booth's repeated calls at this middle-class domicile which was one hardly calculated to attract an eminent stage star. He told of the actor conferring with Mrs. Surratt behind closed doors. Of her son, John Surratt, going on clandestine trips to lower Maryland. Of nocturnal visits from a Southern agent who called himself Gus Howell, and from a veiled lady known as Mrs. Slater. Of the furtive comings and goings of a local drugstore clerk and an oaf from Port Tobacco, down the Potomac, and a strapping backwoods youth who had come from Baltimore and who posed as a Baptist preacher. These men were armed with pistols and daggers. They used some kind of code. Wiechmann had discovered a false mustache on Surratt's bureau. One night there had been an angry scene with Surratt stomping into the parlor brandishing a pistol, Booth entering the house in a rage, the "Baptist preacher" storming in. They had gone upstairs to hold a secret conference.

"By God, that is strange!" exclaimed Captain Gleason. "There is something wrong going on there."

Then "it was suggested that probably it would be a good thing to go and tell the Secretary of War." But Gleason tempered the suggestion. Why not wait until something further developed? Wherewith they did delay until after the assassination.[22]

The historian Oldroyd did not have at his disposal an unabridged set of records when he wrote the foregoing in 1901. At that date the War Department was still holding much of the data on the Lincoln murder case in files marked "Secret." Since then, a few more details have come to the surface.

We learn from modern historian Otto Eisenschiml that "Gleason undertook to see that Stanton was informed through Lieutenant Sharp, an assistant provost marshal on the staff of General Augur." Gleason volunteered this effort ten days after Wiechmann first confided in him. And Wiechmann himself told his story to a United States enrolling officer, one McDavitt, who notified his own superiors.[23]

Drawing on War Department files finally released from closed archives, and basing his account on an article published by Captain Gleason in 1911,[24] Eisenschiml states that *on February 20, 1865,* Wiechmann informed Gleason that an attempt would be made to kidnap Lincoln on Inauguration Day.

The War Department itself revealed that it was informed in February or March, 1865, of Booth's abduction plans—not in so many words, but by action which spoke louder than words. This action drew the notice of

---

22 *Ibid.*

23 Eisenschiml, *op. cit.,* p. 46.

24 D. H. L. Gleason, "Conspiracy Against Lincoln," *Magazine of History,* February, 1911.

Booth's uneasy little gang. In a post-war lecture, John Surratt recalled: "We understood that the Government had received information that there was a plot of some kind on hand. They had even commenced to build a stockade on the Navy Yard bridge, gates opening toward the south, as though they had expected danger from within and not from without."[25]

Wiechmann must have furnished descriptions and names: Booth, Mrs. Surratt, John Surratt, Atzerodt, Herold, Paine. Wiechmann had become acquainted with them all. He would hardly have informed Captain Gleason of the subversive plot without naming the suspected subversives. There can be little doubt that he turned in the whole H Street establishment, including the Confederate spy, Howell, and the mysterious Mrs. Slater. But it is not necessary to deduce this as a logical conclusion. The fact that arrests followed immediately after the assassination reveals the Government's informed hand.

In fact, the Secret Service jumped the gun. On March 24 the Confederate agent, Augustus (Spencer) Howell, was arrested. He was committed by Colonel Ingraham to Old Capitol Prison, charged with being a "blockade runner."[26] Here was a visitor to the H Street boardinghouse promptly in the bag. But he was kept there like the proverbial cat.

War Department records go shy on the subject of Howell's arrest. During the eventual conspiracy trial, the fact of his capture was mentioned in connection with Mrs. Surratt. It seemed that she tried to have the man released—a friendly attempt to help a family friend. What the Government did not indicate (or intend to indicate) was that Howell's arrest undoubtedly stemmed from a tip from Wiechmann.

Nor did the Government advertise the fact that the arrest of the spy Howell substantiated Wiechmann's communiqué concerning conspiracy in the house on H Street. Howell himself must have contributed a word or two on the subject. The Old Capitol, a tough prison, heard many a confessional. Lafayette Baker had ways and means of eliciting confessions. When the Secret Service wanted information, the extractions were usually wrought, however painful the methods might have been.

The questions then arise: Why did the War Department fail to act? Why were not Army detectives immediately dispatched to trail Booth night and day? Why did not the Federal Secret Service promptly descend on Mrs. Surratt's boardinghouse? Given far less warrant (and actual paperwork warrants were not needed by the Military Police), Secretary Stanton in the year just past had ordered the arrest of thousands of suspected subversives. Here was a house openly "Secesh," a family that entertained a Confederate spy, a mysterious gang of men, reportedly armed, plus the

---

[25] Surratt lecture, Rockville, Md., December 8, 1870. Quoted in Eisenschiml, *op. cit.*, p. 41.

[26] National Archives, War Dept. Records, File "W," Doc. 1914, JAO.

ambush of the Presidential carriage on March 20. With one swoop the entire gang could have been bagged. Nothing was done.

A final warning came on April 5. The President was at that time on board the flagship *Malverne* in the James River just below Richmond. The Confederate capital was toppling. On the morning of the 5th, Brigadier General Edward H. Ripley called on Lincoln to deliver urgent and personal information.

Ripley brought with him a Rebel enlisted man, a soldier who had been in the Confederate Secret Service, and, believing the cause lost, had come over to the Union side. This informant confided that he had served in a "special bureau" under command of the brilliant G. J. Rains. As Federal intelligence had long been aware, the Rains organization conducted topsecret operations of a type known to the military as *missions extraordinaires*. The informant from this bureau swore out a deposition stating that a party had been dispatched from Richmond on secret mission aimed "at the head of the Yankee Government." He could give no further information, but he said he was convinced President Lincoln was in mortal danger.

Historian Carl Sandburg notes that Lincoln refused to see the informant at City Point, and quotes General Ripley as saying the urgent visit was "all to no purpose." To Ripley, the President remarked: "I cannot bring myself to believe that any human being lives who would want to do me harm."[27]

In line with that type of anecdote (or out of line with it), history was seeded with a crop of vignettes representing Lincoln as too whimsical, too indifferent, too war-burdened, or too fatalistic to care about his own safety.

Lafayette Baker told a typical story of this genre, as related by Oldroyd: "On one occasion General Lafayette C. Baker . . . carried to Mr. Lincoln two anonymous communications, in which he was threatened with assassination. In a laughing, joking manner the President remarked, 'Well, Mr. Baker, what do they want to kill me for? If they kill me, they will run the risk of getting a worse man.' "[28]

Booth's biographer, Francis Wilson, repeats the oft-quoted statement attributed to Lincoln: "I cannot possibly guard myself against all dangers unless I shut myself up in an iron box."[29]

Manufactured by such anecdotes is the impression that President Lincoln persisted in an utter disregard of danger. That he refused to take ordinary precautions and rejected proposed security measures. That Lincoln himself was to blame for the fact that he went unprotected on the night of April 14, 1865.

Some of the stories concerning Lincoln's whimsicality or his unconcern or his fatalism are unquestionably true. Some are fireside legends. But

[27] Sandburg, *op. cit.*, p. 242.
[28] Oldroyd, *op. cit.*, p. 218.
[29] Francis Wilson, *John Wilkes Booth* (Boston: Houghton Mifflin Company, 1929), p. 29.

whether truth or fable, they do not alter the fact that Lincoln's attitudes, his preferences in the matter of protection, are beside the point. Whether the President liked it or not, it was the Government's business—specifically the business of the War Department—to furnish him with physical and material security.

And the truth is, Lincoln saw and appreciated the necessity for protection. Occasionally he walked or drove without a guard, but more often he went accompanied by an armed escort. Existing records show that Lincoln personally applied for protection when he thought it urgent. He requested a military bodyguard on April 14, 1865—a guard to go with him to Ford's Theater! Moreover, Lincoln went straight to the War Department with this request.

The request was refused!

The remarkable story comes from one of the White House guards, William Crook, and from David Homer Bates, a telegrapher in the War Office. On the afternoon of April 14, Lincoln walked from the White House over to the War Office to call on Secretary Stanton. Crook accompanied the President. On Pennsylvania Avenue a group of drunken brawlers blocked the pavement. Crook had to clear these hoodlums out of the way, and the President, in passing, heard a mutter of obscenity and snarled epithets.

Lincoln seemed disturbed by the incident. "Crook," he said a few minutes later, "do you know, I believe there are men who want to take my life. And I have no doubt they will do it."

The guard stammered protests.

Lincoln shook his head. "Other men have been assassinated." He added soberly, "I have perfect confidence in those who are around me. In every one of you men. I know no one could do it and escape alive. But if it is to be done, it is impossible to prevent it."[30]

Here is the fatalistic Lincoln, but also the Lincoln walking with a protector to the War Department where he asked for a military guard— a strong escort for the evening.

Lincoln put the request directly to War Secretary Stanton. He told (or, rather, reminded) Stanton of the theater party in prospect that evening. He intended, he said, to take Mrs. Lincoln to Ford's to see the comedy *Our American Cousin*. Lincoln asked Stanton for the services of Major Thomas T. Eckert, one of the Secretary's aides.

"I have seen Eckert break five pokers, one after the other, over his arm," Lincoln said. "And I am thinking he would be the kind of man to go with me this evening. May I have him?"[31]

---

[30] William Crook, *Through Five Administrations* (New York: Harper and Brothers, Publishers, 1907), p. 66.

[31] David Homer Bates, *Lincoln in the Telegraph Office* (New York: Century Co., 1907), p. 367.

Previously Lincoln (or Mrs. Lincoln) had invited the Stantons to this theater party. Stanton had declined, pleading pressure of official business. General and Mrs. Grant had also been invited. Stanton knew that the Grants, too, had declined. In fact, as noted by David Homer Bates, Stanton had urged Grant not to go "and, if possible, to dissuade Lincoln from going." According to telegraph-operator Bates, Stanton thought the public appearance of the two eminent leaders would be dangerous in a city infested with "evil-disposed persons."

As Bates tells it, Stanton was deeply concerned for the security of Grant and Lincoln. Bates adds that when Lincoln saw Stanton on the afternoon of the 14th, "the stern and cautious Secretary again urged the President to give up the theater party, and when he found that he was set on going told him he ought to have a competent guard."

Bates does not offer the immediate reason behind the War Secretary's refusal and Grant's refusal to join the theater party. In all likelihood, the telegraph operator remained unaware of it, since it involved a personal matter between Mrs. Stanton, Mrs. Grant and Mrs. Lincoln. But Bates should have known that General Grant, surrounded by military guards and aides, would have had no reason for anxiety over a theater appearance. Stanton, had he so desired, could have packed the house with soldiers and Secret Service men.

Knowing that neither he nor General Grant would be in attendance, the War Secretary was fully aware that the theater party would be deprived of the full-dress military escort customarily furnished for the public appearances of high-ranking Army leaders. Stanton also knew (since Lincoln was there telling him) that the President intended to go to Ford's Theater for all of his, Stanton's, warnings. Stanton must have realized those warnings would be in vain. Stanton knew Mary Lincoln. He knew the party had been announced. He knew—and he knew that Lincoln knew—the domestic White House storm that could arise if this social event were canceled. In spite of this knowledge that Lincoln would go—and go without Grant's military entourage—Stanton refused Lincoln's request for the loan of Major Eckert as a special guard.

Stanton said that "he had some important work for Eckert that evening and could not spare him." He insisted that Eckert, who was chief of the War Department Telegraph Office, had the duty that night, and his work could not be put off.

Here again Bates interprets Stanton's motive, declaring the War Secretary "still unwilling to encourage the theater project." What other motive could Bates attribute to Stanton's otherwise inexplicable turn-down of a Presidential request? But Bates was merely interpreting. One of Stanton's men, he naturally treated the War Secretary with deference. When he wrote his story in 1907, Bates was doubtless still awed by Stanton's reputation as the "Mad Incorruptible." At that date Stanton's aura had not dimmed.

Bates, of course, was not a trained writer. He may have been a fair observer with a retentive memory, but we are left, for instance, to guess Stanton's manner, his tone of voice, his facial expression during the episode in question. Bates calls him "stern and cautious." Other contemporaries, with keener eyes and insight, called the War Secretary bumptious, officious, inconsiderate, caustic, self-important. Grant would say of Stanton: "It seemed to be pleasanter to him to disappoint than to gratify."[32] This, evidently, was the Stanton who denied Lincoln the loan of Major Eckert that day.

Lincoln may or may not have been inwardly offended by this brusque refusal from his War Secretary. The Secretary's unwillingness to oblige the President constituted, of course, a violation of protocol. Lincoln cared little for the formal punctilios of protocol. From the height of his great stature he could look down on Stanton's discourtesies with the tolerance of the gentlemanly person who ignores ill-breeding in the crude.

But on this occasion Lincoln's sensitive ear seems to have detected in Stanton's tone an unusually petty brassiness. This time Lincoln persisted in his request.

Lincoln sauntered into the cipher room where Major Eckert superintended. Lincoln spoke to Eckert about the theater party that evening, and voiced the wish that Eckert would come as a personal bodyguard. He said that both he and Mrs. Lincoln would appreciate it. As for the important work mentioned by Stanton, couldn't it wait until tomorrow?

Lincoln's reference to Eckert's poker-breaking may have been Lincolnian humor. Eckert did, however, embody the physique for such a performance—forearms like a blacksmith's, and the chest and shoulders of a circus strong man. However, he was only a major.

Given the negative lead by Secretary Stanton, the Major behaved with soldierly circumspection. Better risk the kindly Lincoln's regretfulness than the splenetic Stanton's displeasure. So, falling in step behind his immediate superior, Eckert said he was sorry, the work could not wait, he was needed that night on the telegraph duty watch.[33]

"Very well," Lincoln said, "I shall take Major Rathbone along, because Stanton insists on having someone to protect me; but I should much rather have you, Major, since I know you can break a poker over your arm."[34]

Walking back to the White House with Crook, Lincoln seemed depressed. Aware that the guard had overheard the interview with Stanton, the President observed that the theater party scheduled for that night

---

[32] Ulysses S. Grant, *Personal Memoirs* (New York: C. L. Webster & Co., 1885–1886), vol. II, p. 380.

[33] *Ibid.*

[34] Crook, *op. cit.*, p. 67.

could not be canceled. "It had been advertised that we will be there, and I cannot disappoint the people. Otherwise, I would not go. I do not want to go."

Crook was distressed. He would never forget that in parting that afternoon, the President said "good-bye" to him instead to the usual "good night."

And so the evening shadows closed around Abraham Lincoln.

At ten o'clock that night Major Eckert was at home, divesting his muscular torso of tie and shirt, preparing to shave. He had been home since suppertime. Had left the War Department Telegraph Office in charge of telegraph operator Bates, a subordinate considerably his junior. What of the "important work" that could not wait until the following day? Historian Eisenschiml, a careful researcher, meticulously tracked down all dispatches received by the War Office telegraph that evening: a smattering of routine messages, two telegrams to Stanton of so little consequence that they were filed, an inconsequential telegram to Lincoln.[35]

At ten o'clock that night Edwin M. Stanton was at home, preparing to retire early. He had quit the War Office about six P.M. In leaving, he had bid Major Eckert "good night." After supper he had paid a brief call on State Secretary Seward, who had been invalided by an almost fatal carriage accident. About nine o'clock Stanton had returned home to pose for a brass band which had come to serenade him. "When Stanton told the President that he expected to do a lot of work that night, he seems to have evaded the truth," remarks Eisenschiml. ". . . it looks as if he had no intention of doing any work at all that evening."

What *had* been the War Secretary's intentions? Bates tells us that Stanton urged on Lincoln the necessity of a "competent guard." But what of Stanton's withholding such a guard when Lincoln promptly conceded the necessity? Bates would have us believe that Stanton's motive in denying Lincoln the services of Major Eckert lay in a desire to discourage the President from going to the theater. Yet when the President, for reasons of his own, insisted on going, Stanton still persisted in withholding the powerful bodyguard. The "discouragement" angle no longer holds, and we know that Eckert was not needed at the War Office. Stanton's conduct in this matter is beyond ready fathoming.

Bates intimates that Stanton was willing to let Lincoln have the services of Major Henry Rathbone, a War Office attaché. About thirty years old, slender, dapper, Rathbone cut a pleasing figure in a drawing room. He knew how to bow from the sash and how to offer a lady his arm. He could *not* have broken a poker over his arm.

In point of fact, Rathbone would have on his arm that night Miss Clara Harris, his pretty fiancée. One may search the voluminous testimony, the

---

[35] Eisenschiml, *op. cit.*, pp. 35–37.

official reports, the news accounts in vain for reference to Rathbone's having a gun on hand. Evidence indicates that the Lincolns had invited Major Rathbone and his fiancée to attend the theater party as guests previous to Lincoln's request for Major Eckert's services. This would explain Rathbone's going unarmed.

Was the War Secretary truly concerned over Lincoln's safety? Carl Sandburg writes in his monumental Lincoln biography: "The two men who most often warned Lincoln about his personal safety were Stanton and [Ward H.] Lamon."[36] It is perhaps significant that Lincoln's good friend Lamon was on a mission for the Federal Government in Richmond on April 14. As for Stanton, Sandburg tells us that the War Secretary had, during the early months of his incumbency, furnished Lincoln with military escorts. "Against Lincoln's open wishes he [Stanton] had thrown cavalry, footguards, and plainclothes attendants around the President."[37] This would seem to demonstrate Stanton's unyielding and anxious solicitude for President Lincoln. But it does not explain (nor does Sandburg offer explanation respecting) the situation on the night of April 14.

At the War Secretary's immediate disposal were all the U.S. military forces in the District of Columbia. At his beck and call were the capital's provost marshals with their companies of Army police and Army detectives. Under him was Lafayette Baker with the forces of a ubiquitous Secret Service. A finger-snap from Edwin McMasters Stanton could have positioned a quiet guard around Ford's Theater, a detail of Army police back stage, Federal detectives throughout the audience, and unobtrusive sentries to watch the corridors to the President's box.

But at ten o'clock that night Lincoln sat in his box unprotected. Of course, Major Rathbone was there—but with a pretty girl to distract his attention. Lincoln's footman, Charles Forbes, was there for part of the time (not as a guard, but as an attendant messenger). One solitary man stood guard (or was supposed to stand guard) over the Presidential box.

His name was John Parker. He was a member of the Metropolitan Police Force. Dissolute, craven, he was a drunken good-for-nothing who had one of the worst records on the Washington Force. And he had been assigned to the White House detail at the special request of Mrs. Lincoln.

To the present day nobody knows why Mrs. Lincoln sponsored this scurvy policeman. When her sponsorship of Parker came to light after the ghastly tragedy enacted at Ford's, nobody wanted to probe that peculiar matter.

Of course—after the tragedy—Parker was investigated. Metropolitan Police Records showed that John F. Parker hailed from Frederick County,

---

[36] *Op. cit.*, p. 242.
[37] *Ibid.*, p. 262.

Virginia. Lived with wife and three children at 750 L Street. Had been a carpenter. Had joined the city force when it was organized in 1861. Had proceeded to accumulate a mass of demerits and reprimands that took him to the foot of the constabulary for insubordination, unbecoming conduct, loafing on beat, drunkenness while on duty, and arresting streetwalkers who had refused him their favors gratis. In March, 1863, he had faced the Police Board to answer charges that he had gone to bed drunk in a house of prostitution and had fired a pistol through the window of said brothel. That charge dismissed, he soon faced others—foul language, sleeping on post, insulting a lady. One black mark after another. This was the character assigned to guard the President's box on the night of April 14.

Where was Policeman Parker at the crucial hour? Days afterward newspaper men and other investigators were asking that question. One fact could not be hushed by official or unofficial censors. Parker had abandoned his post. The door of Lincoln's box had been left unguarded.

Parker, then, was a key figure in the murder case. Perhaps *the* key. This possibility was not lost on the authorities. Nor was Parker lost, for he turned up at Police Headquarters next day. But the facts concerning John F. Parker were promptly "lost" in the files of official investigation, and so were lost to history. The reason: Mrs. Lincoln's strange involvement with John F. Parker?

Just the week before the murder, Mary Todd Lincoln had written a letter to Provost Marshal James R. O'Beirne declaring her sponsorship of Parker's transfer to the White House guard. Penned on White House stationery, her note read as follows:

EXECUTIVE MANSION

Washington, April 3d, 1865

This is to certify that John F. Parker, a member of the Metropolitan Police has been detailed for duty at the Executive Mansion by order of,

Mrs. Lincoln

It seemed that Parker had come up for the Army draft—a type of selective service he evidently wished to avoid. Provost Marshal O'Beirne responded with a query concerning Parker's exemption and that of another White House guard. On April 4, Mrs. Lincoln endorsed the Provost Marshal's note: "Please have them both exempted from the Draft."[38]

What conceivable interest could Mary Todd Lincoln have had in this slovenly roundsman from a back-street beat? Here was an enigma at once hustled under the censorship veil. That veil has never been lifted.

The First Lady was guilty of a number of peculiar indiscretions. She became involved in a miserable scandal with the White House gardener, an unsavory jackdaw suspected of being a Confederate spy. Another scandal

---

[38] Both letters quoted in Eisenschiml, *op. cit.*, p. 14.

—with an adventurer named Wikoff—evoked a Congressional inquiry. Extravagance plunged Mary Todd Lincoln into a nightmare of debt, and her unbridled tongue led the unfortunate woman into a morass of difficulties.

She openly criticized Seward, Chase and other members of Lincoln's Cabinet. She snubbed Andrew Johnson, treating him as poor white trash. She derided the war effort, scorned McClellan, and called Grant a "butcher." So it was rumored (not unnaturally) that Mrs. Lincoln was a Southern sympathizer. Finally it was alleged that she sent information to relatives in the Confederate command.

Family friends and Lincoln's advisors did their best to shield her. Her critics were denounced as scandal-mongers and slanderers, as no doubt some of them were. The stories about her were denied. Censorship stepped in. But, as is always the case with censorship, some of the story emerged—distortions and fragmentations worse than the whole truth might have been. By 1865 a fog of suspicion shrouded Lincoln's wife. Some of Lincoln's closest friends feared and mistrusted her.

Superimposed on other follies, Mrs. Lincoln's involvement with John Parker proved too distressing for contemporary investigators. Mrs. Lincoln had requested Parker's services shortly after her return from City Point where, during a review, she had staged an appalling scene, publicly raging at Mrs. Grant, at the wife of General Ord, and at the President. In the wake of that episode, the Parker matter (perhaps a mere kindness on the part of Mrs. Lincoln) would undoubtedly have created a storm. So investigation of the delinquent policeman was smothered.

But in the effort to hide Mrs. Lincoln behind censorship, the censors had perforce to hide John F. Parker. In concealing this skeleton in a closet, they may have effectually abetted the concealment of the person or persons responsible for Lincoln's betrayal.

Two American Presidents were accused of having had a hand in Lincoln's murder.

Jefferson Davis, President of the Confederacy, was named as a leading assassination conspirator in an official indictment set forth by the U.S. Government. While held as Federal prisoner in Fortress Monroe, Davis was found guilty as charged by a United States Military Commission trying Booth's accomplices in Washington, D.C.

But Davis himself was never put on trial. All efforts to bring him to court were eventually quashed. Although he had been found guilty *in absentia,* the Confederacy's President was finally granted official amnesty.

Stanton's Bureau of Military Justice had claimed there was a great deal of evidence linking Jefferson Davis to the assassination conspiracy. But this evidence, like the indictment, somehow dissolved. In the end a cloak of censorship was thrown over the whole Davis case. The modern historian endeavoring to investigate the records finds himself groping in a vacuum.

No less mysterious than the Davis cover-up was the cloak thrown over Andrew Johnson of Tennessee.

In the specific absolutes of dictionary definition there is no compromise between "patriot" and "traitor." There are degrees of patriotism, perhaps, and degrees of treachery, but the terms are completely antithetical. Andrew Johnson was called both. He could only have been one or the other.

The treason accusation was hurled at Johnson from the Senate floor. Impeached, he won a hairline acquittal. But he was never fully acquitted in the public mind. For behind the impeachment charges lurked another charge—one that should have been (and probably could have been) satisfactorily answered, but never was. The charge: that Johnson was involved in the assassination conspiracy.

Listen to the roaring of Congressman Benjamin Loan of Missouri: "An assassin's bullet wielded and directed by Rebel hand made Andrew Johnson President. . . . The price that he was to pay for his promotion was treachery to the Republicans and fidelity to the party of treason and rebellion!" Loan promised the Congress that "the proofs . . . will be furnished to . . . satisfaction."[39]

Congressman J. M. Ashley of Ohio denounced "the man who came into the Presidency through the door of assassination." He calls attention to a "dark suspicion which crept over the minds of men as to his [Johnson's] complicity in the assassination plot." The nation demands, roared Ashley, that "the incubus which has blotted our country's history with the foulest blot should be removed."[40]

The baleful charges were dismissed. Loyal men who knew Andrew Johnson denounced his accusers as slanderers and said he was the victim of a monstrous cabal. But the charges left a blot.

Lincoln's own Vice President accused of conniving in the President's murder? Good Americans recoiled, aghast. Recoiling, they refused to inquire into the facts. Which is to say, they feared the facts that might be found. Of course, this was tantamount to mistrusting Johnson.

Such mistrust on the part of Johnson's friends played directly into the hands of his enemies, who cherished private reasons for desiring the ruin of Johnson by a smear campaign. They, too, were against a fact-finding inquiry, for they well knew that official censorship would leave in its wake the shadow of a doubt.

Could Johnson conceivably—just conceivably—have had a hand . . . ?

The question stems from three others.

Was Andrew Johnson personally acquainted with John Wilkes Booth?

Where was Andrew Johnson during the dark hours Lincoln lay dying?

---

[39] *Congressional Globe,* 39th Cong., 2nd Session, pp. 444–46.

[40] *Congressional Globe,* 40th Cong., 1st Session, pp. 18–25.

Why did Johnson himself never answer those questions? Or, if he did answer them, why were the answers withheld from the public?

Eventually, unable to trust Andrew Johnson, the public mind belittled him. Tennesseans might come to revere him, but he would not be awarded national recognition as one of the great patriots who preserved the Union. Censorship condemned him to a sort of historical mediocrity. Today's American histories and standard biographies do not answer the questions which compose the "incubus" that haunted Andrew Johnson. If honest, the historians confess they do not know the facts because the facts were never fully disclosed.

Gloss over the Stanton-Eckert episode, veil Mrs. Lincoln's involvement with Parker, secrete evidence concerning Jefferson Davis, bury two hours in the life of Andrew Johnson, and a vast cover-up is under way. Attribute the purest motives to this official censorship, and it still amounts to the concealment of facts. And whatever the motive, such concealment—by its very nature deceptive—tends to be misleading and to obscure the truth.

The military censors had a field day with the Lincoln murder case. From the outset Stanton held that many of the facts relating to the assassination were "not in the public interest." Eventually so much of the truth was tampered with that no one could learn the truth. Thus an immense deception was imposed and a stupendous crime was covered.

Today the cover-up is conceded by at least one Government agency which tells us in its official literature that "confusion and mystery" cloak Lincoln's assassination and "we probably shall never know all the facts."[41]

But the case is an omnibus of mysteries, wherein the Eckert puzzle, the Parker riddle, the Davis paradox, and the Johnson enigma are merely incidental bafflers in a labyrinthian anthology. Not the least of the mysteries is the persistent Government secrecy which shrouded the case history.

For seventy years the War Department kept the official files on the assassination conspiracy, the pursuit and capture of John Wilkes Booth, and the trial of Booth's accomplices under lock and key. One might assume that during the Reconstruction Era some legitimate purpose was served in this. But in decades long after the Civil War, what "national security" was protected by the military censors? As of 1890, for example, what strategic plans, operations, or weapons were safeguarded by this secrecy?

In 1925 the War Department was still withholding the records of the Lincoln murder case from the public domain. The U.S. generals now in command were not Civil War, nor even Spanish-American War, generals. They were World War I generals, who (one must suppose) were busy with the direction and administration of a veteran army of Doughboys recently back from France. The Secretary of War, a Coolidge appointee,

---

[41] See Chapter 25, "Curtain Call."

was (one might think) more concerned with Billy Mitchell than with John Wilkes Booth. A lock of secrecy on the assassination conspiracy of 1865 certainly withheld no vital information from the "enemy," for the Confederacy had long since gone with the wind and the only rebels troubling the U.S. Army were a handful of *insurrectos* in a little shooting war way down in Nicaragua.

But no, perhaps there was one last troublesome Confederate. At turn of the century the press had featured a story that Lincoln's assassin had escaped. Now a mummy was in circulation with the story—a cadaver represented as Booth's. It should have been easy enough for the War Department to explode both story and mummy; yet, in 1925, when interested magazine writers and journalists wanted to examine the records they were put off.

In addition to dossiers on the conspiracy, the Army Judge Advocate's Office held in its files numerous items presumably taken from the captured assassin. These included weapons, a compass, a diary, a little bevy of photographs, and a riding boot. With public interest aroused by the Booth escape story, people wanted to see these relics.

As George M. Battery, Jr., noted in the current Washington *Star:* "The requests have reached the thousands of late. . . . So persistent have visitors and correspondents become that the matter is a source of much embarrassment to the War Department, and the relics are literally a 'white elephant' of considerable proportions."

The Army authorities would show the items to insistent inquirers, but censorship withheld information on one of the photographs (portrait of a lady), and the conspiracy files were not open for public inspection. Obvious discrepancies appeared in those briefs on the case which were made available.

". . . These are a few of the things," wrote the *Star* correspondent, "that have made it difficult for the War Department to convince certain credulous persons that Booth was duly dispatched. The Department has insisted on treating the matter as a *fait accompli* and has steadfastly refused to go beyond the records as written."[42]

In 1932 the "white elephant" relics were at last relinquished by the Army and placed on display in the Government's Lincoln Museum. A few years later the dossiers on the assassination conspiracy were released to the public domain. That is, the files were at last transferred from the Judge Advocate's Office in the War Department to the reliquary of the National Archives. There they are today—or what is left of them after sedulous "screening"—bales and boxes of yellowing dossiers and dusty documents entombed in secluded recesses where they may be examined by the modern researcher.

---

[42] Washington *Sunday Star,* May 17, 1925.

But do the Archives now hold *all* of the War Department records on Lincoln's assassination? It would seem there are still gaps in these mysterious files.

According to the Washington *Post*, a Congressional sub-committee in 1957 endeavored to learn just when the Defense Department was "going to erase the secret labels" on a mountain of old Army records stored in St. Louis. The *Post* article reported this secret data was locked in "some 100,-000 file drawers . . . spanning 180 years of military activity. . . . Although most of them [the secret files] cover the World War II period, many go back to World War I, the Civil War, and even the Revolutionary War."[43]

Question: Not to mention Revolutionary War records, why are Civil War records still marked "secret?" One may presume, of course, that these records have to do with secret intelligence. But what security, today, could be compromised by Civil War intelligence reports? What possible activities conducted by the Federal bluecoats, what devices or artifices of 1865 intelligence could, if revealed, give aid or comfort to a modern enemy possessed of all the means of scientific espionage?

In respect to the Lincoln murder case no modern intelligence device could be compromised. What could be compromised is the security of a myth, or the reputation of an institution, or the concealment of some figure or group who had been party to a heinous crime.

Did military censorship conceal the survival of John Wilkes Booth? Did it hide the truth concerning a $200,000 swindle by an unscrupulous Secret Service Chief? Was it designed to preserve the reputation, the prestige of some group or faction supposedly upholding symbols of national virtue? Did it sustain the "dignity" (a favorite military shibboleth) of the War Department and the Army?

All who write about him tell us that Edwin M. Stanton was a devious man. And some of the Civil War's general officers were devious officers. "The bullet-headed generals," noted Nathaniel Hawthorne, as he sat in the lobby of Willard's Hotel in 1862, ". . . one will succeed another in the Presidential chair; and veterans will hold office, at home and abroad, and sit in Congress and the state legislatures, and fill all the avenues of public life. . . ."[44]

However, to promote that end—the end being to save face in order to keep their own ends high in the saddle—did it become imperative for those "bullet-headed" generals to censor certain facts and suppress certain records? Those who bid for authoritarian powers must pretend to infallibility—captains and kings cannot admit to error. Much less could the Union military leaders have confessed a failure to bring to justice the criminals responsible for the greatest crime in the nation's history.

---

[43] Article by Thomas J. Foley, INS, Washington *Post*, November 17, 1957.

[44] Quoted in Thomas Beer, *Mark Hanna* (New York: Alfred A. Knopf, Inc., 1929), pp. 49–50.

And what other end than military face-saving could have motivated almost a century's censorship of the records pertaining to the assassination conspiracy? If Booth had been brought to justice as the Army claimed— if there had been no $200,000 swindle—if the conspirators were fairly tried and justly convicted—if Stanton's War Department had clean hands— then *why the secrecy?*

But the Lincoln murder case remains an unsolved mystery.

War Department secrecy covered a betrayal.

The betrayal of Abraham Lincoln is as obvious as the situation at Ford's Theater on the night of April 14, 1865.

As the curtain goes up, the President is posed like a target—a perfect setup for assassination.

There are no soldiers policing the front of the house, no Secret Service agents in the audience, no Army police backstage.

No sentries guard the door of the Presidential box. Even the scarecrow policeman, Parker, has wandered away.

Not a single military guard is watching Lincoln there at the theater.

But Booth is.

CHAPTER 2

Enter John Wilkes Booth

THE ASSASSIN of Abraham Lincoln was the ninth of ten children born to Junius Brutus Booth and his "wife," Mary Ann Holmes. Named for the revolutionary Lord Mayor of London who cheered for Yankee Doodle in the War of Independence and helped many an American captive escape through the secret underground, John Wilkes was handsome and beloved. Great and yet terrible things were foretold about him by his mother's visions and a gypsy's predictions. He was the darling of a large, eccentric family.

His father, generally considered to be the greatest actor of his time, was also generally conceded to be a drunkard and half, if not completely, insane.

By the time of Johnny's boyhood, the Old Man was a graying alcoholic, battered, bruised in body and soul, an artist with the reputation of a circus freak. Mama was middle-aged, weepy, plaintive. More or less self-supporting, the family acres at Bel Air, Maryland, had become the rough equivalent of a gentleman's farm, the cabin grown into a house called Tudor Hall.

Could a clue to John Wilkes' errant character be traced to environmental influence? This does not seem unlikely. During his boyhood the household scene shifted in wintertime from Bel Air to Baltimore, where the family had a home on Exeter Street.

The Monument City had much to offer. A hustling seaport. A thriving public market. Four-story buildings. Theaters. Oyster houses. Saloons. Barnum's Hotel. A world of excitements and enticements for the teen-age juvenile.

Young Johnny found a friend in a quick little Irish boy, Mike O'Laughlin, who lived across the street. Johnny soon was leader in the neighborhood. The youngsters climbed fences, hitched wagon rides, and whooped down to the waterfront to see the big sailing ships sidle in, cracking the ice. Healthy enough pursuits. What was it about Johnny?

He was moody at times, sometimes sullen. He became resentful when corrected for ill manners, might refuse to tell his mother where he'd been that afternoon, or might squabble with his favorite sister.

Is this the portrait of any fifteen-year-old boy? On the face of it, yes. But John Wilkes Booth may have had unique problems of his own. One can only surmise his reactions.

At that age he knew the tangled skein of his father's affairs. Relatives had come over from England—a swarm of grubs named Mitchell. Jimmy Mitchell (uncle by marriage) had blackmailed Junius Brutus, Sr., for family support in exchange for silence concerning the Old Man's legal wife and son in London. The desperate actor paid for a time, then ordered Mitchell to leave Bel Air. The Mitchell tribe settled in Baltimore, and the ratty uncle sneered the story—all the American-born Booth kids were bastards.

Mary Ann Holmes wept, and the children raised their chins, determined to preserve the fiction of aristocratic breeding. But in 1846 the true wife, Adelaide Booth, had turned up in Baltimore. The Old Man had stormed in despair—there'd been a family scene when "the woman" visited Bel Air.

Adelaide took up residence in Baltimore with the son, Richard Junius. In March, 1851 (when John Wilkes was thirteen), the case boiled to a head. Now the cat was out of the bag—a law suit in the local court—all the neighbors on Exeter tongue-wagging. The Old Man did not contest. Adelaide Booth won a divorce. And in May of that year Junius Brutus Booth and Mary Ann Holmes were finally married.

For John Wilkes, living on Exeter Street, the affair and its consequent publicity may have been extremely painful.

Adelaide Booth's continued presence in Baltimore must have upset the family on Exeter Street. A skeleton from a closet, she took to haunting the saloons around the public market. If she chanced to spy the Booths, she would shake a fist and rail in public denouncement of the Old Man. John Wilkes certainly heard about her (she died of drink in 1858) and he may have encountered her on occasion.

It appears that something marred the relationship between young John Wilkes Booth and his father. Was it stark disillusion with the parent? This has turned more than one unhappy adolescent against his father's authority —against his philosophy, his politics, his way of life. Youth, idealistic, can be exacting and unforgiving, and savagely resentful.

Was such disillusionment a clue to the future conduct of John Wilkes Booth? Could it have been the seed of the plant that flowered into an obsessional hatred of Abraham Lincoln? They called the wartime President "Father Abraham."

Thousands of teen-age boys have been disillusioned by inebriate, shift-less, or otherwise unworthy fathers and have taken the blow standing up. This was common enough in candlelight America. Denounced as "bastard son of a Scotch peddler," Alexander Hamilton had lived through it. Similar ostracism had not downed John Paul Jones. Abraham Lincoln had little use for his own worthless and sponging father. Lincoln, too, had to bear the rumor of illegitimacy.

Moreover, John Wilkes was supported by a staunchly loyal family, and by the knowledge that his father was one of the more celebrated figures in America. The Booths were never ostracized.

Still, the Baltimore scandal hurt. Johnny's older brothers were affected by the situation. Junius, who had married the actress Clementine De Bar, suddenly deserted his wife and small daughter, Blanche, and took off for California with the actress Hattie Mace. Solid "Juney!" Presently the Old Man and Edwin sailed for a West Coast tour. The Gold Rush. Escape. Edwin Booth would later admit that he almost went to pieces on the Barbary Coast. He never forgave himself for this period of wild de-bauchery. All this upheaval in the family must have left young Johnny, just entering his teens, emotionally disturbed.

At about this time young Johnny was sent to St. Timothy's Hall, an Episcopal academy at Catonsville with a semimilitary curriculum. There he donned the gray of an artillery cadet and took the field with new class-mates to learn mathematics, moral philosophy, English grammar, and the manual of arms.

Legend: One day the boys are grouped around Johnny, exchanging glory dreams. Classmate Morris Oram says he would like to be a greater orator than Webster, a greater lawyer than Reverdy Johnson. Johnny stares off with a far-away look. He hopes to do something big. Really big. Some-thing like pulling down, single-handed, the Colossus of Rhodes.

Years later Oram would remember Johnny saying: "Suppose that statue was now standing, and I should by some means overthrow it? My name would descend to posterity and never be forgotten, for it would be in all the histories of the times, and be read thousands of years after we are dead, and no matter how smart and good men we may be, we would never get our names in so many histories."

"But suppose the falling statue took you down with it?" Oram countered. "Then what good would all your glory do you?"

Johnny smiled. "I should die with the satisfaction of knowing I had done something never before accomplished by any other man, and something no other man would do."

In another hint of things to come, John Wilkes associated at St. Timothy's with a fractious lad named Samuel Arnold.

And he may have begun his sexual experimenting there. Gaslight historians would eventually dwell on his reckless "amours" as an actor. But, for Victorians, sex in the schoolboy realm simply didn't exist.

However, John Wilkes exhibited some signs of delayed adolescence. So, for that matter, did the whole country.

During the Mexican War period the populace was swept by a wave of chauvinistic nationalism. Eagle-screaming and flag-waving gave rise to so-called "Americanism" which found its culmination in an anti-English, anti-Catholic movement led by a secret organization of self-styled Super Patriots who, when asked about it, would answer, "I know nothing." Born was the idiotic Know-Nothing Party, sponsored by rabble-rouser Ned Buntline. "Sailor Ned's" curbstone brotherhood had a high old time. They broke up political meetings, badgered innocent priests, burned opposition leaders in effigy. In 1849 they incited the murderous Astor Place riot which drove Charles Macready, the great English tragedian, out of New York and off the American stage.

It is interesting to find juvenile John Wilkes Booth entering the Know-Nothing ranks. A first heady taste of underground secrecy, after-dark clanship, passwords, clandestine oaths. An early indoctrination in the fun of anonymous threats and thrilling conspiracy.

Asia Booth doted on her exciting brother. Would recall him as having "Father's finely shaped head and beautiful face—he had the black hair and large hazel eyes of his mother." She also wrote of his "perfectly shaped hands . . . across the back of one he had clumsily marked, when a little boy, his initials in India ink."[1]

We will have reason to remark this sister's description of John Wilkes' eyes. And it is a pity she did not specify which hand bore the tattooing. Both subjects would contribute to a mystery.

Sandburg informs us on the early venture into the clandestine, drawing on Asia's recollections. "They sang together, or he played the flute to her

---

[1] Asia Booth Clarke, *The Unlocked Book* (London: Faber & Faber, Ltd., 1938).

piano accompaniment. She saw him ride away to secret meetings of a boys' Know-Nothing Society."

A step indicative of character? Many a lad joins a secret fraternity, and grows up—and out of it—afterward.

Another of Asia's recollections (quoted by Sandburg):

"She saw him once put on a girl's petticoat and bonnet, walk past a group of workmen and win the respectful salutes they would give a well-behaved young girl."

This last could mean anything, or nothing.

Abruptly John Wilkes Booth went on the stage. The year: 1856. He was seventeen. Scene of debut: the St. Charles Street Theater in Baltimore.

The Old Man had died in 1852 while returning from California. When Rufus Choate, renowned orator, heard of it, he exclaimed, "Now there are no more actors!"[2]

John Wilkes may have decided to show the illustrious Mr. Choate and the world that there *was* another actor!

He walked on in a minor role in *Richard III*, given this opportunity by comedian John Sleeper Clarke who was showing at the same playhouse in an afterpiece. Johnny muffed his lines, choking in stagefright. Afterwards his mother blamed Clarke for pushing Johnny's debut. She insisted that the comic had wanted Booth's name on the billboards.

After his laughingstock debut, John Wilkes sulked for days. Meantime, he had picked up some rowdy companions around the Bel Air neighborhood. By one account, he became an oyster pirate, joining a gang that was looting oyster beds in Chesapeake Bay. He seems to have found, too, that he could loot beds of another kind. The family had to hush up several affairs. At a predatory age, Johnny roamed Baltimore with a predatory eye. He must have been familiar with Barnum's Hotel. It would be interesting to know if he became acquainted with the barber, Cipriano Fernandina.

But the stage was in his blood, and Johnny's mother and sisters pushed him on. Two seasons after the Baltimore fiasco he appeared at the Arch Street Theater in Philadelphia—minor roles in Sheridan Knowles' *The Wife* and Hugo's *Lucrezia Borgia*. He won a modicum of praise. Philadelphia dazzled him. Which is to say he dazzled himself in Philadelphia. There, it seems, he discovered three of the world's most dangerous intoxicants—audience applause, brandy neat, and flattering women.

Here, perhaps, was the beginning of the "change" in Johnny.

In the summer of 1858, Edwin Booth starred in a benefit at Baltimore's Holliday Street Theater. *Richard III*. John Wilkes appeared in the role of Richmond. That autumn the two brothers performed together in Rich-

---

[2] Quoted in Eleanor Ruggles, *Prince of Players: Edwin Booth* (New York: W. W. Norton & Company, Inc., 1953), p. 62.

mond, Virginia. *Hamlet*. Edwin in the lead, John Wilkes as Horatio. Johnny bungled, but at the final curtain Edwin graciously presented him to the audience for a round of applause. John Wilkes did not hesitate to use a steppingstone when one was offered.

"I don't think John will startle the world," Edwin wrote Junius, ". . . but he is improving and looks beautiful on the platform."

John Wilkes joined a Richmond stock company that paid $20 a week. The salary proved far too meager for the luxuries he was learning to enjoy. Southern hospitality was delightful, but expensive. "John is doing well in Richmond," his mother wrote to Junius proudly. "He is very anxious to get on faster. When he has a run of bad parts he writes home in despair."[3] Generous Edwin returned to Richmond to play a second-lead Iago in a benefit starring John Wilkes as Othello. With such support in the cast, Johnny played to standing room only. But he could not compare with Edwin, and he must have known it.

John Wilkes was a star made, not born. His precocity had another bent. Every other woman in the Virginia capital took notice of him. They chirped and screamed when he walked onstage. Thronged after him on the street. Pawed him for his autograph. Clustered about him like pins drawn to a magnet. Overnight John Wilkes Booth became that great American phenomenon—the personification of a woman's dream.

At the height of this season John Wilkes Booth was appearing on the street as Beau Brummel in a claret-colored coat with velvet lapels, a fawn waistcoat, tight dove-gray trousers with elastic heel-straps. Add jabot shirtfront, cameo, bushel-sized straw hat with wide brim, and bamboo cane. The glass of fashion.

J. Wilkes Booth (as he now signed himself) doffed this garb on one occasion, exchanging it for the uniform of the Richmond Grays. The episode is significant.

The year: 1859. The big headline: John Brown. "God's Angry Man" had come out of blood-stained Missouri to settle the slavery issue in Virginia. The Abolition Champion had his hour of destiny at Harper's Ferry where he lost to Colonel Robert E. Lee, who led United States military forces to squelch insurrection and protect Federal property. In December the flaming Messiah of Freedom was to go to the gallows. John Wilkes Booth wanted to see the show.

Temporarily enlisting in the fashionable Richmond militia, Booth borrowed a uniform and proceeded with the company to Charles Town. The outfit formed the hollow square. The drum snared the fatal long roll. The sword of Robert E. Lee flashed. John Brown dangled in the scaffold.

Asia would recall that Johnny told her he felt sorry for the old gray-

---

[3] Quoted in Wilson, *op. cit.*, pp. 17, 18.

beard. Brown had peered about, desperately, as the noose was adjusted. Booth thought him "a brave old man" who "had been deserted."[4]

It is generally assumed that Booth received the virus of war propaganda while circulating in the drawing rooms of Richmond. That his upbringing as a Marylander disposed him to Southern sentiments. That he became a blazing Southern patriot. And that the war fever aroused latent psychotic tendencies (inherited) which finally went to his head.

War fever he undoubtedly had, but there is something lacking in the "Southern patriot" diagnosis.

To begin with, one might wonder how the slavery issue, the States' Rights issue, or the Secession principle would concern, or even interest, a Beau Brummel of the theater. Booth was not born a "deep Southerner." He had neither an emotional nor a monetary investment in slavery. The average Secession advocate was a narrow provincial who posed as a Georgia man, or an Alabaman, or a Virginian. Booth's family were cosmopolites, his world the stage. One might think he would have been immune to a pro-South mania.

Ever since 1865 historians have speculated on the motives which impelled John Wilkes Booth to adopt the Confederate cause and end up as a rabid zealot. Dealing with such abstract terms as "patriotism," "martial fervor," and "zeal," they grope in vapor. Booth himself employed many of these high-sounding abstractions. But rationale can offer a multitude of specious reasons.

In 1860 John Wilkes Booth left Richmond for a tour of the "deep South." He "had resolved to become a star when he read in the papers that Edwin had got five thousand dollars for a month's engagement in Boston."[5] The date of Johnny's determination seems questionable—he had been stagestruck for some time before this. But his interest in lucrative reward is the point. John Wilkes Booth wanted money.

Thus in October, 1860, he was starring in Montgomery, Alabama, as the wicked Duke Pescara in *The Apostate*. Montgomery applauded his playing as sensational, and compared him with his father. He was a hit.

(Note: It was apparently in Montgomery that some fire-eater displayed a trick rifle, vowing he would murder Lincoln. Booth may have been there at the time, and found the town's boiling sentiments to his taste.)

He remained in the South until February, 1861. Then, with war threatening, he accepted theatrical bookings in the North, perhaps at his mother's urging. At any rate, the Northern theaters paid bigger box-office returns than those in the South. Then, as today, New York City was the actor's El Dorado.

---

[4] Asia Booth Clarke, *op. cit.*
[5] Ruggles, *op. cit.*, p. 123.

John Wilkes was playing Pescara at the Gayety Theater in Albany, New York, when Lincoln passed through on his way to Washington. By some accounts, Booth trailed the procession, glaring hatred at the "Rail Splitter." However, he had another Albany interest, it appears—an actress, Henrietta Irving.

When cannon fire at Sumter exploded the war, John Wilkes told an Albany crowd that the attack on the Federal fort characterized the "most heroic deed of modern times." A mob threatened the theater, and he was ordered to leave the city. Soon after that he almost died playing Romeo— not on the stage, but in a drunken brawl in Madison, Indiana, in a hotel room with Miss Irving. He was stabbed in the face; she tried to commit suicide.[6] He scuttled out of town.

He did not rush south to join the Confederate Army. Thousands of Southern patriots died for the Stars and Bars before the year was out. John Wilkes Booth remained on the stage, dying as Hamlet, Macbeth, and Othello, to the tune of five hundred a week. Like Joseph Choate, Jay Gould, youthful Mr. Vanderbilt, and some other distinguished young gentlemen of that day, he did his fighting verbally. And while the battlefield boomed gunpowder, the business field boomed money. Theaters were crammed by workmen and soldiery with pay to burn. Show business was never better. John Wilkes Booth would make $20,000 that year.

He had projected himself into a stupendous repertoire, one that would stagger a young actor today. It included starring roles in *Romeo and Juliet, Money, The Robbers, The Apostate, The Stranger, The Lady of Lyons, The Corsican Brothers, Lucrezia Borgia, The Wife, The Marble Heart, The Merchant of Venice, Katharine and Petruchio, Julius Caesar, Othello, Richard III, Hamlet, Macbeth.* Had he contented himself with a slower start in roles that were naturals—Romeo and Raphael, for example —he might have won the laurels he hungered for. Obviously he had bitten off more than he could chew.

He seems to have played Hamlet as a pacing madman, Richard III as a bawling monster, and Macbeth as a jumping-jack. In March 1863 he made his New York debut as Richard. Historian Ruggles tells us that after the performance "he slept smothered in oysters to heal the bruises got during a stage battle."[7] The type of onstage violence that sent him to an oyster bed did not evoke critical approval. The New York *Herald* scolded: "Youth may be an excuse for his errors, but it is no excuse for presenting them to a Metropolitan audience."[8] William Winter thought John Wilkes' acting "raw, crude, and much given to boisterous declamation."[9]

---

[6] There are several versions of the stabbing incident. Ruggles, in *Prince of Players,* says it occurred in Albany. However, the story broke in the Madison (Ind.) *Courier,* May 10, 1861.

[7] Ruggles, *op. cit.,* p. 124.

[8] New York *Herald,* March 1863.

[9] Quoted in Sandburg, *op. cit.,* p. 313.

He was stung. Particularly by criticism that called him a "comer," offered suggestions for improvement, and compared his performances with his father's or Edwin's. He refused to be taken for second-fiddle. When he appeared in Baltimore, his billposters blared in heavy block type: *I am Myself Alone!* Baltimore critics were amused. The *Sun* (his home town paper!) caustically dubbed him "the gymnastic actor." Others gently rebuked him for leaping about on the stage like a circus acrobat.

Richard Cary, one of Edwin's intimate friends, watched John Wilkes play Macbeth in Baltimore. Edwin wanted an honest opinion. Cary wrote unhappily that Johnny delivered some speeches in good voice, but his facial expression remained wooden. Cary observed that the performance smacked of an old-time "blood-and-thunder melodrama full of sheet iron and burnt resin and ghosts and other horrors."[10]

That was in 1863. And unbeknownst to the actor's critic (much less to Edwin), John Wilkes Booth had begun to play an off-stage melodrama which more than matched the critical description of his stage performance.

Impelled by reasons perhaps obscure even to himself, John Wilkes Booth had joined the Rebel underground.

He had reached the point of departure.

In St. Louis he spoke openly against the Union war effort. At the McVikers Theater in Chicago he muttered to some of the actors, "What a glorious opportunity there is for a man to immortalize himself by killing Lincoln."[11] Reeling into some bar, he would suddenly burst out singing a salacious ditty entitled, "When Lincoln Shall Be King."

He began to quarrel with his brothers, who were for the Union. He would call on Asia, at that time a housewife in Philadelphia, and deliver impassioned denunciations of the North and all its works. Asia listened sympathetically, but finally, in some exasperation, asked her brother why he didn't fight for the Stars and Bars. A promise to Mother, he told Asia. She had made him give his word he would not enlist.

But he had enlisted, and in the most dangerous of all services—the service that admits to no formal enlistment. The service that deals in code messages, shadow signals, forged papers, veiled missions, cover stories. The service that acknowledges none of the diplomatic legalities of warfare, none of the military rules. If caught, the very side you were on might disown you. Exposure meant a firing squad, unless you talked. Talk, and the forces you betrayed would promise to track you down and slay you, if it took a lifetime.

The Confederate Secret Service was highly organized, and its complex operations went far underground. It embraced a military espionage corps and a sabotage corps. Rebel spy rings worked in every major city of the

---

[10] Quoted in Ruggles, *op. cit.,* p. 123.
[11] Quoted in Sandburg, *op. cit.,* p. 316.

Union. Gray agents burrowed through the Knights of the Golden Circle, played politics in Washington, penetrated Wall Street. Uniformed combat troops who thought campaigns were won or lost on the battlefield would have been astonished to learn of the coincident underground activity. Probably a field general like Stonewall Jackson never heard of Tom Hines or G. J. Rains. The old-school soldier would have been shocked at the thought of arson raids and the use of poison as a weapon.

The depth of Booth's involvement, where he began, and the extent of his early operations pose questions beyond answering. Secret missions go deep. While guns were thundering on the Peninsula, while Blue and Gray armies were locked in bloody conflict at Shiloh, Antietam, Gettysburg and Vicksburg, he was playing theaters in Chicago, Buffalo, Cleveland, St. Louis, Pittsburgh. Backstage he met with messengers and secret agents.

He had a pass (perhaps a forgery) bearing the signature of General Grant.[12] He moved across State lines and front lines at will. Will-o-wisp, he showed up in Tennessee, in Kentucky, in Kansas. He told his sister, "My profession, my name is my passport." His actor role made a perfect disguise.

In 1864 he played the St. Charles Theater in New Orleans. Later he played several engagements in Niagara Falls—a Confederate spy center. Documentary evidence shows him in communication with Rebel intelligence in Canada. He had a girl there who signed herself "Jenny." Of her we shall hear more later.

The wonder is that the Federals failed to trap him. Touring the country, he danced between the raindrops. He was reckless about it, too. He looked the part and behaved like a spy. He had begun to drink heavily—a dangerous indulgence for a man in that game. Heated up by brandy, he would curse the North or leer sneering remarks about "King Abe." He was arrested and fined in St. Louis for declaring that he "wished the whole damn Government would go to hell!"[13]

On a train his brother-in-law, "Sleepy" Clarke, made a derisive remark about Jeff Davis. Johnny caught Clarke by the throat, raging, "If you value your life never speak that way to me again of a man and a cause I hold sacred!" Fellow passengers had to loosen Booth's fingers and drag him off. Gasping, Clarke stared at Johnny dumbfounded. According to Charles Wyndham, Asia's husband "passed the matter off as a harmless and temporary aberration. . . . No one pretended to have an understanding of the strange man [John Wilkes Booth]. It was just another queer prank such as his father used to play."[14] But what of the other passengers who heard Booth's outburst? At that period of the war citizens were being jailed for the mere rumor of disloyalty.

---

12 Asia Booth Clarke, *op. cit.*, p. 112.
13 Quoted in Ruggles, *op. cit.*, p. 155.
14 Wyndham, article in New York *Herald,* June 27, 1909.

Probably Booth's utter recklessness, plus the theatrics and the brandy breath, proved his best protective coloration. A Rebel agent wouldn't be flaunting the fact on his sleeve. The fellow was drunk. Besides, he was "strange" (wasn't his father a lunatic?). All the Booths were "crazy."

And John Wilkes Booth was an idolized celebrity. He was said to be rich. Government detectives often displayed an aversion to arresting prominent persons with impressive bank accounts.

By 1864 John Wilkes had acquired the grand manner and wardrobe of a millionaire. For public consumption he posed as the gentleman and dasher, the drawing room Lothario dispensing romance, gallantry and largesse. His stage costumes were the talk of the theater. For street attire he favored a dove-gray coat with astrakhan collar, gloves, soft hat and stick. A diamond stickpin flashed in his cravat. He sat an elegant saddle on horses groomed as smartly as he was.

At the National Hotel in Washington, D.C., he set up housekeeping with a dainty strawberry blonde, Ella Turner, a prostitute who had consorted with his sporting friend Patrick Barron. In the capital city Booth spent money like a drunken sailor, and he acted like one. When he wasn't dazzling some socialite drawing room, or dallying with pretty Nell, he was touring the houses of "Hooker's Division" with customers of a lower order—stable-hands, roustabouts, waterfront loafers. The social set thought him a Bohemian, a gay blade—as was to be expected of an actor starring in the stock company at Grover's. Theater people who saw him associating with shabby riffraff thought him laudably amiable and democratic.

But under the surface John Wilkes Booth was neither so democratic nor so amiable. An ugly side of him had begun to show.

He is playing in a theater, a star role, with E. L. Tilton in second lead. The script calls for a sham battle, which Booth ends by hurling Tilton into the orchestra pit. The climax wins tumultuous applause, at the expense of a painfully injured fellow actor.

A company is rehearsing *The Taming of the Shrew*. Booth dislikes the members of the cast. He walks on stage and smears each player in the face with a slab of ham scrubbed with lampblack.

At another rehearsal the prompter is slow in feeding the lines. John Wilkes Booth snatches up a wooden wedge and flings it like a thunderbolt, just skimming the prompter's head. The players stare aghast. That block of hickory could have killed the man.

Old friends began to avoid him. Edwin Forrest called him a "damned spad!"

The savage temper, the vicious pranks, the libertine gaming and cheap debauchery hint at moral deterioration indicative of mental disease. They could also have expressed a swollen and frustrated ego—the ego of an actor unable to win top dramatic laurels—or of a Super Patriot unable to run the world to his satisfaction.

A feral restlessness possessed Johnny. His moods were unpredictable. Visiting Edwin or "Juney" in New York, he wanted to argue about the war. When they disagreed with him about Lincoln, he flew into rages. Edwin, saddened by the recent death of his beloved wife, found Johnny's violences unendurable, and for a time would not permit him in the house.

He frightened Asia. He would show up in Philadelphia in the garb of a stage villain—black riding cloak, slouch hat, quirt, with pistols in his pockets and a dagger in his waistband. "He could come and go at our house unobserved," Asia wrote. "He often slept in his clothes on the couch downstairs, having on his long riding boots. Strange men called at late hours, some whose voices I knew, but who would not answer to their names. . . . They never came farther than the inner sill, and spoke in whispers."

One night (apparently in the winter of 1864) he stormed to Asia, "So help me Holy God, my soul, my life, all my possessions are for the South!"

Again she chided him. "Why not go fight for her then?"

He blurted, "I have only one arm to give; my brains are worth twenty men; my money worth a hundred! I have free pass everywhere. . . . My knowledge of drugs is valuable. My beloved precious money—Oh, never beloved til now!—is the means, one of the means, by which I serve the South." He said he was smuggling quinine and other drugs to persons who took them South in "horsecollars and so forth."

He was smuggling drugs. Had he begun to use them? One might think so from this excited outburst, this admission that he is a secret agent with the Rebel underground. In breaking secrecy he violates the cardinal rule, indeed the *only* rule, of the deadly game.

For a time, in the war's fourth year, Wilkes Booth was rolling in opulence. He could make $100 a night for stage appearances. (A brigadier general at the front with the Union Army didn't make that much in a month, and a Confederate general in 1864 was paid about $20 a month.) But Wilkes Booth's income soared above his box-office returns. To the despair of his agents, he rejected theatrical bookings in the autumn of 1864, and rushed to hinterland Pennsylvania to visit the newly discovered oil fields. Plunging into oil stocks, he told friends he'd struck it rich.

According to the press, he made a wildcat fortune. What happened to the profits? Early in 1865, John Wilkes Booth was borrowing to pay livery bills. One historian says he squandered his money on riotous living and women. Some of it, perhaps. But most of it disappeared down other drains. You can hardly dissipate a fortune in one or two months.

He may have been buying protection—bribes are costly. Or paying blackmail—subversive operators are subject to extortion. We know he was spending heavily for something behind the scenes in Washington.

Coincident with his oil strike, John Wilkes Booth was enlisting recruits for his cherished Lincoln-abduction "enterprise." In October, 1864, he dodged from Pennsylvania to Canada. In Montreal he consulted with Jacob Thompson and other Confederate leaders in charge of the Rebel underground there. He may have met with John Yates Beall, Bennet Burleigh, and other Confederate raiders who planned to harry the North with a sabotage campaign.

Before leaving Canada, Booth paid $300 for a London bill of exchange. He told the Canadian bankers that he planned to run the blockade. He deposited $550 in gold in a Canadian bank. By one account he then slipped across the border to Niagara Falls to consult with Rebel agents there.

Did Booth propose his kidnap scheme to Jacob Thompson? Ask for underground aid? Probably. Did he suggest Lincoln's assassination, and contrive arrangements *via* the secret line from Montreal to Richmond? The underground connection between Richmond, Canada, and Booth is still of controversial import.

On the return trip to Washington, John Wilkes Booth paused in New York City. The date: final week in November 1864—the month of President Lincoln's re-election. On the night of November 25, John Wilkes joined his two brothers in a gala performance of *Julius Caesar* at the Winter Garden. Edwin played Brutus, Junius played Cassius, John Wilkes played Mark Antony.

Top tickets were $5.00, and the house bulged with a sellout. Mrs. Booth, Rosalie, and Asia sat in a box. As the brothers came on in their Roman togas, cheers, stamping and shouted *bravos* shook the proscenium. Again and again one or another of the Booths "stopped the show." John Wilkes, who had shaved his fierce mustache, presented a profile that could be taken for the very picture of manliness and firm integrity. Like Edwin and Junius he was awarded an ovation.

Suddenly the play was interrupted by a clamor in the street. Fire bells. Muffled shouting. Voices from the lobby. As the audience turned and craned, Edwin Booth sensed possible panic and stopped it with a quiet apron speech. The fire wasn't in the Winter Garden.

Quitting the theater after the show, the playgoers learned the blaze had been in a neighboring building. Then they discovered midtown Manhattan seething with excitement. A dozen hotels, including the Astor House, the Fifth Avenue, the big St. Nicholas, the Belmont, and the huge block-long Metropolitan were afire. The United States Hotel at Broadway and Maiden Lane was gutted. So was the Bancroft at 12th Street. Several vessels at the Hudson docks were burning. Men, women, and children were trampled in a fire-riot and panic that wrecked Barnum's Museum. All night long the city was in wild turmoil.

Headlines in the New York *Herald:*

ATTEMPT TO BURN THE CITY
Discovery of a Vast Rebel Conspiracy
Twelve Hotels Fired by Turpentine and Phosphorus
SIMILAR ATTEMPTS ON THE SHIPPING
Prompt Frustration of the Scheme
GREAT PANIC AT BARNUM'S
Excitement at Niblo's and the Winter Garden[15]

One can only believe that something more than coincidence found John Wilkes Booth in New York City on this night of alarm and conflagration. That he had a hand in the arson raid was never proved, but the fires were set by Confederate saboteurs. That much was known within a matter of hours. Several of the Rebel incendiaries were caught in a prompt roundup of suspects—fast work by city detectives and New York's hard-hitting Police Chief. One of the captured arsonists, Lieutenant Robert Cobb Kennedy, C.S.A., an escapee from Johnson's Island, confessed the entire plan was originated by Confederate leaders in Canada.[16] And just before the fire raid, John Wilkes Booth had been in Canada with those leaders. Could he have carried secret messages to underground agents in New York? Could he have aided in mapping out the back streets or in directing the arsonists? It is not far-fetched to suppose that he might have signalled to secret agents from the stage.

The morning after, a violent quarrel broke out in the Booth house on 19th Street.[17] Junius said the hotel burners ought to be lynched. Edwin declared he was glad he'd voted for Lincoln.[18] John Wilkes stormed out of the house in a crimson fury. And left for Washington.

Did he carry in his mind instructions received in Canada? Had he been advised to bide his time, or to push the abduction enterprise? Had he been told to go ahead on his own? Nobody knows with certainty. The Richmond leaders, of course, officially disavowed all connection with Booth, and so did the Confederate agents in Montreal. But Booth was on the path that would take him, finally, to Ford's Theater.

He had reached the point of no return.

So much for the legend that John Wilkes Booth was a madman, a lunatic fanatic who went berserk and assassinated President Lincoln.

John Wilkes Booth was a Confederate operative, a secret agent.

---

[15] New York *Herald*, Nov. 27, 1864.
[16] War Dept. Records, "Confession of Robert Cobb Kennedy," at Fort Lafayette, March 25, 1865.
[17] Ruggles, *op. cit.*, pp. 165, 166.
[18] Edwin Booth to Nahum Cap, quoted in Asia Booth Clarke, *op. cit.*, p. 196.

CHAPTER 3

The Conspirators

B OOTH CHOSE for himself the leading role in that fatal production.
Here are the supporting players—the *dramatis personae* destined to
stand trial as accessories to the murder of Abraham Lincoln.

Mrs. Mary Eugenia Surratt. Née Jenkins. Widow. Age about 45. Washington boardinghouse keeper.

Descriptions of Mrs. Surratt are as various as the opinions of those who
have written about her. She is described as "fair, fat and forty" (by a
sympathetic witness)[1]; "buxom-looking with feline gray eyes" (by an
unsympathetic journalist)[2]; and widow with "plain, unlovely face who
parted her mousy hair in the middle" (by a modern historian).[3]

Needless to say, she did not look like the grim-jawed steel engravings
printed in that Victorian day when censors considered indecent the publication of a female's photograph in the periodical press. Nor did she
resemble the appealing gentlewoman portrayed in several modern plays
dramatizing the tragic story of Mrs. Surratt.

Contemporary accounts leave us with the distinct impression of a
woman of something near medium height, plump in the approved fashion
of the period. The age which has softened her body has hardened her countenance; her features, made severe by the part-in-the-middle hair-do, are
loaned additional severity by the frown of middle-years' nearsightedness.

Mrs. Surratt was rather stiff in carriage and demeanor—again reflecting
the Victorian mold. Raised to be a "lady," she was as conscious of her
social position as of her posture, the one going hand-in-glove with the
other. Unhappily for Mrs. Surratt, her physical hand had been compelled
to work for a livelihood; the glove of gentility had become a little frayed.
She ran a boardinghouse—shopping for bargains, keeping a shoestring

---

[1] Colonel Henry Kyd Douglas, C.S.A., *I Rode With Stonewall* (Chapel Hill, N.C.:
University of North Carolina, 1940).

[2] Ben Perley Poore, *op. cit.*

[3] Jim Bishop, *The Day Lincoln Was Shot* (New York: Harper and Brothers, Publishers, 1955).

budget, patching last season's bombazine—an occupation that must have been uncongenial to a woman who liked to refer to herself as "a Jenkins." If one suspects that domestic adversity had tightened her lips, it is fair to assume that the war had hardened something in her mind.

The Jenkins family had not been rich, but they had enjoyed a considerable prestige in Prince Georges County, Maryland, where Mary E. Jenkins was raised and bred. She was born in 1820 near Waterloo—a rural area bordering the District of Columbia. Although her parents were Protestant, they sent her to Miss Winifred Martin's School for Young Ladies—a Catholic school in Alexandria, Virginia. While there she adopted the Catholic faith.

So Mary Eugenia enjoyed a modicum of education in a day when higher learning for females was frowned upon as radical, and the average curriculum for young girls stopped somewhere near the level of pious scriptural passages and Mother Goose. She was probably a limited reader, and her spelling remained faulty—perhaps her scholastic accomplishments never ranged far beyond grade school. Even so, they would have been outstanding in a region where many of the natives signed their names with the illiterate's "X."

Of course, Miss Jenkins could hardly have comprehended the great sociological cross-currents which swept America in the years immediately preceding the Civil War: the Missouri Compromise, States' Rights, the slavery issue. If, or when, she heard these matters argued by her elders across the table, her response must have been purely emotional. Southern Maryland was for States' Rights, including the right of secession. Southern Maryland was pro-slavery. Miss Mary E. Jenkins was bred a Southern Marylander.

She was married when she was fifteen to John Harrison Surratt, a swain considered a "good catch." He was handsome (at least in the eyes of his young bride), dashing (in the way of a Marylander), and possessed of a few acres at Condon's Mills—land left him by an uncle. The Surratts were of Huguenot extraction, and the inherited acres fringed the District of Columbia. Thus endowed, Surratt settled down to enjoy the life of a gentleman farmer.

When the blush of romance wore off, Mary Surratt found herself wed to an indigent whose interests seemed limited to a hunting rifle and a bottle. From the first there were economic troubles. Domestic troubles and disillusionment soon followed.

Mary Surratt lived in a day when the wife was expected to be subordinate to her husband. The husband might be a fool, an incompetent, a drunkard, a sadist, but—so ruled the civil and the religious laws—he was household dictator. The legal status of the Victorian American wife placed her on a footing only a little above that of the Indian squaw—a situation intolerable to an intelligent woman.

The wife in this case bore three children: two sons, Isaac and John Harrison, Jr., and a daughter, Anna, much beloved by her mother and brothers. There is evidence which suggests that mother and children were in close-knit alliance against the improvident father.

Mrs. Surratt was a strong-willed woman. Left the burden of farm management as well as family rearing, she shouldered a heavy responsibility, and kept the family together when hard times came a-knocking.

Surratt seems to have taken out his distempers on the bottle and on the slaves. One night the house was set afire—a costly conflagration that left the family all but dispossessed. According to historian Oldroyd, the blaze was set by a slave in revenge for cruel treatment.[4] Surratt decided to leave Condon's Mills.

The disastrous fire may have sobered Mr. Surratt. Squaring up, he obtained commission as a contractor for the Orange & Alexandria Railroad, then extending its iron trail across central Virginia. For a time he made good money, and the family enjoyed a brief prosperity. In the wake of the railroad venture, Surratt purchased from the Calvert family a sprawling farm in Prince Georges County, Maryland. At a backwoods crossroads about thirteen miles below Washington, he established a roadside store. The place was a stage-stop on the turnpike to Bryantown. Surratt procured the Post Office concession, with job as Postmaster. He called the store Surratt's Villa. The stage-stop presently acquired the name of Surrattsville.

The establishment of Surratt's Villa seems to have set the family fortunes again on the decline. Perhaps local real estate deteriorated in value. Possibly the threat of war between North and South sapped the commercial vitality of the area. Or perhaps the store's handy whiskey barrel undermined the character of an incompetent already beset by infirmities. The store failed.

The store was turned into a tavern. The change might have helped but for the taproom. Presiding in the drab barroom, Surratt played seedy host, dispensing drams to the customers and to himself—drinks and loud conversation . . . big talk . . . politics. Postmaster Surratt declared himself a Union man. Most of the customers declared for the South. While debate loudened in the bar, Mrs. Surratt, in a back room, figured over the shabby account books, trying to make ends meet. The farmlands were mortgaged to the Calverts, and the Calverts began to press for payment.

Mrs. Surratt was worried about the children. About Anna's future. But mostly about the boys. She didn't like them hanging about the tavern. Isaac needed schooling. So did John, the secretive one. Where did they go nights? She didn't like them riding off and coming back late. Their manners needed mending. They must go into business, become gentlemen. They mustn't be like their father.

---

[4] Oldroyd, *op. cit.*, p. 129.

These thoughts and troubles were revealed by Mrs. Surratt in a letter to her pastor. Posted at Surrattsville, January 17, 1858, this appealing missive said in part:

> As Mr. Surratt will not send Isaac to school and I have sent him as long as I have any means I must now put him to doing of something to get his liveing and it seams impossible to get him a place in Washington. . . . O I hope Dear Father you will try and get him something to do as it will be so much better for him to be out of the sight of his Pa as he is drunk almost every day. . . . O, I could not tell you what a time I see on this earth. I try to keep it all from the world on account of my poor Children. . . . I hope I shall be able to send John to school next year. . . .[5]

The letter contains this mournful note: "I have not had the pleasure of going to Church on Sunday for more than a year." Was she compelled to mind the tavern? Or did she feel she lacked appropriate front-pew apparel? That, to an ambitious and prideful lady, could have been the ultimate despair.

Isaac Surratt did obtain some higher schooling, studying to become an engineer. By dint of scratching and scraping, Annie was sent to a seminary near Bryantown, Maryland. Apparently through the efforts of a relative and a Father Waldron, John Harrison, Jr., was entered in St. Charles College, not far from Baltimore—a divinity school run by the Sulpician Fathers.

But then, just as her prayers seemed answered with Isaac and John and Anna in school, Mary Surratt's private world came crashing down, ruined by the thunder of national disaster.

Just before the war's outbreak, Isaac went to Texas. There he enlisted in the Confederate Army. Then the cannon roared at Sumter. Lincoln called for volunteers. Virginia seceded. The war came close to home.

Anna came home, frightened, from Bryantown.

John wrote that he wanted to leave divinity school.

Relatives went away, angry, excited, tearful. Neighbors quit the county. Stage travel slowed to a trickle as the road to Richmond was closed off at the Potomac. Prices went up. Income went down. Anxiety walked into the tavern at Surrattsville. And so did Poverty, shabby, pinching every penny.

For John Surratt, Sr., the quickest way out was through the bottom of a glass. At the bottom there was a coffin. He died in July, 1862.

Widowed, Mrs. Surratt donned conventional black, and, recovering from the shock of a freedom that was unexpected (but never to be admitted as such), set about repairing her household. Anna was there to help her. John had quit St. Charles College and come home. Probably he wanted to go South and enlist; some of his Baltimore friends were in gray uniform.

---

[5] Excerpts in Eisenschiml, *op. cit.;* also in Helen Jones Campbell, *The Case for Mrs. Surratt* (New York: G. P. Putnam's Sons, 1943), p. 270.

His mother prevailed upon him to wait—he was only eighteen. She procured for him the Postmastership, and he took over in his father's stead.

But the tavern could not be resuscitated. Nor could the Surratt farm, with field hands at a premium. After Lincoln's Emancipation Proclamation the slaves walked away, leaving the crops untended.

A plague of renegades entered the locality. Nobody's home was safe, and farmers slept in barns to guard the horses.

Then Federal bluecoats marched in, bringing with them military domination. The soldiers tore down Mrs. Surratt's fences for firewood. They raided the chicken runs, and stole livestock. They brought women to the tavern, and some of the officers winked at Anna. For Mrs. Surratt this Yankee invasion, coupled with the loss of her few slaves, must have seemed unbearable.

The tavern at Surrattsville became an after-dark oasis for Southern sympathizers. In time it came to harbor Confederate agents, Rebel spies, and blockade runners from Richmond. One can only believe that Mary Surratt was well acquainted with the character and purposes of these guests. The family entertained a secret agent named Augustus (or Spencer) Howell and a woman spy named Mrs. Slater.

But here the face of Mary E. Surratt becomes indistinct behind her widow's veil. Did she work with these espionage agents as an active operator? Was she, herself, in direct contact with Richmond as a Confederate agent, under instruction of the Confederate Secret Service and supported by funds from the Confederate Government? Or did she serve merely as an unofficial partisan, offering her home as a way-station on the Rebel underground? On the one hand, her activities would have come under the category of military spying. On the other, they would have been considered by the United States authorities as subversive.

Historians do not know the answer. Mystery shrouds Mrs. Surratt's activities during the last year of the Civil War. But known facts and their continuity offer circumstantial evidence pointing to the widow's direct involvement in a complex Confederate underground apparatus.

In the fall of 1864 the Confederates unleashed their all-out underground campaign to explode a Copperhead uprising in Ohio and Indiana, break the Federal prison camps, seize control of Lake Erie, raid New England, set fire to New York City and generally disrupt the North with riot and sabotage. In that same autumn, Mrs. Surratt rented her Surrattsville farm and tavern to one John M. Lloyd, and removed her household to Washington, D.C. There she acquired a residence at 541 H Street, N.W.—a "three-story brick" containing ten rooms. This was a sizable establishment for those days, and it was located in what was then considered a good residential neighborhood. Mrs. Surratt placed advertisements in the papers and opened the residence as a boardinghouse. (Minus its Civil War front stoop, the house exists today, its number changed to 604 H.)

Where did Mrs. Surratt obtain the funds for this move to the national capital?

A housing shortage in Washington had sent realty and rentals soaring. Mrs. Surratt was debt-ridden at the time. She owed a painful sum to the Calverts, and she could not collect money owed her husband's estate by a certain John Nothey. She could have expected or realized little from the lease of her farm and tavern to John M. Lloyd, a shiftless no-account with the reputation of a soak. Who subsidized the expensive move to Washington?

Odd, too, the setting of Mrs. Surratt's Washington house. Located near 6th Street, it was only four blocks away from a playhouse frequently attended by President Lincoln—Ford's Theater.

First of the male boarders was Louis Wiechmann, a school friend of young John Surratt. Wiechmann had visited the family at Surrattsville. He was a very courteous and solicitous young man with a model reputation, although he had flunked out of St. Charles. In Washington he had a wartime job in the Office of the Commissary General of Prisoners. He moved into the H Street house at Mrs. Surratt's invitation.

Then came Mr. Holohan with wife and two children to occupy the two rooms, second story front. John Holohan was a tombstone-cutter of good Irish-American stock.

A Miss Honora Fitzpatrick had been staying with the Surratts since September. At 541 H Street she roomed with Miss Anna Surratt. When the house was crowded, Honora shared a double bed with Mrs. Surratt in the widow's commodious room, second floor back.

Another paying inmate was Miss Appollonia Dean, aged nine, who was boarded out by her mother.

Respectable lodgers, these—a quietly inconspicuous group such as might be found at any establishment open to boarders. As noted by Oldroyd, the house at 541 H Street "was full from the start, and was a paying institution."[6]

Yet anyone acquainted with wartime underground operations must know that respectable boarders could make a very respectable cover for the subterranean and the clandestine.

Mrs. Slater visited the H Street house. So did the Confederate agent, Howell. Other shadowy persons entered Mrs. Surratt's parlor: a Major Somebody, a vague Mr. Downing—persons unknown to the permanent lodgers, callers glimpsed from the corner of the eye.

Late in December, 1864, John Wilkes Booth visited the house.

We do not know when the H Street address first came to Booth's attention. Was the rendezvous arranged through Richmond? Or was the Widow Surratt involved unintentionally, as her defenders would insist, drawn in by the drift of a capricious fate?

---

[6] *Op. cit.*

Soon after John Wilkes Booth called at the H Street house, a grubby transient applied for a room, giving his name as George A. Atzerodt.

Presently another stranger arrived—a hulking young fellow who at first called himself Wood, then said he was a Baptist preacher, the Reverend Paine.

Not long after that, a quail-hunter, David Herold, called. Earlier in the war he had stopped on several occasions at Mrs. Surratt's tavern.

By February, 1865, John Wilkes Booth was a frequent caller at 541 H Street, where he was seen to confer in private with young John Surratt and with the widow. By March she must have known that Atzerodt, Wood, and Herold were engaged with her son and Booth in some underground activity. Evidence indicates that she was aware of a plan to abduct the President of the United States and carry him prisoner to Richmond.

Andrew Johnson called the house on H Street "the nest where the egg was hatched."[7]

Did the Widow Surratt participate in that fatal incubation? So the Federal Government would contend. And even her most ardent defenders could not deny the facts in evidence: The conspirators met at her house and tavern. Her son, John Surratt, had operated for months as a Confederate spy and message-bearer in direct contact with Richmond. And one of the assassins was caught at her door red-handed.

Yet, to the day of her death, Mrs. Surratt would deny any complicity in Lincoln's murder.

John Harrison Surratt, Jr. Age 21. Ex-divinity student. Ex-Postmaster at Surrattsville. Confederate spy and underground message-bearer.

Photographs show a tallish young man, sparely built, with deep-set eyes, a domed forehead under receding hair, and a silky mustache drooping under a nose which seems about one-third as long as his face. The features seem to lack any particular character, and the eyes appear rather expressionless.

Official records on John Harrison Surratt, Jr., are similarly devoid of depth. His personality seems to have been as elusive as his physical presence on a given scene. He passes through Washington like a shadow. His appearances in the house on H Street are shadowy. Now he is glimpsed in Richmond. Next he is glimpsed in Canada. The authorities can never quite lay their hands on him, and neither can the historians. Of the immediate members of Booth's coterie, least is known about John Harrison Surratt, Jr.

Young Surratt made a good impression when he first entered St. Charles College. "He was tall and slender, dignified in manner, genial in nature, and at once won many friends among the students. He was a very pro-

---

[7] Quoted in Wilson, *op. cit.*, p. 63.

nounced Southern man, but in no instance did he make himself offensive to anyone by his views."[8] John Surratt at this time was sixteen years old.

He is harder to visualize as Postmaster at Surrattsville. He received this appointment in September, 1862, and retained the position until November, 1863, when it went to a Mr. Andrew Roby (or Robey). By some accounts a quarrel arose between Roby and Mrs. Surratt's brother, "Zad" Jenkins. Young Surratt was dismissed out of spite.[9]

But in 1862, John H. Surratt was a spare eighteen. Older men probably coveted the Postmastership, and wondered why this youngster didn't up and enlist.

The appointment was under Civil Service—a Union job. As Postmaster, John Surratt perforce took an oath of allegiance to the United States Government. Perhaps loyalists in the neighborhood (and there were a few Unionists in the locality) recalled his pronounced Southern views. Perhaps Surratt voiced a pro-South opinion or two while selling stamps across the counter or distributing the U.S. Mail.

A village post office could be a key point for dangerous subversion during the Civil War, especially a post office in an area subject to enemy infiltration. Government letters could be steamed open. Enemy mail could be sent through, code messages delivered. Marked stamps, tricky handwriting—these and other devices were employed at the time. A Postmaster under the faintest suspicion might well be dismissed. At any rate, young Surratt lost the job.

The loss was a blow to his widowed mother. Although the local Postmastership was picayune and the pay a pittance, the loss came at a time when every penny counted. Moreover, the position kept the boy home. Out of Civil Service, he was now subject to conscription, and, as she later testified, Mrs. Surratt made every effort to keep her youngest son from being drafted.[10] In this, her motives would seem entirely maternal were it not for her avowed Confederate sympathies and John H. Surratt's enlistment as a Confederate agent.

In 1864 young Surratt made a secret trip to Richmond, crossing the Potomac by underground route. Thereafter, he operated as spy and as message-bearer, conveying Confederate dispatches between Richmond, Washington, and Montreal, Canada. By the time Mrs. Surratt's boardinghouse was well established in Washington, John H. Surratt had become a well paid and highly adept operator in the Secret Service of the C.S.A.

This was extremely dangerous work, demanding agile wits, steely nerves, and the ability to remain unseen, anonymous. That John H. Surratt was a most adroit operator in secret intelligence is attested by the dearth of available information on his activities. Speaking of those activities after

---

[8] Oldroyd, *op. cit.*, p. 155.
[9] H. J. Campbell, *op. cit.*, p. 51.
[10] National Archives, War Dept. Records, File "S," Doc. R.B.P. 79, JAO.

the war, he offered personal impressions, but carefully sidestepped details relating the operation to the Confederate war effort.

In a lecture delivered at Rockville, Maryland, in 1870, John Harrison Surratt, Jr., stated:

> I left [St. Charles College] in July, 1861, and, returning home, commenced to take an active part in the stirring events of that period. I was not more than eighteen years of age, and was mostly engaged in sending information regarding the movements of the United States Army stationed in Washington and elsewhere, and carrying dispatches to the Confederate boats on the Potomac. We had a regularly established line from Washington to the Potomac. And I, being the only unmarried man on the route, had most of the hard riding to do.
>
> I devised various ways to carry the dispatches—sometimes in the heel of my boots; sometimes between the planks of the buggy. I confess that never in my life did I come across a more stupid set of detectives than those generally employed in the United States Government. They seemed to have no idea whatever how to search me.
>
> In 1864 my family left Maryland and moved to Washington, where I took a still more active part in the stirring events of that period. It was a fascinating life to me. It seemed as if I could not do too much or run too great a risk.[11]

We have John Surratt's own word for it, then, that he was engaged in military intelligence, a Rebel spy, while serving as U.S. Postmaster at Surrattsville. His contempt for Federal counter-intelligence, his enjoyment of cloak-and-dagger missions provide a few clues to the young man's character.

Some of the cloak work must, indeed, have included fascinations. Exciting visits to New York City. The companionship of veiled ladies. Several trips to Richmond with the mysterious Mrs. Slater. The ex-divinity student, evidence shows, found time to indulge a taste for romance. What more could a young swain want? Swords and roses. A chance to write love letters in disappearing ink.

It would appear that John Surratt was enamoured of his New York cousin, Belle Seaman. In ink that did not disappear he wrote her from Washington, New York and Montreal. In one letter he calls her his *"very dear cousin Bell,"* underlining the term of endearment. Again he writes: "I have the shakes so badly by seeing a certain young Lady pass by."[12]

His sister Annie, too, was romantically inclined. To Cousin Belle, John Surratt wrote (on February 6, 1865): "I have just taken a peep into the parlor. Would you like to know what I saw there? Well, ma was sitting on the sofa, nodding first to one chair and then to another, next the piano. Anna is sitting in a corner dreaming, I expect, of J. W. Booth. Well,

---

[11] Lecture at Rockville, Md., December 8, 1870. Also quoted in Oldroyd, *op. cit.*, pp. 238–239.
[12] Quoted in Wilson, *op. cit.*, p. 103.

who is J. W. Booth? *She* can answer the question. But hark! The doorbell rings and Mr. J. W. Booth is announced. And listen to the scamperings. Such brushing and fixing."[13]

Booth calls, and the ladies primp. John Surratt notes his sister's blush and flurry. Some historians have wondered about Mrs. Surratt's "brushing and fixing." Lloyd Lewis suggests that Mrs. Surratt was "fascinated, probably to the point of romantic love, by Booth's matinee-idol manner."[14]

Lewis's suggestion seems somewhat improbable. But Mrs. Surratt would not have been the first middle-aged woman to sigh over the exciting Mr. Booth. Too, the landlady had reached that stage in life wherein maternal instinct may become confused with romance. As for Booth, he would not have hesitated to flatter Mrs. Surratt with a show of gallantry. He could use Mrs. Surratt. He wanted the aid of her son—aid that would be assured by her blessing, or at least her acceptance, of a certain enterprise. No doubt he paid her a few exaggerated compliments.

Louis Wiechmann beheld the cozy scene reported in John Surratt's letter. The boarder had a habit of peering into the parlor whenever the celebrated Mr. Booth called. Wiechmann, it seemed, had an eye for Anna Surratt. His interest was not reciprocated. Family legend would eventually have it that Anna slapped his face on one occasion. And some historians would conclude that jealousy of Booth led the rebuffed Government employee to bear false witness against the Surratts. This conclusion, however, is pure conjecture.

Wiechmann did subsequently testify that Mrs. Surratt and son retired with Booth into the privacy of her room for a secret conference that February night. Wiechmann may have erred on the date, but apparently such conferences did take place between Mrs. Surratt, John Surratt and Booth in the house on H Street. Witness to these privy "retirements" were Anna Surratt and Honora Fitzpatrick, as well as young Wiechmann. They did not, of course, hear what was said behind Mrs. Surratt's back-room door. Nor would anyone ever learn the substance of those private conversations. Mysteries, they would remain on record to embarrass Mrs. Surratt and her defenders.

According to Louis Wiechmann, Booth was first introduced to John Harrison Surratt, Jr., by Dr. Samuel Mudd of Bryantown, Maryland. Wiechmann would testify that this occurred in Washington in January, 1865, while he and John Surratt were strolling down 7th Street. Near Odd Fellow's Hall, Surratt was hailed by the doctor, an old friend, who was walking in company with a stranger.

Surratt introduced Wiechmann to Dr. Mudd. The physician, in turn, introduced his companion as a "Mr. Boone." The pleasant "Mr. Boone"

---

[13] National Archives, Correspondence, Surratt-Belle Seaman, War Dept. Records.
[14] Lloyd Lewis, "The Four Were Hanged," *Liberty Magazine*, February 11, 1928.

invited Surratt and Wiechmann to the National Hotel for refreshments. Surratt accepted the invitation, and Wiechmann tagged along. "Mr. Boone" served expensive brandy, suave cigars. Small talk revolved around Maryland neighbors and the war.

Nothing led Wiechmann to suspect the party of subversive intent (or so he later averred). But when he saw "Mr. Boone" again, at the house on H Street, the engaging gentleman seemed very friendly with John Surratt. And the name was John Wilkes Booth.[15]

In post-war recollection, John Surratt intimated that he had met Booth late in 1864. Booth had heard of him from Southern agents in Canada and had gone to some lengths to meet him and cultivate an acquaintance. As Surratt recalled it, the meeting was in Washington, on Pennsylvania Avenue, with Dr. Mudd making introductions at Booth's request.[16] Aside from the date, this coincides with Wiechmann's story. But in 1898, in an interview with the writer Hanson Hiss, Surratt stated that Booth was never introduced to him by Dr. Mudd. Surratt declared, "Booth came to me with a letter of introduction from a valued and trusted friend."

In his Rockville lecture Surratt said he responded cautiously to Booth's overtures. "We met several times," Surratt remembered. "But as he seemed to be reticent with regard to his purposes, and very anxious to get all the information out of me he could, I refused to tell him anything at all."

One is left to imagine the conversational sparring, with Booth nosing around the subject of back roads through lower Maryland—from Surrattsville, say, down to Pope's Creek or Port Tobacco on the Potomac. John Surratt's neck prickled. A Union counter-spy might ask such questions.

Finally, after guarded answers, Surratt asked Booth what the hinting meant. Booth agreed to confide his plans, saying, "First let me make known the motives that actuate me."

Before divulging his motives, the actor went through an elaborate pantomime. They were closeted in Booth's hotel room. According to Surratt's recollection, Booth tiptoed to the door, peeked out into the hall, then crossed the floor to glance into the wardrobe, then peered under the bed. "We must be careful," he warned melodramatically. "The very walls have ears."

Then the actor confided that his motives had to do with "thousands of men in Northern prisons whom the United States Government refuses to exchange." Booth reminded Surratt that the Confederacy was desperate for troops, whereas the Union leaders were willing to let Federal soldiers languish in Southern prisons because the U.S. did not need them. Booth whispered: "I have a proposition to make to you which, I think, if we can carry it out, would bring about the desired exchange."

---

[15] National Archives, Wiechmann testimony, War Dept. Records, JAO.
[16] Surratt lecture, Rockville, 1870.

The proposition was to kidnap President Lincoln and carry him south as hostage to Richmond! Surratt declared that the "unparalleled audacity of the scheme" left him "aghast."

In justification of his joining the enterprise, Surratt, in his post-war lecture, posed the question: "Where is there a young man in the North, with one spark of patriotism in his heart, who would not have joined with enthusiastic ardor in any undertaking for the capture of Jefferson Davis. . . . So I was led on by a desire to assist the South in gaining her independence."

Surratt thus asked historians to believe that Booth's proposal contained a flash of brilliant strategy, that the concept radiated patriotic fervor. It would seem that Booth did cherish glory dreams, and in young John Surratt he found a kindred soul. But in Booth's case, at least, the compulsive motive may have stemmed from some other and more twisted roots. It is even possible that the Holy Grail in view was gold-plated. John Surratt, too, may have been spurred by the gleam of prize money.

In this respect, one may wonder if Booth himself dreamed up the abduction scheme, or if it emanated from somewhere in the Confederate High Command. The South's military and governmental leaders would make austere denial of sponsoring such a plan, and a generation of ingenuous historians would accept the denial in eager faith. But the Confederacy's leaders also denied sponsorship of the Northwest Conspiracy, the Lake Erie strike, the New York fire raid. The Lincoln abduction plot may have been equally subject to diplomatic falsehood.

For Booth's plan coincided with the underground sabotage campaign led by Confederate Captains Hines and Beall. It is highly unlikely that the stage star would, for all his flamboyance, risk so desperate a venture without assurance of underground support and the approval of Richmond. Nor would it seem that actor Booth was so naive, so selflessly dedicated, as to scorn monetary award. Prize money was a common incentive to both sides in the Civil War.

Then there was John Surratt. When he met Booth he was operating as a Confederate courier and spy. Agreeing to team up with Booth, he took a job in Washington on December 28, 1864, with the Adams Express Company.[17] The job was a blind to keep him on hand in the capital. It is inconceivable that Surratt could have quit the Confederate Secret Service to join Booth in an independent venture, without the permission or cognizance of Richmond headquarters. So leaders in Richmond must have known of the abduction plot.

However the truth in respect to John Surratt remains obscure. He himself remains elusive, indecipherable.

John H. Surratt would outlive all nine of the other so-called Lincoln Conspirators. As late as 1906 he could be found in Baltimore, working as

---

[17] Oldroyd (from Wiechmann testimony), *op. cit.*, p. 164.

an auditor for the Old Bay Steamship Line—an elderly man, wispy-haired, with blue-veined hands, given to shadowy reserves and silences. Few who saw him on the Baltimore streets were aware that he had once been hunted by the U.S. Government as a notorious criminal. In age, as in youth, John Surratt maintained his obscurity.

When he died in 1916, John Surratt took with him to the grave the answers to many questions concerning the Lincoln murder case. But perhaps by that date he had forgotten them.

David E. Herold. Age 23. Former drugstore clerk. Drifter. Addicted to night-owling and quail hunting.

Contemporary photographs show David Herold as an individual with two faces—a surprising duality of countenance.

The full-face portrait presents a young man with reasonably well-molded features and an expression of at least average intelligence. The eyes are expressive. The mouth is normally composed. Given sympathetic study, this countenance may be seen as containing a suggestion of sensitivity. If the gaze seems faintly troubled, under other circumstances it might express amusement. Contemporary young ladies might have rated the portrait as handsome.

Herold's profile photograph bears scarcely a family resemblance to the full-face. The forehead is canted, the nose curved like a sabre, the mouth small and tight, the chin receding. The cheek has a pouchy sag, and the eye, under a heavy lid, looks beady and moronic. This Herold might be the other's half-wit cousin.

These are police photographs, taken without the benefit of studied pose and artifice. Both are taken by the same camera, presumably at one sitting and by the same cameraman. But by a mere shift in focus the camera finds two Herolds: the one who is a competent horseman, a good shot, an adept field scout, a trustworthy lieutenant; and the Herold described as a fatuous and irresponsible dunce, an over-age juvenile delinquent.

The Herold family were Marylanders who had moved to Washington long before the Civil War. The family resided on 8th Street, S.E., not far from the Washington Navy Yard, where Herold's father was chief clerk in the Navy Yard store. By all accounts, the family upheld the rules of Victorian respectability. With the exception of young David, the problem child.

Problem he may well have been, for he was brought up in the mutual lap of seven sisters who probably babied, spoiled, teased, chided, flattered, cuffed, and petted him to distraction. Too late his father sent him to Charlotte Hall Academy, some distance below Bryantown, in St. Mary's County, Maryland.

Herold's aspirations did not include scholarship. Soon he was back on

8th Street, returned to what could certainly be called the bosom of his family where seven sisters and their ma fussed over him.

Old enough to wear galluses, Herold sought to escape this petticoat tyranny. No doubt his love of bird-hunting developed as a compensation. He took to hitching rides down to lower Maryland. His conversation—he was a talky boy—chattered constantly of guns, dogs, and horses. Because he hung around blacksmith shops and stables, his neighbors thought him shiftless and scatter-brained. But he was amiable and inoffensive.

In 1860 or thereabouts, David Herold went to work for a druggist. When the war broke out he was clerk in the pharmacy of Francis S. Walsh, on 8th Street near the Navy Yard. He worked there for about a year, lodging with Mr. Walsh. Eventually questioned about Herold, Walsh said he found "nothing objectionable in his character," but "very little reliability could be placed in him."[18] Again we have the dual countenance of David Herold.

In 1863 Herold obtained a clerk's job in the pharmacy of Wm. S. Thompson, located in the heart of Washington at 15th Street and New York Avenue. Druggist Thompson considered Herold reliable enough to be trusted with an errand to the White House.

Herold met President Lincoln. He delivered a bottle of castor oil, and Lincoln—probably with some appropriate, thigh-slapping joke—asked to have it charged. On a day for afterthought, David Herold would recall the President's sense of humor.

Herold's father died in 1864. Family and friends would state that this bereavement set "the boy" off on a fatal course. But he had already steered into the ominous current. Wiechmann saw David Herold at Surratt's Tavern in 1863.[19] Herold himself eventually testified that he had known John Surratt before the war, perhaps from schooldays at Charlotte Hall. But his visiting the Surratts in 1863, when the tavern catered to a Secessionist clientele, suggests Herold's initiation into the Confederate underground.

Herold shook his head when subsequently questioned on his first meeting with John Wilkes Booth. For the record, he said:

> I do not remember exactly. I think I was a clerk with Wm. S. Thompson. . . . It was the night Booth played the "Marble Heart" . . . the time when Booth had a ball taken from his neck by some surgeon in Washington. I met Mr. Booth [after that] off and on, sometimes once a week, or maybe two or three times. We would always stand and have a chat.

Sometimes they chatted over ale and oysters in various restaurants. Occasionally they repaired to the National Hotel to chat in Booth's room. Booth presented Herold with complimentary tickets to the theater. He

18 Oldroyd, *op. cit.*, p. 137.
19 National Archives, War Dept. Records, File "W," R.B.P. 99, JAO.

invited Herold "to go behind the scenes at different times." Herold went backstage to see him. They chatted again, in the star's dressing room.

One might wonder (as did Herold's inquisitors) what the celebrated stage star saw in the tacky drugstore clerk. Herold implied these intimate chats were about nothing in particular. But one time, at the National Hotel, "I went there to see him about some coal oil. He said he was in the coal oil business."[20] A more likely topic would have been horses and guns and the roads of lower Maryland.

Apparently Herold's responses were somewhat sluggish until Booth, perhaps by accident, touched the Jack-in-a-box trigger: the complimentary theater tickets. After the show, Herold babbled in excitement.

Herold was stage struck. Booth must have wanted to laugh. Now he had this errand boy hooked on a lure that had held far bigger fish. And Herold could be very useful with his knowledge of lower Maryland. Besides, as a pharmacy clerk he would have a handy acquaintance with drugs.

Probably Booth handled the line with consummate skill. Small promises, but big hints. No reason a smart man, with the right coaching, couldn't achieve a theatrical career. No quicker way in the world to fortune and fame.

Booth's biographer, Francis Wilson, called this "feeding Herold's fledgling fancy for the stage with golden dreams of public applause."[21]

So the stage star acquired the understudy. David E. Herold. With *his* profile!

Samuel Bland Arnold. Age 28. Ex-Confederate soldier. Commissary clerk at Fortress Monroe, Virginia.

Soft, dark eyes in a youthful face with a soft, full-lipped mouth—Arnold's is hardly the countenance one might associate with the resolution, resourcefulness, stamina, and intrepidity usually supposed to be the attributes required for cloak-and-dagger work. However, secret agents seldom look like secret agents. Arnold's face, as photographed, strikes one as intelligent. And a fairly perceptive intelligence seems to characterize the man.

The files of the Bureau of Military Justice contain an odd little brief on Arnold. It reads:

> Samuel B. Arnold was born at Georgetown, D.C., of highly respectable parents. . . . He was first sent to be educated at Georgetown College, from there he was sent to the Reverend J. H. Dashills, [in] Baltimore County, his parents having removed from Georgetown to Baltimore. He was one year in Rockingham County, Virginia, under the charge of the Reverend Mr. Gibbins, and afterward sent to Saint Timothy Hall, Catonsville, Maryland, and place (*sic*) under the Rev. L. Vanbakelin. Lately was engaged

---

20 National Archives, War Dept. Records, File "H," R.B.P. 38, JAO.
21 *Op. cit.*, p. 61.

in Clerking. He is now between 30 and 31 years of age. On his approach to manhood he was a restless and wayward youth, inclined to bad associations. He had been in the Rebel Army.[22]

The foregoing tells us about as much of Arnold's character as a tintype would tell us about the character of a neurotic. The subject's age is incorrectly given, and the usual official moralizing comes by way of a biased military report. Arnold's "waywardness" would probably not have been reported had he joined the Union Army.

However, Arnold caught the prevailing war fever. In company with some other Baltimore swains, he entered Virginia to enlist.

Service drudgery may have dampened his ardor. By 1864, Arnold was out of uniform, drifting aimlessly and impecuniously around Baltimore. In the summer of that fourth year of the war he was merely one of a million young civilians destined to live out his days in the comfortable role of a nonentity. This secure, if mundane, anonymity seemed assured by his employment as a harvest hand on a farm near Hookstown, Maryland, a village not far from Baltimore. But there he received a letter.

A companion farm hand had reason to remember Sam Arnold's letter. Months later, Mr. L. P. D. Newman visited the Baltimore office of Provost Marshal McPhail to volunteer the following testimony:

> I was threshing at the Julius Graham's farm [September last] on the Reister town road. Samuel B. Arnold was one of the hands. While there Arnold received a letter I think delivered by his brother William. He broke open the seal in my presence, read it, and remarked he was flush.

In support of this interesting announcement, Arnold handed Newman the letter to read. As Newman recalled it:

> The letter was ambiguous, exceedingly so. Had either a fifty or a twenty dollar note enclosed, and spoke about business, but what kind I could not tell. I asked what it meant. He replied, you will know all about it some of these days through the newspapers.[23]

Surely Booth assembled in his train some of the most loquacious undercover men in the history of clandestine operations. With the possible exception of John Surratt, all connected with the Lincoln enterprise seemed determined to compromise the plan. Sam Arnold's display of a letter obviously written in code, his dark hint concerning "some of these days"—these gestures were typical. Booth himself led the mummery with exaggerated whispering, furtive peering and theatrical posturing as obvious as the acting of a showboat villain.

If the context of events is indicative, the code letter, which left Arnold "flush," summoned him to a Baltimore meeting with Booth at Barnum's Hotel. Oldroyd dates this rendezvous as taking place in "the first part of

---

[22] National Archives, War Dept. Records, File "S," R.B.P. 554, JAO.
[23] National Archives, War Dept. Records, File "N," Doc. 209, JAO.

September, 1864."[24] The historian's prose style seems to set the tone of this meeting:

"The two [Booth and Arnold] were engaged in conversation upon their former school days while they sipped their wine and smoked cigars that Booth had ordered. They were interrupted by a knock at the door. When opened, Michael O'Laughlin stepped in, and after an introduction to Arnold the trio sipped and smoked. It was here that Booth ventured his proposition to kidnap the President." Arnold and O'Laughlin showed the proper "politics and feelings" and, after some more sipping and smoking, "Booth invited them to join him in the conspiracy."

As in Herold's case, the actor seems to have offered the two Baltimoreans some incentives a little more substantial than a mere chance for glory. Arnold's advance payment included a new suit of clothes. O'Laughlin also seems to have benefitted by way of haberdasheries.

On the strength of this meeting at Barnum's, it would appear that Arnold and O'Laughlin were Booth's first abduction recruits. Later that autumn, Booth journeyed to New York, Boston, and Montreal, where he conferred with Confederate agents in Canada. He did not see Arnold and O'Laughlin again until January, 1865. Calling another Baltimore meeting, he entrusted to their care a trunk containing two guns, ammunition, a brace of revolvers, some knives, and a pair of handcuffs "to shackle the President." Arnold and O'Laughlin were instructed to smuggle the firearms and other items into Washington after Booth went on ahead.

Historians usually link the names Arnold and O'Laughlin as though the two were Tweedledee and Tweedledum. The comparison does an injustice to Sam Arnold. As the abduction plot matured, Arnold had sense enough to see it as a dangerously ramshackle contrivance. To his credit, he would risk Booth's malice by protesting the jerry-built scheme. In the end he would sensibly try to back out.

But by then it was too late, and his letter of resignation came close to being a death warrant.

Michael O'Laughlin. Age 27. Clerk in Baltimore feed store.
The biographical brief on O'Laughlin in the files of the Bureau of Military Justice reads as follows:

Michael O. Laughlin (*sic*) was born in the City of Baltimore. . . . He was educated at a School conducted by a highly respectable Teacher at the corner of Front and LaFayette Sts., and after leaving School learned the trade of manufacturing ornamental Plaster work, and also acquired the art of Engraving. The company he was in the habit of associating with was not of a character that a person indisposed to evil would have made choice of. His appearance was generally of a genteel character.[25]

24 *Op. cit.*, pp. 56–57.
25 National Archives, War Dept. Records, File "S," Doc. 554, JAO.

The appearance registered by glass-plate camera might be character-ized either as genteel or as foxy, depending on semantic interpetations and on points of view. O'Laughlin faces the official photographer defiantly, with a thrust to his small-boned jaw and a faint pugnacity in the eyes. The heavy mustache and light imperial are deceiving.

Like Arnold, O'Laughlin had known Booth since boyhood. The O'Laughlins lived at 57 N. Exeter Street, Baltimore. The Booths moved into a house across the street. Mike O'Laughlin tagged after the narcotic-eyed John Wilkes—a willing little terrier trotting at the heels of a high-strung show dog.

O'Laughlin probably imbibed of politics at the bar in Barnum's Hotel. He, too, may have joined the secret band which was captained by the barber, Fernandina. O'Laughlin's older brother joined the Knights of the Golden Circle, and another Knight would testify that he "thought" Michael did, too.[26]

When the war exploded, O'Laughlin journeyed to Virginia to don Confederate uniform. According to report, he was discharged from the Confederate Army in June, 1862.[27] The report does not define the discharge. He may have served out a short-term enlistment, or he may have been dismissed as unfit. In either case, his service with the Rebel Army probably evoked the bad character rating in the official (Federal) report.

When Booth found him in Baltimore, Mike was working for his brother in the feed and produce business. He was a dapper little fellow with a taste for expensive cheroots and plaid vests. O'Laughlin was delighted to get into Booth's scheme. But that was in September, 1864. As of March, 1865, he would have been delighted to get out of it. But the high sign was on him. This adult game of stump-the-leader would cost him his life.

George Andrew Atzerodt. Age 33. Port Tobacco carriage painter. Boat-man on the Potomac underground.

In 1832, at Seebach, in the district of Langensalza, Prussia, George Atzerodt was born. When he was eight years old, he was wafted by fate to the shores of Maryland, but he never became an American, legally or intellectually. He could not even pass muster as an apprentice blacksmith.

Of Booth's co-conspirators, Atzerodt was probably the earthiest. And much of that earth seems to have been on his wrists, on the nape of his neck, in his ears, and in the pores of his nose. Still, by all accounts, he was a good-natured sort of clod—an amiable animal with the face of a dancing bear. That is, until the war routed him out of his den. Then he emerged, so to speak, scratching and grinning, attracted by the scent of battlefield carrion. In his habitat, Port Tobacco, Maryland, the scent was strong.

---

[26] National Archives, War Dept. Records, File "S," Doc. 81, JAO.
[27] National Archives, War Dept. Records, File "C," Doc. 316, JAO.

Through this Potomac village drifted all kinds of war supplies. From across the river came the echo of gunfire. There was money, Atzerodt learned, in warfare. A smart operator could cash in on the black market or the flea market. Atzerodt's ursine instincts took him into the flea market.

Some years before the shooting started, he had arrived in Port Tobacco with his older brother John. The little town showed promise as a shipping center. Boasting an artesian well, it invited a tourist trade—pleasure steamers from Washington. Business was brisk. (It was by no means limited to tobacco. The town's name, incidentally, was originally Indian— "Potobac"—a variation of "Potomac." Today, the town exists in memory only, a few cottages and a sunken pier at the end of a lonely road.)

The Brothers Atzerodt set up a carriage repair shop in Port Tobacco. John, the more intelligent, worked as mechanic. Thick George applied the varnish and paint. For a time the two prospered. Then George and his brother separated. There may have been trouble over beer bills and a local seamstress who caught George's eye. At any rate, John Atzerodt packed up his tools and moved to Baltimore, where he married in strict accordance with respectability. Later, John said the trouble with George concerned politics.

Early in the war, George Atzerodt took to rowing his Secessionist friends back and forth across the Potomac River. He was actively engaged in blockade-running (he probably would have done it for either side, were the prices right) when John Surratt arrived in Port Tobacco via the underground. Atzerodt knew all about available horses, back roads, hidden boats. In time, he was invited to Washington City to meet a Mr. J. W. Booth.

Atzerodt was also introduced to the boarding house on H Street. Mrs. Surratt did not like this crude specimen who snuffled with a German accent and ate with his knife. When she found a bottle in his room, she told John Mr. Atzerodt would have to lodge elsewhere; she would not permit liquor on the premises. In deference to her wishes, Atzerodt removed to the Pennsylvania House (or Kimmel House, as it was known), a low hostelry more in keeping with his habits and habiliments.

Many historians have since wondered how Booth came to tolerate the loutish Atzerodt, inviting him into his secret camarilla. As an oarsman for a furtive rowboat, he might blend into a musky riverside littoral. Why did Booth fetch him out of his element, risk him on a mission in Washington City?

One answer might be that there were many boorish louts in Washington, D.C., at that date. Thousands of navvies and rough roustabouts worked on supply jobs or defense projects in the nation's war-busy capital. The man who was nicknamed "Port Tobacco" (or "Plug Tobacco," as some called him) mixed with reasonable congruity in this floating populace of shovel hands and muleteers.

But Atzerodt was extremely conspicuous in a hotel parlor. Booth invited him to the National, took him to dine at Gautier's Restaurant, and finally selected him for a sensitive post at the Kirkwood House—an establishment catering to a top hat clientele that included the Vice President of the United States. There the uneasy "Port Tobacco," installed as a guest, was left with instructions to murder the Vice President.

What did Booth have in mind?

In the Machiavellian chess of secret intelligence one finds a pawn called the "fool spy," who is sent into enemy country on a mission known to be fatally impossible. In short, this operator is used as a decoy, deliberately planted to divert the enemy's counter-intelligence. While counter-intelligence is diverted by the "fool," who walks, blindfolded, straight into a firing squad, the master spy slips over the border with impunity.

One of Booth's favorite words was "sacrifice," and George Atzerodt could have been a handy pawn.

Dr. Samuel A. Mudd. Age 32. Country physician on family farm near Bryantown, Maryland. Probable Rebel partisan.

Oldroyd describes Dr. Mudd as "the most inoffensive and respectable in appearance" of the Lincoln Conspirators.[28] Bishop pictures him as "tall, thin, [with] a bald forehead, blue eyes and brick-colored hair and whiskers."[29] To General T. M. Harris, U.S.A., a contemporary, Dr. Mudd "had the appearance of a natural-born liar and deceiver."[30] Eisenschiml tells us Dr. Mudd was a "gentle, kindly country practitioner."[31] The dim photographic portrait which dominates the parlor of the ancestral Mudd home today is a ghost that tells us nothing. Who, what, was Dr. Samuel Mudd?

One of a numerous and highly-respected clan, Samuel Mudd existed as a quiet man on a quiet farm in the interior of Charles County, Maryland. As a student he had attended Georgetown College in the District of Columbia. Had studied medicine at the University of Maryland, Baltimore. Had married in 1857. With the onset of the Civil War he had slowed an active practice as a physician to devote his time to farming. He was not, therefore, the busy horse-and-buggy doctor sometimes pictured. Kindly he may have been, but he was also rather humorless and exacting. He owned ten slaves. It is on record that when one of these refused to work, Mudd shot the Negro through the leg.

Some considered him a Secession sympathizer. He may have joined the Jarboes, Colonel Samuel Cox and others in the county as an active anti-

---

[28] *Op. cit.*, p. 138.
[29] *Op. cit.*, p. 276.
[30] T. M. Harris, *Assassination of Lincoln* (Boston: American Citizen Co., 1892), p. 23.
[31] *Op. cit.*, p. 259.

Union partisan, working with the secret underground. Of this, the evidence hints rather than proves.

One Sunday in November, 1864, Booth attended services at St. Mary's Church near Bryantown. He was guest in the pew of Dr. Queen. In a neighboring pew sat Dr. and Mrs. Samuel Mudd. After Mass, the handsome actor, a nominal Episcopalian, asked an introduction to the Mudds. The doctor responded by inviting Booth to his farm to spend the night.

Dr. Mudd would eventually state that the visit had to do with a potential horse sale. But the physician's recollection of Booth's overnight stay seems vague as to detail, and one might think that the visit of a famous stage star would have been most memorable to this country household. Evidently Mrs. Mudd did not cotton to the distinguished guest. One detail she recalled with clarity. After Booth's departure she found in his room a letter, apparently dropped by accident. Long afterward she wrote that a glance at the missive "convinced me that some poor man's home had been wrecked by the handsome face and wily ways of Booth."[32]

Early in December Booth again visited the Mudd farm. While there, he rode about the countryside, inspecting land and stables as a prospective buyer. A deal with Dr. Mudd failed to materialize. But the celebrated visitor did purchase a carriage horse from a neighbor, Squire Gardiner. The horse was a dark bay, blind in one eye.

The authorities would contend that Booth's visit to the Mudd home involved something more than a horse deal. And what of Dr. Mudd's visit to Booth's hotel in Washington during the ensuing winter? Louis Wiechmann would say he saw Dr. Mudd draw some lines on the back of an envelope and hand the envelope to Booth. Was it a map?

In the spring of 1865 Dr. Mudd would be called upon to answer these and other questions. An inability to answer them to the Government's satisfaction would condemn the doctor to many months in Purgatory. Subsequently he would win amnesty and national respect by a display of monumental heroism. Still, the questions would remain unanswered. And so would a final question. Did he or did he not belong on the Government's list as one of Booth's co-conspirators?

The face of the ghostly portrait which overlooks the parlor of the Mudd home today is an enigma, and its features are fading.

Edward Spangler. Age about 40. Assistant stage carpenter and scene shifter at Ford's Theater.

A composite of ignorance, incompetence, poverty, sloth, turpitude, distemper and alcoholism, the face of Edward Spangler is a stereotype. It was one doubtless seen by the tipstaffs on the opening day of Newgate. It is

---

[32] Nettie Mudd (ed.), *The Life of Dr. Samuel A. Mudd* (Marietta, Ga.: Continental Book Co., 1955), p. 30.

seen today on the street we call Skid Row. It will be seen tomorrow in any police line-up.

It was seen in the company of John Wilkes Booth in the winter of 1864 and the early spring of 1865. A journeyman carpenter from Pennsylvania, Spangler had worked on the Booth estate at Bel Air when the family was repairing Tudor Hall. He was coarse, foul-mouthed, lazy, shabby, undependable. But Booth liked him. Spangler could down a "spider" at one quaff, and he was an expert hand at crabbing. Booth had a taste for dram drinkers and Maryland crabs.

Probably through Booth, the tramp carpenter obtained employment as a stage hand at Ford's in Washington. There he became the actor's devoted horse holder. Booth paid him off in drinks.

It would be contended that Ned Spangler did more than hold Booth's horse. Authorities would have it that he opened doors for Booth, closed doors for Booth, obliged Booth with little odd jobs.

And then there was the matter of rope. It seemed the abduction plan demanded a heavy coil of rope, and some eighty-one feet of rope were found crammed in a carpetbag belonging to the sleazy stagehand.

That rope came close to hanging Edward Spangler.

Lewis Paine. Age 20. Paroled Confederate soldier. Possible secret agent.
His full name was Lewis Paine Powell. He preferred aliases. Sometimes he used "Wood," or "The Reverend Wood." Sometimes he called himself "Hull." Usually he signed himself "Paine." This last almost won him execution as member of a band of Western desperadoes by that name, or as one of the Payne brothers who participated in the Confederate raid on St. Albans, Vermont. At the time he enlisted under Booth, he carried a parolee's Oath of Allegiance signed "Paine."

Father was the Rev. George C. Powell, Baptist minister with flock at Live Oak Station, Florida. One of nine children. Reared in backwoods Alabama, country school. So read the historical biographies on Lewis Paine.

One might believe this stripling developed the muscles of his body and mind wrestling king alligators in the swamps below Tallahassee. We can only guess at his adolescent pastimes, but we know he possessed the biceps of a junior giant and the combative instincts of a panther. He was a handsome young primitive. As he listened to hard-shell Southern sermons, his nostrils would flare and a chill intensity would stare from his eyes.

> *Arise for the day is dawning, and you lie slumbering on;*
> *Your father has buckled on his armor, and off to the war has gone.*

In this case, it was the father's sons who went—Lewis, aged sixteen, and his two older brothers. They enlisted soon after Sumter. Serving with the Second Florida Infantry, Lewis was baptized by fire early.

Young Paine fought in the Valley. He fought on the plain. He fought in the Peninsular Campaign, at Antietam, at Chancellorsville. By the time he was eighteen he was as inured to blood, fury and agony as a Carthaginian.

His two older brothers were slain at Murfreesboro.

Out of the crucible, Lewis Paine emerged as a front-line soldier's front-line soldier. Private Paine was a good workman. He was neither afraid of being killed nor afraid to kill.

Yet this boyish Neanderthal was not entirely drained of emotion. Once, on leave in Richmond, he betook himself to the theater, the first he had ever attended. The gilt boxes, the gleaming chandeliers, the gaslit stage, the actors striding about and declaiming—this world of make-believe stirred the combat veteran as battlefield reality never had. After the play, Lewis Paine waited at the stage door to see the star. Most case histories have it that this was the means of Paine's introduction to John Wilkes Booth.

At Richmond Paine's regiment became part of Lee's army and was attached to the corps of A. P. Hill.[33] Paine marched to Gettysburg. He charged with Pickett's men, fell wounded on the field, was captured on July 3, 1863, by counter-charging Federals. Taken as prisoner to the Gettysburg General Hospital, he soon recovered and was put to work as a male nurse. "Imagine," writes Francis Wilson, "the humiliation, the outraged feelings of this fire-eating Confederate set to nursing the enemies of his country."[34] But evidence, perhaps unknown to Booth's biographer, inserts another angle into the case. A defiant P.O.W. might go to prison. A cooperative male nurse might escape, especially if given underground aid.

In Gettysburg Hospital, Paine became acquainted with two sisters from Baltimore. The Misses Margaret and Mary Branson had volunteered as temporary nurses to care for Confederate wounded. Both spoke a Southern accent, but the authorities shrugged—let the girls fuss over the Rebs if they wanted to; it gave the Sanitary Commission people more time with the Union boys. So the Misses Branson fluttered over Lewis Paine, at that time answering to the name of Private Powell. Presently Private Powell was transferred to the West Buildings Hospital in Baltimore.

While in Baltimore, Paine paid a visit or two to the Branson girls. Their mother ran a boardinghouse at the corner of Fayette and Eutaw Streets. This establishment had a gray Secessionist tinge, not unlike a certain H Street boardinghouse in Washington. Perhaps that attracted Paine to the address. The girls preferred to say that they were the attraction.[35]

Now Paine's movements are hard to follow. In October, 1863, he slipped away from Baltimore and disappeared. But historians are uncertain about

---

[33] J. E. Buckingham, Sr., *Reminiscences and Souvenirs of the Assassination of Abraham Lincoln* (Washington, D.C.: Rufus H. Darby, 1894), p. 39.

[34] *Op. cit.*, p. 96.

[35] National Archives, War Dept. Records, File "B," Doc. 187–8, JAO.

it. Bishop writes: "There is an unexplained hitch in his [Paine's] record."[36] According to Oldroyd, Paine "deserted, returning to the Confederate Army, remaining at Fauquier, Va., until January 1, 1865, when he again deserted and returned to Baltimore."[37] Mystery is only compounded by this inexact usage of the term "desertion."

Paine escaped to Virginia—not exactly a defection. And although official records in the U.S. War Department files call Paine a Confederate deserter, one may doubt that this young warrior deserted the Confederate camp. Evidence suggests something more devious.

Early in January, 1865, Paine showed up at the Branson house in Baltimore. He came to call on Miss Maggie Branson. As she testified later: "He was dressed in black clothes. He said he was from Fauquier County, Virginia, and had just moved in town. . . . On his second [next] visit to the house he said his name was Paine. . . . He talked a lot about Mosby. . . . I went to church with him."[38]

Paine was also attentive to Miss Mary Branson. She, too, gained the impression that he had been with Mosby's command. She also gathered that "he was a short time since with Harry Gilmore, but he said they were such a rough class of men that they did not suit him."[39]

Paine produced a Federal parole of some kind signed in Fauquier County, Virginia. It seemed he had, indeed, been with Mosby. A man named Paine, serving with Mosby in the summer of 1864, captured the famous Union scout, Dick Blazer and took him to Richmond.

One would also like to know Paine's connection with the raider Gilmore, whose men were too "rough" for his sensibilities. If overly rough for Lewis Paine, they must have been rough indeed.

On January 19 Paine transferred his address from Miller's Hotel to the Branson boardinghouse. Quiet, unobtrusive, he seemed an exemplary boarder. Then one day a colored servant girl exhibited what he took to be impudence. Paine smashed her in the face and, as she fell, kicked her in the groin. The girl swore out a warrant. Arrested for assault and battery, Paine appeared before Provost Marshal Colonel Woolley. The Federal Provost, more concerned by the parolee's presence in Baltimore than by his penchant for mayhem, ordered Paine to stay two hundred miles north of the war front.

Paine, apparently, did go to New York. It would seem he even visited Canada. Meantime, he had visited Washington.

One February night a stranger rang the doorbell of Mrs. Surratt's boardinghouse at 541 H Street. Boarder Wiechmann answered the door. He saw before him a "six-foot man who wore a big, black, shabby overcoat with

36 *Op. cit.*, p. 77.
37 *Op. cit.*, p. 137.
38 National Archives, War Dept. Records, File "B," Doc. 187, JAO.
39 National Archives, War Dept. Records, File "B," Doc. 186, JAO.

his hands buried deep in the coat pockets." The stranger asked to see John Surratt. Told Surratt wasn't home, he asked to see Mrs. Surratt, giving the name of Wood—Lewis Wood. Mrs. Surratt invited Wood in. He said he had not eaten that day. The widow hurried to the kitchen. At table, Wood "ate voraciously, as if very hungry. He had the eye of an eagle, and his hair was jet black." Wiechmann asked him where he was from. He said he was from Baltimore, "a clerk in the china store of a Mr. Parr." When the meal was consumed, the visitor at once retired. In the morning he was gone.[40]

On the evening of March 13, Wiechmann again answered the door. There stood Mr. Wood. "A complete transformation had been effected in his appearance." Wood was now attired in a new gray suit, a jaunty hat and a "pretty black necktie." To Wiechmann's further surprise, Mr. Wood announced himself as the Reverend Paine. Wiechmann found himself confused. The ladies in the Surratt parlor accepted the Reverend politely. He joined Miss Anna Surratt at the piano. "Then he sat down to a game of euchre, and one of the ladies (Miss Fitzpatrick) called him Mr. Wood." Oldroyd speaks the question for Wiechmann. "What was at the bottom of it all?"[41]

At the bottom of it was a meeting between John Wilkes Booth and Lewis Paine. Early that February, Booth had flitted to Baltimore for a conference with Arnold and O'Laughlin. As Wilson tells it: "One day in front of Barnum's Hotel, Booth saw Payne (sic) passing by. He recognized and hailed him."[42]

Wilson would have it that the actor had never forgotten the six-foot athlete who saluted him at a stage door in Richmond. Other accounts follow this line. The Baltimore meeting was sheer accident. Booth immediately recognized Paine, was delighted to see this handsome admirer, took him into the bar for a drink. Then—and only then—did he find in Paine a firebrand, seething with hate for Abe Lincoln. Here was just the champion he'd been looking for! An old front-line soldier who boasted (as Paine apparently did) that he had drunk pre-battle toasts from the skull of a dead Yankee!

Did mere chance bring Paine and Booth together in front of Barnum's Hotel that day? The odds of such a meeting are long. Would a stage star be liable to remember a soldier he had seen but once, on a night long past? It is easier to believe this meeting in Baltimore came through design.

Design or chance, the meeting occurred. When the two parted that day, they had formed a lethal bond. Paine lacked mental capacity, but the capability of his muscled hand was impressive. The actor, his own hand swamped by the athlete's, knew a deadly grip when he felt one.

---

[40] Oldroyd, op. cit., pp. 166–167.
[41] Ibid., pp. 167–168.
[42] Op. cit., p. 95.

So the murderous corporation was formed. And a day would come when the United States Government would charge John Wilkes Booth, Mrs. Mary Surratt, John H. Surratt, David E. Herold, Samuel Bland Arnold, Michael O'Laughlin, George A. Atzerodt, Dr. Samuel A. Mudd, Edward Spangler, and Lewis Paine with the assassination of Abraham Lincoln and the attempted assassination of Secretary of State Seward, Vice President Johnson, and General Grant.

The indictment left out one accessory.

On February 20, 1865, Louis Wiechmann informed a fellow clerk in the War Department that a conspiracy was brewing in the house on H Street. The clerk—a Captain Gleason—informed his superior officer of the matter. The War Department did nothing.

CHAPTER **4**

To Kidnap or to Kill?

BOOTH'S ORIGINAL abduction plans were masterpieces of folly. Had they been spur-of-the-moment contrivances, there might have been some excuse for patent defects, but Booth confided to his diary that the kidnap plot (he called it "capture") was months in the making. Booth's biographer, Francis Wilson, says he devoted four years to the scheme.

During the autumn of 1864 Booth spent hours and days in feverish planning. For weeks he pored over maps, charted roads, studied the lay of the land. When he wasn't scouting the Maryland back country or seeking recruits in Baltimore and New York, he was prowling around Washington, or pacing his hotel room in the National, scheming, pondering, his brain simmering.

The strategic objective of the abduction plot had just enough in it to make it seem valid. The capture of the United States President would deal a staggering morale blow to the North. Lincoln's impoundment in some Confederate stronghold would certainly inspirit the desperate South. Too, there was the possibility that Lincoln could be used as hostage for a massive prisoner exchange.

Contrary minds might argue that the President's abduction would arouse the North to volcanic fury; that savage reprisal might be visited on Southern territories occupied by Federal troops; that Washington might order the shooting of captive Confederate officers unless Lincoln were returned unharmed. Still, all grand strategic plans involve degrees of risk. Perhaps in objective Booth's abduction plan was as valid as the move that took Lee to Gettysburg or Grant to Cold Harbor.

Considerably less valid were Booth's tactical schemes, the *modus operandi* for attaining the strategic objective. In common with all lofty Jominis and Clausewitzes, he not only designed a master plan, he devised several alternatives to be employed if preferentially opportune. But then he committed the error of failing to make provision for operational setbacks. Master plan and alternatives lacked that strategic mechanism which permits defeated generals to withdraw their forces to the safety of what is known as "a previously prepared position." The actor strategist invented withdrawal mechanisms for the high command—namely, Booth—but his troops, in event of defeat, were to fend for themselves.

Booth's master plan projected the "capture" while President Lincoln attended a Washington theater. Preferably Ford's Theater; Grover's if necessary. Lincoln patronized both.

Booth was well acquainted with the two playhouses. In 1863 he had headed the Grover Stock Company, and he had played at Ford's. He favored Ford's for the abduction ambush, apparently because of its location and accommodations.

Booth arranged to receive some of his mail at Ford's, a step which gave him an excuse for frequent visits. He patronized Taltavul's saloon next door where he could meet, prime, and pump the stage crew. Whenever opportunity presented, he would stroll into a dressing room to chat with some fellow thespian or lounge in the wings watching rehearsals. By December, 1864, he had the stage, the boxes, the corridors, the backstage spaces, every alcove and cranny blueprinted on his mind.

At Ford's the State box—the President's box—consisted of upper boxes 7 and 8 which could be made into one compartment by the removal of the interior partition. In the fashion of Victorian architecture, the boxes flanked the apron of the stage, so that patrons in an upper box looked directly down on the players behind the footlights.

Booth proposed to trap Lincoln in the State box at Ford's by the simple expedient of charging in on him during the second or third act of a play. At a given signal, a hand would turn off the main gas valve. As the theater was plunged into darkness, the abductors would dash into the box. Booth would manacle the President while Surratt, Arnold, and O'Laughlin held others in the box at bay. Lincoln, trussed, would then be lowered to the stage (a good ten feet). The captive would be rushed through the wings to the backstage exit, thrown into a carriage waiting at the stage door, and spirited out of the capital.

At least seventy things could go wrong with such a complex plan. Unquestionably the audience would riot when the lights went out. What was to prevent some of the rioters from mobbing up on the stage, thereby blocking an escape through the wings? Naturally the actors on stage would panic. What if the ingénue fainted and fell against the scenery, bringing a flat crashing down on the kidnapers? What if Lincoln's guests put up a fight? What if the President himself fought back? Brawny, sinewy Abe Lincoln was tall as a tree compared to Booth, and had arms that had once split rails. Booth gloried in the title of "gymnastic actor," but a battle with this President of the United States would not be a simulated combat with some grease-painted Macduff.

These were petty hazards compared with those that could wreck the long-haul abduction procedure. The kidnap coach had to get out of the District of Columbia. Plans called for a run down the lower Maryland peninsula. This meant the carriage must either make a roundabout run through Upper Marlboro or cross the Anacostia River by way of the guarded Navy Yard (Eastern Branch) Bridge.

Presumably when the carriage reached the Maryland side of the river, fresh horses would be waiting. Another relay would wait near Piscataway. From there the equipage would race on down to Port Tobacco, where the underground would have a barge in readiness to ferry the kidnap party across the Potomac to Mathias Point, Virginia. One more river remained to be crossed—the Rappahannock—Port Conway to Port Royal. Then away, full gallop, down through Bowling Green to Richmond.

To make time, the kidnap coach must stay on the main turnpikes, on which it would pass through a number of towns and villages, and be as visible as a circus wagon. Even harder to conceal would be a big, slow, getaway barge. Federal gunboats patrolled the Potomac and might be encountered up the Rappahannock. And as a final, a truly panoramic obstacle to this abduction run, Grant's United States Army stood in a giant sector overlooking Richmond. All main roads leading down to the Confederate capital were hazardous. Blue cavalry patrols probed the city's outskirts. If the abductors ran this gantlet into Richmond, they could thank nothing short of a miracle.

Booth's second abduction plan, an alternate, at least had the virtue of containing an easier "capture." Lincoln frequently visited the Soldiers' Home, a military hospital some three miles out of Washington at the rural end of 7th Street. Usually the newspapers announced an intended visit, and the abductors had only to read the morning editions to discover the President's itinerary. Woods shadowed the winding road as it approached the hospital grounds. There were a number of likely places where armed horsemen might ambush the Presidential party. Here the chances of waylaying Lincoln were relatively good. A holdup at gun point could conceivably catch the President's coachman off guard. The Presidential carriage could serve as the getaway vehicle for the first lap of the race. But again there remained the marathon gantlet-run to Richmond.

Plan Number Three entailed a "capture" method simple and direct. It had been Lincoln's habit to leave the White House of an evening and stroll down the block to 17th Street. Sometimes he turned left at the corner and obliqued across to the Winder Building, which had housed Grant's Washington Headquarters. There Lincoln stopped in to read dispatches from the fighting front. After Grant went to City Point, Lincoln took to going over to Stanton's office in the War Department. The walk, a breath of fresh air, braced him, if the interviews with Stanton frequently did not.

Often Lincoln made this stroll unaccompanied, a solitary figure passing under the streetlamps in unmistakable silhouette.

What could be simpler, then, than to waylay the lonely stroller on an evening when the moon was down, or on a rainy night, say, when the avenue would be free of pedestrians? A slingshot could extinguish the light at the corner of 17th. Shadows could dart from nearby shrubbery. A muffled blow, a gag, a rush to a waiting hack, and the bird would be in hand.

At the distant foot of 17th Street stood an old, dark mansion—the Van Ness House. A two and one-half story brick, its mansards warped with age, it had been built in 1820 near the sight of the pioneer homestead of David Burns, one of the earliest settlers in the area. It was neither so venerable nor so distinguished as the classic Octagon House a few blocks away, but it possessed some interesting features.

Thick as the battlements of a fort, the walls of the old house were built for secret passages. The basement was a honeycomb of cellars and vaults. A trapdoor opened into one of the deeper vaults. Booth seems to have negotiated with the inmates of the mansion for the use of this sub-cellar; it was to serve as a dungeon for Lincoln if he were seized at night on the street.[1] The house had the virtue of being located near the Potomac River. Just how the abductors were to spirit Lincoln across the heavily guarded Potomac at that point was never clarified for the record.

So far as is known, Booth never attempted to operate Plan Three. Perhaps he was unable to clarify the river-crossing detail. More probably he disliked the simplicity of the "capture." Like most grand strategists, Booth savored the complex. Reduce the game to a scuffle on the street, and it lacked dignity.

In mid-January, 1865, Booth believed that the supreme hour had arrived. He learned that Lincoln and two guests were to attend Ford's Theater on the night of Wednesday, January 18, to see Edwin Forrest in *Jack Cade*. Lincoln was a great admirer of Forrest, and saw this celebrated tragedian whenever he played in Washington City.[2]

One can imagine Booth striking fist in palm when he heard the news.

---

[1] Oldroyd, *op. cit.*, p. 58.
[2] Wilson, *op. cit.*, p. 13.

Forrest had been so jealous he wouldn't let Booth substitute for John McCullough in Philadelphia when McCullough was ill. Here was a prize turn of events. Booth could steal the show from Forrest here in Washington!

Moreover, *Jack Cade* was made to order for the enterprise. A drama dealing with the Kentish revolution, it was full of fury and shouting, bound to engross the audience, who, if the play were good, usually gave the Union President precious little attention.

On the weekend prior to the 18th, Booth pulled the high-gear lever of the abduction machinery: code signs, passwords, secret orders. Herold was rushed to Prince Georges County, Maryland, to procure a team of horses. He was to wait with these relays on the southern bank of the Anacostia at a point near Navy Yard Bridge. Arnold and O'Laughlin were sent for. Booth contacted John Surratt, who was to ride at once to Port Tobacco and have that Dutchman down there secure a flatboat that could hold a carriage and fifteen men.

Here a curious hitch grated the gears. Surratt had held his job with the Adams Express Company less than a month, and now he must ask the Washington manager for a few days' leave, lest his absence arouse suspicion. So, on January 15, he told Mr. Dunn, the express agent, that his mother intended to drive down country and she wanted him along as escort. Dunn, a negative soul, frowned over cold spectacles with a disapproving no. The appeal refused, John Surratt returned to the express office with his mother. Mrs. Surratt begged leave for her son, stating her wish for an escort to the country.[3]

Now Dunn's refusal (promptly given) provided Surratt with an excuse to quit. He had, with his mother's help, established a logical cover story. He galloped south to Port Tobacco on his pressing business with Atzerodt.

For Mrs. Surratt, the horse would one day assume another color. Express Agent Dunn was the picky type who remembered office episodes. In this instance, his memory would insert another doubt as to the widow's probity when her activities in Washington came under investigation.

But the abduction machinery was in motion. At Port Tobacco the bumbling Atzerodt hustled among the rivermen, inquiring about boats. By one account, Atzerodt purchased a scow from a James Brawner at Goose Creek, and moored it in a convenient cove in Nanjemoy Creek. Years later (in 1904) one Richard Mitchell Smoot published a little booklet on the conspiracy. Describing himself as a "successful planter" who joined the underground in lower Maryland, Smoot asserts that he sold the getaway boat to Atzerodt and John Surratt.[4] We will refer to this boat transaction in a later chapter.

[3] Oldroyd, *op. cit.*, p. 164.

[4] R. M. Smoot, *The Unwritten History of the Assassination of Abraham Lincoln* (Baltimore: John Murphy Co., 1904), pp. 2, 3.

At Piscataway, at Pope's Creek, at Allen's Fresh, and at Mathias Point, Virginia, the Rebel underground was alerted. One of the more bizarre aspects of the abduction enterprise was the advance publicity given the event. For some weeks Booth had been dropping dark hints to friends that "something big" was pending. Giddy with excitement, the acolyte Herold uttered similar predictions to bartenders and stable hands.

As courier for the underground, John Surratt conveyed cautious word to partisans in Prince Georges and Charles Counties. But he did confide some reckless hints to Joe Knott, the barman at the Surrattsville tavern.

Atzerodt talked all over Port Tobacco. Setting up drinks in the local hotel, he announced to all and sundry that he would soon be rich enough to buy out the whole *verdammt* town. He even hinted to a traveler from New York, a Mr. Eddy Martin, that a mysterious equipage was soon to be rushed in secret across the river. Fast relays were to bring it all the way down from Washington. Martin stared. "What does this mean?" Atzerodt shook his head enigmatically.[5]

Even Spangler, last and least of Booth's associates, got in his two cents' worth. Down the alley behind Ford's Theater (known colloquially as "Baptist Alley"), the unkempt stagehand was constructing a horse stall in an abandoned shed. A stable, he told inquisitive onlookers, for Mr. Booth.

Rumors of a plot to abduct the President leaked to Capitol Hill. Congressmen voiced their concern. Senator Willard Saulsbury of Delaware direfully predicted that Lincoln would not be inaugurated.[6]

Then, with the wheels racing full speed ahead, a hard jolt shook the kidnap contraption. Arnold and O'Laughlin failed to answer the summons to duty. John Surratt raced back to Washington to find Booth in a barbarous temper, but determined to go ahead.

In his headquarters at the National Hotel, the master planner readied the props: handcuffs, gags, ropes. Someone—perhaps stagehand Spangler—was prepared to turn out the theater lights at a given cue. Booth steeled John Surratt for the hot work in the Presidential box. A vehicle with appropriate side-curtains was stationed in the alley behind the playhouse. At a signal, this delivery cart would pull up to the stage door.

With everything in readiness, the conspirators keyed up to performance pitch, Booth and Surratt repaired to the theater. The anticlimax came as a stunning flop. The night was stormy, and the President stayed at home.

Thwarted, the chief abductor drained the vials of bitter wrath, washed down with shots of high-proof brandy. Clad in black riding coat and boots, Booth stalked the streets of Washington. Wintry fog and drizzle did noth-

---

[5] Oldroyd, *op. cit.*, p. 274.
[6] National Archives, War Dept. Records, File "S," JAO.

ing to sweeten the devil's broth in his mind. Nor did hours in Deery's bar above Grover's Theater, and in Taltavul's next door to Ford's.

Booth's determination to go on with the enterprise after the *Jack Cade* fiasco has been widely interpreted by historians as manifesting an *idée fixe*. This implies a compulsive drive beyond rationality. Unquestionably the actor was obsessed with the idea of kidnaping Lincoln. Booth's hunger for fame was a fox gnawing at his vitals. He would blurt out this truth on an evening when brandy loosened his tongue. He saw the strike at Lincoln as a masterstroke calculated to make the name of John Wilkes Booth a household word.

Nor can it be doubted that the *Jack Cade* miscarriage cut Booth's skin to the quick. All that mobilizing and alerting, all that rushing and girding to spring a trap on nothing but air. He could imagine the confusion, the resentment among the partisans of lower Maryland—gentlemen who had saddled up and gone to certain rendezvous points, only to wait in vain. People in Washington, in Montreal and in New York would know about it too, not to mention Richmond. How could he face their questions, their possible derision?

However, there may have been other drives behind the compulsion. Booth had a monetary as well as an emotional investment in the abduction project. Conspiracies are expensive. For some weeks he had been subsidizing Herold and Atzerodt, sending cash to Arnold (and probably to O'Laughlin), tipping Spangler, buying their loyalty and the loyalty of other useful individuals with rounds of drinks, dinners and oyster suppers.

Even more costly were the tools of conspiracy: the purchase or rental of horses, carriages, boats; the procurement of ammunition and firearms. These items Booth had been paying for out of pocket.

Then there were travel expenses—Booth, himself, always traveled on red plush—and other necessary disbursements—his room at the National Hotel, for instance, plus his social activities in Washington's champagne circles. He must finance his affair with a gentle "Eva" because this daughter of a Union Senator was good for tidbits of information. He must invest in his betrothal to another Washington socialite—a handy girl and a magnificent cover for his prolonged stay in the capital.

At any rate, Booth had to act quickly if he wanted to salvage the project. For events far beyond his control threatened to deprive the exploit of its ostensible objective as a stroke to save the Confederacy. Unless the stroke were swiftly delivered, there would be no Confederacy to save. This was the news from Richmond, by press report and by underground code. At Petersburg Grant's armies were constantly being reinforced, while Lee's last reserves were desperately holding the forts below the Confederate capital. Federal forces were now in possession of Wilmington, North Carolina—the Confederate Army's last major supply base. Sherman was coming up from Savannah.

Booth wept at the headlines in the Washington papers. In February, his brother Junius happened to visit him. The hard-headed Junius could never quite fathom Johnny's moods. On this occasion some chance remark reduced Johnny to near hysteria. Tears rushed to his eyes. Features contorted, cheeks streaming, he faced in the direction of Richmond and sobbed, "Virginia! Virginia!"[7]

One cannot help wondering (as Junius Booth doubtless wondered) how much was acting, how much the voice of sincerity. Did Booth mourn the entrapment of Richmond, or mourn the possible ruination of his own grand war plan?

Booth whisked off to Baltimore to take care of Mike O'Laughlin and Sam Arnold. We do not know how those two worthies placated the infuriated actor. Somehow they talked their way out of the *Jack Cade* affair, evidently promising to be on hand the next time. Aside from that, this February junket to the Monument City proved productive. For it was then that Booth procured the bulk and biceps of Lewis Paine for the enterprise.

Apparently Booth experienced some trouble introducing Paine into the Surratt menage. Mrs. Surratt may have been uneasy about the hulking stranger who came to her door as "Wood." Or perhaps she merely lacked accommodations for the handsome stalwart with the voracious appetite. Arrangements were ultimately made for him to lodge at the Herndon House when he came to Washington as the "Reverend Paine." Located on 9th Street, the Herndon House was just one block from Ford's Theater.

Encouraged by reinforcement, Booth ached for action. However, White House schedules were not arranged to suit the convenience of Lincoln's hidden enemy. February slipped away on the calendar. Neither wishes nor oaths nor incantations could stay the arrival of March, and, with it, Inauguration Day.

Inauguration Day was on March 4. On the evening of March 3, Booth called at the house on H Street. As was usual, he spent an hour or so basking in the warm admiration of the Surratt parlor. Later that evening he and John Surratt and Louis Wiechmann paid a visit to Capitol Hill ostensibly to watch the closing night session of Congress.[8]

Could Booth have gone there for another reason? Reconnaissance, say? A chance to scout the visitors' gallery, the plaza, the Capitol rotunda? Too, Lincoln was there that night signing late bills. Could Booth's dream have included an abduction from the United States Capitol? That, indeed, would be a grandstand play. Evidence exists that the Government was informed an attempt to abduct Lincoln would be made on Inauguration Day.

[7] Ruggles, *op. cit.*, p. 176.
[8] Oldroyd, *op. cit.*, p. 167.

"The 4th of March, 1865, was rainy and unpleasant," Ben Perley Poore noted in his journalistic memoirs. "The streets and sidewalks were encrusted with from two to ten inches of muddy paste, through which men and horses plodded wearily."[9]

Mire and drizzle notwithstanding, a "multitude" assembled at the steps of the recently completed Capitol to see President Lincoln sworn in for his second term. A procession (Poore thought it "very creditable") paced up Pennsylvania Avenue with undampened enthusiasm. Marchers included a delegation of Fire Zouaves from Philadelphia, "the Washington City Fire Department, the Colored Grand Lodge of Odd Fellows, and . . . many other civic bodies. . . ."

But the umbrella weather was inauspicious. And so were two incidents which occurred in the hour before Lincoln's inauguration.

Upon arriving at the Capitol, Lincoln was escorted to the President's room. There, in accordance with tradition, he signed the final bills of that session. Meantime Andrew Johnson, the newly elected Vice President, was shown to the Vice President's chamber across the hall, where he was formally welcomed by Hannibal Hamlin, the retiring Vice President. It was here that a most unfortunate occurrence took place.

As reported by journalist Poore: "The usual courtesies being exchanged . . . , Mr. Johnson asked Mr. Hamlin if he had any liquor in his room, stating that he was sick and nervous. He was told that there was none, but it could be sent for. Brandy being indicated, a bottle was brought from the Senate restaurant by one of the pages."

By Poore's account, Johnson gulped two tumblers of brandy straight. According to Hamlin's grandson (who eventually wrote an account based on the retiring Vice President's version), Johnson gulped three.[10] Whether two or three, they had an effect on Johnson. When escorted to the Senate Chamber to take the oath of office, the Vice President-elect was staggering.

"To the surprise of everybody," Poore wrote, "the Vice President . . . made a maudlin, drunken speech. . . . The Republican Senators were horror-stricken, and Colonel Forney vainly endeavored to make him conclude the harangue; but he would not be stopped; the brandy had made him crazily drunk, and the mortifying scene was prolonged until he was told that it was necessary to go with the President to the eastern front of the Capitol."[11]

Johnson's wretched inaugural performance threatened to ruin his public career. Apologists would say that he was "ill" that morning. He may very well have been. He had attended a supper party the previous night, and the wassail bowl had gone 'round.

---

[9] *Op. cit.*, pp. 157–159.

[10] Charles E. Hamlin, *Life and Times of Hannibal Hamlin* (Cambridge, Mass.: The Riverside Press, 1899), p. 497.

[11] Poore, *op. cit.*, p. 160.

Johnson, however, was known for his stamina. It would be remarked (by Lincoln) that the Vice President was not an inebriate. How came it that he collapsed as he did?

Curiously enough, it does not seem to have occurred to the authorities that Johnson might have been poisoned or drugged. It could have happened at the soiree the night before, or on the morning in question when the bottle (apparently) came from the Senate dining room. This is sheer speculation, but it would have been in keeping with contemporary cloak-and-dagger operations.

If a veiled lady, a secret agent, could enter the White House to give President Lincoln a poisonous kiss that left him infected with varioloid, why not a pill or powder in Andrew Johnson's liquor? There were, in Washington, men who carried drugs on their persons. Men wise in the bribery of household servants and page boys. Men who might have relished a chance to dope Lincoln's Vice President in order to sabotage the inaugural ceremonies.[12]

Such a man was there in the rotunda of the Capitol on that Inaugural Day.

The story of this, the second ominous occurrence of that dark morning, comes from O. H. Oldroyd. Its authenticity has been questioned by some historians. Oldroyd offers "proofs . . . given in a dozen or more affidavits" —documents preserved in the Oldroyd Lincoln Memorial Collection.

After the miserable ceremony in the Senate Chamber, the Presidential procession formed to escort Lincoln to the eastern portico of the Capitol where the President was to be inaugurated. In the rotunda under the great dome an expectant crowd shoved and jostled, craning for a glimpse of the President. Capitol guards struggled to clear a path for the line of march across the rotunda. Then, as Lincoln's party passed, the crowd surged forward in an effort to follow the dignitaries out to the portico.

Ordered to hold the exit against persons trying to tag the procession, the Capitol guards fought against the crush. One man, however, "persisted in forcing his way through the ranks against the earnest endeavors of John W. Westfall, one of the policemen." Westfall grappled with the recalcitrant, and shouted, "Shut that door!" In an eddy of tousled heads and bonnets, a hot scrimmage ensued. The outer door was closed (says Oldroyd) and "the procession stopped until the officers, after a severe struggle, overcame the intruder, and placed him in custody below stairs in the guardroom, from whence he was released after the ceremonies of the day were over."

---

12 In a little book published in 1866, one John Smith Dye asserts that at his inaugural James Buchanan *was* poisoned. Dye names the poison as arsenic, and lays the attempt to Confederate "slave owners." He fails to produce evidence, and weakens the case by asserting that Presidents Harrison and Taylor were murdered by Southern poisoners. Thus propaganda may bury facts. (See Bibliography for Dye's book.)

Who was the brawler in the vortex of this melee? Oldroyd tells us that he was not identified until six weeks later when Westfall and his fellow guards were shown a significant photograph. At once the Capitol policemen recognized the countenance "of the man who had forced his way through their ranks on the day of the inauguration." It was John Wilkes Booth.[13]

If the story be true, the actor staged an ugly scene on the threshold of Lincoln's inaugural. Historian Eisenschiml doubts the Oldroyd account, remarking that Washington police records do not contain the name of Officer Westfall and that the story is supported by relatively few sources.[14]

But perhaps the chief defect in Oldroyd's account lies in the statement that the intruder was held under guard below stairs until the "ceremonies of the day" were concluded. Booth attended Lincoln's inaugural; that fact has been long substantiated. In *Prince of Players,* Eleanor Ruggles tells us that the actor was on hand that day "wearing a slouch hat, gauntlets, spurs, and a satanic scowl." And that he "had a ticket for the platform, where he stood quite near the President."[15] The ticket Booth had obtained through the medium of his fiancée, who had an entrée in Senatorial circles. Thus provided, there was no need for him to force his way out to the portico.

Obviously, if Booth stood near the President on the platform, he was not the man held in the Capitol guard room until the ceremonies were over. In a recently uncovered photograph of the inaugural scene, one may discover Booth's scowl (or so the experts declare) among the faces grouped behind Lincoln.

Yet there are the affidavits in the Oldroyd Collection. And Oldroyd states that Officer Westfall, by special order, was made Lieutenant of Police in recognition of his services in stopping the intruder on March 4—a commission held by Westfall until 1876.[16] What of this conflicting historical evidence?

Explanation could be simple. A garbled report (eventually lost). Officer Westfall's name in some long-dead file. Booth glimpsed during the disturbance in the rotunda (and suspected of being its author), but the brawl incited by another man, presumably an accomplice. The riot act failing, Booth settles his collar and stalks out to the inauguration stand to witness the ceremony.

Lincoln kissed a Bible open at the fifth chapter of *Isaiah,* and began a speech which would live in mankind's memory as a sermon only a human step below the one delivered on the Mount.

"With malice toward none; with charity for all; with firmness in the

---

[13] Oldroyd, *op. cit.,* 216–217.
[14] *Op. cit.,* p. 210.
[15] *Op. cit.,* p. 177.
[16] *Op. cit.,* p. 217.

right as God gives us to see the right, let us strive on to finish the work we are in; to bind up the nation's wounds . . . to do all which may achieve and cherish a just and lasting peace among ourselves, and with all nations."

Listening to Lincoln's second inaurgural, John Wilkes Booth tasted hatred in his mouth. It may be that he slid his hand into his coat to grip the hilt of a concealed dagger.

In New York City a few days after the inaugural, Booth confided to his reluctant friend, Chester, that he had missed a chance to kill Lincoln on March 4. No doubt discretion stayed his hand out on the portico over-looking the packed plaza. Out in the open, before massed thousands, there could have been no escape from the platform. Booth had no desire to be torn to pieces by a mob.

Booth left the Capitol that day in company with Walter Burton, night clerk at the National. The occasion called for a drink. Burton would not forget a round with the actor at the National bar. Conversationally Booth remarked that his tickets to the inaugural ceremony had been procured through a lady friend, a Miss Hale, his current betrothed.

The next morning (March 5) Booth was occupied with another lady. Little is known about her, other than the fact that she was daughter of a U.S. Senator. Booth addressed her as "Eva."

He sat with her at dawn, and jotted sentimental fluff on the back of an old envelope.

> *Now in this hour that we part,*
> *I will ask to be forgotten never,*
> *But, in thy pure and guileless heart*
> *Consider me thy friend dear Eva.*

Gullible, if not guileless, the young woman endowed with this scrap of verse added her own inscription to love's epitaph.

> *For of all sad words from tongue or pen*
> *The saddest are these—it might have been.*
>
> *March 5th, 1865*
> *In John's room*[17]

One can only imagine the lady's dismay if she saw these lines when they subsequently found their way into history's scrapbook, via a police dossier. Or her possible mortification, or fury, at their publication in connection with a dozen similar items combed from Booth's effects: notes from Ella Turner, a *billet-doux* signed "Etta," a letter from someone named Jenny. But "Eva's" name was secure. Government censors joined Booth in keeping it from the public.

---

[17] Quoted in Sandburg, *op. cit.*, p. 331.

Booth must have been finding more intramural games in Washington than he could conveniently handle. He became incautious. Ella Turner he escorted more or less openly. He was seen at the National with a veiled lady later identified as Mrs. Slater. This doubling as Petruchio and the Pimpernel was dangerous. Jealousy talks. And aside from that aspect, events were catching up with Booth's abduction plan.

All the news from Richmond spoke of urgency. Lee's lines were crumbling. Yankees in Washington bars were boasting the South would soon surrender. Newspaper editorials mentioned the "Ides of March." Booth savored the phrase and liked the Roman sound of it.

Brutus had felled Caesar during the "Ides."

On March 13—a Monday—Booth set the wheels of conspiracy once more in motion. The first move: a telegram to Michael O'Laughlin.

MR. O'LAUGHLIN
57 NORTH EXETER STREET
BALTIMORE, MD.
DON'T FEAR TO NEGLECT YOUR BUSINESS; YOU HAD BETTER COME AT ONCE.
J. BOOTH.[18]

Either by wire or grapevine, similar summonses went to the other out-of-towners in the band. Atzerodt drifted up from Port Tobacco. Arnold came riding into town. Paine appeared early on the scene, clad in his new gray suit and his new character as Baptist preacher.

Booth took Paine in tow to acquaint him with Ford's Theater and its environs. Paine called him "Cap." Crude though it was, this simple acknowledgement of subordination from the veteran soldier doubtless flattered Booth's ego.

On March 15 the Lincolns attended a performance of *The Magic Flute* put on by the German Opera Company at Grover's. The President had been ill and would not have gone to the theater but for Mrs. Lincoln's importuning.

Booth's abduction machine was unready. The press had reported the President bedridden from influenza. Lincoln's surprise appearance at Grover's Theater drove the actor into a frenzy of conspiratorial maneuvering. Another chance must not be allowed to go by the board.

It could be surmised that Lincoln would presently attend a play at Ford's. With all members of the band on hand, Booth was confident that the original abduction trap could be sprung. He called for an emergency meeting at Gautier's Restaurant, 4½ Street and Pennsylvania Avenue.

Meantime, he had already arranged to introduce Lewis Paine to Ford's Theater by means of a little theater party. John Surratt had box seats. Paine was spending the afternoon in the house on H Street where he could not

---

[18] National Archives, War Dept. Records, JAO.

wander off. Surratt had been instructed to invite two of the lady boarders to the show as a "cover."

Paine's reappearance in the H Street boardinghouse occasioned some odd little sleights-of-hand, disturbing to the routines of that establishment, or, at least, disturbing to the routines of star boarder Louis Wiechmann. But for a number of days Wiechmann had been noticing oddities. Some of these were so palpably peculiar, so manifestly out of line with normal boardinghouse doings, that one cannot help wondering at Wiechmann's casual acceptance of the happenings at the time.

For instance, one time late in February, John Surratt, who had been out of town, arrived at the door with a lady in a closed carriage. The lady (Wiechmann perceived she was young) wore the type of nose veil known to the current stylists as a "mask." Wiechmann did not enjoy the privilege of meeting this intriguing guest, although she remained in the house over-night. By morning she was gone.

Not long after that, the H Street house played host to another mysterious arrival, Mr. Augustus (sometimes Spencer) Howell. This gentleman remained on the premises for two days. Wiechmann deduced he "was also engaged in running the blockade."

Blockade runner and spy were synonymous terms when applied to Civil War agents, and the nature of Howell's activities could hardly have been considered unimportant by a loyal Union citizen. Moreover, this interesting Mr. Howell spent part of an evening teaching Wiechmann a secret cipher "which investigation showed was the same as used by Booth and by the Confederates." Evidently Wiechmann took the exercise as a demonstration of some sort of innocent acrostic. That is, if he can be credited on the point. Later Wiechmann said he did not know the cipher had to do with Confederate spy communications and "the only use he ever made of it was to translate into it Longfellow's 'A Psalm of Life.'"

It seems that on the afternoon of March 15, Surratt showed Wiechmann the brace of box-seat tickets for that night's performance at Ford's. Wiech-mann expressed a desire to go. Surratt shook his head. Wiechmann remem-bered that.

Then there was the false mustache. On his return from work that evening, Wiechmann found this ridiculous article on a table in the room he shared with John Surratt. He tossed it into a receptacle on the bureau, intending to have a little fun with it later—or so he would say.

Presently the star boarder went upstairs to the back attic on some errand. Opening the door, he was surprised to see Surratt and the Reverend Paine seated together on a cot "surrounded by spurs, bowie knives and revolvers." As Wiechmann entered the room, Paine sprang to his feet and Surratt made an effort to push the weapons out of sight. Hastily Wiechmann backed out of the room. Now he was most disturbed. According to his subsequent statement, he hurried downstairs to tell Mrs. Surratt that the boys were playing with guns. Mrs. Surratt did not appear to be concerned. She told Wiechmann "that he must not think anything of that, as he knew her son was in the habit of going to the country, and he had to have these things as a protection."[19] Wiechmann loaned Lewis Paine his military cloak to wear that night to the theater—a curiously generous gesture, considering his evident pique at not being invited.

Another odd feature of the party: John Surratt offered to take Miss Honora Fitzpatrick, and Miss Appollonia Dean, aged nine. It would not have occurred to little Appolonia, but Miss Fitzpatrick, given acuity, might have wondered why Mrs. Surratt and Anna were not the favored invitees. Wondered, too, how a Baptist preacher happened to be going to the theater—a practice deplored by most ministers of that persuasion. No, Miss Fitzpatrick was wholly dazzled.

They sat that night in the President's box! During the intermission, the celebrated John Wilkes Booth looked in on them, for good measure. John Surratt and the Reverend Paine stepped out to the side corridor to chat with the famous actor. Nora and Polly shone in reflected glory.

Both girls would have cowered in terror had they guessed the purpose behind the theater party, or envisioned the scene staged in Gautier's Restaurant soon after the curtain-fall at Ford's. History has left us several versions of this midnight conference. We know that Booth foregathered there with his henchmen. In a private dining room the little band consumed a lusty supper. When the meal reached the point of surfeit and cigars, Booth outlined his cherished project of abducting Lincoln from a local theater. Arnold and O'Laughlin spoke up in uneasy objection. Official reports, courtroom testimony, and formally transcribed "confessions" offer only the bare bones of the episode. Years later Arnold wrote a newspaper article[20] on the conspiracy, but he wrote defensively, avoiding embarrassing details. Exactly what transpired at the meeting, what was said in boast or anger, cannot be related with certainty.

A serious quarrel threatened during the Roman feast. Arnold argued with Booth, no doubt of that. The others, Paine excepted, were inclined to shift position, like jurymen persuaded by the debate of a lone dissenter. His leadership openly defied, domination slipping from his hands, Booth's temper suffered an explosion of internal combustion. He accused Arnold of being a quitter.

Arnold could not quite meet this menace. No, he said, he did not want to quit. His protest was aimed at the theater exploit. He would be willing to go along with the plan to capture the President in the woods near the Soldiers' Home.

Perhaps warmed by nods of approval from some of the listeners, Arnold

---

[19] Oldroyd, *op. cit.*, pp. 166–169.
[20] Samuel Arnold, "The Lincoln Conspiracy," *Baltimore American*, December, 1901.

was encouraged to go on. He said he had seen a notice in the paper that Lincoln would attend a matinee at the suburban hospital the following Monday. If the trap could be sprung that day, he, Arnold, could be counted in. But he couldn't wait much longer. He'd applied for a job in a store at Fortress Monroe. He expected to go down there soon. If the abduction trap wasn't sprung within a week or so, he'd have to drop out of the venture.

Booth's face went milky white. He said savagely, "Any man who talks of quitting should be shot!"

Arnold met his fixed stare. He said with a bleak smile, "Two can play at that game."

By another account (Francis Wilson's)[21] Mike O'Laughlin answered Booth's threat with the "two can play" retort. Others in the group protested this heady talk. Out-voted, Booth became conciliatory and apologetic. A little limelight would be better than none. He seems to have told hearers that he would be playing at Ford's Theater on Saturday night (March 18). If Lincoln was going to a benefit at the Soldiers' Home the following Monday, the players at Ford's would know about it. They could set their trap with certainty, then.

That Saturday night John Wilkes Booth played what would prove to be his last professional role: Pescara in *The Apostate*. Between the acts of this favorite, which was staged at Ford's as a benefit for actor John McCullough, the star learned from dressing-room gossip that Lester Wallack and E. L. Davenport were going to appear at the Soldiers' Home on Monday. So was his friend, stock actor John Matthews.[22] The play programmed for the Soldiers' Home was *Still Waters Run Deep*. Lincoln was scheduled to attend the matinee.

To Booth, with his love of the melodramatic, the drama's title must have seemed inviting. By all means, Lincoln must be snared on Monday. Reluctant though he was to abandon the theatricals of an abduction in a playhouse, Booth again threw the kidnap machinery into high gear.

Electrified, Booth's co-conspirators went scuttling about Washington in a fever of activity, darting in and out of the Surratt house on H Street, dodging in and out of the National Hotel, whipping from this bar to that, and slipping around corners like weasels on ice.

David Herold galloped south to Surrattsville. He was soon joined at the tavern by John Surratt and George Atzerodt. Together, the three drove five miles down the road to Teebee. When they returned to the Surrattsville tavern an hour later, they deposited with tavern keeper Lloyd a bundle of guns and gear that had nothing to do with hunting. Surratt ordered Lloyd to hide the articles upstairs.

---

[21] *Op. cit.*, p. 48.
[22] *Ibid.*, p. 25.

Afterward Lloyd would swear he did not know what the items were for. The delivery men could have told him (if they hadn't already). The two army carbines were combat weapons. The big monkey wrench could be used for emergency repairs on a carriage. The long coil of heavy rope could be stretched across the turnpike between two trees—a device which could unsaddle a squad of hard-riding cavalrymen.

Booth doubtless expected hot pursuit by Federal horsemen. And at that date he seems to have feared the shortcut across Navy Yard Bridge. Plans called for the kidnap party to race across Benning's Bridge and gallop to Surrattsville by a roundabout swing through Upper Marlboro.

By Monday noon everything was set. Booth went around to the alley behind Ford's Theater for the two horses he kept stabled there—his saddle horse and the one-eyed nag he had purchased the previous November. O'Laughlin, Arnold, Surratt, and either Atzerodt or Paine were on livery mounts. All hands were charged up with brandy. Slouch hats over eyes, pistols under coats, the abductors started out of town, filtering out 7th Street two by two, so as not to attract attention.

Rendezvous was made in a stand of timber well beyond the city's outskirts. The road bent abruptly there, and a holdup would be screened from both directions. Blustery wind and gray sky set the mood.

Booth issued final orders. When Lincoln's carriage rounded the bend, Surratt and he were to canter out ahead of it. As soon as it had passed this grove, the other four were to come out behind. Surratt would grab the coachman, get into his livery. Mike, Sam, Atzerodt, were to handle the President's escort. Paine and Booth would handle Mr. Lincoln.

They sat in saddle with pistols cocked.

Presently they heard a carriage coming.

Booth edged out into the road, standing in stirrups, craning his neck, expectant.

A smart team, a polished carriage flashed into view.

But it was not President Lincoln. Booth's exclamation of rage stopped his henchmen in their tracks. Rearing horsemen. Rearing team. The coachman lashing out with his whip as the carriage swerves. Then, like frightened highwaymen, the would-be abductors are gone, larruping off up the road.

And where was the President? Lincoln at that hour was reviewing a regiment of battle veterans—the 140th Indiana—unexpectedly in town to present him with a captured Rebel flag. In order to honor those troops, Lincoln (according to some accounts) had made a last-minute decision to cancel the Soldiers' Home visit.

Most historians take Surratt's word[23] for it that the occupant of the carriage was Treasury Secretary Salmon P. Chase, for Chase seems to have attended the matinee at the Soldiers' Home. According to one

---

[23] Surratt Lecture, Rockville, Maryland, December 8, 1870.

account, the actor E. L. Davenport later that day told Booth as much. Yet Chase's attendance would not prove he was in the intercepted carriage.

Probing deeper sources than those made available to period historians, Eisenschiml doubts that the gentleman in question was Chase. "Surratt thought he recognized Chase, but he was probably in error." And Eisenschiml notes: "Who took his [Lincoln's] place that day the authorities have never disclosed."

The government withheld some other facts concerning the Soldiers' Home episode. As Eisenschiml remarks, the party victimized by the holdup must have been badly frightened. Certainly the coachman would have been scared. "The chances are the horses were whirled around and driven top speed back to Washington, where the adventure must have been reported to the secret service with telling effect."[24]

But existing War Department files contain no reports of the adventure. The affair did not come to light until the conspiracy trial many weeks later, at which time, strange to say, the Bureau of Military Justice introduced vague testimony dating the holdup as March 16.[25] Years later (1906) Colonel Henry L. Burnett, who had held a key post in the Judge Advocate's Office in 1865, dated the abduction attempt as "about March 20th."[26]

Censorship . . . confusion . . . obfuscation . . . these are classic devices for keeping something under cover. The affair on the road to the Soldiers' Home—a serious attempt to kidnap Lincoln—was a red-flag warning that the President was in danger. And the Government (meaning certain responsible leaders in authority) did nothing.

In wake of the failure on the open road occurred a furious squabble among the empty-handed kidnapers. Surratt was certain their trap had been betrayed. "Chase" had been sent as a decoy. Frantic, Sam Arnold blurted that the game was up—the sooner they were out of the District the better. O'Laughlin agreed, and the two Baltimoreans quirted off in the dusk, hitting for home. Atzerodt departed for Port Tobacco. The kidnap machine tumbled down around Booth in absurd, irreparable wreckage.

Late that afternoon there was a stormy scene in the house on H Street. Booth strode the parlor, lashing his boot with his quirt. Paine came in, gritting and cursing. Declaring himself through, John Surratt flung up his hands. "I'm going down to Richmond, by God!" When boarder Wiechmann, arriving home from work, happened in on the scene, the raging trio

---

[24] Op. cit., p. 45.

[25] Wiechmann Testimony, noted in Oldroyd, op. cit., p. 171.

[26] Henry L. Burnett, "Assassination of President Lincoln and the Trial of the Assassins," in James Henry Kennedy, *History of the Ohio Society of New York* (New York, 1906).

slammed into Surratt's room upstairs. Later, Wiechmann came across Mrs. Surratt weeping. "John is gone away! John is gone away!"[27]

Mrs. Surratt referred to her son's promised departure, not the departure of John Wilkes Booth. Doubtless she wished by that time Mr. Booth had never crossed her son's path.

CHAPTER 5

The Tragedy

WHEN DID Booth finally determine to slay Lincoln? Booth's apologists chose to believe the urge to homicide flowered in his soul during a feverish drinking bout induced by Lee's surrender on April 9, 1865. This bit of biographical mind reading was bound to please a various audience. Booth's friends could blame the act on liquor. Temperance advocates were glad to adopt the story. Southern historians were glad to accept it as evidence that Richmond had nothing to do with an assassination which *ipso facto* resulted from a drunken spree. The swords-and-roses sentimentalists could say that if the South had not been overthrown, Booth would not have been compelled to drown his grief in alcohol, and Lincoln might have lived.

The Government authorities in Washington were not averse to the foregoing line, because for purposes of propaganda it gave them a subject with two heads. One head: Booth the cunning enemy agent, the arch-criminal in a vast subversive conspiracy manipulated by Richmond. But if the public asked embarrassing questions—why did the Federal police fail to stop this Confederate assassin?—the populace could be shown the other head: Booth, the crazed maniac who struck with the unexpectedness of sudden frenzy. Congressional investigating committees (and American history) could have it both ways.

No one knows exactly when Booth arrived at his fatal decision. But it is clear that Booth's determination to murder Abraham Lincoln did not spring impulsively from a drinking spree which supposedly purged him of all restraint. The spree merely watered a *fleur de mal* already full-blown.

A significant body of evidence shows that Booth had cherished homicidal intentions for days. Moreover, he had urged a co-conspirator to slay the

---

[27] Oldroyd, *op. cit.*, p. 170.

President some weeks before he committed his own hand to the crime.

One afternoon in March (the date is uncertain) Booth took the mastiff Paine on a tour of the White House grounds. As they scanned the Executive Mansion, the actor abruptly turned to his companion and suggested that a man who really wanted to kill "that tyrant" could do it easily. Simply go to the front entrance, there, and present a calling card. Lincoln always sees petitioners. Anyone could walk into his office and shoot him on the spot.

Booth apparently phrased it in terms of suggestion. So the mastiff hesitated. (Although aching to please a master who wants him to jump, a dog may recoil from the rim of an abyss.) It seems that Booth eyed Paine coldly, and asked him if he'd lost his nerve. The account comes from a police statement made later by Lewis Paine, a dubious deponent. Yet the goading sounds like Booth.

Goaded or not, the battlefield veteran rejected all thought of a frontal assault on the White House. Perhaps the stately mansion awed him. Perhaps he caught a glimpse of uniformed guards. Every soldierly instinct was against it. Experience teaches a combat trooper to use every available means of cover.

Those bushes at the side, then. Right by the path. A man could lie in those shrubs at dusk and pick off the President when he came back from his usual visit to the War Department. "If you have the nerve," Booth said, in effect, "you could waylay the tyrant there."

Paine agreed. An outdoor ambush he could understand. Either that night or an evening or two later, the hulking twenty-year-old crouched in the shrubbery in front of the White House conservatory and waited for Lincoln's customary return from Stanton's War Office. A light rain had frozen on the ground, and the bushes glittered with diamonds. Presently footsteps crackled on the sidewalk. Lincoln and a heavy-set man approached. Paine heard the President warn his companion, "Major, spread out, spread out, or we shall break through the ice!"

Reporting this episode, Sandburg notes that Lincoln's warning bore jocular reference to an incident which occurred back in Illinois, when some of his neighbors were crossing the frozen Sangamon.[1]

But there on the White House grounds, Lincoln's whimsical jesting may have saved his life. "Spread out!" A startling utterance. Paine's clutch must have frozen on his revolver. Then the footsteps and voices faded, and the moment was gone. That night in the boarding house on H Street, Paine, miserable, told Booth he'd lost his nerve.

Some historians question the foregoing story, doubting the validity of the source. For the source was Lewis Paine himself, speaking in ultimate confession extracted by military duress. But Paine made this eventual confes-

[1] Sandburg, *op. cit.*, p. 328.

sion to Major Thomas T. Eckert, who was Lincoln's companion on that icy evening. The Major, therefore, could verify Paine's recollection of Lincoln's words.

The story, thus substantiated, reveals Booth's malice aforethought in respect to the murder of Lincoln. It also strips from Booth the shining armor of gallantry in which he tried to pose as a Brutus or a William Tell. For what could be more ignoble than this imposing star of rank and distinction, this cultured cavalier, urging a brainless and worshipful vassal to attempt an atrocious and suicidally dangerous crime, and taunting him for cowardice when he hesitated.

After the abduction fizzle of March 20, Booth went to New York. Some accounts say that, raging in disappointment, he left Washington that very night. Records are lacking on his movements around Manhattan at this time. Probably he plunged into a lost weekend with some of his feminine playmates on lower Broadway.

But amours with the *demi-mondaine* sort could not salve Booth's excruciated ego. Nor could a wild fling repair the shattered abduction contrivance that was so costly in time, effort and money. Booth must have gone into a fury every time he thought of it. His band had taken to its heels. Atzerodt, Arnold, O'Laughlin—away like rats from a sinking ship. Surratt was going to Richmond with Mrs. Slater. Herold had slunk home, frightened. Only Paine had stood by him, and Paine was a brainless clod.

Acting on a new resolve, Booth returned to Washington on March 25. That day (a Saturday) John Surratt, his mother and Mrs. Slater were seen by Wiechmann leaving the H Street house in a fast carriage drawn by a matched team of whites. Mrs. Surratt returned home alone that evening, and when Wiechmann asked her if John would be in, she said her son "has gone to Richmond to secure a clerkship." Next day (Sunday) Mrs. Surratt sent Wiechmann to the National Hotel to ask Booth to call on her that afternoon. On his way to the National, Wiechmann encountered Atzerodt. "Port Tobacco"—in town for the day, it appeared—was also on his way to visit Booth. After delivering the message from Mrs. Surratt, the obliging Wiechmann returned to H Street to observe eventualities. Booth arrived in due course, and Mrs. Surratt "had an interview with him near the head of the kitchen stairs."[2]

Apparently Wiechmann's ear missed the stairway interview. His testimony breaks off at that point. But it seems a fair surmise that Mrs. Surratt whispered a message from her son. Did it have to do with another abduction try?

On Monday, March 27, the Washington *Star* contained an item reporting that the President had reserved the State box at Ford's Theater for the night of the 29th. Billed for that night was the Italian opera *Ernani*. Booth

---

[2] Oldroyd, *op. cit.*, p. 176–177.

at once dispatched a telegram to Mike O'Laughlin, instructing him to be in Washington on Wednesday, bringing Arnold with him if possible.

Booth's wire concluded: *We sell that day sure. Do not fail.*

O'Laughlin failed. So did Arnold. The "sell" was off. Booth's cup of bitterness overflowed a day or two later when he received a letter from Sam Arnold dated March 27. Writing from Hookstown, Baltimore County, Arnold advised Booth to defer the "undertaking" for a time. He cautioned: "Why not, for the present, desist, for various reasons, which, if you look into, you can readily see, without my making any mention thereof. You, nor anyone, can censure me for my present course. . . . Suspicion rests upon me now from my whole family and even parties in the country. . . . I am, as you well know, in need . . . you may say, in rags, whereas to-day I ought to be well clothed. . . . Time more propitious will arrive yet. Do not act rashly or in haste. I would prefer your first query, 'Go and see how it will be taken at R——d.' . . . Do not in anger peruse this. Weigh all I have said, and, as a rational man and a *friend,* you can not censure or upbraid my conduct. . . ."[3]

Booth flung the letter into his steamer trunk. Arnold was out of the conspiracy. If Booth's reaction was typical, he probably paced his hotel room, damning his former friend with Shakespearean vituperation. But that letter (could Booth possibly have planned it that way?) would damn Arnold as no cursing of him *in absentia* ever could. The police were going to find the epistle signed "Sam," and the writer would live to regret the day he wrote it.

Ernani proved the swan song of Booth's abduction dream. As a final barb in his tortured ego, he learned the President and Mrs. Lincoln remained at City Point, Virginia, that week, reviewing the Union troops besieging Richmond. Once more Booth had triggered off a kidnap machination when the target was nowhere in the vicinity. With Lincoln out of the city, Booth could not bear to stay in the capital. Besides, his bank account had drained to such a low ebb that he had had to sell his horses. Restless, driven, he went to New York on April 1 to borrow from his family and squeeze fifty dollars out of Samuel Chester.

Richmond fell to Grant's forces on April 3. On that day Booth was in Newport, Rhode Island, engaged in an *affaire d'amour.* He broke it off, and went on to Boston to see his brother Edwin. Edwin Booth expressed satisfaction at the war news. Johnny retorted hotly, and packed to return to Washington. Edwin's loyalty to the Union became intolerable. "Good-by, Ned," Johnny said. "You and I could never agree on that."[4]

On his southward journey Booth again paused in New York to root Chester out from behind the scenes and demand repayment of the fifty

---

[3] National Archives, War Dept. Records, JAO.
[4] Ruggles, *op. cit.,* p. 177.

dollars "loaned" in January. In foul humor, Booth declared that the "oil business" had left him strapped.

On Saturday, April 8, Booth checked in at the National in Washington, D.C. Room 228.

Late Sunday evening he heard shouts in the street. Lee had surrendered to General Grant.

The next day Booth began to drink steadily at Deery's.

While in Boston, Booth had missed John Surratt, who had returned from Richmond on April 3, then gone scurrying north to Montreal, carrying secret Confederate dispatches.

Surratt's furtive passage through Washington had not been missed by Louis Wiechmann, whose memory registered some interesting details for future reference. Wiechmann was sitting in Mrs. Surratt's parlor when John Surratt unexpectedly walked in. "Why, Surratt, I thought you'd gone to Richmond!" Wiechmann exclaimed. He added some comment about the news that the Confederate capital had just been evacuated. "No, it has not," Surratt snapped. "I saw Davis and Benjamin in Richmond, and they told me it would not be evacuated."

So John Surratt had been in personal contact with Jefferson Davis and Confederate State Secretary Judah P. Benjamin! Wiechmann was further impressed when Surratt showed him a handful of clinking twenty-dollar gold pieces. Could Wiechmann make change? Wiechmann couldn't. However, tombstone-cutter Holohan obliged. That evening Surratt treated Wiechmann to an oyster supper on Pennsylvania Avenue. Upon parting, Surratt confided that he was spending the night at the National Hotel and going next day to Montreal.[5]

An extraordinary business, surely. For Surratt did go to Montreal. There he delivered dispatches from the Confederacy's leaders to the Rebel leaders in Canada. The content of those dispatches is a mystery. They were probably burned immediately after they were read by Jacob Thompson or some other leader who received them. John Surratt subsequently stated that the secret dispatches he carried from Richmond to Canada had to do with a "money transaction." One could believe his story or not.

Historians have since done a good deal of guessing concerning Surratt's mission to Montreal. Some suppose he carried advices from Davis warning Thompson and Clay the Canada game was up and they should run for it. This surmise negates Davis' expressed determination to fight "to the last man" (and Lee at that time was still fighting). Other historians suggest the dispatches may have concerned the release of Rebel prisoners then held in upper New York State.[6] This guess stumbles because Hines, Beall,

---

[5] Wiechmann Testimony, quoted in Oldroyd, *op. cit.*, pp. 177–178.
[6] Bishop, *op. cit.*, p. 94.

Cole, Grenfell—captains who might have led such a raid—were no longer in Canada. Sandburg gives up on the doings of John Surratt after Surratt's visit to Richmond. The scholarly historian writes: "Surratt leaves . . . and disappears forever from Booth's plan to save the Confederacy by the device of abduction."[7]

True, but did Surratt "disappear forever" from Booth's other plans? Slipping over the border like quicksilver, he reentered the States during the second week of April. Witnesses would claim they saw him in Washington on April 14. He would say he was in Elmira, New York, on that date.

From this welter of contradictory evidence, the truth has never emerged. In *Confederate Agent*, James D. Horan writes, "The mists of history have hidden two important links between the Confederate mission in Canada and the assassination of Lincoln."[8] One of the "links" the writer discerns as having to do with that secret courier-run from Richmond to Montreal by John H. Surratt.

The mists are not dissolved by the fact that the War Department had been fully informed on the underground trail to Montreal. Where, one wonders, were the forces of United States Army Intelligence? Where were the Secret Service agents of Colonel Lafayette C. Baker?

We know where one informer was. He was right in the center of a spy ring, an abduction gang. And as he sat there of an April evening in the house on H Street, he must have been sweating under the collar. Away back in February, he had told his friend Gleason about this gang, and Gleason had taken the story to a Lieutenant Sharp, an Assistant Provost Marshal. Also Enrolling Officer McDavitt had been informed under cover. Yet Booth and the others were still free. Nobody had stopped Surratt's trip to Canada. Louis Wiechmann's scalp must have prickled, unless someone in the War Department had assured him the situation was well in hand, unless someone at Headquarters had promised him personal protection.

Without such a promise of protection, a man in Wiechmann's situation ought to have been scared out of his wits. Somewhere he must have been assured backing in this most dangerous game.

On the evening of Monday, April 10, Wiechmann discovered John Wilkes Booth and a Miss Ward (friend of the Surratt family) enjoying the hospitality of Mrs. Surratt's parlor. Miss Ward displayed a letter from John Surratt, postmarked Canada. Booth read it with interest, and departed. That same evening Mrs. Surratt begged a favor of Wiechmann. Would he drive her on the morrow down to Prince Georges County? She wished to call on Mr. John K. Nothey to collect a debt. Wiechmann was happy to oblige.

---

[7] *Op. cit.*, pp. 329–330.

[8] James D. Horan, *Confederate Agent* (New York: Crown Publishers, 1954), pp. 265–266.

According to Oldroyd: "He [Wiechmann] then went and asked the permission of his superior officers to be absent for the day."[9] Permission was granted. And the somewhat ingenuous historian takes the granting of this permission as a matter of course. So, it seems, did trial lawyers and military judges and persons who should have known better. We surmise that Wiechmann's "superiors" instructed him to go ahead.

Tuesday morning, April 11, Mrs. Surratt sent Wiechmann to the National Hotel to borrow Mr. Booth's horse and buggy. Running this errand, the obliging Wiechmann learned that Mr. Booth had sold his rig. However, the actor handed Wiechmann ten dollars, with which Wiechmann rented a conveyance at Howard's Stable on 7th Street. By 9:30 he and the widow were jogging on their way through rain and mud to Surrattsville.

Their route took them across Navy Yard Bridge, where they had a glimpse of the Anacostia River and a war vessel or two at the naval wharf. Then, at Uniontown, on the Maryland side, they had a glimpse of something else—a buggy coming toward them, containing John Lloyd and his sister, Mrs. Emma Offutt, on their way to Washington.

Mrs. Surratt pushed aside the oilcloth curtains and leaned out to call a greeting. Lloyd pulled up his rig, climbed out, walked over to chat with Mrs. Surratt. Wiechmann's ear, although pricked up, failed to catch their low-voiced confab. John Lloyd would eventually testify that it bore reference to the "shooting irons" concealed in the Surrattsville tavern; he was told to "get them ready." Mrs. Surratt categorically denied this statement.

Mrs. Surratt did continue to Surrattsville that day. There, before witnesses, she conferred with the indebted Nothey, who owed her $479 plus thirteen years unpaid interest. A threat to sue wrung from Nothey a promise to settle. But he had been making such promises for over a decade. So one might wonder why the widow chose that particular day to press this bad debtor for a settlement. A pretext to take her to Surrattsville? A cover story for another errand—a chance to see innkeeper Lloyd and convey a message from Booth? That became the Government's contention.

Formal celebration of Lee's surrender was scheduled for the night of Tuesday, April 11.

The capital had been celebrating since the fall of Richmond on the 3rd. Although heads ached and throats were sore, the crowds could not seem to weary of fireworks, brass bands, parades, bonfires, spectaculars and "grand illuminations." Between Capitol Hill and the White House throngs churned along Pennsylvania Avenue, excited, hunting excitements. Soldiers chain-danced along the curbs. Drunks slept against walls. A confetti of humanity surged in the public squares. Paper lanterns glimmered in dooryards. The Capitol dome was illuminated. Across the

---

[9] *Op. cit.*, p. 179.

Potomac, in Arlington, Lee's former home was alight. Through windows of the city's grand mansions one could glimpse ladies with plumed head-dresses waltzing with lion-maned gentlemen under flaring chandeliers. Amazed ex-slaves wandered the streets, looking on. This was Millennium, the Year of Jubilo.

Shouldering their way up Pennsylvania Avenue that evening, John Wilkes Booth and Lewis Paine did not partake of the carnival jubilance. Booth glared at the celebrant lights and flags, and muttered through his teeth. Paine, his face a handsome and dull block of wood, plodded beside the master.

They followed the erratic bend of the Avenue around the Treasury Building, and proceeded toward the White House. There, they merged with a dense throng crowding the White House lawn. "Lincoln!" men in the crowd were chanting. "Speech!"

A French window opened and the tall, stooped figure of the President could be seen facing the crowd in silhouette. An aide handed him a candle, and the President's face came into view. A multi-throated roar went up. When the tumult subsided, the President, holding the candle, began to read an address.

"Fellow citizens, we meet this evening not in sorrow, but in gladness of heart. The evacuation of Petersburg and Richmond, and the surrender of the principal insurgent army, give hope of a righteous and speedy peace, whose joyous expression cannot be restrained. . . . To General Grant, his skillful officers and brave men, all belongs. . . ."

But if the crowd had hoped to hear a "hang Jeff Davis" and "punish the conquered enemy" speech, it was in for a disappointment. The President's keynote was Reconstruction—the restoration of self-government to the ex-Confederate States.

"Let us all join in doing the acts necessary to restore the proper practical relations between these States and the Union," he appealed. He wanted no military dictatorship imposed on the conquered South, no huge penalties exacted of the Southern people. He thought that as soon as possible the local governments should be returned to the hands of those Americans.

He spoke of giving ex-slaves the right to vote. "It is . . . unsatisfactory to some that the elective franchise is not given to the colored man. I would myself prefer that it were now conferred on the very intelligent and those who serve our cause as soldiers."

According to Booth's biographer, Francis Wilson, that utterance of Presidential policy sealed Lincoln's doom. For the actor and his henchman, there on the fringe of the crowd, went livid upon hearing the President's words. Booth's hatred galvanized, as it were, into a sudden iron resolve.

Wilson's conclusion is, of course, sheer mind reading. The biographer forgets Paine's testimony of a previous visit to the White House grounds, with Booth in a murderous mood. And Wilson overlooks some other facts, including the one that nobody knows or could ever know the actual motive behind a secret determination in a mind as devious as Booth's.

Nevertheless, most historians tell it that way—that Booth resolved to kill Lincoln when he heard the President propose "elective franchise" for the colored man.

Historical accounts also state that Booth, in a transport of rage, urged Paine to shoot Lincoln on the spot. And that Paine demurred because the risk was too great.[10] Days later Paine himself related this episode to Major Eckert. As Paine recalled it, Booth pressured him to shoot, but the hazard proved too frightening. They edged their way out of the crowd, and walked off. As they left the White House grounds, Booth snarled, "That is the last speech *he* will ever make!"

The big, not too nimble-witted Paine probably lacked the imagination to compose fast fiction. The curtain line sounds like Booth, and so does the byplay preceding it. A smart operator would try to get a fool to do the job for him, if at all possible. And while the mob destroyed the servant (and all chances of the servant's talking) the master could quietly walk off and claim the fame—perhaps even claim a lucrative award.

Still, no one could say what lay in Booth's mind that night. It seems far-fetched to assert that mention of the Negro vote decided Booth, but Lincoln's White House speech on the night of Tuesday, April 11, may indeed have sealed the President's doom. In announcing a policy of amnesty and peaceful restoration, Lincoln set a course exactly 180 degrees opposite from that favored by the most powerful faction in Congress, a faction dedicated to punishing—or (to give it the right word) plundering—the Southern states. Thaddeus Stevens, Ben Wade, Benjamin Butler, Wendell Phillips—these and their ilk were dangerous men to cross, especially when the issue involved control of a vast empire, millions of acres of rich cotton country, millions of dollars in commerce and trade.

Lincoln's announced policy was also opposed by many bridgadier generals and lesser warriors who saw their chances of ruling over occupied territories fading away. Peaceful restoration of the South would mean disarmament, demobilization. Peace would reduce the military to a nub, and what militarist could vote for that? No one would stand more opposed to Lincoln's declared policy than the Secretary of War, Edwin McMasters Stanton.

"That will be the last speech *he* will ever make."

If Booth did, indeed, speak those words on the night of April 11, he may have voiced a determination that was not his alone. Historians generally recognize (because evidence indicates) that Booth did not play a lone game. Many believe another player moved behind the scenes—a powerful ally (perhaps one unknown to Booth, himself)—a conspirator never unmasked, never detected.

---

[10] Sandburg, *op. cit.*, p. 330.

Few of Booth's Washington friends or intimates knew him better, or had known him longer, than John Deery. American billiard champion, Deery ran a billiard saloon which was located above the lobby of Grover's Theater, corner of E Street and Pennsylvania Avenue. Deery's was a high-class establishment, noted for its handsome tables and its excellent bar and cuisine.

Booth, a devoted customer, stopped in on the morning of Wednesday, April 12. His interest lay neither in billiards nor in edibles. He ordered a quart of brandy.

Deery, cordial, tried to invite conversation. Booth muttered a few remarks, rejecting his friend's camaraderie. Dour, uncommunicative, he drained the bottle, glass after glass. Then, flushed and holding himself erect, he walked out.

Next afternoon (Thursday, April 13) Booth was back. He asked Deery for two things—a quart of brandy and a favor. Deery would recall the favor as having been easily satisfied. Booth wanted him to reserve a right-hand box at Grover's for the following night, the opening of *Aladdin, or the Wonderful Lamp.* "If I try to buy a ticket," Booth said in effect, "Mr. Hess, the manager, will insist on giving me the box, and I prefer to pay for it."

Afterward, Deery learned the real reason behind the request. Booth had been watching a rehearsal of *Aladdin.* From Charlie Hess he'd heard that the President and his family were to be invited to the opening. If Lincoln decided to go to Grover's, Booth wanted to be in the next box. And he sought to "cover" the move by having Deery make the reservation.

A typical Booth maneuver, this usage of John Deery. That the innocent Deery would end up in a maelstrom of trouble if the box were used as gunman's blind meant nothing to the scheming assassin. His oldest friend, or anybody else, could take the lumps if it suited Booth's purpose.

Exemplary, too, of Booth's disarming character is the fact that Deery harbored no resentment when he ultimately discovered the truth about the dangerous favor Booth imposed. Deery blamed Johnny's conduct on alcohol. Years later the billiard champion penned a reminiscent portrait of Booth which gives us, at least, the views and reactions of a devoted friend:

> He [Booth] was, like many another brilliant man who has been overfond of his glass, one of the most charming of men. He was as handsome as a young god with his clear, pale, olive complexion, classically regular features, and hair and mustache literally as black as night; but his appearance was not more seductive than his manners. . . .
> John Wilkes Booth cast a spell over most men with whom he came in contact, and I believe all women without exception. . . . In liquor, of which he could absorb an astonishing quantity and still retain the bearing of a gentleman, he would sometimes flash out an angry word, but it was a hard matter to provoke him to a quarrel.

For a period of about ten days before the assassination, he visited my place every day, sometimes in the afternoons, sometimes in the evenings. . . . During that last week at Washington he sometimes drank at my bar as much as a quart of brandy in the space of less than two hours. . . . It was more than a spree, I could see that, and yet Booth was not given to sprees. . . . I believe Booth was as much crazed by the liquor he drank that week as by any motive when he shot Lincoln. . . .[11]

Here, perhaps, in this portrait by Deery can be found the source of the story that brandy, rather than Booth, was responsible for the President's murder. But Deery, too, indulges in mind reading. Manifestly a quart of brandy a day for five days (and the Civil War product was liquid flame) could fill a man's skull with molten lava. Yet Booth proceeded to carry out the murder with ingenuity, with attention to detail, and with an unerring aim not usually associated with berserk alcoholism.

With brandy Booth merely bolstered an intent to homicide already decided upon.

On the night of the 13th, Booth conveyed the word in person to the male members of his residual camarilla. Grant had arrived in the capital that day, could be seen (if one could get near the place) at Willard's Hotel. The coming of the Hero of Appomattox had touched off another fireworks celebration. It may have spurred Booth's assassination schedule.

Through a city cheering, singing, tossing up its hat in pyrotechnic razzle-dazzle, the dark stage star wended his way on secret business. He located Herold and told the drugstore clerk the hour had come. He found Atzerodt in the slovenly Pennsylvania House on C Street and ordered the startled "Port Tobacco" to move to the first-class Kirkwood House on Pennsylvania Avenue. Paine awaited the master at the Herndon House on 9th Street. Booth closeted himself with the husky "Reverend" and issued explicit orders and instructions. O'Laughlin was somewhere in town with a party of Baltimore sports, spreeing through the "Hooker's Division" brothels. Apparently Booth was unable to get in touch with him.

Before going to bed that night, Booth dashed off a letter to his mother. Nothing about his socialite fiancée. Nothing of interest.

. . . indeed I have nothing to write about. Everything is dull, that is, has been until last night. Everything was bright and splendid. More so in my eyes if it had been a display in a nobler cause. But so goes the world. Might makes right. I only drop you these lines to let you know that I am well and to say I have not heard from you. Excuse brevity, am in haste. . . . I am your affectionate son, ever. . . .[12]

An incredible letter from a writer who knew that by the time his mother received it he might be either dead or a wanted fugitive. A letter that

---

[11] Article in New York *Sunday Telegraph,* May 23, 1909.
[12] Quoted in Sandburg, *op. cit.,* p. 333.

baffles ready analysis. It suggests a dual personality—Jekyll Booth and Hyde Booth. Hyde plotting a blood bath at 11:00 P.M. Jekyll, some time later that same night, writing quietly to his mother.

Was the letter a calculated deception somehow aimed to mislead the police? If so, why bring anguish to his mother with such a note? Why write this offhand letter to her in any case? Was Booth deceiving himself? Pretending that tomorrow would never come? Telling himself, as well as her, that "everything is dull," and hoping that somehow the words on paper would make it so? Such self-deceptions have been practiced by frightened men unable to face some inescapable and horrifying reality, caught in deep commitments from which they cannot or dare not disengage.

Had Booth, at some time before Good Friday, 1865, bound himself by such a commitment?

April 14, 1865. Good Friday.

A day that began like other days for President Lincoln.

A day that began like other days for John Wilkes Booth.

Historians have chronicled Lincoln's every known move on that fateful day.

Booth's movements, too, have been followed by historians trailing through the documentary evidence accumulated on the subject. But there are blanks in the record on Booth: an hour missing here, twenty unaccounted minutes there. He steps into a bar. Did he pass a signal to some messenger? He shuts himself in his room for a time. To write code letters which are later slipped, unnoticed, into a postbox? We cannot trail these concealed moves and hidden motives.

In any event, the tabulation of Booth's known actions throughout that day tells us little more about the assassination conspiracy than a railroad timetable would tell us about the character of the road's Board of Directors and the quality of its rolling stock. Invisible forces worked behind the visible that day. They do not show on the timetable.

But here is the continuity, so far as it is known.

Booth rises in midmorning, breakfasts, and saunters into a barber shop, Booker & Stewart's, on E Street near Grover's Theater.[13] Barber Charlie Wood would subsequently testify that Booth was in the shop between 9:00 and 10:00 A.M.—and so were John Surratt and Michael O'Laughlin.

Booth returned to the National Hotel. There, around 10:30 (reports are confusing) he was visited in his room by the dapper little Irishman from Baltimore. O'Laughlin told friends he was seeing Booth to collect a debt. Something about the "oil business." Nobody knows, of course, the private words exchanged between the two.

---

[13] Oldroyd, *op. cit.*, pp. 236–237.

Shortly before noon, Booth left the National Hotel and, alone, strolled over to Ford's Theater to pick up his mail. Standing at the playhouse entry with some friends, Harry Ford sighted Booth approaching. Ford called attention to the jaunty stage star. "Here comes the handsomest man in Washington."[14]

In the manager's office, Ford handed Booth some incidental mail. Booth chatted amiably for a moment and was turning to go when James Gifford, stage carpenter, walked in. What about tonight? Did Mr. Ford want the State box ready?

Harry Ford nodded. Yes, they'd received word from the White House that the President, General Grant and party were coming.

Booth looks up. Here? To see *Our American Cousin?*

That's right, Ford bobs his head. He tells Booth that James Ford has just rushed the announcements to the press. Maybe the stale old comedy will do business. Grant will be a whale of an attraction. It ought to be a gala evening.

With some indifferent comment or other, Booth went out front to sit on the step at the entry and read his mail. A witness recalled him laughing over one letter. Thomas Raybold, the ticket-seller, remarked nothing extraordinary in Booth's demeanor. Here was a truly marvelous actor!

For in a trice his plan to kill Lincoln at Grover's Theater was dissolved. Lincoln had shifted the game to Ford's. And with that shift the plot whirled back full circle to the starting point. The stage was waiting. The props were handy. Stagehand Spangler and other friends were on the scene. Was that why Booth, perusing a letter, suddenly paused and laughed aloud? Did he continue a pretense of reading, his face a mask, while his mind raced through lightning calculations? So it would seem.

Now the continuity swiftly unfolds.

Booth reenters the theater unnoticed, crosses the parquet and takes the stairs, comes down to the dress circle (today's mezzanine), and slips into a side passage that leads to Boxes 7 and 8—the right-hand tier of upper boxes that will be joined to form the Presidential box.

He enters Box 7 (the rear box), and sits for a time watching the actors under the proscenium gibber through the abbreviated business of a rehearsal.

Laura Keene is on stage, running through her lines as Florence Trenchard. This will be "Red Laura's" last appearance in *Cousin* (the show is closing) and, mindful of the President's promised attendance, the English actress strives for a flawless reading. On stage, also, are Mrs. Muzzy as Mrs. Mountchessington, Miss Helen Trueman as Augusta, and Mr. Harry Hawk as the comic Yankee Asa Trenchard. Bit players stroll on and off,

---

[14] Quoted in Ruggles, *op. cit.*, p. 178.

tightening up on cues. Voices sound hollow in the empty house. Side remarks and instructions punctuate the dialogue. Then——

There comes a point in Act Three, Scene Two, where Mrs. Mountchessington (comic dowager) bawls out Asa Trenchard (the rube) and sweeps offstage. Left with apron to himself, "Trenchard" flares: "Don't know the manners of good society, eh? Well, I guess I know enough to turn you inside out, old gal—you sockdologizing old man trap!"

Harry Hawk, as Trenchard, recited the line with gestures. It could be counted on to bring down the house.

Booth, shadowy listener in Box 7, came alert. Hawk, there, alone on stage. The audience would be guffawing. This was the time!

You sockdologizing old man trap!

Tom Taylor, English playwright, never imagined when he composed that burlesque line that it would cue a great American tragedy.

Having settled on the place and time, Booth quietly left the empty theater. Joining a midday flow of pedestrian traffic, he headed crosstown. At the corner of 12th and E, he exchanged a few words with James R. Ford, who had halted in a buggy to say hello. Ford was returning from the Treasury Building where he had procured some large flags with which to drape the Presidential box. Ford said he anticipated a sellout. They would come to see Grant.

Booth hurried on up to G Street, cut back along G to 7th, and went into Howard's Stable where he kept the one-eyed roan he had purchased the previous December. He asked the liveryman to take the big horse over to the shed in "Baptist Alley" behind Ford's Theater and leave it there in a stall.

Walking fast now, Booth went down to the Mall and over to Pumphrey's Livery Stable. From James Pumphrey he engaged a saddle horse—a lively little bay mare with black mane and tail and a starred forehead. He told Pumphrey he'd like her saddled and ready to go at 4:00 P.M.

Now we lose Booth for an hour or two. He may have gone directly from Pumphrey's to his hotel. He may have made a prearranged contact with George A. Atzerodt.

Atzerodt had transferred his address from the sleazy Pennsylvania House to the Kirkwood, on the Avenue at 12th. He had signed in just like any gentleman. Most of the morning he had tippled in the bar, asking questions about "Vize Bresident Johnson." The bartender would remember this accent, but at the time Atzerodt was taken for another barfly.

Booth may have made a midday check on the fellow and on David Herold, who had things to do. At some time that morning Herold had visited Atzerodt's room at the Kirkwood and stowed therein some garments and sidearms. Presumably some of this gear was to be used on Vice President Johnson.

About 2:00 P.M. Booth appeared in the lobby of the National. He was smartened up, now, for riding. But he would not be mounted until 4:00 P.M., and he still had some errands to do on foot.

First errand: go to Mrs. Surratt's. Booth rang the bell of the house on H Street about 2:35. Wiechmann was just leaving on an errand for Mrs. Surratt—another drive down to Surrattsville to call on Mr. Nothey. Good Friday having been declared a holiday for Government employees, the amiable civil servant had agreed to accompany his landlady "down country." He was starting for Howard's Stable to rent a rig when Booth walked in.

Wiechmann would recall that, looking back, he saw Booth posed at the parlor fireplace, one arm draped across the mantel (always good theater). The widow faced the actor, her expression attentive.

When Wiechmann returned with horse and buggy, Booth had gone. However, he had left a little package for Mrs. Surratt to deliver to Lloyd at the Surrattsville tavern. Mrs. Surratt handled the parcel carefully. She told Wiechmann it was "glass."

While star-boarder Wiechmann was setting out with Mary Surratt for Surrattsville, stage star Booth was hurrying to the Herndon House to call on Lewis Paine. He found the "Reverend" obediently waiting for him. They talked in Paine's stuffy little room—about what no one can say with certainty. Paine's story: Booth handed him the mission of killing General Grant. Booth also assigned him the one-eyed roan for a mount, told him to check out of the Herndon House, and promised to meet him later.

Now Booth walks in seemingly tireless boots down to the Kirkwood House. At the desk he inquires for Mr. Atzerodt. Out? Booth shrugs and steps into the bar. A quick glass, and he is back in the lobby.

And here he makes perhaps the strangest move in all that complex day-long gambit. Time: about 3:30 P.M. Action: Booth asks the desk clerk if Vice President Johnson is in. Told Johnson is out, he requests a blank card. On this card he scribbles *Don't wish to disturb you Are you at home?*, signs his name, and asks the clerk to deliver this item to Mr. Johnson. To this day no two historians can agree on the meaning or import of that card.

After this bit of wizardry, Booth scribbled a note to Atzerodt which (according to some accounts) he carried to the Dutchman's room and slipped under the door. Satisfied, the author of these mysteries left the Kirkwood. Another brisk walk took him down the Mall to Pumphrey's Livery Stable, where he picked up the snappy little mare.

Mounting, Booth tested the lively bay. Skittery, she danced and wheeled, tossed her head and snorted. The actor-horseman trotted her up 6th Street, swung her into Pennsylvania Avenue, and let her race a few blocks.

Charley Warwick, coming up the Avenue, would not forget a glimpse of Booth "sitting his horse like a Centaur." Warwick recalled: "He was faultlessly dressed, elegant riding boots with a slender steel spur were on his feet."[15]

Booth cantered on toward Willard's, made a horseshoe turn, came back east, and reined up in front of Grover's Theater. He dismounted, tethered the mare, and walked in to see Mr. Hess. Finding the manager's office vacant, he went upstairs to Deery's Billiard Saloon. Deery said he had Booth's tickets for *Aladdin*. Booth said he'd pick them up later. Just now he wanted a bottle of brandy.

After consuming the brandy, the actor descended to the theater lobby and revisited the manager's office. As Hess was still absent, Booth sat himself at the theater man's desk and scribbled a letter. He addressed the envelope: "Editor, National Intelligencer." He sealed the envelope, stamped it, put the letter in his pocket: another mystery in the making.

Next stop: Ford's Theater. Some time between 4:30 and 5:00 P.M., Booth cantered into 10th Street and pulled up before the playhouse.

James Maddox, property man, stood out front, taking the air. Through the window of a neighboring restaurant James Ferguson, restaurant-keeper, saw Booth chatting with Maddox.

After a moment Booth settled himself in the saddle. "See what a nice horse I've got," he said to Maddox. "Now watch. She can run just like a cat."[16] He jabbed a spur into the mare's flank and she shot down 10th at racetrack pace.

Turning right on Pennsylvania, Booth slowed the mare, trotted her toward the busy 14th Street corner—Willard's. There he sighted stock actor John Matthews. Booth veered over and dismounted. He asked Matthews to do him a small favor.

Matthews expressed himself as eager. Probably the expression was genuine. Not every day were you seen on the Avenue in cordial conversation with the elegant Booth. (Matthews did not know that this elegant Booth had, a short time ago, denounced him as someone who deserved to be "sacrificed.")

Booth drew from his pocket the letter addressed to the editor of the *National Intelligencer*. He told Matthews the letter was important. Would Matthews oblige by delivering it by hand to the newspaper office tomorrow forenoon?

Matthews was puzzled, but glad to accommodate. Or so he said later.

Booth had foot in stirrup to go on when he suddenly paused, glaring. Across the corner, blocking traffic, swung a company of Union troops conducting a file of tattered prisoners.

"Great God! Matthews, I have no longer a country!"[17]

A moment later Grant rode by in an open carriage. Booth angled the

---

[15] Quoted in Ruggles, *op. cit.*, p. 178.
[16] National Archives, War Dept. Records, Maddox Testimony, JAO.
[17] Sandburg, *op. cit.*, p. 334.

nimble mare over for a close look at the General. As the carriage pulled away under cavalry escort, the actor sent his horse skittering back to the curbstone in front of Willard's. Where, he asked, was the General off to? Curbstone loungers (who knew everything) said the General was off to the railroad depot. He and his wife were going north to New Jersey.

Could Booth have been previously advised on Grant's departure? Here is another blank in the record. Grant had attended the Cabinet meeting earlier that day. At that time he had explained to Lincoln that he and Mrs. Grant were going up to New Jersey to see their children at Burlington. Stanton, of course, had previously declined the theater-party invitation.

Booth does not seem to have been thrown by Grant's departure from Washington. Probably he was delighted, for Grant with his staff would have been a stupendous problem at the theater. Possibly Grant's departure settled Booth's determination to strike.

The afternoon blended into early evening. John Wilkes Booth had spent a busy day. During his hectic comings and goings crosstown, downtown, uptown, he had been noticed by scores of people. He had made, in fact, a great show of himself, waving to friends, tipping his hat to ladies, calling to passersby from the saddle. Mountains of witness testimony would follow him through these labyrinthine ways but would prove next to nothing concerning motives behind moves—even open moves.

One item of eyewitness testimony (never entered in police dossiers, and, perhaps for that reason, heretofore overlooked by historians) may hold a significant clue to motive. At some hour during that day, Booth encountered Mr. Thomas B. Florence, editor of the *Daily Constitutional Union*. Editor Florence noted in his Saturday edition:

> We met him [Booth] yesterday on the Avenue, and in a short conversation with him he stated . . . that he had lost about $6,000 in oil by the recent floods at Oil City. He appeared to be perfectly sober, though we now recollect that at times he seemed abstracted. . . .[18]

To a plunger on the brink of bankruptcy, a possible award might be a compelling murder motive.

At 6:00 P.M. or thereabouts, Booth walked the mare into "Baptist Alley" behind Ford's Theater. Stopping at the stage door, he shouted for Ned Spangler.

Mary Jane Anderson and some of her colored neighbors down the alley saw Spangler emerge, followed by Maddox. The men took the fancy little bay down to the improvised stable, watered and fed her, left her in the stall. Booth then steered Spangler, Maddox and stagehand Jake Ritterspaugh around to Taltavul's, and left them there with a bottle he bought them.

---

[18] *Daily Constitutional Union*, Washington, D.C., April 15, 1865.

Booth then disappeared. As far as he can be traced, he circuited back into "Baptist Alley" and entered the theater by the stage door. Presumably the house was dark and deserted—the *Cousin* cast out for supper, the stage crew (including the hands next door) away.

We are left to imagine Booth, a lone figure, emerging on stage. He drops into the orchestra pit, obliques to the front of the house, goes up to the mezzanine, and makes his way down the side passage where he enters the little corridor leading to the State box. Here he works in solitude (or so it is presumed). He has with him a small slab of wood (part of a music stand he picked up, apparently, in the orchestra pit). Booth will use this piece of pine as a wedge to bar the outer door of the box corridor.

Working swiftly with knife, the actor carves a niche in the plaster wall just inside the corridor, to hold the wedge. He hides the stick in a dark recess of the corridor. Now he goes to the door of the box, opens it, looks in. After giving the seating arrangements a swift inspection, he turns his attention to the door panel. It would seem he had provided himself with some tool, perhaps a gimlet. He uses this to bore a small hole in the upper panel, a little below eye level. The hole is enlarged by whittling with a pocket-knife. The shavings are scooped up. The plaster at corridor entry is brushed away. Booth leaves the theater by the stage door.

Did he actually work alone, or did one of the hands secretly aid him? Afterwards it was contended that he bribed some stagehand to place the President's rocking chair in line with the peephole in the inner door. Spangler, of course, was suspected; also stage carpenter Gifford and property man Maddox. Perhaps Gifford left a gimlet handy for Booth. Perhaps Spangler fixed the chair for a price.

Nobody saw Booth there at his secret carpentry. The evidence is circumstantial.

By 7:00 P.M., Booth was in the dining room at the National Hotel, completing a repast. After a last liqueur, he went up to his room. Another blank in the record. Historians assume he remained there for about an hour—perhaps pacing, perhaps napping, perhaps studying a map or chart.

Someone may have visited him. He may have dashed off some code letters. He may have dodged out of the building, and come in again. Guessing games do not constitute evidence.

But we know Booth was in his room for a brief time. He picked up a dark shawl or muffler. From his trunk he procured a wig, a false mustache and a false beard. He buttoned a steel dagger under his coat. He wrapped a pair of revolvers in the shawl. Finally, he loaded a little brass derringer— a six-inch, single-shot model with the name "Deringer" inscribed on the handle. It would fire a lead ball about as big as a small marble. The target was waiting.

Armed for murder, Booth left the National about 8:00 P.M. In passing he asked the desk clerk if he was going to Ford's that evening. No? Booth told him he ought to. "There'll be some fine acting there tonight!"[19]

Again Booth disappeared for an hour or so. Evidence indicates a final conference somewhere with his henchmen. No minutes were kept for the convenience of historians.

Some suppose the conferees met at the Herndon House. Others guess another locale. As for business, it seems that Booth armed Paine and Atzerodt with service revolvers. Ordered Paine to go to Seward's house to assassinate the Secretary of State. Ordered Herold to accompany Paine. Ordered Atzerodt to waylay and slay Vice President Johnson. Last-minute instructions—the time to strike—getaway details.

The conspirators scattered, each to his appointed rendezvous with criminal history.

About this time, Mrs. Surratt and Louis Wiechmann were entering the outskirts of Washington City. The widow's afternoon junket to Surrattsville had been (it would appear) futile; that is, her debtor, Mr. Nothey, had not been at home. Depressed by this disappointment and the tiring buggy-ride, she gazed dourly at the festive lights crowning Capitol Hill. A Cassandra mood, colored by religious rationale, darkened her mien.

"I am afraid all this rejoicing will be turned into mourning," she prognosticated for Wiechmann's benefit. "The people are too proud and licentious, and God will punish them."[20]

Unhappy Mrs. Surratt was not the first individual to mistake man's intentions for God's. If she did make such an utterance.

Time: about 9:30 P.M. Booth reined up at the stage door in "Baptist Alley." Dismounting, he called out, "Spangler!" Mary Jane Anderson looked from her shanty door and saw the black-clad actor there in the dimness. So did John Miles, Negro, peering down from a high window in the theater's back wall.

Presently they saw Spangler step from the stage door. He talked with Booth a moment, reentered the theater, returned with Joseph Burroughs, called "Johnny Peanuts," a helper. "Peanut" held the horse. Booth and Spangler went into the playhouse.

Inside, Booth learned that he was well ahead of time. He took a basement passage to a side exit, walked out to 10th Street. There he saw the Presidential carriage waiting at the curb. He stepped into Taltavul's saloon.

Presently, his cheekbones flushed by successive drinks, Booth turned to go. Someone at the bar flung a taunt. "You'll never be the actor your father was!" Booth wheeled around, nettled. Then, smiling abruptly, walk-

---

[19] Ruggles, *op. cit.*, p. 179.
[20] Oldroyd, *op. cit.*, p. 183.

ing out, he called back: "When I leave the stage, I'll be the most famous man in America."[21]

"You'll not want a ticket from *me!*" he ogled Joseph Buckingham, the doorkeeper.[22]

Buck laughed. Young Mr. Booth could be real comic.

Booth borrowed a chew of tobacco from Buck, let the flattered fellow present him to some bystanders. Then, bowing to all, Booth stepped inside.

For a second he scanned the audience, and listened to the voices echoing from the stage. A moment later he was up the stairway to the dress circle. There he paused again to scan the audience. He made no effort to conceal himself from the patrons in the mezzanine. A number (including two Army officers) noticed Booth as he walked to the passage leading to the State box.

Did Booth hand somebody a card, there, at the head of the passage? An Army officer in the dress circle, half watching, thought so. Nobody else seems to have glimpsed the gesture. Could the man encountered have been Lincoln's attendant, the messenger Charles Forbes? Forbes claimed he was there at that hour. Occupants of the box claimed he was not.

If Forbes *was* there, what of the card from Booth? Why did the attendant fail to stop the intruder? Or, if some other man was on hand, why didn't *he* stop Booth? No, the sum of all known evidence shows that the door from the corridor into the box went unguarded. An empty chair stood there. The appointed guard, John Parker, was not in it.

Nobody stopped Booth. He slipped into the corridor, quickly closed the door, found the piece of wood and wedged it fast between doorknob and wall-niche. Having sealed the entry, he moved softly to the inner door, peered through the peephole.

A perfect bead on the back of Lincoln's head!

The President sat in an upholstered rocker with an overcoat over his shoulders. Changing position, squinting, Booth could make out Mrs. Lincoln at the President's side, and an Army officer seated on a divan against the inside wall of the box. A young lady sat forward in an armchair.

Booth tense, listening.

Voices. Faint but distinct. The artificial tones and diction of stage dialogue.

No heir to the fortune, Mr. Trenchard?

Oh, no!

What? No fortune?

Nary a red . . . barking up the wrong tree. . . .

---

[21] Ruggles, *op. cit.*, p. 179.
[22] Wilson, *op. cit.*, p. 112.

Augusta, go to your room!

Yes, ma! The nasty beast!

I am aware, Mr. Trenchard, that you are not used to the manners of good society. . . .

Pause. Then—

. . . manners of good society, eh? Well—!

Booth drew his pistol. Turned the doorknob—one quick, quiet turn—opened the door.

. . . you sockdologizing old man trap!

The audience roared with laughter.

Booth stepped forward swiftly, aimed the derringer at the back of the President's head.

A flash. A muffled explosion.

Lincoln's chin dropped to his chest, and he sat very still, as though fallen asleep.

Major Henry Reed Rathbone looked around, startled. He saw a shadow man behind the President's chair. A little cloud of smoke drifted over the President's head. A hoarse voice barked at Rathbone. He thought he caught the word "Freedom." Then something like: *"Sic Semper Tyrannis!"*

Rathbone sprang at the demonish figure. Desperately Rathbone grappled. The steel blade flashed. The officer raised a defensive elbow, and the arm that never could have broken a poker took a savage gash to the bone.

Rathbone reared back, lunged again, and clung. Wrestled to the ledge of the box, Booth flung the officer off and got a leg over the rail. Rathbone made another grab as Booth rolled himself over the ledge and hung for a second by his hands.

Cloth tore through Rathbone's grasp. He tried to shout. His clutch grabbed air.

Audience laughter was dying out as Booth let go for the drop to the stage. In dropping, he hooked a spur in the Treasury Guards flag which draped the face of the box. Bunting ripped, and he fell through a blur of red, white and blue. He felt a sickening little *snap!* as he tore free of the flag.

Afterwards, Rathbone testified: "The time which elapsed between the discharge of the pistol and the time when the assassin leaped from the box did not exceed thirty seconds."

Rathbone also testified that there were no guards in the box. Just the President, Mrs. Lincoln, Miss Harris, himself, and *no other person.*[23]

No John Parker at the door. No Secret Service men. No soldiers. No military police.

And Lincoln—a fixed target.

---

[23] National Archives, War Dept. Records, File "R," Doc. R.B.P. 74, JAO.

A few hours after the murder, War Secretary Stanton dispatched an urgent warning to General Sherman.

> ... I find evidence that an assassin is also on your track, and I beseech you to be more heedful than Mr. Lincoln was of such knowledge.[24]

CHAPTER **6**

Conspirators Amuck

SECRETARY OF STATE William H. Seward lay propped in bed, his right arm in a sling, his chin fixed in a rigid tilt by a leather and steel brace cupping a broken jaw.

Beneath a patrician head of white hair, his features wore the chalky pallor, the strained expression of endured suffering. The side of his face was puffed, the sockets of his eyes discolored. His left hand, listless on the counterpane, looked feeble, bony, the skin unnaturally white, as though powdered. The bedding below his knees was loosely bunched to accommodate a sprained foot.

At the start of a carriage drive on April 5, 1865, with his daughter, Fanny, another young lady and his eldest son, something had frightened the span of blacks.

The carriage bounced, reeled as the runaways swerved around a corner. Frederick Seward, nursing a recently broken arm, could not hold them. He shouted to the girls to hang on, and vainly tried to check the team. Secretary Seward swung out over the carriage step in an endeavor to grab the harness. His heel caught, and he fell awkwardly—a 64-year-old man, no athlete— and sprawled in the road.[1]

Somehow the horses were reared up to a stop. The figure lying inert in the road was sorely hurt. Doctors would find Mr. Seward's lower jaw broken, his right arm fractured below the shoulder, ligaments torn in his twisted foot, his body mottled with bruises. For a time they thought the Secretary might not recover.

The Sewards lived in a four-story mansion on the east side of Lafayette Square, cat-a-corner from the White House. During Buchanan's administra-

---

[24] *Official Records, U.S. Army, War of The Rebellion*, Series I, Vol. 47, Part 3, p. 221.

[1] Letter from Mrs. Seward to a Mr. Alward, May 11, 1865.

tion the mansion had housed a fashionable gentleman's club, and it retained the name during Seward's occupancy—the "Old Club House."

In the Secretary's third-floor bedroom, now converted into a hospital room, Sergeant George Robinson, colored veteran only recently recovered from war disablement, presided as male nurse. Mrs. Seward had arrived on April 7, returning from Auburn, New York, where she had been recuperating from a long illness. An invalid, she could do little to aid, but could bravely try to comfort, her stricken husband.

Frederick Seward and his wife resided there, and Major Augustus Seward and Fanny were on hand. Doctors, messengers, visitors constantly came and went. Lincoln called on April 9, solicitous, cheerful. Lounging at bedside, he related the happenings at City Point, told Seward the war was almost over. Then, seeing the Secretary was asleep, he tiptoed out.

Nights, when the front door finally closed, Fanny and Augustus took turns with other members of the family at the bedside watch. By April 10 their father showed signs of a good recovery.

Seward was a patient sufferer. His injuries pained him whenever he moved, and his neck ached from the brace supporting his fractured jaw. He was too weak to withstand heavy sedation. He bore his pain with the patience and fortitude of an elder who found spiritual strength in philosophy, a wise man who could say with Lincoln, "This, too, will pass," and leave the way and time up to Providence.

On the evening of April 14, 1865, it was the inscrutable way of Providence to burden Seward with a round of tiresome callers. Dr. Verdi and another physician stepped in. Stanton was there for a time, robust, bustling. Dr. Norris, last of the physicians to call that evening, found Seward exhausted and in pain. He administered a mild sedative.

By 10:00 P.M. the visitors were gone, the family retired, the house quiet. Seward's daughter Fanny sat by the bed anxiously watching for the relaxed breathing that would mean her father was asleep. George Robinson sat at a corner table, at ease but ready to act and serve at the slightest sign from the patient or from Miss Fanny.

A clock ticked somewhere, audible in the deepening hush. The gaslights, turned low, fluttered occasionally and dimmed, then revived, as pressure in the lines varied somewhere in the feeder system. Shadows faded and came back on the wall when the light waned and waxed. The Secretary of State dozed.

History is a record of improbable coincidences, random indeterminates, boomerang turns, and O. Henry twists.

In 1846, William H. Seward, prominent lawyer and ex-Governor of New York, risked his public career by volunteering to defend two homicidal maniacs who faced trial at Auburn. Convinced the killers were lunatics, Seward pioneered the cause of the insane by entering insanity pleas for the friendless defendants. He could not defeat the prejudice of the time, but his lucid and humane defense of the mentally irresponsible stood as a landmark on humanity's road.

Now, as the injured Secretary dozed in a haze of pain, a sudden disturbance broke the quiet of the outer hall. Fanny Seward moved, frowning, to the bedroom door.

Abruptly the door burst inward, hurling Fanny back to the wall.

A figure rushed across the threshold.

Seward roused in alarm. He found himself staring into the blazing eyes of a madman!

David Herold knew where Seward lived. He had passed the Old Club House many times. When Booth assigned him as guide to conduct the "Reverend" Paine to the Seward home, Herold came up Johnny-on-the-spot.

All day the soiled drug clerk had been dashing around town on exciting errands. To the Kirkwood House to hide weapons and gear in Atzerodt's room. To the Herndon House with a word for Paine. To the National Hotel, looking for Booth. In company with Atzerodt to Allison Naylor's Livery Stable, opposite Grover's Theater on E Street, where Atzerodt stabled a dark bay mare. To Willard's with an acquaintance (Mr. Cipriano Grillo), covering a private errand with the pretext that they might glimpse Robert E. Lee (who wasn't there). To Taltavul's and to Ford's, seeking Booth. Then, around 4:15 P.M., back to Naylor's to obtain a mount.

Earlier in the week Herold and Atzerodt had patronized Naylor's Livery. Stable Foreman John Fletcher did not take kindly to the pair; Atzerodt reeked of booze, and a drunk was liable to abuse a horse. Herold struck Fletcher as shifty-eyed and simpering, untrustworthy. Still, when Herold fished five dollars from his vest on this Good Friday afternoon, Fletcher trotted out the specified horse. Herold selected a roan mare of the type known as a "single-footed pacer."

Herold also chose a smart English saddle with ring-type steel stirrups. As he swung into saddle, the stableman reminded him that the horse must be returned at nine that night, no later. Herold agreed.

About 5:00 P.M. Herold halted at Howard's Livery on 7th Street. After some pointless chatter, he walked with Mr. Howard into Shreve's Bowling Alley, where he set up drinks for the house. Later he cantered over toward Willard's. A witness would testify to seeing Herold in earnest conversation with several men in front of the Bank of Washington.

And now, in the dusk of supper hour, Herold rode into byways untraceable. Still later, as the evening darkened, he trotted to that meeting place (the Herndon House? some alley?) where Booth waited with final instructions.

No outsider would ever learn the detail of those secret instructions. So far as can be deduced from the evidence, Herold was ordered to lead

Paine to the Seward mansion, to stand lookout while Paine went in, and to see that the strike was timed for quarter after ten. By some accounts, it was Herold who suggested that they pick up a bottle of medicine at some pharmacy so that Paine might pose as a messenger from Seward's physician, Dr. Verdi. It was a smart idea, quite possibly Herold's.

The conspirators separated. Herold on the roan led Paine on the one-eyed horse here and there for a spell, marking time. He probably had no particular liking for Lewis Paine, for with that perception common to gamins and street arabs, he must have perceived that Paine disliked him.

Paine seems to have regarded Herold much as a warrior would regard a camp-follower. The big Confederate had little use for such as this drug-store clerk. He referred to Herold as a "blab." After he was caught, Paine would contemptuously describe the others in Booth's band as "women and babies."[2]

Did Paine think of Herold as "woman" or "baby?" Herold did, perhaps, have in his make-up a womanish streak. His sisters thought him silly. This may have been more than vapidity. His shallow glibness, his slyness, his harum-scarum insouciance, his slavish devotion to Booth suggest the androgyne. Boastful of his own masculinity, Paine would not have liked the type.

To Herold, Paine doubtless seemed a backwoods moron. At least six times that evening Herold described for Paine the escape route across the city. Paine couldn't remember it. As they approached Lafayette Square the numbskull had to be told Dr. Verdi's name over and over; he kept forgetting it.

Booth had shown perspicacity in teaming these two for the mission. The ferret craft of one would get them to their destination; the mastiff brawn of the other would do the job.

They rode on under the streetlamps. Crossed the deserted square. Reined up in front of the Seward residence.

Ten minutes after ten.

Features set in a scowl of resolution, Paine dismounted and stalked to the door.

Waiting in saddle at curbside, Herold watched in a transport of excitement. The door opened. Paine stepped in. The door closed.

Statement of William H. Bell, servant at Secretary Seward's:

> I was at Mr. Seward's house Friday night 14th of April 1865, when the man came. . . . He rang the door-bell and I answered. I opened the door and he walked in about two feet, when he stopped and told me he wanted to see Mr. Seward. He said he must see him—that he was sent there by Dr. Verdi with a little package which he had in his hand with a label on it. I told [him] he could not see him and he had better send it up by me.

---

[2] Paine Confession; quoted in Wilson, *op. cit.*, p. 99.

He seemed to be excited and talked very fast and very loud. He started up a few steps and I followed him. He met Mr. Frederick Seward on the steps. . . . He asked Mr. Frederick if he could see Mr. Seward and he told him he could not. . . . [The man] said he must see him as he was directed by Dr. Verdi to give the package to him. . . . Mr. Frederick told him that he could not go in, and if he could not leave the message with him he could not leave it at all. He then said "Well, if I can't see him!"—and he made a little mumbling, and started to go down stairs, and came down two or three steps after me.

I was in front of him and his boots made a great noise. I asked him not to make such a great noise. About the time I said that, he [turned and] struck Mr. Frederick, I think with a knife. I saw the last time he hit Mr. Frederick and Mr. Frederick fell. He then ran into Mr. Seward's room and I ran down to the door to give the alarm.

I am not certain of the time when he came to the door . . . it was about five minutes after the Doctor had gone away. . . . He was a tall man, I think full six foot and a little taller than Mr. Frederick . . . had a red face, dark complected, and no whiskers or moustache. His hair was black and turned a little behind. . . . He had [on] an overcoat and black pants. The coat came down below the knees. He had very thin lips and in talking used his upper lip but didn't show his teeth.

I am pretty certain it was a knife he struck Mr. Frederick across the head with. It was about fourteen or sixteen inches long. He had [on] a light brown, broad-brimmed, soft left hat. I can't tell how long he was in the Secretary's room because I ran downstairs as soon as I saw Mr. Frederick fall. . . . I went down to the door and hollered "Murder!" and then ran over to General Augur's office to give the alarm.[3]

Paine did not strike Frederick Seward with a knife.

Hearing the commotion in the lower hall, Frederick Seward, in dressing gown and slippers, had hurried to the stairhead to see what it was about.

As Frederick Seward recalled the episode: "There seemed nothing unusual in the occurrence when a tall, well-dressed, but unknown man presented himself below; and informing the servant that he brought a message from the doctor, was allowed to come up the stairs to [toward?] the door of Seward's room. . . . [I] refused him admission, explaining that the sleeping invalid must not be disturbed. He paused, apparently irresolute. When advised to leave his message and go back to report to the doctor, he replied, 'Very well, sir, I will go,' and turning away, took two or three steps down the stairs.

"Suddenly, turning again, he sprang up and forward, having drawn a navy revolver, which he levelled, with a muttered oath, and pulled the trigger. . . ."[4]

The Colt misfired.

Enraged, Paine charged. And before Frederick Seward could fend the

---

[3] National Archives, War Dept. Records, File "B," Evd. B.P. 4, JAO.

[4] Frederick W. Seward, *Reminiscences of a War-Time Statesman and Diplomat* (New York: G. P. Putnam's Sons, 1916), pp. 276–277.

blow with his injured arm, big Lewis brought the pistol-barrel smashing down. As the stunned victim sank against the bannister, Paine struck him again and again—terrific blows that broke the pistol. Paine hurled the useless gun at his victim's head, stepped back and drew a bowie knife.

Ribbons of blood streaming down his face, Frederick Seward slumped over, unconscious.

Paine threw himself at Secretary Seward's door. The barrier burst inward, and the killer on the threshhold glared straight at his defenseless prey.

Paine flung himself at the helpless figure in the bed. The action was instantaneous—faster than the leap of the panther which crouches, measures distance, and studies its victim before the spring.

Seward barely had time to see the knife. Recoiling, rolling to evade the blow, he gasped as the blade slashed the side of his face from cheekbone to jaw—a barbarous cut that laid his cheek open in a cruel slice. But not fatal.

Uttering a choked cry, Seward tried to escape from the bed. Paine was on him, kneeing him, clutching him by the hair in an effort to jerk his head back and expose his throat. Bedsprings creaked and twanged, and the bedstead swayed and jounced like a runaway carriage as murderer and victim wrestled in a tousel of quilts, pillows and counterpane. Twice and again the killer slashed as the invalid heaved from side to side, fighting to duck the knife. Two stunning blows struck Seward's broken jaw. Each time the blade flashed sparks and the knife was jarred in Paine's grip.

Through the heat of animal rage, the lamp-haze, the sweat, Paine saw that his victim wore some kind of surgical collar—an appliance of leather and steel embracing his throat. Infuriated, blood-maddened, Paine slashed at the neck-brace. Crimson spattered Seward's tossing shoulders. Paine slashed again and again. Somehow Seward rolled from the mattress and slid to the floor in a tumble of bedclothing.

Hands grabbed Paine's arm, yanking him back. Somewhere behind him a girl was screaming and screaming. Intent on his work, he had hardly been aware of others in the room. Whirling from the bed, he found himself fighting two men—a Negro, a white man—interferences to be disposed of. Now the warrior was in his element, lunging, kicking, stabbing blindly in pitched battle.

They fought across the floor, stumbling over chairs. Paine slammed the white man against a table, gashed him with the knife, spun around and cut at the Negro joyously. A rocker fell over backward. Bedroom bric-à-brac crashed. Rampaging, Paine downed his foes, kicked furniture aside, and charged out into the hall to the stairhead, bellowing, "I'm mad!"

Behind him the killer left a scene of carnage and gore as bloody as any in the annals of crime.

Frederick Seward lying unconscious in a crimson welter.

Augustus Seward, staggering with hands to head, half scalped.

George Robinson maimed, his stabbed chest and shoulders streaming blood.

Fanny Seward fainting, hysterical.

And Mrs. Seward, frail with invalidism, shaking with terror, groping into the wrecked bedroom to the side of her husband, who seemed to be dead.

On the bloodstained carpet, William H. Seward, American Secretary of State, lay prostrate, his broken arm grotesquely bent, his head askew, his broken jaw unhinged, his face a crimson death-mask.

An old front-line soldier, aged twenty, had come and gone.

Throughout the day and evening of Good Friday, 1865, Michael O'Laughlin roamed Washington City with a party of Baltimore friends. They were, as O'Laughlin phrased it, "in liquor."

The party included Lieutenant James B. Henderson, U.S.N.; a tailor named Bernard Early; a plumber, Edward Murphy. Part of the time they were accompanied by George Grillet, an employee of the New York Excelsior Cracker Co.[5]

The Baltimoreans had come to Washington on the previous afternoon (April 13) to see the "illuminations." They wanted to whoop it up, and they did. They set out from the Lichau House, and let 'er rip from there.

They kept it going all night of the 13th and were still at it Good Friday morning. Afterwards, O'Laughlin would have a hard time remembering where he had been that Thursday night. The police eventually acquired statements from Murphy, Early, and Naval Lieutenant Henderson giving a fairly comprehensive review of O'Laughlin's doings and whereabouts.

A police brief on Edward Murphy characterizes the other briefs and also Mr. Murphy:

> Edward Murphy, one of the company ... who left Baltimore on the afternoon of April 13, 1865, is a man about 25 years of age, said to be a Plumber by trade. He a few years ago was unfortunate in causing the death of a young lad named Patterson. He has been in the habit of keeping bad company, and has the appearance of being fond of drink. The statement obtained from him places him in company with the [other] parties, from the time they left Baltimore in the 3½ o'clock train for Washington, up to the hour that O'Laughlin and Early left Washington on the afternoon of the 15th April, going the rounds about Washington with them, visiting Hotels, Restaurants, Houses of ill fame, &c, and remained in Washington [after] O'Laughlin and Early had left him there.[6]

Murphy's statement provided Mike O'Laughlin with an alibi—one duly supported by Bernie Early and Lieutenant Henderson, and in part by

---

[5] National Archives, War Dept. Records, File "S," Doc. 554, JAO.
[6] National Archives, War Dept. Records, File "S," Doc. 554, JAO.

George Grillet. O'Laughlin was roistering with all or a couple of these sports from the time he entered the capital on the 13th until he quit the city on the 15th.

However, an examination of the witness record serves to shade the surface picture. On several occasions during that hectic weekend, O'Laughlin was off on private errands. At least twice he went to John Wilkes Booth's hotel.

According to the deposition sworn by Bernard Early, the celebrants arrived in Washington about 5:30 P.M. on the 13th:

> We all walked up the Avenue together as far as Rullman's Hotel, or the Lichau House, went in and took drinks. . . . O'Laughlin asked me to walk up as far as the National Hotel to see a party. . . . He went in the National Hotel and I with him, and he inquired of the clerk for some one, I did not hear the name. He went upstairs and returned immediately, saying the party he wanted to see was not in, but that he would see him the next morning about ten o'clock. . . . We went to the Canterberry, stayed a considerable time, came out all together, and went down the Avenue . . . and visited a Dutch Ball at Riddle's Lager Beer Saloon.[7]

After frolicking through the red-light district, they ended up at the Metropolitan Hotel. A night of wassail and concupiscence did not faze the group, although O'Laughlin seems to have felt "seedy" that morning. Early goes on:

> After breakfast went out and walked down the Avenue as far as the National Hotel. O'Laughlin went upstairs in the Hotel, to see his friend who he had been looking for the evening before. I, Henderson and Murphy went to the water closet of the Hotel, when I came out of the closet, Henderson was setting upon a Lounge or Settee, and told me he was waiting for Mr. O'Laughlin, who had gone upstairs to see Booth. We waited an half hour. . . .
>
> We then went out of the Hotel and down the Avenue as far as Lichau House. Mr. O'Laughlin afterward joined us there. I don't recollect whether I asked him or not, if he saw his friend Booth, or not, while in Lichau's. Mr. O'Laughlin went out on the pavement to speak to his brother who was passing by, and held a conversation with him some five or ten minutes. We all four then took a strole (*sic*) around the City, until dinner time [noon], and brought up at Welch's, and dined there. After dinner we took another strole until about 4 o'clock of the afternoon. We separated. . . . O'Laughlin and I went to see a friend of mine named Mrs. Dugan, 496 D Street.[8]

Grillet added that he thought he glimpsed Booth having a private drink with O'Laughlin at the Lichau House that day. At what hour Grillet did not state.

Supporting O'Laughlin (or perhaps O'Laughlin supporting them), Early and Henderson staggered into Welch's at suppertime. After oysters and

---

[7] National Archives, War Dept. Records, File "E," R.B.P. 15, JAO.
[8] *Ibid.*

brandy, the indomitable trio went reeling down to Lichau's. This was the crucial hour, insofar as an alibi for O'Laughlin were concerned. For the police would eventually contend that this Baltimore hooligan participated in the assassination strike, that he "laid in wait," that his target may have been General Grant, or possibly Edwin M. Stanton.

John R. Giles, bartender at Lichau's, spoke for O'Laughlin an almost unbreakable alibi: "O'Laughlin was at the Lichau House the night of the assassination the whole evening. . . . Barney Early was there . . . several boys from the Express Company were there."

As Giles recalled it, a soldier came in about 11:15 P.M. (perhaps earlier) and announced that the President had been murdered and Booth was the assassin. O'Laughlin looked startled and said, "It can't be so."

The bartender added this caveat: "I cannot swear that he was there all evening, but he appeared to be. I saw him pretty nearly all the time. He could not have been away more than twenty minutes or half an hour any time. He was in liquor that night, pretty tight. I was no great friend of his [but] he was a good jovial kind of fellow."[9]

The good jovial kind of fellow was too intoxicated to assess the full import of the news. Or so it would appear. According to Early, O'Laughlin left Lichau's before midnight with John Fuller, a man who tended bar in a saloon near the depot. They spent the night carousing in the Franklin House on D Street. Evidently O'Laughlin was in no shape to recollect anything the following morning.

But he did recollect. And his memories were highly unpleasant. If he had any sense at all, he must have wished he had never stopped in to see Booth at the National the previous day. He must have regretted he hadn't gone to Fortress Monroe with Sam Arnold instead of answering Booth's final summons to Washington.

George Atzerodt was scared sick. He couldn't go through with it.

Acting on Booth's orders, he had gone to the Kirkwood House at 12th and Pennsylvania soon after breakfast. There he paid one day's lodging in advance, signed the register, went clumping up the stairs to Room 126.

Red carpets, polished brass spittoons, plush armchairs—the place frightened him. It was not as *gemütlich* as the so-called "Kimmel House," the five-in-a-room flophouse he had just left on C Street. He knew no one here, and the one person he had to acquaint himself with frightened him.

Vice President Andrew Johnson—Atzerodt swallowed lumps in his throat at the thought of it. He stayed but a few minutes in his scary room, then went to the bar to wash down the lumps with whiskey. A few whiskeys and he was encouraged to ask the bartender off-hand questions about Mr. Johnson.

---

[9] National Archives, War Dept. Records, File "G," R.B.P. 96, JAO.

At midmorning Herold showed up at his elbow, and Atzerodt felt better. He gave Herold the key to Room 126. Herold went up and left some things. He said he'd meet Atzerodt around one o'clock. Atzerodt was to rent himself a horse at Kelleher & Pywell's Stable.

The Kirkwood room clerk would remember that Atzerodt stopped at the desk around noon and inquired the number of Vice President's Johnson's room. He obliged by pointing out the room to the Dutch fellow, and he told the Dutchman that Mr. Johnson had just come in. Whereupon the Dutchman hurried back into the bar. Perhaps Atzerodt had been alarmed to learn that his room was directly over the one occupied by the Vice President.

About 1:00 P.M. Atzerodt, now "in liquor," visited Kelleher & Pywell's on 8th Street. He paid money down and hired a dark bay mare. At an appointed corner he met David Herold. They went on down E Street and over to Naylor's Livery, where Atzerodt stabled the dark bay. A strategem: you took a horse from one livery and stabled it in another a few blocks away, and then you could duck off somewhere on foot. Later, if an alibi were necessary, you could say you'd spent the afternoon horseback riding.

Midafternoon, and Atzerodt could again be seen at Kirkwood bar. Fidgety, he did not stay long. He was out at 4:00 P.M. or thereabouts when Booth called to see him and, finding him absent, left a calling-card for Vice President Johnson, who also was out.

Did Booth encounter George Atzerodt on the street later that afternoon? So some historical accounts would have it. Booth, mounted, spied "Port Tobacco" scurrying along the curb, hailed him, and pulled up alongside.

In a whispered conference, Booth told Atzerodt the showdown had arrived. He assigned to Atzerodt the mission of assassinating the Vice President that evening. George Atzerodt was to go to Johnson's room about 10:15 P.M., knock on the door, push in when the knock was answered, and shoot Johnson point-blank. Then hit for Navy Yard Bridge and Surrattsville.

According to this story, Atzerodt declined the mission then and there. He reminded Booth that the plan had been to abduct. Said he hadn't promised to enter a murder scheme. Told Booth that he wanted no part of an assassination job. Whereupon Booth, blenching in fury, advised that it was "too late to back out now." Menacingly he assured Atzerodt that he had "already gone too far." If he knew what was good for him, he'd carry out the mission.

"I am in trouble," Atzerodt presumably countered mournfully. "And I will never be shut of it."[10]

There are several flaws in the foregoing story. Perhaps the major flaw is that it was based on a "confession" extracted from Atzerodt by extreme

---

[10] Oldroyd, *op. cit.*

duress. Under the circumstances, he tried to put a good foot forward and tried to tell his inquisitors that he'd been caught in a vise with Booth turning the screw.

Aside from that manifest weakness—the source—the story reveals obvious fictioneering in substance. Atzerodt did not make it clear in his confession just where or when this encounter with Booth took place. Nor did he offer such details as how Booth could know Mr. Johnson would be in his room at the Kirkwood that evening at the appointed hour, or how he, Atzerodt, was to escape from a crowded hotel after firing a shot bound to wake the whole place.

Finally, Atzerodt sputtered another and differing account. In this version he said that he met Booth and Paine at the Herndon House that evening, and it was there that Booth saddled him with the murder assignment.[11] These flaws have led many students of the case to assume that the story is so much linsey-woolsey.

Several noted historians believe that Booth never assigned an assassination role to Atzerodt. Detecting fallacies in the set-up, they reject the entire story as fable. Eisenschiml observes that "the man supposedly selected by Booth was notoriously unfit for the task allotted to him. Such flaws in the plans of this brilliant plotter are unlikely; they become unbelievable on closer examination of the clues left in Atzerodt's room. . . ."[12] He refers to the weapons and wearing apparel later found abandoned in Room 126 at the Kirkwood.

Eisenschiml develops the theory that the clues were deliberately planted by Booth "in his contempt for the intelligence of the police, and perhaps in a spirit of bravado." Why else would he have had Herold deposit in Atzerodt's room a bundle of articles easily identified as belonging to the various members of his band?

But inevitably the stuff subsequently found in Atzerodt's room at the Kirkwood linked Atzerodt to the assassination conspiracy like a length of chain. Could Atzerodt himself have been the target of this little game? Undoubtedly Booth realized the Port Tobaccan might panic at the showdown and flee. Bolting, he would never stop to clean out his hotel room.

But, in the wake of Lincoln's assassination, the police would surely throw a protective screen around Johnson. Detectives, swarming over the Kirkwood, would soon hear of the clown Dutchman who'd made himself conspicuous in the place. Sooner or later, the officers would search Atzerodt's room, then take off after him like hounds after a varmint.

So the key to the Atzerodt puzzle possibly lies in a device not known to scholarly researchers, historians and other honest persons unacquainted with the trickeries of the espionage trade—the "fool spy." Here, perhaps,

---

[11] Official statement quoted in full in Buckingham, *op. cit.*, pp. 33–37.
[12] *Op. cit.*, p. 168.

is the only logical explanation for the plant in Atzerodt's room, for the planting of dull George himself in the Kirkwood. Atzerodt was to draw the chase. Atzerodt was to be "sacrificed." If the "fool" went ahead and tried to shoot or did shoot Johnson, so much the better. In any event, he would divert the manhunt while the master assassin made a getaway.

Poor, muddled Atzerodt had no intention of shooting Mr. Johnson, especially after a noontime glimpse of Mr. Johnson in the Kirkwood dining room. He saw a hearty eater with napkin under chin—a square-faced, rugged-looking individual who refused to hide his features behind the hirsute adornments in current vogue. Andrew Johnson looked a hard man to surprise, a tough customer to deal with. Watching him from under cover, George Atzerodt evidently experienced a sinking sensation. Booth or no Booth, he couldn't beard this lion in this den.

Yet Atzerodt, too, apparently went to the secret rendezvous that evening for final instructions from Booth. Scared to go. Scared not to go. There it would seem that Booth applied a last twist of some kind to Atzerodt's wrist—perhaps a savage threat—perhaps a dollar for the purchase of some more Dutch courage. The miserable conspirator returned to the Kirkwood bar where he asked a few more questions about the habits of Vice President Johnson. Then, about 10:00 P.M., he went to Naylor's Livery for his horse.

Stable Foreman Fletcher would recall the transaction, Atzerodt's flushed face and whiskey breath, his fumbling and mumbling. When Fletcher trotted out the dark bay, Atzerodt mumbled something that sounded to Fletcher like, "If this thing happens tonight you will get a present."

The Dutchman mounted clumsily. Fletcher warned him the horse seemed skittish. "*Ja,*" Atzerodt nodded, "but she is good upon a retreat."

Herold had not returned at the designated hour with the roan, and Fletcher, frowning, asked Atzerodt if his friend would be out much longer. Atzerodt mumbled, "Oh, he should be back after a while."[13]

Suspicious, Fletcher watched the Dutchman ride down the block to the Kirkwood. He saw Atzerodt tie up the horse, clump into the hotel, and soon come clumping out. After clambering again into saddle, Atzerodt started off in the direction of 10th Street. The stable foreman did not know it, but he was witnessing the "retreat" Atzerodt had mentioned.

By one account, the retreat became galloping fright after Atzerodt heard the explosion of sudden tumult on 10th Street, and, passing the corner, glimpsed the riot spilling out of Ford's Theater.[14] Shouts that the President had been murdered. Cries for vengence. Atzerodt saw a knot of men struggling under a lamppost, and a desperate figure struggling in the center

---

[13] Oldroyd, *op. cit.,* p. 47.

[14] Philip Van Doren Stern, *The Man Who Killed Lincoln* (New York: The Literary Guild of America, 1939), p. 152.

of the knot. Someone shouted, "Bring the rope!" Atzerodt's Dutch courage ebbed in a gush. Wheeling the horse, he fled.

He galloped the animal to its home stable—Kelleher & Pywell's. People who had seen him ride away from the Kirkwood House would expect him to be mounted; in ridding himself of the horse, Atzerodt made an almost intelligent move.

His next move was not so intelligent. He went into a bar (apparently one on 12th Street known as the "Oyster Bay"), then to another, and so on for several blocks, hoping to drown his fears, to forget his miseries, to drink himself out of his difficulties.

Later, slinking down a dark street, he slung away his unused bowie knife.

Still later, sweating, panting, George Atzerodt reeled on foot across the brow of Capitol Hill. He would never find a way home. The authorities would contend that George A. Atzerodt was one of at least five persons who knew of Booth's plot to kill Lincoln in Ford's Theater, a witness who could have gone with what he knew to the police an hour before the murder and thus saved the President's life.

Who were the others acquainted with Booth's intentions? Herold, when captured, would testify that Booth told him there were 35 men in the conspiracy.[15] Surratt would confide to a friend that the directors of the conspiracy were "men who are not yet known."[16] Evidence strongly hints that more than five persons knew of the impending assassination strike.

Did Mrs. Mary E. Surratt know?

Mrs. Surratt beheld the world through unhappy eyes upon her return from Surrattsville on the evening of Good Friday, April 14, 1865. During this, her second junket "down country" to see the insolvent Nothey about unpaid debts, she had left a package for Mr. Booth at the Surrattsville tavern, and had conveyed some sort of message from Booth to John Lloyd. Or so Mr. Lloyd would subsequently state. Mary Surratt would say otherwise.

She would state that her visit to Surrattsville that fatal day had its source in a letter from Mr. Calvert, who was dunning her for money. She, in turn, had to wring some money out of Nothey. A logical story were it not for the parcel and message delivered for Mr. Booth. The parcel, it seemed, contained a pair of field glasses belonging to Booth. The message (so Lloyd eventually testified) had to do with readying the weapons and escape gear hidden at the tavern. Mrs. Surratt could deny delivery of the secret message, but she could not deny delivery of the binoculars. Her escort, Louis Wiechmann, saw the package. Just as they started off for

---

[15] National Archives, War Dept. Records, File "H," Doc. R.B.P. 38, JAO.
[16] Quoted in Oldroyd, *op. cit.*, p. 229.

Surrattsville that afternoon, Mrs. Surratt had exclaimed, "Stop! Let me get those things of Booth's."

En route home she hurried the drive, saying to Wiechmann that she wanted to be back by nine o'clock as she'd made an engagement to meet a gentleman at that hour.

"Booth?" Wiechmann casually asked.

Mrs. Surratt did not answer directly. Some time later she remarked, "Booth is done acting. He's going to New York very soon, never to return." She added vehemently, "Yes, and Booth is crazy on one subject, and next time I see him I am going to give him a good scolding."

Mrs. Surratt and Wiechmann drew up at the H Street house about 8:30 P.M. Wiechmann returned the rig to Howard's Stable. When he got back to the boardinghouse, Mrs. Surratt invited him to join her in a bite of supper. At table she showed him a letter which, she said, had just come from her son John. For some unexplained reason the letter had been delivered by John's friend Annie Ward. It was postmarked St. Lawrence Hall, Canada, April 12, 1865. (Of course, it could have been posted by a friend.) Surratt wrote that he liked Montreal and the French Cathedral. He had purchased a French-style jacket. He might go on to Toronto. Mrs. Surratt later claimed that this letter proved her son's whereabouts as Canada on the night of the assassination. Unfortunately she was never able to produce the letter as evidence—when she wanted to find it, it could not be found.

Just as the supper dishes were being cleared, there was a ring at the door. Wiechmann started to answer. Mrs. Surratt said she would go. From the downstairs dining room, Wiechmann heard a murmurous conversation in the upper hall. Or perhaps Mrs. Surratt took the caller into the parlor. The visitor did not stay long. Was this the gentleman she had expected at nine? Could it have been John Wilkes Booth? Or John Surratt?

Already depressed by the drive to Surrattsville, the widow seemed wrapped in gloom after the caller's departure. Her countenance darkened as the evening wore on. Going up to the parlor, Wiechmann found her with her prayer beads in her hand. Looking up from the Rosary, she asked him to "pray for her intentions." Wiechmann expressed bafflement. He told her he had no idea what her intentions might be. Whereupon as Oldroyd relates the incident, "She then asked him to pray for them, anyhow."[17]

This view of Mrs. Surratt and her demeanor comes, of course, from Wiechmann. One finds it in the testimony volunteered by the Government employee in the dark period following the assassination strike. Critics are constrained to wonder at the accuracy of Wiechmann's observations, if not their veracity. Other witnesses in the house that evening did not, apparently, notice anything unusual in the widow's behavior.

She did, however, make one rather peculiar move, to which the lady

---

[17] *Ibid.*, pp. 181–184.

inmates of the establishment bore witness. About ten o'clock she hustled the distaff side of the household, Anna Surratt, Nora Fitzpatrick and Mrs. Surratt's niece Olivia Jenkins, up to bed. Wiechmann, too, went to his room. The widow traveled through the house, turning out the oil lamps. Not often did the household retire at so early an hour.

The little boardinghouse would never again go peacefully to its rest. The ladies were hardly in their nightgowns and curl papers when sounds of disturbance and alarm aroused the night.

Did three breathless men enter the Surratt house about midnight and hastily change their clothes? Did they mutter ominously about murder? Did one of them tell Mrs. Surratt that her son had been at Ford's Theater that night?

Such would be the story told by the colored servant girl, Susan Jackson. Few historians believe Susan's tale. In the ensuing game of truth and consequences, it would incur dire consequences, but the truth would never be determined.

Unhappy Mrs. Surratt. As was the case with Atzerodt, it was too late for her to back out now. The trap that had sprung would spring another trap—the deadliest trap of all—under her.

Mrs. Surratt's protestations of innocence were hopelessly compromised by Susan Jackson's testimony. There were incongruities in Susan's story, and glaring incongruities in the official recording of that story and in the War Department's handling of the matter. The gist of the tale, however, was that Susan overheard one of the three midnight visitors say John Surratt had been at Ford's Theater with Booth on Good Friday night. That statement was to make more trouble for Mary Surratt than it ever made for her conspirator son.

For Mrs. Surratt swore on the Bible that her son was in Canada that night. Or, at least, to her knowledge, he was not in Washington City.

Two years later John Surratt would testify that he spent the night of April 14 in New York State.

Yet an abundance of eyewitness testimony placed him in Washington during the daylight hours of the 14th. He was seen by an acquaintance near Willard's Hotel. A detective who knew him glimpsed him on Pennsylvania Avenue. A neighbor saw him hurrying down H Street. The authorities, naturally enough, assumed that he would hardly visit Washington and be in the vicinity of his mother's boardinghouse without stopping in to see his mother, or, if she were out when he called, at least leaving a message for his mother.

If he was, Mrs. Surratt must have known her son was in town. It followed that, possessed of this knowledge, she must have lied to the investigating authorities. One breach in the widow's testimony and she became immediately suspect. Alas for Mary Surratt, she could not thereafter guarantee her word on any of the many answers to be demanded of her.

But where *was* John Surratt on the night of Lincoln's murder?

If he was in Washington during the day, he must have quit the capital early that evening, before the assassination. A train left at 6:00 P.M. for Philadelphia. General and Mrs. Grant were on this northbound train. Some historians surmise that John Surratt had been assigned the mission of assassinating General Grant.

At noon that day Mrs. Grant had been alarmed by a wild-eyed individual who glared at her as she entered the dining room at Willard's. She mentioned the incident to Grant when he returned to the hotel after attending a Cabinet session at the White House.[18]

Then, as the General and his wife left the hotel and headed for the railroad station, a horseman had cut across the avenue, drawn up alongside the carriage, and scowled ferociously at the departing celebrities. Grant's carriage, of course, was escorted by a cordon of cavalry. The intrusive horseman was edged aside in the press of traffic. Had his scowl meant a curse for the General, or had it meant poor eyesight—the grimace of some rubberneck with myopic vision? Evidently the General thought nothing of the incident. But some time afterwards, studying photographs, he thought he recognized the scowler in Booth's camera portrait. Who could say? Could it have been John Surratt?

The Grants were not disturbed on the train to Philadelphia. But the General eventually found in his mail an anonymous letter concerning the matter. The writer declared that he was a conspirator who had been assigned to murder Grant. He had boarded the train with that intent, but had been unable to force a barred door and enter Grant's compartment. The writer said in conclusion that he thanked God he'd been unable to carry out the murder.

Official mails were flooded with freak correspondence at the time. Perhaps the oddest part of this confessional letter to Grant—as remarked by Eisenschiml[19]—lies in the fact that the Government authorities never revealed its existence until years later. So far as is known, no attempt was made by the Secret Service or the Military Police to analyze the handwriting, trace the postmark, or otherwise track down the writer.

Very possibly the letter was a fake. However, it may have been intended as a troublemaker, or as a decoy to divert the police effort. It seems unlikely that John Surratt could have been the writer. The authorities had in their possession many examples of Surratt's penmanship. Had the handwriting matched this letter's, surely the letter must have been recognized as Exhibit A in the evidence against John Surratt.

---

[18] Jesse Grant, *In The Days of My Father* (New York & London: Harper and Brothers, Publishers, 1925), pp. 36–40.

[19] *Op. cit.*, p. 165.

Unless the War Department did not want to produce such an exhibit in evidence against John Harrison Surratt.

Vice President Andrew Johnson found time on his hands during the day of April 14, 1865. The Government offices were closed for Good Friday, and so he had nothing much to do that morning but sit in his room and read.

Lincoln had called a Cabinet meeting for the forenoon, but the Vice President was not invited. Commentators took this to mean that Andy was on the "outs" with Lincoln, who had not seen him since the inauguration fiasco.

After that unhappy episode Johnson had gone to stay for a few days in the home of Frank Blair out at Silver Spring, Maryland. Lincoln's attitude toward the inaugural affair was clearly recalled by Treasury Secretary Hugh McCulloch. Two or three days after the Vice President's unfortunate performance, Lincoln said to McCulloch: "I have known Andy Johnson for many years. He made a bad slip the other day, but you need not be scared. Andy ain't a drunkard."[20]

On his return to Washington, Johnson had remained in semi-seclusion at the Kirkwood, probably hoping that the inaugural storm would blow over. If that were, in truth, his hope, he sadly misjudged the character of his political enemies.

The Gray underground menaced Andrew Johnson in Washington City. As he sat reading in his two-room suite at the Kirkwood on the morning of April 14, 1865, he was unaware of the shadows around him. In the hotel dining room he did not know he was under surveillance. Early in the afternoon Johnson walked over to the White House to keep an appointment with the President. So he was out when Booth called at the Kirkwood, leaving his card.

Booth gave that mysterious card to desk clerk Robert Jones. Later that afternoon (according to witness testimony) Jones gave the card to Johnson's secretary, William A. Browning. Whether Browning handed the card to Johnson that evening or forgot it until the following day is a question never answered. By one of those freakish twists which contorted nearly every angle of the Lincoln murder case, investigators would hear that Booth's card ended up in the mailbox of Edward Salomon, ex-Governor of Wisconsin, whose room at the Kirkwood adjoined Johnson's. To this day nobody knows if Johnson ever saw the card.

On the evening of April 14, Andrew Johnson was visited in his suite by a second ex-Governor of Wisconsin—Leonard J. Farwell. Johnson said he was very tired, planned to retire early. By all accounts the Vice President did retire at the unusually early hour of nine o'clock.

Two hours later, roused by pounding on his door, Johnson woke to find

---

[20] Hugh McCulloch, *Men and Measures of Half a Century*, p. 373.

himself in the grip of nightmare. Lincoln had been assassinated, and there was this early retirement and—worse—Booth's calling card to explain.

Neither card nor early retirement were ever satisfactorily explained. They composed ugly question marks which remained to haunt the career of the new American president.

PART

II

Exeunt Assassins

Thou sure and firm-set earth
Hear not my steps, which way they walk, for fear
Thy very stones prate of my whereabouts.

—*Macbeth*

Nay, but make haste, the better foot before.

—*King John*

CHAPTER **7**

Booth Rides

Booth entered the wings on a stumbling run. Charging into darkness, he almost collided with Laura Keene. She had been poised there, in the first entrance, awaiting her cue. Behind her stood actor William J. Ferguson, costumed as a Royal Navy officer, the Lieutenant Vernon of the cast. Both players had been dumfounded by Booth's appearance on stage. Now they gaped at him in frozen astonishment.

Blindly Booth charged, brandishing the dagger. According to some accounts he shouted, "I've done it!" as he rushed into the wings.[1] Afterward, neither Miss Keene nor Ferguson could remember exactly what happened. Laura Keene raised her hands in a defensive gesture.[2] She caught an alcoholic hiss from Booth's teeth as he struck her arm aside. His rush carried him between the actress and the stupefied Ferguson. Then he was gone like a shadow absorbed by the backstage gloom.

In the cavernous dusk behind the flats, John Matthews waited to make his surprise entry on the scene. Matthews was costumed as the Mr. Coyle of the play. When he heard the shot he thought it some sort of extemporized stunt introduced to enliven the comedy.[3] A moment later he would hear the scream of ghastly tragedy. But by that time the assassin was gone.

Down the dim passage to the stage door Booth fled, apparently unaware of a crippling injury. A few days later he would boast to one Thomas Harbin that courage alone propelled him across the stage after his sprawling jump from Lincoln's box. "If I hadn't been very courageous, I'd have given up right there. I thought for an instant I was going to faint."[4] Such self-glorification was typical of him. He was more probably anaesthetized by brandy and excitement, and propelled by the urgency for action, the animal instinct for getaway.

In the dim backstage passage Booth encountered a shadowy figure—

---

[1] Poore, *op. cit.,* p. 172.

[2] Ruggles, *op. cit.,* p. 181.

[3] Wilson, *op. cit.,* p. 115.

[4] Ella V. Mahoney, *Sketches of Tudor Hall and the Booth Family* (Belair, Maryland, 1925), p. 34.

William Withers, Jr., orchestra leader. Booth cut at the musician, flinging him aside. Afterward Withers asserted that Booth knifed him twice.

"He had a dagger in his hand and he waved it threateningly," Withers recalled. "He slashed at me, and the knife cut through my coat, vest, and underclothing. He struck again, the point of the weapon penetrating the back of my neck, and the blow brought me to the floor. I recognized him as J. Wilkes Booth, and watched him make his exit into the alley."[5] One historian says Booth grappled frantically with the door handle,[6] implying that he found the door closed and had to open it. Another tells us that he opened the stage door and shut it behind him.[7] But a witness who lived on "Baptist Alley" testified that she saw the door standing open, saw Booth come plunging through the exit,[8] still brandishing the dagger, and lunge out into the night.

In the alley Joseph Burroughs waited with Booth's horse. Unknowing pawn in a game beyond his comprehension or imagination, little "Johnny Peanuts" expected a tip. His award was a brush with death which may have been closer than he knew. Like orchestra leader Withers, he was lucky.

The following day, Burroughs testified:

> I heard a pistol go off in the direction of the stage, I then went up towards the door leading the horse, when here comes Mr. Booth out of the door. He holerd (sic) give me that horse, when he had one foot on the stirrup. I had hold of the bridle and Mr. Booth struck me with the butt of a knife or dagger he had drawn in his hand. He struck me on the breast and knocked me down. He then kicked me. When he got on the horse, the horse was about four feet from the door.[9]

In concluding his statement, "Johnny Peanuts" declared that when Booth "hopped out" of the theater "he left the door open." Here is another of those weird discrepancies that seem inevitable to eyewitness reports and historic accounts of an episode.

Booth mounted with a skip, a buck and a twist. The nervous mare shied and danced. As she curveted away, a man burst from the stage door, shouting, "Stop! Stop!" This was Major Joseph B. Stewart, a Washington attorney.

From a front seat of the orchestra Stewart had glimpsed the scuffle in the President's box. Booth's leap to the stage had brought the lawyer to his feet. Reflex action carried Stewart up and over the footlights and across the stage in a dash after the assassin, crying: "Stop that man!" Had anyone backstage possessed similar perception and gumption, the killer would never have made the exit. But just as Stewart reached the stage door, it

---

[5] Oldroyd, *op. cit.*, p. 21.
[6] Van Doren Stern, *op. cit.*, p. 136.
[7] Bishop, *op. cit.*, p. 211.
[8] National Archives, War Dept. Records, File "A," Doc. 527, JAO.
[9] National Archives, War Dept. Records, File "B," Doc. "Ev.B.R.7." JAO.

was slammed in front of him.[10] By someone in the darkness there? A stage hand? One of the carpenters? No one could tell with certainty who barred the way of the only pursuer on Booth's heels.

It was Stewart, then, who had to grapple with the door handle. On the delay of those few seconds hinged a nightmare of history. Later, actor Ferguson declared that "possibly a minute had passed between the time of the pistol report and the moment when Booth rode out of sight."[11] Undoubtedly those seconds which stalled the pursuit gave Booth his chance to ride.

Stewart started to grab for the bridle just as Booth drove a spur into the mare's flank. Stewart's grasp missed. The little horse shot down the dark alley. Booth had to clutch the pommel to hold on. Ahead of him loomed the gateway to F Street. Did he race from "Baptist Alley" into F? Or did he head for E and gallop over to 9th Street? Again accounts vary.[12] But according to Oldroyd, Stewart saw Booth ride "out on F Street,"[13] which would imply the gate at alley's end was either ajar or wide open.

On F Street or 9th Street, Booth raced from darkness into deeper dark. Nobody saw him charge down the broad canyon of F, or gallop down 9th. It was conjectured that he cut back to Pennsylvania Avenue a block or two east of Ford's Theater. Then he raced toward Capitol Hill.

The weather was gusty with a threat of rain. The moon was trying to sail into the clear. Pennsylvania Avenue was dim-lit by pale lamps. Night mist had settled on midtown. Riding like a steeplechaser, Booth headed for the blackout of the city's fringes.

On the south side of the Capitol, a horseman cantering toward midtown was passed by another horseman going hell-bent toward the outlying Navy Yard. Perhaps the hard-riding horseman was John Wilkes Booth, perhaps not. Apparently Booth raced out New Jersey Avenue to Virginia Avenue, and galloped through a dark shanty-town where lamps burned low in windows and the denizens stayed indoors after nightfall—a sprawling warren made for a game of hide-and-seek. But that night the lamps seem to have been lower than usual. Nobody saw the assassin ride through this warren. Nobody knows or will ever know his exact route from Ford's Theater to Navy Yard Bridge.

For, back at the fatal playhouse, all minds had but a single thought. Lincoln! Lincoln! Lincoln! In that star-spangled box the President of the United States had been shot.

The playhouse shook with mounting tumult. The audience was in riot.

---

[10] Oldroyd, *op. cit.*, p. 27.

[11] Quoted in Wilson, *op. cit.*, p. 116.

[12] Van Doren Stern, *op. cit.*, says Booth headed down the alley "out into the broad expanse of F Street" (p. 137). Bishop, *op. cit.*, says Booth avoided the gate and turned "out through Ninth Street" (p. 211).

[13] *Op. cit.*, p. 27.

Uproar swelled until the walls seemed about to burst. Men broke from their chairs in the orchestra and fought to reach the stage. Seats were overturned. Women and children were trampled. In the frenzy and crush people shrieked, fainted, shouted, wailed in agony. There were wild cries. "Burn the theater!"—"Hang the assassin!"—"Kill the actors!"—"Hang them all!" Someone screamed that the playhouse was mined. Mob fury stampeded into terror as panic swept the house. The riot grew as soldiers burst in from the street with fixed bayonets.

Witnesses would never forget that terrifying scene which brought down the curtain on *Our American Cousin*. As perhaps to no one in the audience, the horror remained vivid to the cast of that unhappy comedy. Harry Hawk wept. Laura Keene made her way to the President's box where she tried to calm hysterical Clara Harris.[14] Dr. Charles Leale was admitted to the box by Major Rathbone. Another physician, Dr. Charles Taft, was hoisted to the box by men on stage. They were joined by a third physician, Dr. A. F. A. King. The doctors worked over Lincoln. They lifted the dying President from the rocking-chair and placed him on the floor. By some accounts, Miss Keene asked if she could hold the President's head in her lap. Young Dr. Leale looked at her coldly, but allowed her to do so. Instinctively she began to bathe the President's temples with gentle hand. An indelible bloodstain spread across the lap of her skirt.

Actor W. J. Ferguson followed Miss Keene into the box. Miss Harris was trying to comfort Mrs. Lincoln. The doctors were loosening Lincoln's clothing. Ferguson stood helplessly by. "I saw what they had been examining so gravely, a little dark spot no larger than the head of a lead pencil, just under the right ear."[15] Ferguson could not recall Miss Keene's action, and expressed it as his belief that she stood by, merely looking on. So the details of that moment remain blurred, as does much of the action which immediately followed the shooting of President Lincoln.

The players in the cast were stunned by the tragedy. Years later, Helen Trueman, who played the role of Augusta, wrote of the ensuing bedlam: "Mrs. Lincoln's scream turned the house into an inferno of noise. There will never be anything like it on earth. The shouts, groans, curses, smashing of seats, screams of women, shuffling of feet, cries of terror created a pandemonium that must have been more terrible to hear than that attending the assassination of Caesar. Through all the ages it will stand out as the hell of hells."[16]

So the curtain descended on a scene of Avernus, and on the heels of an assassin who rode out of Washington City like a black wind unseen in pitchy night. Booth had played out his murderous role with a precision

14 Buckingham, *op. cit.*, p. 15.
15 Wilson, *op. cit.*, p. 130. (Ferguson's memory erred. Lincoln was shot behind the left ear.)
16 New York *World*, February 17, 1924.

that might have been perfected by the schooling of a thousand rehearsals. One flaw had marred the performance—the *faux pas* of a penny-sized spur. But the rest was faultless black magic. Booth reached the getaway bridge.

"Booth! Booth! Booth!" Many persons in the theater recognized the assassin. His name was shouted by witnesses in the audience soon after he rushed off stage.

Both Laura Keene and Ferguson had recognized him. So had Harry Hawk, who was alone on stage when Booth sprang from Lincoln's box. "I had only one glance at him as he was rushing toward me with a dagger," Hawk testified later, "and I turned and ran. After I ran up a flight of stairs I turned and exclaimed, 'My God, that's *John Booth!* '"[17]

James C. Ferguson, restaurant keeper, sat in the dress circle. He had chatted with Booth that afternoon, and he recognized him the moment the assassin landed on stage. Ferguson fought his way out of the rioting playhouse, and hurried to a nearby police station. He told a gaping officer, "John Wilkes Booth has shot the President!" An almost simultaneous report was made to the police by an ex-Army officer, John Deveny.

James Maddox, property man at Ford's Theater, identified the assassin at once. So did William Withers, Jr., felled by Booth backstage. So, of course, did "Johnny Peanuts" at the stage door. As the assassin plunged out of the rear exit, Jacob Ritterspaugh, assistant scene shifter, had dodged from under the backstage flies and bumped into Ned Spangler.

Ritterspaugh cried, "That was Booth who ran out!"

"Shut up!" Spangler struck at his assistant. "What the hell do you know about it?"[18]

Mary Jane Anderson, domiciled on "Baptist Alley," saw and remembered the getaway episode in wide-eyed detail. Here are excerpts from her deposition in the War Department files:

> . . . About 8 o'clock in the evening I saw Booth lead a horse up to the stage door & heard him call in a low voice, "Ned!" three or four times. John Myers, a colored man employed in the theater looked out of the window & called into the theater, "Mr. Ned, Mr. Booth wants you." Ned Spangler . . . then came out of the door, and I heard Booth say in a low voice, "Tell Maddox to come here!" Maddox came & took the horse from Booth . . . A little time afterward Maddox gave the horse to some other person who came up, and then went into the theater. The horse was standing there altogether about an hour and a half. At the end of this time I was looking through the open door, & noticing the people moving about behind the scenes from time to time, when all of the sudden I saw Booth burst into the passage as if coming from the stage, and rush to the back door like lightning. He had his right arm up above his head and held something in his hand that glittered in the gaslight. His other arm seemed to be held at back of him. He had no

---

[17] Quoted in Eisenschiml, *op. cit.*, p. 69.
[18] National Archives, War Dept. Records, File "R," JAO.

hat on. As he came out of the door to his horse, I saw him strike at somebody & then leap on his horse & gallop down the alley. . . . There was
immediately a great excitement and people ran out into the alley.

I saw Maddox come out of the theater looking as if he was scared to
death, and Spangler, too. . . . I went up to Spangler and said to him, "Mr.
Ned, you know Mr. Booth called you out." He said, "No, he didn't!" in a
squeaky sort of voice as if he didn't want anybody to hear what he said.
I said, "Yes, he did . . . you must know something about this." He said
nothing, then, but sneaked away down the alley, putting on his coat and
looking as guilty as he could.[19]

An important police official in the theater audience had recognized
Booth at once. This was no less an authority than Major A. C. Richards,
Superintendent of Washington's Metropolitan Force. Richards left the
theater almost immediately after the shooting. He spent a few minutes
trying to find John F. Parker, the policeman who had been assigned to
guard Lincoln's box. Unable to locate the missing guard, Richards hurried
to police headquarters to muster his detective squad.

Major Richards was a capable officer, tough and exacting. He briefed
the duty force on what had happened, dispatched messengers to summon
the reserves, rushed detectives to Ford's Theater to round up witnesses,
and sent word of his emergency action to General Christopher C. Augur,
commander of Army forces in charge of the national capital. Unquestionably, Richards gave Augur detailed information on the assassination and
named John Wilkes Booth as the fugitive assassin.

But now a fog of confusion settled on the nation's military headquarters.
This fog seemed to bind the Federal authorities with ropes of lethargy. It
slowed the manhunt, obscured the assassin's trail, and did everything to
abet an escape.

Booth had fired the deadly shot about 10:30 P.M. Within fifteen minutes
of his flight from the theater alley, witnesses were blurting his name to
the police. By 11:00 P.M., the blotter at Washington police headquarters
contained the names of seventeen witnesses. They were listed under the
following notation:

> At this hour the melancholy intelligence of the assassination of Mr.
> Lincoln, President of the United States, at Ford's Theater was brought to
> this office, and the information obtained . . . goes to show that the assassin
> is a man named John Wilkes Booth.[20]

At that hour, then, there was no doubt whatever about the assassin's
identity. Yet the military authorities sent out no general alarm for John
Wilkes Booth. No flying squad was immediately dispatched to Booth's
hotel. A couple of cavalry patrols were ordered to scout the city streets.

[19] National Archives, War Dept. Records, File "A," Doc. 527, JAO.
[20] Records of Metropolitan Police Dept., Washington, D.C.

Aside from that, General Christopher C. Augur seems to have made empty gestures. Between 10:30 and midnight, most of the significant detective work was done by the Metropolitan Police.

Apologists blame Augur's inertia on the lateness of the hour, on the lack of available duty forces, on fatigue, and on whatnot. Critics maintain that the general was a tin soldier all tied up in red tape; it would appear that he awaited concrete orders from higher up—from the War Department, from Stanton.

Probably Augur was badly rattled. Wild rumors raced through midtown Washington. News of the President's assassination was followed by word that Vice President Johnson had been slain, Grant shot dead, Seward killed. Hotfoot across the city ran the story that Lee's surrender had been a ruse to disarm the North—the capital was under attack by Rebel partisans. Alarmed citizens armed themselves with shotguns, pistols, and knives, preparing to defend their homes. Runners sprinted through the residence districts, rapping on pavements and curbstones a sharp tattoo— the secret signal of the Union League society. Members of this clandestine fraternity grabbed rifles and darted to a rendezvous, determined to take over the city's defense.

Augur's headquarters became the center of a whirlpool of hue and cry. In the midst of hubbub and frenzy, the General must have been sorely tried. Nobody seemed to know what was in the wind, and reports were blowing from all directions.

Of course, an Army commander is supposed to be prepared for surprise situations, especially when a war is on. Apologies for Augur's fuddlement appear rather flabby under the circumstances. Only that afternoon Federal Headquarters had been alerted to the possibility of a Confederate raid on the District of Columbia by Mosby's forces operating in nearby Loudon County. Military intelligence was also aware that the President's safety was menaced.

Yet Augur's apathy was not the only freakish angle to that night's riddle. By midnight the nation's military leaders seemed in doubt concerning the assassin's identity. Although scores of people had recognized John Wilkes Booth, the War Department cautiously withheld the killer's name from official dispatches.

Representing the Associated Press in Washington was Mr. L. A. Gobright, reputedly one of the nation's leading news correspondents. His coverage of the President's murder added an element of mystery which remains unsolved to this day. Gobright was just locking up his office for the night when news of the shooting at Ford's Theater reached him. At once he ran to the nearest telegraph office and flashed a wire to New York: THE PRESIDENT WAS SHOT IN FORD'S THEATER TONIGHT AND PERHAPS MORTALLY WOUNDED.

From the telegraph office he raced to Ford's Theater. He was there before eleven o'clock. Therefore he must have sent his wire around 10:45 P.M. But only a few papers received his headline news flash.[21]

Gobright made his way into the President's box. A good reporter, he wanted to see for himself. His efforts were well rewarded—in the box he found Booth's derringer. Certainly he heard the story from eyewitnesses. On all sides he must have heard Booth's name. Then Gobright's next action was one of the weirdest in the annals of journalism. Shortly after his visit to the theater he filed a second telegram. This appeared in the morning edition of the New York *Tribune*: OUR WASHINGTON AGENT ORDERS THE DISPATCH ABOUT THE PRESIDENT "STOPPED." NOTHING IS SAID ABOUT THE TRUTH OR FALSITY OF THAT DISPATCH.[22]

Why did Gobright try to cancel the headline news? Four years later he wrote an account of his doings that night. He described his visit to the theater and mentioned a conversation with Major Richards at Police Headquarters. But it was not until the following morning that he filed a news account identifying the assassin. In his memoirs he did not divulge the reason for his cancellation of the first news flash.[23]

Gobright's extraordinary reticence won mention at the subsequent conspiracy trial, but no explanation. He merely stated that he was "satisfied" the assassin was John Wilkes Booth, but, "I did not so telegraph that night."[24]

A number of newspapers published Booth's name on the morning of April 15. The New York *World* carried the sub-head, "J. Wilkes Booth suspected!"[25] Washington papers named the assassin, but the great Associated Press syndicate delayed the story. From the distance of the present one can only surmise that someone in top authority in the War Department held Gobright's hand. For a guess, War Secretary Stanton?

And was the Gobright mystery linked to a mysterious silencing of the commercial telegraph in the hour after Lincoln's murder? About fifteen minutes after Gobright filed his first dispatch, the commercial lines out of Washington City went dead. Only the military line to Old Point Comfort and City Point, Virginia, remained operative. The commercial wires did not function again until one o'clock next morning. Then they revived as mysteriously as they had expired.

A generation of researchers would be stymied by the interruption of the telegraph communications on that fateful night. Official records avoided the subject. It was censored from contemporary reports. Major

---

[21] Eisenschiml, *op. cit.*, p. 73.

[22] New York *Tribune*, April 15, 1865.

[23] L. A. Gobright, *Recollections of Men and Things in Washington* (Philadelphia: Claxton, Remsen & Haffelfinger, 1869), p. 348.

[24] Benn Pitman, *Trial of the Conspirators* (Cincinnati: Moore, Wilstach & Baldwin, 1865), p. 213.

[25] New York *World*, April 15, 1865.

Eckert, Stanton's telegraph chief, was queried on the matter by a House investigating committee in 1867. Eckert admitted the commercial lines had been scotched. He said he thought they had been short-circuited by grounding. Asked if there had been an immediate investigation, Eckert replied, "It did not at the time seem sufficiently important, as the interruption only continued about two hours."[26]

For years, historians believed Booth's gang had scuttled the telegraph lines. But why would enemy agents restore dead communications?

Again it would seem that extraordinary efforts were made by someone in Washington command to keep Booth's name under wraps. Years later, Colonel Harry L. Burnett, who served as assistant judge advocate at the conspiracy trial stated: "When I entered upon the duty of assisting in the investigation of the murder of the President, on the 19th of April . . . it was not positively known who had assassinated the President. . . ."[27]

That the War Department Judge Advocate's Office could not positively name Lincoln's assassin five days after the murder strikes us as more than astounding!

One man might have stopped the fugitive assassin dead in his tracks: Silas T. Cobb, U.S.A., sergeant of the guard at Navy Yard Bridge.

Sometimes called the "Eastern Branch Bridge," this long wooden span crossed the Anacostia River to link the District of Columbia with the road into lower Maryland. The Washington end of the bridge stood at the end of 11th Street SE. At the left, the access was shadowed by tall trees. At the right, a frame house served as the guard station. The ramp to the span could be barred by a swinging boom or gate. As a wartime measure, this gate was supposed to be closed at 9:00 P.M.

Sergeant Cobb and two men served as the bridge guard. Sentry duty had been dull as ditchwater since Lee's surrender. Nobody expected an enemy assault on the Navy Yard. So wartime restrictions had been somewhat relaxed, and an occasional after-dark traveler who could prove legitimate business had been allowed to cross the span.

Of course, all travelers who wanted to cross the bridge after 9:00 P.M. claimed their business legitimate. Very probably if that business were urgent or at all pressing, travelers backed their claims with a slight gratuity. It is also probable that Cobb had been briefed on certain illegitimate travelers, such as Confederate secret agents, message bearers and the like. That these individuals might also back their claims of legitimacy with a five- or ten-dollar bill went without saying.

The gratuity implication may be unjust in respect to Sergeant Silas T. Cobb, or it may understate the peculiar matter. Insofar as motives or pos-

---

[26] House Impeachment Investigation, p. 673.
[27] Quoted in Eisenschiml, *op. cit.*, p. 265.

sible machinations were involved, the answer to Cobb's conduct that night will never be known.

At 10:30 on that evening of April 14, 1865, Sergeant Cobb was a cipher among the half million men wearing the blue uniform of the United States Army. By 11:00 o'clock he was a question mark in the riddle of America's greatest murder case.

Some time between 10:30 and 10:45 on that Friday night, Cobb heard fast hoofbeats coming down the dark reach of 11th Street. The Sergeant alerted his men, and stepped out in front of the bridge gate to challenge the rider.

A bay mare raced up. The rider reared the horse, and brought her to a standstill as one of the sentries grasped the bridle rein. The sentry led the horseman over to the light for Cobb's inspection. Sergeant Cobb squinted up at a hatless man whose face seemed the bleaker for a curved, black mustache. The man wore riding costume and smart black boots. His appearance was that of a "gentleman." Cobb noted the expensive boots, the patrician features of the pale countenance.

In subsequent statement the Sergeant testified to the following dialogue between himself and the horseman:

"Who are you, sir?"

"My name is Booth."

"Where are you from?"

"The city."

"Where are you going?"

"I'm going home."

"Where would that be?"

"Charles."

Cobb took him to mean Charles County, and asked: "What town?"

"No town," was the answer.

"Look here, you must live in some town."

"I live close to Beantown, but I don't live in the town."

Cobb asked the rider why he was on the road at that hour. "Don't you know that travelers aren't allowed to pass after nine o'clock?"

The rider said evenly: "That's new to me." He added that he'd had an errand in the city. The early night being dark, he had waited for the moon to ride home by.

Cobb went on to state that he thought the horseman some rich man's son who had been "pleasuring" in the capital. Scrutinizing rider and mount, the Sergeant sauntered around the animal. Then he stood back and nodded. "All right, you can pass."[28]

The sentries swung the barrier. The rider urged the nervous bay out on the bridge. The mare's hoofs danced on the planking as she sidled forward,

---

[28] National Archives, War Dept. Records, File "C," Evd., JAO. Also quoted in Oldroyd, *op. cit.*, p. 243.

then she went ahead at a walk. About half way across the span, the little horse quickened pace. Cobb heard the hoofbeats fade as the horseman galloped her away from the far end of the bridge.

So Lincoln's murderer escaped from the nation's capital. Investigators would wonder about Booth's getaway across Navy Yard Bridge. Sergeant Silas T. Cobb would be severely censured for allowing the assassin to pass.

But Cobb would not be censured by his Army superiors. Investigation of his conduct was not ordered by the War Department. Booth's escape across Navy Yard Bridge did not bring an avalanche of military discipline down on the bridge guard. And, of course, a guard at the bridge would have had no reason to suppose that a late-going horseman had just murdered the President of the United States. Navy Yard Bridge was about three miles from Ford's Theater, and word of the assassination could not have preceded the hard-riding assassin.

However, Sergeant Cobb had certainly been lax, as indicated by his own admission that the rider's proffered excuse for crossing at that late hour was a desire to travel by moonlight. Cobb did not ask the horseman to specify his business in the capital. He did not ask the man to show papers to verify his name. He accepted a vague reference to a distant village as the traveler's destination. The man's elegant dress meant noth-ing. For all Cobb knew, he could have been a secret emissary of Jeff Davis, or a sharp highwayman. The guard's challenge, then, amounted to no more than token formality.

And Cobb's allowing Booth to pass was not his sole blunder that night. A few minutes later the Sergeant let a second nocturnal horseman (Herold) ride across the bridge to lower Maryland. Finally, he was responsible for the turning back of a third horseman—a man who had urgent business at that dark hour.

As will be seen, Cobb came under some barbed questioning in respect to the second and third horsemen. But again he was not officially censured for his action. Evidently his Army superiors accepted his "decisions" as unfortunate but militarily excusable as errors of judgment. What soldier during the war had not committed errors of judgment?

If Sergeant Cobb erred, what of the Headquarters failure to alert the bridge guard immediately after the murderous shooting at Ford's Theater? No message was rushed at 10:30 P.M. to the guard station at Navy Yard Bridge. In fact, when the guard changed at midnight, Cobb apparently was still uninformed on the assassination. Nor did Augur rush military police to the bridge to inquire if the fugitive Booth had crossed into Maryland.

The records of history contain many "holes." John Wilkes Booth rode through one of them on the night he killed Abraham Lincoln. Was it there through "error in judgment"—meaning military blunder? Or was it there through deliberate design?

CHAPTER **8**

Escape

1. PAINE VANISHES

Paine hurled himself down the staircase, bellowing, "I'm mad! I'm mad!"
With his blood-smeared coat and crimson hands, he looked as gory as
a Roman gladiator.

A man had come out of a lower room and started up the stairs. He saw
Paine charging down on him. The man stood transfixed.

Paine flung himself at this victim, drove his bowie knife to the hilt in
the man's chest. The man's body crumpled as the gladiator wrenched out
the knife. Paine shoved the body off and bounded down to the street door.

He had expected David Herold to be waiting. Herold wasn't there.

Paine realized in an instant Herold had deserted him. From an upper
window of the house a woman was screaming, "Murder! Murder!" Paine
spied his own horse tethered to a curbside tree. An insane man, abandoned
by a friend, might have taken fright and fled to the first cellarway. Or sat
down and wept. Paine deftly untied the horse and mounted. Then, with
the cry of "Murder!" alarming the night, he calmly walked his horse up
the street.

Augustus Seward reached the door just as Paine started off. Young
Seward brandished an immense revolver. "Murder!" he shouted hoarsely.
But he was too dazed to shoot. Blood streamed from his scalp into his
eyes. Perhaps it blinded him. Possibly, in his numbed condition, he
hesitated to fire at a horseman who casually moved off in such fashion.
Paine's leisurely retirement certainly displayed a steel control. He could
not have contrived a more deceptive retreat.

"Murder! Murder!"

Now the cry was echoing across Lafayette Square. Shadows were
running under the street lamps, Boots pounding on the cobbles. Still Paine
held his horse to a walk.

He was heading in a wrong direction—north toward H Street. He did
not know what direction he was taking, and one way seemed as good as
another, now that his guide was gone. Paine reined up for an instant's pause

to mop his mouth and cheek. Then he drew the bowie knife from his belt, and cast it to the curb.

William Bell came running from the building which housed the headquarters of General Augur. Bell pointed at Paine and wailed, "Murder! It's him!"

Paine touched his horse's flank, and walked the animal forward.

"Murder!" Bell wailed.

The little Negro cried the alarm over and over again. Stubbornly he followed Paine's horse, keeping about twelve paces behind. That took courage, for the horseman might turn and shoot. It was like a bad dream—crying out, and help running the other way. He could hear people sprinting toward the Seward house.

The gory gladiator in the saddle heard the voice wailing close behind. Turning his head, Lewis Paine glanced contemptuously at his lone pursuer. Then, with a snort, he kicked his mount into a trot toward the lighted corner.

A group of soldiers spilled helter-skelter from the entry to Augur's headquarters.

William Bell danced and pointed. "Murder!"

The soldiers rushed past Paine, past Bell, and past an irretrievable chance for promotion and pay. To a man they charged up the steps and into the lighted entry of the Old Club House.

Bell followed the murderous horseman for another half block. Then his breath gave out. He saw the horseman trot around a corner. Panting, streaming perspiration, he turned and ran back to the Seward house.

The whole town seemed to be at the door, crowding the inner hall, jamming the stair. Mr. Augustus Seward struggled against the intruders, his face like death. Bell saw them holding up another man near the newel post whose chin bobbed horribly on his chest. It was Hansell, the messenger from the State Department.

"I saw him!" Bell wailed. "On a dark bay horse! He done went that-away! I followed him up past 'I' to Vermont Avenue! He went up Vermont Avenue. . . . !"[1]

Nobody listened. Nobody paid attention to the little Negro. More people came crowding in. William Bell was swept aside. Make way for War Secretary Stanton!

Little William Bell gave up. Of all the people involved in that night of tragedy and frenzy, he remains as the ultimate personification of abject futility and frustration.

Surgeon General J. K. Barnes was driving down Pennsylvania Avenue. His carriage was about opposite Willard's Hotel when he was startled by a shout. A Blue cavalryman galloped up.

[1] Based on National Archives, War Dept. Records, File "B," Doc. "Evd. B," JAO.

"General! Go to Ford's Theater! The President has been shot!"

General Barnes ordered his driver, "Take me to my office!"

The carriage careened up the Avenue. As the horses pulled up, Barnes sprang out. In another moment he had his instrument case. Just as he was leaving his office, a soldier rushed in.

"Secretary Seward has been stabbed! He's dying! His son is stabbed! They want you to come at once!"

The Surgeon General thought the report about the President had been a mistake. He drove at once to Seward's home. He found the house a shambles. A mob of pedestrians, neighbors, soldiers and servants crowding, elbowing and shouting.

General Barnes forced his way up the blood-spattered staircase. In the upper hall Miss Fanny Seward was fainting on her mother's arm. Mrs. Anna Seward stood in a pose of rigid control. At her elbow Augustus Seward clutched a handkerchief to his bleeding head. Men hovered over the prostrate form of Hansell, the Department messenger.

"It's Frederick," Mrs. Seward told Barnes. "And Mr. Seward. Robinson, too." She pointed. "In there."

Barnes had his work cut out for him. He found the Secretary semi-conscious, a cloth over his forehead, an improvised bandage masking his cheek and jaws. The gashes in his throat were not fatal. The steel neck-brace had saved his jugular vein. If he came out of shock, he would probably live.

Robinson, the male nurse, had been painfully injured. But his wounds looked superficial.

Emerick Hansel, the man who had been stabbed on the staircase, miraculously might pull through.

Frederick Seward was a serious case, unconscious, breathing stertorously, his face gray, cold and moist. Barnes diagnosed a "double fracture of the cranium, profuse bleeding, no pulse, inability to speak." The surgeon gravely advised the household that Frederick's wounds might prove mortal.[2]

Barnes was working over Frederick Seward when a Negro hack driver brought a message from Ford's Theater.

"It's President Lincoln! He's dying!"

Desperate, the Surgeon General concluded his work at the Sewards, packed his instruments, and raced off to tend the President.

At about this time Lewis Paine galloped his horse into the East Capitol section of Washington. "Cap" had told him to make right turns. He had been making them. Somehow they got him headed in the general direction of the Navy Yard.

Paine had been lost from the moment he left Lafayette Square. In the

---

[2] Quoted in Bishop, *op. cit.,* p. 235.

East Capitol section many of the streets were unlighted. Where could he spend the night?

But sleeping accommodations didn't trouble a six-footer with the physique of a blacksmith. Nor would conscience trouble this old frontline soldier who had been killing Yankees ever since he was sixteen years old.

Secretary Stanton was in his bedroom undressing. He had enjoyed a pleasant evening—the Arsenal band had treated him to a serenade. Stanton liked brass bands. What he did not like was someone banging on his door just as he was going to bed.

Patient Mrs. Stanton heard the commotion: something about Lincoln and Secretary Seward. Stanton looked in to tell her the town was full of wild rumors. He started back to bed.

A minute or two later there was more banging at the door. This time the callers convinced Stanton—as the soldier messenger had been unable to do—that terrible emergency was in the wind. Stanton flung himself into his clothes, summoned a hack, and drove to Secretary Seward's home. He arrived there almost simultaneously with Naval Secretary Gideon Welles.

"Uncle Gideon" looked winded and grim. There was deviltry afoot this night, and "Uncle Gideon's" jaw was set to meet it.

The Naval Secretary's impressions of the Seward episode are best told in his own words.

From the *Diary* of Gideon Welles:

> I had retired to bed about half past-ten on the evening of the 14th of April, and was just getting asleep when Mrs. Welles, my wife, said some one was at our door. . . . I arose at once and raised a window, when my messenger, James Smith, called to me that Mr. Lincoln, the President, had been shot, and said Secretary Seward and his son, Assistant Secretary Frederick Seward, were assassinated. . . .
>
> I immediately dressed myself, and, against the earnest remonstrance and appeals of my wife, went directly to Mr. Seward's, whose residence was on the east side of the square, mine being on the north. James accompanied me. As we were crossing 15th Street, I saw four of five men in earnest consultation, standing under the lamp on the corner by St. John's Church. Before I got half across the street, the lamp was suddenly extinguished and the knot of persons rapidly dispersed. For a moment and but a moment I was disconcerted to find myself in darkness, but, recollecting that it was late and about time for the moon to rise, I proceeded on. . . . Hurrying forward into 15th Street, I found it pretty full of people, especially so near the residence of Secretary Seward, where there were many soldiers as well as citizens already gathered.
>
> Entering the house, I found the lower hall and office full of persons, and among them most of the foreign legations, all anxiously inquiring what truth there was in the horrible rumors afloat. . . . The servants were frightened and appeared relieved to see me. I hastily asked what truth there was in the story that an assassin or assassins had entered the house and assaulted the Secretary. They said it was true, and that Mr. Frederick was also badly

injured. They wished me to go up, but no others. At the head of the first stairs I met the elder Mrs. Seward, who was scarcely able to speak but desired me to proceed up to Mr. Seward's room. I met Mrs. Frederick Seward on the third story, who, although in extreme distress, was, under the circumstances, exceedingly composed. I asked for the Secretary's room, which she pointed out,—the southwest room. As I entered, I met Miss Fanny Seward, with whom I exchanged a single word, and proceeded to the foot of the bed. Dr. Verdi and, I think, two others were there. The bed was saturated with blood. The Secretary was lying on his back, the upper part of his head covered by a cloth, which extended down over his eyes. His mouth was open, the lower jaw dropping down. I exchanged a few whispered words with Dr. V. Secretary Stanton, who came after but almost simultaneously with me, made inquiries in a louder tone till admonished by a word from one of the physicians. We almost immediately withdrew and went into the adjoining front room, where lay Frederick Seward. . . . Doctor White, who was in attendance, told me he was unconscious and more dangerously injured than his father.

As we descended the stairs, I asked Stanton what he had heard in regard to the President that was reliable. He said the President was shot at Ford's Theater, that he had seen a man who was present and witnessed the occurrence. . . . "Then," said I, "let us go immediately there." He said that was his intention, and asked me, if I had not a carriage, to go with him. In the lower hall we met General Meigs. . . . General Meigs begged Stanton not to go down to 10th Street; others also remonstrated against our going. Stanton, I thought, hesitated. . . . I said we were wasting time, and, pressing through the crowd, entered the carriage and urged Stanton, who was detained by others after he had placed his foot on the step. I was impatient. Stanton, as soon as he had seated himself, turned round, rose partly, and said the carriage was not his. I said that was no objection. He invited Meigs to go with us, and Judge Cartter of the Supreme Court mounted with the driver. At this moment Major Eckert rode up on horseback beside the carriage and protested vehemently against Stanton's going to 10th Street; said he had just come from there, that there were thousands of people of all sorts there, and he considered it very unsafe for the Secretary of War to expose himself. I replied that I knew not where he would be more safe, and that the duty of both of us was to attend the President immediately. Stanton concurred. . . .[3]

The Naval Secretary's *Diary* leaves us with something more than a hasty sketch of his emergency call on the Sewards. That little incident on the Square; shadowy figures under a lamp-post; the light going out—the Naval Secretary's spunk may have scattered an ambush. The city teemed with buckos and bully-boys ready to hire for any enterprise. But we know no more of that street-corner incident than that it failed to extinguish the grit of Gideon Welles.

Then "Uncle Gideon's" account draws a sharp picture of Stanton. The War Secretary does not appear overly heroic in this unvarnished profile.

[3] Gideon Welles, *Diary* (Boston: Houghton Mifflin Company, 1929), Vol. II, pp. 283–286.

Of course, Stanton's "loud voice" at the Sewards' may have boomed from extreme emotion—his shock at beholding the havoc wrought upon a fellow Cabinet member. Or it may have been the voice of anxiety for the national welfare. But Gideon Welles did not miss Stanton's bluster on that fearful night, or his officious fluster, or his timidity, or his finicky stickling—"This isn't our carriage!" No doubt about it, the great War Secretary was badly scared.

Gideon Welles could not abide Edward M. Stanton.

Of the many persons who beheld that scene of horror at the Seward home, one witness, the wife and mother in the stricken household, leaves us a most vivid picture.

Herself a convalescent invalid, Mrs. Seward underwent an ordeal experienced by few other women in history. Historians have concentrated on Mrs. Lincoln's ordeal, but Fanny Seward's extremity must have surpassed Mary Lincoln's. Nearly a month would pass before she could bring herself to recall the details of that excruciating night.

Mrs. Seward wrote, on the 11th of May, to Mr. Alward at Auburn:

> Though the scenes of horror through which I have passed have neither hardened my heart nor paralyzed my hand, I still find it difficult to guide my pen. I came here the 7th of April, two days after Mr. Seward was injured in falling from the carriage. I found him a great sufferer—so bruised and swollen was his face that it was difficult to trace any resemblance to his features as they were. . . . Mr. Seward was still in the condition I describe when his assassination was attempted the night of the 14th. . . . Robinson, the nurse, tried to prevent his [the assassin's] entrance, was struck a number of times with a large bowie-knife, but still kept hold of the murderer while he sprang upon Mr. Seward's bed. Mr. Seward . . . says he knew the man sought his life, still he feared for Fanny, and, with great effort, rose up in his bed to interpose his shattered frame as a protection.
>
> His throat was cut on both sides, his right cheek nearly severed from his face, when he fell upon the floor. . . .
>
> In the meantime, Fanny's screams had awakened the family. Augustus, with the aid of Robinson, succeeded in getting the man out of the room. Augustus received three wounds from that fearful knife. His head was cut twice to the bone, and one hand severely cut. . . .
>
> I will not attempt to describe what I witnessed of this scene of horrors. Mr. Seward and Frederick both insensible; and Augustus, Robinson and Hansell covered with blood. Anna, with remarkable presence of mind, sent the servants for surgeons, who soon came.
>
> One hour after Mr. Seward's wounds were dressed I thought him dying, but he revived, and, thanks to a merciful God, is still alive.
>
> Frederick lay forty-eight hours motionless and unconscious. His skull was badly fractured in two places. There were marks of five blows with the pistol, which the assassin vainly attempted to fire. Partial consciousness returned to Frederick about the fourth day; but not until three different examinations by the surgeons, were all the pieces of bone (eight in

number) taken from the brain. . . . His chief danger now arises from hemorrhages from his wounds, which produce such prostration that we are constantly apprehensive that he will die.[4]

Where, that night, was the perpetrator of this untrammeled butchery?

About an hour after the assassination strike a riderless horse was found on the outskirts of the East Capitol section, a brown horse, heavy in the haunches, blind in one eye.

When found, the animal was shuddering its flanks, streaming sweat. Some brute had ridden the beast almost to death. The finders judged the horse stolen, then abandoned. The supposed thief had left behind a flat, black English saddle. Excited, the finders turned the horse over to the Army authorities.

But General Augur had more to do that night than try to identify stolen horses. Several hours would pass before the brown, half-blind animal was identified. Then, confusingly, the saddle would be recognized as belonging to a roustabout named Atzerodt.

So the perpetrator of the butchery at Seward's slipped away. Some time between midnight and dawn he crossed an open meadow and entered a patch of dark woods just north of Fort Lincoln. The undergrowth embraced him; the trees closed in behind him. Lewis Paine was unaware of the fact, but his lair that night was less than a mile from Navy Yard Bridge.

South of the bridge, some sixteen miles distant, the true author of the carnage at Seward's found haven. Paine himself was only a human weapon. Booth had loaded him, sent him to the front, directed him on the target as though he were some sort of soulless cannon. He had gone into action with monstrous effect.

No one knows exactly where this human battery spent the Saturday and Sunday of that black Easter weekend. When subsequently queried, Paine declared that he had crouched for three days in the top of a cedar tree.[5] More probably he huddled in some nest of underbrush, as sunk in inertia as an abandoned piece of heavy artillery, but loaded still and dangerous to any chance finder who might kick the firing mechanism unaware.

By early Saturday morning hundreds of soldiers, policemen, Federal agents and aroused citizens were hunting the man who had assaulted the Sewards. Nobody knew his name. Nobody possessed his recognizable description. It was reasoned he was one of Booth's accomplices. By 2:00 A.M. of that day General Augur had acquired the names of David Herold, Atzerodt and John Surratt, but nobody had heard of a Lewis Paine.

So the hunt for Paine charged off on a left foot. First, the garbled reports

---

[4] Frederick W. Seward, *op. cit.*, pp. 278–80.
[5] Doster, *op. cit.*, p. 269.

John Wilkes Booth.

Recd 25 April

65

Somerset Perry Co   Ohio   April 21

To the Honorable Secretary of State

Dear Sir

In looking over some old papers yesterday my eye
came in contact with the enclosed extract which, under the existing state of affairs I thought was worthy
of being pointed out to you specially as the State
(Ala) is now in our possession and the authors of the
proposition can be hunted out and brought to justice
even provided they are innocent of the Murder.

I have the honor to be Your Obt Servt

Henry C. Grimes

Allan Pinkerton.

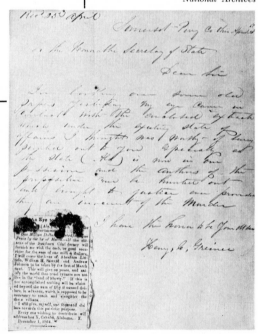

AN EYE TO BUSINESS

The Salem (Ala.) Dispatch has the following advertisement:

One Million Dollars, Wanted, to Have Peace by the 1st of March.—If the
citizens of the Southern Confederacy will furnish me with the cash, or good
securities for the sum of one million dollars, I will cause the lives of Abraham
Lincoln, William H. Seward and Andrew Johnson to be taken by the first of
March next. This will give us peace and satisfy the world that cruel tyrants
cannot live in the "land of liberty." If this is not accomplished nothing will be
claimed beyond the sum of fifty thousand dollars, in advance, which is supposed
to be necessary to reach and slaughter the three villains.

I will give, myself, one thousand dollars towards this patriotic purpose.

Every one wishing to contribute will address box X, Cahaba, Alabama. X.
December 1, 1864.

Mary Eugenia Jenkins Surratt.

Mrs. Surratt's boardinghouse about the time of the Civil War.

Anna Surratt.

Louis Wiechmann.

DAVID HEROLD

Lewis Paine.

George Andrew Atzerodt.

Michael O'Loughlin.

Samuel Bland Arnold.

Edward Spangler.

Dr. Samuel A. Mudd, as he appeared while imprisoned in Fort Jefferson.

Ford's Theater.

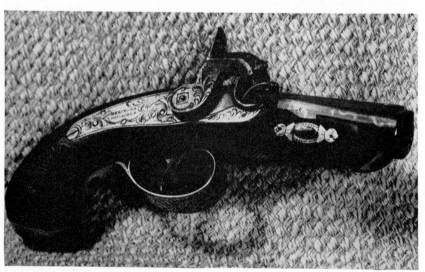

The pistol Booth used to shoot Lincoln.

Box in Ford's Theater where Lincoln was assassinated.

The Treasury Guards flag in which Booth caught his leg when leaping from Lincoln's box.

The livery stable where Booth kept the one-eyed roan procured for Paine.

"Baptist Alley" behind Ford's Theater.

The Kirkwood House, at Twelfth Street and Pennsylvania Avenue, Washington, D.C., where Andrew Johnson and George Atzerodt stayed.

Andrew Johnson, 17th President of the United States.

William H. Seward, Secretary of State in Lincoln's Cabinet.

Edwin M. Stanton, Secretary of War in Lincoln's Cabinet.

sent the Army looking for John Surratt as Seward's assailant. At 9:40 that morning Brigadier General N. L. Jeffers sent a message (for Stanton) to the border stations. It began: "It is believed the assassins of the President and Secretary Seward are attempting to escape to Canada. . . ."[6] That evening, Assistant War Secretary Dana dispatched a message to the police of Baltimore, Philadelphia, and New York naming "G. A. Atzerodt, the assassin of Mr. Seward."[7] Dana provided a reasonably fair description of the slovenly German carriage-painter, who bore no resemblance whatever to the hulking Lewis Paine.

This faulty identification came through a stableman's recognizing as Atzerodt's the saddle found on the abandoned one-eyed horse. Naturally, General Augur put two and two together. This time they did not make four because the basic premise—that Atzerodt had been in the saddle—was erroneous.

Meantime, any of six people at the Sewards' had glimpsed Lewis Paine. Little William Bell, in subsequent deposition, furnished a most observant description of the invader. "Full six foot . . . red face . . . no whiskers or moustache . . . shaved very close . . . coat came down below the knees . . . thin lips . . . light, broadbrimmed, soft felt hat. . . ."[8] But that Saturday nobody listened to the plaintive servant.

By Easter Sunday all reports on the "Seward assassin" were garbled beyond recognition. Most of the War Department dispatches confused him with John Surratt. Governor Curtin of Pennsylvania came up with a fantastic guess that was to involve an Army lieutenant and his wife in a Chinese puzzle of difficulties.[9] But the authorities were in the dark about Lewis Paine.

Paine himself remained in the dark. Nobody saw him during that time, so far as is known. Perhaps he clung to his woodsy dell. Perhaps he emerged from cover several times to raid a barnyard or two. Old soldiers are good at forage.

In the woods he shed his bloodstained coat. That much is known. He probably scrubbed his hands in some stream, cleaned the blood from his face, and then rubbed in some dirt so that he would look like a farmhand or workman.

The coat was eventually found by an Army private going through the woods. But not until the evening of Monday, April 17, were the authorities to learn the name of the killer Booth had unleashed on the Seward home.

For the Sewards the nightmare proved of long duration. Flowers, gifts,

---

[6] New York *Evening Post*, April 15, 1865.
[7] *Official Records*, Series I, Vol. 46, Part 3, p. 782.
[8] National Archives, War Dept. Records, File "B," Doc. "Evd. B," JAO.
[9] National Archives, War Dept. Records, File "B," "Evidence," JAO.

and messages of sympathy and encouragement came to the stricken home. And then, inserted into this profusion of expressed good will, came notes like the following, which arrived in a bright yellow envelope addressed to the Secretary of State. It was postmarked, "Cincinnati, Apr. 24, 1865."

> Wishing to inform you as soon as possible that you and the God dam Yankee government, their detectives and M P searchers can save their selves the trouble and expences and perhaps also their lives—that any further search is unnecessary and will all avail nothing for Booth my dearest and best friend J W Booth is now safe forever. He is by now over 500 miles from Washington. With my friends our company is over 800 strong in the dam Yankee states and will commence to operate very soon [Symbols here, suggestive of skulls, etc.] You Sonofabitch.
>
> [Signed] Blackheart.[10]

The following week, an envelope postmarked "Lewistown, Ill.," was another shocking intruder in the morning mail. This venomous letter began:

> I wish I had cut your dam head off while I was at it instead of only half doing it. If I only had you and Johnson and Stanton out of the way I would feel as if I had done my duty to my Country. . . ."

There was more of it, ending with "*Sic Semper Tyrannis.*" It was signed, "Jorgen."[11]

Had some madman authored this screed? Or was it the work of some conspirator? The mails by this date were flooded with frenzied correspondence addressed to the leaders in Washington. Many historians assume these letters emanated from crackpots.

Yet some of these vicious missives may have been conspiratorial contrivances designed to go with the assassination strike. Booth had friends in many cities who could have been primed to launch a terror campaign through the mails. For that matter, some of the letters could have been composed by the Booth gang. The "Jorgen" specimen sounds like a soldier who had fashioned a drinking cup of a Yankee skull.

Most accounts of the assassination strike concentrate on the killing of President Lincoln. The public mind could hardly accept a dual picture of two leaders lying at death's door. Accordingly many Americans, particularly those of the ensuing generation, came to believe the attack on Seward did not end tragically.

But the assassin did not fail. The strike at the Seward home did claim a tragic fatality. Mrs. Seward, convalescent at the time of the attack,

---

[10] National Archives, War Dept. Records, File "A," "Anonymous," JAO.
[11] National Archives, War Dept. Records, File "A," Doc. 179, JAO.

sustained a shock from which she never recovered. In the spring of 1865 her reserve strength ebbed away. She died that summer in Auburn.

So Lewis Paine left death in his wake.

2. HEROLD LIGHTS OUT

Weak-chinned David Herold watched Paine enter the Seward house. Two minutes later he heard from within a muffled scream. Quickly he dismounted and tied Paine's horse to a tree. He sprang back into saddle, and took off. History has left us the impression of a fleeing coward.

Yet Herold subsequently displayed sufficient nerve. He even showed a sort of dogged "devotion to duty."

Was it possible Booth's toady had been instructed to desert Paine? Once the brainless giant struck the target his usefulness was over; thereafter he became a drag on high-speed escape. Herold had wits. Booth liked wits. Besides, Herold knew the back trails of lower Maryland. His guidance was part of the getaway scheme. If Atzerodt failed to show up, Herold could lead the way. Booth was not counting on the services of "Plug Tobacco."

Under these known circumstances it seems possible—even probable— that Booth instructed Herold to ditch Paine at Seward's. The dull gladiator was expendable.

Spurring his roan, Herold headed southward down 15th Street, came into Pennsylvania Avenue where it makes its freakish bend to avoid the Treasury Building.

Herold reined up.

The usual idlers were on the next corner in front of Willard's Hotel. The last thing Herold wanted was to attract attention. He trotted the roan along the outside traffic lane, hugging the darker side of the avenue. But someone noticed him.

A man disengaged himself from the group in front of Willard's, and darted out into the avenue. Inadvertently, Herold slowed.

The man waved at him and shouted, "*You!* I want that roan! You been out on that horse long enough!"[12]

Herold gave a start of recognition. It was the stable man from Naylor's— Fletcher. Atzerodt knew him! The horse had been out over-time!

The livery man ran at Herold with outstretched hand. As Fletcher grabbed for the bridle, Herold danced the horse aside. The roan reared as Herold dug heels into flanks. Then, jerking the bit, Herold sent the animal on a gallop to the left, up 14th Street to the corner of F.

Fletcher sprinted down to his livery stable, saddled up, and galloped up 13th to F in an effort to intercept the hare-brained boy, but there was no sign of Herold or the roan on F Street.

---

[12] National Archives, War Dept. Records, File "F," "Evidence," JAO.

Wheeling his mount, Fletcher galloped back to the broad reach of Pennsylvania Avenue. It looked as if the boy had been heading for East Capitol, where the streets were dark. It was a good area to disappear into with a stolen horse.

Fletcher, who knew the ways and means of horse thieves, headed for the East Capitol section. There had been a deal of horse wrangling out there on the fringe of town. Get an animal across the Anacostia into Maryland, and those people over there could paint a black horse white and sell him back to the rightful owner without batting an eye.

Stable-foreman Fletcher spurred up Capitol Hill. The streetlamps were only occasional out there, but a green moon drifting through scudding clouds cast a faint light on the avenue's path.

On the south side of the Capitol, Fletcher saw a horseman coming toward him. He swerved into the path of this equestrian, thinking it might be Herold coming back with the roan, but it was not.

"Seen any horsemen heading east?" Fletcher inquired.

"Why, yes." The man turned in saddle to point. "Few minutes ago. Two of them—one following the other. Both racing."[13]

Fletcher thanked him, and rowelled his mount. The first must be that Dutchman from Port Tobacco. The second must be his pal. They were probably working together, cutting and running for the Navy Yard Bridge.

Stable-foreman Fletcher headed for the bridge in determined chase. By sheer happenstance, he was the first man in Washington on the trail of the assassins.

About the time irate John Fletcher queried the horseman under the shadow of the Capitol, a similar meeting occurred on the crest of Good Hope Hill on the Maryland side of the Anacostia River. Riding toward Washington was a gentleman named Polk Gardner. Riding southward (out of Washington) came this other gentleman, low in saddle on a lathered horse.

Polk Gardner pulled well aside to give the oncoming rider the road. But the stranger, cresting the hill, let his horse slow to a walk. Polk's horse shied and snorted as the other animal approached. Polk saw the stranger was riding a small bay mare.

"Good evening," the stranger said, swerving across the road and coming up. He halted, intercepting Gardner. "Could you tell me if you passed anyone down the road? Any horsemen riding out of Washington City?"

"No," Gardner said. "Not in the last few miles. I've been on this road about an hour."

The stranger inquired the way to Marlboro, then thanked Gardner and spurred on.

---

[13] *Ibid.*

Many hours later Polk Gardner would wake up to the realization that he had encountered the man who assassinated the President of the United States.

Sergeant Silas T. Cobb, U.S.A., leaned in the door of the sentry house. Perhaps he was scanning the night sky, trying to predict the morrow's weather. Perhaps he was wondering about the other side of the moon.

Then Cobb looked up. Hoofbeats. Here came another rider from town. Automatically, Cobb squared up with his rifle, and moved out to the gate to the bridge. One of the sentries came out of the house to join him.

Out of the long moon-gloomed canyon of 11th Street galloped a young man on a lathered roan. He reined up when he saw the soldiers barring his way.

"Who goes there?"

The rider said in an uncertain tone, "Friend."

Cobb walked up to the horse, grasped the bridle, and led it over to the sentry light. The rider blinked in the lantern-shine. Cobb demanded his name.

"It's Smith."

"Well, now," Cobb said caustically. "John, I suppose."

The young man in the saddle avoided the Sergeant's eye. Then he said sullenly, "My name is Thomas."[14]

"All right, Thomas. Where you bound for?"

"White Plains."

"What you doing out so late?"

The young man exclaimed, "I been seeing a woman. I gotta get to White Plains! I gotta get home!"

White Plains was a town unfamiliar to Cobb, but the rider seemed innocent enough—at least, as far as the war was concerned. So Cobb nodded to the sentry. They swung the wide gate, and the young man on the roan walked his horse out onto the bridge. The Sergeant and the other Boys in Blue watched the horseman fade across the span.

Sergeant Silas T. Cobb didn't know it, but he had just made the second biggest mistake of his life. The rider on the roan was David E. Herold, on his way to join Booth.

Stableman Fletcher reached the bridge only a few minutes behind Herold. Sergeant Cobb stepped out to meet this third rider. Fletcher asked the Sergeant if a roan had gone across. Cobb allowed as much.

"Rider give you his name?" Fletcher asked.

Cobb nodded. "He said his name was Smith."[15]

Fletcher was excited. He was satisfied now that the young man on the

[14] Van Doren Stern, *op. cit.*, p. 155.
[15] Poore, *op. cit.*, Vol. I, pp. 329, 333.

roan was David Herold. No doubt, now, about him stealing the roan. Fletcher told Cobb he was after a stolen horse. "I've got to get across the bridge!"

"How," Cobb asked, "do you expect to get back?"

Fletcher glared, and wanted to know what Cobb meant.

Cobb informed him that if he crossed at this late hour, he would not be allowed to return that night. Fuming, Fletcher headed his horse back to town.

Sergeant Cobb had just made the third biggest mistake of his life.

When he reached the Maryland bank of the Anacostia, David Herold dug his heels into the roan's flanks. Once he got over Good Hope Hill, no manure-pitching hostler would ever find him. He'd be as safe as home in bed.

Herold started the roan on a run up Good Hope Hill. Then he glimpsed a wagon coming downhill toward him; a teamster hauling a load of produce to Washington market. Herold "Whoa-ed!" up. Sparks splashed as the teamster applied brakes, pulled up his horses, and the market wagon skidded to a halt.

Herold asked the teamster if he'd seen a horseman on the road, heading away from Washington. The teamster reckoned he had. He pointed uphill with his whip.

While Herold exchanged words with the teamster, Polk Gardner came loping down the grade. Herold wanted no words with this gentleman riding toward Washington. Veering to the right side of the road, he sent the roan upgrade on a burst.

The moon was low, the road dark. Herold spurred past Gardner and on up Good Hope Hill. The teamster had convinced him Mr. Booth was only half a mile or so ahead.

Mr. Booth was not quite that far in the lead. The little mare that could "run like a cat" was windblown. Spur her as he would, Booth could not urge her into another dash. Besides, the Maryland road was potholed in places, and it wouldn't do to let the mare stumble and break a leg. The fugitive let her jog in a tired canter.

Booth himself had begun to feel the pace. Exultation had borne him out of Washington like a gale-blown feather. But then the actor must have experienced a depressing letdown, once he reached the security of Maryland in night. The thrill was gone, and there was something wrong with his left ankle. On the climb up Good Hope Hill it had seemed numb, but now he could feel heat in his foot and up to his knee.

Booth did not know it at that hour, but, in sprawling on the stage at Ford's, he had twisted his left leg under him and snapped the tibia bone. Accounts vary, but it seems he thought he had wrenched a ligament or sprained his ankle. Characteristic would have been a moan of self-pity.

He may have been indulging in self-commiseration when he heard a spatter of hoofbeats in the night behind him. Quickly Booth turned the mare aside and walked her into a screen of black saplings. Holding the little bay quiet, he drew his revolver and waited, masked by the darkness.

Booth let the rider pass. Then he raised the revolver and shouted, "Halt!" The dimly-seen horseman had looked familiar.

The horseman reared up and turned a white face toward the thicket. Booth saw it was David Herold.

As the bay mare emerged from the saplings, Herold must have gulped in relief.

"Mr. Booth!"

The two were content.

But historians have only guessed this nocturnal meeting of Booth and Herold on the road to Surrattsville. Tradition tells the story just related, but nobody knows the facts. Herold may have joined Booth at some pre-arranged rendezvous. There were no witnesses.

One of the extraordinary turns of the escape story hinges on the invisibility of Booth, Paine, and Herold on that Friday night. Booth went through Washington like an unseen wind. Paine disappeared two blocks from the Seward house. David Herold seemed equally possessed of a power to evade the eye.

Only two witnesses would swear that they had seen Herold ride out of Washington. Even then one of the witnesses became doubtful. Stable-foreman Fletcher remained hand-on-Bible certain he'd seen Herold pass Willard's on the roan. Sergeant Silas T. Cobb, of the bridge guard, was sure about the horse. But when the time came to testify, he hedged a little about recognizing Herold.

In fact, when called upon to report on the episode at Navy Yard Bridge, Sergeant Cobb spoke candidly enough about Booth, but he would have side-stepped Herold entirely had the interrogator not pinned him on the point. And at that time Sergeant Cobb was not at all sure he could identify David E. Herold.[16]

As for David E. Herold, a fortnight later he would flatly deny he had been in Washington on the night of April 14. Here, in part, is his statement to Special Judge Advocate John A. Bingham. Herold was a prisoner when he made it, and in any case his word was hardly reliable. But his declaration offers a verbal self-portrait perhaps more revealing than a Brady photograph.

Q. Where were you living last year?
A. I lived with F. S. Ward, druggist, Washington City.
Q. How long did you live with him?

---

[16] Eisenschiml, *op. cit.*, p. 253. Also Pitman, *op. cit.*, p. 85.

A. I lived with him eleven months exactly. I left him in the early part of the fall, and went to Maryland. I do not remember the exact time. I am passionately found of partridge shooting, and nearly every fall take two or three months for that purpose. I came back home to my mother, and have been endeavoring to obtain a situation. I did not wish to do anything until after January. . . . Previous to this I went to the country, and was fox-hunting. In jumping a fence I knocked my ancle (*sic*) out of place, and was in bed two weeks. This happened in Prince George County, Maryland.

Q. At whose house were you?

A. I was stopping with a gentleman named Walter Edelin. I stopped there once or twice. I have numerous acquaintances—indeed know nearly every one in Maryland, especially in Piscataway District. I sometimes would board in a hotel. . . .

Q. At what other houses did you stay, beside those named?

A. I stopped with James B. Burch, who sold his place. . . . I also stopped with Mr. Walter Griffin, Mr. Wm. A. Jarboe, Mr. Phil Beale, Mr. John Steed, & Mr. John Roberts. I went through the lower counties.

Q. What counties?

A. Charles, down to Port Tobacco. I stopped with Mr. Patrick and with Peregrine Davis. . . . They are persons I have known five or six years, and whom I have been in the habit of visiting for a long time.

[At this point, under questioning, Herold admitted he knew Booth and had met Atzerodt in Booth's room at the National Hotel about the first of April.]

Q. What was said at that time, if anything, by Booth, to either of you, about the President?

A. Nothing at all, sir.

Q. What was said about anything?

A. We were talking about horse-trading, the coal-oil business, theatrical performances.

Q. Did you see Booth on the day of this occurrence? [The assassination.]

A. I don't think I did.

Q. Did you see anybody else that spoke to you upon this subject that day?

A. No, sir; I never had any idea of it that day.

Q. Where did you see Booth after the occurrence?

A. I was in the country, & was coming home.

Q. Where were you?

A. I had been in the country, trying to sell a horse.

Q. When did you go to the country?

A. Friday afternoon.

Q. Was it the day of this occurrence?

A. Yes, sir.

Q. Whose horse were you trying to sell?

A. A horse belonging to Atzerodt. . . .

Q. Where did you go?

A. I went to Lloyd's country tavern, on the road going to T. B. in Prince George County. It was late in the night when I arrived there. I believe I took one or two drinks.

Q. What time did you start from Washington on that journey?

A. I don't know. I was tight. I had been tight nearly all day.

Q. Who asked you to go?

A. No one; I asked myself. Atzerodt wanted to sell a horse, and loaned him to me at Shreve's stable. . . . He had two horses he wanted to sell. Mr. Greenawalt, the proprietor of the Pennsylvania House, bought one of them for $140. . . . It was when the circus was here.

Q. What I want to know is, who asked you on Friday evening to take that horse and sell him? . . . How did you come to go that Friday afternoon?

A. I don't know how, any more upon that afternoon than any other.

Q. Did nobody tell you anything about going that day?

A. No, sir; it is nothing unusual for me to leave home seven or eight o'clock at night to go to the country. As I have said, I took one, if not two drinks. I owed Mr. Lloyd two dollars. I gave him a bill—I think it was either one or two dollars—and told him it was all the money I had in change. I said, "Mr. Lloyd, here is a bill; you need not give me any change, let it stand." On my way home, at the foot of Soper's Still, between seven & eight miles from Washington, I met Booth. He spoke to me.

Q. What time was that?

A. I think it must have been about half-past eleven o'clock at night.

Q. The same Friday night you went down?

A. Yes, sir; the same Friday. Says Booth, "Come go back down the country; we will have a gay old time." I told him I was obliged to go back home. He said it was impossible to cross the bridge, for the gates were shut, & he had had difficulty in getting over himself. I think Booth must have been drinking; I am quite confident that he had been. He insisted upon my going down to Bryantown with him.

Q. How was he travelling?

A. He was riding a bay mare, which I saw in the morning.

[He was shown a photograph of a man with scrubby mustache and goatee.]

Q. Who is that?

A. Why, it's old "Plug Tobacco"—G. A. Atzerodt from Port Tobacco. I rode his horse Friday night—the same night the President was murdered. . . .

Q. What kind of clothes did Atzerodt have on when you saw him that Friday evening?

A. I don't remember. As near as I can describe, he wore a black slouch hat, with a tolerably broad band upon it. . . . I am confident as to the black slouch hat. He used to wear a kind of black pantaloons—a kind of a zig-zag white. I don't know whether he had those on that Friday evening. I don't believe he had but one pair of pants that evening when he came up from the country.

Surely Herold's testimony exhibits a remarkable talent for detail, even to such an item as Atzerodt's pants. Not the ones with zigzag white stripes— enough to etch themselves on anyone's memory—but the fact that the Port Tobaccan had brought to the city only one pair.

Herold went on to say that after meeting Atzerodt, he treated him and some other friends to drinks at a "ten-pin alley." The interrogators wanted to know where he had gone after he left the ten-pin alley. Where was he at suppertime on April 14?

HEROLD: When I started from Shreve's stable I went directly down Seventh St. I took the horse from that stable about four o'clock. . . . I rode one or two squares around the city, but where I don't remember. I rode finally to my mother's house. . . . I don't remember how long I staid (*sic*) at mother's house—not more than ten minutes. My sister asked me where I was going. I said I was going on a bust, or made some such foolish remark. I went immediately out of town, & before sundown I was on Good Hope Hill.

Q. Did you not drink that evening in town with Booth?

A. I did not. I did not see Booth that evening. . . .

Q. Is there any other statement in regard to your conduct or your connection with this matter, or in regard to the conduct or connection of anybody else with the murder of the President or the attempted murder of Mr. Seward, that you wish to make?

A. I do not know of any. I had no idea that there was any such thing in view, by any party at all. I knew nothing of all of it. I never knew any party in existence that had the slightest idea of injuring the President or any of the Cabinet.[17]

That was Herold's story of his meeting with Booth on the night of April 14—a chance encounter on the road to Surrattsville, long after dark, when he, Herold, was returning to Washington after an evening in the country.

But another witness testified to seeing David Herold in Washington on the evening of April 14.

This was Mr. B. H. Strother, a clerk in the Commissary Department. Eight days after the assassination—while the police were seeking a "Harold," "Herrod," or "Harrold" as Booth's accomplice—Mr. Strother decided his acquaintance, David Herold, was the party wanted.

Strother hurried to the police. His deposition does not bear eyewitness evidence to a getaway, but it injects an interesting angle to escape possibilities—namely, the great open spaces of Idaho!

Statement of B. H. Strother (April 22, 1865):

I know David Harold. Have known him 4 or 5 years, and very well. Saw him, I think, on Friday Evening (April 14) in front of the Bank of Washington in company with two others and spoke to him. . . . He appeared sullen. He introduced me to a young man with him—but I did not hear the name. It was done with rather bad grace; so I made some casual remark. I asked him when he was going to start to Idaho. He was at my house two or three weeks ago with a tall dark fine looking man, to see about getting up a party to start for Idaho; but I declined to go.

Neither of the young men [with Herold on the street] were tall, but the taller of the two I would suppose to be 5 feet 9 or 10 inches. . . . They were not conversing at all—just standing still. He had on rather a worried look. Do not know who were his associates in this city. I have been told by parties who knew the family intimately that this young man has given his mother a good deal of trouble since his father's death.[18]

---

[17] National Archives, War Dept. Records, File "H," Doc. R.B.P. 38, JAO.

[18] National Archives, War Dept. Records, File "S," R.B.P. 31, JAO.

So it was noised about by the conspirators that they had Idaho in mind. It was a good trick to play on the authorities, contrived by a devious mind. Who owned it? John Wilkes Booth?

Aside from the mention of Idaho, Mr. Strother's testimony sheds no light on David Herold's whereabouts on the night of April 14. Strothers says he saw Herold in Washington that evening. But "evening" can mean the latter part of the day or early part of the night. As was the case with hundreds of depositions taken by the military during the Lincoln murder case, word usage was as fuzzy as the official comprehension of good English.

At least Mr. Strother's deposition came close to a correct spelling of Herold's name. The transcript came up with "a" instead of "e." But this was hairline accuracy compared with such War Department versions as "Herod" and "Harrod." One extraordinary dispatch went as widely wrong as "Harriott."

What difference did it make? Only enough to waste the time of the police in such cities as Toronto, Canada, and Buffalo, New York. Only enough to create a mystery where there should have been no mystery, confusion where there should have been no confusion.

One of the smartest detectives in Washington was an officer named Rosch. Bigwigs would overlook him; historians would never hear of him. His name would not make the index of any popular text devoted to the Lincoln murder case. He seems to have been one of those hard-plugging, thorough, capable underlings who so frequently do the job for which the high-ranking figureheads modestly accept the credit.

Rosch was listed as one of Olcott's men. Somehow—available records do not say how—this operative got on Herold's trail the night of the assassination. Perhaps he knew Herold or had seen him in Booth's company. Perhaps he acted on word from stable-foreman Fletcher when the hostler, empty-handed and nettled, returned from the bridge.

Officer Rosch caught the scent like a beagle. Within 24 hours, he placed a report on David Herold in the hands of the Provost Marshal General: Herold's name, his home address, his previous employers, his subversive views. Contained in this comprehensive memo was a slip of paper bearing David Herold's signature. With the notation: *Herolds handwriting obtained from Mr. Vincent, Druggist—near Navy Yard—by Officer C. H. Rosch/14th Apr. '65.*[19]

All this before midnight of April 14—straight to the target!

So far as is known, Officer Rosch did not receive even a platitude of commendation.

On April 20, six days after Rosch procured Herold's name, the War Department issued the following notice:

---

[19] National Archives, War Department Records, File "R," R.B., JAO.

War Department, Washington, April 20, 1865

$100,000 REWARD!

THE MURDERER

of our late beloved President, Abraham Lincoln,

IS STILL AT LARGE

$50,000 REWARD!

will be paid . . . for his apprehension, in addition to any reward offered by Municipal Authorities or State Executives.

$25,000 REWARD!

will be paid for the apprehension of
JOHN H. SURRATT, one of Booth's accomplices.

$25,000 REWARD!

will be paid for the apprehension of
DANIEL C. HARROLD, another of Booth's accomplices.

All persons harboring or secreting the said persons . . . or aiding or assisting their concealment or escape, will be treated as accomplices . . . and shall be subject to trial before a Military Commission and the punishment of DEATH.

Let the stain of innocent blood be removed from the land by the arrest and punishment of the murderers. . . .
—EDWIN M. STANTON, *Secretary of War*

Could "DANIEL C. HARROLD" have been a printer's error? An editor's? "SURRATT" is correctly spelled.

This garblement must mean one of two things. Someone in the War Department deliberately altered Herold's name—which seems improbable —or the military leaders, ignoring the Rosch report, were still groping for Herold's name and identity. The latter seems highly probable in the light of their subsequent handling of the Lincoln murder case.

3. ATZERODT WALKS AWAY

Befuddled Atzerodt boarded a horse car at East 6th and A Streets in southeast Washington at about 11:15 P.M. As this conveyance went clop-clop-clopping through the dim-lit streets, driver and passengers remarked the raffish man in the long coat and battered "round hat" as an odd customer. According to the testimony of witnesses: "His manner at that time was very much abstracted."[20]

The term "abstracted" was probably a euphemism for inebriated. He had been drinking to reupholster his nerves, and the liquor had evidently backfired, exciting his fears while dulling his perceptions. Now, his eye dilated, his mind a Halloween of apprehensions, he moved uncertainly up the jumpy aisle toward a seat.

Fleeing on slow, unmanageable feet to the center of the car, Atzerodt was so engrossed with his anxieties that he failed to recognize an acquaintance standing in the aisle. This was Washington Briscoe, a sophisticate of sorts, who clerked in a store at 8th and "Eye" Streets. Briscoe was on his way home to lodgings in the Navy Yard district. Accompanying him was a fellow employee, John S. Yates.

As Atzerodt groped past, Briscoe gave him an amiable push. Next moment the roustabout from lower Maryland had the store clerk by the lapels and was breathing and hiccuping into Briscoe's face.

"I spoke to him," Briscoe testified later, "asking him if he had heard the news [about the shooting at Ford's Theater]. He said in a very feeble manner that he had. He was very much excited. Was trembling."

The tremors may have come from a fusion of fright and alcohol, or from a sudden, exaggerated hope. Atzerodt had been heading for the Navy Yard with the vagueness of a drunk who remembers a destination but has forgotten the purpose of the errand. Now he wanted only a place to take cover, a rabbit-hole. He clung to Briscoe. Briscoe could put him up for the night. Briscoe might even become an alibi.

But Briscoe looked down his nose at the distraught supplicant. "He asked me if he could spend the night in my store. Told him he could not. Wanted to come home with me, but I refused."[21]

Atzerodt grew insistent. When informed there was no spare bed available at Briscoe's lodgings, he asked if he might share Briscoe's bed. Mr. Briscoe showed a decided lack of enthusiasm for this proposal. Atzerodt was behaving like a "loafer"—Briscoe's word for him in subsequent deposition—and the exasperated clerk finally pushed him off.

They got out of the horse car at the Navy Yard end of the line. Sullenly Atzerodt asked Briscoe if the car could take him back to the city and on out to Georgetown. Briscoe supplied information in the affirmative. Later he declared that he was happy to be rid of the fellow from Port Tobacco.

The futile ride out to the Navy Yard had done nothing to clear Atzerodt's head. He decided to return to the "Kimmel House"—the drab Pennsylvania House on C Street. He rode the "owl car" back to the East Capitol section.

---

[20] National Archives, War Dept. Records.
[21] National Archives, War Dept. Records, File "B," Doc. 31, Evidence 304, JAO.

About 2:00 A.M. he arrived at the door of the back-street hostel. He found it locked for the night, and he had to rouse the house boy, James Walker, whose job, as he testified later, was to "make fires, carry water, and to wait on gentlemen that come in late and early."

Waiting on the gentleman with the Dutch accent, the house boy called the proprietor. John Greenawalt, hotel keeper, turned up the gas and gazed upon the night owl with jaundiced eye. Atzerodt mumbled something about paying him on the morrow. Greenawalt said the house was full up, but grudgingly offered to bed Atzerodt in company with another nocturnal transient if the latter was willing. This second party, a bearded man who registered as "S. Thomas," grunted assent.

Atzerodt scrawled his own signature in the ledger and followed S. Thomas to the proffered room. The accommodations could hardly have been fastidious, but apparently Mr. Thomas was not fussy. His willingness to share on this occasion was going to win him subsequent mention in the press and in official dispatches issued by the War Department.

Atzerodt must have been on the verge of exhaustion when he flopped into a bunk at the "Kimmel House." It was then about 2:30 A.M. Yet, according to his own testimony, he was up and out on the street at 5:00. Something revived and energized him. Unshaven, unwashed, unkempt, unfed, he set out on foot in the rainy dawn, shaping an erratic course for Georgetown.

He must have made a conspicuous figure even in a city crowded with the vagrant backwash of war. The streets were alive with excitement. Yet Atzerodt walked through Washington and on out to the vicinity of the Georgetown Canal Docks as unnoticed by soldiery and police patrols as though he were invisible.

Kitchen smokes were thinning from the chimneys, and good citizens were through with breakfast and on their way to work on this dark Saturday morning when Atzerodt shuffled into Georgetown and headed up High Street (now Wisconsin Avenue). He had relatives out in the country. If he could only raise the stage fare. . . .

Statement of John L. Caldwell (recorded May 8, 1865):

On Saturday morning, April 15th, about 8:00 o'clock, Atzerodt came into the store and told me he was going to Montgomery County and asked if I did not want to buy a watch. I said I had a watch of my own and did not want any. "Well," said he, "I want to borrow $10; I have not any money; I am going to my uncle's; you let me have the $10 and I will leave my revolver with you and will send you the money or bring it to you next week. . . ."

I let him have the $10 and kept the revolver. The revolver was No. 499, Cooper Fire Arms Manufacturing Company, Frankford, Philadelphia. After I gave him the money I remarked to him that the assassination of the President was a right bad affair. He said, "Yes, it is a pretty bad thing for the country," or something to that effect. He did not seem to be the least excited. I had never been intimate with him; was only acquainted with him.[22]

Lucinda A. Metz, who lived at the corner of High and West Streets in Georgetown, was also visited by the ambling itinerant, as she testified to the interested authorities a few days later:

> I know a man called Atwood whom I have since learned is named Atzerodt. He came to my house on Saturday morning [April 15] somewhere between 7 and 8 o'clock, I think, and said he was going to Cunningham's Tavern to take the stage.[23]

Atzerodt probably begged breakfast, although Lucinda's official recollections did not include mention of hospitality asked or given. Nor did she vouchsafe any other reason for Atzerodt's call, or just where she had previously heard of him or known him as "Atwood." However, there are other Metzes in the case, as will be seen. They, too, knew Atzerodt as "Atwood."

Lucinda Metz asked the early-morning visitor if he had heard about the President's assassination. The topic seemed to distress Mr. Atzerodt. He did not linger on her doorstep. In concluding her subsequent testimony, she stated to the officers that he "looked guilty and talked in such a way."[24]

While Atzerodt may have "looked guilty" to Lucinda Metz (and it is odd how conspirators invariably look the part to simple souls who sign their depositions, as did Lucinda, with an "X"), he bore no such appearance to the customers at Cunningham's Tavern, where he boarded the north-bound stage for Rockville, Maryland.

About 9:00 A.M. the Rockville stage rattled up to the "Forts" which guarded the turnpike north of Georgetown. These were little more than "picket lines," three in number, spaced a mile or so apart, so as to span the road on either side of the village of Tennellytown. Anyone acquainted with the Rockville pike (and Atzerodt had traveled it before) must have known he would come up against this road-block.

So the stage came up against it—a "whoa!" from the driver, a grinding of wheel-brakes—and the passenger with face to window could glimpse Union blue, the gleam of bayonets and a soldier with gauntlet upraised.

Everybody out!

Everybody was George A. Atzerodt. The stage, after brief palaver, was ordered to go on. The lone passenger was told to stand and wait. Only a bear would have blundered into such a trap.

By this hour of the morning after the assassination, the military forces in and around the nation's capital were aroused to frenzies of endeavor.

---

[22] National Archives, War Dept. Records, File "C," "Evidence."
[23] National Archives, War Dept. Records, File "M," Doc. 544 JAO.
[24] *Ibid.*

Since midnight the War Department had been issuing orders to detain all travelers leaving the District of Columbia. General Augur had anticipated a possible escape in the Rockville direction. To the commander of Army forces garrisoned at Darnestown above Tennellytown, Augur had dispatched the following message an hour or so before midnight of the 14th.

> An attempt has been made to assassinate President Lincoln and Secretary Seward. The assassins are supposed to have escaped toward Maryland. Send all your available people at once to scout north of Washington, and arrest all suspicious persons. Report.[25]

Augur's message to Darnestown was probably the first of the many dispatched that night to U. S. troops outside of the capital. The Darnestown commander answered immediately, wiring Augur's Chief of Staff.

> I have sent three squadrons on as many different roads. The country will be thoroughly scoured before morning. Will report result.
>
> J. L. Thompson
> Colonel, Commanding

Having thus acknowledged the alarm from Washington Headquarters, the Darnestown commander sent a later, supplementary reply, reporting in detail the action taken.

> Sir: I have the honor to report that your dispatch was received last evening at 11:30, directing search to be made for the assassins. At 12 o'clock three squadrons were on the different roads. One squadron was directed to search the country between the telegraph road and the river as far down as Tennellytown. Another moved on the telegraph road with instructions to scour well to the left, and the third took the road to Barnesville and will make a wide circuit toward Frederick. Extreme vigilance has been enjoined on the whole line. . . .[26]

So, long before reveille Saturday morning, the "Forts" at Tennellytown north of Georgetown had the word. And at nine o'clock Saturday morning they had more than that. They had the fugitive George A. Atzerodt. But at three o'clock that afternoon they let him go!

The Army's explanation for the bungle remains almost as fantastic as the episode itself.

> On reaching the Forts [says the officially prepared report] in obedience to orders then issued, he [Atzerodt] and others . . . were detained there from 9 o'clock until three in the afternoon. During that time he treated the guard to several drinks, and finally induced them to allow him to proceed in a wagon of one John Garther, who took him as far as Rockville, when he left and proceeded to his own house.[27]

---

25 *Official Records*, Series I, Vol. 46, Part 3.
26 *Ibid.*
27 National Archives, War Dept. Records.

Forwarded from Colonel John A. Foster, USA, the report in question appears almost unrelievedly frank and open-handed, at first reading. On second reading it becomes so casually candid as to seem implausible. It must have been extended with apologies, but they do not appear in the record.

Throughout the District of Columbia and neighboring Maryland and Virginia all available soldiers, sailors and police had been ordered on the manhunt. Yet the military post on this northbound pike out of Washington remained so unvigilant that it allowed a character who looked like a Balkan anarchist to wheedle his way through the barrier after "treating the guard to several drinks."

It seems that Atzerodt went through the lines as "Atwood." A more unlikely name for the piratical derelict could not have been invented. In no way did it suit the grubby costume, the *Plattdeutsch* accent, the face like a dancing bear's. Yet he carried it off, we are told, actually clowning, burlesquing the role of innocent with ingratiating winks and back-slaps and nervous jocularity.

At the road-block waited a traffic-jam of market wagons, buggies and drays. Atzerodt circulated through this tie-up, slapping the horses, climbing over wagons, making himself as ostentatious as a master of ceremonies at a fair.

Witness to the shenanigan performance was no less an observer than "John Garther," the man who gave Atzerodt a lift. This citizen's name, it evolved, was actually Gaither—a substantial one if its adoption by a Maryland village means anything. Questioned by authorities five days late on the trail, Gaither offered the following testimony, duly sworn.

My name is William R. Gaither. I live about four miles above Rockville. My business is farming. Do not know a man of the name of Atzerodt. Know a man who I since have heard was Atzerodt.

The first time I ever saw him was when he got out of the stage up there at the pickets. It was last Saturday morning. I was going home. I had a light two-horse springer wagon [and was] alone. He was on the Rockville stagecoach. There was no person else besides him in the stage except the driver. . . .

The man who was taken from the stage [Atzerodt] passed about among the 40 or 50 wagons which were there and talked with them very familiarly and jovially in a familiar way. He asked me how I was traveling, and I pointed to my wagon, and he asked me if he could get a seat up with me. I told him I saw no objection, that some company was better than none.

One of the pickets came back [our] way and fetched up. . . . to search the wagons and let the citizens pass through. He [Atzerodt] then got up into the wagon with me and made a very polite bow to the Captain and said, "It's all right so fur!"

Up to this time I was off the wagon in a little store. . . . They did not let us through until 3 o'clock, as near as I can guess. During this time the Officer of the Guard was in the little store, and they [the officer and

Atzerodt] drank cider together. They did so twice—nothing but cider that I saw. I do not know the soldier who commanded the picket. He was the one he [Atzerodt] talked with mostly. I do not recollect particularly what he said to him. Sometimes they were in my hearing and at other times not. He appeared to be very familiar with him. He finally got on my wagon and I drove him off. . . .[28]

Here is one shaft of daylight on the mystery of the porous road-block that let Atzerodt seep through to Rockville. Some "Officer of the Guard," after detaining him for six hours, let him go through. This "officer's" name is not to be found in available War Department records. Evidently the War Department preferred to say that the "guard" had been diddled by a round of drinks—thus conveying an impression that a non-com and some privates were donkeys.

Yet it remains hard to believe that bribery by bottle was the answer to the business. George Andrew Atzerodt had been high on the "wanted" list since early morning. Long before sun-up the authorities had discovered him as an accomplice of Booth and Herold and as the renegade slated to murder the Vice President.

The Army police may not have been hunting a jocular Merry Andrew, but they were certainly seeking a roustabout with scraggly locks and a goatee, with a German accent and a menagerie personality, and Andrew somewhere in his name. Yet in broad daylight of that Saturday afternoon, Atzerodt, as "Andrew Atwood," went through the military road-block with all of these possessions.

About one-thirty in the morning after the assassination, stableman John Fletcher, frustrated in his chase of Herold's horse, reported the loss to General Augur's office.

As Fletcher testified later: "I went around to Dorsey's stables and inquired if the horse had got back, and he said no. I went down to 10th Street to the police office, by the direction of a sergeant, I went up to General Augur's office and identified a saddle and bridle which they had found. . . ."

Fletcher identified the black English saddle and bridle as belonging to George A. Atzerodt.

> General Augur asked what kind of a horse had that saddle and bridle been on. I told him a big brown horse, blind of one eye; a heavy horse, with a heavy tail; a kind of pacing horse. He asked me did I know the man's [Atzerodt's] name. I told him that I did not know his name, but I had it at the office. He sent the detective, Charley Stone, with me down to the office; and I went into the office, and got his name right upon one of our cards, and brought it up, and gave it to the general.[29]

---

[28] National Archives, War Dept. Records. File "G," Doc. 539, JAO.
[29] National Archives, War Dept. Records, File "F," JAO.

Having furnished a photographic description of the other stolen horse, Fletcher went on to describe the rider, Davy Herold. It is only reasonable to believe that the sharp-eyed stable foreman also supplied General Augur with a good description of George A. Atzerodt. Fletcher had reason to recall Atzerodt, for Atzerodt had been in and out of Naylor's Livery Stable several times in the past week.

Augur made no immediate move to send troops in pursuit of the two horsemen who had crossed Navy Yard bridge in spite of the 9:00 P.M. regulation. Nor did the General take immediate steps to locate and apprehend Atzerodt. Extraordinary, under the circumstances. Shortly after the President is murdered in a midtown theater, two mounted men—one on a stolen horse—go through a bridge-block on the city's southerly outskirts. A third man, an unprepossessing character, obviously an associate of the second horseman, is reported in the midtown area. Yet the Army general in charge of the manhunt does nothing. As Colonel Lafayette Baker of the Secret Service wrote in retrospect: "Here begins the first series of blunders in [the] attempted search for the assassins. Fletcher's statement was entirely disregarded. No steps were taken to follow up the clue thus given until sixteen hours afterward."[30]

However, by 2:30 A.M. of the 15th, Atzerodt's name was linked with that of Booth, John Surratt and Herold on the Provost Marshal's blotter. And the blotter was hardly dry before military headquarters had indelible proof that Atzerodt was one of Booth's accomplices.

This information came from the Kirkwood House at 12th and Pennsylvania—the hotel where Atzerodt had registered on the afternoon before the assassination. He had never slept in his room at the Kirkwood. But he had signed in as "G. A. Atzerodt," and his appearance as a guest was remembered when word of the bloody work at Ford's echoed through the capital.

Some time after midnight, Major James O'Beirne sent a special detective, John Lee, to the Kirkwood to mount guard over the room occupied by Vice President Johnson. One of O'Beirne's better men, this Lee, had his wits about him. After locating and visiting Johnson's door, he had the management show him the roof of the building, where he remarked a skylight and a fire escape to be guarded. When the guard was posted, Lee went down to the taproom, always a fount of information.

Detective Lee turned the spigot on bartender Michael Henry, and was rewarded with a spate of brass-rail intelligence well worth an alert detective's hearing.

Lee called for the night manager; he asked to see the registry. What about this barfly Dutchman who'd signed in? The manager opened the

---

[30] General Lafayette C. Baker, *History of the United States Secret Service* (Philadelphia: Privately published, 1867).

register. There it was—G. A. Atzerodt—but, no, he hadn't noticed him around the lobby tonight.

Atzerodt's second-floor room was the next stop—room 126. The door was locked. When knocking failed to elicit an answer, Lee demanded the housekey. It seemed there was only one key, and the guest had not returned it to the desk. Lee persisted. With permission of the management, he forced the door to Atzerodt's room—and walked into a veritable reliquary of evidence.

Hanging on an inner door was a black coat at first believed to be Atzerodt's. However, one pocket divulged a bankbook bearing the label of a bank in Ontario, Canada, and made out to *J. Wilkes Booth*. Detective Lee's eyes must have widened as he held this signature under the gas jet for a confirmative look. Understandably he thought he had found the assassin's coat. (The coat was later identified as belonging to David Herold.)

The bed looked lumpy. Lee groped under the pillow and pulled out a Colt revolver. He told Sprague, the night manager, to remain in the room, while he himself reported to headquarters immediately.

Lee was rushing through the Kirkwood lobby when he encountered Major O'Beirne. Dispatched with a message from Stanton, O'Beirne had just notified Vice President Johnson that Lincoln was dying. The major was evidently too excited to pay full attention to Lee's blurted report, and told him to go on searching Atzerodt's room and come back to headquarters when finished.

Detective Lee's efforts proved more productive than the findings of any fictional detective. Shaking out the black coat, ripping up the bed, yanking bureau drawers, and literally prying into every cranny of the chamber, he came up with a fantastic assortment of items and oddments, all handily traceable through size, markings, or initialling to Booth, Herold, or Atzerodt.

Lee dutifully listed the items. The list, filed with the War Department, reads:

> One Colt revolver with six chambers, loaded and capped.
> Three boxes of Colt's pistol cartridges, Caliber .44.
> One bowie-knife, blade 12 inches long, 1½ inches wide, ⅛ inch thick, somewhat stained. . . .
> One black coat. In its pockets were found a bankbook with J. W. Booth's name written both outside and inside, and a war map of the Southern states.
> One handkerchief, marked Mary R. E. Booth.
> One handkerchief marked F. M. Nelson.[31]
> One handkerchief, marked H.[32]
> One brass spur.
> One pair of gantlets (new).

---

[31] F. M. Nelson was the name of one of Herold's sisters.
[32] For Herold.

One plain envelope franked "Hon. John Conness."
One pair of socks.
One unmarked colored handkerchief.
One stick of licorice.
One toothbrush.
One collar, size 16.
One collar, size 17.[33]

Every item in the room was linked to the known assassin or to an accomplice yet to be identified. But the room itself bore registry to "G. A. Atzerodt." Thus in signing the hotel register, Atzerodt had signed his own death warrant.

And while his name was high on the "wanted" list at General Augur's headquarters, Atzerodt went clowning through the road-block at Tennellytown.

It is a good wagon ride from Tennellytown to Rockville. What with the morning's rain, the road was muddy and the going slow, but Gaither's wagon was not pursued. Plodding uphill and jogging downhill, the team took its time and Atzerodt's, but there was leisure to spare.

"On the way," Gaither recalled in deposition, "he was talking about fine horses and girls and dogs and trifling things."[34]

Gaither brought up the subject of the President's assassination. "I asked him about this affair, and he said there was a man by the name of Booth who was suspected of the deed, and that was pretty much all he said about it. . . . He did not appear to be on the subject at all—appeared as if he didn't care anything about it."

Near Rockville they were passed by the Washington-bound stage. Atzerodt should have taken alarm, for the stage driver, Francis Kerns, had a most observant eye. He remarked Atzerodt in the wagon, and later recalled he had on "sort of salt-and-pepper clothes. . . . Appeared to be in conversation with Mr. Gaither. . . . They were driving along very moderately."[35] But Kerns' keen eye was wasted, for the authorities did not question him that day concerning possible travelers on the Rockville pike. He was not queried until days later.

Gaither's wagon rattled along in the cool twilight. From the fields came the smell of fresh-ploughed earth; bottomland mist brought the smell of a swamp's rich compost. They clattered across a small stone bridge, past a mossy mill.

"Atzerodt," says DeWitt (that early authority on the case), "was going back to the home of his boyhood . . . poor, pitiable creature of a conspirator."[36]

---

[33] National Archives, War Dept. Records. Also Pitman, *op. cit.*
[34] National Archives, War Dept. Records, Doc. "G," 539, JAO.
[35] National Archives, War Dept. Records, File "K," JAO.
[36] David M. DeWitt, *The Assassination of Abraham Lincoln and Its Expiation* (New York: Macmillan Company, 1903).

One can agree with DeWitt that Atzerodt was a poor conspirator. But the picture of a man as a "pitiable creature" returning like the prodigal to a Stephen Foster homestead fails to conform with his performance at the "Forts" and his otherwise miscreant conduct. It is difficult to believe that the scenes of his childhood or any fondness for an Old Oaken Bucket drew this renegade back into the folds of Montgomery County.

Afterward he told a different story. But evidence suggests that the bumbling conspirator may have hoped to reach Confederate forces which had been operating in the Virginia hills to the west: Mosby somewhere around Winchester, or, more likely, Mobberly's guerillas bushwhacking in the back country of Loudon County. Atzerodt might well have been welcomed by such a band as Mobberly's.

But time and history and Federal forces in the field were all against an escape to some Confederate camp or guerilla lair in upper Virginia. From Winchester headquarters, General Hancock directed an army which had already closed in around Mosby. Even as Atzerodt drifted toward Rockville, Federal contingents in Loudon County were trapping and shooting the last of Mobberly's marauders.

So Atzerodt had no place to go.

Yet, paradoxically, he got there.

Unquestionably the headline news from Washington had arrived in Rockville with the morning stage, and the press dispatches had been supplemented by a chattering telegraph. Good townsmen were therefore clustered in excited groups before the bulletin boards. All in-bound traffic would have been hailed for the latest tidings. Gaither's wagon must have attracted attention. Yet, again, George Atzerodt became somehow invisible. Gaither recalled, under inquisition: "He went with me two miles past Rockville to Mulligan's shop. I left him at the shop, and he said that his father's wagon was behind and that he would stop there till he came up. I have never seen him since. . . ."[37]

Atzerodt, grounded at Mulligan's, was on his own (his father's wagon was, of course, a myth). Records do not exist on Mulligan's shop. It may have dealt in horseshoes, general merchandise, or grog. But whatever its business, this road-fork establishment would have had its own Saturday night clientele. And that Saturday night in particular it would have been a scene of coming and going, a hub of talk and excitement.

Atzerodt burrowed through this minor turmoil as a badger burrows through underbrush. Somewhere beyond Mulligan's he spent that Saturday night with impunity, while detectives scoured Washington, frantically hunting his trail, and the War Department issued dispatches advising Baltimore and the North to be on the lookout for him. The first of these

---

[37] National Archives, War Dept. Records, File "G," Doc. 539, JAO.

disptaches went out about the time Atzerodt was wagoning through Rockville. This dispatch erroneously identified him as the man who had attacked Seward.

Honorable E. G. Spaulding, Buffalo:
The assassin of the President is J. Wilkes Booth, well known to all theatrical people. He is about five feet six inches tall; of a slight, graceful figure; black hair, and eyes rather close together, and pale complexion; about twenty-six years old.
The assailant of Mr. Seward has been known here by the name of G. A. Atzerodt. He is twenty-six or twenty-eight years old, five feet eight inches tall; light complexion, brown from exposure; brown hair; long and rather curly mustache and goatee, dark from being dyed; rather round shouldered and stooping; wore dark pants, vest and coat, with a long gray overcoat, and a low, slouched hat, much worn. Atzerodt has been here in company with a man named S. Thomas, about thirty years old; poorly clad in a dark suit; wore a heavy beard and mustache—a rough, weatherbeaten looking man. Atzerodt is believed to have left this city this morning at 6:30 in the Baltimore train.

C. A. DANA
Assistant Secretary of War[38]

At 9:00 P.M. the War Department issued dispatches to the Police Chiefs of Baltimore, Philadelphia, New York. While these contained, verbatim, the description of Atzerodt telegraphed to Buffalo, they did not mention the Baltimore train. Nor did they mistakenly name him as Seward's assailant. And although the inclusion of "S. Thomas" was sufficiently misleading (the police would be on watch for a pair of fugitives rather than one), Atzerodt was sketched fairly accurately. Just how he remained undetected by Army patrols in the Rockville area that Sunday adds still another mystery to the case.

Atzerodt's cousin, Hartman Richter, resided in Germantown. And, as of Sunday, April 16, Atzerodt was there at his cousin's. But by no means in hiding. His experience with the Tennellytown pickets must have convinced him that exposure was the best protective coloration. At church-time he was out on the road. His course that morning took him up-country toward Barnseville on the pike leading toward Leesburg and Harper's Ferry.

Shortly before eleven he arrived at the farmhouse of Hezekiah Metz. Atzerodt went in. The house was full of people.

The Metz family had two other guests—the brothers James and Somerset Leamen. A neighbor, Mr. Purdon (or Burton), dropped in and out. Dinner was served.

When the meal reached the toothpick stage, it was time to go. Metz's door stood wide, and the road to the West lay open. All George Atzerodt had to do was keep on walking.

Instead of that, he went on talking.

---

[38] *Official Records*, Series I, Vol. 46, Part 3.

As in every household in the land, the topic that Sunday revolved around Lincoln's assassination. At Metz's table somebody mentioned the fact that General Grant had been missed by the assassins.

"*Ja*," said Atzerodt sagely, "but if they had done as they were supposed to do, they would have got General Grant."

After that remark, instead of heading West he went back to his Cousin Richter's.

The man's luck remained incredible.

He had been seen that weekend by at least a thousand Washingtonians, dozens of citizens in Georgetown, and scores of farmers and villagers around Rockville—an area scoured by Federal cavalry ordered to exert "extreme vigilance" and arrest all suspicious strangers.

Yet the question asked by the nation's police that Sunday night—and for three days afterward—was this: *Where is George A. Atzerodt?*

CHAPTER 9

The Trail to Doctor Mudd's

BY MIDNIGHT Booth was in agony. The night had gone chill, and the cold throbbed in his broken leg. His tired mare kept slipping in the road's soft gravel. Every jolt of the stirrup rubbed the broken bone above his left ankle. The pain was making him sick at his stomach. He thirsted for brandy.

He and Herold, who was riding alongside, could procure liquor at the tavern in Surrattsville. But the eleven miles to Surrattsville had never seemed so far. When they rode into the small village shortly after midnight, Booth's injured foot had begun to swell in the boot, and the leather seemed to be tightening like an iron vise.

The inn stood in black silhouette at left of the highroad—a low-roofed, two-story building set on a rise of ground a little back from the roadway. A gravel drive curved up through shrubbery to the front verandah. The tavern was dark except for a single light burning in the barroom.

Booth stopped his horse in a bay of shadow near the verandah. Herold dismounted and went up to the door. He found the place locked for the night. He peered into the entrance hall, then began a peremptory pounding.

After a minute, flabby John Lloyd appeared. He had been asleep on a sofa. His shirttail was out in front and his carpet slippers slapped loosely. As usual, he was drunk.

Some accounts say Herold darted in and got the secreted articles: the carbines, binoculars, cartridges, rope. Lloyd eventually testified that he himself went upstairs to procure this gear from the hiding place under the eaves. The fugitives left the rope, the monkey wrench, and one of the carbines behind.

While Lloyd was groping upstairs, Booth called to his companion, "For God's sake, bring me some brandy. This damned foot is driving me crazy!"

Herold came out with a bottle. "There's no brandy here. Only whisky."

Booth clutched at the bottle. Tilting it, he drank greedily. The whisky warmed him. He drank again, coughed, handed the bottle to Herold. They had to get away from the lighted doorway, clear out of there.

Herold was reluctant to leave one of the guns. He stripped the cloth from the carbine Lloyd had given him. "Good gun," he admired.

"Government issue," Booth warned. "It could be recognized. Better take the other one. I can't carry one, damn it! I'm hurt."

Wobbling against a verandah post, Lloyd looked at Booth inquiringly. Booth demanded, "Where's the nearest doctor? I've hurt my leg."

"Doc Hoxton," Lloyd hiccuped. "Down the road a piece. But he's old and don't want to practice any more."

"Never mind, we'll get another." Booth turned on Herold impatiently. "We've got to get started and—wait. Give me another drink."

Herold passed the bottle. While Booth drank, Herold busied himself, unwrapping the second carbine and ripping the cloth to make a sling for the gun.

Booth drained the bottle and flung it savagely into the brush. "Do you want to hear some news?" he said, glaring abruptly at Lloyd. "We've just killed the President. And some of his curst Cabinet!"

From the verandah, John Lloyd mumbled something that sounded as if he wasn't interested or didn't care to hear more—something like that.

"Pay him," Booth snapped at Herold. "Let's be on our way!"

Herold handed the innkeeper a dollar bill. He swung into the saddle and turned his horse down the curving drive. Booth followed. Darkness enfolded them as they galloped southward down the dim stretch of open road.

Behind them, John Lloyd stood in an inebriate daze. According to his subsequent testimony, he was "much excited and unnerved at the time."[1] Perhaps he stared at the dollar bill in his soiled grasp. Stared dully, and then blinked and turned bloodshot eyes to the dark gulf of night which had swallowed the fugitives.

About two o'clock in the morning of April 15 the fugitives galloped

---

[1] Testimony quoted in Oldroyd, *op. cit.*, p. 197.

through the roadside hamlet of Teebee. Herold maintained the lead. Booth rode askew in saddle, his posture contorted, his face white as bone.

The sedative effect of the whisky had drained away, leaving Booth sick. His whole body ached, and the throb in his left leg had become intolerable. Like many high-strung egotists, he could not bear pain with stoicism. Self-concern exaggerated his anguish.

According to one version of the escape story, Booth's horse fell with him somewhere on the road near Teebee. Pitched to the ground, Booth lay for a moment chewing his fist, sobbing in agony. The always-solicitous Herold picked him up tenderly and seated the injured actor on the broad-backed roan. Herold then mounted the nervy little mare and rode as escort alongside the exhausted Booth.[2]

Some authorities contend the story of Booth's fall from the horse a fabrication invented by the fugitives to deceive the doctor. Unable to endure the pain of his broken leg, Booth's nerves collapsed as they galloped through the night. He told Herold they could never make it to Port Tobacco, as planned. He couldn't stand it. They had to find a doctor who could ease his leg.

The nearest physician, a Dr. Samuel Mudd, lived on a back road near Bryantown. Presumably he was a Southern sympathizer. Booth had tested this doctor's sentiments the previous winter. Apparently he wasn't too sure of the man. But they'd have to risk Mudd's sentiments, and hazard a ten-mile detour off the main route to Port Tobacco where, if Atzerodt had prepared the way, an escape boat was ready and waiting.

Nobody knows the conversation that passed between Booth and his toady on the road that night. Historians can only conjecture at the discussion that may have preceded the visit to Dr. Samuel Mudd. Most historians accept the popular conclusion that the visit to this backwoods physician was dictated by accident—Booth's injury. It was a fatal detour from a well-planned escape route to a Potomac crossing.

The fugitives turned off the road near Beantown. A wagon trail dipped and wound through woods. On this woodsy trail the two riders headed east by south toward Bryantown. Booth had been in the neighborhood before, but whisky-muddled, pain-wracked as he was, he would doubtless have gone astray had not Herold been there as guide.

The seedy drug clerk knew Charles County like the back of his hand. He seems to have been as instinctively oriented as a cat. All his nocturnal senses were alert that night. Probably he was enjoying himself—the escape, the excitement, the fact that Mr. Booth, his idol, in this crisis had to rely on him. This was a big hour in David Herold's life. He rode toward a bright mirage of fame and fortune.

About 4:00 A.M. Herold led Booth up to a roadside gate, ghostly in the

---

[2] Version in Van Doren Stern, *op. cit.*, p. 175.

wooded gloom. Far back from the gate a large farmhouse stood in dark silhouette against night sky. Herold opened the gate. He took Booth's bridle and the bridle of his own horse, and led the animals up the long, dim drive.

It seems the visitors had decided on a cover story. They would use assumed names. Herold was to do the talking. According to some accounts, Booth paused to don a makeshift disguise. From his pocket he drew a false beard which he had salvaged from his theatrical trunk. He had brought with him a shawl. He fastened on the beard with some sort of adhesive, then pulled the shawl up around his ears, and contrived the appearance of "an old man."[3]

Skeptics doubt this story of Booth's disguise, and the doubt may be justified. He must have known the doctor would ask him to remove shawl and coat. And false whiskers are as obvious as dyed hair. It is possible, however, that Booth wished to hide his countenance from servants or house guests who might be on hand. The doctor and his wife asserted later that the injured visitor wore a beard.

Herold hammered on the front door. The pounding aroused an excited dog. Several dogs took up the clamor in the rear barnyard. Presently a light glimmered in the house. A voice called from within. "Who's there?"

Herold answered something or other about a man who had been hurt by a fall from a horse. Dr. Mudd appeared in the doorway, looked out uneasily.

Herold went on with the story. His friend had a broken leg. Was in great pain. Could the doctor fix him up?

Dr. Mudd descended to the driveway where Herold had tethered Booth's mount to a tree. The doctor aided Herold in lifting Booth from the saddle. Between them they helped the limping man into the house. Booth groaned and panted. Dr. Mudd procured a lamp. The light showed a stairway going up at the right of a hall. At hall left a door opened into a neat parlor. Dr. Mudd and Herold helped the patient into the parlor, and Booth sank moaning on a sofa.

Gently the doctor took hold of Booth's left boot and tried to work it off. The injured actor gasped, cried out, and nearly fainted. Mudd told him the boot would have to be cut from his foot. The doctor said he could work better upstairs where Booth could be placed on a bed. He went out to summon his wife.

Presently Mrs. Mudd arrived in wrapper and nightcap. They carried Booth up the stairway to a bedroom, the same one he had occupied during his previous visit to the Mudd homestead as Dr. Mudd's invited guest.

Now Booth sprawled on the bed. Mumbling, he complained of pain in the back. He kept his face turned aside, his shawl pulled up to his eyes.

---

3 Bishop, *op. cit.*, p. 276.

Or so Dr. Mudd would testify. Afterward, the doctor and his wife would have some explaining to do. Authorities could not believe their sworn statements to the effect that they failed to recognize the injured fugitive. Conceivably the doctor and his wife, roused from sleep, could have been at first bemused. Lamplight and shadow could have abetted Booth's disguise. The doctor's attention could have been centered on his patient's leg.

But that Booth could or would have maintained a masquerade after the physician got him upstairs seems highly implausible. He must have whispered his name or otherwise revealed his identity to the doctor. Possibly he did so before he entered the house.

Mudd found Booth's foot badly swollen. He got his medical kit and chose a sharp knife. Carefully he cut the tight boot open, slitting the leather down the shin to the instep. Booth groaned through clenched teeth as the doctor drew the loosened boot from the puffed foot. Again he almost fainted as Dr. Mudd manipulated the broken limb, feeling for the snapped bone.

Mudd told Booth the injury was nasty. A splint would be necessary. It might be two weeks before the patient could be up and about. Then he would have to use a crutch for a time.

One can only surmise Booth's despair at this information. He knew the Federals would be on his trail within a matter of hours. Whatever cover had been promised by the underground, pursuit could not be permanently blocked.

Herold, too, seems to have been alarmed. He said something about going on as soon as the leg was splinted.

Nobody can state with certainty the words exchanged at that hour in the upstairs bedroom at Dr. Mudd's. But the doctor did his best for the patient. Medical supplies were lacking. A makeshift splint was contrived of an old bandbox. This was pasted to Booth's left shin. While the splint was being applied, Booth complained again of pains in his back. He sank into a sort of stupor. The homemade splint apparently relieved him greatly and exhaustion put him to sleep. The doctor covered him with a quilt and let him lie. Herold went down to take care of the horses.

After setting the patient's leg, Dr. Mudd, wakeful and restless, had gone out to the barnyard. Day was breaking. The doctor pottered around at farm chores until breakfast time. Then he went in and offered breakfast to the patient's friend. The injured man remained upstairs asleep.

In the gray light of a rainy morning Booth awoke to find Herold standing over him, an uneasy sentinel.

The fugitives were whispering when Mrs. Mudd knocked at the bedroom door. Quickly Booth covered himself with the quilt and turned face to wall. He was lying bundled up, inert, when the doctor's wife came in with a tray. Or so she would state.

"He ain't feeling so good," Herold told Mrs. Mudd as she entered the room. "If you have some brandy, that might perk him up."

Kindly Mrs. Mudd shook her head. She could not provide brandy. But there was whisky in the house. Good homemade whisky.

Corn liquor. Booth declined it with a muttered thanks. Mrs. Mudd set down the tray and quietly withdrew. Doutbless she was uneasy about this strange, uninvited guest. She could not have liked his manner, and she had even more reason to dislike his companion's. At breakfast table Herold had chatted in a glib and braggart fashion that countryfolk instinctively mistrust. The doctor had thought him a "fast young man." There was something wrong with this couple. Mrs. Mudd's intuition must have told her that her husband had been upset by their arrival.

Host and hostess were themselves suspect of anti-Government sentiments. The doctor was a quiet, moody man, probably embittered by the war, disappointed by the South's defeat, worried about the future. He had friends among the "Secesh" element, and his deportment suggested contact with the Rebel underground. Or was he an honest neutral?

Not long after breakfast Herold came downstairs to request the loan of the doctor's razor. It seemed the patient thought a shave would spruce him up. Obligingly the doctor offered his shaving kit.[4]

At noon time there was another uncomfortable repast in the dining room with Herold chattering like a magpie. According to Dr. Mudd, the "fast young man" gave his name as "Henston" and confided that the injured man was named "Tyson." Now he rattled off the names of numerous people known to him in the neighborhood of Bryantown and nearby Beantown—the Robys, Major Thomas, Parson Wilmer and others.

Herold now (according to Dr. Mudd) confusingly asked the way to Bryantown. This inquiry did not make sense. When the visitors had arrived at the house at 4:00 A.M., the young man had said they were on their way to Washington *from* Bryantown.

One wonders why Dr. Mudd brought up this point in his eventual statement to the authorities. Was the doctor trying to cover himself in the matter? That is, trying to say that when he admitted the fugitives to his home he believed they were going to Washington (hence, innocent travelers). Then endeavoring to explain how he came to direct the fugitives southward (as he did), declaring himself bewildered by a garbled story from Herold.

Anyway, the young man now wanted to go to Bryantown to obtain a carriage so that he could take his injured friend over to Parson Wilmer's. But if Herold's conversation seemed confusing to Dr. Mudd, so would the doctor's testimony on this point seem confusing to the authorities.

---

[4] National Archives, War Dept. Records, File "E," 315, JAO.

Fatally enough for his own plea of innocence, the doctor later admitted that he went out to hunt up a conveyance for Booth and Herold.

Dr. Mudd made other gestures to help the patient and his "fast" companion. After the noontime meal he went upstairs to examine the patient's leg. Booth (or Tyson) kept his face turned away. That, in itself, should have troubled any inquiring physician, but Mudd (according to his statement) asked no questions. He noticed that the patient had shaved his mustache while retaining a beard. Although the doctor remarked this peculiar fact, it did not trouble him at the time.

If Mudd's word may be believed, he said little to the patient that morning. He examined the splints, asked a question or two. Booth answered in monosyllables. The physician told him he would have to keep off the injured foot. The break would need time to knit together, perhaps three or four weeks. Undue movement or strain would aggravate the fracture.

Herold followed Dr. Mudd downstairs. Could the doctor fix up some crutches for "Mr. Tyson"? Mudd nodded, and went to the barn on this errand. There was an old Englishman, John Best, around the place—a sort of family retainer. With this hand's assistance, the doctor carpentered a crude pair of crutches—a couple of sawed-off lengths of wood with crossbars screwed on top. A Negro boy, Frank Washington, took them up to Booth's room.

Shortly after noon Dr. Mudd saddled up and trotted over to his father's home to see about borrowing a carriage for the patient. Herold accompanied the doctor on this errand. It proved a futile one. Patriarch of the numerous Mudd clan, the doctor's father answered the request with something less than enthusiasm. He said that his several conveyances were under repair. The only buggy in use would be needed on the morrow— Easter Sunday—to take the family to church. Nor did he know of an available rig in the immediate vicinity. Perhaps the strangers could procure a vehicle in Bryantown.

Dr. Mudd pointed out the road to Bryantown, and Booth's henchman set off by himself on what he must have known was a risky gallop. Dr. Mudd trotted over to the homestead of a Mr. Hardy. Later, he recalled that he spent an hour at the Hardy place "in conversation" with this farmer. What did they talk about? Inconsequentials, according to the doctor. Yet it seems odd that he would spend so much time away from home that afternoon, leaving his wife unguarded with a wounded and sullen stranger in the house. Dr. Mudd must have wanted to discuss something more than yams and fertilizer with Mr. Hardy.

Then Mudd returned home "leisurely" (the doctor's word for it). He found the injured man and his young friend "just in the act of leaving." Herold inquired the way to Parson Wilmer's. Mudd gave the directions. "I did not see them leave the house. The man on crutches had left the house when I got back . . . I do not know how or where Booth got a conveyance away from my house."

The doctor's reference to a "conveyance" is most confusing. Surely he recalled Booth's arrival that morning on horseback. Apparently he forgot the horses, even as he found it expedient to forget a number of details concerning Booth's stay at the Mudd homstead.

But it does appear that Herold had returned from Bryantown before Dr. Mudd concluded his visit with Mr. Hardy. Hurrying upstairs, Herold burst into Booth's room probably with the news that word of the assassination had reached Bryantown. Herold appears to have been frightened. He blurted the information that a carriage couldn't be had. They must be off at once, ride for cover. Booth, alarmed and flustered, immediately made for the front stairs.

Mrs. Mudd heard the cripple and his companion come floundering down the stairway. Surprised by the commotion, she hastened into the lower hall. Later, she said that as Booth lurched down his shawl went askew, and she noticed that his beard seemed to fall away from one side of his chin.[5] He kept his face averted as he and his companion hustled to the front door. Mrs. Mudd expressed bewilderment about this flurried departure. To inquiring Federal officers, her recital of the false-whisker incident must have sounded unconvincing.

Herold hurried out to fetch the horses. Booth did not wait. He mumbled a thank-you-ma'am and goodbye over his shoulder to Mrs. Mudd, and hobbled on his crutches down to the front gate.

According to Dr. Mudd's account, the cripple was some seventy yards down the road when he, Mudd, cantered home from Hardy's. The doctor did not speak to the departing patient. The "fast" young man approached him and asked him the nearest way to Wilmer's. Mudd pointed out two roads. The public road which went through Beantown. And a little-used shortcut which traversed a stretch of dense swampland.

Herold nodded curtly. He pressed a wad of bills into the doctor's palm. Twenty-five dollars.

Dr. Mudd went around to the barnyard, then into the house. That was the last he saw of his uninvited guests. But he would see Herold in a cell.

Dr. Samuel Mudd was going to pay and pay dearly for setting Booth's leg. The Government would contend that this taciturn country doctor was an arch conspirator. That he was a member of the Booth gang, and party to the assassination plot. That his home was a hideaway on the Rebel underground. That in aiding the crippled assassin and putting him on a back-road trail, the physician acted as a prime accomplice, a subversive agent, a traitor.

---

[5] Nettie Mudd (ed), *op. cit.*, p. 32.

Mudd may have been guilty on one or several of these counts. **Evidently** his sentiments had been pro-South, therefore anti-United States (hence treasonable). Evidence indicates that he had engaged in subversive activities. He had met John Wilkes Booth the previous winter, entertained Booth in his home, conversed with the actor in Washington. He must have recognized the fugitive who dragged a broken leg into his parlor. He could not deny giving shelter to Booth and Herold. He splinted Booth's fracture.

Mudd's defenders made too much of the fact that Booth arrived at Mudd's door at night. That Booth wore a disguise. That the doctor had never seen Herold before. That, in any event, the physician was duty-bound, to aid, in the Hippocratic tradition, a man who was badly injured and suffering.

Such a defense for Dr. Mudd was, and remains, flimsy. He himself stated that he did not recognize Booth that night. But even in candlelight and shadow he must have known false whiskers when he saw them. He must have sensed something familiar about the groaning patient. He must have talked to the patient, if only to ask professional questions about his leg. But if Booth were a stranger, would Mudd have offered him a room?

Assume this actor hid his face, disguised his voice, and all the rest of it. The doctor would have realized something criminal was afoot. The two at his door were wind-blown, saddle-rumpled, haggard. Booth carried pistols. Herold wore a carbine. A carbine is not an ordinary hunting rifle. A carbine is made for bigger game. And bandits were known to be about.

In subsequent testimony, Dr. Mudd failed to remark the fact that his visitors resembled renegades; that Herold carried a carbine. Unfortunately, he hedged on other matters. When the Federal officers eventually knocked at his door, he muttered evasive answers, told half-truths. Typically ambiguous was his account of the fugitives' departure from his farm.

To the last, Dr. Mudd told a confusing and garbled story to the authorities. There are holes in his testimony which remain unfilled to this day.[6] We see him as a shadowy figure caught in a tangle of ugly events, not sure, perhaps, of his own feelings.

Examine the doctor in the light of certain evidence, and his features become even more indistinct. In this light he is not the ardent pro-Southerner ready and waiting to aid Lincoln's assassin. Neither is he the innocent bystander, the humane physician who felt it his professional duty to aid a sufferer.

The evidence in question exists in the War Department files. Two items serve to blur the stereotyped, partisan views of Dr. Mudd.

Consider the testimony of Thomas Davis, an intimate of the Mudd household. On the night after Booth and Herold visited the house, Davis

---

[6] See Appendix D for Dr. Mudd's full statement.

sat with Dr. and Mrs. Mudd at supper. All were probably thinking of the crippled man and his sleazy companion.

Then (according to Davis): "Dr. Mudd remarked that the setting of this man's leg didn't pay him for his trouble." Davis asked the doctor if he had been paid at all. The doctor replied shortly, "Only twenty-five dollars."

Mrs. Mudd observed, "It takes a lot of cotton to bandage a man's leg."[7]

From this vignette it can be inferred that the Mudds were hard-up, and that the doctor was beginning to regret services rendered. Dr. Mudd, it would seem, was weighing values.

On Easter Sunday morning, April 16, Dr. Samuel Mudd paid a surprise call on his cousin, Dr. George Mudd. An older man, Dr. George Mudd was known throughout the area as a staunch Union loyalist, patriotic to the core. Samuel Mudd told this Unionist cousin that he, Sam, was worried. Two suspicious characters had been at his house the day before. He confided that he was afraid to report them, for fear of reprisals from "Secesh" zealots in the neighborhood. Would George Mudd inform the Federals about the fugitives?[8]

Evidently Dr. Samuel Mudd had done some serious overnight thinking. Either Booth or Herold had told of the assassination strike, or Mudd, hearing by neighborhood grapevine of the assassination (perhaps Saturday evening) had put two and two together. Now he was caught between Federal Law on the one hand and Rebel vengeance, if he talked, on the other.

So Dr. Mudd took steps to have the fugitives reported. He did not tell the entire story, but he met the Federals half way. His tip, relayed to the authorities on April 17, was the first definite word they had on Booth's presence in the locality.

From a pro-North standpoint, then, he acted as a loyal patriot, risking his neck to turn Booth in. From a pro-South standpoint, he was a traitor to the dying cause—an informer. In trying to play it safe, he lost the game.

John Lloyd, the dissolute Surrattsville innkeeper, would deliberately mislead the police. Yet the Government eventually treated him as a favored witness, and he went unpunished.

The doctor who risked his neck to put the man-hunters hot on Booth's trail eventually came close to being hanged on a Federal gallows.

---

[7] National Archives, War Dept. Records, File "D," JAO.
[8] Noted in Eisenschiml, *op. cit.*, p. 260. Also Pitman, *op. cit.*

CHAPTER 10

The Barn Is Locked

O N THE NIGHT of April 14, 1865, Edwin M. Stanton took charge of the United States of America. In terms of stamina, energy, volubility, determination and initiative it was an astonishing performance.

For more than ten hours, while Lincoln lay dying in the next room, the War Secretary ruled in the back parlor of the Petersen house, issuing a nonstop torrent of orders, instructions, decrees, mandates, directives and commands. Making a desk of the top hat on his knee, he scribbled high-speed dispatches to the Army. He rushed emergency orders to the United States Navy. He advised the State Department. He ran the Adjutant General's Office. He bossed the Cabinet members who had gathered at Lincoln's deathbed. He reigned over the city of Washington.

Stanton took charge of the national defenses. Believing the capital threatened by Confederate forces from without, he called for the 8,000 Army troops in the District area to man the forts and battle stations. To quell possible internal uprising, he ordered 500 military police, squads of city constabulary, Federal detectives, Secret Service agents, and all available guards to protect the public buildings, patrol the avenues and scour Washington's back streets.

Stanton took charge of the hunt for the assassins. He flung commands at the District Provosts Marshal, sent directives to the Metropolitan Police. He ordered the seizure of Ford's Theater, the detention of all its personnel, the arrest of everyone in the cast of *Our American Cousin*. He placed Justice Cartter in charge of a drumhead court of inquiry. He himself played chief interrogator, examining witnesses and suspects who were hustled in from the street.

He sent for Robert Lincoln. He conferred with generals and statesmen, senators and journalists, doctors, lawyers, clergymen. Shouting, snapping, beckoning, gesturing, he rushed messengers out of the house, ordered people into the house, detained some and dismissed others pellmell. When Mrs. Lincoln became hysterical, the War Secretary went so far as to order her away from her husband's bedside.

One might believe that after this night of furor and frenzy Edwin M.

Stanton would have been exhausted, his voice hoarse, his collar wilted, his forehead dripping. Perhaps his mien and habiliments were mussed, but he went on going like a steam engine until well into the ensuing forenoon. Edwin M. Stanton was generalissimo, Commander-in-Chief, National Dictator, Supreme Police Superintendent, High Judge, Captain, King, all in one. A one-man junta, in effect he was acting President of the United States.

Some awed observers and a following of historians considered Stanton's assumption of supreme command a remarkable demonstration of leadership at an hour of crisis. Others considered it a remarkable demonstration of an assumption of supreme command. Either way, Stanton's performance was astounding. Some aspects of it were seen as little short of amazing. And they remain so in the long view of history.

One of Stanton's first moves at the Petersen house was to send a peremptory summons to Vice President Johnson.

No one could have asserted that Andrew Johnson understood the situation. Least of all, Andrew Johnson. Had he been discerning, he would have immediately explained his early retirement on the evening of April 14. He would have realized few would believe that tough, vigorous Andy Johnson, normally a late retirer, went early to bed on this, of all evenings, without a motive.

Suddenly there had been ex-Governor Farwell pounding on the door of Johnson's hotel room. To quote Farwell's testimony: ". . . I rapped, but receiving no answer, I rapped again and said in a loud voice, 'Governor Johnson, if you are in the room, I must see you.' I believe the door was locked but am not certain. . . ."[1]

Finally Johnson had opened the door. Farwell blurted the tidings— Lincoln had just been shot at Ford's Theater. What did Johnson do then? By one account, he paced the floor, roaring in fury. Farwell locked the door, and Johnson did nothing but storm until Major O'Beirne came with word from Stanton demanding the Vice President's appearance at the Petersen house. Another account says Johnson volunteered to go at once to the President, but was restrained by anxious friends.

However, not long after midnight Johnson walked with escorts to the house across from Ford's Theater and remained at the President's side for about half an hour. Then he headed back through the drizzling dark for the Kirkwood.

Johnson's brief watch over the dying President would contribute a load of ammunition to enemy political snipers who claimed it exhibited a callous disregard for Lincoln. Friends could and did retort that Johnson's call was abbreviated by shock and grief; a man of strong emotions, he could not

---

[1] Pitman, *op. cit.*, pp. 151–152.

bear the deathbed scene. Something might be said for this last. At Lincoln's bedside there were some persons who apparently made the most of drama and publicity.

Nevertheless, the Vice President's conduct seems to have been peculiar. By one account he paused for a few words with Stanton, and the War Secretary "dismissed" him. Another story has it that he could not wait to get back to the Kirkwood House for a conference with his private secretary who briefed him on the procedures of accession to the Presidency. Strangest of all, it appears that Johnson left the Kirkwood some time before dawn and went somewhere in the night and rain—nobody knows whether accompanied or alone—and did not turn up again until daylight. Where did he go? Nobody could say. But something weird must have occurred, if Senator William M. Stewart of Nevada is to be believed.

About eight o'clock in the morning after the assassination, Senator Stewart called at the Kirkwood to see Johnson. According to Senator Stewart, he found Johnson in a drunken stupor, his clothing in disarray, his hair matted with mud. He looked as though he had fallen headlong in a gutter. A doctor and a barber were hustled into the suite to ready him for the office he was soon to inherit.[2]

So still another cloud darkened the overcast which formed over Andrew Johnson.

First a strange message from Booth. A little card on which Booth had written: *Don't wish to disturb you Are you at home?*

Then an unexplained early retirement—two hours unaccounted for.

Then a seemingly reluctant glance at the dying President.

Finally, a disappearance and a drunken sprawl somewhere in the dark before dawn.

Such elements comprise the tenebrous mystery which shadows the record of Andrew Johnson.

Are there plausible answers to these Johnson enigmas? If so, they are not in available literature. On the subject of Booth's card, Johnson seems to have shut his mouth like a trap. Most historians believe the leaving of the card was an evil trick to implicate the Vice President in the conspiracy. But could his refusal to discuss the card have rested on a former acquaintance with the actor? In 1867 detectives sent out to investigate Johnson's past reported that when he was governor of Tennessee he had met Booth in Nashville on a local level hardly recommended for a public official.[3]

If the detective reports were reliable, one might wonder if a related situation accounted for the mystery of Johnson's early retirement on the night of April 14. This is pure, unsubstantiated hypothesis. But neither

[2] Senator William M. Stewart, *Reminiscences* (New York: Neale Publishing Co., 1908), pp. 194, 195.

[3] Hamilton G. Howard, *Civil War Echoes—Character Sketches and State Secrets* (Washington, D.C., 1907), p. 84.

Farwell, O'Beirne, nor anyone else who visited Johnson's room that night mention his wife. Evidently Mrs. Johnson was not there. Was someone else? Could that explain the mystery, the reportorial confusion, the censorship? Farwell knocks on the Vice President's door, and discussing the next eight hours Johnson's biographers stammer and stutter. In his massive volume on Johnson, Lloyd Paul Stryker avoids the matter entirely and leaves perhaps the most important night in Johnson's life a complete blank.[4]

But how possibly explain Johnson's before-dawn disappearance, his discovery in a state of stupor and muddy dishevelment at 8:00 A.M.? Is one to suppose that the Vice President went out on a 4:00 A.M. spree? As Senator Stewart tells it, yes. Yet, what incredible folly on the heels of the inaugural fiasco! The Vice President drunk while the President lay dying?

Andrew Johnson was no rumpot drunkard. Nor was he a blind fool. Andrew Johnson was a hard-headed politician. How then did he come to end up sick, stupefied, mud-spattered in his hotel room that fateful morning?

Did someone at the Peterson house offer him a flask? Out on the street did he meet some acquaintance who held out a bottle? Was he invited in somewhere for a bracer? Answers are lost to history. But Andrew Johnson had been marked by the Confederacy's secret underground. A few drops of chloral or a pinch of nightshade seem more probable on this night of terror than his plunging off on a spree.

Lincoln died at 7:22 A.M. on April 15, 1865.

At ten o'clock of that dark Saturday morning Andrew Johnson was sworn in as the seventeenth President of the United States. Had he, too, been marked for assassination? It is an open question. One fact, however, comes clear. Johnson entered office with his character assassinated.

Meantime, Edwin M. Stanton played Chief Executive. And if Andrew Johnson wandered the night, semi-solitary, in a fog of mystery, his actions were open and revealing compared with some of Stanton's. From around midnight of April 14 to midmorning of the 15th, the War Secretary ruled as Supreme Commander of Army, Navy, Police. As dictator, Stanton and Stanton alone was responsible for the crucial opening moves of the man-hunt for Booth and Booth's fellow conspirators. To this day some of those dictatorial moves remain inexplicable.

Consider the cloak of censorship immediately thrown over the identity of the arch assassin. Not only was an effort made to withhold Booth's name from the press, but for some hours after the assassination it was ruled out of military dispatches. Between midnight of Good Friday and 3:00 A.M., Saturday, the War Secretary and his subordinates issued a spate of

---

[4] Lloyd Paul Stryker, *Andrew Johnson* (New York: Macmillan Company, 1929), p. 194.

emergency messages to outlying Army, Navy and police posts. Filed on official record, these War Department dispatches make interesting reading. Most of them flash word of the deadly attacks on Lincoln and Seward. Military and police are alerted, ordered to be on the lookout for fugitives. But only two or three or these out-of-town dispatches flash the name of John Wilkes Booth.

Yet dozens of witnesses at Ford's Theater had recognized Lincoln's assailant. Around 11:30 on the night of the 14th Assistant Adjutant-General J. H. Taylor had rushed an order to Colonel G. W. Gile of the District's First Brigade. Gile was to detail an officer and ten men to take the next train for Baltimore. The order continued:

> Shortly after leaving the city the officer in charge will search every car in the train and arrest, if found, J. Wilkes Booth, and other parties whom you may deem it in the interest of the service to apprehend . . .

But at 12:20 A.M. Stanton rushed the following message to "Agent, Military Railroad, Alexandria [Va.]":

> It is reported that the assassin of the President has gone out hence to Alexandria, thence on train to Fairfax [Va.] Stop all trains in that direction. Apply to military command at Alexandria for guard to arrest all persons on train or on the road not known. By order of the Secretary of War.[5]

No reference to John Wilkes Booth. Nothing to suggest that the wanted assassin was the celebrated actor. Thereafter no official mention of Booth until a message telegraphed more than an hour later. Why the prolonged delay? Historians are left to grope for plausible answers.

It has been supposed that Stanton was, as the military put it, "exercising caution." Some apologists presume that he must have heard reports which conflicted with the shouts of recognition that had rocked Ford's Theater; the War Secretary wanted no hue and cry after the wrong party. Such suppositions do not conform with the story told by Corporal James Tanner, U.S.A. Tanner was there. Adept at shorthand, the Army corporal had been pressed into duty at the Peterson house where he was called upon to record the statements of witnesses brought in for interrogation by Stanton, Judge Cartter and other presiding officials. Tanner started in around midnight. Later he recalled that in fifteen minutes he had recorded enough testimony to hang John Wilkes Booth.

Meanwhile, on his own initiative Provost Marshal O'Beirne had sent a detective to Booth's hotel. Official reports of this action are hazy. Someone forgot to note the exact time and just who went. Nor did anyone record exactly what transpired when Booth's room was entered.

Out of the haze came the story that O'Beirne dispatched Detective William Eaton to the National Hotel. This account credits Eaton with entering Booth's room shortly after midnight, discovering the actor's abandoned

---

[5] *Official Records*, Series I, Vol. 46, Part 3.

trunk, and promptly rushing this prize and other vital finds to O'Beirne. As one modern historian tells it, O'Beirne turned this evidence over "to Lieutenant William H. Terry to assess."[6]

However, War Department files not released to public domain until the 1930's contain an odd communique from Major A. C. Richards of the Metropolitan Police to Colonel H. L. Burnett of the Army Judge Advocate's office. Dated May 17, 1865, the message (apparently answering a query) reads:

"I am *informed* that Lieut. Brown of Major O'Beirne's force searched Booth's room at the National Hotel on the night of the assassination."[7] One wonders why Richards emphasized the word "informed."

The long-secreted files contain another interesting document. Evidently pigeonholed in the autumn of 1865, this brief introduces a third party into the search picture. Presenting a reward claim, the item states that "Asahel Hitchcox of Fabius, N.Y., says that April last he served as Detective at Provost Marshal General's Office, Washington, D.C. . . . Went to Booth's room at hotel in Washington, found his photograph, articles of disguise, cartridges, etc., and took them to the Provost Marshal General."[8]

Still another long-secreted item indicates that the officer assigned the task of examining Booth's trunk was "Lt. W. H. Tyrrell, A.A.D.C."[9]

So mists obscure the details of this important search episode. The probability is that half a dozen Army detectives from various District posts converged on Booth's hotel. But why the ultimate secrecy?

In any event, the "who" in this puzzle was not so vital as the "what." Just what did the detectives discover in Booth's deserted room? Again the records go hazy. There was filed no meticulous on-the-spot inventory such as Detective John Lee made when he uncovered the cache in Atzerodt's room at the Kirkwood House. The Federal police who eventually raided Mrs. Surratt's boardinghouse listed every item in the place down to "2 buttons, 1 sponge, 1 pincushion, 1 paper of needles and 1 needle threaded."[10] The detectives who searched Booth's room itemized nothing.

Apparently Eaton went in one direction with Booth's trunk while Hitchcox raced elsewhere with costumes, wigs or whatever. Possibly a scrimmage ensued among the other competing sleuths, and it was first come, first served, and finders keepers. Although Booth had left his theatrical costumes and regalia in Canada for shipment to the Bahamas, he had brought to Washington his fashionable street wardrobe. What became of the smart attire he was seen in on the morning of April 14? What became of his haberdasheries, his dressing gown, his underclothing? Not to men-

---

[6] Bishop, *op. cit.*, p. 254.
[7] National Archives, War Dept. Records, File "R," Doc. 323, JAO.
[8] National Archives, War Dept. Records, "Trunk 10."
[9] National Archives, War Dept. Records, File "T," Doc. 287, JAO.
[10] National Archives, War Dept. Records, File "S," Doc. 732, JAO.

tion his caracul-collared overcoat and his jewelry, including a cherished signet ring? It would seem that someone turned in the actor's cravat. But, so far as records go, no other shred of Booth's street apparel, no particles of jewelry were delivered to the Government authorities.

As for Booth's trunk, it appeared that a Paul Pry had been in it ahead of the detectives. During the subsequent Conspiracy Trial, Mr. G. W. Bunker, night clerk at the National, testified to finding a large gimlet in said trunk and giving it to Mr. Hall "who was attending to Mr. Ford's business."[11] What else, one wonders, did Mr. Bunker filch from Booth's luggage? (And why was he never prosecuted for making off with a most important piece of evidence?)

However, the trunk did reach O'Beirne's office soon after midnight of April 14. There a Lieutenant Tyrrell (or was it Terry?) combed the contents. Some of the contents presently went to the Bureau of Military Justice under a manifest reading: "Package of Private Papers belonging to J. Wilkes Booth, seized at his room at the National Hotel by order of Col. J. H. Taylor, Chief of Staff. This package contains the secret cypher of the Confederate States Department of the Confederate Govt., and letter to Booth from 'Sam.' "[12]

The "Package of Papers" contained some other interesting items. An official list would have enumerated the following:

1. Letter to Booth from his mother mentioning his engagement to a Washington belle.
2. Billet-doux to Booth, signed "E.T."
3. Telegrams re various theatrical engagements.
4. Prospectus of the Fuller Farms Oil Company, featuring Booth's name as an investor.
5. Business letter to Booth from J. H. Simonds, oil broker of "Franklin, Venango County, Pa."
6. Letter postmarked New York, February 20, 1865, addressed to "John W. Booth, Fords Theater, Washington, D.C.—*Important*," and signed "J. J. Redford." Writer advises that he "could not find out Mr. Edwin Booth's house as his name is not in the Directory." Discussing a shipment of horses, he adds: "I may say the desire of the owner of the horses is to send them to Paris. He is a strong Union man and in a good position here." Remainder of the letter is jargon, probably code.
7. Ambiguous map sketched on face of small envelope addressed to "T. Zizinia, Box 1314, N.Y., 10 South William Street."
8. Scrap of paper bearing notation, "71 West 45th St., New York, 10 April '62, Thursday."
9. Memo reading: "Send me a program also once in a while, it helps a man's imagination, makes him believe he is still in a city of civilization. Hoxie."
10. Bill for "one hair ring" made by Tiffany's.

---

[11] National Archives, War Dept. Records, Trial report in contemporary news account (undated).
[12] National Archives, War Dept. Records, File "F," JAO.

11. Letter signed "Jenny."
12. Confederate secret cipher—an alphabetic acrostic.
13. Letter from "Sam."[13]

By way of evidence of skulduggery what more could the Federal authorities have wanted? The Fuller Farms brochure, the Tiffany bill, and some of the other scraps may have signified nothing. But the missive mentioning a shipment of horses to Paris surely invites attention. So does the mysterious map. So does the letter from "Jenny" in Canada informing Booth that she is sending him a "rubber coat"—or is it a "rubber boat"?

The "Sam" letter with its guarded wordage reeks of an underground plot. Especially the lines: "You know full well that the G———t suspicions something . . ." and, "Do not act rashly or in haste . . . go and see how it will be taken at R———d. . . ."

The Confederate cipher settles it. Here, certainly, is confirmation that Booth was up to his neck in conspiracy. And in addition to the items enumerated, Lieutenant Tyrrell found a pair of handcuffs in the actor's trunk,[14] and there were the "disguises" and whatnot confiscated by Detective Hitchcox.

Was there more? Even as the disappearance of Booth's wardrobe indicates that his luggage was scavenged, holes in the record induce a suspicion that some of his effects may have proved too hot to handle (which is to say, too hot after hasty consignment to War Department coffers marked for burning). However, if further evidence were needed, the clincher came from Atzerodt's room at the Kirkwood. By one o'clock or shortly thereafter in the morning of April 15, the authorities knew that John Wilkes Booth was a ringleader in the Confederate underground and chief of the assassins.

Still, no general alarm went out for John Wilkes Booth. Around the time the detectives reported from Booth's hotel, Stanton called an emergency conference at the Petersen house. In attendance were General Augur, Judge Cartter, Major O'Beirne and Assistant War Secretary Dana. Major Richards of the Metropolitan Police and Captain William Williams, a Federal detective officer, also sat in.

This conference took place behind closed doors. Stenographic notes were not permitted, so no historian knows exactly what was said or left unsaid. It seems that Stanton reviewed the criminal assault at Ford's. He stated that a "bullet hole" in the panel proved the murderous shot had been fired through the door of Lincoln's box. He conceded that the great bulk of evidence pointed to John Wilkes Booth as the assassin. Even so, the War Secretary clamped a silencer on the alarm system. Sound the disaster tocsins, rouse the national police, but let no one give tongue to the assassin's name.

---

[13] National Archives, War Dept. Records, "Trunk 10."
[14] National Archives, War Dept. Records, File "T," Doc. 287, JAO.

In *The Day Lincoln Was Shot,* Jim Bishop remarks that Stanton "gave no reason" for this censorship.[15] One is constrained to wonder what possible reason he could have given.

At 12:20 A.M., Major T. T. Eckert flashed a message to General Grant's northbound train. "The President was assassinated at Ford's Theater at 10:30 tonight and cannot live. . . . Secretary Seward and his son Frederick were also assassinated. . . . The Secretary of War desires that you return to Washington immediately."[16] Grant was advised that Lincoln's wound was "a pistol shot in the head," and that the Sewards were attacked at their residence. Minor details, but no description of John Wilkes Booth.

To New York Police Chief John H. Kennedy went an urgent dispatch at 1:00 A.M. "Send here immediately three or four of your best detectives to investigate the facts as to the assassination of the President and Secretary Seward." No word that the assassin was a well-known stage star with relatives residing in New York.

To Generals Morris at Baltimore and Cadwalader at Philadelphia went 2:00 A.M. telegrams ordering the arrest of all travelers from Washington. But no word on *the* traveler, the bad actor, the known killer, who might conceivably switch tickets with some accomplice at a way-station and thereby pose as a passenger from anywhere but the nation's capital.

To General Ord at Richmond went a 2:00 A.M. telegram reading: "Attempts have been made to assassinate the President and Secretary of State. Arrest all persons who may enter your lines by water or land. Particulars will be given hereafter." But no person from Washington could conceivably have reached Richmond at this hour, and if Ord obeyed the directive scores of innocent persons would be subjected to false arrest.

At 2:15 A.M. an order similar to the one sent Ord was flashed to General Barnes at Point Lookout at the mouth of the Potomac. "Stop all vessels going down the river and hold all persons on them until further orders." Again too much, and much too early, and no particulars on the party wanted.

The same sort of vague directive to General Gamble at Fairfax Station, a few miles southwest of Washington. A similar order to General Slough in command at Alexandria, Virginia. Then a follow-up flash to Baltimore advising the authorities there that the War Department now offered "a reward of $10,000 for apprehension of the assassin of the President and Secretary of State. Please communicate this to the police and detectives of your department." Pitch into a haystack, find the needle, and win a fortune! But nothing to guide the search or identify the needle. No such clue as might send Baltimore's sleuths to Barnum's Hotel or Bel Air.

Then someone must have awakened to the situation. Time: 3:55 A.M.

---

15 *Op. cit.,* p. 255.
16 *Official Records,* Series I, Vol. 46, Part 3.

To the Army command at Baltimore went the following wire: "Make immediate arrangements for guarding thoroughly every avenue leading into Baltimore, and if possible arrest J. Wilkes Booth, the murderer of President Lincoln. . . . [Signed] Edwin M. Stanton, Secretary of War."

So at long last, five hours after the shooting at Ford's Theater, the alarm was flashed to Booth's home area. But there was still no description of the actor—no word on his height, weight, looks, the horse he was riding, his apparel when last seen. Had Booth been aware of Stanton's belated wire, he might have been the first to laugh. *What's in a name?* At stage stops and Army outposts, city stationhouses and railway depots, soldiers and constables were rushed into a game of blindman's buff.

Yet Stanton's 3:55 A.M. message alerted one police official who was on the job. Apparently this Baltimore officer flashed the first description of the wanted fugitive. One may note that in the Army records this telegram is not timed, but its posting in the continuity indicates an early morning dispatch, and it was probably sent soon after receipt of the message which named the assassin. Author of the informative wire was Baltimore Provost Marshal McPhail, and it was sent to the commander of the Navy station on the Potomac at St. Inigoes, Maryland.

> The President murdered; Mr. Seward and son nearly so. One of the murderers J. Wilkes Booth, actor, played at Holliday Street a year ago. Twenty-five years old, 5 feet 8 inches high, dark hair and mustache. He took the direction from Washington toward St. Marys and Calvert Counties. Use all efforts to secure him.[17]

Through the fog raised by the muddled alarms from the capital, this dispatch from distant Baltimore shines like a spotlight. How did the Baltimore Provost know that Booth *"took the direction from Washington toward St. Marys and Calvert Counties"?*

Perhaps McPhail's long-distance intelligence derived from sheer supposition. In Washington City the authorities had more to go on. That no one went stems from the fact that no one was allowed to go. Thus another strange situation developed under the military dictatorship of War Secretary Stanton.

At 10:30 P.M. the President's assailant had vanished in midtown Washington. Simultaneously the vandal who assaulted the Sewards had disappeared. It was only reasonable to assume that the fugitive assassins would meet at some prearranged rendezvous and lose no time in getting out of the national capital.

Washington was a barn with many doors. Eight highroads radiated from the District area. All were potential escape routes for the mounted felons. The fugitives might abandon their mounts and try to get away by railroad —the northbound B. & O. to Baltimore, with a junction at Relay, Maryland,

[17] *Ibid.*

giving access to points west on the Ohio line; the southbound Orange & Alexandria trailing down to Lynchburg, Virginia, with westbound connections to the Shenandoah country. Escape might also be made by water— across the Potomac to Arlington and Fairfax, or down the Potomac by boat to the open Chesapeake or to any of a dozen clamshell ports in lower Maryland or tidewater Virginia. In addition there were capillary backroads going everywhere. A fugitive might even take the towpath of the C. & O. Canal bound for the Cumberland region of West Virginia.

But the problem of blocking these escape routes, while considerable, was by no means insuperable. The railroads could be easily covered by police work at the terminals, and the lines out of Alexandria, Virginia, were under Federal military control. Naval forces stationed along the Potomac and based at the Chesapeake outlets could readily block the channels of water escape. A guard post up the river at Chain Bridge covered the towpath of the C. & O. Canal. Bad to begin with, the back roads out of Washington City had gone to worse from spring thawing; no desperate horseman would risk the chance of flooded fords, or miles of mud on some detour ending in Nowhere with bloodhounds at his heels. So the eight post roads, the main turnpikes, offered the likeliest avenues of escape, and thus constituted the major blockage problem. Yet the means to block these overland routes were readily available.

The eight highroads out of Washington roughly boxed the compass. Due east out of the District via Benning's Bridge ran the post road to Upper Marlboro, Maryland. Flanking this road were Army camps—troops which were roused by one of the early alarms from Augur's headquarters. Booth and his henchmen would have surely been trapped had they taken the route for Upper Marlboro.

Northeast from Washington City ran the old Blandensburg Pike, the ancient post road to Baltimore, with a branch to Annapolis. Early alarms flashed to Baltimore and relayed to Annapolis served to block escape through Blandensburg.

Due north the Montgomery County Turnpike headed into central Maryland, then bent eastward to intersect the Frederick-Baltimore post road. This turnpike, too, was blocked by the alerts dispatched to Baltimore.

Northwest out of the District, through Georgetown, wound the Rockville Road, the main route leading to Frederick, Maryland. Augur's initial dispatch to the cavalry station at Darnestown was calculated to close this escape route.

West of Washington, across the Potomac and through Arlington, wound the road to Falls Church, Virginia, where a branch bent northward up to Leesburg in Loudon County. Westerly the main pike extended to Fairfax Court House, and thence to Manassas—the old road out to Bull Run. Warnings dispatched to the Army Commander at Fairfax threw a military blockade athwart the Falls Church and Leesburg highways.

Due south of Washington, across Potomac (Long) Bridge, ran the post road to Alexandria—main highroad into the heart of Virginia. First stop, Occoquan. Next stop, Fredericksburg. Then on down to Richmond. One of the nation's vital arteries, and Augur's headquarters sent a dispatch to General Slough at Alexandria ordering a roadblock there and another at Occoquan.

There remained two southbound post roads which trailed down the lower Maryland peninsula—escape routes which horsemen could reach by crossing the Anacostia via Navy Yard Bridge. First and fastest of these pikes was the one that headed down through Piscataway to Port Tobacco. At Chapel Point just below Port Tobacco a Federal cavalry force was garrisoned. As of three o'clock in the morning after the assassination strike, this force at Chapel Point had received no alert from Washington. No urgent alarm roused the military in the strategic Port Tobacco area.

In fact, Army Headquarters in Washington took no notice of the highroad to Port Tobacco until about 4:00 A.M. Then, as will be seen, a Federal cavalry troop was dispatched from Washington to Piscataway. Hard riding would bring this troop down the pike to that point around 7:00 A.M. Meaning the Piscataway-Port Tobacco route remained wide open throughout the entire night of the assassination.

Peculiar as seems the Port Tobacco situation, it squares to normal in comparison with the War Department's disregard of the other escape route through lower Maryland. Traversing the hinterland of Prince Georges County, this was the turnpike leading from Navy Yard Bridge to Surrattsville, Teebee and Bryantown. At Teebee and at Bryantown side roads branched westward to Port Tobacco. From Bryantown a woodsy trail wandered down through Charles County to Allen's Fresh, while the post road meandered eastward across St. Marys County through Leonardtown to St. Inigoes and Point Lookout on Chesapeake Bay.

Shortly before Good Friday midnight, General Augur's Chief of Staff had flashed an alert to the Navy commander at St. Inigoes. "An attempt has been made this P.M. to assassinate the President and Secretary of State. The parties may escape or attempt to escape across the Potomac."[18] Then at 2:15 A.M. Stanton alerted the Point Lookout garrison at the road's Chesapeake extremity. But Stanton specifically ordered the stoppage of river boats. And the earlier flash to St. Inigoes had said nothing of highway traffic. Nor was any effort made to throw barriers across the route at Teebee and Bryantown, the chief points for strategic roadblocks. Like the post road through Piscataway, the Surrattsville-Bryantown-Point Lookout pike was left wide open on the night of April 14–15.

In the light of past as well as immediate circumstances, this failure to block the turnpike through the lower Maryland hinterland appears fantas-

---

18 *Ibid.*

tic. As early as the spring of 1862 the War Department had been made aware that this Maryland region was "pro Secesh" to the core. Stanton himself had sponsored several campaigns to stamp out subversion in the area. But it was known that anti-Union sentiments smoldered hot in the villages and backwoods hamlets of this peninsula.

Moreover, the U.S. Government had only recently been advised that the Confederate underground burrowed through Prince Georges, Charles and St. Marys Counties. Advice had come from Canada in a letter addressed to Secretary of State Seward by R. J. Kimball, U.S. Consular Agent in Toronto. (Years after the Civil War this letter was placed in National Archives files open to "public domain." It was super secret at the time it was posted.) Dated January 3, 1865, Kimball's communique reads:

> The following facts have been given to me; I hasten to transmit them directly to you. . . .
> The Rebels in this city have a quick and successful communication with Jeff Davis and the authorities in Richmond in the following manner— Having plenty of money at their command, they employ British Subjects, who are provided with British passports and also with passports from Col———— [probably Jacob Thompson] which are plainly written; name and date of issue on fine silk and as ingeniously secreted in the lining of the coat. They carry dispatches which are made and carried in the same manner.
> *These messengers wear metal buttons, which, upon the inside, dispatches are most minutely photographed, not perceptible to the naked eye, but are easily read by the aid of a powerful lens.*[19]
> Letters are written, but are closely interlined with imperceptible ink (as they term it) which, when a certain chemical is employed, is easily deciphered.
> The messenger arriving at Baltimore receives additional instructions from "B————" and proceeds to Washington. Here he undergoes a thorough examination, is searched and permitted to pass—he takes a south-easterly course to "Port Tobacco" where he is sheltered by a widow, "Mrs. F————" and at dead of night crosses in an india rubber boat to the south side of the Potomac, thence he goes to "Bowling Green" where his Rebel passport is used (*sic*) to "Guerilla B————" who hastens him on to Richmond—he returns by the same route. The last trip was made in fourteen days (Dec. 14–28). . . .[20]

Of parenthetical interest is the italicized sentence concerning the metal buttons worn by the secret message bearers. After World War II much excitement and publicity was elicited when the F.B.I. revealed that Nazi agents had used "micro-photography" for spy communications. As this letter shows, the idea was not new. The ingenious Confederates seem to have invented "mini-cam photography" with tintypes!

Of interest, too, the mention of a "rubber boat" (another Civil War invention!). We are reminded of "Jenny's" letter to Booth, and also reminded

---

[19] Italics supplied.
[20] National Archives, War Dept. Records, File "K," Doc. 12, JAO.

that detectives should not filch an assassin's wardrobe when the very buttons of his dress coat may convey spy messages.

But more to the point than the detail on the gimmicks used by Confederate agents is the information on their route through lower Maryland. And the margin of the Kimball letter bears a significant State Department endorsement: "A copy of this was sent to the War Department in January on the 7th or soon after."[21]

So Stanton's office was fully informed on the underground trail to Port Tobacco and points south. And on the night of Lincoln's murder that subterranean road should have come to mind as a possible, and even probable, escape route. It must also have been apparent that the backwoods road through Surrattsville, Teebee and Bryantown might be used. Endeavoring to avoid traffic, fugitives would be liable to go around Robin Hood's proverbial barn.

Furthermore, after the assassination strike two nocturnal horsemen had gone south across Navy Yard Bridge, as reported to the authorities by irate Stableman Fletcher. Yet Fletcher's report was ignored by the Army's leaders. It was not ignored by Superintendent Richards of the Metropolitan Police. But Richards was not an Army leader, and when he proposed to act in his offical civilian capacity he was put, and literally kept, in his place.

The frustration of the Washington Police Superintendent adds another baffler to that night's sorcery. For Stableman Fletcher had darted into Police Headquarters on 10th Street before he went to General Augur's office. Whether he told Richards of the chase to Navy Yard Bridge or blurted his story to an attendant officer remains a question. But Fletcher's name was recorded on the police ledger as one of the witnesses interviewed before Good Friday midnight. Which means that the city constables had Fletcher's vitally important testimony at least an hour before it reached the ear of General Augur.

Sooner or later (and probably immediately) the stable foreman's story was assessed by Police Superintendent Richards. Apparently Richards at once put two and two together, connected the pair of southbound horsemen with the shooting at Ford's and the mayhem at the Seward residence, and decided the assassins had fled into lower Maryland. Perhaps Richards had some background information to conjure with—reports of Secessionist activity in Prince Georges County—prevalent tales of Rebel groups around Surrattsville, Teebee and Bryantown, Richards made some swift calculations. Soon after midnight he applied to General Augur for horses to mount a posse. It seems that he wanted to send a flying squad down the road to Surrattsville.

Horses for a posse of city police? Army Headquarters would not con-

---

[21] *Ibid.*

sider such a request. Richards was informed that mounts were not available for his men. Not only was his request turned down, but he was told, in effect, to sit tight at Police Headquarters and let the military handle the pursuit for the time being.

Oldroyd attributes this astonishing impasse to bureaucratic fuddling. "Major A. C. Richards . . . being satisfied that Booth . . . had taken flight across Navy Yard Bridge, was ready to pursue the assassin as soon as the Government would furnish the horses; but owing to red tape, *to which our Government is so prone* (*sic*), the posse could not leave Washington till twelve hours after the shooting."[22] Other historians blame General Augur for stalling Richards. Richards himself thought the military were jealous of the police.

But the refusal to mount Richards' men was given at the time that Secretary Stanton sat in the saddle as national dictator. General Augur served as one of Stanton's top subordinates, but he was only a general.

Given horses, Major Richards might have overtaken Booth and Herold before morning. On the War Secretary's shoulders must rest the blame for the tie-up that prevented an immediate police pursuit of Lincoln's assassin.

President Lincoln lies dying. Andrew Johnson is temporarily superseded, and Edwin M. Stanton grabs the reins of government. Under Stanton's supreme authority the manhunt for the assassins is launched. If the fugitives are to be traced the initial moves are vital. Here is a resumé of the opening moves.

Military censorship is imposed; the press is not allowed to publish Booth's name; for several hours the identity of Lincoln's assassin is withheld from War Department dispatches to outlying Army and police posts.

Even after Booth is positively identified as Rebel agent and assassination ringleader, his description is not broadcast in general alarm. A screen of fog obscures the searching of his hotel room. No record is made of the findings. Garments and other objects belonging to the assassin are allowed to disappear.

Five hours after the shooting at Ford's, the assassin's name is finally flashed by Stanton to the authorities at Baltimore. But the War Department offers no follow-up information, although it proffers a reward for the fugitive's capture.

North, south, east and west, authorities near and far from Washington are advised to arrest passengers on boats and trains and to hold travelers attempting to enter their specified lines. Yet John Wilkes Booth is as vague and faceless as John Doe in all War Department dispatches issued on the night of April 14–15. Only one military dispatch—an alert issued by a provost marshal in Balitmore—carries Booth's description.

---

[22] Oldroyd, *op. cit.*, p. 66. Italics supplied.

Washington is a barn with many doors. Haphazard efforts are made to block the numerous escape routes, particularly those going northward, westward and southwestward. Southward and south by east through the lower Maryland counties lie two roads, both previously marked as trails used by the Confederate underground. One of these roads is belatedly blocked. The other—going through Surrattsville—is left wide open throughout the entire night of the assassination strike. And when a Washington police official proposes to send a posse down the Surrattsville road, his request for horses is refused.

Headquarters blunders? Or so-called "errors in judgment"?

Accidental oversights? Or red-tape tangles and bureaucratic confusion?

Downright bungling and blind bobbles? Or was there method behind the muddlement? Edwin M. Stanton was in charge, and to suppose the last would be to attribute to his mind and hand a Machiavellian craft almost too sinister for credence.

Yet if the fantasia which permitted Booth's escape was unintentional, one must attribute to War Secretary Stanton a head of almost solid bone, a plethora of unadulterated stupidity. True, he was noted for snap judgments. Some of his contemporaries considered him a mussy-minded muddler, a hysteric. A maelstrom of furor swirled around him at the Petersen house. But it is hard to believe that the former "King of Steubenville," the supposed iron man of the War Office, could have lost his wits completely, and made blunder after blunder.

Witless blunders? Intentional craft? Whatever the answers, they remain unknown. But the moves are on record, and the record stands.

As of Saturday noon, April 15, Lincoln's assassin was somewhere in limbo.

At three o'clock that afternoon Stanton dashed off a wire to Colonel Lafayette C. Baker, Astor House, New York City:

Come here immediately and see if you can find the murderer of the President.

This was the cue that brought to the scene the nation's master manhunter.

CHAPTER **11**

Manhunt on a Checkrein

COLONEL (sometimes General) Lafayette C. Baker was one of the more powerful figures behind the scenes of the Civil War. Yet his name was (and is) almost unknown to the American public. Emerging from the wings, as it were, at the time of Lincoln's assassination, he performed briefly in the spotlight as a sort of wizard. Then, as though by the aid of mirrors, he disappeared from the national stage. The fadeaway of this warlock constitutes one of the major thaumaturgies of American history.

The fact that Baker, as Chief of the National Detective Police, operated in a realm of deliberately contrived obscurity, does not explain his ultimate exit into oblivion. Nor can it be said that this historical obliteration was due to any desire on his part for anonymity. As soon as he retired from active duty, General Baker published a *History of the United States Secret Service* which was not presumed to hide his light under a bushel.

But even as Baker portrayed himself as a figure deserving of an equestrian statue in Valhalla, Albert Gallatin Riddle saw him as "a man of little culture, dark, taciturn, square-shouldered, and of powerful frame, who had seen service under the Vigilance Committee of San Francisco."[1] And a House of Representatives Report pronounced him a "miserable wretch" entitled to "an unenviable immortality."[2]

Baker's star ascended on the strength of one of his exploits as a spy in Confederate territory. Awarded an Army commission, he was installed in Washington as a military intelligence expert. For a time he served with the State Department detective corps. By way of additional duty he became Colonel of the District of Columbia Regiment of Cavalry. While in this saddle in the winter of 1861–1862, he led several scouting expeditions into lower Maryland on the hunt for subversives.[3]

While working as a military detective, Baker tried to pin a liquor

---

[1] Albert Gallatin Riddle, *Recollections of War Times, Reminiscences of Men and Events in Washington* (New York: G. P. Putnam's Sons, 1895), p. 306.

[2] Impeachment Investigation, 40th Congress, 1st Session, Representative Committee No. 7.

[3] Baker, *op. cit.*, p. 102.

smuggling charge on a young officer who was serving in Washington under General Wadsworth. The officer, Major William E. Doster, hit back hard. Able to prove the evidence against him was forged, he brought counter-charges against Detective Baker. Someone shielded Baker who "could not be found" at the time, and the forgery charge was allowed to evaporate. Recounting the incident years later in *Lincoln and Episodes of the Civil War*, Doster recalled that Baker was mistrusted by many of the Army commanders in the capital. But the former Vigilante leader won rapid promotion under War Secretary Stanton.

When the State Department detective corps was transferred to the War Department in 1862, Baker was transferred with it. Serving under Stanton, he climbed the ladder as a Provost Marshal. The post gave him a chance to demonstrate his talents for Vigilantism. His roughshod tactics pleased the vigorous War Secretary. Someone was needed to head the newly authorized Federal Secret Service. Stanton appointed Baker.

Without precedent in American history, Baker's force introduced the nation to midnight raids, entries without warrant, summary arrests and imprisonments without bail. Worse, it indulged in some of the ugliest police corruption, some of the worst injustices on national record. From the outset Baker's Federals engaged in everything from bribery to blackmail. Center of all this infamy was Washington's Old Capital Prison, crammed to the locks with men, women and children, innocent and guilty alike incarcerated without recourse to *habeas corpus* or due processes of law.

Screened by the smoke and excitement of the Civil War, Baker's operations fastened a secret grip on the North, and, according to critics, threatened to sabotage the very liberties and freedoms the nation was fighting for. As described by Chittenden: "The Detective Bureau was established as one of the regular bureaus. . . . By some means, never clearly understood, his [Baker's] jurisdiction was extended to the Army, and he exercised his authority in all the departments and throughout the United States. . . . Corruption spread like a contagious disease wherever the operations of these detectives extended. It soon became known that impunity for frauds against the government could be procured for money. Men who, but for the detective system, would never have thought of such enterprises, went into the regular business of illicit distilling, bounty-jumping, smuggling . . . and other similar practices. . . . The dishonest rapidly accumulated wealth. . . . Good citizens became discouraged and ceased to take any interest in the administration of justice. . . ."[4]

At least one modern writer on secret service tells us that Baker was a wonderful organizer, "an artful officer, one of the few spies and managers of spies in America whose career and methods have engaged the studious

---

[4] Lucius E. Chittenden, *Recollections of President Lincoln and His Administration* (New York: Harper and Brothers, Publishers, 1901), p. 346.

appreciation of European experts."[5] Baker would have been the first to concede that such appreciation was fully warranted.

But historian Albert Gallatin Riddle has a different opinion. Although he acted for a time as Baker's attorney, Riddle vaguely identifies General Baker as a Washington Provost Marshal. Then he writes: "The secret history of the Provost Marshal General's office at Washington, and its connection with the War Office, of which it was an agency, never can be written, perhaps never should be."[6]

It never was. The censors and launderers of history saw to that. But is was impossible to eradicate Lafayette Baker entirely from the records. For one of the missions assigned to the Secret Service was the protection of President Lincoln. That Baker and his agents failed this duty was signified by the death shot at Ford's Theater.

Could Baker's failure to protect Lincoln be laid to bungling, to gross negligence? Or could it be attributed to something worse? Modern historian George Fort Milton suggests something worse in describing Lafayette C. Baker as "one of the worst rapscallions of an age in which rascality paid high dividends."[7]

This was the man selected by Stanton to play Avenger, the officer chosen to head the manhunt for the assassination conspirators.

In prose as deplorable as his reputation, Baker subsequently composed an interesting account of the manner in which he received word of Lincoln's assassination.

"On Saturday morning, April 15, while in my room at the Astor House, having just risen to dress, Lieutenant Luther B. Baker, who had come on from Washington the evening previous, rushed into my room and announced the fact that President Lincoln had been assassinated. This announcement called to my mind at once the various communications containing threats of assassination that he had for nearly two years received."[8]

Baker does not remark that the persistent threats should have spurred his Secret Service organization to exert the utmost in preventive endeavor. Nor does he explain why he, the Secret Service Chief, acutely aware of the menace, failed to provide a shield of surveillance over the President. Obtuse, the general goes on to say that he received Stanton's emergency summons that Saturday noon. Baker's memory errs on this point. Official Records show that Stanton's wire to Baker was dispatched on April 15 at 3:00 P.M.[9] But perhaps the three-hour disparity is of little moment. Even

---

[5] Richard Wilmer Rowan, *The Story of Secret Service* (New York: Garden City Publishing Co., 1939), p. 285.

[6] *Op. cit.*, p. 308.

[7] George Fort Milton, *The Age of Hate, Andrew Johnson and the Radicals* (New York: Coward-McCann, Inc., 1930), p. 193.

[8] *Op. cit.*, pp. 524–525.

[9] *Official Records*, Series I, Vol. 46, Part 3.

had it been sent at high noon that Saturday, this message from the War Secretary to the head of the Federal detective force seems to have been delayed.

Baker's account continues: "No train left New York by which I could reach Washington the following morning. On Sunday, April 16, I arrived in Washington. My interview with the Secretary of War was a sad one. As I entered the Secretary's office and he recognized me, he turned away to hide his tears. He remarked, 'Well, Baker, they have now performed what they have long threatened to do; they have killed the President. You must go to work. My whole dependence is upon you.'"

A number of observant critics and historians were jarred by this alleged comment of Stanton's. From it they were compelled to infer that the War Secretary, too, must have been extremely lax in regard to the President's protection. However, one cannot accept the quote without remarking the source. Lafayette Baker was hardly a fountainhead of unimpeachable veracity.

Baker closes the account of his late-Sunday interview with Stanton on a line that, if true, damns the War Department dictator for something more than mere laxity.

"I made some inquiries with reference to what had been done toward the capture of the assassins, and ascertained that no direct clue even had been obtained, beyond the simple conceded fact that J. Wilkes Booth was the assassin of the President."[10]

Again we have only Baker's word for this intimate detail. But in the light of another's testimony it appears that Stanton at that time did withhold vital information from his supposedly trusted subordinates. Years later Colonel Henry L. Burnett of the Judge Advocate's Office wrote that "while it was rumored and generally believed that J. Wilkes Booth was the assassin, *for some days this rested only upon the statements of some of the persons at the theater* . . . they thought that they recognized him as he ran across the stage, but could not be certain about it."[11] If the War Secretary thus withheld information from the Office of the Judge Advocate General, Baker's story sounds entirely plausible.

And, of course, as of Sunday, April 16, Stanton's office had something more to go on than the "simple conceded fact" that John Wilkes Booth was the assassin. Not to mention clues more substantial than uncertain statements from "some of the persons at the theater."

There were, for instance, the numerous items of evidence found in Booth's hotel room on Good Friday night. There was the mass of evidence discovered in Atzerodt's room at the Kirkwood. There was Stableman Fletcher's testimony concerning the two horsemen who had crossed Navy Yard Bridge. There was Officer Rosch's report on David Herold.

---

[10] *Op. cit.,* p. 525.
[11] Quoted in Eisenschiml, *op. cit.,* pp. 265–266. Italics supplied.

On Saturday, April 15, the clues had led directly to Surrattsville. By Saturday night John Surratt was marked as a conspirator, and suspicion hovered over Mrs. Surratt's boardinghouse on H Street.

Baker's account, seemingly verified by Colonel Burnett's, contributes another jigsaw to the puzzle involving the manhunt for Lincoln's assassin. Why did Stanton summon his Secret Service Chief to Washington so late in the day? And why, when Baker finally arrived on the scene, did the War Secretary fail to inform him immediately on the known details of the assassination strike and on the probable escape route of the arch assassin?

The police were actually on Booth's trail as early as seven o'clock in the morning of Saturday, April 15. On record is the fact that Major Richards of the Metropolitan Force directed the initial pursuit of Lincoln's assassin. His men were the first to cross Navy Yard Bridge on Booth's track; the first to follow the getaway road to Surrattsville.

Major A. C. Richards had been right on target from the outset. His early request for a mounted posse having been frustrated, he had determined to act on his own initiative. Possessed of the names of Booth, Herold, and John Surratt, he had put a prompt finger on Mrs. Surratt's H Street boardinghouse. When his detectives came in with word from Louis Wiechmann, the astute Washington Police Superintendent made a lightning calculation. Two and two added up to the Surrattsville tavern. Mentally Richards got there about three hours behind Booth and many hours ahead of the U.S. Army.

Physically Richards was still delayed by War Department red tape during the pre-dawn hours of Saturday morning. One can only imagine the impatience of this resolute public servant. He was certain he knew the assassin's trail. But protocol and discipline chained him to his desk at Police Headquarters while Army Headquarters tried to make up its mussy mind. About 3:00 A.M. that Saturday morning Richards received a typical directive from the War Office. Dutifully the Police Superintendent relayed the order to his subordinate constables:

> In view of the melancholy events of last evening, I am directed to cause all places where liquor is sold to be closed this entire day and night. The sergeants of the several precincts are instructed that this order is enforced.[12]

From then until sunrise, Superintendent Richards continued to interview witnesses and grill suspects brought in by his busy detectives. About seven o'clock in the morning Richards finally procured mounts and was enabled to dispatch a police posse. His constables immediately headed for Surrattsville. By 8:00 A.M. these officers were knocking on the door of the roadside tavern.

---

[12] Records of the Metropolitan Police.

The knocking roused the alcoholic innkeeper. Blinking and no doubt hiccuping in alarm, John Lloyd faced the constables on his doorstep. He was
immediately battered by a barrage of questions. Verbatim records of his
responses do not exist. But in substance John Lloyd told the police that he
had not seen hide nor hair of Booth and Herold. To this deliberate falsehood, he added another lie. Misleadingly he sent the police posse on a false
trail toward Piscataway.

So the misdirected officers ended the morning in a fruitless cross-country
gallop. It was not a fast gallop, either, for the Government horses which had
been grudgingly loaned to Richards were spavined old plugs already slated
for the boneyard. By noon these ancient nags were lathered, limping and
blown. Virtually dismounted, Richards' posse returned to Washington.

Later that Saturday Richards missed again by a hair's breadth. About
the time inebriate Lloyd was misdirecting the constabulary in the field,
Louis Wiechmann and John T. Holohan entered Richards' office on 10th
Street near E. After five minutes of interview, Major Richards knew he
held an ace card in his hand. The Police Superintendent at once determined to maintain his hold on this card. He treated Wiechmann with the
utmost courtesy. Instead of placing him under arrest, he held Wiechmann
as a sort of special witness informally deputized to aid the police.

The records are vague as to what Louis Wiechmann told the Police
Superintendent that Saturday morning. It is certain, however, that Mrs.
Surratt's star boarder volunteered much information on the doings of John
Wilkes Booth, John Surratt and company. Undoubtedly he detailed the
several plots to abduct Lincoln. Probably he furnished the Police Department with excellent descriptions of Paine, Herold, Atzerodt and the other
conspirators. He must have told about his carriage drive to Surrattsville
with Mrs. Surratt, and described the various comings and goings of John
Surratt on the underground route between Richmond and Canada.

It seems that Holohan corroborated much of Wiechmann's original
story. After the interview the police permitted Holohan to leave. A second
police squad set out for lower Maryland before noon. Wiechmann went
along with Major Richards as a "personal prisoner."

The flying squad spent the remainder of that Saturday junketing through
the interior of Charles County and Prince Georges County. They stopped
at taverns, crossroads post offices and remote farm houses. According to
Oldroyd, they "secured little information of any account."[13]

So far as Booth's trail through Prince Georges County was concerned,
the first clues of any consequence seem to have been uncovered by a
Special Officer Cunningham who arrested the barman at Lloyd's tavern,
one Joseph Thomas Knott.

Knott (or Nott, according to simplified spelling) worked at the Surratts-

---

[13] *Op. cit.,* p. 187.

ville tavern when the spirit moved him. By trade he was a bricklayer. By repute he was a shiftless fellow who kept bad company. The War Department files contain this notation: "Jos. Thomas Knott, Prince George County, Maryland. Arrested Apr. 15 and committed to Old Capitol, May 1, 1865."[14]

The files of the Judge Advocate's Office divulge this brief on Lloyd's bartender:

> Knott lives at Lloyd's. Heard Surratt say going to Europe. Heard Lloyd or wife a week or 10 days before assassination say that *guns* were concealed there. Had suspicions that Mr. Lloyd would not be fairly dealt by—he had a great many enemies. Lloyd always appeared to be a miserable man—said he was.[15]

Because Major Richards did not trap Booth he received little credit for his hard-riding police work. He deserved a Government commendation, and he knew it. That Saturday night he held Louis Wiechmann incommunicado at the station house on 10th Street. Easter Sunday he rushed Wiechmann to Baltimore for a secret conference with Marshal McPhail. Richards then procured from the War Department a special order which enabled him to dispatch Wiechmann with a detective squad to New York City. From there Wiechmann was rushed by the police to Canada in an effort to track down John Surratt. Major Richards did not fully apprise the military authorities on the motives behind these moves. During the trial of John Surratt two years later, the Washington Police Superintendent was questioned on the point. It was hinted that he had "appropriated" the services of the key witness. Police Superintendent Richards made no bones about the reason why.

> RICHARDS: . . . we wanted to use him [Wiechmann] to pursue the suspected assassins of the President. . . .
> Q. You had him in charge?
> A. Yes, sir; but not to his knowledge. It was our intention to hold him as a witness, *for the reason that certain other parties were monopolizing all the information, and we wanted to hold him, as we thought we had not been treated altogether proper.*[16]

Obviously the head of the Washington Police Force did not trust the military authorities who had delayed his posse to Surrattsville and then had mounted his men on spavined nags. Interesting is his comment on certain other parties "monopolizing all the information."

So we have it from the Washington Police Superintendent that information on Booth was being monopolized. And the records indicate that as of Sunday, April 16, there was a good deal of information to monopolize. The Army, too, had found Booth's trail.

---

14 National Archives, War Dept. Records, File "R," Doc. 746, JAO.
15 National Archives, War Dept. Records, File "K," Doc. R.B.P. 98, JAO.
16 Surratt Trial, Vol. II, p. 988. Italics supplied.

Coincident with the time Booth and Herold reached Dr. Mudd's—about four o'clock in the morning of Saturday, April 15—a troop of Federal cavalry had been dispatched by General Augur from Washington to Piscataway, Maryland. Someone in the War Department had awakened to the fact that the road south from Navy Yard Bridge—the main turnpike to Port Tobacco—had been left wide open.

General Augur placed this particular cavalry troop under command of Lieutenant David D. Dana, younger brother of Assistant War Secretary Charles A. Dana.

Some historians would credit young Dana with being the first Army officer on Booth's trail. Ordered to operate out of Piscataway, he was directed to patrol a triangular area cornered by Piscataway, Accokeek and Surrattsville—a triangle lying athwart the old Port Tobacco underground. Belatedly, the military were at last on the track of Lincoln's assassin.

Dana's cavalry troop reached Piscataway about breakfast time. At 7:00 A.M. the young lieutenant dashed off a telegram notifying the War Department of his arrival. To this wire he amended an odd postscript.

> I have reliable information that the person who murdered Secretary Seward is Boyce or Boyd [Boyle], the man who killed Captain Watkins in Maryland. I think it without doubt true.[17]

Dana's information on Boyd was, of course, incorrect. But his report indicates that at seven o'clock of that dark Saturday morning Blue cavalrymen were in the upper reaches of Charles County, scouring for the fugitives.

Dana also sent off a dispatch to alert the military garrison at Chapel Point, just below Port Tobacco. Then the young officer made a curious move. Official records contain no explanatory word on the matter. But Lieutenant Dana abruptly abandoned Piscataway and led his cavalry troop from there to Bryantown.

Reaching Bryantown that Saturday forenoon, he set up temporary headquarters in the local hotel. And at the hour when Dana arrived in that village, John Wilkes Booth was still asleep, his head wrapped in a shawl, in the upstairs bedroom of the Mudd house less than five miles away. David Herold was in Mudd's barnyard fussing with the horses. Had Lieutenant Dana launched an immediate scouring operation he might have handily trapped Lincoln's assassin.

Dana did nothing of the kind. When Booth awoke that Saturday noon and sent Dr. Mudd in search of a carriage, Lieutenant David D. Dana and his men were lolling in Bryantown at their ease. Undoubtedly Herold spied the "bluebellies" when he scouted around the village, and the glimpse of Federal cavalry sent him racing back to Mudd's in panic. There in Bryan-

---

[17] *Official Records*, Series I, Vol. 46, Part 3, p. 767.

town Dana's troopers remained in inertia throughout that Saturday afternoon while the fugitives, forewarned, gave them a wide berth.

Dana's conduct adds still another mystery to the escape puzzle. Augur dispatches him to Piscataway on the main road to Port Tobacco. From there he makes a sudden tack to Bryantown, planting his cavalry troop squarely across Booth's path. But then the plant takes root. Instead of searching for the fugitives, Dana holds his troop immobile.

No critic has since made a point of the fact that the Army officer first put on Booth's trail was the brother of Stanton's Assistant Secretary. The relationship suggests that a singular importance must have been attached to Lieutenant Dana's mission. General Augur would hardly have dispatched the Assistant Secretary's brother on a routine hit-or-miss patrol.

As for Lieutenant Dana's sudden move from Piscataway to Bryantown, one can only assume that he picked up information which inspired the move, or he received secret (and unrecorded) orders which spurred him to that strategic locale. In either case General Augur's headquarters must have been privy to the matter. An Army lieutenant would not abandon a designated patrol area on his own initiative unless he were able to justify the action. If Dana uncovered a clue which routed him to Bryantown, he must have reported it. If, on the other hand, the move was ordered, Augur's office must have found some straw in the wind.

Then did someone in the War Department intervene? Had Lieutenant Dana (or General Augur) come too close to the target? Did someone higher up issue a secret directive ordering Dana to stand pat?

Existing War Department records do not contain the answer to the Dana mystery. But there it is. As of midday Saturday, April 15, the U.S. Army in the person of Lieutenant David D. Dana was almost on top of Booth's hideout near Bryantown. Something or someone must have sent Dana there, and General Augur's office must have known about it. Then, for reasons never divulged, Dana hobbled his patrol.

That same afternoon, belatedly, War Secretary Stanton summoned Lafayette Baker to Washington. And when Baker arrived the following afternoon (Easter Sunday), Stanton left the Chief of the United States Secret Service groping in the dark.

Repeat: "I made some inquiries with reference to what had been done toward the capture of the assassins, and ascertained that no direct clue even had been obtained. . . ."

According to Baker, then, he was not briefed on any of the pertinent developments or significant details. He was told nothing of the Surrattsville posse, nothing of Knott's arrest, nothing of the H Street house, nothing of Wiechmann's testimony. Possibly Police Superintendent Richards had not as yet confided his store of information to the War Department. But Army detectives in Washington had acquired much information on the

Booth gang, and Baker was apparently denied this information. Too, he was evidently left in the dark concerning Lieutenant Dana's mission to Bryantown.

Baker was utterly mystified when he left the War Department that Sunday evening—or so he avers:

> I could learn but little more than that John Wilkes Booth was the supposed assassin and Harrold (*sic*) was his accomplice. I asked if any photographs of the supposed assassins, or descriptions of their persons, had been secured or published. To my surprise I learned that nothing of the kind had been done; during the afternoon of Sunday rumors were freely circulated throughout the city connecting the name of John Surratt with the other assassins. I immediately secured pictures of those mentioned above, and on Monday the 17th had them copied with a full and accurate description of each assassin printed in a circular, in which I offered a reward of Ten Thousand Dollars. These . . . I dispatched to a number of detective agents in all parts of the country. I also mailed large numbers to different localities. These photographs and descriptions were the first ever published or circulated.[18]

So Lafayette Baker plunged into action. Unscrupulous, brutal, addicted to mendacity he may have been—a smalltime corporal elevated to giant stature by seven-league boots. But Stanton's Secret Service Chief was neither entirely incompetent nor brainless. Ruthless self-interest motivated most of his moves. That interest alone was enough to spur him on the hunt for Lincoln's assassin; an officer of Baker's proclivities would let no grass grow where prize money was involved. Hence the insistence in his memoir that his handbills were the first to be put in circulation—a statement written with an eye on ultimate reward claims.

But again one cannot take General Baker entirely at his word. He implies that he circularized photographs of the wanted fugitives on Monday, April 17. Actually the first circulars bearing these photographs are dated April 20, 1865—Thursday. Headlined are pictures of Booth, Herold and presumably John Surratt. As will be seen, an element of mystery shadowed the issuance of these pictures and cast doubt on the validity of Baker's reward demand.

Doubt of another color shadows Baker's assertion that he distributed an "accurate description of each assassin." True, his office issued the first handbill announcing a reward for Booth's capture. The handbill carries a description of Booth and of the "Person who Attempted to Assassinate Hon. W. H. Seward." This police flyer is an interesting item. Analyze the text, and it becomes a most peculiar article.

One is at once struck by the lengthy profile on Lewis Paine. Although his name was at that time unknown and only a few witnesses had glimpsed him—a frightened house servant, persons dazed by his maniacal onslaught —the fugitive is described in Dickensian detail. Height, features, com-

---

[18] *Op. cit.,* p. 526.

plexion, carriage, mannerisms, wearing apparel—from head to footgear Paine's appearance is delineated. "Upper lip protruded when he talked" . . . "manner vulgar" . . . "sack overcoat, pockets in side and one on the breast"—these minor touches are most definitive and remarkably accurate. Even the tone of voice is described: "small and thin, inclined to tenor."

Compare this excellent portrayal of Paine with the description of John Wilkes Booth. Whereas ten lines of text describes Seward's assailant, a scant three are devoted to Lincoln's assassin. And in this slapdash coverage of Booth, only the height, weight, hair and build are roughly accurate —features, incidentally, possessed by a large segment of the adult male population, and therefore not at all distinguishing.

Nothing on Booth's facial features except the eyes and brows. Nothing on his apparel except a signet ring. Nothing to characterize him except an alleged mannerism: "when talking inclines his head forward, looks down." Could any delineation of a wanted fugitive be more vague, more uninformative? In this handbill Booth is not even identified as a well-known public figure, Booth the Actor, Booth who has been seen on the stage in New York, Boston, St. Louis, Philadelphia.

Not only do the brief three lines on the assassin contain ambiguous inconsequentials. They emphasize at least one doubtful particular. "When talking looks down"—this is nonsense. So is reference to a signet ring— the first thing a desperate fugitive would be rid of. But in particularizing "eyes black, and heavy dark eyebrows"—the only distinguishing features reported—Baker's handbill may be the source of an error which came to be perpetuated in popular literature. Of course the arch assassin must have had black eyes. All fiends in Victorian novels had eyes like jet beads. Villainy's eyes are always black and glittering. But according to Booth's sister Asia, *his eyes were hazel!*[19]

In respect to Booth's description, then, the handbill issued by Secret Service Chief Baker was a hollow sham. The country was flooded with this circular. Was its falsity deliberately contrived?

Baker would insist that the military authorities refused to provide him with information on Lincoln's assassin. But the Secret Service Chief, then in Washington, had his own sources of information. From any of a dozen agencies he could have procured Booth's picture. Equally available were reams of testimony on the actor's appearance when last seen at Ford's. Conclusion: Baker deliberately contrived the misleading handbill.

Why?

One can only believe that Colonel-General Lafayette Baker had his eye on the main chance. Booth had not yet been apprehended, and big rewards were in the offing. Baker did not want some competitor, even one of his own field agents, to snare the jackpot before all the bids were

---

[19] Asia Booth Clarke, *op. cit.*

in. The Secret Service Chief intended to reserve the grand prize for himself.

General Augur holding out on Police Supertindent Richards; Richards holding out on General Augur; city detectives competing with military detectives; Army Provosts striving to out-do each other; and both military and civilian authorities mistrustful of Baker and his Federal secret agents—in this atmosphere of rivalry and mutual suspicion the manhunt for Booth and his fellow assassins got under way.

Inject the goad of a fortune in prize money, and the competition and mistrust become as ugly as the glares of jealous relatives about to read a will. (By Monday, April 17, Booth had turned into a coveted legacy, a bonanza. Within the week he would be worth a king's ransom.)

Add an element of treachery or conspiratorial complicity in the War Department. (If not in Stanton's office, somewhere behind the scenes someone was abetting the escape of Lincoln's killer.)

Result: cross-purposes, double-dealing, contrived confusion and misdirection—a hindrance that would hold the manhunt on a checkrein for days. At the outset this situation gave Booth and Herold a long lead on their pursuers. By Monday, April 17, Lincoln's assassin and his accomplice were snugged down in a hideout deep in the recesses of the Zekiah Swamps.

CHAPTER **12**

Zekiah Swamps Underground

WHEN BOOTH and Herold quit Dr. Mudd's, the hour was somewhere between 4:30 and 5:00 in the afternoon of Saturday, April 15.

In Bryantown, not five miles distant, Lieutenant David D. Dana and his cavalry troop took their ease. At that same hour, in Washington on the Potomac, a vast, ponderous complex of machinery was grinding as the Government mustered forces for a mammoth manhunt.

Meanwhile in a mudhole patch of swamp, less than thirty crow-flight miles away, the midget author of this monstrous turmoil disappeared in evening mist. On the pages of authenticated history Booth and Herold do not turn up again until that day's midnight. They might have vanished from known history for good and all, had they followed escape directions and reached their destination without undue delay. But the night that covered them proved a dual blindfold. The swamp that sheltered them enmeshed them in a snare. Soon after nightfall they lost their way.

Because the fugitives lost the swampland trail, their track at this point remains lost to history. To begin with, they were on a secret route, and secret routes may defy the best of trackers.

After quitting the Mudd farmstead, the fugitives followed a cart road which wound southwestward through the upper reaches of the Zekiah Swamps. These swamps occupy a narrow belt extending southward from Bryantown to Allen's Fresh, a minuscule settlement at the point where the Wicomico broadens into a wide backwater of the Potomac River. Oldroyd attributes to Major O'Beirne, who eventually scouted a section of this region, a vivid word picture of the terrain. In respect to the authorship, Oldroyd probably errs, for the empurpled prose smacks of the journalese of ghostwriter George Alfred Townsend.

> The swamps tributary to the various branches of the Wicomico River, of which the chief feeder is Allen's Creek, bear various names, such as Jordan's Swamp, Atchall's Swamp, and Scrub Swamp. These are dense growths of dogwood, gum, and beech, planted in sluices of water and bog. Frequent deep ponds dot this wilderness place, with here and there a stretch of dry soil, but no human being inhabits the malarial expanse; even a hunted murderer would shrink from hiding there. Serpents and slimy lizards are the only living denizens.[1]

Actually, the Zekiah Swamps were no worse than miles of territory covered by Grant's troopers and Sherman's "bummers." Here and there in the swampland stood a Negro's cabin. Squatters and woodcutters lived along Allen's Creek. Trappers entered the bogs after coon and possum and muskrat, the latter a favorite for "swamp-rabbit stew." This region was not the Amazon. Near Allen's Fresh, Confederate blockade runners concealed their small craft. And up the Wicomico, not far from the farm of one Samuel Cox, Rebel secret agents hid their boats. Throughout the war the natives in the area had stealthily participated in this underground activity.

The writer exaggerated when he said that "even a hunted murderer would shrink from hiding there." John Wilkes Booth hid there. So did onion-chinned David Herold. It would seem Dr. Samuel Mudd had advised the fugitives that they could find a haven on Cox's farm and a boat in the vicinity of Allen's Fresh, whence they could escape down the Wicomico and across the Potomac. The "Parson Wilmer" story Herold had told Mudd was obviously a blind. For Booth and Herold headed for

---

[1] Oldroyd, *op. cit.*, p. 67.

Cox's as soon as they left Mudd's farm. Had they stayed on the cart road through the swamps, they could have made good time to Cox's house.

But after nightfall the thickets went murky black. Somewhere near Brice's Chapel, a tiny church in the wildwood, the fugitives lost their way. Rather, they were presented with a choice of wagon tracks which seemed to lead nowhere. At this point they were not far from the village of La Plata, southwest of Bryantown.

Herold was puzzled. He peered at the dimly discernible road-fork and squinted at a fragment of map which he had been carrying. Never before had he seen the little church, ghostly in the night.

It seems that Booth huddled on the church steps while Herold probed ahead in the moonless dark, trying to locate a hog's-back through the swamp-bottom. To the actor, softened by city luxuries, the wait at the rustic chapel, marooned in desolation, must have been frightening. Less than twenty-four hours ago he had made his grandstand play; now his solitude in the night was like oblivion.

Herold finally materialized out of the darkness, to report that the road ended nearby in a marsh. They would have to follow the other trail through the dogwood. Treading these thickets, the fugitives proceeded at snail's pace. Booth's left crutch sank in muck, throwing him full weight on his injured leg. Again, as he toiled through mire, the crutches slipped from his grasp and he sprawled cursing. In moonless gloom they slogged forward through the gluey swamp.

At length Booth could stand the trudge no longer. Riding would bruise his leg at every jog, but they would make better time. Faithful Herold hoisted his strange master into the saddle. He himself felt better with horseflesh under him, for the horses could sense the trail and lead the way.

The horses picked their way through sloughs and dense undergrowth. Suddenly Herold reared up his mount, his hand lifted in warning. Booth pulled up. On the path ahead of them stood a man, his face darker than the night. They could just discern the whites of his eyes.

"Who's there?"

"Yessuh, yessuh, it's only me."

"Who's that?"

"Only me, suh. Oscar Swann."

At the Negro's voice they relaxed. But Oscar Swann was scared wide-eyed. He has reason to be. This swamp was a haunt of ghosts. During the war, it harbored Army deserters, bad men, murderous renegades. Only last month there was a guerrilla marauder around here—Boyd—who would kill a black man as soon as spit!

Tonight old Oscar was close to such a killing. He did not know it, but the two who confronted him that Saturday evening were in moods as vicious as Death itself. They asked him to guide them to the home of a Mr. Burtle. Trembling, Oscar agreed to lead the way.

So Booth and Herold faded from the neighborhood of Bryantown. In that one-horse village, Lieutenant David D. Dana settled down with his cavalry troop for the night. It seems the young lieutenant thought he had accomplished a good day's work, but insofar as apprehending Lincoln's assassin was concerned, Dana's acomplishment that Saturday amounted to less than zero. Not only did he fail to block Booth's escape, but Lieutenant Dana's endeavors assured the getaway. For he informed the natives in the Bryantown area *that John Wilkes Booth was still in Washington City!*[2] Thereby Dana completely disarmed the Marylanders in the region. Loyal citizens who might otherwise have been on the lookout for the fugitives would for that day at least ignore strangers in the neighborhood. Another inexplicable in the tangled skein of the Lincoln murder case.

About seven miles below Bryantown lived Colonel Samuel Cox, planter. This Cox was a period piece, descendant of the Maryland cavaliers. One pictures him with beeswax mustache and goatee, and with character to match. However, one historian has described the Colonel as "about forty-five, thickset and stern-visaged," with a "powerfully muscled face." Still, he seems to have been the stereotype of the class-conscious cavalier. He was, of course, an avowed Secessionist.

Cox had two sons: Harry, a Confederate soldier, who had been badly wounded at Petersburg, and Samuel Cox, Jr., an adopted son, who attended Charlotte Hall Academy. Samuel was home that Easter weekend with his father. They had planned a journey to Washington City, where the Colonel hoped to obtain a pass to visit his wounded boy. As Samuel Cox, Jr., remembered it:

> On Saturday evening, April 15, when we received the mail, we were shocked to learn of the assassination of President Lincoln. It was particularly shocking to us, for besides the deed itself, in which none of us sympathized, we realized that it would prevent our rendering such aid to my stricken brother as his condition required, as we would not be permitted to leave the vicinity of Washington, which would naturally have been thrown into great excitement by the insane act of John Wilkes Booth.[3]

The junior Cox voiced these recollections years after the Saturday in question. Undoubtedly he editorialized to suit opinion that prevailed long after the war. For John Wilkes Booth and David Herold found refuge on the Cox farm that Saturday midnight. Down through history have come two completely different versions of the fugitives' reception. Version One (the traditional): far from regarding Booth as the perpetrator of an insane deed, Colonel Cox admitted him with open arms, and entertained him

---

2 Eisenschiml, *op. cit.*, p. 267.
3 Quoted in Oldroyd, *op. cit.*, p. 266.

royally. Version Two: the Maryland Colonel cold-shouldered the assassin and refused him the house.

We cannot rely on the word of the principals involved, but a measure of truth may be gleaned from the recorded testimony of two witnesses who were eventually called upon to talk: Oscar Swann, innocent swamp guide; and Mary Swann, slavey on the Cox domain.

Statement of Oscar Swann (taken as Government witness):

> I met two men on Sat. night, 15 April—about 9 o'clock. I had heard of the murder of the President. These men asked me the way to Mr. Burtle's; in dark, and could not see their faces. . . . They told me to get my horse and show them the way. . . . Before I got to Burtle's they asked me if I could take them to Capt. Cox. . . . One was a small man. The other was lame and had a crutch. The small man said the other man broke his leg. I saw it was the left leg that was broken.
>
> When they got to Cox's they got off. It was near midnight. Cox came out with a candle. He said, "How do you do." They went in and remained 3 or 4 hours. I remained outside.
>
> When they came out they were alone. Cox did not come out with them. The small man went some little distance when the lame one said, "Don't you know I can't get on." The small man then came back and helped. The small man told me to put my hand under his fork and lift him up, which I did.
>
> One said when they were mounted, "I thought Cox was a man of southern feeling."
>
> They did not come out of the gate as far as I saw. The gate is quarter of a mile from the Cox house. Before I got to Cox's, the small man said, "Don't you say anything. If you tell that you saw anybody, you will not live long." I saw nothing more of them. I got back home, which is 12 miles from Cox's, about sunrise.
>
> In all they paid me $12.00.[4]

Swann was in the hands of the Federal authorities when he made the foregoing statement. He may have been under duress at the time. He may have been cajoled. His account seems singularly sparse. But he was a colored man talking of white folks *to* white folks, and he came from an area where a colored man was warned to guard his tongue.

There are two significant lines in Oscar Swann's brief statement. The first concerns an important time element. *"They went in and remained 3 or 4 hours."* The second reflects on Cox's sentiments as remarked by one of the fugitives. *"I thought Cox was a man of southern feeling."* The scared Negro probably thought these details of little consequence, but they were weights in the balance so far as Colonel Cox was involved. On the face of it, they seem contradictory. The one implies hospitality; the other, chilly indifference.

The girl, Mary Swann, confused the issue. When questioned by the authorities three weeks after the event, her memory faltered. Or perhaps her courage needed bolstering. Like Oscar Swann, she had been schooled

---

[4] National Archives, War Dept. Records, File "S," Doc. R.B./r 79, JAO.

in reticence. Moreover, she was a servant in a household that would hardly have tolerated an independent Topsy. If she was frightened into talking to the police, it seems equally likely that she withheld information, covering for her master.

Transcribed under the auspices of Secret Service Chief Lafayette C. Baker, the colored girl's statement follows:

> Three men came to the house [Cox's] on Easter Saturday night. Do not know who they were. The people had all gone to bed. Someone rapped at the door, and Capt. Cox got up and put on his pants and went to the door.
>
> I was in the dining room, where I sleep. . . . I got up and looked out at the window and saw three men in the yard. I could not see their faces, only their forms. They did not come in the house, as he refused to let them in. . . . If they came in I did not see them. Did not put on my clothes. I did not lay awake long. I heard Capt. Cox shut the door on them. Nobody got them anything to eat or drink that I know of.
>
> The next morning Mrs. Cox asked Master who they were, and he said he did not know—that they were strangers. The next night some persons came & stayed all night. I was not in the house when they first came. I saw a man standing in the front yard with a stick in his left hand. That was the first night when these people came. I did not see any horses at all.
>
> It was almost daylight when they went away.[5]

Now the facts are blurred. Oscar Swann says the fugitives entered Cox's house and stayed several hours. Mary Swann, who slept (or said she slept) in the dining room, swears the visitors were turned away from the door.

A third witness may be referred to, namely, Samuel Cox, Jr. As the younger Cox recalled it, Colonel Cox demanded the names of the midnight visitors ". . . which they declined to give." The Colonel "thereupon refused them admittance, and in a short time they left, incensed at his want of hospitality. . . . It was Booth and Herold who were seeking admittance, but he did not know either of them."[6]

Like Mary Swann, Samuel Cox's adopted son can hardly be credited as a disinterested party. Too, he did not testify under oath, but scratched his memory years later for the benefit of an interested historian (O. H. Oldroyd). So he probably re-hashed a tale which had been edited by family consent for reasons peculiar to the case.

In *The Man Who Killed Lincoln*, historian Philip Van Doren Stern tells it this way: Colonel Cox admitted the fugitives at once. They talked for a time. Then, learning Booth's identity as Lincoln's assassin, the Colonel damned Booth for a murder that was bound to bring reprisals down on the beaten South. Booth left the Cox house in a fury, cursing the Colonel as a traitor to the Cause.[7] But Stern advises that this scene is an assumption based on the testimony of the Negro who led the fugitives to Cox's

---

[5] National Archives, War Dept. Records, File "S," JAO.
[6] Oldroyd, *op. cit.*, p. 266.
[7] *Op. cit.*, pp. 203–13.

house.[8] A nice blend of the implication of hospitality and the implication of cold-shouldering.

Booth's biographer, Francis Wilson, recounts the "hero's welcome" story. Wilson asserts that Booth identified himself to Cox by displaying the initials "J. W. B." on his hand. Then: "Cox pretended before the Negro [Oscar Swann] to be afraid to receive them. The Negro was in no wise fooled. Once the door was closed, Booth was smothered with praise and congratulations! According to Baker of the Secret Service, by peeping through the window the Negro Swann saw Booth, Herold, and Cox feasting at table for hours."[9]

Two holes drain the validity from Wilson's account. In Swann's officially recorded statement, he makes no mention of "peeping through the window" at a congratulatory feast. And the word "according to Baker" is as invalid as a quote from Ananias. The Federal Secret Service Chief was never noted for veracity.

So the truth of what happened at Cox's house on the occasion in question remains locked behind closed doors. Yet, winnowing the known testimony, we may glean one glimmer of light. There is the colored girl's curious statement, introduced as though by an afterthought, about two visitors *Sunday* night—one *with a stick in his left hand*. These nocturnal arrivals were received as guests. They stayed until daybreak. Could it be these shadowy guests were Booth and Herold, and Easter Sunday night the date of the Roman banquet? Apparently the Federal investigators never followed this lead.

However, the matter of cordiality seems rather beside the point. For Samuel Cox did harbor the desperate fugitives. What difference if he did so willingly or grudgingly, with gracious courtesy or with sour reluctance? In either case, the upshot was the same. On the Cox domain Booth and Herold disappeared. Cox abetted their disappearance, saw that they were liquored and fed, raised a verbal smoke-screen over their lair. And failed to inform the United States authorities on their whereabouts. While thousands of soldiers and police spent thousands of hours on the manhunt, the fugitives played possum and Cox stayed mum.

The Government never followed this lead, either.

Sunday, April 16, 1865, was perhaps the grimmest Easter in American history. A day of mourning, of national grief and national bitterness, and of mounting national wrath.

Few pastors in Northern pulpits told the ancient story of man's hope for life eternal, of immortality symbolized by the stone that was rolled away. Sunday congregations wore black. The flowers on the national altar were

---

[8] *Ibid.*, p. 381.
[9] Wilson, *op. cit.*, p. 153.

funeral flowers. The national mind was fixed on the Tomb rather than the Resurrection.

In Washington, Father Abraham lay dead.

In the White House, a widow tore her hair.

The nation heard that Mrs. Lincon lay in her bedchamber, stricken. Her frenzy at this time approached madness. Elizabeth Keckley, her companion and confidante, wrote:

> I shall never forget the scene. The wails of a broken heart, the unearthly shrieks, the terrible convulsions, the wild, tempestuous outbursts of grief from the soul. I bathed Mrs. Lincoln's head with cold water, and soothed the terrible tornado as best I could.[10]

Mrs. Lincoln's anguish characterized the convulsive grief of the stricken populace. If her agony stemmed in part from thrusts of conscience and remorse, so did some of the nation's sorrow.

The New York *Herald*, for example, reminded its readers that certain elements in the North had jeered at Lincoln and traduced him during the war. The *Herald* demanded the "halter and the gallows" for the assassins. But in an Easter editorial, the paper observed: "There is an ominous muttering in the streets; a general feeling is abroad that the lives of the wretched assassin or assassins in this horrid business will not meet the requirements of justice, and that justice should now take its course against treason and traitors wherever found."[11]

Perhaps the *Herald's* commentary was too broad. Had the *Herald* chosen to be specific on that Easter morn, it might have asked questions concerning John Wilkes Booth's escape.

On that same Sunday morning, Dr. Samuel Mudd (individual with troubled conscience?) told his cousin Dr. George Mudd, in Bryantown, that a crippled fugitive with an unprepossessing companion had been at his house the day before. Dr. Sam must have told Dr. George a good deal more. The village hotel was crowded with Blue soldiery, and Lincoln's murder was on every tongue. One can believe the older cousin asked Samuel Mudd some searching questions. They must have had a grim discussion, with personal security and family reputation involved. The upshot was Sam Mudd's appeal: would his cousin inform the Federal police?

Dr. George Mudd could not have relished this responsibility. But he was a loyal Unionist, a man with a strong sense of duty. He agreed to inform the Federal officers, although he must have warned his cousin that the consequences might be painful.

Dr. George Mudd did not relay the word that day. There were Easter services to be attended, family doings, perhaps he was burdened with

---

[10] Elizabeth Keckley, *Behind the Scenes, or Four Years in the White House* (New York: G. W. Carleton & Co., 1868).

[11] New York *Herald*, April 16, 1865.

professional calls. Possibly he put off the matter, hoping that the fugitives —if they were Booth and an accomplice—would be caught by the soldiers in the vicinity. Moreover, Lieutenant Dana, at the Bryantown Hotel, had published the statement that Booth was still in Washington. George Mudd may have believed his cousin overexcited or somehow wrong.

And Dr. George Mudd had other worries on his mind. Official records fail to detail the matter, but on that Easter Sunday evening, Dr. George Mudd learned that Guerrilla Boyle and two companion renegades were in the near locality. Boyle had uttered threats against George Mudd. The local grapevine brought him this disturbing news, and George Mudd spent an uneasy night at home.

However, on Monday, April 17, Dr. George Mudd informed the Federal commander at Bryantown about the two fugitives who had been at Samuel Mudd's home on Saturday.

The Federals did not get around to visiting the home of Dr. Samuel Mudd until Tuesday afternoon, April 18—more than thirty hours after Dr. George Mudd conveyed the word to Lieutenant Dana.

By that time, of course, Booth and Herold were in the lower recesses of the Zekiah Swamps, snugged down in a hideaway provided by silent Colonel Cox.

If, in truth, Colonel Cox did not know Booth's identity that Saturday midnight, he was certainly aware of it by Easter Sunday morning.

Cox took steps to have the fugitives concealed and provisioned. He screened their whereabouts with a veil of silence. He furnished them with an accomplice to serve as guide and lookout. For six days he harbored Booth and Herold, and kept his peace.

As Samuel Cox, Jr., recalled it:

> When they [the fugitives] were dismissed from our door, they discharged the Negro Swann, and during the morning while riding out on his farm Colonel Cox came upon them secreted in a gully about half a mile southeast from his house. The . . . suffering condition of Booth appealed to his humanity, and he then carried them into the pines, some two miles from his house, where they were secreted by him and Thomas A. Jones until Friday night, April 21. . . . On Monday the 18th of April I was dispatched by Colonel Cox to Jones. Jones responded to the appeal of Colonel Cox, who besought him to aid him in getting them across the Potomac.[12]

Thomas A. Jones was Cox's stepbrother. (Some say foster brother.) He had been an active member of the Confederate underground. As Samuel Cox, Jr., tells it, Jones was most reluctant to aid the fugitives and "would not have done so but to aid his friend Colonel Cox, who had gone into it without reflection and without realizing the full meaning of what he was doing until it was too late. . . ."

---

[12] Quoted in Oldroyd, *op. cit.*, pp. 266–67.

This sounds like stuff and nonsense as an alibi for Cox's action. The patrician Colonel, aged 45, was as acute as a cocked pistol. As for Thomas Jones's reluctance, we have his own word on the matter. Thirty years later he recalled the episode clearly:

> On Easter Sunday morning, 1865, a boy came to my house and told me Samuel Cox . . . wanted me to come over to his place, as he wished to see me about some seed corn. I knew that was not the real cause for his sending for me, but I saddled my horse at once, and went with the boy. . . . Cox met me at the gate, and we walked quite a distance out from the house, so that our conversation could not be heard. Cox said: "There were two men called at my house this morning before daybreak, and I think one was Booth. Now, we want you to take charge of them, feed and care for them, and get them across the river as soon as you can. We must help them as they are on our side." . . . I knew to assist in any way the assassin of Lincoln would jeopardize my life. . . . After weighing the matter a few moments I said: "I will see what I can do, but must see these men first; where are they?" Cox then told me that his overseer, Franklin Robey, had piloted them to a thick piece of pine and advised them to keep perfectly quiet. . . . I left Cox and rode toward the spot, fully realizing the risk I was undertaking; but I did not hesitate. . . .[13]

Jones found Booth and Herold cowering in a thicket not far from a wagon road. Here the ground was swampy. Underbrush formed a dense screen. Near this jungle nest stood an aged, gray stump—a huge stump with three long gnarly roots which gave it the appearance of a giant bird foot, its talons gripping the soil. This landmark no longer exists, but Samuel Cox, Jr., remembered it well. It was used as an underground "letter box." In a cavity of the stump secret mail was deposited—"mail that was going to Richmond and Southern points during the war, and from South to North. . . ."[14] United States stamps would be placed on northbound spy letters left in the stump. They would then be posted at Allen's Fresh or Bryantown, and the U.S. Mail would obligingly deliver them to unsuspected Rebel agents in the northern States.

The younger Cox declared that this stump and Booth's nearby hideaway were on the land of Captain Michael Robertson. But it seems probable the hideout and its marker were on or just inside the border of Cox's plantation.

The Cox estate was named "Rich Hill." The house lacked the manorial elegance implied by the name, but in that sparsely settled district it was imposing. Thomas Jones lived down the road at a little place called "Huckleberry." There he dwelt in a small, frame cottage. "Rich Hill" and "Huckleberry" aptly suggest the difference in status between a Maryland squire and an impoverished dirt farmer.

It is apparent that Colonel Cox burdened his stepbrother with the dirty

---

13 *Ibid.*, pp. 101–02.
14 *Ibid.*, p. 270.

end of the stick—direct contact with the fugitives. The Colonel warned Jones to be extremely cautions in approaching their hideout. A secret signal had been agreed upon by Cox and Booth. Jones was to whistle in a peculiar way. "As I drew near the hiding place of the fugitives," Jones recalled, "I stopped and gave the signal."

Presently Herold stepped out of the thicket. Scowling, he aimed his carbine at Jones. He demanded in a menacing tone: "Who are you, and what do you want?"

Jones said, "I came from Cox. I'm a friend. You have nothing to fear."

After a hard scrutiny, Herold lowered the gun and told Jones to follow him. Pushing through the undergrowth, he led Jones to a patch of clearing in the bush. For the first time, Thomas Jones saw John Wilkes Booth.

"He was lying on the wet, cold ground," Jones recalled, "his head supported by his hand. His weapons of defense were close beside him; an old blanket was partly drawn over him. His slouch hat and crutch were lying by him, he was exceedingly pale, and his features bore traces of intense suffering. . . ."

Booth did not have a slouch hat and blanket when he fled from Washington. Either one or both of these articles must have come from Dr. Samuel Mudd or from Colonel Cox.

Jones' sympathies were won by Booth's demeanor. "Murderer though I knew him to be . . . I determined to do all I could to get him into Virginia, and so assured him. . . . He held out his hand and thanked me; also said: 'I killed President Lincoln, and knew the United States Government would use every means in its power to capture me; but John Wilkes Booth will never be taken alive.'"

Heroically declaimed with theatrical gesture, no doubt, this sentiment was sufficient to enlist the aid of Thomas A. Jones.

"I visited them [Booth and Herold] daily, giving them food and newspapers and any information that I could. . . . Each day I made it my business to gain any information I might, and the following day to report to Booth."[15]

For the better part of a week, then, the farmer from "Huckleberry" supplied and sustained the fugitives. Every morning he brought them a basket of food. Cox sent liquor. The mission was a dangerous one for Jones. By midweek, Federal soldiers and detectives were scouting the fringes of the swamp. Jones never knew when he might be caught scuttling through the underbrush. He made a pretense of feeding livestock. As he went through the thickets he uttered shrill hog-calls.

Not only did Jones feed Booth and Herold. He spied on the Federal police in the area. On one occasion he visited Port Tobacco with an ear cocked for information. At length, he advised the fugitives when the

---

15 *Ibid.*, pp. 102–104.

coast was clear for a Potomac crossing. He procured a boat for the venture. No one of the subsequently accused conspirators gave Booth a bigger hand in the getaway than Thomas A. Jones.

The Federals finally arrived with inquiries on Jones' doorstep. They had been informed on Jones' subversive endeavors. But the authorities showed a strange disinterest in the doings of this shadowy farmer. As was the case with Cox, the United States Government was to award Jones an inexplicable exemption.

The popular version has it that Booth, at this time, huddled in the swamp in woeful misery, half starved, feverish from his untended injury. Vintage historians played on the conscience theme. Contemporary artists pictured him as languishing with head on hand, his face drawn with sadness, his eyes on a vision of limbo, his pose a combination of Hamlet and the Dying Gaul.

Undoubtedly Booth experienced miseries. His injury was painful. Probably he ran a temperature. The night mists were chill, the hard ground uncomfortable. But Booth had been known as a muscled gymnast. It would have taken more than a few days in the open to reduce him to the pallid invalid pictured by the sentimentalists. In the hideout he did not want for food. Cox supplied him with brandy. The devoted Herold, experienced in wood-lore, probably arranged a comfortable lean-to. As Dr. Mudd had advised, so long as Booth remained off his leg the pain would be bearable.

If Booth was starved, then, the hunger was for luxuries and for news. He was avid for news.

Jones brought him copies of the *National Intelligencer*. Booth spread out the big sheets, reading the columns with the eagerness and self-interest of an actor scanning first-night reviews. It would seem he feasted on every detail. The black-barred stories of the shooting at Ford's. The descriptions of Lincoln's death. The raging editorials. But where was the name of John Wilkes Booth? Only a word or two! In the early editions he was scarcely mentioned.

Where was the letter he had written to the *Intelligencer?* The screed he had given to John Matthews? It wasn't there. And they had the story all wrong. He had shouted "Sic Semper!" before he fired.

In *The Man Who Killed Lincoln,* Van Doren Stern builds a dramatic scene around Booth's disappointment at the newspaper's failure to publish his letter. But dialogue between Booth and Herold remains in the realm of supposition. We do not know Booth's spoken reaction to the press accounts of the assassination. We have only the evidence that he read the papers with that egocentric fascination which seems common to even run-of-the-mill criminals who enjoy press notoriety.

Booth did record some of his thoughts in a little red book he carried.

These febrile jottings contain an expression of resentment at the news reports.

> I struck boldly and not as the papers say. . . . I walked with a firm step through a thousand of his [Lincoln's] friends, was stopped, but pushed on. A Colonel was at his side. . . . In jumping broke my leg. I passed all his pickets. Rode sixty miles that night, with the bone of my leg tearing the flesh at every jump.

Booth wrote a good deal in the little red book. If one takes his writing as that of confidante to diary, it stands as a masterpiece of self-pity, self-interest, self-glorification. He sees himself as a heroic figure abandoned by the Fates. He finds himself unappreciated by a people *"too degenerate"* to comprehend his superior mission.

> . . . if the world knew my heart, that one blow would have made me great, though I did not desire greatness.

This from the Booth who coveted star billing, the actor who thirsted for notoriety.

> . . . I have too great a soul to die like a criminal.

But no thought for Lewis Paine, for John Surratt, for others who, if caught, would certainly face the gallows, or stand before the firing squad as his henchmen.

On Thursday, April 20, an attempt to cross the Potomac was frustrated by the appearance of a gunboat downstream. At this, Booth almost drowned himself in self-commiseration. He wrote:

> After being hunted like a dog through swamps and woods, and last night being chased by gunboats till I was forced to return, wet, cold, and starving, with every man's hand against me, I am here in despair. And why? For doing what Brutus was honored for—for what made William Tell a Hero; and yet I, for striking down an even greater tyrant than they ever knew, am looked upon as a common cutthroat.

In the underground hideout near Cox's, he was neither hotly hunted nor chased. He may have been wet and cold, but he was not starving. Nor was "every man's hand" against him. In Colonel Cox he had a powerful ally. In Thomas A. Jones he had a staunch accomplice. In David Herold a faithful Sancho Panza. Furthermore, it seems clear that remnant elements of a Confederate spy organization were operating for him.

But: *". . . I struck for my country, and her alone. A people ground beneath this tyranny prayed for the end, and yet see now the cold hands they extend me!"*

He had read that Southern leaders deplored his act. The official disavowals of the crumbling Confederate Government. Did he actually expect the applause and acclaim of a grateful South? Such an expectation could have been logical enough. For four years Southern leaders had raged at Lincoln. The Richmond press had called Lincoln "monster" and "fiend." Militarists of the Beauregard school had called upon the populace to fight the tyrant whose cruel armies fought under the banner of "Beauty and Booty."[16] Branding the Yankees as rapists, barbarians and murderers, Southern orators had made Abraham Lincon the symbol of all the forces of evil.

Young men with impressionable minds are unable to see through the perfervid violence of war propaganda. If Lincoln were tyrant, monster and fiend, then his assassination was in order as a war measure and a boon to humanity. Did Booth *believe* this propaganda? If so, his act to eradicate the tyrant was indeed heroic and self-sacrificial. And his denouncement by Southern leaders was so much base hypocrisy.

We do not know what Booth believed.

He may have been writing when he was half drunk. He may have been indulging self-deception. He may have been practicing another kind of deception.

As a secret agent he should have known, and perhaps did know, that Headquarters would disown him if he were caught. Governments invariably disavow the acts of saboteurs and espionage personnel. Richmond had denied any hand in the Northwest Conspiracy, in the Johnson Island plot, in the St. Alban's raid, in the underground attempt to burn New York. From Captain Tom Hines and C. C. Cole and St. Leger Grenfel and John Yates Beall (or word from their directors), Booth should have known that the secret agent is on his own.

> The little, the very little, I left behind to clear my name, the Government will not allow to be printed.

Did he mean the U.S. Government or the Confederate Government? Apparently he referred to the letter he left for the *Intelligencer*, but we cannot be certain.

> So ends all! For my country I have given up all that makes life sweet and holy—to-night misfortune upon my family and am sure there is no pardon in the Heavens for me, since man condemns me so. . . . God, try and forgive me and bless my mother."
> . . . I do not repent the blow I struck. . . . I think I have done well, though I am abandoned with the curse of Cain upon me. . . . To-night I will try once more to escape these bloodhounds.
> God's will be done.
> Let me die bravely.
> I have never hated nor wronged any one.

He does give a thought to David Herold:

> And for this brave boy, Herold, here with me, who often prays (yes, before and since) with a true and sincere heart. . . .

---

[16] Douglas Southall Freeman, *Lee's Lieutenants* (New York: Charles Scribner's Sons, 1942), Vol. I.

And finally: "I do not wish to shed a drop of blood, but I must fight the course. 'Tis all that's left me."

If these are the declamations of a psychotic, his mind excited by fever and brandy, some of the lines are pitiful. There is a baffling duality in Booth. Yesterday full of schemes and exciting plots and dreams of glory and an obsessional hatred of Abraham Lincoln. Today the ascetic sufferer, the unsung hero, the humble man who never hated anyone. This is a small boy who weeps as he pictures his own funeral. Or this is a madman.

Booth may have been all of these things. He may have been something else. The writing in his little red book would puzzle a generation of investigators. One line is especially baffling.

> To-night I will once more try the river with the intention to cross; though I have a greater desire and almost a mind to return to Washington, and in a measure clear my name, which I feel I can do.

How did the assassin feel he could in a measure clear his name by returning to Washington? Did the thought occur that if he gave himself up he might appear in a dazzlingly heroic light? Did he picture himself addressing the Senate, delivering a brilliant oration in his own defense? Or did he mean to insert the implication that he might expose certain backers, name sponsors who had conspired in the assassination?

Several historians have read a sinister hint in this line. It is possible that Booth intended it as a hint, that he intended to leave the little red book where it might be found. Booth knew how to leave false clues.

For six days and five nights Booth and Herold remained in hiding. The bay mare and roan were led into the swamp and killed. Herold is said to have shot the animals—the police had their description, hence they were done away with. According to Samuel Cox, Jr., Colonel Cox's overseer, Franklin Roby, got rid of the horses.[17]

This Roby (sometimes spelled Robey) lurked in the background as another person who abetted Booth's getaway. Like Cox and Thomas A. Jones, he shielded the fugitives from the Federal police.

Eventually Army detectives arrested Cox and Jones as suspects. Interrogated, Colonel Cox did his best to mislead the authorities. On May 8 he was grilled by Colonel H. H. Wells at Bryantown. Before the Army officer could wring a semblance of truth out of Cox, he had to threaten the Maryland planter with coercion.

Says the military report: " . . . Cox denied all knowledge of either of the two persons named [Booth and Herold] being or having been at his house; and on being told by Colonel Wells that he could make a statement if he pleased, but if he did make one it must be true, and that if he made a false one the Colonel would tie him up by his thumbs, he asked

---

[17] Oldroyd, *op. cit.,* p. 269.

time for reflection. Colonel Wells told him he could have until 4 o'clock the next morning to reflect. At 4 o'clock in the morning he was brought in by the guard . . . and the first expression he made use of was that it was no use concealing the fact that two men were at his house, but he did not know who they were."[18]

The denial saved Cox a pair of sprained thumbs. But why did the Federal authorities swallow his feeble disavowal? Why did they eventually free Cox and Jones when they had every reason to believe these two had engineered Booth's escape across the Potomac?

Ten days before Colonel Cox's belated arrest and interrogation, Federal agents had picked up Henry Woodland (sometimes called Woodlawn), an ex-slave who worked for Thomas A. Jones. Woodland had told how Jones harbored "suspicious men." How Jones had ordered him, Henry, to procure a boat at Allen's Fresh. How the boat had been hidden near "Mr. Dent's . . . about half a mile from Mr. Jones's."

Woodland informed the Federal men that he had "often seen signal lights at night across the Potomac." That Jones had signalled back, and surreptitious boats had crossed. That "Dr. Dent and George Dent, neighbors, seemed to be engaged in carrying the mail or any other thing that was needful on the other side." The Negro added: "Whenever men came and wanted to go across the Potomac, they would come and stay a day, and the next day I would miss them."[19]

Historians have assumed that this testimony implicating Jones must have implicated his prominent stepbrother, Colonel Cox. But there exists indelible evidence which shows that the authorities had something more on Cox than guilt by association.

Woodland talked to the Federal police on April 30—after Booth had crossed the Potomac and entered Virginia. The files of the Bureau of Military Justice contain a remarkable document which tells us that the Federal Government was previously advised on the activities of Colonel Cox and Thomas A. Jones. This evidence is recorded in the statement of a Washington physician, Dr. James G. Coombe.

Unfortunately, Dr. Coombe's sworn statement is undated. But the wordage indicates that he went voluntarily to Colonel Lafayette Baker *while the manhunt for Booth was still going on in lower Maryland;* that is, while Booth and Herold were still in hiding on Cox's farm. Coombe pinpointed places and named names. He put his finger squarely on Booth's hideaway. And also on something else.

Here is Coombe's extraordinary (and hitherto unpublished) statement:

> I live in Washington City, 3rd St. East No. 783; on the Eastern Branch near where they land the marble for the Capitol. I can be found there easily.

---

[18] National Archives, War Dept. Records, JAO. Also Eisenschiml, *op. cit.,* p. 299.
[19] National Archives, War Dept. Records, File "W," R.B., JAO.

I want to state that I have heard from Wise the Constable, that Booth Friday night at three or four o'clock, went to the house of Dr. Alexis (*sic*) Mudd, with a broken leg, which he set; that Booth remained there the following day & Saturday night gave a negro five dollars to take him to the house of Samuel Cox, & that Mr. Cox could give information where Booth went afterwards.

Now comes my surmise, & that is what brought me. I am well acquainted with the neighborhood. Within a few miles, say 10 or 12, there is an elegant place for hiding & I am satisfied Booth has gone there. It is another four miles to Allen's Fresh about 10 or 11 miles from Bryantown. He has gone there for advice, I think, to see a person who is capable as he is a Doctor. The person I suspect is Dr. Stoughton Dent, a man queer in every respect. He would not tell, because he would consider it a breach of hospitality. That is my idea.

I went last night to Col. Baker, but found that he was a $200,000 man, & I want the Government to have the information, & to save the reward.

Dr. Dent lives upon the road from Allen's Fresh to Bryant's town, four miles from Allen's Fresh. . . . By making a dash, taking 20 or 25 men, surrounding his house and beating the adjoining thicket I think Booth may be captured. Such is my surmise.[20]

In one neat package this affidavit wrapped up the whole subversive apparatus that harbored Booth in lower Maryland: Cox's plantation, the underground to Allen's Fresh, Dent's meadow, where the getaway boat was concealed, the fugitives' hideaway near the road (in an "adjoining thicket"). Coombe's statement also reveals that he mistrusted Secret Service Chief Lafayette C. Baker, that he divulged his information, under oath, to some other Federal official, and that the authorities were fully aware of Booth's visit to the Cox plantation even before Dr. Coombe put the matter on record.

For Coombe heard the word from a certain Constable Wise. *The constable must have heard it from some one of the Federal officers who had scoured lower Maryland.*

The Federal police did not raid Cox's farm on a red hot hunt for Booth and Herold. While Booth and Herold lay concealed on or near Cox's farmland, the Federals concentrated on Bryantown, Port Tobacco, Leonardtown.

Colonel Cox was never indicted for aiding and abetting Lincoln's assassin. Nor was Thomas A. Jones. Nor was Cox's overseer, Franklin Roby. As for mysterious Dr. Stoughton Dent, it is not on record that he was so much as detained for interrogation.

A strange and impenetrable curtain of immunity was lowered by the War Department on Colonel Cox and his underground associates. For reasons known only to someone high in authority, the Federal Government chose to prosecute Dr. Samuel Mudd, who was arrested on April 22. No effort was made to trap Booth and Herold at Cox's. In consequence, they were able to escape across the Potomac to Virginia.

---

[20] National Archives, War Dept. Records, File "C," Ev. B, JAO.

P A R T

III

Pursuit and Capture

There's villainy abroad; this letter shall tell you more.
—Love's Labour's Lost

Not a soul
But felt a fever of the mad, and played
Some tricks of desperation.
—The Tempest

CHAPTER 13

First Catch

O NE of the first assassination suspects arrested by the military police in the nation's capital was Mr. (sometimes Major) Benjamin F. Ficklin. An anomalous individual of Southern extraction, mysterious antecedents and shadowy dealings, Mr. Ficklin came and went in an obscurity which has left him all but invisible to history.

On the day after Lincoln was shot, one A. E. Fitzpatrick, a clerk in the Philadelphia office of the American Telegraph Company addressed a confidential letter to War Secretary Stanton. Fitzpatrick advised that "Major Benjamin Ficklin" was in the nation's capital, and the War Department would do well to apprehend him and question him in regard to the assassination.

Fitzpatrick wrote: "He has, in my opinion, the ability to plan and the courage to carry out the villainous act just consummated. . . . I have no personal knowledge of anything done by him upon which I could base the supposition that he would be party to such a foul proceeding. He has been kind to me. . . . But he was agent for the Confederate Government, making much money for himself."

The writer contributed a verbal tintype of Benjamin Ficklin which remains the only recorded picture of that interesting individual. "[He is] about 6 ft., dark hair cut short, sallow complexion, small black eyes, thin features altogether, more muscle than flesh, and on the whole presenting the appearance of a refined pirate. . . ."

In closing, Fitzpatrick added a cautious postscript: "I request that my name be kept from the officers, etcetera."

The public-spirited employee of the American Telegraph Company needn't have worried about a possible libel action with Ficklin as plaintiff. The gentleman who presented the appearance of a "refined pirate" had already been reported to the War Department in Washington.

On the night of the assassination, a Mr. Leach, citizen of Washington City, hurried into the office of the Deputy Provost Marshal, corner of 18th and "Eye" Streets, and asked to see Lieutenant Samuel K. Brown, Deputy. Brown jotted the detail in a memo.

"Leach told me there was a man in Washington by name of Benjamin F. Ficklin, as he had been seen at the Kirkwood House [that] morning. Leach stated that Mr. Ficklin owned a reputation far from savory. He was notoriously 'Secesh,' had gone south from Washington at the outbreak of the war, and was unquestionably a Rebel blockade runner."

Leach further stated that the sinister Ficklin had been "recognized by Barney Green, who keeps a Segar Stand in the hotel." According to Green, Ficklin had come to the Kirkwood House on the morning of April 14 "and entered the saloon." Remembering Ficklin as a pre-war customer, the seneschal of the cigar stand had followed him into the bar for a sociable chat. Ficklin adjured Mr. Green not to mention to anyone that he'd seen him. Citizen Leach thought Ficklin's conduct warranted investigation.

So did Deputy Provost Marshal Brown. Taking Leach along to assist, he spent much of the night of April 14-15 touring the midtown hotels on a hunt through the registers for Mr. Ficklin's signature. The signature could not be found. However, on Sunday, April 16, the subject himself was sighted on the corner of Pennsylvania Avenue and 11th Street. Whereupon Ficklin was taken into custody by Provost Marshal O'Beirne.[1]

Ficklin found himself facing an angry officer who wanted facts and brooked no shilly-shally. Here was a known Richmond agent in the parlor of the Kirkwood House in Washington on the day of the assassination!

One can visualize pallor on the cheek of the "refined pirate" caught in this Washington trap. Under the gaslight in O'Beirne's office, the prisoner lost no time in volunteering a deposition. Benjamin F. Ficklin swore, to wit: That he was born and reared in Charlotte (sic), Virginia; that he "left there" and went to Alabama and points West, was in Washington in 1860 and in the "first quarter" of 1861, where he "stayed at the Kirkwood House," and went to Richmond in March 1861 "to start an express company." He said he had served three months as Quartermaster, State of Virginia, but "never held appointment under Rebel Government."

Reluctantly Mr. Ficklin admitted he had owned "an interest" in the steamer *Coquette,* purchased from the Rebel Navy Department. He stated:

> I was engaged in running the blockade from Wilmington and Charleston. . . . I plead guilty of the charge of shipping cotton to Europe. I lost all the money I made in it. . . . In the early part of the Rebellion, I had some difficulty with the Rebel Government, and never had anything more to do with them, or they with me. The Government persecuted me on every occasion possible, and if it had not been for some friends there, they would have treated me worse than I am treated here.

And how did he come to be here? Ficklin shrugged. He had, he deponed, left Richmond on March 28, 1865, and had arrived in Washington City on Saturday, March 31. "I decline telling how I crossed the Potomac or where.

---

[1] National Archives, War Dept. Records, File "F," Ficklin Dossier, JAO.

. . . [In Washington] I went to see General Singleton, as part of my business was to take some papers to him."

Ficklin carried an abundance of papers on his person. The man was a walking postoffice. Detectives searched the sweatband of his hat, the lining of his coat, the underside of his pantaloons. From concealed pockets and flaps they fished some interesting reading.

For instance, Ficklin was carrying an introductory letter to a Dr. George A. Laithrop of New York City. The letter advised that "Major Ficklin" was on his way to Europe "for his health."

A tiny envelope addressed to "Maj. B. F. Ficklin, 7th Street" contained a note from a lady asking Ficklin to procure for her a number of articles and feminine dainties. As listed:

1 Black Silk.	*1 Ditto Checked Muslin.*
2 Calicoes.	*Gloves, Shoes, Handkerchiefs.*
2 Cossets.	*1 Muslin Dress.*
1 Hoop Skirt.	*1 Black Lace Veil.*
1 Piece Long Cloth.	*1 Piece Flannel.*

Appended to the list was a charming little note in dainty handwriting.

"The list of articles needed by a forlorn *Spinster* who *contemplates matrimony,* but is obliged to forego that *bliss* on account of not being able to obtain the above named articles."

The note was signed: "Matilda Slaughter."

A pretty story, Miss Slaughter's note—if one was a romanticist. But if one were, instead, an Army Provost Marshal wise in the ways of enemy strategems? If you were a soldier detective, an agent of the Intelligence Corps, versed in the tricks of code and cipher, the devices of secret communication? Then you would be loath to believe that an enemy agent of the Ficklin stamp would take time out from a hazardous mission to go trousseau shopping.

The astute intelligence officer is a born skeptic. He might see in Ficklin's list a complex message "locked up" in a lavender-and-old-lace vocabulary. "Black Silk" might mean Booth. "Calicoes" and "Cossets" might mean accomplices. "Hoop Skirt" could refer to a boardinghouse landlady. Such messages keep military intelligence agencies burning the midnight oil year 'round. Major James R. O'Beirne—no romantic—would not have taken that detailed listing at face value. Not when it was signed by the name "Slaughter." It was probably innocent, but you never knew.

Found on Ficklin was still another intriguing letter. Addressed to the Archbishop of New York, this epistle read as follows:

Most Rev. Dear Sir:

Mr. B. F. Ficklin who has been a most liberal friend of our little orphans during the past years of difficulty, although not a member of our church, and who, as I am informed visits the North on business of his own not connected with the troubles of the day, will present you these lines of introduction. Any courtesy you may be able to extend to him will be well bestowed, and will be appreciated by yours very truly in Xt.

J. McGill
Bp of Richmond

Richmond
March 28th 1865
To Most Rev Dr McCloskey
    Archbishop of New York

Here, again, the military intelligence agents would have been suspicious. Reference to "our little orphans" could mean almost anything. Ficklin, with his piratical appearance, hardly looked the type to play benefactor to a genuine orphanage. Was the letter itself genuine, or was it a forgery to serve as a blind?

A final item: the following notation on a scrap of Kirkwood House stationary.

Mr. Browning, Near Mr. Whitney's on Capital Hill.
Lncljn Hughes, at Mrs. Whitney's.
Gen J. W. Singleton, Metropolitan Hotel.
    Will either of you call at the Kirkwood House to see me.

B. F. Ficklin.[2]

Who was "Lncljn Hughes"? How came this Rebel agent to be in contact with General Singleton? And this "Mr. Browning"—who was he? O'Beirne undoubtedly intended to follow this line of inquiry. Until a routine question produced one surprising answer:

Q. When you came to Washington, did you or did you not take the Oath of Allegiance?
A. I did not, and desire to state to the following reason.—Ex-Senator Browning from Illinois, whom I knew, was to apply to the President for a permit for me to return south without taking the Oath of Allegiance, in order that I might not impair my influence which I wished to exert in pacifying the country and restoring peace.[3]

O'Beirne might have laughed at Ficklin's posing as an influential emissary. But he did not laugh at mention of Senator Browning! Nothing stumps a military officer faster than the mention of a Senator. Orville H. Browning posed as one of Abraham Lincoln's best friends.

The Ficklin grilling was discreetly terminated. Ficklin's deposition went into the special-treatment files of the Bureau of Military Justice. Memo: Senator Browning must be consulted.

Ficklin himself was filed in a comfortable detention cell for future reference.

Operating with independent initiative, Major A. C. Richards of the Metropolitan Police was, on the night of the assassination strike, a long

---

[2] National Archives, War Dept. Records, File "O," R.B., JAO.
[3] National Archives, War Dept. Records, File "F," JAO.

jump ahead of the military. While General Augur groped and floundered, deploying 8,000 soldiers where they did the least good, Superintendent Richards shot to the target with some 155 men.[4] By two o'clock in the morning of Saturday, April 15, Richards had interrogated dozens of witnesses, listed several suspects, and come up with three vital names: *John Wilkes Booth, David E. Herold, John H. Surratt.* By that hour, too, Richards had on his desk a vital address—*541 H Street.*

Two years later, during the Surratt Trial of 1867, District Prosecutor E. C. Carrington would state that "the officers of justice, by a sort of intuition, made their way to 541 H Street."[5] On the surface of it, this is shallow nonsense. Under the surface, the statement deliberately conceals the fact that the War Department had known about "541 H Street" since February, 1865, and had failed to act. Also, the "officers of justice" were not military police, but city police who struck with the speed of lightning as soon as Superintendent Richards learned John Surratt's local address.

Richards summoned Detective John A. W. Clarvoe and told him to pick up a detective squad, raid this boardinghouse on H Street, and arrest the actor Booth and his friend John Surratt.

Clarvoe and ten men scouted up to the H Street house about 2:15 A.M. Clarvoe deployed six officers at the side and back of the building. Then he led Detective James McDevitt, Detective Donaldson, Lieutenant Skippon and Officer Maxwell up the steps to the dark front door. Clarvoe did not know it, but he sounded a tiny tocsin of doom when he jangled the bellpull.

Lodger Louis Wiechmann answered the bell. One might wonder at his alert door-tending, for he slept in an upper back room, and others were nearer at hand. Historian Oldroyd, however, provides an explanation for Wiechmann's readiness at the hour in question. It seemed that early in the morning of the 15th, "he [Wiechmann] being slightly indisposed, had gone to the yard, returned to his room, and was hardly in bed again when the front doorbell was pulled very violenty. Hastily drawing on a pair of trousers, for he was the only man in the house, he ran downstairs. . . ."

Oldroyd errs in this account, for tombstone-cutter Holohan was also in the house at that time. Nevertheless, it was Wiechmann who answered the ring.

Wiechmann: "Who's there?"

Clarvoe: "Detectives come to search the house for John Wilkes Booth and John H. Surratt."

Wiechmann: "Neither of them are here."

Clarvoe: "Let us in anyhow, we wish to search the house."

Wiechmann: "Before doing so, gentlemen, I will have to get the permis-

---

[4] Statistic noted in Eisenschiml, *op. cit.*, p. 446.
[5] Surratt Trial, Vol. I, p. 688; also noted in Eisenschiml, *op. cit.*, p. 273.

sion of the mistress of the house."[6] Wiechmann went to Mrs. Surratt's bedroom door at the rear of the parlor. A polite knock roused the landlady. Wiechmann informed her the police were calling. As stated in Wiechmann's affidavit, Mrs. Surratt made a most injudicious reply: "For God's sake, let them come in! I expected the house to be searched."[7]

If Wiechmann quoted her accurately, Mrs. Surratt's expectations were swiftly realized. Clarvoe and his men crowded into the parlor, then moved swiftly through the house. At the door of Mrs. Surratt's bedroom, Clarvoe announced his business: We've come for your son! You'd better open up!

From behind the door the widow retorted that she had not seen her son for two weeks. Clarvoe wheeled on Wiechmann. Take us to *your* room! Wiechmann obligingly led the detective up to the second floor.

After searching Wiechmann's room, Clarvoe woke John Holohan and his wife. While the officers examined Holohan's room, Clarvoe went on up to the third floor where Anna Surratt and Honora Fitzpatrick cowered in bed. A quick glance at the corners of the room and at the shy young ladies satisfied Clarvoe. He called his officers together in the lower hall. There, Louis Wiechmann presumed to scold the detectives.

"Gentlemen, what do you mean by searching this house so early in the morning!"

Clarvoe stared. "Do you mean to tell us you don't know what happened last night?"

The boarder blankly shook his head.

Clarvoe drew from his pocket "a piece of black cravat." He held it out. "Do you see the blood on that?"

Wiechmann stared at what appeared to be an ugly stain.

Clarvoe nodded grimly. "That's Lincoln's blood! John Wilkes Booth has murdered the President, and your friend John H. Surratt, the Secretary of State."[8]

Afterward Wiechmann testified that the news stunned him. In all probability, he spoke the truth. He may have wondered just what had happened to the information he had passed to the War Department, and he must have been in some anxiety as to what, now, might happen to his own skin. On tenterhooks, he followed the detectives down to the parlor.

Mrs. Surratt, properly clad, had come out of her bedroom. When he saw her, Wiechmann blurted: "What do you think! John Wilkes Booth has murdered the President!"

The widow raised both hands in a startled gesture. "My God, Mr. Wiechmann! You don't tell me so!"

Clarvoe would recall that her shocked expression seemed genuine. He

6 *Op. cit.*, pp. 184–185.
7 Pitman, *op. cit.*, p. 421.
8 Oldroyd, *op. cit.*, p. 185.

questioned her at length about Booth. Readily she admitted knowing the actor, and she told Clarvoe that she'd seen Booth "at two o'clock yesterday [Good Friday] afternoon." But Mrs. Surratt insisted repeatedly that she had not seen her son John for about two weeks. Detective McDevitt took over the interrogation, grilling her on her son's whereabouts. Mrs. Surratt shook her head. She did not know where he was, she declared.

Clarvoe was stalled. His orders had been to arrest Booth and John Surratt if they were in the house.[9] They weren't in the house. But a good detective could scent more than the smell of midnight musk in Mrs. Surratt's parlor. There was, for instance, this peculiar Mr. Wiechmann.

Wiechmann volunteered to report at police headquarters at 8:00 A.M. in order to assist the officers in making an investigation. "With this assurance the detectives left the house."

Wiechmann then returned to the parlor and informed the household that, in consequence of Booth's visits, "everyone living in the house would be held to accountability."

Anna Surratt exclaimed, "Oh, Ma, Mr. Wiechmann is right! Just think of that man Booth having been here an hour before the murder!"

Mrs. Surratt's reply was somber. "Come what will, I am resigned. I think that John Wilkes Booth was only an instrument in the hands of the Almighty to punish this proud and licentious people."[10]

Unfortunately history has only Wiechmann's word for the foregoing dialogue. Or historian Oldroyd's word for Wiechmann's word. A careful study of the evidence indicates that neither the witness nor the historian was entirely trustworthy in the matter of quotes.

Yet a family facing strenuous police interrogration may also hedge a little when it comes to the absolutes of truth. Many of the critics quick to mistrust Louis Wiechmann were prepared to believe any statement at all from the Widow Surratt, her daughter Annie and her niece Olivia Jenkins. Such are the ready sympathies of public sentiment and the inherent repugnance for the "informer."

But the Metropolitan Police on this occasion were dealing with a murder case. The victim happened to be the President of the United States. With the killer and his gang at large, Police Superintendent Richards could afford neither sentiment nor delicacy. Undoubtedly he was happy to find and use an informer in the house on H Street.

But the serious trouble that came to Mary E. Surratt did not actually begin with Wiechmann. We find it tucked away in an affidavit furnished the War Department by an O Street neighbor, Mr. J. H. Kimball. This curious document did not come to light until years after its making. Evidently it was never seen by Police Superintendent Richards, and it seems

---

9 Surratt Trial, Vol. I, p. 688.
10 Oldroyd, *op. cit.*, pp. 186–187.

to have been overlooked by subsequent historians who delved into the case.

The affidavit bears no date. From the context, however, it is apparent that it was sworn some time on Sunday, April 16.

Statement of J. H. Kimball in the matter of the Murder of the President:

> Q. Where do you live?
> A. Corner of 11th and O; I think the number is 3420.
> Q. Now just go on and state this transaction in relation to Surrat (*sic*).
> A. Well, Mrs. Griffin yesterday was called out by a girl named Susan Mahoney who is a servant with Mrs. Surrat. She said that Saturday night there were three men drove up to the house of Mrs. Surrat. . . . . These men came there and had a little conversation with Mrs. Surrat.
> Q. What time?
> A. She did not tell the hour, but it was late Saturday. She was lying on the floor apparently asleep, with a cloth thrown over her head. She said that they had some low conversation with Mrs. Surrat; and amongst the others she heard them say that Surrat was in the theatre Friday night with Booth, she called it.
> Q. That was her son?
> A. Yes, sir, that was her son. Then she inquired of the men if they had seen their friends. They said they had seen their friends, but were afraid to speak to them—"afraid to let on,"—that is the expression she heard. They called for a change of clothing—one of them at least, and left the room and apparently got the change of clothing. She did not know whether they did or not. After that they drove away.
> Q. Did the girl feign sleep?
> A. She feigned sleep. She said Mrs. Surrat came & listened to see whether she was asleep, and she breathed hard to pretend to her that she was asleep. This girl understood her to say that the young man, her son, had not been home since Friday night . . . I have not seen this colored girl. I do not know how old she is, for I have not seen her and did not ask Mrs. Griffin.[11]

Kimball's statement concerning the servant girl's story poses two riddles, one of them mystifying. He names the girl "Susan Mahoney." Her right name was Susan M. Jackson. Perhaps her middle name was Mahoney, and, in keeping with prevalent custom which referred to colored help as "Mary Lou" or "John Henry," she was addressed in the condescending familiar. The mystification begins with the reported time of the nocturnal visit by the trio. Kimball states that the girl said this occurred on Saturday night— at least twenty-four hours after the assassination. By her own testimony, sworn on April 17, Susan Jackson timed the visit as occurring "on the night of the assassination."[12]

The 24-hour variation remains highly significant. Evidently the military authorities wanted to believe that Booth and John Surratt and another member of the band had escaped immediate capture on the night of the

---

[11] National Archives, War Dept. Records, File "K," R. B., JAO.
[12] Noted in Eisenschiml, *op. cit.*, p. 271.

murder by dodging into the Surratt house and donning disguises. Publication of this story would furnish the military with an alibi for its failure to snare the assassins before morning. Aside from that angle, the girl's remarkable story would pin accomplice guilt on Mrs. Surratt, thereby saving a lot of detective work and legal effort.

Federal officers would grill Mrs. Surratt for hours on the business of the midnight visitation. To the last she would protest ignorance of such a visit. Mrs. Surratt appeared utterly bewildered when queried on Susan's story. Her interrogators were unable to develop the theme.

If Susan's story were true, the three men must have entered the H Street house only two hours or so before Detective Clarvoe and his squad arrived. One naturally wonders why the girl did not inform Clarvoe of the mysterious visitors. One might also wonder why the visitors conferred in the basement where this girl slept, instead of, say, in the privacy of the kitchen.

Yet it seems incredible that this colored girl, who had been in Mrs. Surratt's employ only two weeks, would concoct such a yarn out of whole cloth. If she did not fear the Surratt family, surely she would have feared to mislead the authorities.

Not the least of the mystery is the fact that two years later, during the trial of John Surratt, the servant girl made no mention of the midnight visitors. But her deposition of April 17, on the heels of neighbor Kimball's statement to the military police, seems to have resulted in the arrest of Mrs. Surratt and—by an amazing quirk of fate—one of the assassins.

In response to this incredible catch, the Government would award Susan Jackson a prize-money allotment of $250. Mary Ann Griffin (the Mrs. Griffin mentioned in Kimball's deposition) also received $250.

Mr. Kimball was awarded $500.

Stagehand Ned Spangler lived in a fool's paradise. Its god was Wilkes Booth. Its atmosphere was composed of whiskey fumes. Its scenery was a wonderland of cardboard landscapes, paper moons and muslin trees. So enamored of the locale was Spangler that he usually spent his nights curled up in some cobwebby cranny backstage, preferring canvas gardens and painted clouds to his room in a boarding house at 7th and G Streets.

Spangler's heaven crashed around him on the night of April 14, 1865. Thereafter he was a soul in Paradise lost.

His descent to Inferno had begun when bit-player J. L. Debonay beckoned him to the stage door and told him Booth wanted him to hold a horse. Spangler sent a worried squint toward the lighted wings where voices echoed from the stage. The "Dairy Scene" was on, and he'd be needed there to break the set. But he left his post. He could not resist the summons of his master's voice.

A few hours later Ned Spangler was writhing in the toils of the law, as he faced the steely stare of Justice Abram B. Olin, a District of Columbia Supreme Court Judge roused from his slumbers to take emergency depositions concerning the assassination.

Of the eight suspects eventually indicted as Booth's accomplices, the shabby stage hand was the first to swear a formal statement. Made on the day following the assassination strike, Spangler's official deposition is presented herewith.

> My name is Edward Spangler. Am attached to Ford's Theater as stage carpenter. I was there last evening.
>
> I know of J. Wilkes Booth and have known him for eleven or twelve years. Mr. Booth came to the theater yesterday afternoon about five or six o'clock with a little bay mare, and put her in a stable which he had been in the habit of using. Booth objected to the bridle being taken off at that time in the stable and said of the mare, "She is a bad little bitch."
>
> . . . I did not see anything of Booth after that until he came back between nine and ten o'clock and holord (sic) for me. I was in the theater on the stage attending to my business. Mr. Debonay said to me, "Booth is calling you." I then went out to the back of the theater in the alley. I saw Mr. Booth holding a mare . . .
>
> Says he to me, "Hold this mare for ten or fifteen minutes." Says I, "I have not time, but I would call Peanut John." I sent word for him to come out and took hold of the mare. . . .
>
> When he [Booth] told me to hold her ten of fifteen minutes, he went into the theater. As soon as Peanut John came out I went back to my work. As near as I could come to it, ten, fifteen minutes after Booth left the horse and went into the house I heard the shot. . . .
>
> Immediately after the shot was fired I saw some person run out at the prompter's side through the exit at the left hand side of the stage, and communicating directly with the door in the rear near which the man was standing when I went into the theater. When I went out I could only hear the clatter of the hoofs in the distance. . . .[13]

Spangler had the remainder of Saturday and all day Easter Sunday to think it over. Evidently he was unaware of the abyss on which he teetered. He made no attempt to skip town, and apparently over the week-end frequented his customary habitats—a point which might have been offered in his favor, had anyone been that interested in the favor of a no-good stage hand.

But Judgment Day was coming for Ned Spangler. The police learned that the grimy stage carpenter was a Booth favorite. From the crew at Ford's they heard Spangler characterized as a ruffian.

According to "Peanut John," on the afternoon of April 14 he and Spangler were assigned the task of arranging the State Box. While engaged in this detail, Spangler began to damn the President.

"Peanut John" remonstrated. "What do you want to damn him for? He never did anything to you!"

---

[13] National Archives, War Dept. Records, File "S," R.B.P. 78, JAO.

Spangler snarled, "Aw, he ought to be shot! For getting all those men killed in the war."[14]

Most historians cite the testimonials in mention as constituting the praecognita which threatened to put Spangler's neck in a noose. But the authorities acquired at least one item of evidence somewhat more substantial than the allegations reported.

The item of substance was produced by Officer Charles H. Rosch, the detective who had come up with David Herold's name, signature and home address on the night of April 14. Attached to a force serving under Colonel H. S. Olcott, Rosch did some high-class sleuthing during the frantic week-end which followed the assassination strike. Official records fail to credit him with working on the Spangler case, but Rosch visited Spangler's seldom-used rooming house quarters. Nosing through the suspicious house, he soon uncovered Ned Spangler's carpetbag.

The carpetbag contained a hempen rope. Uncoiled, the rope stretched (according to account) a good 81 feet. The bag also divulged "some blank paper and a dirty shirt collar."[15] It could hardly have contained anything more. But the rope was sufficient. Someone in the Bureau of Military Justice would recall that Booth planned to stretch ropes across the turnpike to thwart cavalry pursuit. The rope in Spangler's bag could have wrung the neck of a whole company of cavalry.

Indeed, it would seem that this rope came close to wringing Spangler's neck. Of course, he could have said he stole it from the theater to sell in the flea market—eighty-one feet of rope could have bought him a good many drinks. Or he could have claimed that he used the rope in his crabbing enterprises up the Chesapeake. Apparently he made no effort to explain the item.

On Monday, April 17, Spangler was arrested by Colonel Olcott, and marched forthwith into Old Capitol Prison. According to the registry of that institution, he was first of the major "conspirators" to go behind bars. He was booked simply as "accomplice."[16]

Early in March, 1865, unhappy Sam Arnold had applied for a clerkship in a civilian sutler's store at Fortress Monroe, Virginia. The storekeeper, John W. Wharton, a former Baltimorean, agreed to hire the applicant. Arnold reported for work on April 2.

Doubtless the Fortress near Old Point Comfort seemed a comfortable distance from Washington City—and John Wilkes Booth. But Arnold had sown dragon's teeth. Now came the unseasonable harvest.

---

[14] Quoted in Wilson, *op. cit.*, p. 110.

[15] *Daily Constitutional Union,* Washington, D.C., May 19, 1865.

[16] National Archives, War Dept. Records, File "R," Doc. "List of Prisoners Committed by Colonels Wells, Foster and Olcott," JAO.

The Bureau of Military Justice in Washington would eventually create the impression that Arnold was identified and traced through the "Sam" letter found in Booth's trunk at the National Hotel. Colonel Lafayette C. Baker did some public preening on this point. But records in the War Department file indicate otherwise. Baltimore's Provost Marshal McPhail registered Sam Arnold as a suspect as early as Saturday, April 15. And on Easter Sunday morning McPhail's men were hounding Arnold's track.

Officers Voltaire Randall and Eaton G. Horner left Baltimore by steamer that Sunday evening. They arrested Arnold at Fortress Monroe on Monday the 17th.

Stoutly Arnold denied association with the Booth gang and any knowledge of the assassination conspiracy. But the arresting officers convinced him the game was up; he was "flushed."

Examining Arnold's carpetbag, they found some letters that needed explanation and a loaded revolver that could not be satisfactorily explained. According to Oldroyd, the despairing prisoner quickly broke down and "made a confession . . . giving the names of certain men connected with a plan for the abduction of President Lincoln."[17]

Arnold was hustled by return steamer to Baltimore, where he did some more "confessing" to Provost Marshal McPhail and to Provost Marshal Colonel Woolley of the 8th Army Corps. From Baltimore, by order of General Lew Wallace, the prisoner was rushed in irons to Washington.

He found Mike O'Laughlin waiting for him—in Old Capitol Prison.

Fast-moving Provost Marshal McPhail was on O'Laughlin's track as early as Saturday morning, April 15.

Just how the Baltimore Provost caught the scent remains a mystery. He did not get the word from the War Department in Washington. The tip-off must have come from someone in Baltimore. Either that, or McPhail sent his detectives to the old Booth house on Exeter Street as soon as he heard that Booth was the possible assassin. Neighborhood urchins could have told the police that Mike O'Laughlin had been chummy with Booth.

When O'Laughlin, bleary from his Washington spree, returned to Baltimore that Saturday afternoon, he was alarmed to hear the authorities had been seeking him. He told a friend it would be "the death of his mother" if he were arrested at home.[18] Yet with the chuckle-headed aimlessness which characterized the actions of most of Booth's co-conspirators, he rode around town for a while. He spent that night and Easter Sunday at the Baltimore home of a friend, one Mr. Bailey. Nemesis in the form of Officer William Wallace caught up with him on Monday.

Wallace delivered the catch to Police Marshal Thomas H. Carmichael. Carmichael reported:

[17] Op. cit., p. 61.
[18] National Archives, War Dept. Records, File "E," R.B.P. 15, JAO.

I ordered William E. Wallace to arrest O'Laughlin. When he first came to my office . . . he said he [had been] to a friend's house up town. . . . He saw Booth in Washington on Friday, the day of the assassination, at the National Hotel—he said that he had loaned Booth $500, and that he had been to Washington several times to see him about it. He confessed to having belonged to the Knights of the Golden Circle about four years ago—that he had not seen them since.[19]

Carmichael delivered the prisoner to Provost Marshal McPhail. Through channels he went to General Lew Wallace. Wallace dispatched him in irons to Washington.

Monday, April 17, a good day for the man-hunters. The bag was growing: Spangler, Arnold, and now Michael O'Laughlin.

But the big game was yet to come.

No character involved in the Lincoln murder case remains harder to analyze and to define than Louis J. Wiechmann. Born in Baltimore in 1842, he attended elementary school at Philadelphia. He was sponsored for a church career by Father E. Q. S. Waldron and the Rt. Rev. John McGill, D.D., Bishop of Richmond, was an exemplary student for a time at St. Charles College, but failed to graduate in divinity, and started teaching in Washington at St. Matthew's Institute. Then he accepted a minor clerkship in the War Department. An odd come-down, this last. Perhaps it could be explained by patriotism. Could an assignment with Union counter-intelligence have been the truer explanation?

In January, 1864, when Wiechmann became a Government employee in the Office of the Commissary General of Prisoners, he lodged in a boarding house kept by a Mr. Purnell. A companion boarder was General A. P. Howe, one of the officers who ultimately served under the Bureau of Military Justice.[20] In all likelihood the affable Wiechmann made General Howe's acquaintance at the excellent table set by Mr. Purnell. Could this general have interested Wiechmann in War Department employment?

Or did Wiechmann enter Government service for other reasons? At this stage of events he was visiting Surratt's Tavern as a family friend, corresponding with John Surratt as a former schoolmate, sending polite regards to Mrs. Surratt. Apparently he needed no second invitation when the widow suggested that he move into her Washington boardinghouse the following November.

We know Louis Wiechmann informed on the abduction plot. Yet he seems to have maintained reservations in passing this information to the authorities. It would appear he told only part of the story. A half way informer, straddling the fence, did he stay friends with each side so that he might play both ends against the middle? He would be so accused.

---

[19] National Archives, War Dept. Records, File "E," R.B.P. 15, JAO.
[20] Oldroyd, *op. cit.,* p. 158.

But on the Saturday following Lincoln's murder the hour for full disclosure had arrived. Wiechmann set out to expose John Harrison Surratt. After breakfast, he and John Holohan reported at Police Headquarters on 10th Street. Major A. C. Richards fastened an iron grip on the volunteer witnesses. As has been related, Wiechmann spent the day with a police posse racing through Prince Georges County, Maryland. That night he slept on the floor at Richards' Headquarters. Easter Sunday morning Wiechmann went with the police to Baltimore to consult with Provost Marshal McPhail. When the party returned to Washington that afternoon, Richards applied to the War Department for clearance papers which would enable him to send Wiechmann and Holohan with a detective party on special mission in pursuit of John Surratt.

Permission was granted by the following dispatch:

Headquarters Department of Washington,
Washington, D.C., April 16, 1865.
SPECIAL ORDERS No. 68.—Extract.
Special Officers James A. McDevitt, George (sic) Holohan, and Louis J. Wiechmann are hereby ordered to New York on important Government business, and, after executing their private orders, to return to this city and report at these headquarters. The Quartermaster's Department will furnish the necessary transportation.
By command of Major-General Augur.
T. Ingraham,
Colonel and Provost-Marshal-General, Defenses
North of the Potomac.[21]

Ingraham's order specifies a journey to New York. A curious specification. Richards' intent was to trail John Surratt to Canada. And his detective party, Wiechmann and Holohan included, kept on going, straight to Montreal.

They reached Montreal on April 20. From the depot the party repaired to the St. Lawrence Hall, the city's leading hotel. There on the register they found the name "John Harrison"—enscribed on Tuesday, April 18. Mr. Harrison, it seemed, had just checked out. It was a close miss. Afterward, John Harrison Surratt declared that he had glimpsed Wiechmann on the street in Montreal. The frightened fugitive lost no time in burrowing under cover.[22]

On the evening of their arrival in Montreal, Detectives James McDevitt and D.R.P. Bigler sent a joint report to Police Superintendent Richards. Their letter informed Richards that they had conferred with the American consul on locale. It went on: "Three parties left here in a carriage last night, one of whom was registered at St. Lawrence Hall as 'John Harrison,' the alias of Surratt. We are convinced . . . that it is Surratt and two of his companions. . . . By taking steamer tomorrow, we shall be able to head

---

[21] *Ibid.*, p. 188.
[22] Clara E. Laughlin, *op. cit.*, pp. 244–45.

them off at Three Rivers. The Chief of Montreal Police accompanies two of our party."[23]

John Harrison Surratt was not headed off, as hoped, at Trois Rivieres. John Harrison Surratt disappeared.

Five days later, Major Richards dispatched Detective Officers Kelly and Harroe to Canada on special mission to bring back the first detective party and (most particularly) Louis J. Wiechmann. Something had soured in Washington.

In the files of the Bureau of Military Justice reposes a statement which was forwarded to the War Department by Detective Officer Kelly. An excerpt:

"I never for a moment hinted to Mr. Wiechmann that he was arrested and I would state that he did not wish to return to the United States until he found John H. Surratt, that he said he knew that from circumstances that he was going to be locked up when he returned, that he did not care what became of him, that he would make a full statement concerning these parties, and that he was disposed to suffer anything to assist the Government. That he stated to me that he could identify the handwriting of John H. Surratt.

"For the truth of the above statement I herewith pledge my sacred honor and word and I am willing to swear to it at any time."[24]

In light of the foregoing, it appears that a shadow of suspicion had fallen upon Louis J. Wiechmann. The cause may have been a letter written to War Secretary Stanton on Sunday, April 16, by Joseph N. Clarke, a clerk in the Adjutant General's Office:

I feel it my duty to make known to you that Lewis J. Weichmann (*sic*), clerk in Gen. Hoffman's office knows something of this "plot," if not one of the accomplices, he has expressed himself to a friend of mine in the last six weeks at different times, in words as follows; he knew a way of making a large sum of money, that Booth was one of the leaders, that it was something by which they would acquire fame, that it was the assassination of the President & C. I just now learned this from my friend.[25]

Admittedly a clerk in one branch of a Government Bureau might be suspicious of a counter-intelligence man in another branch. It is Wiechmann's statement to Officer Kelly, that he expected to be locked up, which wraps puzzle within enigma.

Upon his return to Washington City on April 29, Wiechmann was closeted for some time with Colonel H. L. Burnett of the Judge Advocate General's Office. The following morning he was seen at breakfast in an élite boardinghouse near the War Department. At his elbow sat Grant's son, 13-year-old Ulysses S., Jr.

---

[23] National Archives, War Dept. Records, File "B," Doc. 47, JAO.
[24] National Archives, War Dept. Records, File "K," Doc. 451, JAO.
[25] National Archives, War Dept. Records, File "C," Doc. 270, JAO.

That afternoon, Wiechmann had a long conference behind closed doors with War Secretary Stanton. At this meeting, Wiechmann protested that he had "done his whole duty to the Government."[26] Stanton advised him that he was to be held in custody for a time. Wiechmann was then committed to the care of Lafayette C. Baker and the Secret Service. Baker conducted him in a streetcar to Carroll Prison. There Wiechmann enjoyed the odd status of "witness."

Strange as was the War Secretary's treatment of Louis Wiechmann, it made sense compared with the treatment dealt Superintendent Richards of the Metropolitan Police. On April 24, Richards was summoned to Stanton's office. Perhaps this energetic policeman expected a pat on the back for his swift pursuit of Booth's chief accomplice. Instead, Richards found himself "on the carpet."

Stanton never preserved memos of such *in camera* meetings. But the substance of this one leaked when Richards was queried, an hour later, in General Augur's Headquarters and scolded for sending Wiechmann and Holohan to Canada on "a wild chase after Surratt." Reporting this incident to Colonel Burnett of the Judge Advocate's staff, Colonel Olcott noted: "Richards said he had been at the Secretary's office just before, and been severely reprimanded for sending the two men off. . . ."[27]

Nothing was said of Richards' loyalty, initiative, resourcefulness, determination and energy. Nor were the Metropolitan Police ever commended for their high-speed raid on the Surratt abode at 541 H Street—an effort which led to the capture of an assassin at that address. Perhaps the reason behind these checkreins and snubs had to do with the jealousy between Army and police—a jealousy spurred by the prospect of huge rewards. The Metropolitan Force had come close to winning the jackpot.

Saturday morning, April 15—bells tolling in sorrow at President Lincoln's death; the sky weeping—it must have been a gray dawn for Mary E. Surratt.

Police were at the house until 3:30 A.M. Her son was a fugitive. And now, after breakfast, her two best-paying boarders gone away. Mrs. Surratt found her private world dissolving around her. There would be no staying the dissolution.

Midmorning, the doorbell announced Mr. William W. Kirby, a neighbor who was an officer of the Criminal and Circuit Court. Another cheerless interview. More questions about her fugitive son.

As reported later by Mr. Kirby: "I talked with her [Mrs. Surratt] about John, and she only told me this. Said she: 'You are the only one I have ever told this to—John is in Canada.'" Kirby called again that Saturday evening. Mrs. Surratt repeated the statement about her son.

---

[26] Oldroyd, *op. cit.*, 189–190.
[27] Quoted in Eisenschiml, *op. cit.*, p. 198.

On Sunday the widow and the ladies of her household attended early services at St. Patrick's. Nowhere in America was this a happy Easter. But no home could have been unhappier than Mary Surratt's. Anna, Olivia Jenkins and Nora Fitzpatrick ventured out to evening vespers. Mrs. Surratt spent the day and evening in an increasingly dreary parlor, her thoughts behind drawn blinds.

Monday morning, Mr. Kirby was back:

> I talked with her at the door . . . and I told her that I would advise as a friend that, if she knew where John was, to let me or the authorities know. . . . Said I, "Of course, if he was away at the time he is innocent." She still told me he was in Canada.[28]

Time was running out for Mary E. Surratt. Having been marked by the Metropolitan Police, by the civil authorities, her house now came to the notice of the military. The Provost Marshal General could delay no longer.

At 11:00 P.M., Monday, April 17, General Augur ordered Colonel H. S. Olcott to mount the raid. Assigned to the mission were Major H. W. Smith, Captain W. M. Wermerskirch, and several detectives, including officer Rosch. At the house on H Street they were joined by Mr. R. C. Morgan, a special War Department investigator.

After posting the lookout, Smith, Wermerskirch and Morgan climbed the porch steps. Smith worked the bellpull. A woman appeared at a window. She called, "Is that you, Mr. Kirby?"

"No," Smith answered. "Are you the mother of John H. Surratt, Jr.?"

"I am."

The Major announced, "I come to arrest you and all your house, and take you for examination to General Augur's headquarters."[29]

Mrs. Surratt woke Anna, Nora and Olivia. Susan Jackson was roused. The officers waited patiently in the parlor while the ladies dressed and hastily packed some things. Outside, the men picketing the house stood in shadow, screened from view. Down the street a carriage stood ready.

Watching the housefront, Officer Rosch would never forget what next occurred. Footsteps sounded on the pavement . . . a shadowy figure approached. This pedestrian—he seemed to be a day laborer—peered at the porch numbers as he advanced. He paused before 541. Rosch would state in an official report: "At about 11:20 P.M. I saw [this] man with a Pickaxe over his shoulder go up the steps, knock, and ring at the door. I saw Captain Wermerskirch and Mr. Morgan let this person in."

Rosch followed. He'd been instructed to let any visitors pass. But that pickaxe troubled him. Inside the door, he found the officers questioning the workman. "I then entered the back parlor and assisted in searching for papers while Mr. Morgan continued to examine this person."[30]

---

[28] National Archives, War Dept. Records, File "K," R.B.P. 83, JAO.
[29] Dialogue quoted in Oldroyd, *op. cit.*, p. 62.
[30] National Archives, War Dept. Records, File "P," R.B.P. 74, JAO.

A remarkable-looking person, to say the least, he was tall, built like a young ox. His workman's clothes were ordinary enough. But he wore on his head what appeared to be at first glance a long stocking-cap, and at closer examination proved to be "the sleeve of a shirt or the leg of a drawers" pulled over his thick hair like a turban.[31]

Balancing the pickaxe, he had glowered at Wermerskirch in the entry. Asked his business, he said he'd come to see Mrs. Surratt. What about? She'd sent for him that morning, to dig a gutter.

"So you come to do the job at 11:30 at night?" Morgan demanded.

"No, to see what time I should begin tomorrow morning."

"Are you a friend of Mrs. Surratt's?"

"Well, I was workin' around the neighborhood. A poor man makin' his livin' with a pick. She offered me work."[32]

At this point Mrs. Surratt, Anna Surratt and Nora Fitzpatrick appeared on the scene. An extraordinary confrontation ensued. Asked if she knew the strange workman in the vestibule, the widow threw up her hands. "Before God, I have not seen that man before; I have not hired him; I don't know anything about him!"[33]

Mrs. Surratt subsequently testified that she thought the workman a "murderer" because her daughter, at sight of him, had begun to cry and had exclaimed that the man with the pickaxe had come to kill them.

By that time, of course, the intruder was relieved of the pickaxe. Cornered, he faced a battery of revolvers while the ladies were hustled out into the night. As the carriage-load of women started away, grim Mr. Morgan and Detective Officers Rosch, Sampson and Devoe set to work grilling the unexpected captive.

Back to wall he stood sullen, muttering. He told the officers he was twenty years old. He said he came from Fauquier County, Virginia. He pulled out an Oath of Allegiance and extended it to his inquisitors.

The certificate bore the name, "Lewis Paine."[34]

Detective Officers Rosch, Sampson and Devoe searched the sullen prisoner. They found on him, among numerous nondescript items, a packet of pistol cartridges and a pocket dictionary.

Why would a workman be carrying a pocket dictionary? Official reports do not give the answer. Nor is one offered by any of the numerous historical accounts of Paine's arrest. But a sharp detective like Rosch would have known that it might be a secret intelligence device, a tool of the trade. Spies often used "Noah Webster" for word-transference, for code translation. (All messages this week: Code 23. If you receive a letter containing underlined words, you count back 23 words in your dictionary. Thus "apple" becomes "apparatus," et cetera.)

---

[31] Oldroyd, *op. cit.*, p. 62.
[32] Dialogue based on Oldroyd, *op. cit.*, p. 62.
[33] *Ibid.*, p. 62.
[34] *Ibid.*, p. 65.

Detective Officer Rosch also gave the Surratt house a fine-tooth combing. Dutifully listed were the items of evidence delivered to Colonel Olcott at Augur's headquarters.

> Sword from the house of J. H. Surratt, 541 H Street.
> Suit of clothing worn by G. J. Hollahan (*sic*) found in the bedroom above the front parlor.
> Pair of boots worn by Weichmann (*sic*).
> Portrait of Lewis J. Weichmann (*sic*).
> Valise from the Surratt house containing sundry portraits, album, acct. books, papers, bullet mould & c. [35]
> And so forth and so on.

Cupboards, trunks, bureaus, handkerchief boxes, every receptacle and container—Rosch did not miss a personal belonging. The Holohan possessions, for instance. War Department files received this inventory:

> 2 pair Pants; 1 Dress Coat; 1 Linen Coat; 1 Knit Jacket; 3 Vests; 7 Shirts; 3 Ladies Dresses; 1 Skirt; 1 Plain Bound Testament; 1 pr. Skates; 1 pr. Ladies Gaiters (worn).[36]

Rosch, it would seem, cleaned out the entire house.

Out of these itemized jackstraws—in particular, the "valise"—the examiners fished some bits and pieces that demanded explanation by the Widow Surratt. Sword and bullet mould were, of course, suspicion-inviting items. So was a camera-portrait of John Wilkes Booth, found in Anna's room. So were several ambiguous letters.

One item found in the H Street house seems especially intriguing. It was not discovered until the following week, when the house was subjected to a second combing, this time by Captain Potts and Officer Newcombe. So far as is known, it was never presented as evidence against the Surratts. We discover it today as a minuscule and seemingly overlooked piece in the Surratt jigsaw puzzle.

The item was merely a scrap of notepaper, folded as though for a ballot. And on this scrap, in spidery handwriting:

> *Gen. Suratt, C.S.A. Present.*

We are reminded of Allan Pinkerton's story of the Baltimore Plot—"the eight red ballots?" And who, we wonder, was "General Suratt"?

But the big find in the house on H Street—the item of evidence most damaging to Mrs. Surratt—was the one delivered in person to General Augur's headquarters by Officers Rosch, Sampson and Devoe—*Lewis Paine.*

Statement of Mrs. Mary E. Surratt interrogated by Colonel H. S. Olcott (April 17, 1865):[37]

---

[35] National Archives, War Dept. Records, File "F," Doc. "Inventory of Property in Possession of Col. Olcott," JAO.
[36] National Archives, War Dept. Records, File "R," Doc. 432, JAO.
[37] National Archives, War Dept. Records, File "S," R.B.P. 79, JAO.

She says her youngest child is John, 21 years old, that she has not seen him since two weeks ago to-day, that is, since the 3d day of April, 1865. She further says:

My son sometime since made the acquaintance of J. Wilkes Booth; I could not say exactly when; he has been coming to our house about two months; sometimes he called twice a day; we found him very much of a gentleman . . . I did not hear him mention how he came to know him. My son is a country-bred young gentleman. I was not surprised that he should make the acquaintance of such a man as Mr. Booth because I consider him capable of forming acquaintants in the best society. I never thought a great deal of his forming Mr. Booth's acquaintance, because he called very frequently when my son was not there; he called upon the rest of us sometimes . . .

Q. What was the bond that brought your son and J. Wilkes Booth together?

A. I don't know, I am sure. . . .

Q. Has not this question occurred to you since the murder?

A. Yes, Sir; but I could not account for it, and I think no one could be more surprised than we were that he should be guilty of such an act. We often remarked that Mr. Booth was very clear of politics; he never mentioned anything of the kind, and it was a subject that we never indulged in.

Q. What are your political sentiments?

A. I don't pretend to express my feelings at all; I have often said that I thought that the South acted too hastily; that is about the amount of my feelings, and I say so again.

Q. Did your son say where he was going when he left you?

A. He did not; when he left he was a little vexed. The draft was being enforced in Maryland, and I told him to go to Mr. Ball, and pay in the fifty dollars for exemption. . . . On Wednesday evening I received a note from him . . . He did not tell me where he was going, but I think he was going to Canada because I heard him say he would leave the country. Last fall he spoke several times of going to Europe. . . . I have hunted my house over, but cannot find the letter he wrote me. When I read it, I felt very much vexed, and pitched it on the window-sill, and have not seen it since. . . . The evening he was at home I saw him have two twenty-dollar gold pieces; he said that he had had them in his pocket some time, and that he would get them exchanged . . . I supposed he exchanged [them] for the advantage of the exchange.

Q. If he expected to go to Canada, why should he sell that money and get its value in greenbacks?

A. He might have wanted it for other uses.

Q. No man on the round earth believes he went to Canada.

A. I believe it.

Q. No one can believe it; they would just as soon believe that a bird could fly if we cut off his wings. If . . . he wanted to travel round the United States, he would use greenbacks; if, on the other hand, he wanted to go South, as he did, and as he had been and back before—

A. He has never been away long enough to go South and back.

Q. How long does it take to go across the [Potomac] River?

A. I don't know the width of the River.

Q. You certainly could go to Fredericksburg and back in four days, to

Richmond and back in a week, and your son had been passing a great many times for a great while longer than that.

A. I don't think he has.

Q. Oh yes, he has. Have I made any error in my record so far as his movements are concerned?

A. No, Sir; that is all correct.

Q. Don't you know of his making the acquaintance of a Mr. Atzerodt?

A. There was a man came to my house from Port Tobacco, looking for board. . . . I found him rather a rough-looking man.

Q. Did he stoop a little?

A. I think he was a little round-shouldered. He was a German, I think. The name he gave was "Port Tobacco." He remained only part of a week, when I found some liquor in his room; no gentleman can board with me who keeps liquor in his rooms, and I told my son that that man could not stay.

Q. What sort of a looking person was he? What colored hair had he?

A. That I don't remember; to the best of my knowledge, he had rather a bushy head.

Q. He used slang words?

A. Not at the table; the only time I ever met the man in the parlor was when I saw him to let him know whether he could board there.

Q. Did you ever see him on horseback?

A. I don't remember.

Q. I want to know if there is another young gentleman who was at your house?

A. Yes Sir; there was a man who staid (*sic*) there for two nights and a day looking for board.

Q. What was the name of the other young man?

A. I think his name was Wood. There were some two or three, one was light complected, who staid about a week.

Q. What was his name?

A. Indeed, I don't remember it.

Q. There was a young gentleman who used to meet your son, whose mother lives over the Navy Yard Bridge, David or Daniel Harold?

A. No such man ever visited my house, I assure you.

[Photograph of J. Wilkes Booth shown to witness]

A. That's Mr. Booth, ain't it?

[Photograph of Harold shown to witness]

A. I don't know that man.

Q. He is a very intimate friend of your son's.

A. Well, Sir; I assure you he is not a visitor to our house, on the honor of a lady.

Q. Speaking of visiting at your house, I will bring the thing down a little nearer. I will be happy to have you give me the names of three men who came to you on Saturday and had a private conversation with you.

A. Last Saturday?

Q. Yes, Madam.

A. No three gentlemen came to my house, I assure you.

Q. How many did come?

A. You mean the gentlemen who came in to search the house?

Q. No; you know who I mean. . . . I mean the three men who came to your house and you had a private conversation with them, and supposed you were alone, but you were not?

A. Last Saturday?

Q. Perhaps Friday. Now, I do not want to occupy your time specially, and I want you to tell me.

A. Upon my word, that I do not know; upon the honor of a lady, I do not remember anybody except Mr. Wicket. [Wiechmann?][38]

Q. I can tell you what you said.

A. Perhaps I can remember, then.

Q. I can tell you what they wanted at your house, too.

A. Well, Sir; if you will please to tell me, if I remember it I will tell you.

Q. You cannot remember anything about it?

A. I don't remember indeed.

Q. There were three men, though.

A. No, I don't think, to my knowledge, if it was the last word I had to say that on Saturday anybody except Mr. Wicket, [Wiechmann?] unless Mr. Wallace Kirby, was there.

Q. Do you make a distinction between day and evening?

A. No, Sir; it is all the same to me.

Q. Or the night?

A. I call it all one.

Q. I don't know but I have misunderstood you. Do you say to me that no two or three or four men ever came to your house the last three or four days—on Friday, or Saturday or Sunday?

A. On Sunday I think three or four men came there while I was at church. I assure you on the honor of a lady that I would not tell you an untruth.

Q. I assure you, on the honor of a gentleman, I shall get this information from you.

A. Whatever it is, I shall tell you.

Q. Now, I know they were there.

A. Well, Sir; if you do, I do not.

Q. I mean men who called at your house and wanted to change their clothes.

A. Mr. Wickman and Mr. Holohan and one of the detectives came there; that might have been Sunday morning; they came in a carriage; that was, I think, on Sunday morning. Mr. Wickman went to his room and changed his clothes.

Q. What time Sunday morning?

A. I think about ten o'clock.

Q. Where were you?

A. I was sitting in the parlor with Mr. Wallace Kirby.

Q. I think you said you were at church.

A. I went out before that; they went up in Mr. Wickman's room.

Q. What did you say to them?

A. Nothing except to say good morning something of the kind.

Q. Will you tell me, in the presence of Almighty God, who first mentioned the name of Mr. Booth in that party?

A. I don't remember.

Q. Indeed you do; I pledge you my word you do. And you will admit it, and I should be very glad if you would do it at once.

---

[38] Possible error in transcript.

A. If I could, I would do it at once.

Q. Reflect a moment, and I will send for a glass of water for you.

[Glass of water brought for witness]

Such little kindnesses as a glass of water are supposed to, and often do, disarm a person under interrogation. But Mrs. Surratt did not break down. Harangue as he would, Olcott could not wring from her an admission concerning the three visitors he had in mind. Possibly those visitors never existed. But one midnight visitor did exist. Inexorably Mrs. Surratt's questioner led the interrogation to this dangerous man.

Q. Did you meet this young man arrested this evening within two or three days and make an arrangement with him to come to your house this evening?

A. No, Sir; the ruffian that was in my door when I came away? He was a tremendous hard fellow with a skull-cap on, and my daughter commenced crying, and said those gentlemen [the officers] came to save our lives. I hope they arrested him.

Q. Did you have any arrangement made with such a person as that to do anything about your premises?

A. I assure you I did not.

Q. He tells me now that he met you in the street and you engaged him to come to your house.

A. Oh! Oh! it is not so, Sir; for I believe he would have murdered us, everyone, I assure you.

Q. Did he have anything in his hand?

A. He had some kind of a weapon.

Q. When did you see him first?

A. Just as the carriage drew up; he rang the door bell, and my daughter said: "Oh! there is a murderer."

[End of interrogation]

The foregoing question-and-answer exchange stands as an exemplary illustration of 1865 police interrogation technique. It also provides a vivid portraiture of Mrs. Mary E. Surratt. One can visualize her sitting in Olcott's office, her mien determinedly calm, her pose as rigid as a dress form.

She seems to speak up smartly and with a considerable show of spirit, considering the circumstances. A pity she did not adhere strictly to the truth, for in effort to shield her son she weakens her own case with statements manifestly implausible.

Mrs. Surratt slips badly in covering Booth's outspokenly subversive sentiments with her declaration that she and her family never heard him mention politics.

She slips again in stating that John Surratt had never been away from home long enough "to go South and back."

Her denial of knowing David Herold does not conform with Wiechmann's memory of meeting Herold at Surratt's tavern in 1863 and evidence that the drugstore clerk had visited the H Street house.

Finally, her denial of knowing Paine when he came to her house as a laborer leaves the gravest doubt as to her veracity. Defense would make much of the widow's nearsightedness. She did not have her glasses; the hour was late, the light dim. She was distracted. And Paine wore that freakish headgear. (A modern playwright makes this the focal point of a drama portraying Mrs. Surratt as innocent.[39]) But Mrs. Surratt's contemporary and modern defenders missed a glaring flaw in this matter.

Poor vision the widow undoubtedly possessed. But her instantaneous denouncement of the man—poor eyesight notwithstanding, she sees him at once as a stranger and a "murderer"—rings false. And she had heard Paine's voice in her parlor on numerous occasions. (She had, according to testimony, recently called on him at the Herndon House.) But Mrs. Surratt's eyesight and perceptions are beside the point. For Anna Surratt and Nora Fitzpatrick were well acquainted with the caller. As the "Reverend Paine" he had joined them at euchre, had turned the music for Annie at the piano, had escorted Nora to the theater. *And Annie and Nora were there at Mrs. Surratt's elbow when she confronted the unexpected visitor that night!*

It would seem that in Mrs. Surratt's panicky outburst (or in her daughter's outburst) the panic was genuine. In all likelihood, Paine was recognized. And in that flash the first word that came to mind was "murderer." What other verification needed for an immediate recognition of Lewis Paine?

Beetle-browed, sullen, defiant, Lewis Paine faced his inquisitors at General Augur's headquarters. Stubbornly he stuck to his "ditch-digger" story. When he saw no one believed him, he shut his teeth and refused to talk. The police brought in little William Bell. Seward's houseboy immediately identified the Spartan captive.

Then the Government shut its teeth on the prisoner. Not many hours after his arrest, Paine was locked in double shackles and cast into "solitary" on board Navy monitor *Saugus*. There he was placed in the special custody of Major Thomas T. Eckert—the officer who could break iron pokers over his arm. It did not take long for this muscular interrogator to break the iron in Lewis Paine.

The War Department soon announced to the world that the Army had captured Seward's assassin.

Immediately following their arrest and preliminary examination, Mrs. Surratt and daughter Anna were jailed in the Carroll Annex of the Old Capitol Prison. They were booked in the prison register:

---

[39] John Patrick, *The Story of Mary Surratt.*

Mrs. Mary Surratt—boardinghouse keeper. Native of Washington. Held for the order of Colonel Foster's Investigating Committee. Anna Surratt—Washington.

Mother and daughter were lodged in the same cell, a concession to housing shortage rather than sentiment on the part of their captors. Ever since the launching of Stanton's anti-subversive drive, cell space in Washington had been at a premium. The dungeons under the Winder Building, the military guardhouses, the Arsenal Penitentiary out on T Street, S.E., and the Old Capitol with its Annex were crowded chock-a-block.

The Old Capitol housed a menagerie of odd suspects. On the roster could be found such prisoners-of-war as General Edward ("Old Allegheny") Johnson of the Stonewall Brigade, spies of the caliber of Augustus (Spencer) Howell, deserters and bounty-jumpers, contraband-smugglers, and persons accused of "disloyal utterance."

As contemporary prisons went, the Old Capitol was not the worst. Many of the prisoners were allowed to mingle in the main detention rooms. Inmates came and went as though at Government whim. Some never knew why they were arrested. Others never knew why they were released. Groups were continuously brought in by the Federal dragnet. As newcomers entered the prison yard the old-timers would shout. "Fresh fish! Fresh fish!"

Sauntering about like an amiable zoo-keeper, plump Warden William P. Wood would address the prisoners with a crude geniality that some found more offensive than hostile bluster. Of a Sunday morning he would make the rounds bellowing, "All you who want to hear the gospel accordin' to Jeff Davis, go down to the Yard. Those who want to hear the Lord God Almighty accordin' to Abe Lincoln, go to Room 16." Or so the story was told.

Conveniently forgetting such purgatories as Richmond's Libby Prison and Castle Thunder, Southern writers would paint the Old Capitol as approximating Dante's Inferno, and Mrs. Surratt's impoundment there as a stark example of Yankee inhumanity to woman. And one modern writer, Helen Jones Campbell, would dwell on the miseries of Mrs. Surratt's dirty cell, the rude cots with straw-tick bedding, the dilapidated chair and table and washbasin, the repulsive food served in greasy tins. Of course, many a present-day jailhouse lacks Kohler and Kohler plumbing and a Savarin cuisine. One is surprised to find on Mrs. Surratt's menu a dab of brown sugar, a cup of milk and a pat of butter, even though author Campbell tells us the butter was "melting."[40]

However, the Old Capitol was not the National Hotel. And after Lincoln's assassination there came an abrupt cessation of jailhouse levity. Through the barred windows Mrs. Surratt and Anna could hear angry shouting from the street as onlookers threatened the prisoners marching

[40] Helen Jones Campbell, *op. cit.*, pp. 30–31.

in. At night the corridors echoed to oaths and sobbing and the clank of leg-chains. No doubt the two women were beset with misery and apprehension. Detectives peered in at them. Federal Army officers paused at the cell door to stare. Then came the intensive interrogations.

Colonel Foster questioned Mrs. Surratt. Colonel Olcott examined her, firing questions. Warden Wood questioned her. Anna had to face a grilling. Over and over again the officers asked them about John Surratt's whereabouts. Neither could say with certainty for the simple reason that they did not know.

One straw Mrs. Surratt probably grasped at—Warden Wood was acquainted with her brother, John Zaddoc Jenkins. Unhappily this acquaintanceship proved little help. Wood interviewed "Zad" Jenkins at Surrattsville at the time of innkeeper Lloyd's arrest. Mrs. Surratt's brother flew into a dazzling fury when he heard her named as a suspect. Eventually neighbors testified that he cursed the Government and threatened potential witnesses. Fiery "Zad" was a liability under the circumstances.

So Mrs. Surratt did suffer ordeal. And it was no relief to have Nora Fitzpatrick brought in to share the cell. Nora told Mrs. Surratt and Anna that the house on H Street swarmed with police and that the city was full of terrifying rumors.

These three were not the only women in the prison. In the cell directly below Mrs. Surratt's, Virginia Lomax lay ill. Miss Lomax had been in prison as a suspected subversive since February, 1863. In her diary she wrote of hearing "Mrs. Surratt's little feet walking up and down, up and down all through the night."[41]

For Mrs. Surratt the ordeal was only beginning.

April 17, 1865, was a red-letter day for the man-hunters. True, Lincoln's assassin and his companion were still at large. So was Booth's chief accomplice, John H. Surratt. But the list of major arrests for that one day remained impressive.

> *Mrs. Mary E. Surratt*
> *Lewis Paine*
> *Michael O'Laughlin*
> *Samuel B. Arnold*
> *Edward Spangler*

And that other who seemed of major importance:

> *B. F. Ficklin*

But mysterious Benjamin Ficklin did not stay on the list. Not long after his arrest the word arrived from somewhere to detain him further but under cover.

---

[41] Elizabeth Lindsay Lomax, *Leaves From an Old Washington Diary* (New York: E. P. Dutton & Co., Inc., 1943), p. 232.

Mr. Ficklin was so detained. Finally, on May 25th, the authorities received a letter from ex-Senator Orville Browning.

Declaring himself "thoroughly satisfied that Mr. Ficklin had no knowledge or participation in the atrocious act and entertaining ... the strongest possible conviction of his innocence," the Senator "prayed" for Ficklin's discharge. The Senator confided that "a lady in whom the President felt a very deep interest" went from Lexington, Kentucky, to Richmond "late in February." The letter continues: "She left Richmond under circumstances of some urgency, and left behind papers which she regarded of very great importance to her, upon an understanding and arrangement with a friend that they should be sent to Washington for her by some safe and trusty agent. Mr. Ficklin came to bring these papers ... to me, and I transmitted them to the lady to whom they belonged, she having left the City before Mr. Ficklin's arrival. I retained copies of them all which I am entirely willing to submit to Mr. Secretary Stanton at any time if he shall desire to see them."

The papers, it seemed, had something to do with a "cotton deal."[42] So wrote Senator Browning.

This B. F. Ficklin apparently engaged in sizable deals. The war Department records contain no note of it, but a few months before Mr. Ficklin's arrest in Washington, the *National Intelligencer* had published the following item:

> SALE OF MONTICELLO: Monticello, the former residence of Thomas Jefferson, in Albemarle County, Virginia, was sold at auction on Thursday under the sequestration act, for $80,500. Benjamin F. Ficklin, purchaser.

The files of the Judge Advocate's Office contain a final reference to Ficklin. On June 12, 1865, Major O'Beirne sent Ficklin's dossier to War Department headquarters with a memo describing Ficklin as one of the "loudest talking sessionists" in Washington before the war. The memo concludes: "He was obliged to leave Montgomery, Ala., on account of killing a man there . . . what disposition shall be made of him?"[43]

Available War Department records do not disclose the disposition made. But there is on record an illicit $7,000,000 cotton deal involving General James Singleton and Mrs. Lincoln's sister, Mrs. Helm, the widow of a Confederate general. It seems that Mrs. Helm had appealed to the President (through Mary Lincoln), begging the salvage of a few thousand dollars' worth of cotton which had belonged to the Helms and was in storage in beleagured Richmond. Kindly Lincoln had dispatched General Singleton to the Richmond front with a "pass" for the captured cotton. Wherewith Singleton had tried to move through Grant's lines a wagon train carrying a $7,000,000 load of cotton.

---

42 National Archives, War Dept. Records, File "B," Doc. 685, JAO.
43 National Archives, War Dept. Records, File "O," R.B.P. 67, JAO.

Advised by Grant, Lincoln realized that he had been misled, and he took steps to squelch the graft. Singleton was recalled to Washington, and the massive cotton transport was stopped. Unfortunately the business exuded a smell that threatened trouble for the White House just before the President's assassination. In the night of appalling national tragedy the shady cotton transaction was lost from view.

But could agent Ficklin have been engaged in some additional criminality? We shall hear of another Rebel secret agent visiting Washington on a "cotton deal." Loreta Velasquez, too, was in the city about that time. Thrown in haste and as hastily pulled in, the Federal dragnet missed these people.

CHAPTER 14

Atzerodt Is Arrested

ALMOST every development of the Lincoln murder case unlatched a Pandora's box of fantasy. No fiction formula would permit such unbelievable improbabilities of coincidence. What, for example, could be more fantastically improbable than the entry of George Atzerodt's brother John in the role of a Baltimore police detective on the force of Provost Marshal McPhail?

John Atzerodt entered the case by accident. Had he not been in lower Maryland at that particular time on a particular mission, he might never have been a party to—and perhaps the principal agency of—his brother's downfall.

Undoubtedly John Atzerodt would eventually have been questioned about Brother George, for the surname was on all police circulars by Sunday, April 16; and since it was not so common as Brown or Jones, it would surely have come to embarrass the law-abiding Baltimore relatives. But the chances are that Police Detective John would have been queried quietly by Marshal McPhail behind closed doors in the Provost's Baltimore office. As a trusted lawman, John Atzerodt would have been given the benefit of privacy and friendly counsel.

Had he been in Baltimore, instead of by chance in lower Maryland, John Atzerodt might have told the authorities little. Indeed, he would have had little to tell. For he had long been separated from his errant younger brother, and had received scant news of him. Baltimore was a long way from Port Tobacco, and George Atzerodt had gone underground. . Had fate been less capricious, then, John Atzerodt would have bowed out of the case as a mere bystander, and George A. Atzerodt might have gone un-hanged. The Army had no inkling as to his whereabouts on Sunday, April 16, and Monday, April 17, 1865. It was not until late Tuesday, April 18 (or early Wednesday, April 19) that the Federal authorities obtained a clue to his trail. Without that clue, he might have remained in hibernation until the worst was over, as did Mrs. Surratt's son. But someone tipped off the authorities. Evidence indicates that the tip came from John Atzerodt.

Improbable coincidence had sent the Baltimore brother on special detail to Point Lookout, Maryland, earlier that month. McPhail had been advised that Confederate blockade runners were operating on this remote beachhead of the Maryland peninsula. The Baltimore Provost Marshal could have ordered any of ten detectives to investigate the region. Luck insisted that he send Detective John Atzerodt.

The shortest road down to Point Lookout was the one through Surrattsville, Teebee, Bryantown, Leonardtown. Some days before the assassination John Atzerodt found himself traveling this road. At the Surrattsville stage stop he put in at Lloyd's tavern. There he encountered his brother. With George Atzerodt were a handsome fellow named John Surratt and an oddish young chap introduced as Davy Herold.

Detective Atzerodt did not cater to his brother's chums, and he was acquainted with the tavern's dubious reputation, for he had been down to Port Tobacco and over around Charlotte Hall on a previous mission in January. His brother acted suspiciously, there at Surrattsville.

John Atzerodt continued on to Point Lookout. He was at St. Inigoes when news of the assassination shattered the doldrums of that April weekend. In this clamshell village at the mouth of the Potomac, anyone named Atzerodt was bound to leap from anonymity to notoriety overnight. Or, at least, as soon as the name came by message to the St. Inigoes naval station.

Records fail to relate just when or how John Atzerodt was advised of the calamitous involvement dealt him by his brother; but on Tuesday, April 18, Detective Atzerodt was under Federal arrest, policeman's papers and loyalty oath notwithstanding.

Again, the records are unclear, but it seems he was held at Chapel Point by the forces operating under Major O'Beirne. . . .

Statement of John C. Atzerodt (April 18, 1865):

> I live in Baltimore, 91 Sharpe Street. I am with Mr. McPhail, and I am down in this part of the country on duty for Mr. McPhail. . . . We were after blockade runners.

I have a brother by the name of George A. Atzerodt. He goes by the name of Andrew. He . . . looks sickly. Is inclined to be consumptive. Has had a cough for several years. Is sallow—not pale, but yellowish. . . .

I met him at Surratt's [Inn], I think about ten miles from here on the Teepee Road. I merely asked him how he was and what he was doing, and he said he was not doing any business in particular. . . .

I [have] heard my sisters say that he had made boasts as to what he was going to do. We would either hear of his being hung or making a good deal of money—a fortune or something like that. He did not state with reference to what it was.

Surratt was there [at the inn]. . . . My brother has always been suspecting me. He took Surratt one side. Surratt went and got into his buggy and drove off. . . . A young man by the name of Herold was there also. . . . [My] brother he had on a brownish speckled coat and pants, also a slack coat. I forget whether it was split up behind; it had flaps on the pockets, a very nice, genteel coat, made at Port Tobacco. . . .

I understood my sister to say that he had a very nice overcoat on in Baltimore—she said a long grey overcoat. . . . He smoked a short briarwood pipe. I do not think there was a silver plug in the bottom of the bowl. I never knew of his having on a black coat . . . while I was down to Port Tobacco he generally wore a pair of buckskin gauntlets. He had a black slouch hat—a pair of cavalry boots with enameled leather, stitched with white. He wore number 7's. . . .

My brother is 29—speaks with a little German accent; carries his head on one side in walking, and one shoulder higher than the other. . . .

I saw him at Port Tobacco two weeks after Christmas; he was riding around with a tall man with black wiskers.[1]

So the Government was presented with a family portrait of George Andrew Atzerodt, complete with canted head, lopsided shoulder, buckskin gauntlets and enameled cavalry boots with white stitching—obviously the Civil War predecessor of the modern motocycle hoodlum with the brass-studded belt, black leather jacket and cap-badge labeled "Wildcat."

The older brother went on to state that "Andy" had never visited his (John's) family in Baltimore, and that Andy's subversive activities were unknown to his respectable relatives. John Atzerodt allowed that he had seen Booth once—he was not sure where—and he offered information on some of Andy's Port Tobacco cronies.

So John Atzerodt talked. Outraged, alarmed by his own arrest, and infuriated at the brother responsible for this hornet's nest of trouble, he must have readily enlarged upon his formal statement. Certainly the troopers asked him where he thought his brother *might* have gone. Surely he supplied the inquisitors with a number of suggestions. He could not have failed to mention the relatives in Montgomery County. He must have made some mention of Rockville and Cousin Richter.

This much is on record. On the day that John Atzerodt was arrested, an urgent dispatch went from Army Headquarters, Washington, to the

---

[1] National Archives, War Dept. Records, File "A," Doc. 541, JAO.

cavalry command at Darnestown Montgomery County, Maryland. Under official heading, the dispatch read:

April 18, 1865

Colonel J. L. Thompson
  Commanding, Darnestown, Md.

Have all canal boats searched at Seneca and at the mouth of the Monocacy, and arrest suspicious persons and such as cannot give a good account of themselves.

By command of Major General Augur
A. R. Sewall
Lieutenant and Acting Assistant Adjutant General[2]

Point of interest: Seneca and the mouth of the Monocacy are only a few miles to the west of Rockville. Of course, Augur may have had only Mosby in mind when he sent the above directive. The Confederate leader was still at large in the area, and strenuous efforts were being made to bag him. However, a War Department dispatch, issued on the morning of the 19th, tells the story without question. Here the point is unequivocal.

War Department, Washington City, April 19, 1865
(Sent 10:45 A.M.)

Major General Hancock, Winchester

There is evidence that Mosby knew of Booth's plan, and was here in the city with him; also that some of the gang are endeavoring to escape by crossing the upper Potomac to get with Mosby or the secesh there. Atzerodt, or Port Tobacco, as he is called, is known to have gone to Rockville Saturday to escape in that direction.

Edwin M. Stanton
Secretary of War[3]

The Mosby reference stemmed from excited rumor. But Stanton had the word on the escape route taken by conspirator Atzerodt.

In vain one may search popular histories of the case for mention of John Atzerodt, the older brother. Contemporary news columns do not contain his name. Federal Army and Secret Service accounts conspicuously "edited out" the brother from Baltimore. War Department censorship thus left the American public with the impression that smart sleuthing by the Army trailed and trapped George Andrew Atzerodt.

But it seems a safe assumption the Officer of the Guard at Tennellytown did not provide Stanton with advice on the fugitive's journey to Rockville. Thompson's Darnestown cavalry did not come across the spoor. The clue could only have emanated from lower Maryland. As witness a final military dispatch.

---

[2] *Official Records*, Series I, Vol. 46, Part 3.
[3] *Ibid.*

Leonardtown, Md., April 20, 1865
(Received 9:20 A.M.)

Brevet-Colonel J. H. Taylor, Chief of Staff

Just reached here with one company; the other three took different roads from the vicinity of Port Tobacco. . . . Major O'Beirne thinks Montgomery County should be searched for George A. Atzerodt. . . .

Jno. M. Waite
Major &c.[4]

Major O'Beirne was at that time operating in the Bryantown-Port Tobacco area. And the one person in that backwoods region who could have informed the Army on the probable Montgomery County haunts of George A. Atzerodt was his older brother.

Sergeant Gemmill, Company D, First Delaware, was stationed with his company at Monocacy Junction, a siding on the B. & O. about three miles south of Frederick, Maryland. The scenery was all right, if you liked scenery; Whittier called this country "fair as the garden of the Lord."

Sergeant Gemmill may or may not have heard of Whittier's poem, but he had been rooting around the countryside, had learned the names of various farmers in the region, and had acquainted himself with the topography—the Barnesville district, for instance, and down around Germantown.

So Sergeant Gemmill was ready for what happened on Wednesday evening, April 19, 1865, when he received a sudden summons from the company commander to take a detail down toward Germantown and pick up a man.

Statement of Sergeant L. C. Gemmill, Company D, First Delaware Regiment, Monocacy Junction (April 21, 1865):

I was detailed on the 19th between 8 and 9 o'clock, and left camp at 10 o'clock to search for Atzerodt. I proceeded to the house of a gentleman named Burton [Purdon] who gave me a description of Atzerodt, and something he had heard him say. He [Atzerodt] was dining at Mr. Mett's [Metz's] and the conversation turning upon the assassination, he stopped eating and said that if all had done their duty who were concerned in it, they would have got General Grant.

I could get no evidence around there to prove that he did say that. Mr. Burton is near the same place—about four miles from where I arrested Atzerodt. Mr. Burton is a good loyal man. He told me the man said that, and it was on the strength of that that I had him arrested.

Mr. Metts is pronounced a loyal man, and Mr. Burton said it was said at Metts' house on Sunday at Dinner, though Burton was not present. He did not tell me how he heard it. I was so certain of catching the man, I did not ask him any questions.

---

[4] *Ibid.*

George A. Atzerodt had violated two imperatives of conspiracy: don't have an older brother on the police force, and don't talk. One of the more garrulous of Booth's gabby henchmen, he had sealed his doom at Metz's dining table.

Even so, there'd been plenty of time to get away. For that was Sunday, and this was Wednesday, and nobody would have stopped him. Instead he hung around Cousin Richter's and got drunk. He went to bed early Wednesday night, sodden.

Luck dealt Atzerodt a last chance. Plugging through the starry dark, Sergeant Gemmill missed the road to Germantown. But Atzerodt snored the night away, and at cockcrow the game was up.

> I got lost, [Sergeant Gemmill reported] and did not get there [to Germantown] before daylight. Did not know a reward was offered then.
> I went to the house of a man named Ricker, I think, and asked him if there was a man there named Lockwood.

Either Gemmill had trouble with names, or the company clerk who transcribed his deposition spelled them phonetically—and so misspelled them. The names in question were Richter and Atwood.

At Richter's door, the blue-coated sergeant found himself facing a sullen householder. Gemmill's report continues:

> I had two men with me at the time. I understood him [Richter] to say that the [Atzerodt, or Atwood] was his cousin, but had left and gone to Frederick. One of my men understood the same, but the other did not.
> I then told him I would search the house. He then said there was a man in the house. He commenced telling me a yarn, and I was suspicious of him. I then searched the house and went up to his [bed]room.[5]

One can picture a dim stairway with a door at the top. The soldier drawing his pistol and going quietly up. He pauses for a cautious second or two to listen, ear to panel, then softly opens the door. He is assailed at once by stale air—countryfolk seldom opened their windows in those days—and the bedroom exhales a breath heavy with the smell of sour quilting and bodies asleep.

Gemmill, his nose wrinkled, peers for a moment blindly. Then, in the dimness under the eaves, a bed takes outline. A washstand comes into focus. A chair. Men's garments are strewn around like soiled laundry—undershirts, pants with suspenders dangling, cow boots. Concentrating on the bed, the sergeant makes out three figures under the blankets. Two of the sleepers rouse and scramble out of bed as the soldier walks in. The third grunts and turns over.

Gemmill has anticipated dealing with one customer, not three. The unexpected bedfellows are a sorry pair, and the man in bed is a nuisance. Any Army non-com with a week's experience can tell when a lug is playing possum.

---

[5] National Archives, War Dept. Records, File "G," Doc. 312, JAO.

The arrest episode is tersely abbreviated in Sergeant Gemmill's report. As worded in the official transcript:

> There were three men in one bed—two of them young men by the name of Nichols, living in the neighborhood, who did not explain how they came there; but as my orders were to arrest Atzerodt alone, I did not arrest them.
>
> When the door opened two of them awoke. He [Atzerodt] did not awake —or at least pretended not to—till I went up to the bed. I asked him his name. He gave me a name which I thought was "Atwood," but I heard it indistinctly as he spoke with German accent.
>
> Mr. Burton gave me a description of him so I knew him. I did not tell him I was going to arrest him, but told him to get up and dress himself. He said nothing, but did as I told him. . . .

Again we can visualize the scene. Frowzy Atzerodt groping for his blouse and blundering into his pants, while the Nichols brothers gawk in a corner and the Sergeant leans in the doorway, casually alert with his gun.

The captive is slow in dressing. He keeps his eyes averted, as though embarrassed at being under observation. The buttons puzzle his fingers. He gets his suspenders criss-crossed, and must patiently slip out of them, un-cross them, and shoulder into them again. Sweat gleams on his forehead as he draws on his boots. Were they the enameled ones, the cowboy numbers with the fancy white stitching? This morning they don't seem to fit.

But it's never easy to put on boots that may walk you to a prison cell. Nor is it easy to find your coat, your neckerchief, your tobacco pouch and loose change and the other possessions which go with you and your apparel. But at last the slugabed was ready.

> I did not iron him [Gemmill's report continues] as I had no irons with me. I went with him up to Mr. Lemons', another loyal man in that section. He went along with me willingly.

The mailbox, here, was labeled "Leamon," not "Lemon." This was either James or Somerset Leamon, one of the brothers who had dined with Atzerodt at Hezekiah Metz's the previous Sunday.

> When we got there a gentleman put his head out of the window. . . . I asked him if he knew a man by the name of Atwood and he said yes—it appears that he went by that name in that section of the country. . . . I then brought the man [Atzerodt] to the door and [had him identified].
>
> He shook hands with Mr. Lemon, but I noticed he held his head down, and I began to suspect him more than ever.
>
> I then sent him back in charge of the two men, and went back to the house where I got him and arrested his Cousin, and left the house surrounded by a guard while I took him away. I asked him [Atzerodt] if he had anything at the house he would like to get, and he said no, only some tobacco and some collars. I brought them down for him at his request.

I told his cousin to get ready as I wanted him to go with me. He said he did not want to go—that he did not know what he was arrested for.

It is possible that Hartman Richter did not know why he was arrested, but not entirely probable. He must have suspected that his cousin from Port Tobacco had been up to something more than painting carriages. Moreover, he had tried to shield Cousin George.

However, Richter's summary arrest offers another picture of what can happen when the military step in to impose the law. A knock at the door, a few gruff questions, and the soldiers whisk you away. But Sergeant Gemmill was by no means so high-handed as some. At least, he went back to fetch Atzerodt's tobacco and celluloid collars.

Atzerodt never asked me a question in relation to his arrest, although he was in my custody several hours . . . did not keep his head down after we left Mr. Lemon's, but was as lively as ever. One of the men told me that Atzerodt told him he had been in the Rebel army for three years. I found upon inquiring around the country that it was not so. He painted carriages.

I then took him to Headquarters. He was there examined by Major Artmer. He said in the examination that he stayed in the Pennsylvania House while in Washington. Do not know that he said he knew Booth— I was not there during the whole of the examination. . . .[6]

By the end of that examination, Atzerodt must have been in need of a fresh collar. If the one around his neck chafed like raw hemp, its discomfort was merely suggestive of what lay in store.

As soon as Atzerodt talked to Major Artmer the authorities set out to round up everyone in the section who had so much as offered "Atwood" the time of day. Some of these subjects came in as arrested suspects. Others were corralled as Government witnesses. The list included:

Caldwell, who purchased Atzerodt's gun in Georgetown.

The Metzes.

The brothers Leamon.

The Nichols boys.

Mr. Burton (who proved to be Mr. Purdon).

Francis Kerns, driver of the Rockville stage.

The Army went scouting to locate a certain Hopkins—no record stating why.

And, of course, William Gaither, the man who had given Atzerodt a lift from the "Forts" to Rockville, was placed under arrest. Gaither was not placed on the witness stand during the subsequent conspiracy trials, however, nor was Atzerodt's breezy escape through the Rockville road-block introduced in the evidence.[7]

---

[6] *Ibid.*

[7] The vacuum is obvious in Pitman's official Trial report.

Atzerodt was not held long at Monocacy Junction. Washington wanted him posthaste. Curiously enough, the Army did not take him under cavalry guard by the short, direct road via Rockville to the capital. Instead, he was shipped by rail eastward to Relay under escort of Major General E. B. Tyler, U.S.A. From this switchyard on the outskirts of Baltimore he went down to the War Department by stagecoach.

The roundabout route, a typical police maneuver, probably represented cloak-and-dagger security. Stanton's excessive fear of Mosby, expressed in numerous directives, doubtless led the Army to extremes of caution. Having bagged this game, the soldiers were not disposed to lose the prize by ambush in Montgomery County.

The Baltimore-Washington post road presented Atzerodt's captors with no problem. Transferred at Relay to the charge of Marshal Robert Murray, the prisoner had no chance of escape. Murray, a tough New Yorker, saw to that, as his official report on Atzerodt clearly shows.

Statement of Robert Murray, Marshal, U.S., for the Southern District of New York:

On the night that Atzerod (*sic*) arrived at the Depot from the Relay House in charge of Genl. E. B. Tyler, I met them there in Company with Col. Ingraham. I found the prisoner Atzerod handcuffed. Genl. Tyler ordered his handcuffs taken off, and I put a pair of our handcuffs on him myself. I happened to pinch Atzerodt in putting the iron in his left hand; and he snapped at me saying "Don't pinch me." I told him I would pinch his neck before he was a week older.

We then got him into one of Willard's Stages with a sufficient guard of Soldiers. I took a seat alongside of Atzerod. After we had proceeded a little ways I enquired of Atzerod where he had slept on Friday, the night of the assassination. He replied at the Pa. House. I then inquired what time did you retire to bed that night? He said between ten and eleven. I enquired of him what time he got up in the morning, he replied at five o'clock. I inquired if five o'clock was his usual time of rising, to which he made no awnser (*sic*).

We rode on for some distance without either of us speaking. I said then you made a great mistake in leaving your things in room 126 in the Kirkwood House. He replied he had no things there. Says I, you lie. You registered your name there. He said yes but simply to get a room for a friend. I asked him, "What is your friend's name." Says he, "It's of no consequence." The conversation here dropped again and we proceeded some distance.

All at once, I turned around to him, and says I, "Where is Booth?" Says he, "I have not seen him since Friday night." "At what hour?" Says he, "It was about six o'clock on the steps of the Theater. I then told him I would have nothing more to do with this thing and backed out of it, and since that time have had nothing more to do with it."

I then turned on him very roughly, told him I did not believe that any man had ever been arrested charged with crime in this country that was fouller (*sic*) than he was. I then said, "We know as much of your operations during Friday night up to Saturday morning as the Almighty does. We know every one you talked to, every one you have seen, traced you to every place you have been, got your coat with the contents in the pocket, which have been identified by your brother as yours. We have got your pistol and the bowie knife. There is not the slightest chance for you, the only chance would be by opening your mouth and revealing to us who the parties were in this conspiracy." He promised me he would do it.[8]

And so the conspirator with the face of a bear came to the final ordeal of his baiting—the Federal Navy Yard. Iron gates clashing at heel. On the double across a compound ominous with anchors, ropes, cannon. A rush across the cobbles to a wharf where a small boat waits. A brisk row to midstream where an iron monitor, black as tar, rides her chain. Then up an iron ladder on the outside of the turret. Then down the dark hatch in the top of the turret—and down an inner hatch—and down through another, this last a manhole to Perdition.

Wrist irons—leg irons—the suffocating canvas bag drawn over his head —probably none of these miseries was as anguishing as the terror of being swallowed alive by a monitor.

Atzerodt was not alone in the bowels of this vessel. It and its sister ship lying nearby had begun to feed well.

The two had shared quite a feast of captives since the night of April 14th. Lewis Paine. O'Laughlin. Arnold. Spangler. These and others had been fed to the iron monitors. Others swallowed by the pair of leviathans were a mysterious Portuguese sea captain, and Atzerodt's cousin, Hartman Richter.

But even company could not dispel the misery of darkness, the grease smell and oil smell, the clank of chain, the gurgle of bilge, the claustrophobia of a monitor's hold. Lewis Paine's steel nerves had broken in this nightmare. Atzerodt had no stamina to begin with. He was hardly below decks before he broke.

Affidavit of Frank Monroe, U.S. Marines, in charge of prisoners on board U.S. monitor *Saugus*:

As well as I can recollect last night, one of my sentries on post over Atzerodt and Richter informed me that the former desired to see me. Atzerodt told me he had sent for me for the purpose of letting me know that he was innocent of any crime and also that he was instrumental in saving the life of the Vice President. Further that he was visited, about three weeks since by a man named John Surrat (*sic*), at Port Tobacco, Md. Surrat informed him that Booth was to open a theatre in Richmond, and also that they [Booth and Surrat] had a vessel to run the blockade and in both enterprises he was wanted.

Atzerodt came to Washington with Surrat and was told by Booth that he must assassinate Mr. Johnson. This he refused to do and Booth threatened to blow his brains out unless he complied. He still refused and returned to to Port Tobacco.

---

[8] National Archives, War Dept. Records, File "M," JAO.

A second time Surrat came for him, and he came again to Washington and took a room at Kirkwood's. He was again asked to murder Mr. Johnson, and again refused.

The day on which the President was killed a man named David Herrold or Harrol brought to Atzerodt's room a knife and revolver, and then left the Hotel. Atzerodt, becoming frightened, locked his door and walked down the street. He knew that the President's assassination was spoken of, but did not believe it would be carried into effect. When he heard the deed had been accomplished, he took a room at the Kimmel House and the next morning went to Montgomery County to the house of his cousin Rickter or Richter at which place he was arrested.

FRANK MONROE
Captain U.S. Marines

WAR DEPARTMENT, WASHINGTON CITY, APL. 23d 1865
Sworn to before me and subscribed in my presence this 23rd day of Apl. 1865.

H. S. BURNETT, JUDGE ADV.[9]

But George A. Atzerodt might as well have saved his breath. His statement to Captain Monroe never got any farther than Judge-Advocate Burnett's file. The wretched cat's-paw from Port Tobacco was left to the digestion of monitor *Saugus*—a Jonah with no hope of deliverance.

The Constitution expressly forbids "cruel and unusual punishments." But Edwin M. Stanton, although posing as a super patriot, apparently had no more use for the laws of the Constitution than he had for the Beatitudes.

On April 23 he issued an order which directed that ". . . the prisoners on board the iron-clads . . . for want of better security against conversation shall have a canvass bag put over the head of each and tied around the neck, with a hole for proper breathing and eating, but not seeing . . . ."[10]

Samuel Arnold would remember this "hooding" as long as he lived. In 1902 he described the punishment as follows:

> The covering of the head was made of canvas, which covered the entire head and face, dropping down in front to the lower portion of the chest. It had cords attached, which were tied around the neck and body in such manner that to remove it was a physical impossibility . . . it being with the greatest difficulty, and frequently impossible, to place food in my mouth, a sentinel kindly volunteering his services to perform that [act] for me. . . . Daylight never lit upon the eye, they not even permitting the cap to be withdrawn for the purpose of washing the swollen, bloated and soiled visage.[11]

---

[9] National Archives, War Dept. Records, File "M," Doc. 26, JAO.
[10] David M. DeWitt, *Judicial Murder of Mary E. Surratt* (Baltimore: J. Murphy & Co., 1895), p. 13.
[11] Samuel A. Arnold, "The Lincoln Conspiracy," *Baltimore American,* Dec. 1901.

The practice of hooding prisoners was not unknown to the U.S. Navy of that day. Back in 1842 the unfortunate boys hanged for mutiny on board U.S. brig *Somers* had been hooded (or "bagged," as it was sometimes called) to put them in the proper mood for confession.[12]

Stanton added some sadistic refinements to the hood. If these refinements were not his own inventions, at least they were applied by his permission. The hoods used on board monitors *Saugus* and *Montauk* were replaced by tight bags which fitted the head and face like certain types of modern gas masks. These head-pieces, of course, were eyeless, and had only slits for nose and mouth. Inside were cotton pads which pressed tightly over the wearer's eyes and against his ears.

Caught in this headlock device the prisoner was stifled, blinded, deafened. The effect on the sinuses alone can be imagined. The effect on the mind defies imagination.

The new hoods were applied after the prisoners were transferred from the monitors to Washington Penitentiary to await trial. The prisoners were also "stiff-shackled" and "leg-ironed," their ankles chained to 75-pound weights.

Military jailors are usually a case-hardened lot, especially after a war wherein third-degree interrogations are routine duty behind prison walls. If the success or failure of a big campaign depends on information, and military interrogators think a prisoner has that vital information, they will stop at nothing to extract it.

While they had raged at Confederates for torturing prisoners of war, the Federal offices had secretly employed brutal methods. They had even tried drugging prisoners with chloroform in the hope they would talk under ether—perhaps the first time in history such brain-washing was attempted.[13]

But the hardened soldiers had seen nothing like the prolonged torture of the captives waiting trial in the Lincoln murder case—nothing like these high-pressure hoods. It was too much for even the calloused prison guards. Dr. George Loring Porter, the prison surgeon, protested to Stanton. He told the War Secretary that the sultry heat (at steam-room temperature in humid Washington) had made the tight headpieces insufferable. He urged that the "hoods" be loosened lest the prisoners suffocate or lose their minds.[14]

Stanton had seen that hooding might be too much for Mary Surratt. It would never do to bring a madwoman to trial. Of the prisoners, she was the only one who was not stiff-shackled and hooded. But Dr. Porter's appeal for the others drew a blank. Arnold said the headpieces, instead

---

[12] See James Fenimore Cooper, *Mutiny of the Somers.*

[13] Old Army Records of the Medical Corps.

[14] Geo. Loring Porter, "How Booth's Body Was Hidden," *Magazine of History*, Vol. 38, No. 1, p. 30.

of being loosened, were actually tightened. Perhaps it just seemed so to the wearers. That is, no one tightened the lacings, but as the wearers' eyes and facial muscles swelled, the pressures increased.

The punishment dealt these prisoners stands as a classic example of what happens when raw dictatorship turns police work into an *auto-da-fé*. All of the victims in this case were civilians. None of them had been tried. Not one as yet had been officially indicted. They had merely been accused and thrown into prison to await trial. But an *auto-da-fé* punishes first and tries afterward.

Only one of the lot suffering pre-trial punishment was unquestionably guilty of attempted murder. Lewis Paine readily admitted the assault on Seward. If he thought confession would ease the hooding, he was wrong.

Even the loose hoods applied on board the ironclads had been terrorizing. The matter was suppressed, but the fact leaked out. Paine, the physical giant of the group, had gone raving mad. He had tried to commit suicide by dashing his brains out against the iron bulkhead of his cell within the monitor.[15]

Looking back on this chapter of history, one sees a weird sequence of reversals. It would seem these were, indeed, the products of a disordered national mind.

On the one hand Lincoln is mourned by a funeral display—and genuine grief—unlike any leader before or since. Yet the funeral is not even started before Lincoln's policies are mistrusted, his plans dispensed with as worthless and unworkable.

The Southerners broke the Union the moment Lincoln was elected. The moment the war is over and he lies slain, they mourn him as a "best friend" lost.

"Beast" Butler, perhaps the war's worst general, and the polar opposite of a saint, orates in the tone of the Old Testament. And is lauded as a great patriot.

Sherman, hard-fighting, hard-swearing, perhaps most capable of the Union generals, and the supposed Attila of Atlanta, writes out the war's most generous surrender terms. Stanton now calls him an inept fool, and the War Secretary brands the patriot a traitor.

The nation that fought for Liberty and Freedom now wants to impose dictatorship on a conquered people. The statesmen who strove to defend the Constitution now regard its tenets as though they were written on a scrap of paper.

But perhaps the strangest reversal of all is the one which attributes Lincoln's death to Providential intervention from On High. So many Northern leaders were convinced that Jehovah had willed Lincoln's murder, it would seem a good defense lawyer could have made some-

---

[15] Trial testimony, Pitman, *op. cit.*

thing of it. If not a Divine Assassin, at least the Supreme Being had been identified as Booth's accomplice.

Of course, the witch-hunters would have considered such talk sacrilegious. Even as they scorned the Christian principles Lincoln had expounded at the last.

"With malice toward none, and charity for all. . . ."

CHAPTER **15**

The Paper Dragnet

B Y EASTER MONDAY the search for Booth and his accomplices had developed into a nation-wide hunt for anyone who might by any stretch of the imagination be connected with the assassination conspiracy.

The imagination could stretch pretty far. It could reach to Richmond, the toppled seat of the Southern Confederacy. It could reach to Canada, the northernmost outpost of the Confederate underground. It could go as far west as the nameless realm of the "American Knights." And it could come as close to home as any Washingtonian's back yard.

That suspicion should fall on citizens who had been anti-Lincoln or had voiced subversive approval of the Confederacy was, perhaps, natural. Also natural was a mistrust of persons whose deportment seemed cloak-and-daggerish. But the conversion of the manhunt into a witchhunt for subversives served to confuse and to scramble the police effort. While civil police, military police and Federal agents went chasing after known or alleged "disloyalists," Lincoln's killer and his partner burrowed deeper underground. So did others who were behind the assassination conspiracy.

If Stanton did not promote the witchhunt for subversives, at least he gave it his blessing and backed it with the forces of the War Department. Baker's Secret Service agents took a leading hand in the game. As has been noted, Baker's initial move was to distribute a handbill which described a featureless and unidentifiable Booth who could have been almost any stranger on Main Street. And while the nation's police agencies were set to arresting such nobodies, Baker launched a roundup of suspected disloyalists.

By Easter Monday the Secret Service Chief was plumbing old "black lists" and the arrests were coming in. During the latter part of the war, Baker had set up a special office in Washington and had established a procedure for the handling of persons accused of disloyalty or some other wartime offense. A graphic report on Baker's police methods comes from L. E. Chittenden, Lincoln's Register of the Treasury.

> He [Baker] dealt with every accused person in the same manner; with a reputable citizen as with a deserter or petty thief. He did not require the formality of a written charge; it was quite sufficient for any person to suggest to Baker that a citizen might be doing something that was against the law. He was immediately arrested, handcuffed, and brought to Baker's office, at that time in the basement of the Treasury. There he was subjected to a brow-beating examination. . . . Men were kept in his rooms for weeks, without warrant, affidavit or other semblance of authority.[1]

In modern setting, Baker's office could be seen as embracing the operations of a police line-up, a night court, a military court of inquiry, a probe by a Congressional committee, a prisoner-of-war interrogation center and a star chamber inquisition. In the days immediately following Lincoln's assassination this mill worked overtime.

A queer medley of prisoners passed through Baker's office: gentlemen in top hats, young women in calico, clerks in alpaca, dowagers in crinoline, merchants in Sunday-go-to-meeting, verminous vagrants, soldiers, sailors, incoherent farmers, glib horse-traders, Northerners, Southerners, scholars, fools, drunkards and teetotalers, penitents and rogues. They were angry, proud, excited, prayerful, belligerent, scared, sullen or worried as temperament might move them.

Hasty dockets were scribbled on these individuals. Preliminary charges ranged from "implicated in assassination" and "accessory" to "suspicious conduct," "Secession sympathizer" and "disloyal utterances." Terms were as loose as ashes, and the effort to sift these charges produced many meaningless clinkers that jammed the screen.

Chittenden deplored the fate of the suspect who had to answer charges levelled by the red-whiskered Secret Service Chief. "If the accused took any measures for his own protection, he was hurried into the Old Capitol Prison, where he was beyond the reach of the civil authorities. . . ."

Warden William P. Wood and his assistant, Captain G. B. Russell, were hard put to find accommodations for the prisoners who began to arrive at the gates of the Old Capitol. Baker's Federal agents were not alone in the field. To expedite military control during the war the North had been divided into military districts, each one under command of a Provost Marshal General. Now these regional or district Army Provosts forwarded conspiracy suspects to Washington. So did Army and Navy officers operating with secret intelligence. With city police and backwoods sheriffs entering the field, the harvest boomed. Then thousands of citizens got into it, and, as might have been expected, the crop swamped the gleaners.

This door-to-door search for "disloyalists" touched off an epidemic of

---

[1] Chittenden, *op. cit.*, pp. 345–46.

neighborhood spying and counter-spying unrivalled in the nation's previous history. Particularly subject to witchhunt contagion was the type of citizen who liked to dance with broomstraws in his hair: "I'll tell you a secret"; "I know a menace"; "Don't quote me, but listen." It was fun to be an informant, and there was no risk to it, either, if you stayed under cover. All it cost was a postage stamp.

In the days following Lincoln's murder, hundreds of informants took pen in hand.

A blizzard of mail descended upon the Government authorities: "I spy" letters, busybody letters, advices, warnings, suggestions, hints, accusations.

Some of the missives were coherent and well-intended. For the most part these were readily recognizable. The writers signed their names and gave their addresses. A number of these advices undoubtedly contained valuable information.

But hundreds of advices were of the anonymous variety easily recognized as crank. Coherent or crank, this correspondence went to Stanton's office or to Baker's for assessment. All informant letters in the Government mailbox were grist for the War Department mill.

Of course, the police can never be certain. Ninety-nine letters may be nonsense. The hundredth may contain a valid tip or a vital clue. So the authorities were compelled to open, read, and study each missive, whatever the fantastic face of it. But the patently fraudulent or libelous or irrelevant, once glanced through, could have been dispensed with. Instead, bushels of this waste paper went through War Department channels to the Office of the Judge Advocate General for further attention. From the first, the overworked clerks in the Bureau of Military Justice had their hands full. In the end, the files were flooded with trash.

The following document, early on Stanton's desk, is typical. It reached the War Department on the Monday or Tuesday after the assassination. It was forwarded as a deposition, but its tone and purport were exemplary of the mail to come.

Joshua L. Henshaw, residing at No. 525 Virginia Avenue, corner of 4th Street East [Washington, D.C.] states:

> The family of Mrs. Cook lives on the same side of the street that I do, with one intervening house between us. The family is notoriously Rebel. The most suspicious circumstance that I know of them occurred on the night of the murder of the President. Mr. James, owner, a brother of Mrs. Cook, and who lives in the house with her, came home about two o'clock in the morning. He was followed by two men at intervals of about ten minutes apart. I had heard of the President's murder and could not sleep and was looking out of the window of my house. I immediately went to a window commanding a partial view of Mrs. Cook's house. . . .
> Mary Cook is by common report a girl of violent temper; a notorious character; swears violently; she is thirty-seven years old. She has been

accustomed to carry food and clothing to the Rebel fruit owners [growers?].

At the time of the siege of Washington by Ewell and Breckenridge Mary Cook said that she had a Rebel flag to throw to the breeze when Washington should be taken. . . .

The family are comparatively wealthy; probably they are worth thirty or fourty thousand dollars, but for the last two or three years they have kept as I have been informed no servants except an idiotic negro boy— perhaps as a measure of precaution.

[Signed]   J. L. Henshaw[2]

On this intelligence from Mr. Henshaw the War Department acted with extraordinary rapidity. On Wednesday, April 19, military police arrested Mrs. Cook. Escorted to Old Capitol Prison, she was booked. The charge was: "Expressions of delight about Lincoln's death. Two strangers came to her house about 2 o'clock, night of the 14th."[3] Her brother was booked for "Disloyal language."

The files contain no further word on the strangers who entered Mary Cook's house around 2:00 A.M. Hundreds of people walked the streets of Washington City that night. Mrs. Cook's visitors may, like neighbor Henshaw, have been guilty of nothing more than insomnia. But Mary Cook and her brother would remain in prison until late June.

An even more interesting (and perhaps more legitimate) deposition than Mr. Henshaw's soon arrived on the War Secretary's desk. This document emanated from the office of the Provost Marshal, 31st District, Dunkirk, N.Y. On April 20 Provost Marshal Crowley forwarded the document to the Provost Marshal General at Elmira. From there it was forwarded on the 21st to Brigadier General James B. Fry, U.S.A., Provost Marshal General, Washington, D.C.

As duly recorded in Dunkirk, N.Y., the deposition reads:

Mr. Simeon J. McKay, a respectable and responsible citizen of the town of Ripley, Chautauqua County, in this District, makes the following statement, To Wit:

That he is in business on Oil Creek near Oil City, Pa.; that he well knew John Wilkes Booth, both in the Oil Region of Pa., & also in Washington, that on the 15th inst. when the news arrived at Oil City, Pa., that the President had been assassinated and that J. Wilkes Booth was the probable assassin, one Robert Fleming of Cherry Tree Township, Vessango County, Pa., declared that while in Washington, D.C. last year he (Fleming) was a member of a secret Society (called the G. D. Lodge).

That he was present at the iniation (sic) of J. Wilkes Booth into said Lodge; that said Booth took a solemn Oath with a sword pointed at his heart, to take the life of Abraham Lincoln under the penality of having his heart torn from his left breast, etc., if both he (Booth) and Abraham Lincoln should be living after the expiration of eight years.

---

[2] National Archives, War Dept. Records, File "A, Ev. B.," JAO.

[3] National Archives, War Dept. Records, File "C," JAO.

Endorsing Mr. Simeon McKay's deposition, Provost Marshal Crowley noted that he had advised the Army Provost at Oil Creek to arrest the said Robert Fleming.[4]

But if the "said Robert Fleming" was subsequently arrested, he must have been held incommunicado. His name does not appear in the various lists of suspects confined at that time to the Old Capitol. Perhaps the Army detectives were unable to trace the man in Cherry Tree Township, Vessango County, Pa. Or he may have been a Confederate agent deliberately stirring up a wild-goose chase. For that matter, he may have existed only in the mind of Mr. Simeon McKay. But those who offer wild fabrications to the authorities usually prefer anonymity. McKay signed a statement. Probably he reported an actual encounter with Robert Fleming who, on his part, reported an actual incident.

For John Wilkes Booth had been in the Oil Creek region. So had the "American Knights." And the bombast and mock heroics seem typical of Lincoln's assassin. Perhaps the personal tragedy of Booth was this: that one of America's leading actors could never resist an opportunity to barnstorm, if only before a handful of imbeciles playing Secret Society in a candle-lit barn.

Although the Oil Creek report, then, remained in the realm of hearsay, the incident as described was not out of character. Another interesting characterization of Booth reached the War Department in the week following Lincoln's assassination. This was a letter addressed on April 17 by the actor Edwin Adams to a Mr. Reakirt, who lost no time in forwarding it to Stanton's office.

Long Beach N. J.

My dear Reakirt

. . . I can only repeat what I said of Booth's manner and reckless habits when I knew him a few years ago. I have not spoken to him since one year ago last January. And that in Louisville, Ky. when he followed me with an engagement at the Theatre in that city. I had not seen him before then for some time. And readily noticed a marked increase of his reckless manners. I heard him boasting over a very long and tedious journey from Leavenworth. Across the prairies in a sleigh to St. Louis, and after having threatened a conductors life, who had stopped his train on account of the great depth of snow, and that by placing a pistol at his head, made him continue his journey. And I am sure that all of his profession (which he has disgraced) will agree with me that he has ever been noted for his love of notoriety. . . .

Your sincere friend
[Signed]   Edwin Adams[5]

---

[4] National Archives, War Dept. Records, File "C," Evidence, JAO.
[5] National Archives, War Dept. Records, File "A," Doc. 31, JAO.

Adams' letter provided the authorities with a glimpse of Booth's personality, but it offered no clue as to the assassin's whereabouts. Nor did it contribute a conspiracy suspect to the Old Capitol. The police wanted tips that led to handcuffs. On April 18 such a tip came in concerning one John D. Reamer, storekeeper in Hagerstown, Maryland. Another typical case. Accused of "disloyal utterances," Mr. Reamer was hustled under military guard to Washington. Arrested with him was his fellow townsman and friend, William Gabriel.

Under questioning, Gabriel denied any friendship with Reamer. Gabriel preferred to blow his own horn as a Union patriot. To prove his patriotism, he denounced Reamer as a Southern sympathizer.

The accused storekeeper (to quote the docket): ". . . in February said 100,000 men were in Canada to incite the North. That $50,000 had been subscribed for the assassination of the President, and that after 1st or 15th of April Lincoln mayn't (sic) be President. He [Reamer] is a violent secessionist. Was with the Rebs in '63 when they were burning buildings in Hagerstown, and his store was left undisturbed at the time the stores of all Union men were being robbed. Reamer says that he only reported the above things as having been published in the paper."[6]

Indeed, as Reamer protested, the "above things" had appeared in newsprint. Sensational stories of Rebel forces in Canada had made front page copy for many weeks. So had tales concerning blood money donated in behalf of plots to assassinate President Lincoln. But the charge that Reamer had abetted the Confederate raiders in Hagerstown was enough to lodge him in Old Capitol Prison where he remained confined until late June. Gabriel, too, was held prisoner, his protestations of patriotism notwithstanding.

"Disloyal utterance" was a common charge during the Civil War. In the wake of Lincoln's murder it became a national byword. That the accusation was usually hearsay mattered little, as did the fact that a drunken denouncement of the Government or of Lincoln might have no bearing whatever on the conspiracy which plotted the President's death.

For instance: the charges levelled against a certain Owens family in a deposition sworn by one Adeline Taskar of Freedman's Village.

> I formerly belonged to Jas. Owens of the City of Bristol Ararundel [Arundel] County, Md. two miles above Pig Point. The house is a large brick, painted blue, stands on the public road. I came from there on Monday. When I was down there, the gentlemen were rejoicing much about Uncle Sam's being dead. Shouting and hurraing (sic). I was there and asked them what they were shouting about. They said Uncle Sam was dead, and that "the Son of Bitch ought to have gone four years ago." Alex Owens, Dennis Owens and Janice Owens all said so; and they were all much rejoiced about it. They said Uncle Sam had brought us all to a

---

[6] National Archives, War Dept. Records; List of Prisoners in Old Capital, JAO.

bad run by attempting to set all the negroes free, and now he has brought you to a pretty drink. By Uncle Sam they meant Abraham Lincoln.

Her
Adeline Taskar   X
mark.[7]

Alex, Dennis, and Janice Owens doubtless learned that Uncle Sam—in the form of Federal soldiery—was not dead. The accused are not registered in the Old Capitol inventories, so they may have escaped from the police. Or they may have been lodged in some Army guardhouse. One can hardly sympathize with their plight. Any jail sounds like a better address than the blue house two miles above Pig Point.

However, odious as such persons may have been, did their babble warrant the attention of Government officials presumably intent on uncovering a giant conspiracy? The War Department wasted much time and effort in investigating such riffraff. Chasing down rabbits far afield, the Federal officers lost sight of foxes in the dooryard.

For example, the Booth gang had frequented the Lichau House in Washington. This fact became known when Sam Arnold and Mike O'Laughlin were arrested Easter weekend. So it might be supposed that the proprietor of the establishment would be taken into custody and held for investigation. He had been seen in confab with Booth, and had possibly overheard subversive talk among the conspirators.

The proprietor of Lichau's was not arrested. It seems the police might have ignored the place entirely, but for an uproar reported during the week of Lincoln's funeral.

There was an unholy row belowstairs: Frank Roth, bar man, slapped Lizzie Batchim, maid, in the mouth; and Julia Ross, cook and washerwoman, stepped in. According to servants William Taylor and Julia Bird, the combatants had said "nearly every day since the assassination of President Lincoln that he ought to have been killed long ago and they hoped he would never be caught (*sic*)."[8] On April 21, Batchim, Ross and Roth were clapped into the Old Capitol. After a twelve-day lodgement these quarrelsome sparrows were released.[9]

Booth had numerous close friends in Washington who, conceivably, might have known more about him and his intentions than did some vagabond miscreant in Keokuk or Pocatello. One of his comrades in the capital was a Billy Barron, drawing-room parvenu and brothel roisterer. Barron was reported as a Secessionist and an associate of Booth's.[10] For reasons unexplained, he remained out of jail. So did John Deery—one of Booth's oldest and closest friends, whose billiard saloon was only a brisk

[7] National Archives, War Dept. Records, File "T," Doc. 617, JAO.
[8] National Archives, War Dept. Records, File "A," Doc. 508, JAO.
[9] National Archives, War Dept. Records, File "R," Doc. 266, JAO.
[10] National Archives, War Dept. Records, File "W," Doc. R.B.P. 102, JAO.

gallop from the office of Lafayette Baker. Guilt by association jailed a number of Booth's business and professional acquaintances. But one man's poison seemed another man's meat.

Overlooking the near, Federal agents groped afar for a mysterious A. U. Minot, a "villian" reported by mail.

"He is a robber and vile Secessionist," wrote D. D. F. Benedict of Piqua, Ohio, in a letter to War Secretary Stanton dated April 22. Identifying Minot as a former night clerk of the Walnut Street House in Cincinnati, the writer went on to describe this party as ". . . a most Desperate man. Has uttered wishes for vengeance on the Government. Is quite a fine looking man, athletic and above Common Size and was last heard of in the city of Baltimore. . . . He appears to be a German. . . . [would] do antying (sic) by which he could be well paid. . . . In a word, I believe him to be an accomplished man and an active athlete, a daring Robber and a vile Secessionist, a Desperado who would love to get revenge on the officers of our Government."[11]

Who was Minot? What became of him? Apparently he was never found.

Meanwhile, an odd married couple, Thomas and Nannie Green, had been booked. Arrested in Washington by Augur's soldiers, they were marched into the grim Old Capitol on April 18. On the 27th a Miss Lomax (otherwise unidentified) was incarcerated, the docket stipulating: "Not to have communication with Mr. Green."[12] Miss Lomax was presently released. As of June 3, the Greens would still be on the list of prison inmates.

And why was this couple thus confined? The initial entry in the prison records is laconic. It reads: "Disloyalty. Lived in VanNess house at foot of 17th Street."[13]

Secretary Stanton and Secret Service Chief Baker liked to keep their captives in the dark. For twenty-two days Thomas Green paced a cell and protested in bafflement at his arrest. At length, given pen and paper, he received permission to compose a statement. He wrote:

> I have had no charges made against me and know not why I am imprisoned—I have committed no offense to justify it—have done nothing and have expressed no opinions that could be offensive.
>
> I know nothing of any of the parties implicated in the recent great assassination—am ready at any time to take the oath of allegiance, and I think I am the proper custodian of my own property. But if I am to be continued in prison and am not allowed to return to my own residence (the old VanNess Square) I desire it may be put in the possession of my friend Mr. Thomas Shankland. . . .

---

[11] National Archives, War Dept. Records, File "B," Doc. 294, JAO.
[12] National Archives, War Dept. Records, File "T," Doc. R.B.P. 101, JAO.
[13] National Archives, War Dept. Records, File "G," Doc. R.B.P. 103, JAO.

Navy Yard Bridge across the "Eastern Branch", Washington, D.C. (circa 1865).

Lloyd's Tavern at Surrattville (1958).

Library of Congress

Washington, D.C., at the time of Lincoln's assassination.

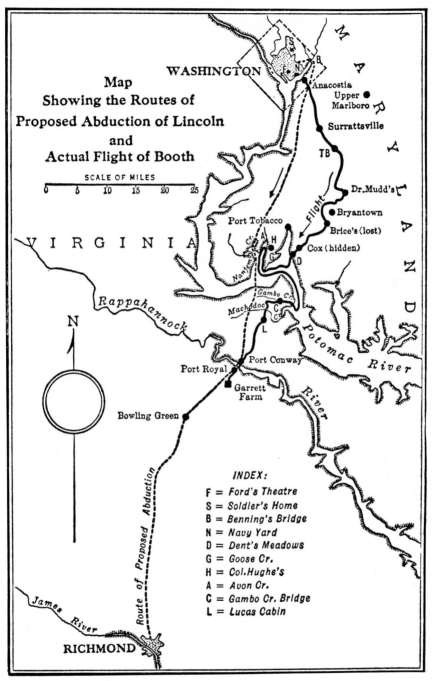

Map
Showing the Routes of
Proposed Abduction of Lincoln
and
Actual Flight of Booth

SCALE OF MILES
0   5   10   15   20   25

WASHINGTON

Anacostia
Upper
Marlboro
Surrattsville
TB
Dr. Mudd's
Bryantown
Brice's (lost)
Port Tobacco
Cox (hidden)
Flight

M A R Y L A N D

V I R G I N I A

Rappahannock

N

Gambo Cr.
Machodoc

Port Conway
Port Royal
Garrett
Farm
Bowling Green

P o t o m a c   R i v e r

River

James River

Route of Proposed Abduction

RICHMOND

INDEX:

F = Ford's Theatre
S = Soldier's Home
B = Benning's Bridge
N = Navy Yard
D = Dent's Meadows
G = Goose Cr.
H = Col. Hughe's
A = Avon Cr.
C = Gambo Cr. Bridge
L = Lucas Cabin

From Francis Wilson, John Wilkes Booth

Booth's escape route.

SURRAT.   BOOTH.   HAROLD.

War Department, Washington, April 20, 1865,

$100,000 REWARD!

Reward poster with false picture of John Surratt and showing Herold as a schoolboy.

SURRAT.   BOOTH.   HAROLD.

War Department, Washington, April 20, 1865.

 # $100,000 REWARD!

THE MURDERER

Of our late beloved President, Abraham Lincoln,

IS STILL AT LARGE.

$50,000 REWARD

Will be paid by this Department for his apprehension, in addition to any reward offered by Municipal Authorities or State Executives.

$25,000 REWARD

Will be paid for the apprehension of JOHN H. SURRAT, one of Booth's Accomplices

$25,000 REWARD

Will be paid for the apprehension of David C. Harold, another of Booth's accomplices.

LIBERAL REWARDS will be paid for any information that shall conduce to the arrest of either of the above-named criminals, or their accomplices.

All persons harboring or secreting the said persons, or either of them, or aiding or assisting their concealment or escape, will be treated as accomplices in the murder of the President and the attempted assassination of the Secretary of State, and shall be subject to trial before a Military Commission and the punishment of DEATH.

Let the stain of innocent blood be removed from the land by the arrest and pu_____ ___urderers.

All good citizens are exhorted to aid public justice on this occasion. Every man should consider his own conscience charged with this solemn duty, and rest neither night nor day until it be accomplished.

EDWIN M. STANTON, Secretary of War.

DESCRIPTIONS.—BOOTH is Five Feet 7 or 8 inches high, slender build, high forehead, black hair, black eyes, and wore a heavy black moustache, which there is some reason to believe has been shaved off.

JOHN H. SURRAT is about 5 feet, 9 inches. Hair rather thin and dark; eyes rather light; no beard. Would weigh 145 or 150 pounds. Complexion rather pale and clear, with color in his cheeks. Wore light clothes of fine quality. Shoulders square; cheek bones rather prominent; chin narrow; ears projecting at the top; forehead rather low and square, but broad. Parts his hair on the right side; neck rather long. His lips are firmly set. A slim man.

DAVID C. HAROLD is five feet six inches high, hair dark, eyes dark, eyebrows rather heavy, full face, nose short, head short and fleshy, feet small, instep high, round bodied, naturally quick and active, slightly closes his eyes when looking at a person.

NOTICE.—In addition to the above, State and other authorities have offered rewards amounting to almost one hundred thousand dollars, making an aggregate of about TWO HUNDRED THOUSAND DOLLARS.

Revised reward poster, faked for history, showing Herold after his capture, and John Suratt about 1867.

Gen. Lafayette C. Baker.

First reward poster.

$30,000 REWARD

DESCRIPTION

OF

JOHN WILKES BOOTH!

Who Assassinated the PRESIDENT on the Evening of April 14th, 1865.

Height 5 feet 8 inches; weight 160 pounds; compact built; hair jet black, inclined to curl. medium length. parted behind ; eyes black, and heavy dark eye-brows ; wears a large seal ring on little finger ; when talking inclines his head forward ; looks down.

Description of the Person who Attempted to Assassinate Hon. W. H. Seward, Secretary of State.

Height 6 feet 1 inch ; hair black, thick, full and straight; no beard, nor appearance of beard ; cheeks red on the jaws . face moderately full ; 22 or 23 years of age ; eyes, color not known—large eyes. not prominent ; brows not heavy, but dark ; face not large, but rather round ; complexion healthy ; nose straight and well formed, medium size ; mouth small ; lips thin ; upper lip protruded when he talked ; chin pointed and prominent ; head medium size ; neck short, and of medium length ; hands soft and small ; fingers tapering ; shows no signs of hard labor. broad shoulders ; taper waist; straight figure ; strong looking man ; manner not gentlemanly, but vulgar ; Overcoat double-breasted, color mixed of pink and grey spots, small —was a sack overcoat, pockets in side and one on the breast, with lappells or flaps ; pants black. common stuff ; new heavy boots ; voice small and thin, inclined to tenor.

The Common Council of Washington, D. C., have offered a reward of $20,000 for the arrest and conviction of these Assassins, in addition to which I will pay $10.000.

L. C. BAKER,
Colonel and Agent War Department.

Mr Wm H Seward

        I wish I had cut
your dam head off while I was at it
instead of only half doing it if I
only had you and Johnson and
Stanton out of the way I would
feel as if I had done my duty to my
country but Knowing that I could
not get at Stanton as he did not come
out of the house untill I saw some one
come for him and Knew that
My Partner had done his part
of the work I thought it best
to "Light Out" of that dam
Abolition hole as soon as I could
and now I have got here I am not
afraid of being Caught by your

National Archives

The "Jorgen" letter.

National Archives

Herold's handwriting.

Map showing the routes of Booth and the Detectives, and the place where Booth
was shot and Harold captured.

Booth's Route —————— Detectives' Route -----

From The American Bastille, *by John A. Marshall*

Booth's escape route and the route of his pursuers. This
map emphasizes Booth's stop at Dr. Mudd's, but fails to indicate his six-day hideout at Cox's farm.

THE FULLER FARM OIL COMPANY.

THIS Company is organized for the purpose of purchasing and further developing the property known as the Fuller Farm, comprising forty acres of land, situated upon the left bank of the Alleghany River, about one mile below the town of Franklin, in Cranberry township, Venango County, Pennsylvania. It is in the heart of the oil region and there are good producing wells both above and below it. Mr. J. Wilkes Booth, a successful and intelligent operator in oil lands, has lately purchased an abandoned well upon the farm adjoining this property on one side, and, although hardly in working order, as yet, the yield has been gratifyingly large. Just beyond its southern limits a new well is being sunk, which already yields ten barrels of oil per day, and about a mile below this is still another, yielding thirty barrels per day. *None of these wells have reached the third sand-rock,* in which the Petroleum of Oil Creek and vicinity is found. There are two wells upon the Fuller Farm, one of which has been bored to the depth of four hundred and eighty feet, and the other five hundred and ten feet, neither, of course, reaching below the second sand-rock. They formerly produced from ten to twelve barrels per day, and, as oil may be dipped from them at any time in considerable quantities, we see no reason to doubt that by pumping they would, to-day, together yield at least fifteen barrels of oil per day,

Fuller Oil Company brochure.

National Archives

MYSTERIOUS ITEMS FOUND

Bill for hair ring bought by Booth.

National Archives

TIFFANY & CO.,
(LATE TIFFANY, YOUNG & ELLIS,)
Importers and Manufacturers,
No. 550 BROADWAY, New-York, and
Rue Richelieu, No. 79 Paris.
DIAMONDS AND OTHER PRECIOUS STONES, SILVER WARE, FINE JEWELRY, WATCHES, CLOCKS, BRONZES, PLATED WARE, DESKS DRESSING CASES, FINE STATIONERY &C.. &C.

Secret cipher.

```
ZABCDEFGHIJKLMNOPQRSTUVWXYZ
ABCDEFGHIJKLMNOPQRSTUVWXYZA
BCDEFGHIJKLMNOPQRSTUVWXYZAB
CDEFGHIJKLMNOPQRSTUVWXYZABC
DEFGHIJKLMNOPQRSTUVWXYZABCD
EFGHIJKLMNOPQRSTUVWXYZABCDE
FGHIJKLMNOPQRSTUVWXYZABCDEF
GHIJKLMNOPQRSTUVWXYZABCDEFG
HIJKLMNOPQRSTUVWXYZABCDEFGH
IJKLMNOPQRSTUVWXYZABCDEFGHI
JKLMNOPQRSTUVWXYZABCDEFGHIJ
KLMNOPQRSTUVWXYZABCDEFGHIJK
LMNOPQRSTUVWXYZABCDEFGHIJKL
MNOPQRSTUVWXYZABCDEFGHIJKLM
NOPQRSTUVWXYZABCDEFGHIJKLMN
OPQRSTUVWXYZABCDEFGHIJKLMNO
PQRSTUVWXYZABCDEFGHIJKLMNOP
QRSTUVWXYZABCDEFGHIJKLMNOPQ
RSTUVWXYZABCDEFGHIJKLMNOPQR
STUVWXYZABCDEFGHIJKLMNOPQRS
TUVWXYZABCDEFGHIJKLMNOPQRST
UVWXYZABCDEFGHIJKLMNOPQRSTU
VWXYZABCDEFGHIJKLMNOPQRSTUV
WXYZABCDEFGHIJKLMNOPQRSTUVW
XYZABCDEFGHIJKLMNOPQRSTUVWX
YZABCDEFGHIJKLMNOPQRSTUVWXY
ZABCDEFGHIJKLMNOPQRSTUVWXYZ
```

IN BOOTH'S TRUNK

"Jenny" letter.

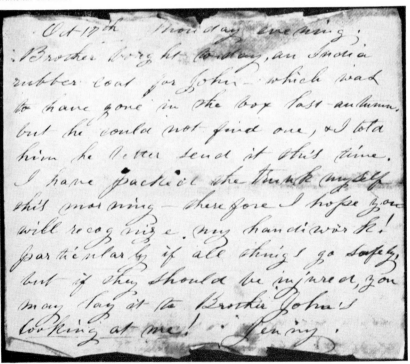

TUESDAY 21

WEDNESDAY 22

After being hunted like a dog through swamps, woods, and last night being chased by gunboats till we were forced to return wet cold and starving with every mans hand against me. I am here in despair. And why? For doing what Brutus was honored for. What made Tell a Hero. And yet I for striking down a greater tyrant than they ever knew. am looked upon as a common cutthroat. My action was purer than either of them. One, hoped to be great himself. The other had not only his country's but his own wrongs to avenge. I hoped for no gain. I knew no private wrong. I struck for my country and that alone. A country that groaned beneath this tyranny and prayed for this end and yet now behold the cold hand they extend to me. God cannot pardon me if I have done wrong. Yet I cannot see my wrong except in serving a degenerate people. The

FRIDAY 24

SATURDAY 25

Page from Booth's diary.

New York April 10th 1865

To J. W. Booth.
    Dear
            I have sent word to
harry to be on the watch for Seward
he has changed his name his
first name to James. You watch
the Box Book of fords theatre
Laura Keene being a great favorite
there there is no doubt but the
President and acquaintances will
visit to see her performance. Do it
either way let me know if you
got the pistol be carefull that
Laura does not see you as she
has a deadly hatred to me and
you have the thing fixed differ
ent among the other actors
George has the plan fixed
for the Secretary and for Stanton

Letter to Booth
"From His Mother."

Drawing by Gilbert Thompson from Oldroyd's The Assassination of President Lincoln

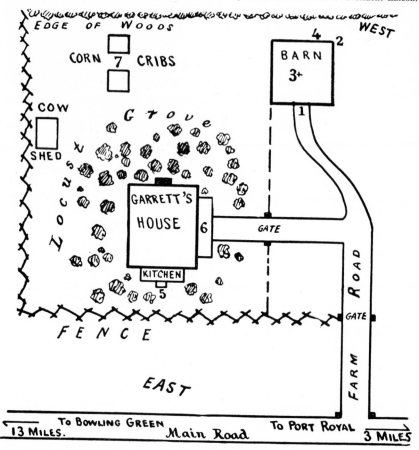

PLAN OF GARRETT'S PLACE.

1. DOOR OF BARN THROUGH WHICH BOOTH WAS BROUGHT.
2. CORNER OF BARN WHICH WAS FIRED.
3. WHERE BOOTH STOOD.
4. WHERE BOSTON CORBETT STOOD.
5. DOOR OF KITCHEN OF HOUSE WHERE BAKER MET GARRETT.
6. FRONT PORCH, ON WHICH BOOTH DIED.
7. CORN CRIBS, WHERE THE TWO GARRETT BOYS SLEPT.

From Harper's Weekly, *1865*

Booth standing in the burning barn.

From Frank Leslie's Magazine, *May 13, 1865*

Booth dragged from the barn.

Capt. Edward P. Doherty,
Booth's captor.

Boston Corbett.

Friend in need, Thomas Shankland submitted the following petition in Green's behalf:

> In respectfully submitting the above, I may be permitted to state that I was the Guest at the house of Mr. Green for two months, that I request all the information [illegible] may be given to the authorities here. . . . Mrs. Green's health has been very much affected by her imprisonment, for the past three weeks, without charges or specifications, as I am informed by Maj. L. C. Turner.[14]

Green's statement and Shankland's petition went into the inactive pigeonhole. The active file on the Greens contained data of more interest to the Bureau of Military Justice. This document consisted of two items which had been forwarded by the arresting officer.

Item 1: "She had a large mail secreted to be sent South. Mrs. Green has two sons in Moseby's (*sic*) band. Is a thorough Secessionist."

Item 2: "Quotation in manuscript from *Hamlet* found lying before Mrs. Green, wife of Thomas Green, when she was arrested at her house on 18th of April."

The quotation from *Hamlet* was penned on a sheet of correspondence paper dated April 15, 1865. The lines (apparently set down by Mrs. Green) were:

> "Alas! poor Yorick! I knew him, Horatio; a fellow of infinite jest—of most excellent fancy; x x x x (*sic*).
> "Where be your gibes now? your gambols? your songs? your flashes of merriment that were wont to set the table on a roar? Not one now to mock your own grinning? quite chapfallen?"[15]

What meaning could be read into this evidence? Of course, secret mail bore evidence to subversive action. But if the Federal detectives were able to make anything of the excerpt from *Hamlet*, the record fails to disclose their deductions.

Shakespeare obviously suggested theater. Theater suggested John Wilkes Booth. Did Yorick's skull suggest the homicidal actor to Nannie Green? The lines omitted by "x x x x" constitute an interesting passage.

> . . . he hath borne me on his back a thousand times; and now how abhorred in my imagination it is! my gorge rises at it. Here hung those lips that I have kissed I know not how oft. . . .

As will be seen, the Greens were members of an underground. But their dossiers, like so many filed by the War Department at the time, cast more shadow than light on the assassination drama. On most of the Old Capitol prisoners, Stanton lowered an iron curtain. Emerging from behind that curtain, mysterious Nannie Green might well have quoted apt lines from *Hamlet's* Ghost:

---

[14] National Archives, War Dept. Records, File "E," Doc. 740, JAO.
[15] National Archives, War Dept. Records, File "E," 740, JAO.

> But that I am forbid
> To tell the secrets of my prison-house,
> I could a tale unfold . . .

One of the suspects questioned at Ford's Theater on the night of April 14 was James Maddox, property man. Grilled by the Washington police, Maddox vehemently protested innocence. Then the Army suddenly stepped in. On April 17 he was committed as an "accessory." The War Department order stipulated: "To be placed in close confinement, in irons, and no one to see or correspond with him under any circumstances."[16]

Probably Maddox never knew the reason for his iron incarceration. The ordeal might have been even more nerve wracking had he known it was ordered by War Secretary Stanton.[17] Stanton's order seems to have stemmed from Secret Service information concerning a Confederate blockade runner named Maddox. That was not all. On April 21 the War Secretary received the following letter:

Hon. Mr. Stanton.
Sir: David Herold's sister married a Mr. Maddox just before the war. Maddox was, I think, from Georgia or Alabama.

David Porter was arrested as a Rebel sympathizer about the first of the rebellion & confined in the Old Capitol—said Porter is the brother of Mrs. Herold—mother of David Herold. I understand that one or two of Herold's sisters have recently married Union naval officers . . .

(Anonymous)[18]

Many loyal Northerners had in-laws in the Rebel service, including Mrs. Lincoln, whose brother-in-law happened to be a Confederate general. That David Herold's sisters were wedded to Union naval officers signified nothing whatever.

The hapless property man somehow managed to clear his name; in May his Old Capitol docket identified him simply as "Witness." Meantime, his wrists had been skinned raw by the irons, his ankles bruised by weights, his nerves shredded by days in solitary.

Acting on another anonymous letter, the Federal police investigated a "Mrs. Duvall, NE corner of 20th Street W." Anonymous stated that Mrs. Duvall draped her house "ostensibly with mourning" on the day Lincoln died. But she had "wept over the fall of Richmond and the surrender of Lee."[19]

Anyone acquainted with the mysteries of human nature, if not those of semantics, might have seen through the Duvall letter. How did the writer know Mrs. Duvall's mourning was merely "ostensible." She had

---

[16] National Archives, War Dept. Records, File "R," Doc. 266, JAO.
[17] National Archives, War Dept. Records, "List of Prisoners," dated April 27, 1865, JAO.
[18] National Archives, War Dept. Records, File "A," "Anon.," JAO.
[19] National Archives, War Dept. Records, File "A," Doc. 552, JAO.

wept at Lee's surrender and the fall of Richmond? So did thousands of Northern ladies, shedding tears of relief.

Wasting footwork on Mrs. Duvall, the military police paid scant attention to a person who must have known a great deal about John Wilkes Booth. This was Charles Dawson, clerk at the National Hotel.

Because he cooperated with the Government authorities, Dawson seems to have divested himself of all suspicion. Yet he had been a confidant of the actor's. Booth had provided him with theater passes and other favors. Dawson's cooperation with the Federals may have been more expedient than patriotic.

In fact, Mr. Dawson may have furnished the police with large doses of misinformation. Leads forwarded by Dawson sent them up several blind alleys. From Dawson's desk came one of the more bizzare correspondence enigmas—a letter presumably intercepted by the hotel clerk, who was keeping an eye out for Booth's mail.

This was the so-called "LEON" or "LON" letter—an item prized by the authorities as one evidence of a nationwide conspiracy to overthrow the Government. The letter itself was meaningless jargon. It read like code. It exuded a tone of menace. It may possibly have been genuine. But in any case its code remained insoluble.

The "LEON" letter was eventually offered as evidence at the Trial of the Conspirators. And it was implied that the Government was able to read such gibberish. The implication was made by Assistant War Secretary Charles A. Dana. When the Union Army entered Richmond on April 4, the vanguard swept into the office of Judah P. Benjamin, Confederate Secretary of State. In Benjamin's office the soldiers found a small decoding machine. This device was rushed to Dana in Washington. Presented at the Conspiracy Trial, the gadget was exhibited to convey the impression that enemy code letters were open books to Union decoders. However, the "LEON" letter defied decoding.

Here is the much-publicized letter:

South Branch Bridge, April 5, 1865

Friend Wilkes:

I received yours of March 12, and reply as soon as practicable. I saw French, Brady and others about oil speculations. The subscription to the stock amounts to $8,000, and I will add $1,000 myself which is about all I can stand now. When you sink you will go deep enough. Don't fail. Everything depends on you and your helpers. If you can't get through on your trip after you strike oil, strike through Thornton Gap, and across by Sapon, Romney, and down by the branch road, and I can keep you safe from all hardship for a year. I am clear of all surveillance now, since that infernal Purdy is beat. I hired that girl to charge him with outrage, and reported him to old Kelly, which sent him in the shade; but he suspects too damn much now. Had he better be silenced for good? I send this up by Tom and if he doesn't get drunk you will get it by the 9th. At all events it can't be understood if lost. I can't half write. I have been drunk for two days.

Don't write so much highfalutin next time. No more, only Jake will be at Green's on the 1st. Burn this immediately. Yours truly. [Signed] LEON.

Guthrie sends much love. Mailed at Cumberland May 8.[20]

Did the "stock subscription" refer to an assassination fund? Was an escape route detailed?

Experts in the Bureau of Military Justice spent hours poring over the "LEON" scrawl and similar specimens of supposed conspiracy correspondence intercepted at the National Hotel after Booth's flight. Yet a most perfunctory study was made of the story told by Mr. Henry E. Merrick, another clerk on the National staff well acquainted with Booth. Early in March this Merrick had gone to Ford's Theater to reserve some seats in the orchestra. Arriving late for the performance that evening, Merrick and party found their seats sold out. Ticket seller Thomas Reybold then ushered them to a front box, only to discover the box was locked. Unable to locate the key, Reybold had then forced the door, breaking the lock to admit the Merrick party. The box in question was Number 8— the one usually reserved for President Lincoln. By oversight, it seemed, the lock went unrepaired.

To a Federal police less interested in woolgathering, Merrick's story might have suggested collusion between Booth and Reybold. Or an arrangement between Booth and the ticket seller, with hotel clerk Merrick acting as go-between. But the long, strong arm of the War Department reached for suspects who never saw the door of Lincoln's box—a circus clown in Philadelphia; a medicine showman in St. Louis; an Army lieutenant who once visited a Washington shooting gallery with Booth. William Donaldson, Dr. Tumblety, Lieutenant Clement Pearson, U.S.A.— one finds these extraneous individuals wandering through many pages of documentation in the War Department files on the assassination conspiracy. The same files contain very little on Henry E. Merrick and Thomas Reybold.

A familiar figure around the Navy Yard and midtown oyster houses and stableyards, David Herold was well known to many persons in Washington City. He had many friends and hallooing acquaintances in Prince Georges County—Forrest Queen, the Jarboe boys and others. His family's neighbors and his several sisters were available for questioning. His ingrown chin and drooping eye could have been readily described and easily recognized.

Under the circumstances it seems strange that Stanton's office bothered to preserve the following communique:

---

[20] National Archives, War Department Records, JAO. (Reprinted in contemporary press releases.)

To
Hon. E. M. Stanton
Secretary of War,
Sir,

I do not know that it is worth while of informing you of it; but the idea strikes me & I cannot get rid of the thought that the Villain Harrod is the same man who escaped from Erie County jail some 20 months since. He styled himself Dr. Harrod, & was living here with a certain Mrs. Laciel, a notorious abortionist.

As I was at that time physician to said jail I could easily recognize him, I think. Booth was playing here in the same time—As these sugestions (*sic*) may lead to some other development bearing on the history of these individuals I thought it my duty to give this information, and subscribe myself

Respectfully yours,
Augustus Jansen
M. D.[21]

"Harrod," of course, could not have been callow David Herold. Nor were the practices of "Mrs. Laciel" exactly War Department business. Nevertheless, Dr. Jansen's letter was added to the midden in the Bureau of Military Justice. That Bureau was fast becoming an Augean Stable.

Sheaves of rumor and hearsay, dossiers of gossip, bales of manifest trivia. Every item demanded reading and endorsement of some kind. Someone had to sift the stuff for possible clues.

The midnight oil burned late in the War Department, where Secretary Dana, Major Eckert, Army intelligence officers and other experts chewed their pencils over unreadable "conspiracy letters" and tried to crank solutions out of the Confederate decoding machine. Some of these weird letters may have been genuine. May have contained meaningful acrostics or alphabet tricks. So far as is known, the Federal cipher experts failed to "unlock" a single code letter bearing on the assassination conspiracy. Probably the experts grew desperate. Crossword puzzles take time. And here came another bag of scrabble from Stanton's office.

Recorded for Bureau attention: From Fond du Lac, Wisconsin, Lieutenant C. R. Potter, late Regiment G. M., 14th Wisconsin, reports that on morning of day Lincoln was shot, one Mr. Larche, Supervisor of Chilton, said to him, "Today Lincoln will be killed."

Recorded for Bureau attention: One C. A. Eldridge said on the cars of the North Western R.R. that "Lincoln lived and died a tyrant and was not assassinated as soon as he [Eldridge] had expected."[22]

And so on.

If the War Department had been able to track down and arrest as subversive every citizen reported for foretelling the exact date of Lincoln's

---

21 National Archives, War Dept. Records, File "Y," Doc. 236, JAO.
22 National Archives, War Dept. Records, File "H," Doc. 260, JAO.

assassination, the seers would have jampacked the Old Capitol. Perhaps the weirdest of many mysteries lurking over the Lincoln murder case concerns the number of persons who presumably prognosticated the assassination to the day.

In St. Joseph, Minnesota, a town without a telegraph office, someone spread the word on April 14 that Lincoln had been slain. Manchester New Hampshire, also received the news on that Good Friday before the press releases were dispatched from Washington. And on the afternoon of the 14th, the *Whig* Press in Middletown, New York, announced that Lincoln had been killed by an assassin[23]—one of the oddest headlines in the history of journalism.

Believers in the occult might credit these divinations to some sort of telepathic influence set adrift at moments of impending crisis. Rationalists might prefer to believe in telegraphy rather than telepathy. But how did advance notice reach far-off St. Joseph, a town without benefit of telegraph? How did the dark tidings reach Manchester before the wires carried the story? Rationale suggests some underground agent—someone advised on what was coming. It could almost look (if anyone looked) as though the news of the impending assassination had been planted here and there in the North.

Official reaction to these phenomena appears to have been apathetic. Stanton's officers filed the name of the citizen reported in distant Fond du Lac. But no sustained effort seems to have been made to locate the source of the pre-event assassination story published in the Catskills not far from New York City. The editor of the Middletown *Whig Press* should have been asked some questions.

In the boil and bubble of witchhunt correspondence, elements or religious prejudice were bound to swirl up in the brew.

Because Mrs. Surratt was a Roman Catholic and her son John had studied at a seminary with boarder Wiechmann, back-fence rumor soon hinted that the Vatican had somehow abetted Lincoln's murder.

Since the Booths were nominal Episcopalians, it would have been as logical to conclude that the Church of England had engineered the assassination. Or to have believed it a Baptist plot because Lewis Paine's father, the Reverend C. H. Powell, was a Baptist preacher.

However, the Catholic whisper, entering the Lincoln murder case by the rear yard, soon occupied the front porch rocking-chair brigade. The Government received advisory letters on the subject from the outset. Some were anonymous. Others bore signature. And a few of the correspondents went so far in their biased convictions as to sign their right names.

Witness a letter addressed to War Secretary Stanton.

---

[23] Noted in Bishop, *op. cit.*, p. 145.

1865
May Sixteenth
Canandaigua, N.Y.

Sir:

John M. Surratt is a Roman Catholic, once patronized and petted by the priests of Georgetown. . . . As he was instrumental in killing a prominent *heretic*, which is considered, at least, a venial offence according to his Church and the spirit of the Pope's late Encyclical letter, may he not find absolution and protection from the Romish priesthood?

As the Papal government only has shown favor to the Southern Rebellion, and as the loyalty of a large proportion of the Catholic clergy is, to say the least, questionable, is not the presumption fair, that Surratt is harbored in some of their secret sanctuaries, more likely in Georgetown? . . .

Yours Respectfully
C. H. A. BULKLEY
formerly Chaplain of 1st
Reg't Excelsior Brigade—
Gen Sickles[24]

Chaplain Bulkley's letter is a curious specimen. The parson's prejudice shines through in descrying the Papal Government as showing a marked favor to the Southern Rebellion—what of England and France? And his reference to Lincoln as a "prominent heretic" shows the other side of an exceedingly odd coin.

For in 1861 Lincoln had been widely denounced as an "atheist." He attended no particular church, acknowledged no creed. It seemed he had never been baptized. All of which brought anathema down on him from the hard-shell Fundamentalists and Bible-belt Sectarians of that day, who were, of course, Protestant.

Lincoln's refusal to adopt a formalized religion outraged rigid conformists and Puritanic pietists throughout his Presidency. His tolerant agnosticism particularly troubled the politicians. Party propagandists contrived to endow him with orthodox views he never possessed, and strenuous efforts were made to bring him to "see the Light." But the light Lincoln saw was of a radiance beyond the visual perception of narrow theologians.

What *was* Lincoln's religion? The question has bothered historians and biographers (not to mention public relationists) ever since it was asked in Springfield. The popular school tries to present him as devout from early youth, ardent in attendance at revival meetings and a member of Springfield's First Presbyterian. "In fact," says historian Tarbell, "Lincoln, all his life, went regularly to church."[25]

Other historians tell us Lincoln was regarded as a skeptic. "If Dennis Hanks is to be believed," says Edgar Lee Masters, "Lincoln did not read the Bible much, though he was always reading something." Masters adds

---

24 National Archives, War Dept. Records, File "B," Doc. 571, JAO.
25 Ida M. Tarbell, *The Life of Abraham Lincoln* (New York: Macmillan Company, 1928), Vol. I, p. 276.

that Lincoln "stood aloof" from revival meetings. And, according to his stepmother, "Lincoln as a boy . . . never talked about religion, and, as far as she could observe, did not even think about religion."[26]

Herndon recalled that Lincoln in Springfield wrote an essay on theology in which he seems to have expressed the view that Jesus, while divinely inspired, was not a supernatural being (the Unitarian philosophy). John T. Stuart, Lincoln's first law partner, called him an "open infidel."

Herndon also wrote that Mrs. Lincoln made the following answer to a query on her husband's religious views: "Mr. Lincoln had no faith and no hope in the usual acceptation of those words. He never joined a church; but still, as I believe, he was a religious man by nature. . . . But . . . he was never a technical Christian."[27] Mrs. Lincoln later denied the statement.

Of course, the most reliable authority on Lincoln's religion was Abraham Lincoln. At the time of his nomination, a canvass was made in Springfield—a sort of trial run to test public sentiment. On reviewing this tabulation, Lincoln was disturbed to find that most of the local clergy were against him. With voting record in hand, he hurried to the State House office of Newton Bateman, an influential Party leader. Closeted with Bateman, Lincoln exhibited the pre-election results.

"Here," Lincoln said, "are twenty-three ministers of different denominations, and all of them are against me but three. Mr. Bateman, I am not a Christian. God knows, I would be one: but I have carefully read the Bible, and I do not so understand this book." He drew from his pocket the New Testament. "These men well know that I am for freedom in the Territories, freedom everywhere as far as the Constitution and laws will permit. And yet with this book in their hands, in the light of which human bondage cannot live for a moment, they are going to vote against me. I do not understand this."[28]

Lincoln's statement, "I am not a Christian," troubled historians for years. As did the fact that twenty out of twenty-three Springfield ministers voted against him. But again, although printed in direct quotes, Lincoln's words were reported as remembered by Newton Bateman. So his tone of voice is lost, his gesture too, an expression, perhaps, of deep humility. His letter to Mrs. Bixby, who supposedly lost five sons in battle, gives us perhaps a more authentic expression of his faith.

> I pray that our heavenly Father may assuage the anguish of your bereavement, and leave you only the cherished memory of the loved and lost. . . .[29]

The truth seems to be that Lincoln leaned to a sort of informal Deism, as did many of America's Founding Fathers. This concept held that the

---

[26] Edgar Lee Masters, *Lincoln: The Man* (New York: Dodd-Mead & Co., 1931), p. 21.

[27] Herndon, Vol II, p. 149.

[28] Abbott and Conwell, *Lives of the Presidents,* pp. 399–40. Also Holland's *Life of Abraham Lincoln,* Masters' *Lincoln: The Man,* and other texts.

[29] *Lincoln's Works,* Vol. II, p. 600.

existence of a Divine Creator is self-evident in nature, that the miracles of sunrise and sunset, of springtime leaf and autumn harvest, are sufficient proof of God's handiwork, without resort to the supernatural revelations of theology.

However, while the Deists rejected literal interpretations of the Bible, they followed the ethics of the Scriptures perhaps more scrupulously than those who insisted on the Biblical letter rather than the Biblical spirit. Moreover, the Deist philosophy was live and let live: freedom to worship as one pleased, or not to worship, if one pleased. This was also the essence of Americanism, a basic root of the tree of Liberty. Franklin, Tom Paine, Jefferson, John Adams (who said religion amounts to four words: "Be Just and Good"), Andrew Jackson, Ulysses S. Grant,—these and other homespun American leaders subscribed to Deist views. Like Lincoln, too, they were denounced by rigid conformists as "atheists," "heretics," "infidels."

But the voices which spoke against Lincoln from the pulpits of Springfield and elsewhere were Protestant. Many liberal Protestant ministers vigorously supported him. But his broad-mindedness was beyond the toleration (and comprehension) of the "hell's-fire-and-brimstone" clergy or those conformists who thought of him as a "heretic." Yet it was just these narrow types (and their parishioners) who saw conspiracy in the Church of Rome when Lincoln was assassinated.

Most of the "anti-Catholic" letters relating to Mary Surratt and her household were so obviously biased that even Stanton must have refused them reading time. Apparently the War Secretary was in no way influenced by the witchhunt reports which pointed a bony finger at the Church of Rome. Evidence is rather to the contrary. Stanton's political target was Richmond, the Confederate leaders. With designs on the South, the astute War Secretary probably wanted no part of an ideological war bound to alienate a large body of Northern voters.

However, the War Department files contain a "Special Order" which indicates at least one military response to information leading to a church institution.

> Head Quarters Department of Washington
> Offices of Provost Marshal General, Defenses North of Potomac
> Washington D.C. May 1st 1865
>
> Special Ordr No. 88 (Extract)
> Special Officer C. Merrill and one (1) assistant on duty at these Hd Qrs will at once proceed to the Convent corner of 10th and "G" Sts this city and examine the baggage of Miss Annie Ward Teacher and arrest her & proceed to War Dpt and deliver her with all letters and papers found in her possesssion to Cl. Burnett without delay.
>
> By Command of Maj. Genl C C Augur
> & Prv Mar Genl.[30]

[30] National Archives, War Dept. Records, File "A," Doc. 317, JAO.

The records hold no further mention of Miss Teacher, her baggage or her alleged papers. It would seem Officer Merrill was misled. As a matter of fact, we know he was if he and his "one (1) assistant" inquired for that name at the G Street Convent. With typical contempt for punctuation and capitalization, the Army garbled Special Order 88 by neglecting to place "teacher" in commas and begin the common noun with a small "t".

The lady's name, of course, was Miss Anna Ward. She was a teacher at the G Street convent. If Officer Merrill missed the first time (and we do not know that he did) he or one of his colleagues soon went back.

The tip came from Louis Wiechmann. And if Mrs. Surratt's star boarder told the truth, Miss Anna Ward was darkly implicated in the doings of Booth and company. During the subsequent Conspiracy Trials, Wiechmann identified Miss Ward as a friend of John Surratt and a confidante of John Wilkes Booth.

On March 23 (said Wiechmann) a strange incident occurred. He, Wiechmann, was busy in his office when the door opened and John Holohan's wife walked in. She brought a telegram which had been delivered to the Surratt boarding house that afternoon. The wire read:

New York, March 23 1865

—Wickman, Esq. No 541 H Street, Washington, D.C.
Tell John telegraph number and street at once.

[Signed] J. Booth

What on earth did it mean? Puzzled, Wiechmann showed the wire to his fellow clerks. Surely his brief acquaintanceship with Booth had not ripened to the joking point. "Wickman, Esquire!" Was this telegram some kind of prank?

Then, as chance would have it, on his way home from work he'd encountered John Surratt at the corner of 7th and F. Wiechmann handed John the telegram.

Surratt glanced at the message. Then he took Wiechmann over to the General Delivery Office. There, Surratt inquired for a letter for a Mr. Sturdy—"James Sturdy," as Wiechmann recalled. A letter so addressed was handed to him. Wiechmann noticed the handwriting because it was peculiarly crude. Somewhere he'd seen that scrawl before. From the corner of his eye he noticed the letter was signed "Wood." Sure! Wood was that fellow who'd been at Mrs. Surratt's house. Called himself "Paine."

After dinner that evening, John Surratt invited Wiechmann out for a stroll. They strolled over to the convent at the corner of 10th and G Streets. Surratt inquired for Miss Annie Ward. The instructress put in an appearance, and Surratt engaged her in a private conversation.

"What the nature of it was," Wiechmann testified, "I do not know."

After calling on Miss Ward at the convent, Surratt led Wiechmann in a saunter over to the Herndon House, corner of 9th and F. There Surratt asked for a Mrs. Murray. When this lady appeared, Surratt drew her aside for a few quiet words. Mrs. Murray couldn't hear. It seemed she was slightly deaf, and Surratt had to raise his voice. So Wiechmann heard the words, too.

"Did not Miss Anna Ward engage a room for a sick man who was to have his meals sent up to him, and who would be here Monday, March 27th?"

(A pretty lengthy speech to issue in a loud baritone, but so Wiechmann's formal deposition reported it.)

Mrs. Murray heard and nodded. Yes, Miss Ward had engaged such a room. A few days later Wiechmann learned that the "sick man" had arrived and was lodged according to room reservations. He gleaned this information from George Atzerodt. The "sick man" at the Herndon House was Lewis Paine.

Some time later Wiechmann mentioned Paine's lodgement at the Herndon House to Mrs. Surratt. When he told her he procured this bit of information from Atzerodt "she was very angry about it." During the week of April 8, Mrs. Surratt, on her way home from St. Patrick's Church, veered aside to call on Paine. (Honora Fitzpatrick substantiated Wiechmann on this bit.) Substance of the interview went unheard by the observers.

Monday evening, April 10, Wiechmann drifted into Mrs. Surratt's parlor. Miss Anna Ward was there. Also John Wilkes Booth. Wiechmann did not say so, but one can imagine the ladies in a flutter, Booth shedding enchanting smiles and presenting his profile. Abruptly the actor crossed the room to Miss Ward and said, "Let me see the address of that lady again." Miss Ward handed Booth a letter. He read it, gave it back. Exit Booth.

After Booth's departure, Annie Surratt read the letter to Wiechmann. "It was too bad," she said, "to practice such deception on him [Wiechmann]." The letter was from John Surratt. Under questioning later, Wiechmann could not recall the contents.[31] Just how Annie Surratt acquired the letter from Anna Ward—and obtained Miss Ward's permission to read it to Wiechmann—is not quite clear in the testimony.

On the evening of April 14—the evening of the assassination strike—Miss Ward reentered the picture. Wiechmann and Mrs. Surratt had just returned from their eventful buggy ride to Surrattsville. The time was about 8:30 P.M. Mrs. Surratt produced a letter from her son John.

This letter was dated St. Lawrence Hall, Canada, April 12, 1865. As Wiechmann recalled it, John Surratt said in the letter that he liked Montreal, had purchased a French pea jacket, was paying $2.50 a day for a hotel room, and intended to go to Toronto soon. Nobody ever saw the letter again. It had not been delivered by the postman; Miss Anna Ward had brought this letter to the house on H Street.

---

[31] Pitman Trial Records. Also Oldroyd, *op. cit.*, p. 178.

Wiechmann doubtless reported all of this within the fortnight after the assassination, when he let his conscience be his guide to the police. Hence Augur's May 1 directive to arrest "Miss Annie Ward Teacher." Surely the police got around to arresting Miss Anna Ward. Or did they? Strange to say, her name is not listed in the inventories of Old Capitol Prison. The prison records are admittedly spotty. She may have been held at some precinct station or Army guardhouse for a time. But major suspects went to the Old Capitol.

A figure of mystery, this instructress at the G Street convent. If we take Wiechmann's word, she made arrangements for Lewis Paine, carried messages for John Surratt, connived somehow with Mrs. Surratt, and knew John Wilkes Booth. Enough to place other necks under the shadow of a hangman's noose. How did Anna Ward escape the shadow?

But for the moment her immunity is beside the point.

The point is, she was not a Presbyterian, Baptist, or Methodist. All kinds of people were in on the Lincoln conspiracy.

Facing trial as a conspirator, Mary Surratt would be defended by counsel who made much of the fact that she was a churchgoer of reputed piety. Catholic churchmen were outraged that a woman of the faith, considered dutifully devout, should be charged with complicity in a shocking crime.

But crime is interdenominational, and the face of conspiracy can be deceiving. In the Lincoln murder case the truth was not to be found in outward appearances.

Nor was much of it gleaned from the mounds of paper work heaped on the Bureau of Military Justice—the harvest of a witchhunt for subversives. There may have been needles in these haystacks, but the higher the stack the more difficult it is to find a needle.

The overloading of files for urgent investigation could have been deliberate. In modern governmentese the device is known as "snowing."

CHAPTER 16

Family Album and Rogues' Gallery

SCENE: the Clarke residence in Philadelphia. Time: Saturday morning, April 15, 1865.

Asia Booth's husband, the comedian John Sleeper Clarke, is shaving. Suddenly the upstairs quiet is broken by a cry from Asia. Clarke hurries to his wife in alarm. Wildly she holds out the morning paper. Clarke stares in shock at the black-barred columns—the latest intelligence from Washington. So begins the ordeal for Booth's sister and brother-in-law.

U.S. Marshal William Millward arrived at the door. Detectives came. Reporters pushed in. Asia Booth Clarke, five months pregnant, almost suffered a nervous breakdown.

The Clarkes were grilled. The servants were grilled. Police prowled through the house, peering into cupboards and closets. Clarke's desk was ransacked. Papers were confiscated. Asia's letters were seized. Incoming mail was intercepted. The Philadephia press enjoyed a field day, describing the venerable Clarke mansion as "mysteriously built,"[1] as though it might contain hidden rooms and secret passages.

Unhappily enough for "Sleepy" Clarke the house did contain that sealed envelope John Wilkes had confided to his sister's keeping the previous winter. After the detectives departed, the comedian and Asia recalled the item. It had been concealed in Clarke's safe. In trepidation they tore open the envelope. Therein they found Booth's explanatory letter to his mother and the open letter addressed "To Whom It May Concern" —the document Booth had dramatically signed with the ostentation of someone processing a last will and testament.

To be characterized by Northern editors as a "Secession Rhapsody," Booth's open letter to the public was purportedly penned as a declaration of intent, a statement of motive, and a valedictory. The modern reader may be surprised by the high-flown phraseology and stilted rhetoric. The

---

[1] Accounts in *Philadelphia Enquirer* and *Washington Evening Star*, April 17–20, 1865.

discerning may detect between the lines a fanaticism and egocentricity amounting to monomania. But Booth's rhetoric simply parroted the platform and pulpit oratory of the time. His fanaticism merely echoed the bombast hurled by both sides during the Civil War—for example, Beauregard's famous "Beauty and Booty" speech, or some of Sumner's perfervid addresses. Indeed, the following excerpts compose a classic in semantic blanks—the standard verbiage of ideological propaganda.

"Right or wrong, God judge me, not man. For be my motive good or bad, of one thing I am sure, the lasting condemnation of the North."

With the above opening line, Booth pits himself against an entire nation —or what he conceives to be an entire nation.

The whole letter contains terrifying balderdash. For it reveals an obsession with symbols and indefinable abstractions so universal that one might see Booth in the throes of a mania which seems the occupational disease of a warring mankind.

But, drunk with rhetoric doubtless laced with brandy, the actor finally gets to his point. He declares: "My love (as things stand to-day) is for the South alone. Nor do I deem it a dishonor in attempting to make for her a prisoner of this man, to whom she owes so much misery. If success attends me, I go penniless to her side. . . ." He signs himself: "A Confederate, Doing Duty upon His Own Responsibility—J. Wilkes Booth."[2]

The reference to making "a prisoner of this man" had to do, of course, with the original plan to abduct Lincoln. The screed deposited with Asia, then, was not composed with Lincoln's murder in mind, and it could not be taken as evidence bearing directly on the assassination conspiracy. Nevertheless, John Wilkes had burdened his sister and brother-in-law with a bugbear.

Furious at being forced to play intermediary, Clarke turned over Booth's epistolary maunderings to Marshal Millward. Immediately the comedian was arrested for secreting evidence. Handcuffed, he went to Washington for lodgement in the Old Capitol.

In the drama of the Lincoln murder case, John Matthews moves on stage and off as one of the more mysterious bit players in the cast. According to his own word—and to the credulity of the Bureau of Military Justice—he was the one man in Washington, outside of Booth's intimate circle, who could have given the authorities the names of the leading conspirators within the hour of Lincoln's assassination.

One would think that an individual with such knowledge in his possession should have rushed straight to the police. And that a failure to do so would have brought Federal charges of complicity so soon as the fact of his delinquency became established. Not only did Matthews fail to go straight to the police, but he secreted his vital knowledge for days on end.

---

[2] Letter published in full in Appendix A.

Then, when he finally told his story, the authorities welcomed him as a key Government witness. Or so the surface facts would make it seem.

The known facts, then, concerning John Matthews are in themselves preposterous. In a long-deferred deposition he declared that he had been accosted by Booth on Pennsylvania Avenue, on Good Friday afternoon. Booth, mounted, had pulled over to the curb and handed Matthews a sealed letter, asking him to deliver it the next day to the editor of the *National Intelligencer*. Obligingly enough, Matthews had thrust the letter into his pocket. He thought nothing of it (or so he said) until the shocking attack on the President at Ford's Theater that night.

Matthews was a member of the *Cousin* cast. Details on his doings at the time of the assassination are confused. By one account, he was backstage behind the flats when Lincoln was shot.[3] By other accounts he had left the theater and gone to a neighboring bar for a quick drink. Matthews told a garbled story. But he did recall that the shooting panicked him. Reminded of Booth's letter in his pocket, he raced from 10th Street back to his hotel. There, in the privacy of his room, he tore open the envelope. The letter was addressed: "To the Editors of the *National Intelligencer*. Confidential and Important."

Afterward Matthews said the letter made him sick. It was a statement by John Wilkes Booth revealing the plan to assassinate President Lincoln. And it contained the names (apparently signatures) of the men who were party to the murder strike. John Matthews' hair went up. Caught with this incriminating screed, he realized he might be held as a co-conspirator.

Frightened, Matthews threw Booth's letter into the grate. When it had burned, he pulverized the ashes. But the letter's closing paragraph was seared into his mind. Months later Matthews could recite it, word for word. It read:

> The moment has at length arrived when my plans must be changed. The world may censure me for what I am about to do, but I am sure that posterity will justify me. [Signed] John Wilkes Booth—Payne—Atzerodt and Herold.[4]

That was the story told by John Matthews. And the Government (and America's historians) swallowed it hook, line, and sinker. The hook was that Matthews told it two years after the assassination, talking as a witness at the trial of John Surratt. The line was that he recalled verbatim the final paragraph of a letter read in panic on the night of April 14, 1865. The sinker was that no one ever saw the letter in question except actor John Matthews; therefore its content rested solely on his dubious word.

Nor was Matthews ever called upon to explain why he failed to report

---

[3] Wilson, *op. cit.*, p. 115.
[4] Quoted in Wilson, *op. cit.*, p. 107.

immediately so important a document—failed to turn it over to the authorities on the night of Lincoln's murder.

While police and Federal detectives combed the city in a game of blindman's buff and the War Department made wild guesses as to the identity of the assassins, actor Matthews quietly walked the streets of the frantic capital.

But Matthews did not remain entirely mum at that time. At some hour during that dark Easter weekend, he entered a police station to swear out a statement. Lodged in the War Department files, this original testimony remained on record. In it Matthews declared that he was professionally acquainted with John Wilkes Booth. Nothing about Booth giving him a letter on Pennsylvania Avenue. Nothing about the names of the conspirators. Nothing at all of any significance.

Except that Matthews did describe Booth to the police as a handsome and personable fellow. And he concluded this initial statement with the interesting observation that had Booth been a woman, he, Matthews, could have loved him.[5]

The shadow fell with stunning violence on Junius Brutus Booth. He was playing in Cincinnati on the night of the assassination. When the news reached the city the following day, an infuriated mob stormed the actor's hotel. Junius Brutus fled by a side exit. He spent the next few days in semiconcealment. Friends sheltered him and he managed to travel east incognito.

Eventually (on April 26) Junius Brutus Booth was arrested in Philadelphia. The War Department muted the matter. But according to the docket of the Old Capitol, the assassin's eldest brother was "committed by order of Secty Stanton."[6]

Long afterward, the reason for Junius Brutus' commitment became known. It seemed the Secret Service had discovered a letter he had written to "Johnny." In this letter the practical Junius had advised John Wilkes Booth to get out of the "oil business." On the hunt for the cryptic, Baker's agents apparently took "oil business" to be a code term for "assassination plot." From supposition they jumped to hard and fast conclusion—a leap too often made in an effort to avoid the drudgery of procuring proof.

But to give the detectives their due, reference to "oil deals" frequently appeared in the correspondence of Rebel secret agents. There was the case of Captain Cole and his mistress "Irish Lize"—the pair who had tried to bribe the crew of U.S. gunboat *Michigan* on Lake Erie. Cole had posed as an "oil merchant," and talked of a big petroleum deal in prospect. Soon after Junius Booth's arrest, the War Department received a letter

---

[5] National Archives, War Dept. Records, File "M," JAO.
[6] National Archives, War Dept. Records, File "W," Doc. 1914, JAO.

from a Canadian physician who advised that shortly before Lincoln's assassination a mysterious young Southerner, a pneumonia patient, had talked in delirium about a big "oil project" in the offing.[7]

Moreover, Booth's loquacious accomplices, Arnold and O'Laughlin, had told a dozen people that they were associated in the "oil business" with Booth. "Oil" was mentioned in the mysterious "LEON" letter. In the devious lexicon of secret intelligence "oil" could mean almost anything. Hence the "assassination plot" translation.

However, John Wilkes Booth actually had been gambling in wildcat oil stocks, as evidenced by the "Fuller Farms" brochures found in his trunk. Reference to these and to business letters from an oil broker should have established the validity of the fraternal advice from Junius Brutus Booth. Apparently such reference was not made.

No use for Junius Booth to protest that wild "Johnny" had been playing the petroleum market. No use for Junius Booth to protest anything. His name was Booth. He was the assassin's brother. Guilt by blood relationship.

A morose figure on the train to Washington, Junius Booth said bitterly to his guard, "I wish John had been killed before the assassination, for the sake of his family."[8] He said little else on the train ride. He must have been dumb with anger when they locked him into an Old Capitol cell. He had supported the North during the war.

Another brother to go to jail was Joseph ("Doc") Booth. After a brief and calamitous appearance on the stage, young Joe had gone to school in the South. Then he had wandered out to California. Returning east in April, 1865, he was astonished when summarily arrested at the steamer landing in New York. As he had just arrived from San Francisco, he could hardly have had a hand in the assassination conspiracy. After a few hours' grilling he was released. But Joseph Booth never forgot the experience. For years he refused to refer to John Wilkes Booth as his brother.

No less beset than the Booth family were the Fords. John T. Ford, the Baltimore impresario, was not in Washington on the night of the tragedy. But Stanton had seized the playhouse; naturally he would seize the theater operator.

Arrested on the weekend following the assassination, John T. Ford vehemently protested innocence. He made no bones about knowing John Wilkes Booth—every theater man in the country knew the Booths. And if Lincoln had been assassinated in the B. & O. depot (Ford might well have asked), would Stanton have seized the terminal and the president of the railroad?

---

[7] National Archives, War Dept. Records, File "Mc," Doc. "Evd." JAO.
[8] Quoted in Ruggles, *op. cit.*, p. 189.

But railroading was respectable business. Theater business had the repute of a shady lady. Solid citizens patronized, but kept their spiritual fingers crossed. On April 19 another of the Fords—James R.—was clapped into the Old Capitol. His docket read simply, "Business man, theater."[9]

Henry Clay Ford, treasurer of the fatal playhouse, was arrested and imprisoned on the 21st. He was promptly released, then rearrested on the 24th, the prison entry reading: "Recommitted. Hold in close confinement until further orders."

The Fords were in dire trouble. Like the members of Booth's family, they were symbols. When Stanton could not lay hands on anything of substance, he was all for jailing the symbolic.

The whole Ford's Theater crew was therefore on the black list. Gifford and Clark, the stage carpenters, were jailed by Stanton's order on April 30. John Slackman, assistant property-man, went protesting into the Old Capitol a week later. Slackman's entry read: "Arrested by order of the President."[10] Which probably meant Andrew Johnson's initials on some slip of paper handed him by the War Secretary.

To be sure, the stage crew and the Fords could hardly have escaped suspicion. Someone in the playhouse had given Booth a hand. Yet there were persons in Washington—John Matthews for one—who stood far more suspect than the assistant property-man. What of the guard, John Parker, who had deliberately walked away from Lincoln's box? What of ticket-seller Thomas Reybold, who had broken the lock on Box 8? But even these individuals were minor cogs in the mechanism. What of the Secret Service Chief, who had failed to post a single under-cover man in the theater audience? What of the War Secretary who had refused the President a special escort?

Imprisoned in the Old Capitol, John T. Ford had a right to protest his treatment by the military.

Socially speaking, all of the assassination conspirators were "Typhoid Marys." An acquaintance with John H. Surratt could prove as unhealthy as one with Atzerodt, Herold, Paine or John Wilkes Booth.

So the bane came to a merchant of substance in Baltimore, Mr. D. Preston Parr. Parr was arrested in the Maryland metropolis on April 18. Unlike many taken into custody by the Federal agents, Mr. Parr immediately managed to procure a lawyer.

Parr's attorney did his legal best with a letter advising War Secretary Stanton that Mr. Parr was a Baltimore citizen who could "produce testimonials from the first men of the city as to his standing in the community;"

---

[9] National Archives, War Dept. Records, File "W," Doc. 1914, JAO.
[10] National Archives, War Dept. Records, File "R," Doc. 266, JAO.

that "no charge has been brought against him;" and that "his health is suffering severely by confinement."[11] And so forth. All of which made no impression whatever on Edwin M. Stanton.

Eight days after his detention in Baltimore, Parr was deposited in Washington's Old Capitol. He was docketed: "Supposed to know something of Surratt—telegraphs to him."[12]

Under prolonged interrogation, Parr reluctantly admitted to an acquaintance with John Surratt. He said he had met young Surratt during a stagecoach journey from Leonardtown to Washington. They had chatted as fellow travelers do. Surratt had been likable. Said he would call on Parr in Baltimore.

The interrogators drew from Parr the admission that he had a son in the Confederate service; that Surratt had said he would "get in touch" with the boy; that he had run a letter for Mr. Parr through the blockade.

Further questioning elicited the admission that Surratt had run several letters through the lines for Mr. Parr. And, finally, that Parr's wife was acquainted with a party in Washington—a certain Mr. Green.[13] A most interesting acknowledgment on the part of the prisoner. For here, extracted from Parr like a bad tooth, is a definite link between the Booth gang and the mysterious Thomas and Nannie Green who lived in the VanNess mansion at the foot of 17th Street.

What did the Federal Secret Service know about the old VanNess mansion? War Department records go shy on the subject. But one can almost be certain that Baker's agents had kept the house under a watchful eye. For Nannie Green's maiden name was Anne Lomax. The family was well known in Washington. Of Southern extraction, they had long been suspected as Secession sympathizers. Old Capitol records show that Anne's sister, Virginia Lomax, had spent many months in prison as a supposed subversive. Nannie's husband, Thomas Green (owner of the VanNess mansion) was a Virginian. Two sons were in the Confederate Army.

If Baker's agents had not been keeping the VanNess mansion under close surveillance, they should have been. Some time after the war, Thomas N. Conrad talked. Conrad had been a Rebel secret intelligence agent. In the winter of 1863 he had built an abduction apparatus in Washington, with the VanNess House as the key element.

Working with Conrad were two other secret agents, a spy named Mountjoy and a hulking fellow known as Frizelle. They had planned to ambush Lincoln's carriage on the road out to the Soldiers' Home, and to smuggle him captive into the VanNess mansion. The plot fell through

---

[11] National Archives, War Dept. Records, File "W," Doc. 433, JAO.
[12] National Archives, War Dept. Records, File "A," "Prisoner Role," JAO.
[13] National Archives, War Dept. Records, File "P," Doc. R.B.P. 68, JAO.

when Lincoln rode out unexpectedly with a cavalry escort, and Conrad decided the enterprise was too risky.[14]

The parallel between Conrad's abduction plot and Booth's leads to the conclusion that Booth, working with the Confederate underground, must have heard of Conrad's scheme and determined to adopt it. It follows that Thomas and Nannie Green were led into Booth's conspiracy. As disclosed by Conrad, the VanNess mansion had been used throughout the war as a spy communications center—a "letter drop." Probably the house was on John Surratt's route when he spirited secret mail through the capital. In any event, evidence indicated that the old dark house featured in Booth's abduction scheme as it had in Conrad's. Did Mr. Parr of Baltimore fit somewhere into the apparatus?

Sweating, ashen, Parr confessed to his interrogators that his wife knew the Greens quite intimately. Before her marriage Mrs. Parr had been a neighbor of the Lomaxes.· Surratt and Parr—Parr and the Lomaxes—Lomaxes, the Greens and the VanNess house—there is a thread running through the warp of all this. One is reminded, too, that when he first visited Mrs. Surratt's boarding house and introduced himself as "Wood," Lewis Paine told Wiechmann that he clerked in Baltimore for a merchant named Parr.

But the thread dissolves. Just as it seems the Government has a strong case against D. Preston Parr, charges against him are shelved. Why? The War Department dossier provides no answer. Shortly after his lodgment in the Old Capitol, Parr suffered an epileptic seizure. His interrogation broke off as abruptly.

Three weeks after his arrest, the prison docket on Parr was altered to read, "Witness."[15] This differs considerably from "telegraphs to Surratt." What happened to the original charge? What happened to the telegrams? What happened to Parr's confessed acquaintance with a family of known subversives? Why was Lewis Paine's connection with a Mr. Parr never closely examined?

The Bureau of Military Justice prosecuted suspected subversives on evidence far less substantial than the evidence mustered on Parr. But the Parr case was dropped. And in equally mysterious fashion, the Greens were eventually cleared of conspiracy charges. Although the Conrad story was not known at the time, Baker's Secret Service agents had a lead of some kind on the doings at the VanNess mansion—hence the arrest of Thomas and Nannie Green. Yet the Greens were to be covered by a cloak of immunity.

Meanwhile, Army police and Federal agents went far afield, rabbit-hunting.

---

[14] Noted in Eisenschiml, *op. cit.*, pp. 12–13.
[15] National Archives, War Dept. Records, File "R," Doc. 266, JAO.

Take the Pearson case. It crowds the War Department files with a clutter of depositions, police reports, official endorsements, Army correspondence and paper-work—thousands of words tied up in Government red tape. Hundreds of dollars and hundreds of man-hours went into the investigation of Lieutenant Clement H. Pearson, U.S.A. Yet from first to last the affair was a comedy of errors so ridiculous that the censors in Stanton's office hastened to hide it from the public. The fact remains that the War Department spent more time and effort on Pearson than it did on Preston Parr or the Greens.

Who was Lieutenant Pearson? He told them at the outset. "I was in the Pennsylvania Reserves, First Pennsylvania Cavalry, promoted from the ranks. Later served with the First New York Cavalry. Was on the staff of General Sigel, Max Weber, General Howe and General Stevenson."

How did a combat veteran on record as a U.S. Army staff officer come to be involved in the Lincoln murder case? For Lieutenant Pearson that seems to have been easy.

It began with Appomattox—victory and cease fire—Grant's army celebrating—Lieutenant Pearson heading for Washington "on private business." He had his mustering-out pay and some other pocket cash, and in Washington he hoped to pick up his bounty money.

Pearson found the national capital in a holiday mood. "I couldn't do any business with all the illuminations and celebrations going on." He could join the celebrants, however. So he, too, became illuminated. Or, as he termed it, "tight." That was Pearson's first step into quicksand.

"Tight," he began to spend his pocket money. He took an expensive room at the National Hotel. So he went in up to his ankle—the room was on the same floor as one occupied by a certain actor.

That week Pearson went on a real spree. His wandering steps led him to a shooting gallery on the corner of 9th and Pennsylvania. While Pearson was firing his mustering-out pay at clay pigeons, the actor from the National Hotel stalked in.

The stranger picked up a pistol and tried a couple of fast shots. He wasn't too expert, as Pearson recalled, but he challenged the Lieutenant to a little contest. Pearson couldn't decline. The fellow acted too cocky. It seemed his name was Booth, but that meant nothing to Clem Pearson. "I beat him twice out of three times in shooting." Mr. Booth grew huffy and walked out.[16]

Pearson did not know it, but he was now up to his knees in trouble. More than one witness had seen the shooting-gallery incident, and it looked as though Booth were practicing with homicidal intent. It also looked as though the Union cavalry lieutenant were practicing as Booth's second. Pearson was a husky young fellow. His pistol skill and his build

---

[16] National Archives, War Dept. Records, File "P," Doc. R.B.P. 68, JAO.

were rememberd on the night of April 14 when the alarm went out for the killer who had invaded the Seward residence.

Naturally enough, the police inquired for Pearson at the National that night. Pearson had left the city. Out went the alarm for a tipsy sharpshooter in the uniform of a Union cavalry officer. What with the Appomattox celebrations going on, every city in the North was probably teeming with tipsy sharpshooters in cavalry-officer uniform. Pearson disappeared.

One week later he was arrested by military police in Philadelphia. The circumstances of his apprehension were odd, to say the least.

Report of Captain W. H. Dunbar, U.S.A. (Philadelphia, Pa., April 22, 1865):

> I arrested Clement P. Humphrey, alias C. H. Pearson, at the Continental Hotel. . . . After the assassination at Washington, Ada McKinsey, alias Ada Pearson, stopped at Lochiel House, Harrisburg, and said that her husband, C. H. Pearson, would be there soon. Governor Curtin had said that this "Pearson" was the supposed assassin of Mr. Seward. . . . He [Pearson] tried to borrow ten dollars from Sgt. Wm. C. Smith, and told him that he could make forty thousand dollars in Washington. When asked how, he said, 'By a simple turn of the wrist.' Also intimated to one Ramsey he could make a fortune—repay a loan to get him to Washington.[17]

Pearson plaintively and indignantly protested his arrest. But under interrogation he became tongue-tied. Where had he been in the past few days? Clutching an aching head, the Lieutenant strove to remember. He'd been on an awful spree, he knew that. He'd gone from Washington to Harrisburg to meet his wife, Ada. But she wasn't there at the Lochiel House when he arrived, so he went down to the bar to pass the time. At the bar he'd met a stranger who introduced himself as Mr. William P. Ashby.

Well, one drink led to another. Then Ashby, friendly, invited Pearson to join him upstairs in a nightcap. They'd had quite a few nightcaps up in Ashby's room. And now it all came back to Pearson's memory. Vague, like a half-remembered nightmare.

They were up in Mr. Ashby's room, drinking, when Ashby suddenly went to a wardrobe and donned a Confederate officer's coat. Pearson should have been surprised, but at that stage of the evening he was too "tight" to raise an eyebrow. Ashby poured him another nightcap (Pearson could raise that), and then Ashby offered Pearson a rather unusual proposition.

"He knew the Shenandoah country," Pearson was able to recall. "And he said there was a man over in Winchester—a man he wanted to kill."

But for various reasons Ashby preferred to have the job done for him. He offered Lieutenant Pearson fifty thousand dollars for the shooting. He said he didn't have the fifty thousand on him. However, he did have a

---

[17] National Archives, War Dept. Records, File "P," Doc. R.B.P. 68, JAO.

"money order," and he offered a down payment of one thousand dollars. He promised to send Lieutenant Pearson the other forty-nine thousand as soon as the job was accomplished.

Pearson stated with much vehemence that he wouldn't have dreamed of taking the down payment had he been sober. As it was, he accepted the thousand-dollar advance. He neither promised nor intended to shoot anybody. The stranger had assured him: "You can take that and spend it, but if you don't do anything, it is all right."[18]

Pearson repaired to his own room, and fell into a deep slumber. When he awoke next day he thought the Ashby confab had been a dream. But, no, there was the "money order" on his bureau. The draft was drawn on "G. W. Johnson & Co. of Washington, D.C." It was made out for a thousand dollars. It bore Mr. Ashby's signature.

The "money order" in question bore something else—something that should have warned Lieutenant Pearson that nightcaps and negotiable notes are not always to be trusted. For the "money order" was scribbled on a scrap of ruled paper as commonplace as any in a schoolboy's notebook. And Mr. Ashby's signature bore the abracadabra countersign: "lla ightr. K.C." Pearson held what was probably the only check in history endorsed in "pig Latin."

One might reasonably have presumed that even an Army lieutenant on a lost weekend would scent the rubber in such a check. Ingenuous Lieutenant Pearson made an effort to cash the paper. When Harrisburgers proved unobliging, Pearson went to Philadelphia. He tried the "money order" on an acquaintance, Mr. Ramsey, and then on a chance-met Army sergeant. Or so the evidence indicates.

Naturally, Pearson did not give the sergeant his right name. No self-respecting Army officer likes to beg a favor of a non-com, and when the sergeant looked askance at the paper, Pearson asked a ten-dollar loan. By way of security, he mentioned a fortune to be made in Washington by a "simple turn of the wrist." The phrase was unfortunate. It hinted of conspiracy, and the sergeant reported it to headquarters.

Pearson assured the arresting officers that he had meant nothing sinister. He'd wanted train fare to Washington where he could present the "money order" to the firm it was drawn on. Mr. Ashby had provided him with the address—G. W. Johnson & Co. at 132 D Street. The M.P.'s had only to consult a Washington directory to learn that this company and its address were authentic.

The M.P.'s did find such a company in the Washington directory. Whereupon they sent Lieutenant Clement H. Pearson to Washington, but to another address. Under guard the unhappy lieutenant went to Old Capitol Prison.

---

[18] *Ibid.*

For it seemed the Johnson firm had never heard of a Mr. Ashby. But Washington detectives had heard of a Lieutenant Pearson, cavalry officer who'd stayed at the National Hotel and been seen at pistol practice with John Wilkes Booth. Nor was that all. Examining Pearson's "money order," Army intelligence people concluded that "lla ightr, K.C." was secret code meaning "all right. Knights of the Golden Circle."[19] A most subversive endorsement!

Worse for Pearson was a report submitted by the Special Commissioner's Office, Philadelphia, on April 21. Colonel Olcott in Washington was informed that ". . . a gentleman named John Lyon, 1203 Citron Street [Philadelphia], states that a neighbor of his named Pearson has made himself conspicuous by his singular conduct. . . ."[20] This Pearson was of Southern extraction. He was often away from home. "He and his wife and children often make disloyal utterances. . . . Recently he gave her $5,000. She was joyous at Lincoln's death . . . seems to come from bloodthirsty stock as she is the sister of Boyle [Boyd?] who murdered a Federal officer at Baltimore."

Moreover, the Pearson in question had told his Philadelphia neighbors he was one of Baker's Secret Service agents. The Philadelphia Commissioner advised Colonel Olcott: "Have to ask if you will ascertain if this Pearson is employed by Col. Baker and telegraph me. In the meantime I am making sure of what facts I can get hold of, and if they prove important and reliable . . . I will lay them before the proper authorities for the arrest of this precious family of vipers."

In Washington, Olcott had rushed the Philadelphia dispatch to Colonel Burnett. On April 22 the Judge Advocate endorsed it: "On conference with Col. Baker directed him [the Philadelphia Commissioner] to arrest both Mrs. and Mr. Pearson and to report result."[21]

Of course, the Pearson of Citron Street, Philadelphia, and Lieutenant Clement H. Pearson, U.S.A., were not synonymous individuals. The latter already in military custody, did his best to identify himself as an Army officer in good standing. While secret intelligence officers were decoding "lla ightr," Pearson sat in the Old Capitol composing an appeal as mournful as anything from the Prisoner of Chillon. He addressed this plea to the son of Secretary Seward.

Brigadier General Seward
    Washington, D.C.
General I have been most unjustly arested (*sic*) at this Post by some officers belonging at Harrisburg as they claim by orders from Washington for my arest as being conected with the assasination of Secretary Seward.

---

[19] *Ibid.*
[20] National Archives, War Dept. Records, File "F," Doc. 6, JAO.
[21] *Ibid.*

All I can say is that I am inocent and know nothing about the affair at all. Please have me released at once. I cannot Stand this any longer.

(Signed) Clem H. Pearson
Late A.D.C.
Genl Stefenson's Staff[22]

Eight days after Pearson's arrest, Secret Service Chief Baker sent the following note to Stanton's office:

"From my investigation in the case I am of the opinion that he P is in no wise implicated in the matter of the assassination of the President and Mr. Seward."[23]

But Lieutenant Pearson's troubles were not over. He had yet to explain Mr. Ashby, the thousand-dollar "money order" and "lla ightr." That explanation was going to take him from late April until late June, 1865. As a matter of record, he would never satisfactorily explain that exotic transaction.

Had Pearson vouchsafed some sensible answer he could perhaps have saved the Government and himself a lot of time. But Pearson adhered to his original story and was accordingly stuck with it. And if Ashby had, indeed, been a figment of his own invention, it would seem the lieutenant should have had more brains than to attach a homicide angle to the fabrication. Much of the involved evidence points to some kind of fraud. But in the tangle the truth was lost.

So was a horse. After two months in prison, Lieutenant Pearson was released. He at once put in a claim for a horse "lost in U.S. service" during the war. The Adjutant General's Office rejected the claim on the contention that "claimant has been arrested on suspicion." The matter went to the Judge Advocate's Office for adjudication. Judge Advocate Burnett finally ruled:

> The within named Clem H. Pearson was arrested for other reasons than his supposed identity with "Paine." After a full examination . . . he was released from custody. *His attitude toward the Government is now the same as any other citizen* and his former imprisonment should be no bar, I think, to adjustment of any just claim. . . .[24]

But what does Burnett mean by reference to Pearson's "attitude toward the Government?" Clearly he implies that Pearson was arrested for disloyalty. He also implies that the lieutenant had actually been disloyal, and had then altered his subversive views. However, the disloyal Pearson was the *other* Pearson; the Philadelphia resident with the "precious family of vipers." The Judge Advocate's decision, then, is tantamount to forgiving a man for a crime he did not commit.

[22] National Archives, War Dept. Records, File "C," Doc. 700, JAO.
[23] National Archives, War Dept. Records, File "C," Doc. 474, JAO.
[24] National Archives, War Dept. Records, File "G," Doc. 251, JAO. (Emphasis supplied.)

Odd contrivances were the scales used in the Bureau of Military Justice for weighing charges of conspiracy and subversion. Innocent of conspiracy, John T. Ford lost a valuable theater. His subversion unproved, Lieutenant C. H. Pearson lost a good horse. In both cases, the confiscated property was eventually paid for. But the theater owner and the Army lieutenant received no recompense for the weeks they spent in jail.

Caught in the anti-subversive dragnet were all kinds of quaint and queer fish. Against many of the arrested individuals the charges were so vaporous that the War Department failed to document them. Fendal McCorbun, Dr. Peter Haskell, Edward H. Wyvill, William Bryon, Walter P. Griffin—they were clapped into the Old Capitol as "suspects," but after a week or two in prison, these five were released.

Who was John Augur Stolt, arrested by Baker's men in Chambersburg? The Old Capitol register shows him as a tenant, but the docket merely labels him "suspicious character." The record is similarly noncommital on Acting Assistant-Surgeon John A. Hall of Lincoln Hospital "to be held for Colonel Burnett." And why was Dr. Robert Neale impounded? The prison docket on Neale remains a blank.[25]

On April 25 the military police arrested one Benjamin Booth Cook in Pottsville, Pennsylvania. Booth could be dangerous, even as a middle name. However, in this instance it proved most misleading. A vagrant who had been on his way through Pottsville, Mr. Cook carried identity papers which named him "Geo. B. Sage, late of 13th Illinois Infantry." Unfortunately for the bearer, Army telegraph soon established that Lieutenant George B. Sage of the 13th Infantry was currently on duty with his regiment in Illinois.

Who was Benjamin Booth Cook? Transferred from Pottsville to the Old Capitol, the man was held for days in solitary as a major assassination suspect. Eventually the prisoner stammered out a lengthy deposition. Among other things, he stated that he had made the acquaintance of Lieutenant Sage "on the Illinois Central Railroad." Traveling to Washington from Illinois, he had then assumed the name of Sage because he "very often used an assumed name." Benjamin Booth Cook, alias Sage, was not quite sure why he'd gone from Washington to Pottsville, Pennsylvania. But finally he came to the point. "I have been in an asylum for several years."[26] So ended the case against Benjamin Booth Cook. Oddly enough, his middle name—the factor that had caused his arrest—proved genuine. But poor Ben Cook was not related to the Maryland Booths.

Another freak specimen in the net was William B. Donaldson, apprehended in Washington by order of Provost Marshal Ingraham. Donaldson was a circus clown. The War Department wanted to know

25 National Archives, War Dept. Records, File "R," Doc. 266, JAO.
26 National Archives, War Dept. Records, File "B," Doc. EB 284, JAO.

what conspiratorial menace he concealed behind his putty nose and painted smile. For the police received word that this itinerant Merry Andrew carried on his person a $100,000 Confederate bond.

Of course, few circus clowns carry $100,000 bonds in their pockets. The $100,000 bond found on Donaldson at the time of his arrest by Captain Franklin and Officer Rosch was guaranteed to pay him dividends of trouble.

Otherwise, like Donaldson himself, the bond did not come up to par as a security. It happened to bear the seal of the Confederacy. As a souvenir it might have been peddled for thirty cents. Still, a pertinent question persisted. How came the unhappy clown into possession of a gilt-edged bond issued by the Confederate States of America?

Colonel H. S. Olcott discovered the answer. "I find that the within named Donaldson is a well known New York gambler and has been indicted as such."[27]

So far as the War Department was concerned, Olcott's endorsement closed the Donaldson dossier. Apparently the Judge Advocate General could find no connection between the assassination conspiracy and a card game in which a circus-lot sharper cheated some victim out of a worthless bond.

Equally tenuous was the connection between the assassination plot and a fantastic character brought in from Missouri. Name: Dr. Francis Tumblety. Residence: A covered wagon. Profession? But the Doctor is best introduced by the report forwarded by Colonel John P. Baker, Provost Marshal General of Missouri, to Assistant War Secretary Dana.

> I have the honor to forward herewith, in compliance with your telegram of this date, Dr. Tumblety, alias Blackburn. All his papers had been carefully examined previous to the arrival of your order, but nothing was found in them tending to implicate him with the assassination.
>
> Tumblety's papers and his own admissions show that he has tramped the continent from Quebec to New Orleans, in the character of an "Indian Herb Doctor"; has gained an extensive notoriety as an impostor and quack; has been compelled to leave several towns and cities in Canada for his rascality and trickery, and is being continually importuned and threatened by those he has deluded and swindled.
>
> Tumblety's principal associates in Saint Louis have been one J. W. Blackburn, his assistant in the "medical profession," and one Oregon Wilson, an artist. There appears to be nothing against them, except they belong to a class of adventurers that encumber and prey upon society.[28]

In light of the Missouri Provost's initial report, what can be made of Secretary Dana's insistence on Tumblety's incarceration and interrogation? Dana advised Judge Advocate General Joseph Holt that he felt the prisoner "should be confined in the Penitentiary." To this advice Dana

27 National Archives, War Dept. Records, File "M," Doc. 264, JAO.
28 National Archives, War Dept. Records, File "B," Doc. 261, JAO.

added the suggestion: "Let the Indian Doctor tell all he knows about Booth and Booth's associates."[29]

What did the "Indian Doctor" know? The files of the Bureau of Military Justice do not confide an answer to that question. Tumblety's name is registered in the Old Capitol inventory, but particulars are not specified. Then he vanishes from the prison records.

So Dana's "let him tell all" endorsement goes unexplained. Yet somehow the Assistant War Secretary had been led to believe Tumblety had something to tell. What could the medicine-show impresario have known?

A hint of Tumblety's suspected knowledge may be found in contemporary newspapers. Issued on the day the doctor was seized, a St. Louis press dispatch referred to him as "J. H. Blackburn, alias Dr. Tumblety, arrested for complicity with Herrold."[30]

A Toronto paper of May 8 elaborated on the St. Louis report with: "Many of our readers will remember Dr. Tumblety, who figured in this city some years ago. From Toronto he went to New York, and at the breaking out of the Civil War he was appointed surgeon in a Union Regiment. The New York papers say that Harrold, Booth's accomplice, turns out to have been the agent and confident of the notorious quack, and that Tumblety lately disappeared from Brooklyn in a mysterious manner."[31]

It remained for the Rochester (New York) *Advertiser* to identify the mountebank.

> The *Telegraph* reports from St. Louis that J. J. Blackburn alias Dr. Tumblety has been arrested charged with complicity with Harrold in the assassination of President Lincoln. The only Dr. Tumblety that we ever heard of was one who lived in Rochester in his younger days and who, taking up the practice of medicine, went elsewhere to astonish the people. He was a tall dandified individual, sported a heavy cane, and was followed by a hound which bore in appearance the same relation to the canine race that his master did to the human. He was a quack all over and nothing else. His name is Tumblety, and we were not aware that he had taken the name of Blackburn. It may be that he has changed his name. We had lost track of him altogether till this assassination scheme brought him to the surface.[32]

Eventually released from the Old Capitol, the doctor returned to his habitat beneath the surface. Did that subterranean area actually extend into the Confederate underground? Did Tumblety, in truth, know David Herold and the mysterious Dr. Blackburn? As he bows out of history— on the tailboard of a covered wagon, with a bottle of medicinal rainwater in either hand—who can say? The War Department records offer nothing further on Dr. Tumblety.

---

[29] National Archives, War Dept. Records, File "B," Doc. 26, JAO.
[30] St. Louis press dispatch, May 6, 1865 (in local papers).
[31] Copied in New York *Daily Tribune*, May 9, 1865.
[32] Rochester *Advertiser*, May 9, 1865.

Three weeks after Lincoln's murder, Captain G. B. Russell prepared for the War Department an inventory of Old Capitol prisoners committed to that date as assassination or conspiracy suspects. To Russell's roster, Secret Service Chief Baker appended a supplementary Secret Service list. In this supplement, Baker's prisoners were identified only by date of arrest.

April 18: John Celestino
April 19: Emile Jarboe
April 21: George Jarboe
April 21: J. W. Wharton
April 24: Jacob Miller
April 24: Oliver Brown
April 25: Edward Chelsey
April 25: R. Condon[33]

Who were these nonentities? Stripped of the usual docketings, their names were entered on the prison roster with less biographical data than one normally finds on tombstones. One must comb the War Department files to clothe these prisoners with the barest scraps of identity.

The Jarboes, for instance, were acquaintances of David Herold. But the Jarboes were small fry. So, apparently, were the others netted by Baker between the 18th and 25th of April. With one exception—the first prisoner listed, namely, John Celestino.

On an Old Capitol roster drawn up by Prison Superintendent Wood on June 1st, the man was registered as follows:

NAME: Celestino, John. Rank or Town: Sea Captain. Regiment or County or State: Cuba. Where Captured: Philadelphia, Pa. Remarks, Charges, &c. &c.: Transferred from arsenal by order of Maj. Gen. Hancock.[34]

Celestino first wormed his way into history in 1864. In April of that year, U.S. gunboat *Vicksburg*, on blockade duty off the North Carolina coast, snared a little two-masted schooner lolling in the approaches to Cape Fear. The craft's aspect was decidedly irregular. Her sternboard bore no name. She carried no freight. Her skipper could not produce a log book. Nor could he reasonably account for her presence off the Confederate seaport of Wilmington, N.C. The skipper's papers identified him as "John M. Celeste."

Questioned on board the *Vicksburg*, Celeste declared himself a Portuguese. He said his true name was Joao Celestino, showed a certificate of British registry for the schooner *Indian* out of Nassau, the Bahamas, and went on to state that he had been sailing to Havana, Cuba, from Belize, Honduras, where he had delivered a cargo of Mexican cotton.

How, then, did he come to be in Confederate waters off North Carolina,

[33] National Archives, War Dept. Records, File "R," Doc. 266, JAO.
[34] National Archives, War Dept. Records, File "W," Doc. 1914, JAO.

hundreds of nautical miles from the West Indies? Muttered in broken English, Celestino's answer did not satisfy the Federal sailors at all. He said he had been blown off course to the Florida Keys, then somehow been carried northward by the Gulf Stream.[35]

Captain D. L. Braine of U.S.S. *Vicksburg* refused to swallow Celestino's sea story. Placing a prize crew aboard the schooner, he sent her to Washington, D.C., as a captive blockade runner. Celestino went north as a prisoner of war.

Braine's report noted that while schooner *Indian* carried no cargo, she was stocked like a pleasure yacht with food, wines, cigars, fresh poultry. To the Navy Department it must have been obvious that little *Indian*, with her gourmet's larder, had been lying off the Confederate coast to pick up special passengers. Rebel envoys, secret agents and spies were frequently spirited to Bermuda or the Bahamas by such craft.

Despite the flagrant evidence, Celestino swore innocence. In Washington he protested to British Ambassador Lord Lyons, who intervened in his behalf. In May, 1864, the Portuguese mariner was released. Somewhat inconsistently, the Federal Government continued to hold the schooner *Indian*. Late in June the craft was auctioned off as a war prize.

Celestino then put in a claim for some $3,000 in gold and silver which he had kept in a strongbox in the schooner's cabin. He swore that this money had belonged to him—his captors had rifled the cabin while he was in jail and filched his life's savings. The Federal Admiralty Court proved unsympathetic.

From June, 1864, to March, 1865, Celestino (sometimes called Zeleste) sulked around Washington, D.C. Undoubtedly he gnawed a bone of resentment against the U.S. Government, and made efforts to regain his money. The record suggests that he may have taken odd jobs on the Potomac waterfront, possibly working with the Confederate underground.[36]

Celestino left Washington to go to Philadelphia on the evening of April 14, 1865. Just before leaving he voiced the comment that Seward ought to be assassinated.

Ninety-six hours later Celestino was back in Washington, confined in the Old Capitol on order of Lafayette Baker. Somehow the miserable sailorman managed to contact the Portuguese minister in Washington. This contact probably caused his abrupt transference on April 25 to the bowels of monitor *Montauk*. Now the alien captain was in double irons and a sea of tribulation.

Early in May the War Department intercepted a letter to Celestino

---

[35] *Official Records.*

[36] Van Doren Stern, "The Unknown Conspirator," *American Heritage*, Vol. VIII, No. 2, p. 58.

from the Hon. de Finagieve of the Portuguese Legation. Official translation read as follows:

Washington, 3 May, 1865

D Joao M. Celestino

As soon as I received a letter of 23 last month (the first of four which you say you had written) I came here to investigate the motive for your detention. The Secretary of War tells me there are proofs which seem to implicate you in the late terrible events—in such case there is no remedy but to wait the judicial investigation which I am told will shortly be proceeded with. . . .

Your obdt Servant
de Finagieve[37]

What were the proofs which (according to Stanton) seemed to implicate Celestino? They must have been strong ones. For he was eventually sent from monitor *Montauk* to the Arsenal Penitentiary, with Paine Atzerodt, Mrs. Surratt and associates to face trial as a major conspirator.

Yet Celestino never went on trial. After weeks in prison he was suddenly released by an order which freed the prisoner "upon condition that he leave the District of Col. at once and depart from the U.S. within ten days. . . ."[38]

Available War Department records contain no explanation for Celestino's sudden release. Nor do they explain the arbitrary time limit attached to his liberation. Nor does anything on record explain the sequel to Celestino's release.

Freed, Celestino ignored the "ten day" mandate. Instead of departing from the U.S., he procured a New York attorney, who petitioned the Government for a sum of money allegedly due Celestino "out of the Secret Service fund." Historian Stern expresses wonderment at this claim. Did it mean that Celestino had been one of Baker's secret agents—a prison spy—a hired informer?[39]

Or was the Portuguese sailor merely promised a fee for turning State's evidence? The evidence could have depended on whatever suited Judge Advocate-General Holt and Lafayette Baker. As would soon be demonstrated, the Judge Advocate's Office was not above fabricating evidence to suit conspiracy charges. Baker tailored such fabrications without scruple. All of this could explain Celestino's reference to the "Secret Service fund," and the War Department's effort to get him out of the country.

Yet if Celestino was a prison spy, why his appeals to the Portuguese Legation? If, on the other hand, he agreed to turn State's evidence, what became of the evidence he presumably turned in?

---

[37] National Archives, War Dept. Records, File "C," JAO.
[38] Van Doren Stern, *op. cit.*, p. 59.
[39] *Ibid.*, p. 103.

Joao Celestino seems to have been the only alleged suspect who was confined for days on board a monitor with Booth's co-conspirators. Or was there still another? In company with official photographs of Paine, Atzerodt, Arnold, O'Laughlin and Herold, there exist in the files photographs of a sixth and a seventh prisoner evidently taken on board a monitor. Mystery shrouds these two police portraits. Long after the Lincoln murder case was officially closed, the War Department placed the sixth "conspirator picture" in public domain. The photograph was tentatively marked "Dr. Mudd."

Here was another puzzle for historians to contend with. In 1900 Oldroyd published a presumably authentic portrait of Dr. Mudd. Comparing this picture with the photograph of the prisoner taken on board a monitor, researchers found a remarkable resemblance between the two. However, the monitor photograph and the later portrait published by Oldroyd could not be pictures of the same man.

Study the pictures, and one can see that the ear of the man in the photograph differs from that shown by the authentic Mudd portrait. The authenticated Mudd portrait shows a left ear with a thin and slanted lobe. The alleged Mudd portrait taken on board a monitor shows a left ear with a bulbous lobe. And, of course, Dr. Mudd was never placed on board a monitor.

Who, then, was this prisoner who looked like Dr. Mudd? Why was his identity withheld by War Department officials who certainly must have known his name? How is it his picture was eventually released as one of Dr. Mudd?

One can hazard a guess. The portrait of this sixth monitor prisoner is a photograph of Joao Celestino?

The seventh portrait bears the simple label, "Unidentified Conspirator." So far as is known, nothing has ever been published in respect to this individual. His photograph is reproduced in this volume as a "find."

But who could he have been, this prisoner with the farcical hat and the soup-strainer moustache? Why was *this* character incarcerated with Booth's co-conspirators? And why did the War Department choose to file his photograph without an identifying tab?

One guess is as legitimate as another. The photograph may be that of Atzerodt's Cousin Richter who spent a brief period on board monitor *Saugus*. Or it *could* be a portrait of a "Sergeant Sheets"—or was it "Street"? A soldier answering to both names was imprisoned on April 15 as a "Sam" suspect. He may have been a detective "plant" in the Old Capitol. After long confinement he was mysteriously released. Whoever it was, the War Department censors had their reasons for concealing the identity of the man in the photograph.

Official records do not divulge the reasons.

CHAPTER 17

Cherchez la Femme

BOOTH was barely on his way through southern Maryland when he was reported in a dozen northern cities at once. Persons in Washington sighted him on Pennsylvania Avenue. New Yorkers glimpsed him skulking down Broadway. Philadelphians saw him at his sister's home in disguise. He was a traveler wearing chin wiskers on a Rock Island train. Furtive "Booths" went through Niagara Falls, Cincinnati, Boston, Chicago.[1] Police closed in on one John Wilkes Booth at Tamaqua, Pennsylvania.[2] Simultaneously they surrounded another at Reading. Army detectives arrested another "Booth" at nearby Pottsville. Still another was chased across Detroit and hunted in Montreal.[3]

And on April 26, the day Fate closed in on the lame man and the youth in Mr. Garrett's tobacco barn, the Pittsburgh *Daily Commercial* reported: J. WILKES BOOTH IN PITTSBURGH BEFORE AND AFTER THE ASSASSINATION OF PRESIDENT LINCOLN!

The *Commercial's* news account dilutes the perfervid headlines. A party registers as J. Wilkes Booth at Pittsburgh's Red Lion Hotel on April 3, 1865. He and his companion, a Mr. McGreggor, depart the next day, presumably for Canada. Shortly after the assassination, "J. Wilkes Booth" is again at the Red Lion in Pittsburgh, coolly catnapping in the public parlor. Honestly (if belatedly) the reporter qualifies the story, admitting it "barely possible" that the party in question "was not *the* J. Wilkes Booth." The fugitive assassin fled through southern Maryland. Assume he escaped in the Zekiah Swamps, and it would draw the long bow to whisk him in a trice from there to Pittsburgh. Then to have him back at the Red Lion, insouciantly dozing "upon a lounge" in public view! But in any event, the Booth previously registered at the Pittsburgh hotel on April 3 could not have been *the* J. Wilkes Booth. For on that particular date, the incipient assassin and a young woman arrived at the Aquidneck Hotel at

---

[1] National Archives, War Dept. Records, Files "Anonymous" and "Miscellaneous," JAO.
[2] New York *Tribune*, April 21, 1865.
[3] National Archives, War Dept. Records, JAO.

Newport, Rhode Island. There the actor signed the register: "J. W. Booth & Lady. Boston."[4]

There could have been no mistaking this Booth at Newport. He had departed that same day for Boston to visit his brother Edwin. This arrival and departure were not lost on desk clerk Alfred Smith, who recognized a lover's quarrel when he witnessed one. The handsome stage star and his pretty companion had arrived by the New York boat. After checking in with baggage, they had gone for a walk in the garden. Later they returned to their room. Weren't those tear stains on the woman's cheek? The actor had worn a Satanic scowl. He had ordered a lavish dinner, then sourly canceled the order, declaring the lady ill. Desk clerk Alfred Smith remembered all of it. When news of Lincoln's murder subsequently reached Newport, he wrote a detailed account of the Aquidneck episode to Stanton.

"They came by steamboat from New York . . . ordered early dinner. . . . He left on the 3.00 P.M. train for Boston."[5]

Answering the letter, War Department detectives visited the Aquidneck Hotel and cut the "J. W. Booth & Lady" out of the register. While this specimen autograph went into the Judge Advocate's file, search was instituted for the lady. Existing War Department records do not identify her. Rumor gave her three names: "Ella," "Eva," "Etta." Possessed with information at hand, the Federal agents should have easily tracked her down. Perhaps they did. As will be seen, the Government chose to veil some of the ladies in Booth's following.

However, Booth's Newport visit settled the question of his whereabouts on April 3. He was *not* in Pittsburgh.

Still, the Pittsburgh report poses some intriguing questions. Although duplication at baptismal fonts remains possible, it seems highly improbable that another J. Wilkes Booth—some legitimate namesake of the assassin—would enter any hotel after April 14 without first introducing himself as an innocent citizen on honest business. Was this second Booth, then, not so innocent? Was some underground agent posing as Booth to confuse the police? And who was the shadowy McGreggor?

The Federal agents assembled an interesting dossier on "W. W. McGreggor." The man's trail led from Pittsburgh to Niagara Falls. At half a dozen hotels his name turned up in the register in company with a "J. Wilkes Booth." Painstakingly the detectives scissored these autographs from the guest books and filed the lot of them in Washington.[6]

---

[4] One modern writer erroneously locates the Aquidneck Hotel in New York City. As stated, however, the Aquidneck was in Newport. Present writer has seen the signatures of the hotel registry.

[5] National Archives, War Department Records, File "S," Doc. 8, JAO.

[6] National Archives, War Dept. Records, File "Mc," Doc. "Evidence," JAO.

Evidently the Federal agents never got far with the "McGreggor-Booth" puzzle. Certainly the elements are baffling. On the surface it would appear that McGreggor and some confederate were dragging red herrings between Pittsburgh and Niagara in an effort to mislead the authorities. Or were they a pair of small-time swindlers up to some confidence game— McGreggor posing as an oil baron, say, and his companion playing J. Wilkes Booth, the famous actor who had struck it rich?

The riddle remains unsolved. So far as can be determined from the records, mysterious Mr. McGreggor and the doubly mysterious "J. Wilkes Booth" disappeared after their last appearance in Pittsburgh. Behind them they left only their dubious signatures.

McGreggor wrote a flamboyant script characterized by capital letters an inch high. The accompanying "Booth" signatures were penned in a variety of hands. In no case did they match the autograph of *the* J. Wilkes Booth.

But at least one ghosted autograph turned up like a spectre in Stanton's mail. Soon after the assassination, letters from "J. Wilkes Booth" began to arrive in Washington. First of this crop of "Booth" epistles reached the War Secretary's desk two or three days after Lincoln's murder. Postmarked New York (date of stamping illegible), the letter read:

New York, April 14, '65

Mr Stanton
Dear Sir
    If you want me you had better send for me.

J. Wilkes Booth

P.S. What do you say?

J W B[7]

The authorities could, and probably did, ignore the substance of this letter. The crudity of "What do you say?" was entirely out of character with Booth's flowery epistolary style. What doubtless startled Baker and his Secret Service personnel was the handwriting. If not genuine, the signature was a remarkable copy. One could only conclude that the writer's hand belonged to Booth, or to an extremely adept forger.

If the hand were Booth's, who posted the letter for him? If a forgery, as seems more probable, who was the felonious penman? In either case, the missive reveals that someone in New York was deliberately trying to mislead the manhunt. The many "Booth" letters which followed are plainly indicative of a wholesale effort to decoy the police.

Unfortunatey for the Federal Government—and lucky for the fugitives from justice—the public bombarded Washington with such a barrage of witchhunt missives that the authorities had neither time nor means to sort the deliberately conspiratorial from the crackpot.

---

[7] National Archives, War Dept. Records, File "A," Doc. 551, JAO.

The following, dispatched on April 17 to General Augur, is typical.

I'm still in your midst. I will remain in this city. God will'd that I should do it. I defy detection.

J. W. Booth, Actor and the Assassin of President Lincoln.

P.S. The ways of the most High are past finding out.[8]

From Canada came a "Booth" letter dated April 26. Its message—"you can't catch me"—added another puzzle to the War Department file.[9]

Every celebrated crime involving a prolonged manhunt produces a crop of clairvoyant letters. Exemplary of this foolishness was a missive mailed on April 26 from Newark, New Jersey. An odd touch was the letter's being addressed to Major General Hancock. The writer advised:

A lady friend is a sort of semi-wakeful dreamer or clairvoyant—she is possessed with the idea that while in this condition she has seen Booth's place of concealment. . . . She says at No 11 J St. second floor back room in a recess from a clothes closet Booth is now concealed & that at No 7 same street some of his accomplices may be found. He is heavily armed & woe to who ever tries to arrest him. She further states that she is totally unacquainted in Washington & did not know that there was a J St until subsequently informed. Signed: P. H. Knapp.[10]

Surely "Knapp" was a wonderfully suitable name for the friend of a "semi-wakeful dreamer." However, the clairvoyant in this case seems to have dozed off entirely. For she dreamed up a thoroughfare non-existent in Washington, where the alphabetized streets hopscotch from "I" to "K."[11]

Astrologers went far afield trailing Booth through the signs of the Zodiac. Second-sighters, tea-leaf readers and palmists offered equally erroneous advices. It would evolve that Lafayette Baker was the only man-hunter on the case who seemed possessed with miraculous powers of divination.

Persistently afoot at the time of Booth's getaway was the rumor that he had escaped from Washington in female disguise. Four days after Lincoln's murder, the New York *Tribune* carried this intelligence:

"Among other arrests today were, it is said, several men in female apparel."[12]

Numerous veiled ladies, who somehow resembled the assassin, were glimpsed here and there. One of the more colorful advices was addressed to Stanton on this subject.

---

8 National Archives, War Dept. Records, File "A," Doc. 548, JAO.

9 National Archives, War Dept. Records, File "A," Doc. 111, JAO.

10 National Archives, War Dept. Records, File "K," Doc. 125, JAO.

11 Tradition attributes the omission of "J Street" to Alexander Hamilton who disapproved of "J" because it might be taken for the Jacobin symbol of the French Revolution.

12 New York *Daily Tribune*, April 18, 1865.

April 20, 1865—West Troy
   Silas S. Jones
To   Secretary of War
Believes J. W. Booth to be secreted in Chicago, Illinois, at a house of ill frame, No. 16 Tenth Avenue—in the disguise of a female.[13]

The Army entered this game of hide-and-seek with a melodramatic telegram from Winchester Headquarters on April 26.

General C. H. Morgan
   Chf. of Staff.
   I have learned from one of Reno's officers that at Mount Jackson last Friday a woman dressed in deep mourning and closely veiled passed up the Valley, and a paroled officer who talked to her said that she had just come from Washington since the assassination. No woman has passed through here from Washington since that time. . . .

A. T. A. Torbert
Brig. Genl.[14]

By curious coincidence the telegram reached the War Department on the same day Stanton's office received from a Washington citizen the following deposition—perhaps the crankiest of the many reports of this genre.

Wednesday, April 26th, 1865.

   Joseph Hill, under oath, living between G & H Streets, on 23d, No. 202, states that he is a printer by trade. He says he is not personally acquainted with John Wilkes Booth more than in seeing him playing on the Stage. As he was going down E Street, between 11th & 12th, he saw a person across the street in the garb of a woman and with a crutch under the right arm whom he took to be a female acquaintance of his named Kate Robinson, and he went across the street and accosted the person thus: "Kate, when did you get hurt?" The person turned her head, and he recognized John Wilkes Booth. He exclaimed "Hullar, Wilkes Booth, that's you, is it?" and the next minute the person addressed disappeared in an instant. The witness then went around to the Kirkwood House and reported the matter to a friend. The person had curls over his head and a black gauze vail (*sic*) over his face, and was dressed altogether in black. Had on a ladies' cap.[15]

While the crutch lends Joseph Hill's deposition an uncanny touch, the "Hullar, Wilkes Booth" and the latter's disappearance "in an instant" reduces the affidavit to the dregs of farce. Although the popular English comedy came a generation later, Joseph Hill's and like reports of the fugitive assassin in curls and petticoats convey the impression that John Wilkes Booth spent the fortnight after Lincoln's murder playing a preview performance of *Charley's Aunt.*

---

[13] National Archives, War Dept. Records, File "J," Doc. 11, JAO.
[14] National Archives, War Dept. Records, File "T," Doc. 138, JAO.
[15] National Archives, War Dept. Records, File "H," Doc. 609, JAO.

The Federal authorities came into possession of one bit of evidence which, if taken at face value, loaned a nuance of validity to rumors that the Lincoln conspirators donned women's garb on occasion. In typically careless fashion, this item went into the Judge Advocate's file undated. Endorsements are unclear concerning its procurement. The code words defy translation. And, as though one "Sam" letter were not enough, this specimen adds another to the conspiracy puzzle. The envelope containing the missive was addressed to "Colonel U.S. Reb—Present." The letter's cloak-and-dagger terminology speaks for itself.

Dear Colonel
I have got things pretty much compleated, *Sall* has got the fruit put up, the *apple* is marked with the compliments of a *lady* as Old *Chase* likes nice things and coming from a lady of course he will take it, one mouthful will land the cuss over Jordan. Bill had on his female attire last night, it was quite becoming to him.
How are you getting along, will you get ready this week: wont Old Mass grone think if her two Nigger wisheper [worshiper?] gone [blurred] under, it is time they went to find their Nigger President.
Meet me tomorrow night at the usual place. I send this by Dan, as I hear that the damn black abolitionists open all of the letters now.
Farewell untill we meet

Off
Sam[16]

The unique handwriting of this letter bore no resemblance to Sam Arnold's. What did the missive mean? It exudes an ugly message of some kind. But the one line of this cabalistic jargon that probably excited Baker's detectives was reference to "Bill" in his becoming "female attire."

To a national mind feasting on sensationalism, the rumor dressing Booth in lady's garb proved an appetizing tidbit. Now no female stranger could drive through town in a closed carriage without creating a stir. No unidentified spinster, wife, or widow could take the steam cars from here to there without at least one bearded passenger offering her a cigar or otherwise trying to extract from her some off-guard, masculine response. Caught in the act, any Peeping Tom could say he was merely looking for John Wilkes Booth.

Or for Jefferson Davis. Or for Jacob Thompson. Or for any of a dozen Confederate leaders soon reported to be nefariously hiding in bonnets and skirts.

The phenomenon of "men in women's clothes" had made its gaslight debut during the Civil War. Probably the aberration was first publicized by stories of male spies in female costume. It was a disguise considered despicably cowardly, although common sense should have seen it as one of the more dangerous in the cloak-and-dagger wardrobe.

Then it seemed that some of the males thus costumed had not been spies.

---

[16] National Archives, War Dept. Records, File "A," Doc. 319, JAO.

There had been whimsical camp shows with soldiers clowning in hoop-skirts and cornsilk wigs, elaborate pranks on the order of "Let's dress up old Joe," and, of course, the deviates inevitable to wartime maladjustment and large military organizations.

The World War II generation would suppose that "transvestism" and "male ladies" were phenomena of modern life—indications of social decadence caused by a departure from the stern and rockribbed virtues of yesteryear. Victorians suffered precisely the same misgivings.

Five years after the Civil War, Mr. John Safford Fiske, the American consul at Leith, became entangled in a frightful row involving his love letters to a "Stella Boulton" and a "Fanny Park," inhabitants of London. The issue was complicated. Both "Stella" and "Fanny," promenading in evening gowns, were arrested at a theater for creating a disturbance. Examination of their fashionable rooms disclosed the *billets-doux* from Consul Fiske. Also disclosed was the fact that "Stella" and "Fanny" were already engaged to, and supported by, Lord Arthur Pelham Clinton, an officer in the Royal Navy. Even diplomatic immunity could not save young Mr. Fiske when further disclosure exposed "Stella" as Ernest Boulton, son of a prominent London broker, and "Fanny" proved to be Frederick Park, scion of a Master of the Superior Courts. The trial before Court of Queen's Bench created a six-day sensation.[17]

The truth seems to be that the good old days were neither so old (meaning far-removed) nor so good. Civil War Americans were well acquainted with certain aspects of the seamy side. The war had demoralized many unstable young men: witness John Safford Fiske, who was probably a Union Army veteran. (Government employ depended largely on "veteran's preference," and ex-Confederates were excluded from Civil Service or State Department jobs.)

True, the war had also demoralized some older men, among them a number of national leaders of supposedly granite character. But the demagogue who wants to dispense with the Bill of Rights, the high-priced grafter who pillages the Treasury, the charlatan who peddles bayonets with giveaway Bibles—these felons are never considered quite so dangerous to society as the unfortunate androgyne or the vapid nincompoop on the "Stella" and "Fanny" level. It was perhaps typical of witchhunt hysteria that the hunt for archsubversives and conspirators in 1865 should degenerate into a hunt for female impersonators.

Modern psychologists might make something of this tendency to dress conspiracy in women's clothes. Of course, every man knows that womankind is up to some sort of conspiracy—the costume itself is conspiratorial. So the symbolism is clear. But it hardly does justice to the fair sex to imagine that plotters planning to overthrow the Government tend to don

---

[17] *Trial of Boulton and Park, with Hurt and Fiske,* Manchester, 1871. Also London *Times,* April-June 1870, and William Roughead, *Bad Companions,* pp. 149–183.

ladies' hats and assume effeminate mannerisms. Instead of mincing around in pinafores and pantalettes, the world's stock of violent revolutionaries and archtraitors has, in common with Benedict Arnold and Napoleon, usually stalked the scene in epaulettes, buckles and spurred boots.

Yet it seems just possible that the Federal detectives (who were probably fairly immune to moralistic propaganda) had picked up a peculiar lead on John Wilkes Booth. Official records do not provide the detail, but soon after the assassination Federal agents must have visited the old Booth homestead at Bel Air. Undoubtedly Provost Marshal McPhail dispatched his Baltimore officers to that locality. Canvassing the countryside, questioning oldsters in the neighborhood of Tudor Hall, the detectives would have heard odd stories about John Wilkes.

Years later Asia Booth Clarke ingenuously recalled some of her younger brother's didoes. "On several occassions he dressed himself in a petticoat and draped a shawl around him for a toga. He put on my long trained dress and walked before the long glass, declaring that he would succeed as Lady Macbeth in the sleepwalking scene. He secretly 'got himself up' after Charlotte Cushman as Meg Merrilies and terrified me and all the darkies who shrieked, 'Ondress Mars' Johnnie, ondress him. . . . !'"

Again Asia wrote of John Wilkes: ". . . dressed in my skirts with a little scarf held over his shoulders he walked the room before the mirror, becoming more and more charmed with himself. . . . He put on the tiny bonnet then in fashion and went out across the fields. The men took off their hats as they passed in their work to salute him . . . [he] came back to the house delighted with his success, which he attributed to his 'elegant deportment.'"[18]

Hearing these or similar anecdotes from the Bel Air neighborhood, the case-hardened Federal police must have made some interesting mental notes. Because the notes went unrecorded, Booth's early propensity for female impersonation has been overlooked by historians. He is pictured, rather, as the drawing-room Adonis, the conqueror of brothels and boudoirs. And by a strange contortion of logic, it is Wiechmann who turns up in history in a dubious psychological light. For rumor eventually hinted that Wiechmann had been infatuated with John Surratt, and it was further hinted that Surratt's friendship with Booth led the jealous Government employee to betray the H Street household.[19]

The Wiechmann tale creates the impression that Wiechmann, Surratt and John Wilkes Booth were, all three, in the embrace of a sickly web. And David Herold? Handsome Lewis Paine? It does seem possible that something more than subversion may have formed the bond between the ill-assorted members of Booth's group.

---

[18] Op. cit., pp. 66–67.
[19] Stanley Kimmel, *The Mad Booths of Maryland* (New York: Bobbs-Merrill Co., 1940).

But the Federals were not concerned with psychological aspects of the case. To them, female impersonation was merely a means of disguise. They would not have wanted to probe deeper into the matter. After all, Louis Wiechmann had been one of the H Street band, and Wiechmann was slated to take the stand as the Government's star witness.

One of the items found in Booth's trunk at the National Hotel was a distressed *billet-doux* from Ella Turner, his local mistress.

> My darling Baby
> Please call this evening or as soon as you receive this note. I will not detain you five minutes—for gods sake come
>
> Yours truly
E T
>
> if you will not come write a note the reason why
> Washington Feb 7th
> 1865[20]

The police had no difficulty in identifying "E.T." as Ella Turner. On Pennsylvania Avenue she was well known as one of the walkers of the primrose path, and she had been seen on Booth's arm at the National.

But the Federal agents seem to have been singularly reticent about Miss Turner. She is barely mentioned in the immense dossier assembled by the War Department on the Lincoln murder case. Her name appears but once or twice in the Judge Advocate's file, and then most shyly and in a cursory way.

This strikes one as a drastic omission, even in the light of Pecksniff Victorianism and War Department prudery concerning any mention in official records of such a subject as prostitution. The Government was bending every effort to uncover a great conspiracy. It would hardly have refused to unveil Booth's lady love because of her disreputable association with the assassin. On the contrary, that relationship presented the propagandists with a fine chance to moralize on the assumed linkage between Confederate doctrine and turpitude. Ella Turner had followed the Rebel camp.

However, the authorities evidently preferred to let the subject lie. In so doing, it would seem the Federal officials sidestepped a potentially important witness. Certainly Miss Turner must have known a great deal more about Booth's ways and means than did the Mary Cooks, Lizzie Batchims and other nobodies hauled in by the random dragnet.

Even the Metropolitan Police appear to have been diffident about booking Miss Turner. Seventeen persons went on the blotter before midnight on the night Lincoln was shot, and as Superintendent Richards noted,

---

[20] National Archives, War Dept. Records, "Letters Found in Booth's Trunk," JAO.

"information obtained . . . goes to show that the assassin is a man named John Wilkes Booth."[21] Nobody was sent to arrest Booth's mistress.

By one o'clock of the following morning, Booth's room at the National Hotel had been searched by military detectives, and Booth's trunk and papers were in the hands of the Provost Marshal's officers. The little note from "E. T." was among these effects. And it is reasonable to assume that the Army and civilian sleuths who swarmed over the National, soon picked up word of Ella Turner from the hotel staff. But Miss Turner was not mentioned in the police reports rushed to Headquarters. Nor was her note to Booth properly inventoried. So it was missed by later historians. Even Jim Bishop's comprehensive study asserts that "the only item of importance" found in Booth's trunk was the letter from Sam Arnold.[22]

Booth's mistress, then, was never booked as a prime "accomplice," "witness," or anything else. The authorities seem to have assiduously avoided her. True, at six o 'clock in the morning after Lincoln's assassination, a city policeman wandered into headquarters with a drunken streetwalker in his custody. The policeman was John Parker, the guard who had deserted Lincoln's box. The bawd answered to the name of Lizzie Williams. She knew a lot about men, but nothing about John Wilkes Booth. The precinct captain released her with an order to get out of town.[23]

Yet the Federal authorities could not wholly ignore Booth's mistress. She herself would see to that. And aside from her own bids for notoriety, Ella Turner was reported by a number of informants. Mr. George Wren of K Street, for one.

Soon after the assassin-hunt was launched, Mr. Wren darted into a police office to tell what he knew. He deponed that he had met Booth here and there, and was convinced the actor belonged to the "American Knights." Wren advised the officers to query a man at Niblo's Garden in New York—Jim Congan—a close friend of Booth. Wren also urged them to apprehend a Billy Barron of the Washington sporting set, one of Booth's gamy companions and an ardent Secessionist.

As stated by Mr. Wren: "Barron was the first man at the house of Booth's mistress on Ohio Avenue after the murder occurred."[24]

Apparently it was this testimony that sent the Federal officers to 62 Ohio Avenue on Saturday morning, April 15. There they picked up the well-known Starr sisters and another inmate of the house. Thence they repaired to a Justice of the Peace for a taking of formal depositions.

Curious fact: the only statement from the ladies in question which went into the Judge Advocate's file was one sworn by Ella Turner's sister, Nellie Starr. Could the police have mistaken Nellie for Ella? Such con-

---

[21] Records, Metropolitan Police Dept., Washington, D.C.

[22] *Op. cit.*, p. 254.

[23] Eisenschiml, *op. cit.*, p. 17. Also Records, Metropolitan Police Dept., Washington, D.C.

[24] National Archives, War Dept. Records, File "W," Doc. "R.P. p. 102," JAO.

fusion appears unlikely. Turner was Ella's married name—the one she used when with Booth. On her professional rounds she seems to have employed Starr, her maiden name, for what might be called her *nom de guerre*. But Ella Starr Turner doubtless declared herself. Ordinarily she made no bones about her trade or her association with Booth. In all likelihood she talked freely to the authorities. Yet the War Department files contain Sister Nellie's deposition, not Ella's.

United States.

vs.   } prelimenary (*sic*) examination

J. Wilks (*sic*) Booth

My name is Nellie Starr, my native place is Baltimore State of Maryland. I have been in Washington City, D.C. since a week before Christmas, I am about ninteen (*sic*) or twenty years of age. I am not married. I have known John Wilkes Booth about three years. He was in the habit of visiting the house where I live, kept by Miss Eliza Thomas No. 62 Ohio Avenue in the City of Washington. The house is one of Prostitution. I have never heard him speak unfavorable of the Presitend, (*sic*) I heard him speak of the Presitend as being a good man just as other people did. I do not disdinctly (*sic*) recollect how he was dressed, when I last saw him. Think he had on dark clothes. I think he wore a Sloneghad [slouch hat?], I do not think it is the one shown me by the District Attorney. I know nothing more about the case. I know not with whom he associates with as I have not been on good terms with him for over a year. The last time I seen Mr. Booth was two weeks ago, at the said house.

Nellie Starr

Sworn and Subscribed before me this 15th day of April A.D. 1865.

[Signature indecipherable]

Justice of the Peace

Washington

Ella Starr   Fannie Harrison[25]

Nellie Starr's brief declaration did not exactly scale the heights of candor. She strayed from the truth in implying that she and Ella were Baltimoreans (meaning Northern girls). According to the Richmond *Whig*, the two Starrs hailed from Petersburg, Virginia.[26]

Too, Nellie's assertion that John Wilkes Booth had spoken favorably of President Lincoln was obvious cover-up for a cherished client. Altogether she swore out an evasive affidavit. But we find appended to the document the witness signatures of Fannie Harrison and Ella Starr—proof positive that the authorities had an eye on Booth's mistress within 24 hours of the assassination.

And an eye, it seems, was all they ever had on her.

With a prime suspect as near at hand as 62 Ohio Avenue, the Washington authorities (meaning War Secretary Stanton and Secret Service Chief

---

[25] National Archives, War Dept. Records, File "S," Doc. "R.B.fi 80," JAO.

[26] Richmond *Whig*, April 1865. Copied in Washington *National Republican*, April 22, 1865.

Baker) spurred a hunt for an unidentified woman in New York City many miles away.

Nobody knew the last name of this charmer. She was to enter the case history simply as "Etta." The effort to locate an "Etta" somewhere in gaslit Manhattan sent the Federal agents into a maze of blind alleys. An extravagant amount of time and Government paperwork was expended on the goose-chase after this semi-anonymous Jezebel.

The lady (if so she could be called) bowed into the Lincoln murder case by way of a letter addressed to "Mr. J. Wilkes Booth, Washington, D.C." Posted in New York City on April 19, this missive was intercepted by the authorities in Washington on the 20th. The dates are key jigsaws of the "Etta" puzzle. Another jigsaw is the abbreviated address.

Here is the letter:

"S.S.T."

New York
April 13th

Dear Wilkes

I received your letter of the 12th (stating you would be in this City on the 16 inst) this morning, and hasten to answer it. On account of a misunderstanding between my Landlady and your humble servant, I have been obliged to leave her hospitable mansion, and am now (for the time being) stopping at the New York Hotel, after your arrival, should you not approve of my present location, it can easly (sic) be changed to suit your convenience.

Yes Dear, I can heartily sympathize with you, for I too, have had the blues ever since the fall of Richmond, and like you, feel like doing something desperate. I have not yet had a favorable opportunity to do what *you* wished, and *I* so solemnly promised, and what, in my own heart, I feel ought to be done. I *remember* what happiness is in store for us if we succeed in our present undertakings, therefor, do not doubt *my* courage, have faith, "for even as you put your faith in me, so will I in you" and Wilkes hath said *vengeance* is mine.

My removal has consumed the means you gave me when we parthed (sic), take this as a gentle hint to bring a good supply, "For money makes the mare go" now a' days. I do as you desired and keep as secluded as a nun, which is not agreeable to me as you have found out ere this, but any thing to oblige you darling. If any thing *should* happen (as I trust there will not) to prevent your coming to the City, please let me know, and I will join you (as agreed upon) at the house of our mutual friend A——s. "Dont-let-any thing (sic) discourage *you.*"

believe me *yours*
and *yours* only
Etta

P.S.

Annie, who is acting the maid to perfection, wishes to be remembered to her dear Ahem!!! Sam.

Au revoir
Etta[27]

27 National Archives, War Dept. Records, File "E" 554, Doc. "B.R.B.," JAO.

Neither the sinister "Leon," the second "Sam," nor the other letters intercepted at Booth's hotel evoked the police reaction aroused by this "Etta" epistle. Placed in charge of the matter, Colonel John A. Foster dispatched a red hot wire to New York Police Superintendent John A. Kennedy. Apprehension of "Etta" was considered so important that this urgent message from the War Department went in the super-secret wrappings of code. We can only guess the substance from Kennedy's reply. Ordered to locate someone named "Etta," the New York Police Superintendent begged a little more detail.

Sent in Cipher

New York City
Apr. 21, 1865

Col. John A. Foster
   Judge Adv. Gen.
What was the date of postmark on "Etta's" letter? Was it in a hotel envelope? If so, what one? Telegraph reply immediately.

John A. Kennedy.[28]

Apparently Foster provided as much of the requested information as could be mined from "Etta's" missive. Kennedy did his best. He combed the New York Hotel mentioned in "Etta's" letter. He combed the city's extensive red-light districts. He combed the files on New York's large population of harlots, demi-mondaines and courtesans. These combings produced no specimen the equivalent of "Etta."

Kennedy reported on the matter with the following dispatch:

SUPERINTENDENT OF THE METROPOLITAN POLICE
300 Mulberry Street,
New York, April 21st 1865

Col. John A. Foster
   Judge Advocate Gen.
      Washington D.C.
         Sir,
Your Telegram in Sypher (*sic*) reached me at 6 o'clock P.M. yesterday, when I immediately commenced enquiry for "*Etta.*" And after eighteen hours constant search, am only able to report that no such personality has had existence in this city. Every public and private house of prostitution of a class such as Booth could visit, has been thoroughly overhauled: from which it appears, that, although a frequent visitor of many of them, at but *one* was regarded as a lover; that of Sally Andrews, No. 67 West 25th Street. And in this Case, he was lover of the landlady. One other person was found between whom and him a close intimacy had existed, but had been broken off by himself, as she admitted that she had, to a very recent period, endeavored to draw him back to her. This person is Anne Horton, No. 3 Clark Street. This woman has undoubtedly had promises for the future from Booth, and seems to be attached to him, but has not seen him within three months or more. Both her and Sally Andrews being landladys, they

---

[28] National Archives, War Dept. Records, File "K," Doc. 125, JAO.

do not meet the case of "Etta"—The name of "Etta" is unknown among the sisterhood.

I took possession of the books of the New York Hotel last evening, on receipt of the dispatch; and a careful examination shews (*sic*) no Woman, or Woman & Maid, had been received in the house since 1st inst. except such as come with other company, or that were well accounted for; nor was any such person or persons in the house on 13th instant, who had remained there from before the first of the month.

I can find no case where a boarder has had a misunderstanding with her landlady, and left in consequence, recently.

From all which, and from the fact that have received no reply to the enquiry made last night, concerning the postal date, and the envellope (*sic*), that the letter is a wicked hoax; got up to distract the attention of the officers from points where their service would be useful.

Several such have been brought to me, by parties who have found them lying around.

Should anything, however, be discovered of "Etta," I will act. And although I have no hope I shall continue to search.

Very Respectfully
Yours
John A. Kennedy
Supert

P.S. Since writing the above, now 1.30 P.M. I receive your dispatch of today. This is nearly conclusive that the whole thing is a sell. A letter written Thursday 13th not posted until Wednesday 19th tells its own story, especially when the tenor of it, and other circumstances have already made it fishy.

JAK[29]

Observant Police Superintendent Kennedy. At first glance he had spotted an incongruity which should have been immediately apparent to the Federal officers: that disparity between the date of the "Etta" letter's composition and the date it was posted. Why the six-day delay between escritoire and mailbox?

And if this bit of business smelled fishy to Kennedy, it should have reeked to the ceiling in Washington headquarters. For the War Department was already in possession of the "From his Mother" letter which had been dated April 10 but postmarked the 17th. Two such procrastinated epistles must have seemed as odoriferous as a breeze from the Tiber Canal.

Moreover, if the "Etta" letter were anything but a hollow fraud, would the writer have addressed it simply to "J. Wilkes Booth, Washington"? It strains credulity to think that one of the actor's paramours would post so revealing a communication to the wide-open box of "general delivery." Could any decoy have been more obvious than the opening line? "Dear Wilkes—I received your letter of the 12th stating you would be in this City on the 16 inst. . . ."

As Kennedy observed, the "Etta" letter smelled of flimflam. But the

---

War Department was not thus easily disillusioned. Rejecting the Police Superintendent's advice, the Federals continued the "Etta" hunt. Non-existent mistresses with non-existent maids being hard to find, the Federal agents ended up holding an empty bag. The question naturally arises: Why were Government detectives sent far afield in pursuit of a phantom when Booth's flesh-and-blood mistress lived within a bracing stroll of the War Office?

"Etta" remained a phantom, though an oddly substantial one. Several modern historians refer to her as one of Booth's playmates. Even Sandburg credits her with existence. Sandburg's text reads: "On April 12, Booth writes to a woman in New York who signs herself 'Etta.' She answers on April 13. . . ."[30] Since the New York police were unable to locate the lady, one must wonder how the historian located the fact that Booth addressed to her a letter. We have only "Etta's" word for such correspondence, but her word is all we have of "Etta." That, and Superintendent Kennedy's opinion that the whole thing was a "sell."

Although Kennedy's report provides no substance to shadowy "Etta," it does add corporeal evidence to the character of John Wilkes Booth. In behalf of historicity, it seems a pity that this evidence was buried by official censorship. Secrecy, propaganda and romanticism eventually combined to create a public portrait of Booth that bore about as much resemblance to the subject as do the profiles of public figures created by the modern artists of Madison Avenue for popular consumption.

During the Reconstruction Era, when American opinion began an about-face on the South, the formerly hated Secessionists were treated to a bath of forgive-and-forget sentimentality. This change of climate brought to flower in New Orleans a scrap of sheet music entitled "Our Brutus." The cover displayed a chromo of J. Wilkes Booth framed in a wreath of laurel.

Several decades later he would be eulogized in *A Tribute to John Wilkes Booth* (probably by a Judge Alexander W. Terrell). A sample:

> He has written his name
> In bright letters of fame
> In the pathway of Liberty's portal;
> And the serfs who now blame
> Shall crimson with shame
> When they have cursed an immortal.[31]

As of 1929, Booth's immortality as a hero on the "pathway of Liberty's portal" was not exactly conceded by biographer Francis Wilson. But Wilson, gentle soul, writes of the actor: "Whatever else John Wilkes Booth was, brutality and vulgarity had no part in his nature." And the kindly

---

[30] *Op. cit.*, p. 332.
[31] *Confederate Veteran*, April 1913.

biographer concludes: "He was a man of refinement and ideals: a man to whom 'the rift of dawn, the reddening rose' meant much."[32]

On the other side of the coin is the Booth profile etched by Police Superintendent Kennedy. A conscientious officer, patient, thorough, Kennedy was hardly a man to invent untruths about an individual, even if the subject was a fugitive from Justice. Unquestionably the New York Police Superintendent (who was there) researched more of Booth's background than did the assassin's later apologists.

That background: the gaslit brothels of New York. And in that soiled littoral of Manhattan John Wilkes Booth seems to have seen "the rift of dawn" in a fashion somewhat inconsistent with idealistic knighthood in romantic flower.

This is the Booth who was stabbed in the face by Henrietta Irving during a scuffle in a hotel room.

The Booth who philandered with soubrettes and leading ladies in one theatrical troupe after another.

The Booth once reported for rape in Philadelphia.

The Booth who fled a beating for adultery in Syracuse.

The Booth so overcome by the fall of Richmond that he dabbled with a lady that day on a junket to Newport, Rhode Island.

The Booth who nested in Manhattan with professional landlady Sally Andrews.

The Booth who voiced "promises of the future" to professional landlady Anne Horton.

The Booth who apparently consorted in Canada with an otherwise nameless "Jenny."

"Eva's" Booth. Nell Starr's Booth. The Booth who could use a socialite fiancée as a cover for his subversive activities, and, while deluding this female pawn, could swear devotion to his Washington mistress, harlot Ella Turner.[33]

Biographer Wilson would have us believe it was "especially the convivial temptations such a handsome young dog would encounter that wrought such havoc in the mind and soul of John Wilkes Booth." Having thus placed responsibility on the "temptations" rather than on the tempted, Wilson tells us the actor was just an immature adolescent. "We scarcely know what Wilkes Booth would have been in maturity," writes Wilson. "He had but reached the formative period."[34]

If he were indeed as described, Booth was surely a retarded grower. Few men cling to a formative period after 21. At the time in question John Wilkes Booth was 26 years old, and some contemporary commentators re-

---

[32] *Op. cit.*, p. 19.

[33] Booth's "chivalrous" sportings are variously recorded in contemporary accounts. The Philadelphia and Syracuse episodes were reported in the New York *Daily Tribune,* April 27, 1865.

[34] *Op. cit.*, p. 19.

garded him as an experienced stag. "Booth," wrote Horace Greeley, "was simply one of the loose-living badly educated young men who infested our country at the time."[35]

However, it seems to remain the tradition that the celebrity who is a cicisbeo and a libertine, with the habits of a Trinidad tomcat, may somehow remain "a man of refinement and ideals" to whom "brutality and vulgarity" are repugnant, vice notwithstanding. The chances are that Booth's women, one and all, would have favored the swords-and-roses portrait of "Our Brutus."

Ella Turner, on the week-end of Booth's flight from Washington, retired to her room, and lay down on a bed, and put his picture under the pillow, and pressed her face into a towel soaked with chloroform.

They found her just in time.[36]

One of the singular incongruities of the Lincoln murder case was the Government's reluctance to lay a glove on a single one of Booth's known inamoratas.

Stanton's Army Provosts and Lafayette Baker were not too shyly Victorian to investigate redlight bagnios or violet-scented boudoirs. Nor did chivalry restrain them when suspicion fell on the distaff side. Mrs. Surratt's cell-bars evince the opposite.

Yet the fact remains that Mistress Ella Turner never endured prolonged confinement in the Old Capitol. Neither did Booth's former Washington favorite, Nellie Starr. No sustained effort was made to locate and apprehend "Jenny," Booth's Canadian attachment. The numerous "landladies" of the assassin's New York harem were never placed on Stanton's Old Capitol list.

Although much time and telegraphy were spent in an effort to track down ghostly "Etta"—a lady Police Chief Kennedy believed to be fictional—a certain "Eva," who had reason to know Booth's intentions, and whose own were known to the authorities, never received so much as a summons to appear in court.

Laura Keene, who had merely a stage acquaintance with Booth, was arrested by the Secret Service the week-end Lincoln died. Undoubtedly Miss Keene would have spent a few weeks in prison but for the timely aid of her lover, a well-heeled Baltimore gambler named Lutz. However, like the other players in the cast of *Our American Cousin,* the English actress was compelled to make a daily parole report to the police.[37]

True, Miss Keene's name appeared in the mysterious "Mother" letter to Booth. But that epistle did not reach the authorities until some time after her summary arrest, and it smacked of poison pen. Moreover, wit-

---

[35] Horace Greeley, *The American Conflict,* Vol. II, p. 749.
[36] New York *Daily Tribune,* April 17, 1865.
[37] Ruggles, *op. cit.,* p. 186.

nesses testified that the assassin had struck viciously at Miss Keene as he dashed off stage at Ford's. Stanton probably ordered her arrest as a sop to public opinion. Or, as he would have euphemized, it was "in the public interest."

The dictator who demanded the arrest of "Red Laura" also found it in the public interest to decree hands off in the case of Booth's Washington fiancée, the socialite mentioned in Booth's letter to his mother. This young lady's infatuation with Booth was early known to the Federal authorities. Another "Eva," she had dallied for some time in a state of betrothal with the amorous actor. As Assistant Judge Advocate Burnett long afterward described her, she "had caught the fever of stage-hero worship." Burnett recalled that it was this young lady who prevailed upon her influential father to procure for Booth a grandstand seat at Lincoln's second inaugural —the seat that put Booth within striking distance of the President on March 4. Here, surely, was a suspect for the Old Capitol interrogators.

But Judge Burnett carefully preserved this lady's anonymity. Gallantly enough, he told a little white lie about her: ". . . she had only a casual acquaintance with Booth."[38] War Secretary Stanton had clamped an absolute censorship on her identity. Even Ben Perley Poore, Washington journalist who knew everything and usually told what he knew, was constrained to withhold the young woman's name. He wrote: "Booth squandered the money received by him in coal-oil speculations and in his attention to an estimable young lady . . . whose name was honorably kept a secret."[39]

Locked up by War Department censorship, this secret was held so inviolate that as late as 1929—almost 65 years after the assassination— the identity of Booth's fiancee remained a mystery. Researchers tiptoed around the subject, and historians gazed at the blank in the record with puzzled frowns. Who was Miss "X"? And why was she so important that the Government refused to divulge her identity?

Booth carried on his person five photographs of lady friends. As will be seen, the Federal authorities came into possession of this miniature collection. Immediate efforts were made to identify the five women. Four proved to be well-known actresses. The fifth (and least attractive, perhaps) was the assassin's betrothed.

The Government made no attempt to withhold the identity of the actresses—their names and photographs were soon made public. Picture No. 5 was not released for publication until 1929 when it appeared in Francis Wilson's biography of Booth.

Biographer Wilson readily names the four actresses: Fanny (Pretty Fay) Brown, Alice Grey, Effie Germon and Helen Western. Wilson captions the fifth picture "A Washington society woman," and advises

---

[38] Quoted in Eisenschiml, *op. cit.*, p. 209.
[39] *Op. cit.*, Vol. II, p. 184.

" . . . the name is withheld out of deference to the lady's descendants."[40]

While a lady's descendants might well deserve biographical deference, it must be remarked that the lady in question had no descendants at the time the War Department censorship was imposed. Her possible future descendants could not have had a bearing on the case.

What, then, endowed Booth's fiancee with a sanctuary denied four actresses who were only passing fancies in his repertoire? What entitled her to a police exemption denied such an innocent bystander as Laura Keene? What etiquette assured her an immunity not granted to such witnesses as Olivia Jenkins, Honora Fitzpatrick and poor Anna Surratt? Scores of women, respectable ladies, too, were arrested and grilled by the Army Provosts in connection with the assassination conspiracy. Many of these innocents were imprisoned in the Old Capitol Prison. Yet Booth's fiancee was impounded only in the Government's secret files.

The truth had to out, for rumor began to associate the name of Mrs. Lincoln with the mystery. Throughout the war she had been suspected of Southern sympathies. It was said she had harbored a Confederate agent in the White House. Could Mary Lincoln have given Booth her picture? Who but the First Lady could have gained such inviolate immunity, such privileged exemption from the public press?[41]

Embarrassed, the War Department finally had to lift the censorship veil. Revealed at long last was the name of Booth's fiancee—Miss Bessie Hale. And why the years of official secrecy? Judge Burnett had provided the historic clue, describing Miss Hale's father as a Washington political leader, ". . . one of the most faithful and earnest of the Union Republican group."[42] One might suppose that the personage in question had been a war leader equal in stature to a Thaddeus Stevens or a Sumner. But John P. Hale was just one of many Senators.

Arrest an English actress who had been on the stage with Booth, yes. Arrest a young lady who had chatted with Booth in the parlor of a boarding house. Arrest and imprison a backwoods farmer's wife who had served a dish of tea to a caller who might have been Booth. Arrest and imprison a scullery maid who had cried, "Hoo-ray for Booth." But do not arrest the society woman who had consorted with him in Washington drawing-rooms. Do not impound this *amourette* who seated the killer near Lincoln at the Inaugural. Never breathe the name of Booth's betrothed. She is privileged, beyond the law, sacrosanct. She is the daughter of a United States Senator!

Senator Hale whisked his daughter to Spain soon after the Lincoln

---

[40] *Op. cit.*, facing p. 12.

[41] The author heard this version in the early 1930's. It was rumored that the Government was holding the picture top secret because it was a photograph of Mrs. Lincoln.

[42] Quoted in Eisenschiml, *op cit.*, p. 209.

tragedy. There the veils that concealed her face were even more impenetrable than those offered by the War Department. Eventually Bessie Hall returned to marry William Eaton Chandler of West Point, New York. According to Philip Van Doren Stern, Miss Hale "was the only one near Booth who did not have to pay a public penalty for having been associated with him."[43]

But there were some others. An almost equally inviolate police immunity was enjoyed by Ella Turner, Nellie Starr and kindred girls at the other end of the social scale.

A wise policeman never raids his own house?

By the end of May, 1865, the big roundup was almost over. During the six weeks following Lincoln's assassination scores of individuals had been summarily arrested and grilled by military police and Federal detectives.

Obviously atrocious injustices were suffered by many of the persons summarily arrested and thrown into the Old Capitol. But there was another side to this brass coin. While it is evident that many of the prisoners suffered false arrest and unwarranted confinement, it remains no less evident that a number enjoyed an unwarranted release from custody.

One might believe that the Bureau of Military Justice indicted or released conspiracy suspects by a drawing of names from a draft wheel. Among numerous shady characters released as by some whim were the dubious Benjamin Ficklin, subversive agents Thomas and Nannie Green, the odd Mr. Preston Parr and mysterious Joao Celestino.

However, the contemporary Northern public was satisfied. There had been a thrilling manhunt for the assassins and every community had been able to participate in the exciting hunt for spies, disloyalists and subversives. Who cared if a few shady suspects walked free? Editorials discussed such things, but the big news was on the front page. The public eye fixed on the easy-to-read headlines.

In May: THE CONSPIRACY TRIAL! MRS. SURRATT INDICTED!

And before that (on April 27): NEWS FROM VIRGINIA! JOHN WILKES BOOTH CAPTURED AND SLAIN!

---

[43] Van Doren Stern, op. cit., p. 394.

CHAPTER **18**

Invasion of Lilliput

O<small>N</small> S<small>UNDAY</small>, April 16, Lieutenant David D. Dana sat in Bryantown, Maryland, like a bump on a log across Booth's escape route. Booth and Herold had easily skirted the log, and the bump made no move in any direction. So most of the literature on the subject dates the all-out manhunt for Booth as commencing on Monday, April 17.

Existing records fail to divulge any specific command decision which finally triggered off the concentrated search. But on that Monday morning Army forces galloped into lower Maryland. By Tuesday a dragnet was cast in Prince Georges and Charles Counties. As the calendar advanced in that third week of April, a mounting tide of Federal soldiery flowed down the Maryland peninsula and lapped across the Potomac to the shores of King George County, Virginia. Dragging the boondocks in Booth's wake, the manhunters caught a large assortment of suspects. The territory was alive with underground game.

But most of the characters snared in this military dragnet were small fry—country folk and river folk who had never been farther from home than the nearest village; villagers with the insular views of Lilliput.

For these backward Marylanders, the advent of Booth in their midst created a sensation akin to the arrival of a Man from the Moon. Then came the Men from Mars. Troops everywhere—in Surrattsville, Bryantown, Allen's Fresh, Port Tobacco, Leonardtown—banging on doors, asking questions, beating the bush. For the Federal soldiers it was uneasy work, scouring the swamps and backlands, knocking on lonely shanty doors. You never knew when a thicket might explode in your face, or the knock might be answered by a shotgun blast. But, surprisingly, few of the native inhabitants showed fight. For the most part they displayed a consuming dread of the Yankees.

A handful of resolute souls resisted—wanted to see search warrants, and demanded lawyers when threatened with summary arrest. But, in general, community resistance took the form of artful dodging—evasive answers; double-talk; loss of memory. And in many instances a servility that was more to be mistrusted than open hostility.

From first cast, then, the Army dragnet in this area snagged in a morass of petty hedgings and deceptions. The Blue troopers and plainclothes military detectives became impatient, and their interrogations roughened to the point of brutality. If not to be exonerated, the blows and threats were understandable. A flock of fibs is often harder to deal with than a pack of lies.

Yet the soldiery should have had little difficulty in uncovering Booth's track. Around Surrattsville and Bryantown they found conspiracy clues as thick as cotton blossoms at picking time. In places like Allen's Fresh and Port Tobacco half the villagers seemed acquainted with John Surratt, David Herold and George Atzerodt. Had they been deliberate marplots, Booth's accomplices—and Booth, himself—could not have made more noise about their intentions and their getaway plans.

One wonders how the Federal men, pursuing Booth's escape route, could possibly have missed the boat.

Special Officer George Cottingham jumped the starting gun. Cottingham was nosing around Surrattsville with Police Superintendent Richards' flying squad on Saturday the 15th. It was Cottingham who caused the arrest of Lloyd's bartender, seedy Joseph Knott.

Cottingham is a vague figure. Accounts vary as to his duties and how he came to be on locale with Richards' posse. He may have been an Army secret intelligence agent—the term "Special Officer" could cover all kinds of operatives. There is no mystery, however, concerning the lead which directed Cottingham to the bartender at the Surrattsville tavern. The tip came from a neighborhood farmer, one Ephraim Smoot.

Eventually called upon to testify as a Government witness, Smoot told of Knott's arrest.

> I had a conversation with Mr. Nott (*sic*) the Saturday after the murder. A young man connected with General Augur's office told me that Surratt was supposed to be the man that cut Secretary Seward, and I asked if he [Knott] could tell me where Surratt was. He said that Surratt was in New York by that time. I asked him why that was, and he said, "My God, John Surratt knows all about this, and do you suppose he is going to stay in Washington and let them catch him? I could have told you this was going to happen six months ago." Then he said, "Keep that in your skin, for if you mention it 'twould ruin me."[1]

Smoot, of course, passed the word to the young man connected with General Augur's office. Special Officer Cottingham promptly arrested the loquacious Knott. By Sunday morning, April 16, Knott was talking his head off to save his neck.

Knott's blurted testimony should have brought a Federal avalanche down on Surrattsville that Easter Sunday afternoon. But, as has been

---

[1] War Dept. Records, "Trunk 10," Press Account, *"The Conspiracy Trial."*

noted, the manhunt was held in check. In Washington that afternoon War Secretary Stanton told Secret Service Chief Baker that no direct clues on the assassination had been uncovered.

According to Baker, his hands were tied that Sunday and Monday.

"At this time it was almost impossible to obtain any information of a reliable character; the unparalleled atrocity of this terrible event and the fact that the assassin had for the time being escaped had seemingly paralyzed the entire community."

The Secret Service Chief's account continues: "The local detective force of New York, Philadelphia, Boston, Baltimore and other cities had arrived [in Washington], and with the entire military force of this Department had reported to General Augur."

Either that Sunday evening or early Monday, Baker galloped crosstown to Augur's headquarters. The Secret Service Chief's account of his interview with the Army general has the tone of official alibi. But in this one instance, at least, Baker's alibi seems genuine.

> . . . A commission, consisting of Colonel Wells, Colonel Foster, and Colonel Olcott, was then in session, and all information, from whatever sources derived, was laid before this commission. The enormity of the crime committed by the assassins, and the anxiety of the public for their arrest, had divested my mind entirely of any thing like rivalry in the investigations going on. I was willing, and indeed anxious, to work and cooperate with any officer or officers in the prosecution of this investigation. I was even willing to place myself under the advice, counsel, and direction of any officer, whether military or civil. Accordingly, I repaired to General Augur's headquarters, and asked some questions with regard to the information already obtained. I was infomed that neither my services nor the services of my force were required; that a positive clue had been obtained as to who the assassins were, and their whereabouts. After making some further inquiries, to all of which I received either evasive or insulting replies, I determined to set on foot an investigation under my own direction. . . .[2]

As has been related, Baker's first move was to procure photographs of the "supposed assassins." Simultaneously he distributed his handbill containing a detailed profile on Lewis Paine and a spurious description of John Wilkes Booth.

Soon after Lieutenant Dana's move to Bryantown, the Army force stationed at Chapel Point stirred action. These troops were under command of Major John M. Waite. By Easter Sunday Waite's force was split into three detachments moving on separate routes eastward across the lower reaches of the Maryland peninsula.

Afterward critics scolded Waite for marching his soldiers away from the Port Tobacco area. A suspicion persisted that the move had been

---

[2] *Op. cit.*, pp. 526–529.

dictated by secret order from Washington headquarters—an order designed to leave Port Tobacco open to Booth. But Waite apparently acted on his own initiative, and his three detachments were not too wide of the mark.

One company headed up the Patuxent from the town of Benedict. Another went to Leonardtown about half way between Port Tobacco and Point Lookout at the mouth of the Potomac. The third company came close to the target. Waite ordered this detachment to scour the country "along the Wicomico River and vicinity."[3] This last detachment must have scouted through Allen's Fresh and come within a stone's throw of Booth's hideaway near Cox's. Unluckily, these soldiers kept on going. They had been ordered to sweep toward Leonardtown and be there on Thursday, April 20.

On Monday morning, April 17, Provost Marshal O'Beirne rushed a cavalry squadron from Washington into lower Maryland. O'Beirne had been told by War Secretary Stanton to "use his own discretion in hunting down the assassins."[4]

The squadron dispatched by O'Beirne was led by Lieutenant Alexander Lovett, U.S.A. With the cavalrymen rode Captain William Williams, one of O'Beirne's special aides.

"Where must I go?" Captain Williams asked O'Beirne.

The Provost Marshal glared. "How do I know? Go, and don't return to Washington until you find Booth. But mind—don't harm a hair of his head."

Williams "mounted a magnificent charger" and shouting "Come, boys!" galloped at top speed for Navy Yard Bridge. The bridge "was successfully crossed by the captain knocking the sentry down by running over him with his horse." Lovett's men raced across the span. As Williams later recalled: "Time was precious."[5]

So the story was told years afterward. One suspects this account of being fictionalized. Lovett's cavalry charged straight to Surrattsville; straight to Lloyd's (or Mrs. Surratt's) tavern. There Lieutenant Lovett, himself, came straight to the point with innkeeper John M. Lloyd. Certainly Williams, detective officer in titular command, must have acted on something more than intuition. Major O'Beirne probably had a substantial tip from Special Officer Cottingham on the tavern at Surrattsville.

The party stopped only long enough to arrest the sniveling Lloyd. Apparently Williams reported back to O'Beirne's headquarters at once. Lieutenant Lovett galloped on down to Bryantown, where he conferred with sleepy Lieutenant Dana. Some interesting off-the-cuff remarks must have passed between these two Army shavetails at the Bryantown Hotel.

---

[3] *Official Records*, Series I, Vol. 46, Part 3, p. 870.

[4] Eisenschiml, *op. cit.*, p. 116.

[5] J. E. Buckingham, *op. cit.*, *p.* 63.

Details are lacking. But on the afternoon of Tuesday, April 18, Lieutenant Lovett got hold of Dr. George Mudd, who guided the soldiers to the home of his physician cousin. So the trap closed on Dr. Samuel Mudd.

On that same Tuesday, Major O'Beirne set out in person from Washington with a party of detectives for Chapel Point. Descending the Potomac by river steamer, O'Beirne and his men reached Chapel Point that evening. They galloped at once to Port Tobacco.

O'Beirne had with him some sharp detectives. His party included officers Lee, D'Angelis, Callahan, Hoey, Bostwick, Hanover, Bevins and McHenry. John Lee was the smart sleuth who had uncovered Atzerodt's hidden reliquary at the Kirkwood House in Washington. Hoey, on loan, was a clever New Yorker. They were soon joined at Port Tobacco by energetic William Williams. These detectives took the town by the scruff, and shook out a lot of information concerning the doings of the Booth gang. Starting from Port Tobacco, O'Beirne then conducted a search that was to come within a hair of catching the fugitives.

Word to the War Department from O'Beirne brought a swarm of military forces to the interior and lower Potomac regions of the Maryland peninsula. By the latter part of that week, Charles County and St. Mary's County were alive with infantry and horse.

At Leonardtown, Major Waite mustered 700 troopers of the Eighth Illinois Cavalry. Colonel H. H. Wells invested Bryantown with the Twenty-sixth Michigan. Lieutenant Edward P. Doherty galloped in with a detachment of the Sixteenth New York. Some 600 colored troops of the Twenty-second arrived on locale. A special party of New York detectives, and a party of Philadelphia plainclothes men joined the search. Provost Marshal McPhail sent Army detectives from Baltimore. Intelligence officers from Richmond entered the hunt.

According to news correspondent George Alfred Townsend, a total of 1,400 Army troops swept lower Maryland and the Potomac bank of Virginia in pursuit of Booth during the third week and the last week of April, 1865.[6] Oldroyd puts the figure at 2,800 soldiers. By some accounts as many as 10,000 men joined the manhunt.[7] If naval brigades and volunteer partisans were counted, the 10,000 figure might be closer than Townsend's estimate.

The Navy forged a strong link in the dragnet chain. The possibility that Booth might escape by water was not lost on Naval Secretary Gideon Welles, who immediately placed his sea and river forces at Stanton's disposal. One of the first alarms from Washington had been flashed to the naval station at St. Inigoes near the mouth of the Potomac. This was the

---

[6] George A. Townsend, *Life, Crime and Capture of John Wilkes Booth* (New York: Dick and Fitzgerald, 1865).

[7] Eisenschiml, *op. cit.*, p. 118.

ambiguous message from Stanton ordering a stoppage of river traffic and the arrest of all passengers outward bound.

On Monday, April 17, the Navy Department in Washington flashed an order to Commander Foxhall Parker at St. Inigoes directing him to set up what amounted to a blockade of the Potomac estuary. Gunboats were stationed at the mouth of the Patuxent River farther north. Naval commands at Annapolis and at Baltimore were put on watch for possible blockade runners. But the Potomac outlet was the more probable escape exit, and the Navy Department exerted a concentrated effort to block the river at St. Inigoes and Point Lookout.

By freakish chance the emergency flash to St. Inigoes caught the commander of the naval station off base. Commander Parker, it seemed, had gone home to Relay, Maryland, for the Easter holiday. Apparently the easygoing naval officer had voted himself an unofficial leave. He was enjoying the bosom of his family homestead near Baltimore when he received a frantic message from his second in command to return at once to St. Inigoes. When Parker failed to do so, he learned that naval duty could be full of surprises. A blistering wire from Secretary Welles ordered him back to base at top speed. Miffed by the order's angry tone, Parker telegraphed a sputtering reply.[8] He begged to excuse his delay by saying that he had thought Relay, Maryland, a strategic point from which to direct a naval hunt for Booth. "Uncle Gideon's" answer to this preposterous excuse sent the fatuous commander racing back to St. Inigoes in a frantic effort to avoid court-martial. But who would have expected an assassination to torpedo a quiet holiday?

Parker would never make admiral. Nor would "Uncle Gideon's" naval forces trap John Wilkes Booth. Still, they tried. The Navy set up a tight Potomac patrol. By midweek following the assassination, armed tugs and belligerent "double-enders" were policing the miles of river between Washington and the Chesapeake. Gunboats stood off Port Tobacco and the river villages lower down. By day, naval shore patrols ranged the riverbanks, rounding up small boats and questioning the tidewater fishermen. By night, iron saurians chugged up and down the broad channel, eyeing the banks with huge and ghostly Drummond lights. But the Potomac is long and wide, with many inlets and bluff-screened coves. The gunboat sailors and monitor men came close. But they missed the mouth of the Wicomico and Allen's Fresh.

By Wednesday, April 19, the Federal dragnet extended from Surrattsville to Port Tobacco to Point Lookout. While the Army scoured overland, the Navy blockaded the Potomac. And at this critical juncture, the Secret Service of Lafayette Baker moved in. Details on the operation are con-

---

[8] *Official Records of the Union and Confederate Navies in the War of the Rebellion,* Series I, Vol. 5, p. 554 *et seq.*

spicuously vague. They come from Colonel-General Lafayette C. Baker. In his *History of the United States Secret Service* Baker states that on Sunday, April 16, Baltimore Provost Marshal McPhail sent a dispatch informing him that a young man named Polk Gardner had seen two midnight riders galloping south from Navy Yard Bridge on the night of the assassination.

> I immediately sent for Polk Gardner, and had his statement taken. The description given of the horses—to wit, one bay and one roan—corresponded exactly with the description furnished by Fletcher of the horses hired from Naylor's stable. This, with Fletcher's statement, furnished to my mind conclusive evidence that the assassins had gone in the direction of Lower Maryland.[9]

Confusingly, at this point in his account, Baker switches to a narrative style wherein he refers to himself in the third person. (If his reference to photographs and handbills seems redundant, we are reminded that when this account was published he was bidding for a Government award of prize money.)

"A careful analysis of all that could be ascertained satisfied General Baker that these parties had fled, and would probably attempt to escape across the Lower Potomac; and his first efforts were directed to securing the accurate likenesses of Booth and Harrold (*sic*), as well as others, and a full and minute description of their persons. These likenesses were taken, and printed—the first and only ones issued of these parties—he caused to be extensively circulated in every direction likely to be taken by the fugitives; in particular, Lieutenant [Luther B.] Baker was detailed, with five or six active and reliable men, to traverse Lower Maryland and distribute them. He [the lieutenant] was also to examine and note every possible indication of the presence of the parties, or other suspected persons, from which labor he returned the Saturday following, having explored the whole region unsuccessfully, while the Chief remained at headquarters, with Colonel Conger and other assistants, constantly, anxiously, and exhaustively collating and exploring every outside rumor, theory, and source of information that sleepless labor, vigilance, and experienced sagacity could compass."

Having delivered his narrative of this windy passage, the General now inserts his reminder that prize money is due. Nothing like the stingy $30,000 offered by the Government as of Monday, April 17, 1865. As of Thursday, April 20, Stanton had raised the ante to a fortune. Baker quotes the reward terms officially issued by the War Department at the height of the manhunt.

"The rewards are special offers for specific services, and qualified by no conditions whatever—$50,000 for the capture of Booth, and $25,000 for the capture of Harrold.

---

[9] *Op. cit.,* p. 530.

"It is assumed that Booth is the murderer, and whether he proves to be or not, $50,000. It is asserted that Harrold was his accomplice, and the Secretary will pay $25,000 for him. The payment in neither case is made to depend upon the conviction of the party, but merely upon his apprehension."[10]

The Secret Service Chief has money on his mind. He had it on his mind when he dispatched Lieutenant Luther Baker to lower Maryland with photographs and descriptions of the fugitives. General Baker's narrative account implies that this was early in the week following the assassination —Monday or Tuesday. But the circulars distributed by Lieutenant Luther Baker bear an April 20 dateline. Which means they were not distributed until Thursday, April 20.

General Baker insists that these circulars were the "first and only." Conveniently he forgets the tricky little handbill put into circulation on Monday the 17th. He prefers the April 20 circular with the headline photographs, and wants posterity to believe that their distribution was a most effective police measure.

Certainly the April 20 circular was most effective in publicizing the $100,000 reward for Booth, Herold and John Surratt. But there is more than meets the eye in this circular. The original—the one distributed by Lieutenant Luther Baker—displays a good likeness of Booth (a stage star portrait) and a quaint parlor photo of Herold, evidently a schoolboy picture. But the photograph captioned "John H. Surratt" is a picture of someone else, perhaps his older brother Isaac. An odd mistake in light of the fact that young Surratt was well known to H Street neighbors eager to furnish the authorities with descriptions of his lengthy nose and wispy whiskers.

As with General Baker's first handbill, then, there is something amiss with this Secret Service circular. It contributes still another complexity to the Lincoln murder case. For someone in the War Department (perhaps General Baker himself) must have detected the flaw after the manhunt was over. At any rate, the War Department eventually placed on record a revised circular featuring a better photograph of Booth and up-to-date pictures of Herold and John Surratt.

This revised circular was released by the War Department for public consumption when public opinion soured after the Conspiracy Trials. The Government continued to display the revised circular when historians dipped into the case. Even today the revised circular is offered the researcher who inquires into the capture of the assassination gang.

But the revised Secret Service circular is as patently fraudulent as a three-dollar bill. Strange that contemporary viewers (not to mention erudite historians) never noticed the fakery. For this new photograph of David Herold was one of a set taken *after his capture*. And the corrected

[10] *Ibid.*, pp. 532–538.

picture of John Surratt shows the "fugitive" in a Brady-type portrait *made long after April 20, 1865.*

Clearly the War Department hedged on the matter of Baker's original circular, embarrassed perhaps by the unrecognizable photograph of David Herold and the erroneous picture of John Surratt. Such a circular obviously contributed little to the manhunt. As Baker himself admits, his relative, Lieutenant Luther Baker, returned from lower Maryland that weekend "having explored the whole region unsuccessfully."

The Army in the field had been more successful.

Lieutenant Lovett and Captain William Williams made the first big catch in lower Maryland when they picked up John M. Lloyd.

Lovett's troop consisted of nine mounted men of so-called Provisional Cavalry. Accompanying the soldiers were Captain Williams and another Special Officer, Simon Gavran. As reported by Lovett, this military group "proceeded to Robey's Post Office [at Surrattsville] for the purpose of arresting such parties as might be suspected of being implicated in the assassination...."

Somewhere en route, Lovett's squad encountered two military detectives with warm information. Or as Lovett's report states it: "I met two more Special Officers of Maj. O'Beirne's force. Named Joshua Lloyd and George Cottingham. Got some information that John M. Lloyd of Surrattsville was an accomplice of the assassins; proceeded toward New Port, passed through T.B. on Tuesday April 18th. Met John M. Lloyd a short distance from that place, returning from Allen's Fresh with his wife who he had sent to that place before the murder of the President. I arrested Lloyd and sent him back under guard to Robey's Post Office where I had established a Guard House or Prison under charge of Special Officer George Cottingham for the purpose of keeping such persons as were arrested untill they could be forwarded to Washington. We went on to New Port and from there to Bryantown."[11]

If the besotted tavern keeper had been chronically miserable (as described by bartender Knott), his miseries were doubled when he fell into the hands of Lovett's Federals. By some accounts, the innkeeper was beaten into talking. It was said that Lovett put a pistol to Lloyd's temple and ordered him to tell what he knew. (In 1897, Lieutenant Dana published a story in the Boston *Globe.* In this he recalled that the troopers hanged an old man to a tree in Surrattsville to make him confess that Booth and Herold had been at the tavern on the night Lincoln was shot.[12])

However, it seems probable that Lloyd broke easily under interrogation. It would not have taken much to snap the will of this boozy pawn.

[11] National Archives, War Dept. Records, File "L," R.B., JAO.
[12] Boston *Globe,* December 12, 1897.

In the improvised jail at Surrattsville, innkeeper Lloyd talked. Removed to Bryantown for grilling, he talked some more. On April 23 he was lodged in the Old Capitol Prison. There, he continued to talk. We do not know the third-degree pressures applied, if any. We do know that John M. Lloyd talked himself out from under the shadow of the noose and into the favor of the Federal authorities as a prime Government witness.

Lloyd told his inquisitors that he was 40 years old, had formerly resided in Washington City, had served as a policeman on the Metropolitan Force under ex-Mayor James Barret, and had removed to Prince Georges County, Maryland, in 1862 to take up farming.

Late in December, 1864, he had (said Lloyd) rented Mrs. Surratt's tavern at Surrattsville. He declared that he was on friendly terms with the Surratt family, but denied any knowledge of a conspiracy to murder President Lincoln. He admitted that John Surratt, David Herold and George Atzerodt frequently visited the tavern to play cards and share a round of drinks—pastimes in which he innocently took a hand.

Then "in the latter part of February or early in March 1865," young Surratt, Herold and Atzerodt came one evening to the tavern. A few minutes after their arrival, Surratt asked Lloyd to step into the parlor.

Here is the conclusion of the statement Lloyd eventually made to the authorities:

> Surratt called me into the front room where on the sofa there lay two firearms or carbines. I did not examine them. He remarked, 'They are something like those that the cavalry use, only heavier.' They were in a kind of woollen cloths. He had a rope from sixteen to twenty feet in length, and a monkey wrench. He showed me where to put them—up in the ceiling of the house in an unfurnished room where the [joists?] were not covered with lathing or plastering, and they were put there.
>
> I understood him to say he would call for them. He did not say when they would be called for. I did not want to receive such things in the house, but he said they would be there only a few days, and I submitted to it.[13]

It is possible that Lloyd thought John Surratt and his pals were running guns. That the tenant of Mrs. Surratt's tavern protested the hiding of such contraband on the premises and "submitted" against his will seems most unlikely.

But now the miserable Lloyd mumbled lines of testimony that proved fatal—fatal for someone else, not for John M. Lloyd. He referred to a meeting with Mrs. Surratt on the road to Uniontown (Anacostia) several days before the assassination.

> Mrs. Surratt was down that day, and in fact had before that met me in Uniontown and asked me in relation to them [the weapons] (sic). It was on Monday previous to the murder. I have been reflecting upon it; I think

---

[13] National Archives, War Dept. Records, File "L," JAO.

it was Monday. [Actually it was Tuesday.] She spoke to me in such a way
in relation to them that I did not understand her. I looked at her and did
not know what she meant. Finally she came out and asked me about the
firearms. I told her they had been shoved back (*sic*), and she asked me
to get them out as they would be called for soon.

She called on the evening of the murder [April 14] with a man by the
name of Wiechmann. I was not at home that day—I had an assault and
battery case to attend to at Baltimore, and got pretty tight. The case was
postponed. I did not get back til five o'clock that evening—I reckon it was
after that. I found Mrs. Offut, my sister-in-law, at home, and Mrs. Surratt
and this young man.

Mrs. Surratt asked me about those things again, and asked me to get
them out for her—saying that they would be called for that night. Mrs.
Offut was present, but nobody else. Wiechmann was not present. I did not
see him until after they had got ready to go. She said her buggy had broken
down and I must fix it for her. She did not tell me who was to call for them,
nor what time they were to be called for. She asked me to have two bottles
of whiskey prepared for them.

She did not mention any names. She did not say that there would be
startling news. The only conversation I had with her was while I was taking some fish and oysters out of my wagon. She gave me a little bundle
rolled up at that time, and asked me to put that there (*sic*). I found it to be
a field glass, a double glass, a large one. It was in a case.

She left as soon as she got her buggy fixed. It was a little before sundown.
I was pretty well in liquor and consequently wanted to retire early. . . .
At midnight Herold was at the door with another man sitting on a horse.[14]

Lloyd's statement ends with a description of Herold demanding the
carbines, the delivery of the weapons and liquor, the fugitives galloping
away in the night. According to Lloyd, just before they raced off Booth
said, "I will tell you some news. I am pretty certain that we have assassinated the President and Secretary Seward." Lloyd swore that Booth was
a complete stranger to him.

The files of the Bureau of Military Justice contain a number of similar
Lloyd statements—the tavern keeper faced numerous interrogators in
the month following his arrest. The statement cited comes from one of
the first transcripts. The theme in all remains susbstantially the same. It
is a theme that points straight to John M. Lloyd as a member of the Booth
gang and an accessory to the assassin's getaway.

Lloyd rents Mrs. Surratt's tavern in December 1864 (an obvious deal
to place the tavern in the hands of someone the gang wanted there).
Lloyd hides the weapons and escape gear. Lloyd has the stuff ready for
the fugitives. Lloyd was up to his neck in the conspiracy. But the War
Department is not interested in the innkeeper's neck.

Lloyd's testimony would be used as a rope—a deadly rope—for the
hanging of Mrs. Surratt.

---

[14] *Ibid.*

The next suspect of any importance to fall into the dragnet was Dr. Samuel Mudd. Accompanied by Dr. George Mudd, Lieutenant Lovett and his men paid a call on the Samuel Mudd homestead. Mrs. Mudd answered the door. The Federals entered the house politely. Upon learning Samuel Mudd was out, Lieutenant Lovett asked that he be sent for. During the wait, he questioned Mrs. Mudd about Booth's visit.

When Dr. Samuel Mudd came in, Lovett questioned him at length. Probably the interview took place in the little parlor where the physician had first examined Booth's leg. It must have been an unhappy hour for the doctor under interrogation—the room crowded with Federals, his wife listening apprehensively, his cousin, Dr. George Mudd, standing grimly in the background.

Here are excerpts from Lovett's official report of the episode:

> We went on to New Port [on Tuesday, April 18] and from there to Bryantown [where we] got information of two strange men being in that vicinity and that one of them had a broken leg and that a man by the name of Dr. Samuel Mudd had set it for him. I then proceeded to Dr. Mudd's farm about four and a half miles from Bryantown. He was not at home, but his wife sent for him. . . .
>
> But in the meantime I . . . questioned his wife concerning the two men who had been there; she stated that they were both strangers to her, that they came there about day brake (sic) Saturday Morning April 15th. . . . I asked her what kind of looking men they were. She stated that one of them was a young man about eighteen or nineteen years of age. The other who had a broken leg was a man over thirty years; she said that when the doctor commenced treating the man's leg she left the room, and didn't see him again until he had his leg fixed, and when she saw him again she missed a moustache that he wore on his face when he entered the house. I asked how that came and she told me that she had since learned that her husband had furnished the man a razor for him to shave it off and when the man was leaving the house in the afternoon she took notice when he came to the foot of the stairs, that his chin whisker became detached and that, she thought it was a false whisker. I asked her how the men got away. She stated that her husband had a pair of crutches made for the injured man, and tried to get a bugay (sic) to help him away. . . .
>
> When the doctor came in, I questioned him about the two men. . . . He seemed to be somewhat excited and said that they were perfect strangers to him, that he had set one of their legs which had been broken by his horse falling on him, and that was all he knew about them. He was then questioned in regard to the appearance of the men and did not give much satisfaction. He stated that the injured man was heavily armed with a pair of revolvers and seemed to be very much excited. Dr. Mudd, seemed to be very much reserved and did not care to give much information. . . . I was under the impression that Booth and Herold were in the neighborhood and that Dr. Mudd knew where they were, and was secretly giving Booth medical attendance. . . .

Lovett posted some of his men around the Mudd homestead to keep it under secret surveillance. His report continues:

I started back to Robey's Post Office where I had Loyd and several other persons confined, to see what information I could obtain from Loyd or others. Loyd made a partial confession and said that he was an accessory after the fact, and if he had thought of it, in time that the *President* would not have been murdered; that he was drew into the plot by a woman, and to save himself would come out on the whole of them. . . .

I procured a fresh squad of [25] mounted men of the 16th N.Y. Cav. and returned to Dr. Samuel Mudd's farm and arrested him. When he saw that we were going to search the house he said something to his wife, she went up stairs and brought down a heavy riding boot which had been split up from the instep and turned it over to me. I examined the inner part of the boot leg and found wrote with ink the makers name and the number of his place of business, beneath that the name J. Wilks. I then demanded from Mr. Mudd, the razor he had furnished Booth to shave off his moustache. He handed me a razor and said that was the one. He was questioned as to whether it was not Booth's leg he set; he said that it was not, and that the young man Booth's companion was not Herold. He was then shown Booth's picture. He said that it did not look like Booth only acrossed the eyes (*sic*). He afterwards stated that Booth had been in his house last fall and was in the neighborhood for some time, and that he was well acquainted with him. He afterwards acknowledged that he was satisfied that it was J. Wilks Booth who's leg he set, and helped through the Swamp. I perceeded (*sic*) with Dr. Mudd to Bryantown where I turned him and the Boot over to Col. Wells.[15]

Lovett's spelling, punctuation and sentence structure are not the only things amiss with this report. It reveals a common military flaw of detailing men to missions for which they have neither training nor aptitude. Lovett was a cavalry officer. Because he was not a skilled interrogator, he probably asked the physician a lot of blunt or clumsy questions which tied the doctor's tongue. And because he could write neither clearly nor grammatically, he doubtless misquoted some of Mudd's answers. But on the whole Lovett did pretty well with his interrogation. His costly error was a bad guess that Booth and Herold were still hiding in the vicinity. In delaying Mudd's arrest for four days, Lovett slowed the manhunt. In fact, it was not until the doctor was arrested and Booth's boot was discovered on the premises that the War Department became convinced Lincoln's assassin was John Wilkes Booth. Or so one learns from Colonel Burnett of the Judge Advocate's Office.

Years after the event Colonel Burnett wrote:

As soon as the boot was received at the War Department, I had ex-Marshal Murray put aboard a special engine and sent to New York to look up the maker and ascertain for whom the boot was made. That night a telegram was received from him saying the boot was made for J. Wilkes Booth. *This settled the identity of the assassin in our minds beyond all doubt.*[16]

---

[15] National Archives, War Dept. Records, File "L," R.B.P. 59, JAO.
[16] Quoted in Eisenschiml, *op. cit.,* p. 266. Emphasis supplied.

Immediately after Mudd's arrest, Colonel William P. Wood, warden of the Old Capitol Prison, appeared in Bryantown. Wood took up quarters in Dr. Samuel Mudd's house, and went over the Mudd farm with a fine-tooth comb. Around the house were posted three young detectives, Wallace Kirby, Aquilla Allen and Bernard Adamson. Booth's whereabouts were still unknown to the Federal soldiery. It was supposed that the assassin might be concealed in the swamp near Mudd's and that the doctor's wife might try to take food or a message to Booth. The detectives were instructed to shoot any suspicious person who tried to sneak up to the house.[17]

As Eisenschiml notes in *Why Was Lincoln Murdered*, the suspicious person who might try to sneak up to the house would presumably be Booth or Herold. Was Warden Wood (Stanton's War Department intimate) given shooting instructions in the hope that Lincoln's assassin might be slain on the spot? Such instructions do not conform with official statements to the effect that the troops were ordered to bring Booth back alive.

While plainclothes men watched the Mudd house and the War Department studied the doctor's statements, military policemen went through the Bryantown-Beantown neighborhood asking questions about Samuel Mudd. On the Mudd farm they picked up John Best, the old Englishman, and the stable hand, Frank Washington. They called on Dr. Mudd's brothers. They interrogated his father.

From a neighbor, Francis R. Farrell, they pried some damaging testimony. Farrell lived about half way between the Mudd farm and Bryantown. He told the Federals that Dr. Mudd stopped by for a chat on Saturday afternoon, April 15. During this visit, Dr. Mudd informed Farrell that the President had been assassinated by a man named Booth.[18] If Farrell spoke the truth, his story completely shattered Dr. Mudd's defensive assertion that he did not know Booth was the assassin until he heard the news Easter Sunday.

The police picked up a farmer named J. B. Thomas. Lafayette Baker interviewed Thomas in Washington and "forwarded" him to Colonel Burnett. Baker noted: "Witness . . . says he will swear that Dr. Mudd (*sic*) told him some 3 weeks previous to the assassination that the President and other Cabinet officers would be murdered."[19]

A serious charge against Dr. Mudd came purportedly from Rachel Spencer, onetime slave in the Mudd household. We find in the Judge Advocate's files a curious document which appears to contain a statement by this colored woman. It reads:

---

[17] Nettie Mudd, *The Life of Dr. Samuel A. Mudd* (New York: Neale Pub. Co., 1906), pp. 35–36.
[18] Oldroyd, *op. cit.*, p. 145.
[19] National Archives, War Dept. Records, File "B," Doc. 243, JAO.

Enter file—Rachal Spencer—in advance—Col.

Dr. Muds wife gave firearms to me and told me to Bury them in the Woods. About ten Guns [illegible], Sowards, Pistoles and ten Bool (*sic*). Doctor Mud told his wife that she ought not to have let Rachal have those things. Mrs. Mud told Rachal she must never Mention about the firearms in the Woods. Mrs. Mud made Rachal take an oath that she should never mention it. Rachal is sick at Present. Will be well Monday.[20]

The foregoing, a crude scrawl on the back of an envelope, presents us with a mystery. Was it written for Rachel by a friend or relative? Or was it written by a detective? The peculiar notation, "Rachal Spencer—in advance" intrigues us. Was her story true? Or did she, or some sponsor, weave it out of whole cloth?

The authorities did not procure Rachel's statement until late in May— *after* Dr. Mudd's indictment. The tip came from an officer, Theodore E. McGowan, who wrote to Colonel Burnett:

The present employer of Rachel Spencer—late slave of Dr. Mudd—tells me that in his family she has spoken ambiguously of arms which at one time she either helped to hide or knew where they were hid in the grounds of Mudd, some time last winter. Rachel is in the family of a Mrs. Day, a clerk in the office of Capt. Camp, A.2.M., at the Soldiers' Rest.[21]

McGowan's note and the "Rachal" statement are both dated May 27, 1865. By that date, Dr. Samuel Mudd was already standing trial as an assassination conspirator.

On April 20, War Secretary Stanton issued a proclamation declaring that: " . . . all persons harboring or secreting the said persons [Booth and Herold] . . . or aiding . . . their concealment or escape, will be treated as accomplices in the murder of the President . . . and shall be subject to trial before a military commission, and the punishment of death."[22]

This decree must have sent a shiver through the counties of lower Maryland. Booth was in hiding there—somewhere—and the grapevine's party line doubtless muted down to a whisper.

Then hair must have risen on many heads in lower Maryland. On April 22, with Booth and Herold still at large, Stanton issued a pronouncement which appeared in the press:

The counties of Prince George, Charles and St. Mary's [Maryland] have during the whole war been noted for hostility to the Government and their protection to Rebel blockade runners, Rebels spies and every species of public enemies; the murderers of the President harbored there before the murder, and Booth fled in that direction. If he escapes it will be owing to Rebel accomplices in that region. The military commander of the De-

---

[20] National Archives, War Dept. Records, File "B," Doc. 406, JAO.
[21] National Archives, War Dept. Records, File "Mc," Doc. 45, JAO.
[22] *Official* Records, Series I, Vol. 46, Sec. 3.

partment will surely take measures to bring those Rebel sympathizers and accomplices in murder to sense their criminal conduct. [signed]: Edwin M. Stanton, Secretary of War.[23]

The dragnet had steadily tightened. East of the Wicomico, Major Waite's troops swept the terrain from the banks of the Patuxent to the beaches of St. Inigoes and Point Lookout.

Among the first suspects arrested in this riparian area was saloonkeeper Walter L. Barnes, an exemplary specimen. A "wanted" on Barnes was issued by Provost Marshal McPhail at Baltimore on the 20th.

> Age about 22 years; height 5 ft. 4 or 5; eyes gray and large; action, quick; walks leaning a little forward; shoulders, a little rounded; hair dark, not black. Very talkative in conversation, free generally, and wears dark clothing.[24]

Aside from the talkativeness (which could be taken for a "conspiracy" characteristic) the records offer no definite clue which links Barnes to the Booth gang. Major Waite's detectives flushed him from the marshes of St. Marys County on April 22. And the Navy shipped him from the Patuxent to Baltimore with "several suspicious persons" in U.S. gunboat *Nansemond*.[25]

The Old Capitol records contain this notation on Barnes: "Supposed to have some knowledge of the plot, but probably no case against him. Was in Baltimore at time of assassination."[26] However, as of June Barnes would still be in prison.[27]

Another suspect sent to Washington to spend long weeks under military confinement was Luther A. Martin, a backwoods muskrat, arrested at Allen's Fresh.

Martin did not know it, but the authorities had been given his name by one John Crampsey. Crampsey told the police that Martin had visited him in Washington the night before the assassination. Had wanted Crampsey to accompany him to Charles County. Had said they "could drive Atzerodt away from there." Also that he, Martin, was going to spend the night "at Surratt's place."[28]

So Luther Martin went from Allen's Fresh to a cell in the Old Capitol. Then, somewhere in the workings of that mysterious mill, Martin's status changed from "suspected accomplice" to "witness." Whereupon it changed again, altering from "witness" to nothing at all. For the War Department files contain a notation on Martin dated one month after his arrest.

---

[23] New York *Daily Tribune*, April 24, 1865.
[24] National Archives, War Dept. Records, File "B," JAO.
[25] *Official Records*, Series I, Vol. V, p. 558.
[26] National Archives, War Dept. Records, File "A," Doc. "List of Persons to be Released," JAO.
[27] National Archives, War Dept. Records, File "W," Doc. 1914, JAO.
[28] National Archives, War Dept. Records, File "B," Doc. 264, JAO.

It reads: "Luther A. Martin will not be detained as a witness."[29]

What did that make Luther A. Martin? In June his name disappeared from the War Department records. Martin walked out of history with it.

Before April was out, Major Waite's forces would arrest some 18 or 20 individuals and ship them to Washington "accompanied by sworn statements and memoranda."[30] The plight of some of these prisoners was typified by the fate which befell Mr. and Mrs. Austin L. Adams.

The Adamses were from Newport, a flyspeck village below Allen's Fresh. Uprooted, dispatched to Washington, marched into the Old Capitol Prison, they were in great distress.

The docket on Adams and his wife read: "Aiding Booth and Herold to escape."[31] According to one police report, this deadly charge was based on the testimony of witnesses who stated that three mounted men had stopped at Mr. Adams' inn on "Wed. night after the Easter holidays."[32]

The Newport innkeeper said he had refused to lodge the three chance travelers who called at his place, and he hotly denied harboring any fugitives. The charge seems to have been a fabrication.

About three weeks after the Adamses were imprisoned, Warden Wood of the Old Capitol dispatched a special message in their regard:

> Austin L. Adams and Wife. They entertained a man named Pat Simpsons who is their neighbor, and who took tea with Mrs. Adams. These parties were arrested for the supposed entertainment of Booth—I respectfully recommend their release.[33]

A man may be known by the company he keeps, but sometimes he himself may not know that company.

O'Beirne and his detectives worked overtime in Port Tobacco. For this the village could thank George A. Atzerodt. Almost every man (and woman) in the locality knew the shambling carriage painter. Yet it seemed they did not know him, after all.

Consider the cases involving Messrs. Bailey, Crangle and Middleton; not to mention a certain lady. How well did they know George Atzerodt? That was the Federal question. Their answers leave us with a tintype of small-town life as quaint as anything in our national family album.

On April 19 a man named Thomas F. Holley, a wood merchant of Baltimore, was picked up in Washington, and identified as a drinking companion of G. A. Atzerodt.

Holley told the police:

---

[29] National Archives, War Dept. Records, File "G," Doc. 44, JAO.
[30] National Archives, War Dept. Records, File "C," Doc. 634, JAO.
[31] National Archives, War Dept. Records, File "R," Doc. 266, JAO.
[32] National Archives, War Dept. Records, File "E," Doc. 382, JAO.
[33] National Archives, War Dept. Records, File "A," JAO.

I last saw George A. Atzerodt about 3 or 4 weeks ago at Goldring's store on 11th Street near the wharf. A fellow by the name of Bailey was with him. . . .

I only know Atzerodt by sight. That day his face looked fat and bloated, as if he had been drunk—a reddish face. . . . They hailed me, and I went back and talked with them a little while. I don't know where you could get a photograph of Atzerodt. Port Tobacco would be the most likely place. I understand that he has taken up with a woman there—not married to her. . . . Do not know of his having a woman here [Washington]. Do not know that he has one in Baltimore. . . . I have not seen this woman that I know of. I do not know how she looks.

There is a reliable Union man there [Port Tobacco] by the name of Hatcher—a shoemaker. He is the only Union man I could name there, I believe.[34]

So trouble came a-knocking for Henry Bailey. Bailey tended bar in Brawner's Tavern in Port Tobacco—a hostel of such unsanitary aspect and sloven repute that self-respecting Port Tobaccans seldom went there.

Bailey had served a year in the Confederate Army, not the only man in the region who had "fit for Gen'ral Lee." The thing was: a short time before the assassination he had gone on a buggy ride to Washington with Atzerodt.

And what was wrong with moseying up to Washington for, as Bailey put it, a "turn around town?" He told the Federal officers: "I was out of business. . . . The three days I was there we knocked around—only visited hotels and bar rooms—part of the time—I met Herold once while we were in Washington, he was then in our room at the Pennsylvania House. . . . I went around with Atzerott (sic)."

Bailey was to learn that a tour of the capital with Atzerodt could lead to a cell in Old Capitol Prison. Trying to be frank, he concluded his statement with: "Atzerott's character is good in Port Tobacco—[but] I think he has no spunk."[35]

This qualifying opinion could not save Bailey. Even as he voiced it, he was on his way back to Washington—in handcuffs.

Mr. Nicholas Crangle was also arrested as a bird of a feather. Mr. Crangle's past association with the carriage painter proved more of an embarrassment than Bailey's. The personification of a small-town nobody (Mark Twain might have invented him and Dickens named him), Crangle was a tailor who had gone threadbare serving a clientele that thought the glass of fashion was an ale mug.

That was before the war. Now times were even harder. Crangle didn't mind. Shabby Port Tobacco suited him fine. There he would have continued to live happily ever after had he been left to his own small vices and devices.

---

[34] National Archives, War Dept. Records, File "H," Doc. 534, JAO.
[35] National Archives, War Dept. Records, File "B," JAO.

But Gulliver in a blue uniform with yellow gauntlets strode into Lilliput, trampling miniature doorsteps, yanking the knobs off doors, kicking up a tremendous dust. The hand of this military giant reached down and plucked Crangle out of the scrambled microcosm and held him up between thumb and forefinger, exposed for examination.

So Crangle, who had met Yankee soldiery before, spoke. Major O'Beirne demanded the truth. He did the best he could, but even with a pistol at his head, it wasn't in keeping with his nature. Too, he had his pride, patched though it was at the seat. He had his loyalties. He could even try for respectability. So the answers came out in squirming half-truths, desperate irrelevancies, twists and turns to escape the subject and introduce happier trends to the conversation.

But Mr. Crangle's testimony speaks for itself. Here are excerpts that might compose a collector's item of Civil War Americana.

Statement of Nicholas Crangle:

> I live in Port Tobacco—have lived there about ten years. Am a Tailor by occupation, worked there at my trade and had "right smart" of work. Know Mr. Bailey who is with me in the Guard House. . . .
>
> I have frequently went in the bar-room of the Brawner House, but can't say whom I usually met there. Citizens of the Town do not usually frequent the bar-room.
>
> Atzerott's (*sic*) shop was about 100 yards from where Mrs. Wheeler [Crangle's lady friend] first lived, and 1½ miles from where she lived last. I *never* worked for Atzerott, nor had anything to do with his shop in the line of working in his business. He had some unfinished business on hand when he went away, and just before he left he asked me to take the key to his shop, and keep it, and if any customers came for their work, and could not wait 'till he returned, to let them have it. . . . I know of nothing against his character at Port Tobacco. He was not very responsible and nobody took much notice of him. He was a kind of trifling kind of man. Never knew anything bad of him, except at to what he did to Mrs. Wheeler. He had a child by her, now over two years old.
>
> He and Mrs. Wheeler had been living together as man and wife—I do not go there for the same purpose as he did. I used to visit the house before he left. I had respect for the three young children, but not for the old lady. I was not so intimate with Atzerott, as with some other people in town. I did not like the way he treated Mrs. Wheeler. Tried my best to get them married to each other, but it was no use. . . .
>
> I have made clothes for Atzerott and he paid me for them; he never appeared to have much money. Mrs. Wheeler did not own the place where she lived, [I] think she paid the rent. Worked at my trade up to the time I was arrested. . . .
>
> Did not have the keys to Atzerott's shop but once, and that was the time he gave them to me, some three weeks before he and Bailey went to Washington. He was then about half-tight, and used to drink "right smart." There are not many men of his calibre here, he bore a very good character, except as to his treatment of Mrs. Wheeler. I married a Miss Adams, which was Mrs. Wheeler's maiden name. Think her husband had been dead two

or three years before I went there. She is about thirty-five years old, and
was a half-sister of my wife, I think, but am not certain but she was full
sister.

Atzerott did not pay me for keeping his key. Only did it as a matter of
friendship. If any one had paid me anything for him, I should have given
it to Mrs. Wheeler. . . .

Mrs. Wheeler solicited me to stay at her house because she was afraid
to stay alone, as she said I was the only single relation of hers around
there. . . .

Did ever testimony contain more irrelevancies and immaterialities? The
odd part of it is the man's social conscience. He can't bring himself to utter
a true word about his mesalliance with the Widow Wheeler. As if the
Federal soldiers would care whether the woman was his wife's half-sister—
or even his wife's sister. But in trying to explain *her* away, Crangle sounds
like nine kinds of a liar.

To the Guard House, then, with Mr. Nicholas Crangle.

And for that night, at least, Mrs. Wheeler was without protection.

Still, there was Edwin Middleton. Arrested on April 20 by O'Beirne's
detectives, he spoke the following testimony:

I know Atzerodt and last saw him I think about two weeks before he
left the village which was two or three weeks before the assassination of
the President.

Don't know with whom I generally saw him in company. He went with
Mrs. Wheeler who was a widow. Atzerodt suspected me of having something to do with her. There are other people about that county of the name
of Wheeler. . . . Atzerodt never made any threats towards me—he has
never spoken to me since he saw me on the bed with Mrs. Wheeler, which
was about two months before he left the village—the general impression
there was that he had gone to Washington.

I have never seen Booth nor any of his pictures. Saw Herold at Port
Tobacco twice and think he visited [the] Pagetts. . . .

Atzerodt is regarded as a coward by the people in the village. . . . I never
heard him express himself—I form my opinion from the fact of his having
a brother in the rebel army. Never had any conversation because I had too
contemptible an opinion of him. . . .

Never heard anyone in Port Tobacco say that if the assassins escaped
they would help them. Never saw Booth there. When Herold came there
he was generally alone. Don't know of his visiting Mrs. Wheeler's house.
Don't know when Atzerodt last visited Mrs. Wheeler. I heard her express
herself before the assassination as being in love with Atzerodt. Visited her
once after the assassination when it was known that Atzerodt was implicated
in it. Stayed there about half an hour. I then told her that it was reported
that Atzerodt had something to do with it which she seemed to regret but
did not express herself as being aware that such was the case. . . .[37]

[37] National Archives, War Dept. Records, File "M."

Out of this tangled syntax (composed of Port Tobacco dialect and Army English) one fact seems clear. Mrs. Wheeler was in for a lonely spring.

Major O'Beirne called on the widow Wheeler. Her garret disgorged Atzerodt's trunk, and the widow herself provided O'Beirne with a candid resumé of Atzerodt's love life interwoven with her own rather pliable affections. But there her candor ceased. Or, as Lafayette Baker assessed O'Beirne's report: "The woman admitted that Atzerodt had been her bane, but she loved him and refused to betray him."

Convinced the widow knew nothing of the whereabouts of Booth and Herold, O'Beirne headed off on another lead. Word had come in from an old lady—a backwoods recluse—who said someone was hiding in her cellar. For the past week she had heard voices belowstairs at night. She told the Federals that she had been frightened by the sinister mumbling. Had been afraid to go down and look.

O'Beirne arranged a lamp-in-the-window signal. Detectives were spotted around the house to wait. Late that night the lamp glowed in alarm. The Federals rushed in. To O'Beirne's consternation, the cellar proved empty. When the old lady insisted she could still hear voices, the Federals realized they were dealing with a madwoman.[38]

Or had the Federals been dealt with? Some of the detective reports suggest between the lines that the military police, for all their parboiled sophistry, were being taken in by a rustic craftiness as sharp as a country horse trade. Superimpose on native guile the veteran cunning of a long-established Confederate underground, and the whole area from Bryantown to Port Tobacco smells foxy.

Operating with O'Beirne, Captain William Williams took a hoodwinking that would gall his memory for years. A special officer on Augur's staff, Williams had been among the first assigned to the manhunt because he knew Booth personally. He had, in fact, met Booth in the street near Ford's Theater on the afternoon before the murder, and had invited the actor to join him in a friendly glass. Now, in Port Tobacco, a bloodhound on the hunt, Williams scouted into Brawners' Hotel.

At the bar Williams struck up a conversation with a farmer from near Allen's Fresh, who answered to the name of Tom Jones. Williams at length identified himself as a Federal officer and quietly informed Jones that a golden reward was up for Booth—all of three hundred thousand dollars. "You could live the rest of your life in comfort on that sum," Williams said in effect. "Just give us a steer to where this crippled assassin is hiding."

Jones stared at Williams with innocent blue eyes. He said he'd like the money, but he hadn't any idea where Booth could be. Not a single, solitary notion.

---

[38] Baker, *op. cit.*, p. 491.

Twenty-five years afterward Williams encountered Thomas A. Jones in Washington. Recognition lit Williams' eye. Introducing himself, he told Jones bluntly: "I can never forget that come-to-the-Lord-and-be-saved expression you wear. . . . If I had known then what I do now, how different things would have been. . . . If you had told me where Booth was, you would have been the biggest man in America!"

Jones told Williams a betrayal of Booth would have given him "a conscience as black as purgatory and the everlasting hatred of the people I love." He said he had been serving as "chief signal agent of the Confederacy north of the Potomac" in charge of underground mail and boats along the river. "I took great chances of being killed," he informed Williams, "and when Richmond was evacuated I was there to collect what was due me, $2,500, and did not get a cent of it."

Williams had to confess Jones had pulled the wool. "Let me say that myself and other officers believed that you knew more than you would tell, but that sanctimonious look of yours saved you."[39]

The Federals tried a few tricks of their own. Satisfied that Port Tobacco was scoured physically if not morally, O'Beirne went over the situation with Major Waite, who rode in empty-handed from Leonardtown. Comparing notes with reports from Colonel Wells at Bryantown, the two officers decided that Booth must be somewhere deep in the Zekiah Swamps. O'Beirne determined to comb the region with his detective force. Apparently he started this operation on Friday the 21st.

Knocking on shanty doors, O'Beirne's party scouted toward Allen's Fresh. The Major resorted to a ruse. Ahead of the party moved Detective Hoey and a cavalry officer named Lafferty. Feigning injury, Lafferty posed as Booth. Hoey assumed the role of David Herold.

The mock fugitives slunk into farmyards and begged for shelter. One backwoods farmer, a character named Claggert, offered to hide the pair in his woods. Claggert was promptly arrested.[40] But he knew nothing of the genuine escapees, and O'Beirne's play would be trumped by an equally deceptive enemy strategem.

That Friday O'Beirne and his men were probing the countryside north of Allen's Fresh. The detectives just missed big game. For they skirted the fringe of swampland bordering Cox's farm. O'Beirne kept a report-book of his party's activities, and therein he jotted a most significant entry: "Sam'l Cox. . . . His mill servant states to another colored man that Cox had been cooking provisions lately & carrying it to persons down in the swamp. . . ."[41]

[39] J. E. Buckingham, *op. cit.*, pp. 63–69.
[40] Baker, p. 493.
[41] O'Beirne Diary, quoted in Eisenschiml, *op. cit.*, p. 120.

Who was the "mill servant" in mention? Who was the other colored man? How did Major O'Beirne obtain this information? And why did O'Beirne neglect to follow up this clue? Especially when the informant offered the opinion that the person in the swamp must be someone of importance, judging from the amount of provisions furnished.

But the clue deals with Colonel Samuel Cox, who seems to have been as elusive as Booth himself. Historian Eisenschiml expresses the belief that O'Beirne "did not have enough men with him to investigate all the reports he received." Yet the region teemed with Federal troops. Something must have diverted O'Beirne's attention from the Cox farm.

Apparently O'Beirne was, indeed, diverted. And by a happenstance as freakish as any in the Lincoln murder case. On Saturday, the 22nd, the hard-riding Major learned that two men had recently crossed the Potomac —two suspicious characters in a skiff. This word came from a man named Mills who had been picked up and identified as a "Rebel mail carrier."[42]

So the story told by Cox's servant seems to have been lost on O'Beirne, whose aim was shifted to the two men who had crossed the Potomac. Certain they were Booth and Herold, O'Beirne led his detective party across the river that Saturday night to Boone's farm, where the fugitives had presumably landed on Virginia soil.

O'Beirne pushed on through the night, reaching King George's Court-House on Sunday morning. At that point he should have learned that the men he chased were innocent fishermen. Instead, he was positive the fugitives were ahead of him, riding toward Port Conway. Top speed, he returned to Chapel Point, Maryland, and rushed from there to Port Tobacco, determined to procure cavalry for the chase.

A fantastic business, this junket of O'Beirne's. For Booth and Herold endeavored to cross the Potomac that same week end. Pursuing the wrong couple, O'Beirne nearly waylaid the right. But that was only a minor phenomenon compared to the remarkable sequence of events that ensued.

When he returned to Port Tobacco, O'Beirne encountered Captain S. H. Beckwith, Grant's telegraph operator, who had just arrived on locale with two Secret Service agents. O'Beirne told Beckwith that he thought Booth and Herold had crossed the Potomac into Virginia. Employing Beckwith as emergency telegrapher, O'Beirne dispatched an urgent wire to the War Department requesting additional men and permission to go to Port Royal, Virginia.

Permission was refused! To O'Beirne's dismay, he was ordered by the War Department to remain on the Maryland side of the Potomac. It would appear that this order emanated from the office of Lafayette C. Baker, who now had assumed charge of the manhunt. As Colonel Baker recalled the episode in his *History of the United States Secret Service:* "He [O'Beirne] telegraphed his information, and asked permission to pursue, promising

---

[42] Baker, *op. cit.*, p. 494.

to catch the assassins before they reached Port Royal. This department refused. . . ."

O'Beirne was stopped in his tracks. Or, rather, he was stopped in what he thought were Booth's tracks. That they *were* Booth's tracks—by sheer accident—is not the least peculiar angle to the episode. Here is one even more peculiar.

Soon after O'Beirne was ordered to remain in Maryland, Secret Service Chief Baker rushed a message to General Hancock.

> General—I am directed by the Secretary of War to apply to you for a small cavalry force of 25 men, well mounted, to be commanded by a reliable and discreet commissioned officer. Can you furnish them? and if so, will you please direct the officer commanding . . . to report to me . . . opposite Willard's Hotel, at once?[43]

Hancock supplied the force. And Baker immediately dispatched this flying squadron of Federals to Port Royal, Virginia. Was it by sheer grab-bag coincidence that the Secret Service Chief picked his cousin, Lieutenant Luther Baker, as one of the detectives to accompany this squadron? Nepotism is an unpleasant word. But we are somehow reminded of the $200,000 offered for Booth's capture.

And it was about that time that a certain Dr. Coombe referred to Lafayette C. Baker as a $200,000 man.

Now occurred perhaps the weirdest episode of the entire manhunt. The day was Tuesday, April 25. Major O'Beirne was stalled in Port Tobacco, Maryland. Across the Potomac River in Virginia, Lafayette Baker's special squadron was hot on the trail of two suspicious travelers who answered the description of Booth and Herold. And on this day O'Beirne received word that a man on a crutch, accompanied by a youthful companion, had just been spotted on the fringe of a swamp *two miles north of Bryantown!* It seemed this furtive pair had stopped at the house of a Mr. Turner to ask for food. Their demeanor had frightened the hired girl, who ran off to find her master. Her fright, in turn, alarmed the cripple and his associate, who ducked into a patch of swamp near the Turner house.

O'Beirne was electrified. Summoning Captain Beckwith, he raced by spur and quirt on the fastest road to Bryantown. An area sweep was immediately launched. While troops converged on the swamp near Turner's farm, O'Beirne and Beckwith went to the Turner house. Two of the excited servants substantiated the story—a man on a crutch had been there with a younger man, begging food. The pair had dodged into a pine thicket twenty yards distant. O'Beirne and Beckwith were told enough to convince them the pair were Booth and Herold.

That night Beckwith wired Major T. T. Eckert at Washington Headquarters: ". . . I proceeded with Major O'Beirne to Bryantown, thence

[43] Cited in Eisenschiml, *op. cit.,* p. 124.

to Turner's house where Booth and Herold were seen by two servants to enquire for food. . . . We at once penetrated the thicket and deployed, after following probable routes. I struck the crutch track and we followed it in a direction circling around a piece of timber, from which they first issued far enough to justify belief they are still in same vicinity."[44]

But O'Beirne and Beckwith soon lost the crutch track. Beckwith blamed the loose deployment of a company of Negro soldiers. "The colored troops . . . upon hearing [a] shout on one part of the line, made a rush in that direction, leaving considerable space uncovered. Cavalry has been operating, and tonight has strong line of pickets around the timber." But the track disappeared. It was presumed the cripple and his companion slipped through the "uncovered space."

That was the night of April 25. And that same night, according to history's record, John Wilkes Booth and David Herold were at a farmhouse miles to the south at a place not far from Bowling Green, Virginia.

Who were the men glimpsed at Turner's house north of Bryantown? Nobody knows. This cripple and his shadowy companion vanished in the woods near Turner's farm like spectres dissolved at cockcrow.

Most historians regard the advent of this second pair of swamp foxes as remarkable coincidence, and let it go at that. If coincidence it was, then the episode is astonishing. That two wanderers resembling Booth and Herold—the older man on a crutch!—should show up and vanish in such fashion at just that time would be a phenomenon as eerie as St. Elmo's fire.

Vagrants who strayed into the dragnet area, appeared for one night only, and departed like phantoms the following dawn? In a woods picketed by cavalry and combed by hundreds of soldiers? There the matter goes beyond the possibilities of coincidence. Something in the picture is beyond focus. The disappearance of this pair in the swamp north of Bryantown is even more fantastic than their appearance.

One answer suggests itself. Decoys. Trickery to draw the Federals away from Booth's southbound trail. Dress up a farmer with a crutch. Give him a suspicious-looking companion. Start a wild-goose chase. Somewhere in the swamps the crutch can be buried, the decoy team can separate and hit for home.

That was the game, according to Richard M. Smoot, the Port Tobacco farmer who, in 1904, published a memoir of the conspiracy. As Smoot recalled it: "When Booth and his party dismounted at Dr. Mudd's house, a man on crutches, accompanied by a second man, was put in the road to make tracks to decoy the searchers in a wrong direction. The ruse was a successful one."[45] Smoot's timing of the stratagem seems beforehand, although the gambit conceivably could have been schemed while Booth

[44] National Archives, War Dept. Records, File "B," JAO.
[45] Smoot, *The Unwritten History of the Assassination*, p. 8.

was at Dr. Mudd's. Evidence shows that Booth had underground support
in the region. Witness the assistance of influential Colonel Cox.

Then, too, there was blue-eyed Thomas A. Jones. And Cox's overseer,
Franklin Robey. Circumstances hint at others unknown, an active sub-
terranean apparatus. But Cox was known—or, at least, strongly suspected.
A memorandum submitted to the War Department by Officer M. A.
Clancey (dated May 1, 1865) contains this notation:

> Captain Samuel Cox is clearly implicated by the evidence of Osborne
> [Oscar] Swann.[46]

The implication seems to have been overlooked by the Bureau of Military
Justice. Belatedly arrested, neither Cox nor Jones was prosecuted by the
Government for aiding and abetting Booth's escape. After a brief imprisonment, the Colonel and his foster brother were quietly released.
Why? An answer comes from Richard Smoot who tells us that shortly
after Cox's arrest the Colonel sold a valuable farm near Washington for
$16,000. "He told me he spent every cent of that amount to secure his
release, and prevent his neck from being cracked."[47]

Hinting at errant bribery, Smoot's story might be discounted were it not
for the mysterious fact of Cox's immunity. For reasons never explained, the
War Department threw a veil of censorship over Cox's farm. When reporters subsequently asked permission to publish the details of the Booth
manhunt, the War Department issued an official map showing the escape
through lower Maryland and adjacent Virginia. Prominently marked as
a key point was Dr. Mudd's. In graphic detail the Potomac crossing was
traced. But the intervening route, as officially charted, showed the trail
as a mere tangent through a point labeled "Cox's Station." The official map
offered no indication that Booth and Herold had stopped there. The War
Department chose to forget Booth's six-day stay at Cox's farm.

The War Department—meaning certain officials therein—also chose to
devaluate the reports submitted by Major O'Beirne. He and his men had
come close to capturing Booth and Herold at Cox's. They had come even
closer when they crossed the Potomac and headed for Port Conway,
Virginia. Having picked up the track, O'Beirne had been deadstalled by
orders from Washington and then decoyed to Bryantown by a weird
double play. But the Major was not to be fully credited for an effort that
directed the Federal pursuit to the ultimate target. Credit meant reward
money. Another claimant bid for the lion's share.

Statement of Colonel-General Lafayette C. Baker (published for the
nation's edification):

---

[46] National Archives, War Dept. Records, File "C," Doc. 634, JAO.
[47] Smoot, p. 9.

I desire to state positively that the information that prompted me to send the expedition to Port Conway, was not, in any way, shape, or manner, derived from the War Department, or from any information or intimation furnished by any one connected with the search for the assassins. I neither saw nor knew the contents, of any telegrams, letters, or memorandums, referring in the slightest manner to the fact that the murderers had crossed the Potomac River. . . . My honest conviction is, and it is the opinion repeatedly expressed by those in authority, that, had not this expedition reached the Garret Farm as they did, on Wednesday morning, before daylight, Booth and Harrold (*sic*) would have escaped entirely.[48]

The veil thrown over Cox's farm, the shelving of O'Beirne, the "doubles" who vanished in the swamp near Bryantown, and the Secret Service Chief's engrossment with prize money would leave some historians to wonder if Booth was actually ever captured in Virginia.

---

[48] Baker, p. 528.

P A R T
IV
Dead End

If I have wit enough to get out of this wood,
I have enough to serve mine own turn.
                    —*Midsummer Night's Dream*

He died,
To throw away the dearest thing he owed
As 'twere a careless trifle.
                    —*Macbeth*

CHAPTER **19**

The Road to
Garrett's Farm

BUZZARDS floated over the woods, a symbol of death. David Herold
sighted the circling scavengers and read the sign. They should never
have shot those animals in the swamp. Every bluebelly in the area would
see those vultures, would come to investigate. They must get out of there
that night. If Jones didn't come, Herold would go fetch him.

Jones came, quiet as an Indian in the dark. Herold collected the guns
and gear, and erased traces of their campsite. Wrapped in a blanket,
Booth limped with hand on Herold's shoulder as they followed Thomas
Jones through the boscage.

Off in the darkness a horse whinnied. The fugitives halted in alarm.
Jones said it was all right—he'd brought a mount for Booth. They found
the animal, a bony mare, tethered in a screen near the road.

Jones avoided the road and guided the fugitives along a trail through
the pines. He told his charges it was "now or never" to cross the Potomac.
Early in the evening he'd been over to Allen's Fresh. From the villagers
he'd learned that the bluecoat patrols had gone on eastward to Leonardtown. Tonight the coast was clear.

Two days before this river attempt, Jones had been "to court" at Port
Tobacco on a scouting expedition. He found the Yankees in that area
thicker than fiddlers in hell. As he recalled the episode years later: "I
knew I would see and hear a great deal concerning the assassination and
the probable whereabouts of the assassin. It was at this time I met Captain
Williams [William Williams], a detective. He was standing in the barroom of Brawner's Hotel in the act of drinking with several gentlemen.
Someone introduced me to him, and he politely asked me to drink. Just
as we were about to take the drink, he said to me, 'I am authorized by
the United States Government to pay one hundred thousand dollars for
Booth, dead or alive.' I looked him in the eye and said, 'That's a good
deal of money to give for one man.'"

Did Thomas A. Jones give a moment's consideration to the hundred-thousand-dollar offer? Not according to Thomas A. Jones. "My word could not be bought for a hundred times that amount. I considered it [sheltering Booth] a sacred trust. The little I had accumulated was irrevocably lost, but thank God, I still possessed something I could call my own, and its name was Honor!"

Then: "On Friday evening, April 21, the opportune time seemed to have presented itself."[1] So Jones (in memory) dated the attempt to cross the Potomac River.

Furtively the little party moved through the night. At length they emerged from the pines. Jones led Booth and Herold across a field to his farm, "Huckleberry." They did not go into the house.

Booth had begun to shiver. He asked for hot coffee. Jones shook his head—too dangerous, no time. But he'd fetch some bread and ham.

As Jones remembered it: "I went to the house and took what I thought would be enough for two men and carried it out to them. . . . After supper we resumed our journey across the open field for the longed-for river. When about three hundred yards from the river, Herold and myself assisted Booth to dismount. The path was steep and narrow, and for three men to walk down it abreast [and one of them crippled] was not the least difficult part of that night's work. At length we reached the shore and found the boat. It was a flat-bottomed one, about twelve feet long of a dark lead color."[2]

One account has it that Jones took the oars and prepared to row the fugitives across the Potomac. They were hardly off shore when they sighted a gunboat in midstream. Rifle shots spanged in the night. The fugitives huddled on the thwarts as Jones, frantic, rowed back to the beach where they hid the boat in underbrush. A naval patrol came in from the gunboat. The manhunters beat the thickets, missing the fugitives by only a few yards. Booth and Herold spent the rest of that night and the following day cowering in a riverside nest of laurels (presumably under the bluffs of Dent's Meadow). Jones came for them on the ensuing night, and they got off on a second try.[3]

However, in Jones' recollection (voiced to Oldroyd) there was only the one attempt, which took place on the night of Friday the 21st. And he did not embark on the river with the fugitives.

> We placed Booth in the stern with an oar to steer, Herold taking the bow seat to row. The night was ink-black. I could not see either of the men, and had to feel for them, and as I was in the act of pushing the boat off, Booth said, "Wait a minute, old fellow." He then offered me some money. I took seventeen dollars, the price of the boat. In a voice choked with emotion, he said, "God bless you, my dear friend, for all you have done for me. Good-by!

---

1 Oldroyd, *op. cit.*, pp. 105–106.
2 Quoted in Oldroyd, *op. cit.*, pp. 109–110.
3 Version in Booth's Diary.

Good-by!" I pushed the boat off, and it glided out in the darkness. I could see nothing, and the only sound was the swish of the waves made by the little boat. . . . I stood on the shore and listened till the sound of the oars died away in the distance, then [I] climbed the hill and took my way home, and my sleep was more quiet and peaceful than it had been for some time.[4]

The unperturbed slumber enjoyed by Thomas A. Jones persists as one of the unexplained mysteries attendant on Booth's escape from lower Maryland. Another mystery: the exact date the fugitives embarked on the river below Dent's Meadow. Still another: Where did they go from there?

Apparently Thomas A. Jones suffered several lapses of memory when, years after the event, he described the river getaway of Booth and Herold.

Evidence discloses that Jones (who knew every secret inlet in that stretch of the Potomac) supplied the fugitives with course and bearings. A five-mile row south-by-west across the river would take them into Machadoc Creek just below Mathias Point. Keep an eye peeled for this and that landmark. Near the creek mouth lives Mrs. Quesenberry, good Virginian. Ask for my brother-in-law, Thomas Harbin. Tom knows the underground from there.

While Jones' lapses of memory concerning these important details could conceivably be attributed to senescence, David Herold's in this respect approached total aphasia. When ultimately queried on the river-crossing, he could recall neither Jones nor the take-off point. His testimony reads:

We staid (*sic*) in the pines, & when anything came along or passed us we would buy bread or meat. On Tuesday or Wednesday night, I forget which, we started to cross the Potomac. It was very foggy. We got along the Maryland shore to Nanjemoy Creek, & went to a man's house and wanted to buy some bread. He said he hadn't any baked, & would not bake any. He said he had nothing to drink either. I said we were wet, and would like to have something to drink. I had a bottle, & asked if he would sell me some whiskey. He said he would not do it. Booth gave the man's little boy a quarter of a dollar for filling the bottle with milk. That night, at sundown, we crossed the mouth of Nanjemoy Creek, passed within 300 yards of a gunboat, and landed at Mathias Point. The boat in which we crossed had one paddle and a broken oar in it.[5]

Following the fugitives' trail, the manhunters on their track picked up (belatedly) a little more detail. True enough, after embarking from the beach under the bluffs of Dent's Meadow, the escapees headed upstream instead of downstream. It is generally assumed that Herold, at the oars, pulled in the wrong direction. Or that the feverish Booth, huddled in a

4 Oldroyd, *op. cit.*, p. 110.
5 National Archives, War Dept. Records, File "H," R.B.P. 38, JAO.

blanket on the stern sheets, steered blindly, fearing to light a match and consult his compass.

Certainly these boatmen in the dark might have gone off course. A flat-bottom skiff on a windy river makes for difficult rowing. Herold was doubt-less an erratic oarsman, and Booth an erratic steersman. Too, the tidewater Potomac presents the navigator with a puzzle of eddies and currents. Yet it seems odd that the two would proceed about five miles upstream with-out realizing they headed up-river instead of down.

Moreover, they clung to the Maryland bank in approaching Nanjemoy Creek. Moonless nights may be dark and misty, but seldom is the black-out so intense that a shoreline's silhouette remains invisible. It seems a fair guess that in traveling five miles upstream instead of down, the fugi-tives made a deliberate try for Nanjemoy Creek, to the west of Port Tobacco.

Why there? Again surmise: in Nanjemoy Creek were the rivermen friends of George Atzerodt. In this backwater had been hidden the big barge procured for the January abduction enterprise. And up Nanjemoy Creek lived Colonel J. J. Hughes, who may have been a "sympathizer."

Oldroyd states that the fugitives "in the darkness of the night lost their bearings and were carried twelve miles out of their way." The historian adds: "During the early morning Herold made his way to the house of Colonel J. J. Hughes, a short distance from where they landed, and there secured something to eat and correct information as to their route back to Machadoc Creek." All of this sounds implausible. Oldroyd's concluding statement makes it appear even more so. "They remained in concealment Saturday the 22nd [of April] and during the night made their way to the mouth of Machadoc Creek."[6]

Colonel Hughes now appears as the man who refused to "bake bread" for Herold—the man whose little son was given twenty-five cents for a whiskey bottle of milk. It seems a reasonable surmise that Herold was acquainted with the Colonel, that the milk story was moonshine, that Booth and Herold visited this riverside planter for a purpose never divulged. In a region teeming with bluecoat soldiery and military detec-tives, fugitives as desperate as Herold and Booth would hardly have dared to approach an unknown farmer who might be loyal to the Union.

Booth and Herold must have wanted something, expected something of Colonel J. J. Hughes. The big barge Atzerodt had purchased for the kidnap enterprise? Money? An underground escort across the water to Virginia? Or had they expected to be smuggled aboard an oyster boat, a fishing smack, some river craft supposedly ready to take them down the Potomac to the Chesapeake?

At this late date, no modern historian could hope to penetrate the Con-federate underground. Records have long since vanished. Much of the

---

[6] Oldroyd, *op. cit.*, pp. 276–77.

contemporary witness testimony is either inaccurate or deliberately misleading. Historical accounts are often confused and contradictory.

Herold seems to have uttered one truth (perhaps by inadvertence)
when he described the night on the river as "foggy." In that fog, assassin
and accomplice remained concealed (by grace of Colonel Hughes) on
the week end of April 22.

Then, in the mist of that Saturday night, the fugitive pair boated across
the Potomac and reached Virginia. Skirting the shoreline of Mathias
Point, they dodged into the mouth of Gambo Creek about a half mile above
Machadoc. There they beached the boat. There they spent the remainder
of the night huddled under the canopy of a monarchial black-walnut tree.

And that was the night Major O'Beirne crossed the Potomac to Boone's
Farm, not ten miles away, and made a high-speed dash to the village of
King George on the road to Port Conway and Port Royal. O'Beirne knew
something. But when he raced back to Chapel Point, Maryland, on Sunday
the 23rd, and telegraphed to Washington for a posse, the War Department
ordered O'Beirne to remain in Maryland.

Not all of the fog was concentrated on the lower Potomac.

Daybreak over the broad Potomac. Venturing to the mouth of Gambo
Creek, and glancing down-river, Herold went tense. A cluster of sailboats
in view. Shad fishermen, heading out of Machadoc Creek. Jones had
warned they might be there.

Herold made his way back to the walnut tree where Booth lay curled
in a blanket. No gunboats, he told Booth. Still, they'd better hide until
later in the morning when the fishermen would be far down the Potomac.
Then he'd roust around and find Mrs. Quesenberry.

At midday Herold located the Quesenberry house near the mouth of
Machadoc Creek, three quarters of a mile from the inlet where they had
landed. As Jones had promised, Mrs. Quesenberry put the fugitives in
touch with Thomas Harbin. Harbin passed them on to a bog-trotter named
Bryan (or Bryant).

Not far from Bryan's cabin was the plantation house of Mr. Benjamin
Arnold, Virginia squire. Apparently the fugitives made no effort to contact
Squire Arnold. Odd, under the circumstances. Years afterward, the Arnold
family admitted that the house was a way station on the Confederate
underground, and that Mister Ben had been a key figure in the Lincoln
abduction plot. In fact, Lincoln was to have been smuggled into his home
when and if Booth brought the President across the Potomac River.[7]

Reminiscing, Arnold's son recalled that his father had said of Lincoln's
assassination: "I'm very sorry the President was shot, but very glad they
never succeeded in kidnaping him, for it let me out of a very dirty job."

---

[7] *Ibid.*, pp. 283–284.

Possibly Benjamin Arnold, entertaining that attitude, refused to harbor the assassin who approached his farm. Or perhaps that Sunday Squire Arnold was not at home. More likely, Booth by-passed the Arnold estate in search of a doctor. Bryan had mounted him on a tottering horse. Every jog of the journey across rough fields and through clawing scrub proved agonizing.

Bryan guided the fugitives to the home of Dr. Richard H. Stewart—an isolated place about half a mile off the public road to Port Conway. They reached the Stewart house that Sunday nightfall.

Booth was all in. Herold, too, stumbled in exhaustion. Called to the door by these visitors, Dr. Stewart regarded them with jaundiced eye. Or so it would appear from the record.

To Booth's appeal for doctoring, Stewart replied that he was a medical practitioner, not a surgeon. Not only did he refuse to tend Booth's leg; he would not offer these travelers a night's lodging. His house, he said, was full. But if the wayfarers were hungry, they could have a bite in the kitchen.

Taken to the rear of the house, the fugitives munched cold fare. Booth took umbrage at their treatment. There might have been a knock-down fight, had not the two been outnumbered by the Stewart family. Booth struggled on his crutches down to the gate. Herold followed.

Bryan waited in the darkness. He told Booth that Dr. Stewart had suggested they go on through the woods to the cabin of a freedman named Lucas. They could spend the night with the Negro.

Bryan guided them along the path to Lucas' cabin—a mean shanty lost in the pines. There Bryan left them. There Booth and Herold spent the night of April 23, 1865.

A few days later, Federal officers, following the fugitives' trail, visited and arrested Dr. Stewart. In his statement to the authorities, Stewart declared that he had turned the fugitives away and had refused to treat the injured man's leg. "I told them I was no surgeon; only a physician. I think he said that Dr. Mudd had recommended him to me. I said that nobody was authorized to recommend anybody to me."[8]

Stewart's deposition closes with an interesting story. The doctor relates:

> I was suspicious of the urgency of the lame man. He desired to tell something I did not care to hear. I did not really believe he had a broken leg; I thought it was all put on, although he was on two crutches. He said he had had a fall & broken his leg; he said Dr. Mudd had set it. The small man had a short carbine, & he had on a satchel. I did not see any arms on; he had a large shawl around him. They were mounted on Bryant's horses. . . . Bryant took them off. . . .
>
> Next Monday evening [April 24] Lucas brought a note over to my house signed "Stranger" with $2½ rolled up in it, & gave it to my wife. I was not at home. He told her that the man who wrote the note had given him the

[8] National Archives, War Dept. Records, File "S," JAO.

note to deliver to me. It was sealed. It was a leaf of a memorandum book rolled around & the money rolled up in it. . . .[9]

Dr. Stewart had preserved the note. It was lucky for him that he did. The note Booth dispatched to Dr. Stewart provided history with a fascinating, if unintentional, self-portrait of the thespian assassin. It read:

> Dea [piece torn out] Forgive me, but I have some little pride. I cannot blame you for want of hospitality; you know your own affairs. I was sick, tired, with a broken limb, and in need of medical assistance. I would not have turned a dog away from my door in such a plight. However, you were kind enough to give us something to eat, for which I not only thank you, but, on account of the reluctant manner in which it was bestowed, I feel bound to pay for it. It is not the substance, but the way in which kindness is extended, that makes one happy in the acceptance thereof. The sauce to meat is ceremony; meeting were bare without it. Be kind enough to accept the enclosed five dollars, although hard to spare, for what we have had.[10]

Apparently Booth scribbled this by candlelight while sprawled on the floor of Lucas' rude cabin. Historian DeWitt remarks ". . . the tone of this letter may serve to show that neither crime, nor wounds, nor suffering, nor banishment, not even imminence of capture and a felon's doom, could quell the vainglorious self-consciousness of this hero of the boards."[11] Some of the vainglory may have been inspired by whisky.

Sensitive, vainglorious, drunk—the crippled fugitive's pride was peeled to the raw by being forced to sleep in a Negro's cabin!

He signs the note, "*Yours respectfully—Stranger.*" Rips it out of the little red notebook in which it was enscribed. Then, instead of a five-dollar bill, he attaches two ones and a 50-center. The reduced gratuity may have been intended as an insult. This was the missive delivered to Dr. Stewart by Lucas.

It would seem, then, that Booth meant to deal Stewart a scathing rebuke for inhospitality. As it eventuated, he provided Stewart with an alibi that may have rescued the physician from a fate similar to Dr. Mudd's. When he exhibited that caustic note from Booth, nobody could accuse Stewart of harboring the assassin.

Statement of William Lucas (colored), May 6, 1865:[12]

> Two men were brought to my house on the night of Sunday, April 23. I was in bed & asleep. . . . My dogs were barking and woke me up. I heard a horse & I thought there might be some one trying to steal my horses. A strange voice called me. . . . I would not open the door, but asked who

---

[9] *Ibid.*
[10] Quoted in Oldroyd, *op. cit.*, p. 285.
[11] *Op. cit.*, p. 80.
[12] National Archives, War Dept. Records, File "L," R.B., JAO, P. 57.

it was. . . . I was frightened at the time. People had been shot in that way, & I was afraid to come out.

I was then asked if I knew old Bryant. . . . I knew him and went out. One of the men said, "We want to stay here tonight." I said, "You cannot do it; I am a colored man & have no right to take care of white people; I have only one room in the house, & my wife is sick." He said, "We are Confederate soldiers; we have been in service 3 years; we have been knocking about all night, and don't intend to any longer; but we are going to stay."

By that time the one with crutches had got into the house. I said, "Gentlemen, you have treated me very badly." The lame man was sitting down then, & he reached behind me, took out a bowie knife, & flourished it, saying, "Old man, how do you like that." I said, "I do not like that at all; I was always afraid of a knife." He said, "We were sent here, old man; we understood you have good teams." I said they could not have my team; I had hired hands to come Monday morning to plant corn. . . . He said to the other, "Well, Dave, we will not go on any further, but stay here, & make this old man get us this horse in the morning."

I was afraid to go to sleep, & my wife & I went out on the step & stayed there the rest of the night. In the morning they ordered the horses, hitched them, & got in. . . . They asked me what I got for driving to Port Conway. I said $10 in gold or $20 in green backs. I asked them to let my son go with them. The lame man refused, saying they might want to go further. . . . Then I said, "I thought you would be done pressing teams in the Northern Neck since the fall of Richmond." The lame one said, "Repeat that again," & I said no more to him. My son, 20 or 21 years old, drove the team. They gave my wife the money when they were starting.

The man who was lame had on one boot & one shoe; the boot seemed muffled around the top; I did not notice whether it was cut in front; I did not go very close to him.

My house is about ten miles from Port Conway, & 3 miles from the Potomac. . . . They started away from my house about 7 o'clock, I think, in the morning of Monday, April 24th.

About two hours by wagon road from Lucas' cabin the southbound travelers came to Port Conway on the Rappahannock. A huddle of cottages, a general store, some warehouses and a wharf—gone to seed since the war and the ruination of the Confederate dollar. Chief activity now was the one-horse ferry plying the three-quarter-mile width of river between Conway and Port Royal, opposite. The larger town, Port Royal, boasted some sizable houses and a remnant tobacco business. But on the morning of Monday, April 24, 1865, both towns seemed dead. William Rollins, Port Conway ferryman, was glad to see passengers in prospect.

The fugitives dismissed Lucas and wagon. On Herold's arm, Booth hobbled down to the ferry landing. No ferry was there. Herold left Booth seated on a piling, and walked over to the house at the waterside where Rollins, repairing a fishnet, looked up.

"Ain't there a ferry in this place?"

"It's over yonder," Rollins said, indicating Port Royal. "Be some time before it's back."

Herold asked for a drink of water for his lame "brother." Rollins obliged. Herold carried the dipper to Booth, then returned to the house with a proposition. Would Rollins take ten dollars, Union money, to drive them down to Bowling Green? Rollins allowed he would. But they couldn't cross until the ferry came back.

Compelled to wait, the two travelers could do no more than make the best of it. His crutches beside him, Booth sat on the ferry wharf, back to a bollard, dozing. Herold nosed around the village, then returned to the landing to squat beside Booth.

Rollins, who later testified to their arrival in Port Conway, offered no detail as to their conversation other than to state: "Herold said they belonged to the Confederate service, had been in Maryland, and wanted to get back to the army. I was asked which route would be the best, but I could not inform them, as they did not want to encounter any Union soldiers."[13]

They did, however, encounter three Confederate soldiers who arrived on the scene in midmorning. On record as subsequent testimony, Herold's version of this meeting at Port Conway typifies his aversion for detail and strict veracity.

> While waiting for a ferryboat, three Confederate soldiers came along. We asked whose command they belonged to. One said to the Ninth Va.; the other two said they belonged to Mosby's command. They stated they were going by Bowling Green. We wanted a man who lives at Port Conway to carry us to Milford. He said he could not start until sundown. We didn't want to travel at night, having lost much rest. The three Confederate soldiers, Booth & myself—five of us—crossed the ferry from Port Conway to Port Royal.
>
> I asked the Confederate Captain who was along his name. He said it was Jett. I told him I once met a gentleman in Baltimore by the name of Westmoreland, & asked if he was any relation. He answered, Yes, he was a cousin. We tried to get a conveyance at Port Royal to take us to Milford. While I was trying to get a conveyance, Booth was talking to this man, Captain Jett. When I came back he said to Booth, "As long as you are a Virginian and wounded, I will carry you up the country, where you can stay." . . . Whether this gentleman knew Booth's correct name or not, I don't know.[14]

Herold did know. He was acutely aware that "Captain Jett" knew Booth's name because he himself had blabbed Booth's name to "Captain Jett"—to the anger and dismay of the fugitive assassin who employed the alias "John William Boyd." And David Herold knew a great deal more than he pretended about this meeting at Port Conway, this crossing of the Rappahannock with three of Mosby's veterans.

The Confederate troopers (or ex-Confederate troopers) are reported

---

13 Oldroyd, *op. cit.*, p. 290.
14 National Archives, War Dept. Records, File "H," R.B.P. 38, JAO.

in most historical accounts as being Captain Willie S. Jett, Lieutenant Mortimer B. Ruggles and Lieutenant A. S. Bainbridge. Some doubt exists concerning their respective ranks, for Willie Jett was only eighteen years old, and Ruggles and Bainbridge were not much older. Official U. S. War Department records list Bainbridge and Ruggles as "privates."[15] Several Confederate sources aver that Jett was never in the army.[16]

But teen-age officers were far from exceptional in the Civil War forces, and particularly in the Confederate Army late in the war. Confusion doubtless stems from the fact that Jett and Ruggles gave up their commissions when they joined Mosby's irregulars. Too, the Federal authorities often listed captives as "private soldiers," and when the trio ultimately fell into Federal hands they may have automatically demoted themselves.

Together, the three young Confederates cantered into Port Conway in the shank of that April morning. They glimpsed the travel-stained couple sitting in a wagon in front of Rollins' house. Jett dismounted at the ferry landing and tethered his horse at the hitching rail. Ruggles and Bainbridge followed suit. The three walked out on the wharf, were standing there when Herold sauntered over.

Jett told him they were men of Mosby's command. Whereupon (according to Jett) Herold became excited, and confided, "We are the assassinators of the President!"[17]

Presently Booth came hobbling over on his crutches. Evidently he was "put out" when Herold introduced him by his right name.

Official records offer no verifiable report of what was said. But the upshot remains in evidence. Booth, Herold, Jett, Bainbridge and Ruggles crossed the Rappahannock together, Booth mounted on Ruggles' horse.

When grilled a few days later by Federal officers, Willie Jett recalled that Booth identified himself at Port Conway by exhibiting the initials "J.W.B." tattooed on his left hand. Similarly eager to prove his "assassinator" identity, Herold rolled up a sleeve to show the tattooed initials "D.E.H."

Years later, Bainbridge stated: "When Booth realized that we were kindly disposed, he threw off all reserve and became quite communicative."[18]

Lieutenant Ruggles would recall that Booth's communicative confidences included the remark that Herold and Atzerodt knew nothing of the "plot to kill."[19] Published in 1890, this exonerative reminiscence came a little late in the day for the drugstore clerk and the carriage painter.

15 Noted in Eisenschiml, *op. cit.*, p. 474.
16 Miss Holloway's article in reference.
17 National Archives, War Dept. Records, File "J," R.B.P. 55, JAO.
18 Quoted in Eisenschiml, *op. cit.*, p. 172.
19 M. B. Ruggles, "Pursuit and Death of John Wilkes Booth," *Century Magazine,* January, 1890.

But it does seem highly probable that Booth disclosed his identity to the three young soldiers at the ferry. Undoubtedly harumscarum David Herold did also, for reasons other than those apparent on the surface.

Around noon the ferryboat cruised up to the Port Conway landing. Horses and men clambered aboard. Herold, who had gone to tell Rollins that his wagon would not be needed, came running. The passengers waved good-by to the disappointed Rollins. Rollins' assistant (the boatman on duty that morning) shoved off.

When the ferry reached Port Royal, Captain Willie Jett guided Booth and Herold through sleepy streets to a quiet house set back from the river— the home of the Misses Sarah Jane and Lucy Peyton. The fugitives were invited in. Booth relaxed on a horsehair sofa. He hadn't seen one since he'd left Dr. Mudd's.

But Booth and Herold (introduced as Confederate veterans named Boyd) were not to remain with the Peytons as guests. One of the ladies, worried, had to explain to Willie Jett. Mister Randolph Peyton was out of town. Under the circumstances, two maiden ladies could not entertain gentlemen visitors overnight. She hoped Mr. Boyd would understand.

Sighing to a stand on his crutches, Mr. Boyd assured the ladies he understood.

One of them smiled tremulously. Perhaps Mr. Richard Garrett, who lived down the road a piece, this side of Bowling Green, would take them in.

Willie Jett nodded. He knew Mr. Garrett. They could go there.

Wearily Booth crutched out to the hitching post. Herold and Jett hoisted him to saddle on Ruggles' horse. Herold mounted behind Jett, Ruggles behind Bainbridge.

As they started away from the Peyton house in Port Royal, it was about one o'clock. At that hour of the afternoon of April 24, Booth—ten days a fugitive—was just 78 miles out of Washington.

In the noon hour of Monday, April 24, Colonel Lafayette Baker sitting in an office in Willard's Hotel, Washington, dispatched a message to General Hancock requesting a cavalry force of twenty-five picked men. Hancock immediately supplied the force. A troop of twenty-five men of the Sixteenth New York Cavalry, detachment under command of Lieutenant Edward P. Doherty, U.S.A.

The cavalrymen galloped down Pennsylvania Avenue, pulled up in front of Willard's Hotel. To quote Doherty's official report:

> In pursuance [of] orders I reported to Colonel Baker, at the time and place specified, and received the following information and instructions. He informed me that he had reliable information that the assassin Booth and his accomplice were somewhere between the Potomac and Rappahannock Rivers. He gave me several photographs of Booth and introduced me

to Mr. Conger and Mr. Baker, and said they would accompany me. He directed me to scour the section of the country indicated thoroughly, to make my own disposition of the men in my command, to forage upon the country, giving receipts for what was taken from loyal parties, and to land at or near Belle Plain at all hazards, to swim my horses ashore if I could not land otherwise, and return when I thought proper . . . .[20]

The Messrs. Conger and Baker, introduced to Doherty at Willard's, were military detectives—Lieutenant Colonel Everton J. Conger and Lieutenant Luther B. Baker. They wore civilian riding garb.

Conger was a hard-bitten combat veteran. He had been shot through the hips in battle early in the war. He would limp a little in rainy weather, but he had accomplished some rough missions on Secret Service duty. Although Doherty remained in charge of the uniformed cavalry troop, Conger assumed "courtesy command" as ranking officer.

Doherty's men were to be also at the disposal of Lieutenant Luther B. Baker—a division of authority which promised difficulty (and made good the promise). Doherty may have been even more disturbed by the fact that this Luther Baker was the Secret Service Chief's cousin.[21] The manhunt for Booth had developed into a fortune hunt. The Government alone offered $50,000 for Booth and $25,000 for Herold. Public-spirited citizens and private organizations had raised the ante to some $200,000. To the cavalry officer, Colonel Lafayette Baker's assignment of a relative to the chase must have smelled of rank favoritism.

After briefing the pursuit team at the Willard, Colonel Baker assured his cousin, "Lieutenant, we have got a sure thing!"[22] The "we" is as significant as the "thing." In reference to both, historian Eisenschiml notes with appropriate irony (in *Why Was Lincoln Murdered?*): "That Baker did all in his power to retain the glory and money for his own family is understandable. . . ."[23]

Less understandable were the marvelous decision with which the Chief of the Secret Service dispatched a flying squadron from Washington that day in pursuit of Booth, and the miraculous way he pinpointed the whereabouts of the fugitive assassin.

Lincoln's murderer and his accomplice had been at large for ten days. "Booths" had been reported here, there, everywhere. Army forces had tracked the actual Booth and his companion into the swamps below Bryantown, Maryland. But there the trail had vanished. So had the fugitives. No Federal officer had seen hide nor hair of them for six days. Now—*mirabile dictu!*—Lafayette Baker snaps his fingers in Washington and announces a "sure thing"!

---

[20] *Official Records,* Series I, Vol. 46, Pt. 1, pp. 1317–1318.
[21] Noted in Eisenschiml, *op. cit.,* p. 124. Also Oldroyd, *op. cit.,* p. 68. Van Doren Stern, *op. cit.,* p. 330, identifies Luther Baker as Lafayette C. Baker's "nephew."
[22] *Impeachment Investigation,* pub. GPO, 1868, p. 487.
[23] *Op. cit.,* p. 129.

How did Colonel Baker in Washington locate the prize? Congressmen and other interested parties eventually came to wonder. And, of course, the question in due time occurred to Government officials in charge of prize-money distributions. A huge reward had to be apportioned, and the Secret Service Chief modestly claimed for himself a $37,000 share.

To support his claim, Colonel Baker said that he "deduced" Booth's whereabouts from information brought to him by an old Negro. He published this detail in his *History of the United States Secret Service*—one of the first and more controversial volumes containing an account of the Booth pursuit.

> There was brought to my headquarters a colored man, who I was informed had important information respecting the assassins. On questioning the colored man, I found he had seen two men, answering the description of Booth and Harrold, entering a small boat in the vicinity of Swan's Point. . . . This information, with my preconceived theory as to the movements of the assassins, decided my course.[24]

Baker's story embodied one grievous lack. He failed to name the "colored man" who offered the vital information. Cousin Luther referred to this Negro in an official report, but he, too, left the name a blank.[25] Nor could records be found naming the alleged informant. Yet anyone who volunteered information which assured Booth's capture should have been on the reward list.

Puzzled by the matter of the "old Negro" was ex-Congressman Albert Gallatin Riddle. A Washington lawyer, Riddle represented Colonel Baker when the Secret Service Chief took his reward claims into court in 1867. After studying the case, Riddle (privately) became skeptical. Long afterward he wrote:

"The old negro informant is to be relegated to the realm of myth. . . . He was a pure creation of the genius of L. C. Baker."

Why did Colonel Baker create this mythical informant? According to Riddle: ". . . to make seeming ground on which the expedition could rest."

Riddle implies that Lafayette Baker located Booth through sheer Sherlock Holmesian deduction—genius insight plus brilliant analysis of clues. Certain he could never convince lesser minds of his long-distance mental wizardry, the Secret Service Chief "invented" the old Negro to simplify his action report and make it readily comprehensible.[26]

Or did the Secret Service Chief create this phony informant for another reason? For the very purpose, say, of convincing the Government that he, Lafayette Baker, owned remarkable deductive powers. That he *could* hear about two men embarking on the Potomac and, coupling this word with

---

[24] Baker, *op. cit.*, p. 527.
[25] Noted in Eisenschiml, *op. cit.*, p. 127.
[26] A. G. Riddle, *op. cit.*, pp. 334–345.

"preconceived theory," go straight to the fugitives' destination. This assertion, of course, served to justify Colonel Baker's reward claim. And it cut a true and valid claimant out of a justified award.

The deserving claimant, it seemed, was Major James R. O'Beirne, the officer who had crossed the Potomac on the night of April 22, and rushed to King George Court-House on the main pike to Port Conway. He had dashed back to Chapel Point, Maryland, to telegraph for a posse, only to be ordered by Colonel Baker to remain in Maryland.

It was conceded that Major O'Beirne in following the wrong quarry had hit upon the right. The concession came from no less a War Department official than Stanton, who congratulated O'Beirne (in December, 1865). ". . . if you did not succeed in capturing Booth, it was, at all events, certainly the information you gave which led to it."[27]

Yet Lafayette Baker persisted in the "pure deduction" fantasy. So did Lawyer Riddle, who pushed the Colonel's reward claim. Presumably for the benefit of posterity, Riddle described (in 1895) the scene at Willard's Hotel—Colonel Baker launching the winning manhunt.

> Before the starting of the party, the Chief spread out a map of Virginia and designated the crossing place of the fugitives and the place where they probably landed. Then, taking a compass, he placed one point at Port Conway, where a road [ferry] crossed the Rappahannock, and drew a circle, which he said included a space of ten miles around that point, and within that territory they would find the fugitives. . . .[28]

Marvelously enough, that circle encompassed Richard Garrett's farm.

Doherty's troop galloped to the Sixth Street wharf to board the steamer *John S. Ide* for the run down the Potomac to Belle Plain. They embarked about four o'clock, heading down river in the pink of the afternoon.

Doherty, Conger and Luther Baker went forward to issue detailed instructions to the steamer's captain. After they landed that night at Belle Plain, he was to moor the vessel at a nearby anchorage. There he was to wait until 6:00 P.M., April 26. If they weren't back by then, he was to return to Washington.[29]

From camp just outside Washington at Vienna, Virginia, these Sixteenth New Yorkers were weary. A fortnight ago they'd thought the war was over, and looked forward to going home. Then they'd been dispatched to scour the Surrattsville-Bryantown area on the hunt for Lincoln's assassin. No sooner back to camp, than they were away again on what was most likely another wild-goose chase.

Among them was Boston Corbett, a fighting evangelist, one of the oddest soldiers in the United States Army.

---

[27] Quoted in Eisenschiml, *op. cit.*, p. 128.
[28] Riddle, *op. cit.*, p. 334.
[29] *Official Records*, Series I, Vol. 46, Pt. 1, p. 1319-20.

Corbett was known as the "Glory to God" man—a nickname from his pre-war career at New York's Fulton Street Mission. Born in London, England, he had come as an immigrant to Troy, New York, where he learned the trade of "hat finisher." Somehow it had driven him to drink. His wife had died in childbirth. He'd become a down-and-outer (or so he liked to shout to "sawdust trail" audiences). Then, one night in Boston, he "saw the light." Whereupon he changed his first name from Thomas to Boston, symbolic of his spiritual re-birth.

No shy-and-retiring salvationist, Boston Corbett went all out to save the world. Soon he was preaching on street corners, wearing his hair down to his waist "because all the pictures of Christ represented Him wearing long locks." In 1858 he conducted a series of revival meetings in Boston. One night on North Square he was accosted by two prostitutes. In despair (apparently at the thoughts aroused) he castrated himself. Records show he spent a month in Massachusetts General Hospital recovering from this self-inflicted operation.[30]

He was, of course, an unbalanced fanatic, not the only one in America of the Civil War period, but one of the more fantastic. He heard voices. He saw angels. Signs in the sky (or in his head) read: "Repent, for the Day is at Hand!" Boston Corbett's God was an angry God who grew "exceeding wroth" with His (and Boston Corbett's) foes. This God had no use for such pallid Biblical admonitions as "Love thine enemies." Especially if those enemies were—as they happened to be in 1861—Confederates.

So, in April, 1861, an extraordinary episode had featured the arrest of Boston Corbett. According to historian Lloyd Lewis, this militant evangelist "had nearly caused a panic among the ladies of his church by declaring in a religious harangue that he was going to enlist and shoot men on sight." Shaking his long tresses, Corbett had worded his resolution most forcefully. "I will say to them, 'God have mercy on your souls'—then pop them off!"[31]

Did Sergeant Boston Corbett receive special instructions from the Almighty as the *John S. Ide* started down the Potomac in pursuit of John Wilkes Booth? Perhaps not then. But when Doherty's cavalry troop reached Garrett's farm, Corbett would say he did. And his declaration to that effect would climax one of the strangest episodes in America's strangest manhunt.

About the time Doherty's troop was boarding the steamer *Ide* for the start down the Potomac from Washington, Willie Jett halted the fugitive

[30] Byron B. Johnson, *Abraham Lincoln and Boston Corbett* (Waltham, Mass.: Privately printed, 1914).
[31] Lloyd Lewis, *Myths After Lincoln* (New York: Harcourt, Brace & Company, 1929), p. 286.

party some three miles south of Port Royal, Virginia, on the public road to Bowling Green.

They drew up at the roadside gate of Garrett's farm. The drive went in at right angles to the highway. A second gate, well back from the road gave admittance to the farmhouse dooryard. Against a wall of pine forest, farther back, stood a small tobacco barn.

The house was screened from the road by locusts and ailanthus trees. Landmarks were a spiny black locust tree which shaded the front lawn, and a paulownia tree.

Willie Jett led the travelers to the inner gate. He dismounted, told Herold to wait, and took the others up to the house. Jett knocked. Mrs. Richard Garrett loomed in the door.

Jett talked with her quietly for a moment. She withdrew to call her husband. While she was gone, Jett beckoned Booth up to the door. Bainbridge and Ruggles idled on the verandah step. Then Farmer Garrett, frowning inquiringly, appeared.

Staying in the Garrett home at this time was Miss L. K. B. Holloway, Richard Garrett's sister-in-law. This Virginia lady was (and would have been first to declare it) a loyal "Southronah." She was a spunky little person and quite literate, too, having done a spell of schoolteaching. Some time after the drama now making at Garrett's doorstep, Miss Holloway took pen in hand. Vividly, if not too accurately, she recalled Booth's visit to the Garrett homestead. Of his arrival that fateful Monday afternoon, she wrote:

> On arriving they were met by Mr. Richard H. Garrett, who was the owner of the house. Upon which Jett addressed him, saying, "This is Mr. Garrett, I presume?" and on securing an affirmative answer, introduced to him this second unknown as his friend John William Boyd, "a Confederate soldier who had been wounded in the battles around Richmond, near Petersburg." At the same time he requested Mr. Garrett to take care of him until Wednesday morning at which time he would call for him. Complying with this request, Mr. Garrett consented to receive him.
>
> By this time it was about three o'clock in the afternoon, so taking leave, Jett and the officers returned to the gate where the stranger (who was none other than Herold, one of the Conspirators) was awaiting them.
>
> How far Herold was conveyed, or how far the two Lieutenants accompanied Jett is not known. . . .[32]

So Booth, forlorn on his crutches, hobbled into the Garrett home. It would be interesting to know the details of his reception in the Garrett parlor, of his meeting with Garrett's young daughters and with the boys— William John (Jack) Garrett, a paroled Confederate cavalryman, and twelve-year-old Robert.

Supper that evening must have had its dramatic moments. Booth could not have resisted a show of the grand manner. Miss Holloway recognized

---

[32] Quoted in Wilson, *op. cit.*, p. 210.

in this guest no ordinary soldier. A knight of old had entered the farm-house. Miss Holloway must have been enchanted.

We know little of Booth's first night there, or of his activities as a guest during much of the following day. Apparently he was given a cot in an upstairs room with the boys. In the morning he was much refreshed, al-though his leg badgered him. Farmer Garrett told him he ought to see a doctor. Booth spent most of that morning reclining on the lawn under the big locust. The household accepted him unquestioningly. They rather liked Mr. Boyd.

Meantime, David Herold spent the night in the house, if not the em-braces, of a Mrs. Clark who lived about three miles outside of Bowling Green. Herold subsequently stated that he was taken there by Bainbridge to see a mutual acquaintance—"a gentleman named Clark, whom I met some three or four years ago. [He] had belonged to Mosby's command." But Herold testified, "I do not know Clark's christian name." He did not seem to know Bainbridge's, either. Although he had spent that day with the man, he consistently referred to Bainbridge as "Bennington."[33] Typical of Herold's word, such samples as these completely devaluate his testi-mony.

In testimony somewhat more reliable than the drug clerk's, Willie Jett stated that "Herold went on to Mrs. Clark's [no mention of a Mr. Clark] . . . remained there all night." Bainbridge remained with him. "Ruggles and myself went on to Bowling Green."[34]

At Bowling Green, the two young soldiers went to the hotel of Henry Goldman, whose daughter welcomed Willie Jett with open arms. It seems she was this young trooper's sweetheart. Jett would later declare that Miss Goldman constituted the sole objective of his mission to Bowling Green. At this point his story frays a little. Jett, too, becomes a man of mystery.

Then, as the sun advances into midday of Tuesday, April 25, Herold and Bainbridge come horsebacking into Bowling Green. Herold's shoes are in tatters. He tries the general store, and comes out proudly exhibiting a new pair.

Jett and Ruggles are waiting at Goldman's. They join up with Bainbridge and "Dave Boyd," and the four ride up the sandy turnpike on a return canter to Garrett's. They show up there in the middle of the afternoon.

And at that same hour three Federal officers are pumping information from William Rollins, ferryman at Port Conway. Those officers, of course, are Doherty, Conger and Luther Baker.

Booth is less than five miles away.

The *John S. Ide* had reached Belle Plain, Virginia, at 10:00 P.M. on

---

[33] National Archives, War Dept. Records, File "H," R.B.P. 38, JAO.
[34] National Archives, War Dept. Records, File "J," R.B.P. 55, JAO.

Monday the 24th. As the steamer snubbed up to the landing, horses were saddled, all hands alerted, ready to go.

Revived by a six-hour boat ride and a round of rations (not to mention stimulating thoughts of reward money), the troop was in lively fettle. Doherty explained the scouring procedure. With a cheer the men spurred their mounts across the wharf.

Action Report of Lieutenant E. P. Doherty, Sixteenth New York Cavalry:

I then proceeded in the direction of Fredericksburg, and after advancing about three miles I turned southwest and struck the Rappahannock River about twelve miles above Port Conway, 6 A.M. There I met two fishermen, who informed me of a number of surgeons living in the vicinity, and having previously learned the fact that Booth was crippled I deemed it proper to visit the different surgeons and search their premises, making such inquiries and examinations as were thought necessary. This being accomplished, and, finding no traces of the assassin or his accomplice, Mr. Conger requested me to furnish him four men and a corporal, which I did, and he moved down the Rappahannock, following its course. I then marched with the remainder of my command, making a detour of some fifteen miles by the way of King George Court-House, forming a junction with Mr. Conger at Conway's Ferry, at 2 P.M.

April 25, 1865—Up to this time we had found no trace of the assassin or his accomplice. I then stopped to feed. It was thought by the detectives that we would not find any traces of the assassins. After feeding, however, I determined to push across the ferry; Mr. Conger, one of the detectives, remained at the house. Mr. Baker, the other detective, accompanied me to the ferry, where I met a negro, who informed me that men answering the description crossed the day before, and that one of them had been into Mr. Roland's [Rollins'] house. Mr. Baker and myself proceeded to the house of Mr. Roland, and there, after exhibiting the photographs [of Booth and Herold] we concluded that we were on their track. I dispatched three men in a small boat to bring over a scow, which was on other side of the Rappahannock River; I also dispatched one man to inform Mr. Conger that we had track of the assassins, and to come down immediately. Mr. Rollins, at the ferry, informed me that two men were brought there from Mathias Point by a negro, to whom they had paid $15, and wanted to engage him, Rollins, to take them to Orange Court-House; that he refused to go so far, but they engaged him to take them to Bowling Green for $10; that these men showed great anxiety to get across the river, and wished him [Mr. Rollins] to use his small boat, and they would pay him extra; that Herold told him that they were brothers, and that Booth was wounded at Petersburg; that he refused his small boat for the reason he was using it putting out his fishing net; that, at about this time, three Confederate soldiers came up and shook hands with one of them. Herold then came to the house . . . and said he had met an old schoolmate, and that they were going to ride in "twain." Mrs. Rollins said the three soldiers were Capt. Willie Jett, Lieutenants Ruggles and Bainbridge; that Captain Jett was courting a young lady by the name of Goldman, whose father kept a hotel at Bowling Green."

The Federals were right on track. In a sweat of impatience, Doherty had to watch the ferry go snail-crawling to Port Royal and back, transporting his troop in sections. Long shadows lay athwart the lazy river when the last squad went over.

> At 6 P.M. my whole command was across, and I moved on toward Bowling Green. On the road, about three miles from Port Royal, I met a negro on horseback. Not wishing to lose time I rode ahead of the column and directed the negro to turn back and ride beside myself. . . . Proceeding along we arrived at a house seven miles from Bowling Green.[35]

The cavalry troop surrounded this tavern which was known as "The Half-Way House." Evidence indicates it was one of those side-of-the-road houses whose inmates watch the race of men go by. Doherty delicately refrains from describing the establishment, but other sources mention the handkerchiefs waved from windows, the yoo-hooing girls not averse to the Yankee dollar.[36]

It seemed a good address to pump for neighborhood information. "Messrs. Conger and Baker entered the house. . . . The house of Mrs. Clark, some four miles distant, was spoken of as a place where some of the party might be. I determined, however, to push on to Bowling Green and secure the said Captain Jett."[37]

Doherty just missed the target that evening. In their ride from Port Royal to Half-Way House, the troopers had raced right past the gate of Garrett's farm.

Booth must have been relieved to see Herold return with Jett, Bainbridge and Ruggles from Bowling Green that afternoon. Herold's irrepressible garrulity was a constant danger. The fellow was a natural liar, glib and smart, but too many lies were hard to sustain, and sooner or later he might trip over his tongue.

Booth may (and should) have been worried over his own nervous talk. He had spent a restless day. At dinner that noon, he couldn't avoid conversation with the Garretts and Miss Holloway. William Garrett, who'd been to Port Royal that morning, came home with word of Lincoln's assassination—the first news of it this simple family had heard. The guest in the house had to say something.

Miss Holloway would never forget that noonday meal. The detail comes from her reminiscent pen.

> While at dinner the tragic event was commented upon, as to the motive which prompted the deed and its effect upon the public welfare. All this time Boyd remained silent, but upon hearing one of the daughters remark that she supposed that the perpetrator had been paid, he turned to her with a smile and said:
> "Do you think so, Miss? By whom do you suppose he was paid?"

---

[35] *Official Records*, Series I, Vol. 46, Pt. 1, pp. 1318–19.
[36] Noted in Van Doren Stern, *op. cit.*, p. 331.
[37] *Official Records*, Series I, Vol. 46, Pt. 1, p. 1319.

"Oh," she replied, "I suppose by both the North and the South."

"It is my opinion," rejoined he, "he wasn't paid a cent, but did it for notoriety's sake."

Soon after, they arose from the table, and as he started out Mrs. Garrett (my sister) asked if he would like to have his wound dressed. He replied by saying that it did not give him the slightest pain. Then thanked her, and with several others went out on the porch commanding full view of the public road and sat down upon the steps.[38]

While "Mr. Boyd" sat there on the verandah steps, one of the Garrett boys brought from the house an old revolver. The guest suggested a bit of target practice, said he wasn't a bad shot. To demonstrate, he fired a couple at a knot in the gatepost. Each time the trigger mechanism dragged. He missed the mark. An odd little incident in that odd day. One that left the marksman chagrined and perhaps uneasy.[39]

There was a wall map in the Garrett house. During that slow afternoon, Booth had the map brought to him on the verandah. He studied it for some time. Then he traced in pencil a winding route from Virginia down to the Mexican border. Whereupon he returned the map to the Garrett wall. On the surface it might seem he was plotting an escape to Mexico. Under the surface, it might appear that he wanted the map's finders to think he plotted an escape to Mexico.

The marked map led several historians to relate that Booth was not only bound for Mexico, but confided as much to Mr. Garrett. Yet if Miss Holloway is to be credited, Booth confided nothing to the Garretts, not even his identity. To the last they thought him a "Mr. Boyd."

Unfortunately Miss Holloway's account cannot be wholly trusted. Loyal to the Stars and Bars, she was even more devoted to the Garrett family. These convictions and sentiments influenced her pen. Some of her story stumbles accordingly. For instance, it is hard to believe that one of the daughters—in this country home where news arrives ten days late!—would make the acute observation that Lincoln's killer might be paid "by both the North and South." Somehow this sounds more like the well-informed little school teacher than her countrified niece.

From this point on, almost nothing written or testified in respect to the doings of the fugitives at Garrett's farm can be taken at face value. Nobody knows exactly what Booth said to the Garretts, or they to him. Nobody knows what passed between Booth and Herold. Or between them and Jett, Bainbridge and Ruggles. Nor can the reports of the Federal officers who scouted the road from Port Royal to Bowling Green be accepted as wholly truthful. Even Boston Corbett's word on what eventuated cannot be taken as gospel.

Only an outline continuity of what occurred that evening and night at

---

[38] L. K. B. Holloway, *The Capture and Death of John Wilkes Booth.*
[39] Related in Oldroyd, *op. cit.,* 203.

Garrett's farm may be constructed—bare bones, so to speak, of the drama that transpired on locale.

Late that afternoon Herold returns from Bowling Green with Jett, Bainbridge and Ruggles. He and Ruggles come up to Garrett's inside gate. Jett and Bainbridge ride on to Port Royal.

Herold finds Booth idling in the dooryard. He dances up the path, exhibiting his new shoes. From the verandah the Garrett family watches this little exhibition. They see Booth and Herold draw aside under a tree to converse together. Miss Holloway notes that the two remain "in close conversation for fully half an hour."[40]

After this confidential talk, Booth and Herold move to the verandah. Herold is introduced as Booth's brother, "Dave Boyd." They sit chatting with the family, taking their ease.

About suppertime, Jett and Bainbridge gallop up to the gate. Jett calls to Booth, advising him that Federal bluecoats are coming across the Rappahannock on the ferry to Port Royal. Ruggles joins his two friends, and the three young ex-Confederates spur away down the road.

Booth is visibly alarmed. (Did he and Herold go in for supper with the family? Miss Holloway does not say so. Another account describes a rather tense meal, with Herold fidgeting and Booth brooding in silence.)

Again the family is on the verandah. Against the west a last streak of sunset dims out like a fading banner. Twilight steals across the wooded slopes. The locusts in the dooryard, the paulownia tree are cobwebbed in dusk. A sudden drum-roll of hoofs echoes through the gloaming. The pounding grows louder. Then, with guidons flying, sabres jangling, shouts —a blurred streak of blue splashed with flecks of chevron yellow—a Yankee cavalry troop batters past the outer gate.

On the verandah young Garrett exclaims, "They must be going to Bowling Green!"

Booth and Herold are going somewhere, too. To the family's surprise, the pair are seen racing for the pine woods beyond the tobacco barn— Booth making grotesque speed on his crutches, and Herold sprinting for dear life. They plunge into the thickets, disappear, and leave behind them a troubled family. And another mystery.

Some accounts say they return to the house in about an hour. Others say they do not return until long after dark. Miss Holloway gives us the shorter absence. At any rate, when the two come back to the verandah they find farmer Garrett suspicious.

We are told that William (Jack) Garrett wanted to know why the two had taken to the woods. If they were paroled Confederates (as claimed) why run and hide from the Federals? Booth mutters something about a brush with the Yankees up in Maryland. Better if he and his "brother" remained out of sight.

---

[40] Holloway, *op. cit.*

As Miss Holloway tells it, her nephew decided to investigate. From neighbors he learned that the house-guests were "wanted." Apparently the neighbors did not know why. But the word was out. The bluecoats were hunting a cripple and companion. "You know what you have done," young Garrett tells Booth. "If you've gotten into any difficulty you must leave at once. I don't want you to bring any trouble upon my aged father."

Booth assures William Garrett that the trouble is over. But he offers him ten dollars for conveyance that night "up to Guinea's Station." Booth says he's heard that a Confederate artillery outfit from Maryland is located near there. If he and his "brother" can reach the place, they'll be safe.

William advises that the journey tonight is impossible. He agrees to go first thing in the morning when the family horse will be rested. To bind the bargain, he accepts the ten dollars in advance.

And now occurs perhaps the strangest episode of that strange day.

> When the hour came to retire [Miss Holloway relates], Boyd saw no place in which he could be made comfortable. He said that anywhere would do rather than go upstairs.
>
> Then he and Herold were conducted to a large tobacco house in which was stored a lot of valuable furniture belonging to the people of Port Royal, covered with hay and other provender.
>
> *After they entered, Jack Garrett locked the door and took the key to the house and gave it to me,* saying he would leave it in my care and that I must not let anyone have it, as it was his opinion that they intended trying to steal their horses and escape. Then, assuring themselves, he [Jack Garrett] and his brother . . . went out into a shed opposite the tobacco house to spend the night.[41]

Here, surely, is a fantastic business. That Booth, his life at stake, would consent to being locked in a barn! One can only believe that the key went into the padlock surreptitiously, after Booth and Herold entered the trap.

However, a surreptitious locking does not seem to have been the case. Here is David Herold's version of what occurred:

> That night Garrett went across to a negro's, living about half a mile distant. He said [upon returning], "I judge, from what I can hear, that these gentlemen [the Federals] are after you." I says, "I don't think they are." Garrett says, "I would sooner that you would not stay here all night." I said, "All right. We would sooner not stay here." Booth had told them that he had shot one or two soldiers in Maryland, and asked them to warn him if the Yankees should come, so that he could escape. It was then after dark. We didn't know where to go. Garrett says, "I don't want you to stay in the house." Booth asked if he could stay in the barn. Garrett said, "Yes." We went down and were locked in the barn.[42]

For what it is worth, this testimony implies consent at being fastened in. Undoubtedly Booth and his sharp-eyed accomplice saw the padlock

---

41 *Ibid.* Emphasis supplied.
42 National Archives, War Dept. Records, File "H," R.B.P. 38, JAO.

on the door. If not, they must have heard the key. Both were heavily armed. Had they feared a trap, they could have shouted dire threats at the Garrett boys, or shot the hasp off the door. Or quietly pried their way through another locked door at the back.

Instead, they entered the barn (probably with a candle) and looked around. They were provided (says one account) with blankets.[43] Stacked furniture offered tables, chairs. Mounds of straw were good for bedding down.

Perhaps Booth thought the locking in a clever trick. If it eased Old Garrett's mind, why not? Who would expect to find desperate fugitives in a padlocked barn?

Afterward Miss Holloway blamed Booth's betrayal on Willie Jett. She had no use for the boy. She describes him as ". . . a young man named William Jett, dressed in a Confederate Captain's uniform."

Miss Holloway suggests that Jett slipped away from his Confederate companions on the evening of the 24th. "It has been conjectured . . . that Jett, leaving the officers, proceeded on to Ashland, a telegraph office, where he sent intelligence to the authorities in Washington as to the whereabouts of the two men."

She also suggests that Jett, on the evening of the 25th, made rendezvous with the Federals, after warning Booth that they were coming. She writes that Jett and Bainbridge "galloped off, *Jett going in the direction of Port Royal to meet, as it is conjectured, the troops who were coming in answer to his telegraphic summons.*"[44]

One wonders why Miss Holloway singled out poor Jett as the Judas informer? Certainly Booth and Herold were conspicuous travelers in the area—Booth on his crutches; Herold with his city-arab air. They had come by public road from Port Conway in broad daylight. Dozens of farmers and villagers could have spied them.

Was Miss Holloway endeavoring to "cover" someone else? No historian could possibly know. A fair guess might be that she suspected her own nephew, perhaps with reason.

Yet the tip-off must have come long before Booth reached Garrett's farm. Evidence indicates that someone up the line put Lafayette Baker (or Major O'Beirne) on the fugitives' trail across the Potomac. Someone directed the manhunt toward Bowling Green.

Miss Holloway was wrong in thinking Willie Jett had not been in the war. His early service record proved authentic, and evidence indicates his connection with the "Gray Ghosts" of Mosby. By his own testimony, Willie was on "secret mission" when he met Booth and Herold at Port Conway. What mission he neglects to say.

---

[43] Van Doren Stern, *op. cit.*, p. 328.
[44] Holloway, *op. cit.*; original italics.

Not all of Willie's statement to the Federal authorities can be believed. But it remains one of the more lucid depositions taken at the time.[45]

On record, too, is Lieutenant Doherty's account of Willie Jett's arrest at Bowling Green on the night of April 25th.

After leaving The Half-Way House, the Federals raced to Bowling Green "to secure Captain Jett." The party scouted up to Goldman's Hotel. Doherty dismounted his troop, deployed his men around the sleeping tavern. "This was about 12 o'clock midnight."

Doherty's action report goes on: "We knocked about fifteen minutes . . . without receiving any reply. At length a negro appeared on the street who showed the way to [a servants'] house in the rear. On entering I asked a negro where Willie was, meaning Captain Jett; he replied that he was in bed. Conger inquired where the room was, & c. In a few moments Mrs. Goldman opened the door, and we asked for her son. She showed us upstairs, and we found Jett and her son in bed, partly undressed. We took Jett downstairs and informed him our business, telling him that if he did not forthwith inform us where the men were, he should suffer; that no parley would be taken & c."[46]

A lad hauled out of sleep by the hair and rushed downstairs with a revolver at his neck may well do some talking.

He requested that two of the party withdraw and leave him with one, and he would make a full statement of what he knew of the assassin's whereabouts. This was granted. Mr. Baker and myself had scarcely left the room when he told Mr. Conger that he would show us the place. On learning this, I took him in my own charge. His horse was got out, he was mounted, and we [started] back to the house of Mr. Garrett, about twelve miles from Bowling Green.

The calendar had turned on April 26th.

---

[45] National Archives, War Dept. Records, File "J," R.B.P. 55, JAO.
[46] *Official Records*, Series I, Vol. 46, Pt. 1, pp. 1319–1320.

CHAPTER **20**

The Shooting at
Garrett's Farm

GARRETT'S farmstead sleeps. Perhaps Miss Holloway stirs on her virgin pillow. The horse in the stable stamps restlessly. Or the cripple in the tobacco barn, shifting his aching limb, utters a half-wakeful moan. Otherwise the nocturne is undisturbed. Wrapped in slumber, the Virginia landscape dreams.

Then, faint in the night from the direction of Bowling Green, the rataplan of hooves pounds the open road. The drum-roll comes nearer, loudening. Then the batter of hoofbeats dead-stops at a muffled command. After a muted burst of orders, a group of shadows rushes through the gate and up the path. The farmyard dog challenges sharply, and a baleful chorus of bloodhounds answers.

Miss Holloway wakens bolt upright to the tumult—sounds of thrashing in underbrush—voices under her window—boots trampling on the porch —metallic jingle of scabbards and spurs—a nasal-twang command, and a sudden, savage pounding on the kitchen door.

"Open up in there! Unlock this door, or we'll smash it in."

Miss Holloway hears a window raised. Mr. Garrett's voice calling down. "Who's there?"

"Never mind who!" a harsh voice answers. "We want to talk to you, mister! Fetch a light and open this door!"

Miss Holloway scurries to the window. Damn Yankees! A whole passel of them—overrunning the barnyard, trampling the flower garden. In the moonless dark below they assume the aspect of an invading legion. She sees them darting toward the barn, pawing through the lilacs, scouting around the outbuildings. The ugly gleam of carbines and buckles and spurred heels is everywhere.

"Open up, you hear? We got the house surrounded! We'll shoot our way in!"

Mrs. Garrett cries out in alarm. There is commotion in the daughters' bedroom. Miss Holloway starts for the hall. From the corner of her eye she sees Farmer Garrett, a rumpled figure in slippers and nightshirt, half tumbling down the stairs.

"Wait! Wait!" Garrett calls out. "Jack! Come quick, it's the Yankees!" The door-latch rattles in his frantic hand. He recoils as the door lurches inward.

On the porch, big as thunder, stands a cavalry officer with pistol aimed straight at the farmer's head. He is the embodiment of Garrett's worst fears for the past four years. A Yankee on the doorstep!

Two soldiers stomp into the kitchen. Muddy boots and yellow gauntlets and U.S. insignia! Old Man Garrett can only stare in vertigo and dread at the officer confronting him.

"We want those two men," the officer says harshly. "We know they're here!"

Farmer Garrett blurts, "No! They've gone!"

To a bellowed, "Where are they?" the farmer can only mutter unintelligibly and nod toward the outer woods.

The officer roars, "So you won't tell us, is that it? By God, we'll show you what it means to harbor men who've killed the President!" He catches the old man by the throat, left-handed, pins him against the door jamb, and holds the revolver to his temple. "Come up here and get this Rebel, boys!" he calls over his shoulder. "Maybe a little neck-stretching will loosen up his tongue!"

Caught by eager yellow gauntlets, the farmer is hustled down the porch steps and across the yard to a chopping block. Forced to stand on this gloomy pedestal, Garrett shivers in his nightshirt, his marrow chilled less by the April cool than by a tree limb arched against the stars.

The officer bellows, "Speak up, Garrett! We know those assassins are on your place! Where they hiding?"

"In the woods," the old man pants. "In the woods!"

"It's your own neck, Rebel! Okay, Sergeant! Bring the rope!"

These Yankees aren't fooling. They are the agents of the grapes of wrath—the men dispatched from Washington by Colonel Lafayette C. Baker. This is the detachment of Sixteenth New York Cavalry under command of Lieutenant Edward P. Doherty and courtesy command of Colonel Everton Conger. The officer threatening Garrett with a pistol and with hanging is Lieutenant Luther Baker.[1]

According to Miss Holloway, Farmer Garrett's wife and two-year-old daughter tearfully appealed for his release. Again and again Garrett was asked to disclose the whereabouts of the assassins. "Again and again did he profess his ignorance."[2]

Mr. Garrett is handcuffed. A coil of manila hemp appears. One of the

[1] Oldroyd, *op. cit.*, p. 70. Van Doren Stern, *op. cit.*, p. 344, says this officer was Conger.

[2] L. K. B. Holloway, *op. cit.*

soldiers hastily fashions a sliding bowline. The noose is dangled before Garrett's face. The shivering figure on the block emits a despairing moan.

But the cat has old Farmer Garrett's tongue. Surrounded by this lynch party, he stands on his pedestal like a speaker who has forgotten his lines. Around him and his house the tumult grows. He sees on the porch his wife and terrified daughters, Miss Holloway arguing with an annoyed trooper. Dogs bark and lanterns flicker. Down at the gate on the fringe of the nightmare stands Willie Jett. Garrett spies him.

"You done this, Willie! You brought these Federals here!"

Baker roars, "Never mind who brought us here! You got one more chance, you old fool! Talk, or be hanged! Where's the two assassins?"

The threat gives Farmer Garrett laryngitis. In fact, Miss Holloway tells us he caught a chill from which he never quite recovered. It would seem that he, too, was about to become one of Booth's dangling marionettes. Miss Holloway cries out aghast as she sees the noose about to be placed around her brother-in-law's neck. The free end of the rope is tossed over the tree limb. Five strong men stand ready to take up the slack.

Fortunately for Garrett, one of his sons has the good sense to intervene. Or, as Miss Holloway states: "At this juncture of affairs, Jack Garrett came up from the shed and, perceiving his father's perplexity, said, 'Gentlemen, if you want to know where those men are, I will take you to the place.' "[3]

Why didn't Garrett speak up? His obdurate refusal to reveal the hiding place of his two unwanted guests would strand him on the block until 8:00 A.M., a shivering statue of misery between the bluecoat guards. And had Stanton's decree been consistently followed, Farmer Garrett's conduct might have cost him a formal hanging as a Booth accomplice.

But the manhunters turn their attentions on Garrett's son. In sixty seconds a cordon of soldiers is thrown around the fateful tobacco barn. Lieutenant Doherty puts his pistol to Jack Garrett's head, catches him by the scruff and runs him to the barn door. It seems to be waiting for them, padlocked and sullen like Old Man Garrett's mouth. A sharp whack on the wood from Doherty's pistol is answered by a deeper silence.

Lieutenant Doherty barks a savage command. "Come out of that! We know you're in there! Can you hear?"

No answer. Ensued the following (dialog based on reports):

Doherty leaves young Garrett in custody of Baker and the others, and circles the barn to deploy his men. Lieutenant Baker takes up the challenge at the barn door. "You're surrounded by Federal troops, you two! You haven't got a chance! We're going to send the Garrett kid in there, and you'll hand your weapons over to him and walk out after him with your arms lifted. Speak up! Do you hear?"

The barn door seems to be deaf.

Baker nudges Jack Garrett. "Unlock the door."

---

[3] *Ibid.*

Trembling, young Garrett opens the padlock. Baker shoves him through the door and dodges aside to duck possible gunfire. Doherty, returning to the front of the barn a moment later, sees young Garrett coming out of the door. The fugitives within won't surrender. According to Jack Garrett, the cripple in the barn snarled and spat at him, "Damn you! Get out of here! You've betrayed me!"[4]

"Look," Conger suggests. "We'll have a little bonfire and burn the bastards out. How about it?" Conger jostles young Garrett roughly as they draw away from the door. "Get a move on and fetch some brush." He shouts at the barn, "If you don't surrender your arms and come out of there, it'll go tough with you."

Behind the barn door there is a rustle of activity. A mutter of oaths. A scurry of hurried movements. The rasp of castors and scraping timber, suggestive of furniture being piled in barricade. A trooper steps up. "Let me go in after them, Lieutenant. I'll get them out!"

Doherty turns on the hovering cavalry sergeant. "Take your position around to the side there, Corbett. Mr. Conger, if you and Mr. Baker take the door, I'll watch the rear. Go on, Corbett! Move! Keep your boys well covered, about ten yards back."

Boston Corbett snaps a salute and races off. One can imagine his eyes dilated with excitement. A not-so-odd soldier, this eunuch with the Mongoloid features, this revivalist with the love of battle in his soul. Military history is replete with warriors who praise the Lord and pass the ammunition.

Jack Garrett returns with an armload of brush. He follows grim-jawed Colonel Conger around to the barn's rear. Cautiously the men stack the brush against the barn wall. They add some old lumber to the fuel. The dry timbering of the tobacco barn will burn like tinder. Satisfied, Conger leads Jack Garrett around to join Baker at the front.

Miss Holloway, now watching with the terrified family on the front porch, sees a whispered consultation.

Lieutenant Doherty is inclined to parley. But Colonel Conger is fretting with impatience. So is Lieutenant Luther Baker. Again Baker warily approaches the barn door.

"Last chance, you two! Surrender, or we'll fire the barn and smoke you out like rats! We'll give you five minutes more to make up your minds!"

A pause while the night waits in bated silence. Then Miss Holloway hears Boyd's high-pitched voice, "Who are you, anyway? What do you want with us?"[5]

"Never mind who *we* are!" Baker threatens. "We know who *you* are. We're ordering you to surrender your arms and walk out here. You're

---

4 Quoted in Oldroyd, *op. cit.*, p. 71.
5 Holloway, *op. cit.*

surrounded by fifty men with carbines and pistols. You don't have a prayer of getting away!"

A pause. Then the voice from the barn: "Captain, this is a hard case, I swear. Perhaps I am being taken by my own friends!" The voice alters to a plaintive wheedle. "A little more time, Captain! Give us a little more time!"[6]

"You've got five minutes!" Baker shouts. "Not a minute longer!"

Five minutes. On the Garrett porch the shawled women stand like Biblical figures in charade. Miss Holloway feels slow tears crawl down her cheek. Propped upright on the block by threatening pistols, Farmer Garrett in his nightshirt poses like an absurd and sagging monument. Around the barn the soldiers in ambush shift restlessly, spit tobacco juice, finger their carbines.

"Time's up!" Baker calls. "Come out peaceable, or you'll be burned out!"

From the trap comes a pleading whine. "Give me a chance for my life, can't you, Captain? I am but a cripple—a one-legged man. Withdraw your troopers a hundred yards from the door, and I'll come out. All I want is a fighting chance."[7]

Although this speech seems stilted, it is possible that the man in the barn uttered some such appeal. Authorities frequently report similar pleas from condemned killers who beg for sportsmanship when facing the executioner for some particularly un-sporting crime. Justifiably enough, the Federal officers on the scene were disinclined to grant the quarry a "fighting chance." Probably Baker and Conger were fuming.

But Oldroyd tells us Baker continued the palaver. "We did not come here to fight, but to capture you. If you do not come out, I will fire the barn."

Another gallery-play is attempted by the high-pitched voice from behind the door. "Well, my brave boys, you can prepare a stretcher for me!"[8] Pause. "I will never surrender!"[9]

This is too much for Jack Garrett's overwrought nerves. Fed up with this guest's mock heroics, the young ex-Confederate lets out a wrathful shout. "For God's sake, Boyd, come out of there! You can't escape! Act like a man and surrender!"[10]

Now the soldiers hear Herold's voice for the first time, in a blurred dialogue within the dark barn. Then a savage outburst. "You're a goddam coward and mean to leave me in my distress. But go, *go!* I don't want you to stay! I won't have you stay!"[11]

---

[6] Oldroyd, *op. cit.*, p. 72.
[7] *Ibid.*, p. 73.
[8] *Ibid.*
[9] Miss Holloway's version.
[10] *Ibid.*, minus the profanity.
[11] Oldroyd, p. 73, minus the profanity.

Lieutenant Doherty tells us the cripple in the barn shouted, "Oh, Captain, there is a man in here who wants to surrender awful bad!"[12]

Gentle Miss Holloway reports Boyd's speech as, "The word surrender is not in my vocabulary. I have never learned the meaning of that. There is one here, however, who will surrender."

This last speech summons to mind a graduation-class elocutionist and "The Boy Stood on the Burning Deck." That a trapped fugitive about to stand in a burning barn might utter such bombast seems a little incredible. Until one recalls that the fugitive is actor John Wilkes Booth—or Miss Holloway's conception of actor John Wilkes Booth. In either case, the theatric lines take on some degree of authenticity.

As for David Herold, he can endure the suspense no longer. There was a time when this seedy drug-store clerk hankered for a role in melodrama. Now the theatricals of reality are too much for him, or so it seems. According to Oldroyd: "A rattle at the door was heard, and a voice saying, 'Let me out! Open the door! I want to surrender!' "

"Hand out your arms, then!" the officers shout.

Herold cries, "I have no arms!"

Baker: "We know what you've got!"

"Boyd's" voice from barn: "On the word of honor of a gentleman, he has no arms with him. They are mine, and I have got them!"[13]

Doherty now orders Jack Garrett to open the padlock once more. Sidling up to the entry, the cavalry officer orders the man who wants to surrender to thrust both hands out the door. The door inches open a little way. Out comes one pale hand. Then the other. Doherty fastens a steely grip on the exposed wrists, and with a savage yank brings his captive lunging from the barn.[14]

Instantly the door is slammed. Herold, thrown offside, is caught by soldiers in a flying tackle. His hat sails off. He is pummeled to the ground. As he struggles in this scrimmage, he cries out that he is innocent of any crime. According to one source, he wails, "Who's that man in there? He says his name is Boyd!"[15]

By another account we are told that Herold whimpered for mercy. He denied any complicity in Lincoln's assassination, and kept repeating, "I always liked Mr. Lincoln's jokes!"[16] Surely the most inane of all lines in that night's fantastic melodrama.

Doherty, lacking handcuffs, hauls the miserable captive across the yard to rope him to a tree. Joyfully the soldiers whoop around this $25,000 prize —a nice fish in the dragnet. The big catch, however, is still yammering in

---

12 *Official Records.*

13 Oldroyd, *op. cit.*, p. 73.

14 Van Doren Stern (*op. cit.*, p. 356) credits Baker with seizing Herold. In his official report, Doherty claimed this exploit for himself.

15 From Trial Report quoted in *Daily Constitutional Union*, May 22, 1865.

16 New York *Tribune*, April 28, 1865.

the tobacco barn. Refusing to come out, he utters all kinds of wild threats, pleas and appeals, ranting and declaiming from his junkshop lair in a nest of sofas, chairs, tables, commodes and whatnots. If the reports of Lieutenants Doherty and Baker and Colonel Conger may be believed, the fugitive in the barn runs through a monologue of claptrap that rivals anything in the library of paperback blood-and-thunder.

He wails, "Give a lame man a show!" He begs the officers to let him come out fighting. He challenges the Yankees to combat, promising to fell them one after another, singly. He assures Colonel Conger that he could have shot him while the Colonel walked about the barnyard with a lantern. He declaims that he did not do so out of respect for a brave officer. His voice breaks in high-keyed emotion. He cries, "Give me fifteen paces and I'll make good my escape!"

Doherty, Conger and Baker are baffled by all this ranting. From the first Conger had wanted to fire the barn without ado. Doherty had been against it. "We ought to wait till morning." But Colonel Conger has the titular command by reason of rank. Now itching with impatience, Conger decides to end this nightmare.

Signalling the troopers to the alert, the Colonel prowls to the barn's rear. There he lights a twist of straw and chucks the firebrand through a crack in the planking. Then he fires the heap of brush. As though ignited by an expert arsonist, the corner of the barn spouts flame. Inside, the fire rushes across a pile of hay, devouring the dry mow in brilliant gulps. It climbs, panting, up and over the jumble of stacked furniture. There is a loud, chewy crackle as though a dozen men were trampling bushel baskets. A snuff of wind, and the crackling becomes a roar. The draught is excellent—the barn walls are loosely boarded, and the timbers are full of knotholes. In a sudden gust of combustion, the barn's interior is revealed in hot light.

Fire glare streams through the wall cracks and knotholes, fanning out through the darkness to splash with crimson bushes, tree trunks, rifle barrels and the tense features of watchers.

The little barn glows in the dark like a kitchen stove. There is a smell of burning pine, hot cedar, blistering varnish, a faint scent of Virginia burleigh. Withdrawn from the barn, like a group of stokers, the troopers stand with their carbines held loosely alert, waiting. They hear above the fire roar a despairing cry. A scarlet haze swims across the barnyard.

Through the openwork planking of the fiery barn, all can glimpse the shadow man within, hopping this way and that, dim and flickering like a figure seen through the slitted cylinder of a magic lantern.

To and fro on his crutch the man hops like an injured raven in a cage. Around him the fires pile up in bright carnival, flowering out of the furniture stack and running in whorls and spirals up the walls. Sparks swirl around the leaping shadow man. He twists, wheels, and dodges in the deadly light. Everywhere he turns his escape is blocked. Finally he stands at bay, gripping his carbine.

Let us peer through a knothole at him with the fascinated eye of Colonel Conger. This Federal officer was kind enough to leave his impressions of the scene for history. We can picture the colonel crouching at the corner of the barn like a boy at the fence of a ballpark. In one hand Conger clutches his revolver. In the other, it would seem, he clutches pencil and notebook, though, of course, he could not have actually been encumbered by writing materials. He must have retained what he saw on the retina of his eye for later composition. But he is a vivid observer, if what he tells of that scene is true. And he tells it with a flair that is deceptively convincing—at first reading.

Here is Conger's description of the man in Garrett's barn. Or, let us say, the description attributed to Colonel Conger.

> Behind the blaze I saw Wilkes Booth standing upright on a crutch. He looked like his brother Edwin, whom he so much resembled that I believed, for a moment, the whole pursuit to have been a mistake. At the gleam of the fire, Wilkes dropped his crutch and carbine and crept to the spot to spy the incendiary and shoot him dead. His eyes were lustrous like fever, and swelled and rolled in terrible beauty, while his teeth were fixed and he wore the expression of one in the calmness of frenzy.
>
> In vain he peered with vengeance in his look; the blaze that made him visible concealed his enemy. A second he turned glaring at the fire, as if to leap upon it and extinguish it, but it made such headway that this was a futile impulse, and he dismissed it. As calmly as upon a battlefield a veteran stands amidst the hail of ball and shell and plunging iron, Booth, shifting his carbine to his left hand and drawing his revolver, turned at a man's stride and, in a kind of limping-halting jump, pushed for the door, and the last resolve of death, which we name despair, sat on his high, bloodless forehead.[17]

Not only is the style lurid, but the account is careless reporting. The first paragraph tells us: "At the gleam of the fire, Wilkes dropped his crutch and carbine." Four sentences later we have "Booth, shifting his carbine to his left hand and drawing his revolver. . . ." We can hardly trust this story, nor can we accredit the Conger version of what happened next.

> As he [Booth] dashed, intent to die not unaccompanied, a disobedient sergeant at an eye-hole draws upon him the fatal bead. The barn was all glorious with conflagration, and in the beautiful ruin this outlawed man strode like all we know of wicked valor, stern in death.

To stride like wicked valor in a limping-halting jump strikes us as impossible, physically as well as metaphorically. And we are not surprised to learn that the man in the barn did not get very far.

---

[17] Quoted in Wilson, *op. cit.*, pp. 179–80.

A shock, a shout, a gathering up of his splendid figure, as if to overtop the stature God gave him, and John Wilkes Booth fell headlong to the floor, lying there in a heap.[18]

This is not honest history. Villains may mime in such fashion on the apron of a stage, but not in a burning barn, a death-trap, blinded and choked by acrid smoke. Not even a Booth could rise to the occasion as described. Not with a bullet shot as this one was through the spinal cord in the victim's neck!

So Conger's account leaves to history another tantalizing mystery. In fact, several mysteries. The man in Garrett's barn was shot, no doubt of that. Conger may or may not have seen him go down. But one thing is certain. From his position at the corner of the barn, Colonel Conger could not possibly have seen the "disobedient sergeant" who was stationed around the corner of the barn. Belatedly, Boston Corbett would declare that he fired the deadly shot. Tradition would accept his statement. But not a single witness offered to corroborate Corbett's word on that night of April 25–26. Twenty-two years later, Robert Garrett claimed he saw the sergeant shoot. But Robert was a boy of twelve on the night in question, and his subsequent statement raised more questions than the one it purported to answer.

The Chairman of the Congressional Committee that dispensed the reward for Booth's capture stated that Corbett, "an insane man," abandoned his post, "thrust a pistol through a crack and fired it without knowing where the ball was going."[19]

The fact seems to be that no reliable witness saw Boston Corbett shoot the man in Garrett's barn. What did Colonel Conger actually see?

Unfortunately, we cannot take the Colonel's word for anything. His original account is riddled with implausibilities. Probably he did not write it in the first place.

Enough for the moment to recognize Conger's report as the stuff, if not the nonsense, of imagination. Conger was the ranking officer at Garrett's farm, and if the ranking imagination is in high gear, who in an Army detachment dares to say it nay?

Grope as one will for the facts, it remains impossible to discern the truth behind the clouds of smoke and mendacity that obscured the shooting at Garrett's farm:

The shot makes a sharp *crack* in the night. The man in the barn goes down "in a heap." The soldiers rush the door. And there is hell to pay. War Department orders are explicit—bring him back alive.

First through the door, according to one version, is Lieutenant Luther Baker, who pounces in and snatches the revolver from the prone man's

---

[18] *Ibid.*
[19] DeWitt, *op. cit.*, p. 277.

hand.[20] Conger's testimony supports this version. But according to Miss Holloway, "As soon as it was discovered that Booth had been shot, Jack Garrett was sent in to bring him out."[21] As will be noted, Lieutenant Doherty's report offers still another version. Little differences, but in the aggregate they add up to a density of confusion that obscures something more than the petty details of individual actions at Garrett's farm.

However, most historians, contemporary and modern, would follow the Baker-Conger version. Thus: Conger darts into the tobacco barn at Baker's heels. Prone on the floor the cripple sprawls like a toppled scarecrow. Immediately there is a squabble over who shot him.

As Conger subsequently testified in court: "I supposed he had shot himself. . . . I stooped over, looked down at him, and said he shot himself. Baker said, 'No, he did not!' He had the appearance of a man who had put a pistol to his head and shot himself, shooting a little too low; and I said again, 'He shot himself.' Baker said, 'No, he did not.' He spoke very positive about it. I thought it a little strange rather, as if he doubted my word when he said so."[22]

Baker did, indeed, doubt Conger's word. Facing a Congressional committee months later during the Johnson impeachment investigation, Lieutenant Baker had this to say about the shooting at Garrett's farm:

> I supposed at the time that Conger shot him, and I said, "What on earth did you shoot him for?" Said he, "I did not shoot him." Then the idea flashed on my mind that if he did, it had better not be known.[23]

There is a considerable variance between these later versions and the gaudy prose account presumably submitted by Colonel Conger.

And another verbal exchange between the two detective officers in the barn merits emphasis.

On the stand at the subsequent Surratt Trial, Baker testified that he said to Conger: "Someone shot him, and whoever it was goes back under arrest." Conger retorted that it was time to carry the dying man out of the barn. Baker then (according to his testimony) lifted the fallen man's head, and said: "It's Booth certainly!"[24]

We would like to know why Baker made that remark, and the tone he made it in. He must have been uncertain if the fallen man, as Conger described, looked a dead ringer for Edwin Booth. But we are now acutely aware of Conger's failings when it comes to veracity. That this wretched cripple, his features distorted by firelight and shadow, blurred by smoke smudge and smeared with grime—that this cripple could have resembled the ascetic Edwin strikes us as improbable. And now, his face in an

20 Wilson, op. cit., p. 181.
21 Holloway, op. cit.
22 Quoted in Eisenschiml, op. cit., p. 156.
23 Quoted in Wilson, op. cit., p. 182.
24 Baker's testimony, Surratt Trial.

agonized contortion, he is recognized with certainty by Lieutenant Luther Baker!

But the fire is closing in. There is no time to argue such a minor matter as identity. The Federal officers act with single-mindedness in this emergency—get that body out of there before one hundred thousand dollars is cremated!

Who carried the dying man out of the furnace? No matter. He was lugged from the burning barn and laid on the grass under a locust tree.

The man under the locust tree began to die in the best opera house tradition. Practically all the principals on the set took a hand in the production.

"Water!" Baker shouted. He carried a tin cup at his hip, and now he snatched the article and waved it at the audience.

Jack Garrett and his young brother Robert were frantically cranking the well. They wanted to save the barn. Conger, who had been half-heartedly forming a bucket brigade, saw that the conflagration was hopeless. The boys took the old oaken bucket to the dying man under the tree.

"I took Booth's head upon my knee and threw some water in his face," Baker reported. "His mouth being open, I poured some in his mouth."

The dying man strangled, blew the water through his teeth, opened his eyes. His breathing whistled and wheezed. His stare at Baker was agonized.

"[He] made his lips go as though he would say something," Baker recalled. "He said, 'Tell mother . . .' and then he swooned again."

Baker revived him with another splash of water. "I was washing his face all the time. He said in a whisper, 'Tell mother I die for my country.' Then I saw his wound. That was the first time I saw it. I saw that he was shot in the back of the neck."[25]

Rather odd that Baker saw the man's wound for "the first time" out there under the locust tree. By his own previous assertion, the detective lieutenant had raised the victim's head while the man lay prone in the barn. And Conger, in the barn, had observed that the victim "had the appearance of a man who had put a pistol to his head and shot himself, shooting a little too low." But the testimony of these two officers remained consistent only in inconsistency.

However, if Baker did examine the wound he must have noted that the bullet penetrated the victim's neck on the right side behind and below the ear. It cut in at a downward slant, drilled three vertebrae, and went clean through the neck, leaving a hole on the left side.[26] Baker, of course, was no physician. But it did not take a physician to see that a man thus shot

---

[25] Testimony quoted in Wilson, *op. cit.*, p. 183.
[26] Subsequent medical reports, Army Medical Museum, Washington, D.C.

through the neck would have had to present his profile to a marksman. Either that, or he had shot himself, pistol to ear, the muzzle slipping just as he pulled the trigger.

In the public view under the locust tree, neither Baker nor Conger bothered with such deductions. Soldiers crowded 'round. Doherty shoved forward. The Garrett boys fetched more water. Conger went to one knee beside the dying man. According to the detective officers, Booth made another agonized effort to speak.

"Tell mother I died for my country."

Conger bent his head to catch the words. To make sure, he repeated them aloud and asked the whisperer, "Is that what you say?"

According to historian Wilson, the dying man answered Conger in the affirmative "with head, eyes and lips."[27] We are not told how he did this "with head"—on a broken neck! One is left with the uncomfortable thought that Baker may have moved his head for him, nodding it up and down in the manner of puppet manipulation. For the dying man is, indeed, no more than a puppet—a dummy figure maneuvered at will by his captors. We know nothing of his thoughts, nothing of his words, if any. We are only certain that a man agonized by a punctured spinal cord does not utter stilted speeches in the best tradition of Victorian literature.

There are at least six versions of the "Tell Mother" speech. We have had the Baker version, and the Conger version. The newspaper version is even more interesting. We do not know which journalist was responsible, but the press telegraph put it this way: "Tell my mother I died for my country. You, Gentlemen, have spoiled my fun in Mexico." So saying, the assassin "died as frivolously and as hardened as he had lived."[28]

But the man shot through the neck took his time about dying. The heat from the burning barn began to sear the April leaves of the locust tree. Soldiers reported the barn beyond saving. One of the Garrett boys ran in to bring out furniture. He came out coughing, carrying one or two small items including the cripple's charred crutch. A wave of scorching wind smote the group under the locust. Conger ordered a retreat to the house.

The dying man was carried across the fire-reddened grass to Garrett's front porch. Miss Holloway noted that he was "to all appearance dead." Someone called for a mattress. Apparently they started to move him into the house. Agony revived him and he gasped, "No, no, let me die here! Let me die here!"

Conger stated that the man was then "laid on an old straw bed or tick or something."[29] Miss Holloway recalled that one of the officers (Doherty?) came up to look at the man. Seeing his eyes starkly open, the officer exclaimed, "The damned Rebel is still living!"

[27] Wilson, *op. cit.*, p. 183.
[28] New York *Daily Tribune*, April 28, 1865.
[29] Pitman, *op. cit.*

But even partisan Miss Holloway remembered the Federals as fairly humane. One of them asked her for a pillow. She flew into the house to fetch it. Wine was offered the dying man. He refused it. They tried to give him water, but it spilled from his mouth.[30]

The nearest physician was sent for—Dr. Urquhart at Port Royal. One of the troopers galloped off on this mission. Miss Holloway knelt over the paralyzed captive. As she would recall this episode: "Presently he protruded his tongue. I took my handkerchief and dipped it in water and moistened his lips. He said, 'Tell my mother I died for my country. I did what I thought to be best.' I again moistened his lips and he repeated the message to his mother."

Dear, romantic Miss Holloway! This is the fourth or fifth "Tell Mother" speech from the man who was shot in the burning barn.

But Miss Holloway did bathe the man's excruciated countenance. She tried to ease his pain with mothering lap and gentle hands. He begged to be placed first on one side, then on the other, then on his face. "We can't put you face down," Conger told him.[31] No position could relieve the pain. He fainted, came conscious again, stared upward.

"I can't stand it!" he gritted. "I want to die!"

But now Dr. Urquhart arrived on the scene, bringing with him (presumably) a medical kit and the voice of diagnostic experience. This physician made a perfunctory examination of the wound. At once he pronounced it fatal. He told the Federal officers the injured man could not live another hour.

Still there was plenty of time. All accounts agree that the dying man seemed to revive. He begged for water. Unable to swallow, he gasped at Conger, "Put your hand on my throat." Conger complied, pressing his fingers against the man's windpipe. An effort to cough purpled the contorted features. He seemed to be trying to dislodge splintered bone from his throat.

"Open your mouth," Conger said. "Let's see if you've blood on your tongue."

The man dropped his jaw and exposed his tongue as bidden. Conger informed him he had not been shot through the throat, his mouth was free of blood. The man's eyes squeezed shut in agony. He panted, "Kill me! Kill me!"

"We don't want to kill you," Conger told him. "We want you to get well."[32]

That speech may have been made out of kindness—a touch of sympathy for the sufferer. The likelihood is, however, that Conger spoke for audience benefit—for Miss Holloway and the press and perhaps Dr. Urquhart, if

---

[30] *Op. cit.*
[31] Wilson, *op. cit.*, p. 184.
[32] Wilson, *op. cit.*, pp. 184–185.

he were looking on. The fact seems to be that Conger itched with impatience to get the dying over with. He wanted to gallop off to Washington to report the big news to Headquarters.

The detective officers permitted Miss Holloway to tend the expiring captive. At end of the porch they paced out the deathwatch. It seems that the question of the shooting came up again. Probably they tried to decide upon some plausible story for Headquarters' consumption.

Accounts of the incident vary, but some historians say Conger launched a brusque inquiry among the cavalrymen, demanding to know if any of them saw a fellow trooper shoot the cripple in the barn. At this juncture, Boston Corbett stood forward to assert that he fired the fatal shot. Conger roared, "What'n hell do you mean, shooting in defiance of orders!" Or words to that effect. Whereupon (according to historian Wilson):

"Corbett drew himself up to his full height, and saluting, said: 'Colonel, Providence directed me.' "[33]

Oldroyd, DeWitt and earlier historians repeat the "Providence directed me" line. Suffice it to say, they are suspicious of Corbett's belated statement (as is Wilson). Delving deeper into the subject than his predecessors, Eisenschiml notes that Corbett's testimony, spoken under oath at the conspiracy trial, makes no mention of divine inspiration.[34] Under questioning on the witness stand, Corbett stated: ". . . one of the men told me that he [the man in the barn] aimed the carbine at me. He was taking aim with the carbine, but at whom I could not say. My mind was upon him attentively to see that he did no harm, and when I became impressed that it was time I shot him. . . ."[35]

Now who was the man who told Boston Corbett that the trapped cripple was aiming the carbine at him? Surely the Sergeant must have known the man's name. Yet he never offered it. To Baker and Conger (and apparently to troopers within earshot) he declared that he pulled the trigger at the urging of Providence.

Corbett's bold admission that he fired against orders must have surprised some of his fellow soldiers, particularly the three or four troopers who had heard from someone on the scene that the man in the barn had shot himself. Years later, one of those Civil War veterans told W. J. Ferguson that the man in Garrett's barn committed suicide.[36] Under oath Conger testified that he himself had believed the man a suicide, thereby contradicting his florid public report.

In light of such on-the-spot confusion, a singularly pertinent question rears its obvious head. Why didn't someone ask it of the victim? *Did you shoot yourself?*

---

[33] *Op. cit.*, p. 190.
[34] *Op. cit.*, pp. 153–54.
[35] Pitman, *op. cit.*, p. 94.
[36] Article in *Saturday Evening Post*, Feb. 12, 1927.

And some other pertinent questions might have been asked the dying man.

Conger dismissed Corbett bluntly. "We'll leave the matter to Providence and the War Department."[37] The Colonel made no pretense of believing the Sergeant's claim. Apparently he regarded Corbett, as did the regulars in the Sixteenth New York Cavalry, as a religious crank.

Conger, fretting to be off, finds the captive's prolonged suffering most uncongenial. So, unwilling to wait for the captive's demise, Conger and Baker begin to search him. Even as he lies snapping his teeth in mortal agony, he is frisked of his belongings as though he were already a corpse. Like his life, the smallest object on his person is now forfeit.

Conger dutifully lists the items. A leather holster. A soldier's knife. A pipe. A nail file. Some cartridges. A spur. A Canadian bill of exchange. A pocket compass smeared with candle drippings. A diamond pin. And a little red booklet—a diary!

Conger finds in a pocket of the diary five little photographs of young women. Then he thumbs through the booklet. Pencilled in hasty scrawl is John Wilkes Booth's own account of conspiracy plans, the assassination, the escape. Under an entry dated "Friday the Ides," Conger reads:

> Until today nothing was ever thought of sacrificing to our country's wrongs. For six months we had worked to capture. I struck BOLDLY and not as the papers say. I walked with a bold step through a thousand of his friends. A colonel at his side. I shouted Sic Semper BEFORE I fired.

This, in the assassin's own handwriting, is Booth's account of how he murdered Abraham Lincoln. Some of the Gascon bravado seems to have evaporated by the time he made his next entry, a week later. Dated April 21, the entry reads:

> After being hunted like a dog through swamps, woods, and last night chased by gunboats till I was forced to return wet, cold, and starving with every man's hand against me, I am here in despair. And why? For doing what Brutus was honored for—what made Tell a hero.

One detects in this diarizing the self-pity and heroics which infected the letters Booth sent to the press, to the authorities, and to Dr. Stewart. The diary goes on:

> The little, the very little I have left to clear my name, the Government will not allow to be printed.

He refers, here, to the missive he directed to the *National Intelligencer*—the screed he had given to John Matthews on the afternoon before the murder?

> Tonight [the diary continues] I try to escape these bloodhounds once more. I have too great a soul to die like a criminal.

---

[37] Paraphrased from quote in Van Doren Stern, *op. cit.*, p. 363.

Conger stares at a later entry: "I care not what becomes of me. I have no desire to outlive my country."

There are other entries. The little red book is full of rodomontade, self-pity and self-justification.

I do not repent the blow I struck. I may before my God, but not to man.

Finally Colonel Conger squints at the cryptic line: "I have almost a mind to return to Washington and clear my name, which I feel I can do."

When he read those last lines, the detective officer should have started asking some fast questions. No astute investigator could have failed to read the implication behind that entry. No quick-thinking intelligence officer would have passed up a chance to interrogate a dying assassin on the meaning of such a notation.

But Colonel Conger closed the little booklet with a snap. Thrusting it into his pocket, he stooped to scoop up the captive's lesser belongings. So far as is known, the detective colonel did not ask the dying man another question. Instead, he wheeled on Lieutenant Baker with a firecracker string of orders.

"I'm going up to Washington! If this man isn't dead within the hour, send up to Belle Plain for a surgeon from one of the gunboats. If he dies, commandeer a wagon and start for the capital. I'm going on ahead!"

With those, or similar, orders Conger sent for his horse. He wrapped the dying man's effects in a paper or a handkerchief. He said nothing about the startling entry in the little red diary.

Roosters are crowing. The flame glow from the barn and the pale gloom that presages sunrise tincture the early morning with an unnatural, eerie light. The officers look haggard, the troopers stir and mutter and yawn. To the saddle-weary, sleepless regulars, their thoughts on breakfast and reward money, the deathwatch is a bore.

To the cripple with the punctured spinal cord, it must have seemed an excruciating eternity. He sees the first red of sunrise streak the morning sky like a bloodstain. It will be a warm spring day. Sluggish pink smoke, thickened by morning fog, surges through the locust grove and stings the eyes of those on the farmhouse porch. "Water!" the dying man gasps. Miss Holloway moistens his shrivelled lips. He moans and clicks his teeth. He thirsts, but he cannot drink. His cheeks bloat and discolor. His eyes distend. He gargles and chokes. The officers, hearing, look down in frank relief. Miss Holloway gently smoothes the sweaty, tousled hair.

One of the witnesses noted that the dying captive wore "a gray woollen shirt, dark cassimere pants; one cavalry, or theater, top boot which drew up above the knees (sic), but was turned down when captured. On the other foot he had an old shoe."[38]

---

[38] New York *Tribune,* April 28, 1865.

A Washington newspaper culled from the death scene this feature story:

> Shortly before he (the captive) died he requested that his hands should be raised up. The request was complied with, and as he looked upon his hands he remarked: "They are useless now. Blood—blood—blood is upon them." These were the last intelligible words that he uttered.[39]

These last words are just too apt. But the story took root in history. It flowered in Oldroyd many years later, and was reverently reprinted by Wilson in 1929. To quote:

" . . . he gazed mournfully at them [his hands] and said, 'Useless! Useless!' These were the last words he spoke."[40]

In *The Death of Lincoln,* historian Laughlin quotes Booth's alleged dying words, and adds: "Whether he bemoaned the uselessness of his hands to fight for him, or the uselessness of their mad crime, God only knows. . . ."[41]

It can be stated with certainty that no other authority knows.

Queerly enough, Miss Holloway, who was with the dying man to the last, did not seem to hear this tidy curtain-speech.

According to her:

> The end was near. Then gasping three times and crossing his hands upon his breast, he died just as the day was breaking and the doctor was reaching the house. A stray curl that had fallen over my fingers while I had soaked the dying man's temples was cut off by Dr. Urquhart and given to me.

Although Miss Holloway seems to have forgotten the timing of the doctor's arrival, she was hardly the romanticist to forget such a dying speech as "Useless! Useless!" We are left to believe that even the last words of the man who died at Garrett's farm were contrived inventions put in his mouth.

Somehow the press dispatches to Europe failed to contain the classic "last words" attributed to John Wilkes Booth. As reported by the *Times* of London:

"The S.S. *Europa* brings news of the death of Booth, who continued to curse the Government to the latest moment. . . . However, [he] found an interval in which to send a message to his mother." But Britain's "Thunderer" insisted on grim death for the assassin who had approximated a regicide. "Such an end [as shooting] was too good for such a miscreant. He dies like a hero of a tragedy, but with execrations on his tongue, still defying the judgment of human tribunals."[42]

He died whispering at his hands, "Useless!"

---

[39] Washington *Daily National Intelligencer,* April 28, 1865.
[40] Wilson, *op. cit.,* p. 187.
[41] *Op. cit.,* p. 153.
[42] London *Times.* May 9, 1865. Also quoted in Wilson, *op. cit.,* pp. 193–94.

He died after gasping three times and crossing his hands on his breast. He died with "execrations on his tongue."

We may take our choice. Moralists chose the "Useless" theme. Romanticists liked the "folded hands" picture. Londoners preferred the lesson in anarchy. Had Tom Taylor written the story, perhaps the victim would have expired with a curtain line from Shakespeare. Had Poe written it, he might have had the dying man expire under the black locust in the front yard, while butcher birds impaled chunks of carrion on the tree's spiny thorns.

But it seems the story was written, in large part, by newspaper men who reported from hearsay. Which means it was slanted to suit the Federal officers on locale and in Washington, D.C. And one officer in particular; namely, Lafayette C. Baker.

Contemporary accounts would make much of the fact that the man shot at Garrett's farm was hit in the back of the neck just opposite the spot where Booth's bullet struck Lincoln. They would also dwell on the fact that he died almost at the same hour that Lincoln died.

Historians, baffled by the shooting controversy, would doubt that Corbett fired the fatal shot, and point to Baker or Conger. As noted by DeWitt, the wrangle could have been settled on the spot by an examination of the dead man's pistol and of Boston Corbett's gun. No such examination was made— whether by oversight, or intent is a moot question.

Strange to relate, no vintage or modern historian asks about Lieutenant Doherty. Where was *he* when the fatal shot was fired? Lieutenant Edward P. Doherty was in command of the cavalrymen on the scene. He was the officer who disposed the troopers around the Garrett farmhouse, collared Jack Garrett and rushed him to the tobacco barn, and planted soldiers around the barn in position to cover the side and rear doors. It was he who snatched David Herold out of the barn. And here is Doherty's action report of what happened next:

> Almost simultaneous with my taking Herold out of the barn, the hay in the rear of the barn was ignited by Mr. Conger, and the barn fired.
> Sergt. Boston Corbett, Company L, Sixteenth New York Cavalry, shot the assassin Booth, wounding him in the neck.
> I entered the barn as soon as the shot was fired, dragging Herold with me, and found that Booth had fallen on his back. Messrs. Conger and Baker, with some of my men, entered the barn and took hold of Booth.[43]

Doherty does not say he *saw* Corbett fire the shot. If his official report may be credited, he, Lieutenant Doherty, was first man *into* the barn. And Herold, dragged with him, was second. Significantly, neither Baker nor Conger mentioned Doherty and Herold as being there when they rushed in.

Could Doherty, then, have slain the man in the barn? According to his

---

[43] *Official Records*, Series I, Vol. 46, Pt. I, p. 1322.

report, the barn was set afire just as he yanked Herold out of the door. Did he swing around, using Herold as a shield? Plunge into the lighted shed, forcing Booth's accomplice ahead of him? And get off a fast shot at the surprised cripple who had turned to glare at the flames?

This seems more probable than Baker's firing the shot while Jack Garrett stood close by. As plausible, at least, as Conger shooting from the blazing corner of the building. And three times as probable as Boston Corbett firing through a crack "without knowing where the ball was going." What of Doherty's statement that Corbett shot the assassin? Easy enough for a fast-thinking lieutenant to pass the buck, especially when the buck could be made to materialize into reward money.

As will be seen, Lieutenant Doherty came in for the second biggest portion of the reward. But for reasons best known to the War Department, Doherty was never called to testify concerning the episode at Garrett's farm.

The Government was satisfied to attribute the shooting to Boston Corbett. When Corbett's self-declared action in violation of orders was reported to War Secretary Stanton, the Washington dictator waved the flag over the Sergeant's delinquency. Said Stanton: "The rebel is dead—the patriot lives—he has saved us continued excitement, delay and expense—the patriot is released."[44] In other words, reward money for Boston Corbett.

Today, the Government-sponsored Lincoln Museum in Washington credits Boston Corbett with killing the man who assassinated Lincoln. But almost no historian who has researched the episode believes that Corbett shot the man in Garrett's barn. Consensus: the trapped cripple committed suicide. But the shooting remains a mystery that has fascinated the experts since 1865.

Yet the question of who fired the shot seems a minor one compared with major mysteries left by the episode at Garrett's farm. Why, for example, did the Federal detectives fail to question the dying man? Any half-astute intelligence officer might have queried him on a dozen vital points. Where is John Surratt? Was Mrs. Surratt in on the plot? Who backed you in Richmond? How many people helped you in Washington? Pressures could have been applied to elicit answers. But for some reason best known to Conger and Baker, the man at Garrett's farm was allowed to die unquestioned.

So it eventuated that the major question was not "Who killed Cock Robin?" but "Who *was* Cock Robin?"

Some authorities who have researched the Lincoln murder case continue to ask that question to this day.

The man who might have answered it died about 7:00 A.M., on the morning of April 26, 1865, at Garrett's farm.

---

[44] Byron Johnson, *op. cit.*

CHAPTER **21**

A Body Is Buried

MOST reports say the bullet that felled the man in Garrett's barn was fired shortly after 3:00 A.M. Oldroyd times the shot exactly "at fifteen minutes past three on the morning of the 26th of April." The military reports are less specific. But the point is, the victim was slow in dying.

As Oldroyd tells it, the man "after lingering two hours and a quarter in terrible agony, died, just as the morning sun brilliantly lighted up the awful scene."[1] By Oldroyd's research, this would time the man's death at 5:30 A.M.

Miss Holloway would recall that "he died just as the day was breaking." Her account substantiates Oldroyd's. And she ought to have known, for she tended the man at the very last while he was *in extremis*.

However, Booth's biographer, Wilson, asserts that death occurred "about 7 A.M., and within twenty-two minutes of the time of day Lincoln died."[2] This was a Government-approved version published in the contemporary press.[3] Many vintage and modern historians accepted it as fact.

In contemporary report, neither Conger nor Baker nor Doherty offered the exact, or even the approximate, time of the captive's death. The point is noteworthy for two reasons. For one: considering the importance of the captive—America's Public Enemy Number One!—it seems extremely careless of these Federal officers not to have recorded the time he died. For another: if he was, in fact, shot about 3:30 and he did live until about seven (the Government-approved version), he was alive for nearly three hours and a half after the shooting. Under such circumstances, the Federal detectives would have had a wealth of opportunity to question the dying captive. If they did not do so, their handling of the case would be fantastically remiss.

All authorities agree that the victim at Garrett's farm lived for a

---

[1] *Op. cit.*, p. 76.
[2] *Op. cit.*, p. 187.
[3] The Washington *Daily Constitutional* (April 27, 1865) reported the shot fired at 4 A.M., death at 7 A.M.

time after he was shot. But the details of his death are so confused, blurred and contradictory that one is compelled to suspect deliberate "cover up."

The reports submitted by the Federal intelligence officers in the "Booth expedition" were as loose as the ashes of Garrett's tobacco barn.

Lieutenant Edward P. Doherty, U.S.A., was not a Federal detective, but a simple cavalry officer. Nevertheless he seems to have been the only one alert to the possibilities of on-the-spot prisoner interrogation. While Conger and Baker had been idling with the dying man on Garrett's porch, Lieutenant Doherty had gone to work on unhappy David Herold.

Undoubtedly the cavalry officer used rough soldier methods. Said one contemporary press account: "Herold is pronounced a mean, cowardly boy. He says he wishes Wilkes Booth had been dead before he had ever seen him. . . ."[4]

When Herold gibbered his fatuous remark about "liking Mr. Lincoln's jokes," one of the soldiers, infuriated, drew a knife. "Shut up, or I'll cut off your goddam head!"[5]

Oldroyd, employing a Victorian prose style, put it this way: "He [Herold] positively and constantly claimed that he was innocent, but was made to cease his talking."[6] But Doherty reported that he "conversed" with Herold,[7] a polite way of saying "interrograted," unless one wants to believe the cavalry officer engaged in a friendly chat.

Unfortunately Doherty left no record of that "conversation," or, if he did, the paper was somehow lost. Doherty's military report on the Garrett farm exploit went into a pigeonhole with some other items of evidence submitted to the War Department.

However, Herold was searched. A "small piece of a map of Virginia with other effects" were taken from him.[8] He blubbered and whimpered. Under pressure, he gave an account of Booth's weapons. He told his captors that Booth had carried two pistols and that the unused firearm must be in the burning barn.[9]

The following day prisoner Herold offered a detailed account of his doings at Garrett's farm to Special Judge Advocate John A. Bingham. Herold's version of the barn episode (or the Government transcript of Herold's version) is interesting. It substantiates some points of the fantastic capture story and skids significantly over others:

> Just before daylight, Booth waked me up & said that the cavalry had surrounded the barn. I said, "You had better give up." He said, "I will suffer death first." Mr. Garrett then came, and said, "Gentlemen, the

---

[4] New York *Daily Tribune,* April 28, 1865.
[5] Incident related in Ruggles, *op. cit.,* p. 193. Also contemporary news accounts.
[6] Oldroyd, *op. cit.,* p. 73.
[7] National Archives, War Dept. Records, File "C," Doc. E.B., p. 7, JAO.
[8] National Archives, War Dept. Records, File "B," Doc. 259, JAO.
[9] New York *Daily Tribune,* April 28, 1865.

cavalry are after you. You are the ones. You had better give yourselves up."
I am confident that he didn't reply to Mr. Garrett, but laid still. I moved
about in the straw. I didn't try to conceal myself at all. Booth says, "Don't
make any noise. Maybe they will go off, thinking we are not here." He
had hardly got the words out of his mouth when the Captain of the party
says, "I want you to surrender. If you don't, I will burn the barn down in
fifteen minutes." Booth then asked who he was and what he was after.
The Captain said he was after him, and wanted him. They passed several
words, which I don't remember exactly; but the amount of it was, he
wanted him to come out and give himself up, and before he came out Mr.
Garrett was to come in and Booth was to give up his arms to him. I had
no weapons at all, only a penknife. I had not even an overcoat. I was
dressed as I am now, except this vest. I traded my vest, which I tore in
getting over a fence, for this one. I traded it with a soldier, whose name
I don't know, on the road, in Virginia.

The Captain called upon Booth a second time to surrender, and told
him there were only ten minutes left. Booth got up, and wanted to know
the officer's authority. I told him, "You don't choose to give yourself up,
let me go out and give myself up." He says, "No, you shall not do it." He
spoke low to me and I to him. I begged him to let me go out. The officers
and the cavalrymen will tell you the same thing. I started for the door once,
when he threatened to shoot me and blow his own brains out.

The Captain then said only five minutes more were left, and the barn
would be burnt down. I said, "I am going; I don't intend to be burnt alive."
I went to the door & knocked. Booth says, "Let him out; that young man
is innocent." The Captain then said to me, "Whoever you are, come out
with your hands up." I did so. He took my gloves and a piece of a map;
that was all I had. The officer says, "Come, stand up by the house." He
caught me by the collar, and as I turned round I heard a pistol shot, looked
around, and saw one corner of the barn in a light blaze.

They jerked the barn door open. Booth was lying there. He tried to
say "Mother," or something of that kind. He [had] said to me, in a low
whisper, "When you go out, don't tell them the arms I have." He had two
revolvers, a bowie knife, and a Spencer rifle. The officers knew what he had.
Mr. Garrett told them. There were also some cartridges. Booth told the
officer that he would not surrender. He told him to open the door, and
draw his men up at fifty yards' distance, and he would fight them all, but
would not come out.[10]

At this point the military interrogator switched Herold's testimony off
on another tack. The prisoner offered no statement (or was not allowed to
make one) concerning subsequent events at Garrett's. No one asked him
if he heard the shooting controversy, or what hour it was when his companion died.

Colonel Everton Conger lit out for Washington just before the captive's
death was announced. The Colonel must have been staggering tired, but
with a $100,000 capture to report, he was off like a steeplechaser.

Lieutenants Baker and Doherty and their men seem to have been

---

[10] National Archives, War Dept. Records, File "H," R.B. (JAO) p. 38.

Bessie Hale.

JOHN WILKES BOOTH'S LADY FRIENDS

Unidentified woman.

Alice Grey.

JOHN WILKES BOOTH'S LADY FRIENDS

Effie Germon.

Helen Western.

JOHN WILKES BOOTH'S LADY FRIENDS

Fanny Brown ("Pretty Fay Brown").

Military Commission for the trial of the conspirators. *Left to right:* Harris, Hunter, Kautz, Howe, Wallace, Bingham.

Judge Holt (seated at left) and his staff.

The hanging of Mary Surratt, Lewis Paine, David Herold, George Atzerodt,
Jul. 7, 1865

Supposed photograph of Dr. Mudd.

Unidentified
conspirator.

Unidentified
conspirator.

Confederate decoding machine.

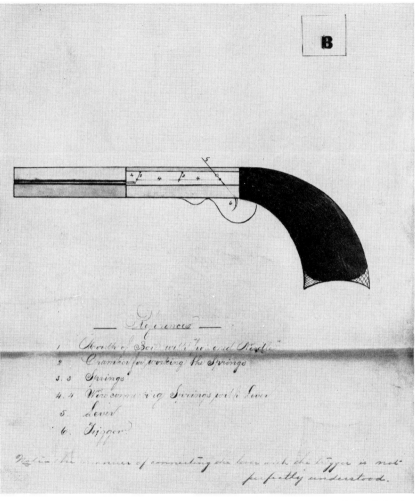

Secret Service sketch of needle gun.

Answer – I do recognize it, though it is very much altered since I saw Booth It looks to me much older, and in appearance much more freckled than he was. I do not recollect that he was at all freckled. I have no doubt it is his body. I recognize the features. When he came to my office, he had no beard excepting a moustache.

Question.– From the nature of this wound, even apart from the general appearance, you could not be mistaken as to the identity of the body?

Answer.– From the scar ~~wounds~~, ~~I think I~~ ~~could not be;~~ ~~but~~ I also in connection with the recognition of the features, which though much changed and altered, still have the same appearance, I think I cannot be mistaken, I recognize the likeness. I have no doubt that it is the person from whom I took the tumor, and that it is the body of J Wilkes Booth.

Jno Fredk. May, M.D.

Sworn & subd at Washington DC this 28th April 1865 before me, and I

A page of Dr. May's testimony.

John Surratt in the uni-
form of a Papal Zouave.

The return of John Surratt, from a contemporary drawing.

Madame Loreta Velasquez
(*The Woman in Battle*,
pub. T. Belknap,
1876)

Madame Velasquez in
military uniform.
(*The Woman in Battle*,
pub. T. Belknap,
1876)

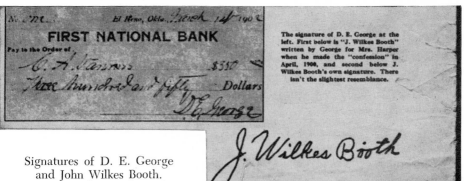

The signature of D. E. George at the left. First below is "J. Wilkes Booth" written by George for Mrs. Harper when he made the "confession" in April, 1900, and second below J. Wilkes Booth's own signature. There isn't the slightest resemblance.

Signatures of D. E. George
and John Wilkes Booth.
Courtesy *Dearborn Independent*
(Ford Motor Company)

Booth forgery.

PUZZLE FOR HISTORY

The photograph of David E. George, from Finis L. Bates' controversial book, *The Escape and Suicide of John Wilkes Booth*, was published with the caption: JOHN WILKES BOOTH, AGED 64 (*11 Days After Death*). *In the Morgue at Enid, Much Swollen from the Poison He Had Taken.* Was George actually Booth? Taking into account the age differential, the variations in pose, in pictorial perspective, in the quality of the photographs and their reproduction, and the fact that George is seen "11 days after death," one may make an interesting comparison of the George photograph with that of Booth (at right).

A Bertillon examination of the George features and those of the twenty-five-year-old Booth discloses some curious similarities. The hairline (George had dyed his hair) may be discounted, for Bates had the undertaker comb the dead man's hair as shown. However, the forehead structure, the general contour of the face around the eyes, and the jawline resemble Booth's. Although the George chin seems heavy, this could be photographic angle, the fleshiness of age, or the "swelling" which Bates attributes (probably inaccurately) to poison.

The George nose seems shorter than the Booth nose, but the top of the nose, the structure of the bridge, the indenture of the left nostril and the distance from nose to mouth bear some resemblance to Booth's.

Features change over the years, and alter in death. But one human facial feature that undergoes relatively little change is the ear (the French police, for example, consider it an infallible means of identification). Unfortunately the left ear in the George photograph is not clearly registered. It seems to show a heavy ridge through the concha (or shell) and the lobe seems thicker than Booth's. If the George head were turned slightly to the right, however, the ear might angle from the head much as Booth's. Its outline is not dissimilar.

Two striking similarities are apparent. George's hands (perspective considered) do seem long-fingered and large—characteristics remarked of Booth's. And the upward lift of George's right eyebrow is notably similar to Booth's.

If nothing else, the George portrait illustrates the fantastic difficulties of body identification in the day before scientific necropsies and fingerprinting.

equally enlivened. All were due to come in for a share of the reward money. Herold was worth $25,000; Booth, $50,000. This was only the Government reward. Numerous states, communities and private organizations had offered huge purses for the capture of Lincoln's assassin. Probably every soldier there was mentally counting and spending a small fortune—even Boston Corbett (though he later denied any mercenary interest).

Doherty jerked a saddle blanket from a horse at the gate and dashed to the porch. "We'll sew up the body in this," he told Baker. "Someone see if Mrs. Garrett can find a needle."

Horse blanket for a winding sheet! Sentimental Miss Holloway wept and turned away. The crude shroud was too short for the body. When Doherty finished the job, the dead man's boot and shoe protruded.

The corpse was treated to vehicular travel, though not out of respect. With four prisoners on his hands, Doherty was short of mounts. Otherwise the cadaver could have gone packsaddle.

The Garrett boys reported that their father didn't own a wagon. The war had stripped the countryside of vehicles, but Ned Freeman, a Negro, had an old ambulance, a quarter mile down toward Bowling Green. Doherty and several of his men went to commandeer it.

Veteran of Lord knew how many battlefields (the owner didn't), Freeman's ancient cart must have been in service since Bull Run. Warped, battered, creaky, with wobbly wheels and moth-eaten canvas top, it looked on its last legs even as it stood motionless in the Negro's dooryard.

But Freeman had a team of sorts, and he agreed to accept two dollars for the haul to Belle Plain. Doherty must have sensed the grim humor in carting a celebrated criminal's body in this wormy old conveyance. Describing that tattered ambulance, reporters subsequently wracked their lexicons for gloomy adjectives.

The body, roped to a board, was chucked into the ancient cart. The cavalry horses were led up to the outer gate. Doherty ordered the men to form up. A sergeant reminded him the platoon was short—they'd forgotten the troopers guarding Old Man Garrett on the block near the kitchen door.

Doherty ordered Garrett released. The agued farmer could scarcely talk when they freed him from his stand on the pedestal. Another delay was occasioned by the business of hoisting prisoners (Jett and the two Garrett boys) to horse.

At the start there was no horse for Booth's accomplice. According to one news account, the wretched Herold was compelled "to run behind a horse, with a rope wound around his neck."[11] Herold "complained bitterly." He said the rope hurt him. Doherty reported that he procured

---

[11] New York *Daily Tribune*, April 28, 1865.

an additional horse "after proceeding some distance."[12] It was too early a date for David Herold to die with a noose around his neck.

From the porch Miss Hollaway watched the ghastly parade form up in the road. The last glimpse she had of the celebrated visitor: the soles of his feet—one boot, one shoe—as the miserable ambulance started away.

One can imagine poor Miss Holloway standing there with a damp, dark curl in her hand, staring with tear-dimmed eyes at the retiring ambulance. Then at the bloodstained mattress, the bloodstained pillow, the bloodstained flooring of the porch, and finally at the curl—all that is left to her of that romantic guest.

Years later she wrote:

> After all had left and the family had become a little composed, I went to the bookcase to get some books for the children, as I was teaching school in the family at the time.
> The first thing that greeted my eyes were the opera glasses. I knew they did not belong to any of the family. I concluded they must be Booth's, so I took them to Mr. Garrett and asked him what I must do with them. He replied by saying: "Take them out of my sight. I do not wish to see anything that will remind me of this dreadful [affair]. . . . And during the day my brother [came] to Mr. Garrett's and [I] gave them to him to take up to my mother, thinking they were too valuable to be destroyed as Mr. Garrett had directed me to do.[13]

Detective Baker returned for those binoculars in forty-eight hours, accusing the lady of hiding valuable evidence. After she surrendered them she was left with nothing but her memories, and the bloodstained pillow case, and the curl.

These cherished mementos were to be taken from her by adversity. According to one account, she finally traded half of the stained pillow-slip for a barrel of flour. The other half of the pillow case apparently mouldered into dust. Robert Garrett came into possession of the curl.

The needy Garretts deplored the tragedy visited upon their homestead, but, ugly though it was, they accepted its dividends. They sold the bloodstained floorboards of the porch to souvenir hunters.[14] They collected on other little items. In July, 1865, John Garrett appealed for a Certificate of Attendance at the Conspiracy Trial so that he might draw his "Witness Fees." Colonel Lafayette Baker endorsed his application on July 18, 1865: "I respectfully recommend that John M. Garrett be paid the amount authorized by law, for attendance as Witness."[15]

Fifteen years later Robert Garrett wrote to the War Department from Louisville, Kentucky, offering to sell some interesting items to the Government. Excerpt from his letter dated January 13, 1880:

---

[12] *Official Records*, Series I, Vol. 46, Part I, p. 1321.
[13] *Op. cit.*
[14] Oldroyd, *op. cit.*, p. 293.
[15] National Archives, War Dept. Records, File "G," Doc. 748, JAO.

. . . I have preserved the relics. Among them are the mattress upon which he died, a piece of the crutch which he used, and a lock of his hair, cut off after his death . . . I can satisfy you that the relics are genuine. I have also a map upon which he traced the route he said he was going to travel from Richmond to Mexico.[16]

One might ask, of course, how the Garretts came to retain in their possession such articles of evidence as the fugitive's crutch and the map on which he traced a proposed route to Mexico.

Edwin Booth reimbursed the Garretts for the loss of the tobacco barn.[17] He was not in any way obligated to do so. This was just one of the many efforts that fine actor made to compensate those who suffered at the hands of his errant brother. The Garretts were doubtless amply paid for the old cedar barn and the furniture it had housed.

Some say the barn's fiery shell collapsed with a muffled crash, sending up a pyrotechnic shower of red sparks, just as the ambulance lugged the dead man away from Garrett's dooryard.

Journalist George Alfred Townsend, who contributed much copy to Lafayette Baker's *History of the United States Secret Service,* probably authored this description of the start for Belle Plain:

When the wagon started, Booth's wound, now scarcely dribbling, began to run anew. Blood fell through the crack of the wagon, and fell dripping upon the axle, and spotting the road with terrible wafers. It stained the planks and soaked the blankets . . . and all the way blood dribbled from the corpse in a slow, incessant, sanguine exudation.[18]

Suspecting this account was colored to suit Government taste, we must regard its purple hue with cautious skepticism. We know, for instance, that no journalist followed the wagon "all the way." We are not certain that Townsend followed it at all, except in imagination.

According to Lieutenant Doherty's official report, he himself "procured a wagon, sewed up the body in a blanket and placed it in the wagon."[19] The start must have been made at about 8:30. Baker and two guards escorted the ambulance cart at the head of the somber parade. With Baker rode prisoner Willie Jett. Doherty, with the rest of the cavalry troop and the other prisoners, brought up the rear. Probably David Herold moved at tag end of the procession.

Meanwhile a Federal officer had galloped into Port Royal with word that the cavalcade was coming. This officer (says Oldroyd) roused up James Thornton, the Negro ferryman.[20] He must have spurred Thornton to take him across the Rappahannock, and then sent the ferryman back

---

[16] National Archives, War Dept. Records, File 45, B.M.J., JAO.
[17] Ruggles, *op. cit.,* p. 213.
[18] *Op. cit.,* p. 505.
[19] *Official Records,* Series I, Vol. 46, Part 1, p. 1320.
[20] *Op. cit.,* p. 303.

to await the others. At any rate, the scow was waiting at the wharf for the processional. The historian does not name the officer who roused Thornton, but it must have been Conger, who was leading the race to Washington.

Up the road, perhaps an hour behind Conger, came the cavalcade from Garrett's farm. Baker's party led the procession, Doherty's troop brought up the rear. This grouping remains important because it bears on a most peculiar episode that presently transpired.

Entering Port Royal, Baker's group galloped down to the ferry landing. As described by Oldroyd (who years later interviewed the ferryman):

> When the procession came along the citizens turned out, surprised at the rude funeral car surrounded by an escort of cavalry. When a stop was made at the wharf, the curiosity of some led them to peer into the vehicle, but they were soon ordered back. All they could see was a pair of feet protruding from under a blanket. It was not long after the passage over the river until every inhabitant in Port Royal knew that the mysterious person was the assassin of the President.[21]

Baker, it seems, was in a ferment to get across the Rappahannock. Without waiting for Doherty's troop to come up, he loaded the ambulance and party aboard the ferry.

Oldroyd's (or the old ferryman's) description of the "funeral car" as being "surrounded by an escort of cavalry" is slightly inaccurate. Actually, only two cavalrymen rode guard on Freeman's antiquated ambulance. The rest of the van party consisted of young Lieutenant Luther Baker and young Confederate prisoner Willie Jett. There was room on the ferry for another man or two, but Baker did not delay. The scow was putting out when Doherty's troop arrived on the scene.

In a fret to get the bulk of the cavalcade across, Doherty had to wait while the ferry crossed to Port Conway with Baker's van, then came slow-poking back. It would take some time to transfer 25 horses and men and three prisoners across the river. Doherty probably had a feeling that the sooner the cavalcade got Booth's body out of Virginia, the better.

Apparently Baker entertained the same feeling. One may believe that the arrival of the body-bearing ambulance in Port Conway awoke this river town as it had roused Port Royal. The detective lieutenant has no intention of waiting in Port Conway for Doherty and the rest of the troop. Not with this body in his charge!

Next stop: Belle Plain on the Potomac.

But something happened before Lieutenant Baker's group reached Belle Plain.

About a mile above Port Conway the road forks. The right branch takes it northward toward Mathias Point. The left branch heads northwestward

---

21 *Op. cit.*, pp. 303–304.

across King George County, skirting the Rappahannock bend known as Skinner's Neck, and meandering on north to Belle Plain.

This Belle Plain pike was not the best road in Virginia, nor the worst; but it was rutted by spring thawing, and in many spots as rough as corduroy. And it was lonely. The region lying between the Rappahannock and the Potomac was (and still is in some areas) a densely wooded wilderness. There were no villages or hamlets on the old pike between Port Conway and Belle Plain.

Baker had reason for caution. The expedition to Bowling Green had come by this lonely route. He must have remembered the mileage through wilderness forest, the rough stretches, the potholes. However, he drove his little party hell-bent. Freeman's cart swayed and jounced on the ruts. The wheels wobbled and screeched in the forested silence.

To quote historian Oldroyd:

> All went well until, about half way between the ferry and the boat at Belle Plain, eighteen miles distant, the old ambulance broke down. There was no time or inclination to stop for repairs, so a new vehicle was pressed into service, and the journey continued, Edward Freeman returning home with his horses, leaving the old ambulance, dripping for the last time with human blood, to decay by the roadside.[22]

The ambulance breakdown should have been expected if the vehicle was as dilapidated as journalist Townsend described it. "Very shaky and absurd . . . wheels that ran in all directions . . . rattled like approaching dissolution."[23]

As ultimately reported in General Lafayette Baker's history, the old cart seemed to dissolve on the roadway. Suddenly a kingbolt snapped. The front wheels ripped out from under the wagon box. The fore end of the cart came a cropper in the dust as the team galloped on down the road. The broken cart slewed and crashed, and the body it carried slid half out of the wreckage "as if in a last effort to escape."

Rival newsmen borrowed this nice writing from the account wherein it originally appeared, and the story became widely featured as "the second escape of John Wilkes Booth."[24] A strange figure of speech, under circumstances which were odd enough to need no literary embellishment.

If the breakdown occurred as described by historian Oldroyd—"about half way between the ferry and the boat at Belle Plain"—it must have happened about nine miles from Port Conway. This would put it somewhere in the vicinity of that Rappahannock bend known as Skinner's Neck, a lonely, backwoodsy spot along the river.

As Oldroyd remarks, ". . . there was no time or inclination to stop for repairs." He might have added that there were no blacksmith forges or

22 *Op. cit.*, p. 78.
23 Baker, *op. cit.*, p. 506.
24 Contemporary press accounts, April 1865.

wagons shops on that side of the forest. So ". . . a new vehicle was pressed into service." This must have taken some doing.

Yet Lieutenant Luther Baker seems to have solved the problem at once. Colonel Lafayette Baker (or Townsend) tells us the lieutenant simply commandeered another wagon. The corpse was placed in this handy new conveyance. Lieutenant Baker's little party resumed the fast push for Belle Plain. Or, as Oldroyd tells it, the new vehicle was "pressed into service" and the old was "left to decay by the roadside." Next sentence: "Belle Plain was reached, and the boat started on its return to Washington."[25]

General Baker's history is equally abrupt in relating the mishap's conclusion. Other contemporary histories offer similarly abbreviated accounts. So the public was led to believe that the incident on the road between Port Conway and Belle Plain was an inconsequential misadventure.

But there is a hiatus here in the story. Three or four hours are skipped, leaving a blank page in the middle of official reports concerning the episode. Bits of information, however, filtered through the blank. Piecing these together, modern historians bridge some of the gaps in the hazy official continuity.

So we learn from Stanley Kimmel (*The Mad Booths of Maryland*) that Luther Baker encountered some Confederate soldiers on the lonely road. They asked him if he was escorting "a dead Yank." Baker assured them that he was. Alarmed by the encounter, he then raced for Belle Plain. Old Freeman was dragooned into continuing the journey. When they finally reached the Potomac, Baker sighted the *Ide* far upriver. He discovered that the Negro had taken him to an old steamer landing which had been abandoned during the war. "Apprehensive that shouts . . . might attract possible enemies, he [Lieutenant Baker] and the Negro hid the body in some nearby willows." Then "Baker ordered Freeman to wait while he rode two miles farther over a wandering road to the landing for aid." Returning with two sailors, he took the corpse upstream to the *Ide*.[26]

Kimmel's account leaves a new hiatus in the record—the blank wherein old Freeman is left alone for a couple of twilight hours with the body hidden in the willows. Understandably the War Department chiefs would not care to publicize the collapse of the ancient ambulance cart or the confiding of the corpse to the hands of a frightened Negro. The delay incurred in locating another vehicle, the fuss and bother on the open road— these were details for military abbreviation. But there was more to it than that. Something "out of the way" happened on that back road between Port Conway and Belle Plain, something Lieutenant Baker or his cousin Lafayette (or the Government) preferred to keep under wraps.

Historians have overlooked the matter because they were not advised that it existed. But tucked away in the War Department (Army) files was

---

[25] *Op. cit.*, p. 78.
[26] *Op. cit.*, pp. 259–260.

the report of Lieutenant Edward P. Doherty, U.S.A., commander Sixteenth New York Cavalry detached on expedition to (and from) Garrett's
farm.

We break into Doherty's report at the point where he starts his cavalcade
on its northward journey from Garrett's farm.

I then proceeded to Port Royal where we arrived at 9 A.M., April 26,
1865, and crossed the river in a scow. While crossing my command Mr.
Baker, without authority, moved off with the body of the assassin, taking
with him the two men who had been detailed as a guard to the body, also
one of the prisoners [Captain Jett, rebel].

I was some time crossing my command, and experienced some difficulty
in bringing Herold and the two Garretts along, having only one horse to
mount the three; thus delay was occasioned. After proceeding some
distance I procured an additional horse.

Fearing some accident might happen to the body of the assassin and the
prisoner Jett, whom Mr. Baker had taken with him, I dispatched an orderly
to tell Mr. Baker to halt. The orderly rode over four miles at full speed,
when, overtaking Mr. Baker, he told him to halt until the column came up.
This, however, Mr. Baker did not do, but continued on, missing me and
the road.

I arrived at Belle Plain at 6 P.M., and found the corpse had not yet
arrived. I felt great anxiety, and was about to apply to Major Bosworth,
Sixteenth New York Cavalry, who was at Belle Plain with his command,
for a detachment of men to go in search of the body when Mr. Baker
arrived. I immediately asked him where the prisoner, Captain Jett, was.
He replied, He did not know; he had escaped.

After a short delay the body of the assassin Booth was placed on board
the steamer John S. Ide, and we proceeded to Washington. . . .[27]

Lieutenant Doherty's report details one of the queerest episodes in the
entire pursuit-and-capture story. Doherty was worried. Not only was the
country between the Rappahannock and the Potomac densely wooded,
but this forested region was in Virginia, hostile territory in spite of Lee's
surrender. The woods were full of vagrant soldiery. Mosby's people were
in the neighborhood. It was no place for a $100,000 prize to "get lost."

Six P.M. brought sundown in April. It must have been after dark when
Baker finally showed up, with the body in a farmer's wagon. But where
is Confederate prisoner Willie Jett?

The answer to this question was never divulged to posterity by Lieutenant Luther Baker, his cousin, Secret Service Chief Lafayette C. Baker,
nor by War Department dictator, Edwin M. Stanton.

The missing Willie Jett was found and apprehended by the Federals
early in May. At that date he made his long and extremely lucid deposition on his original meeting with Booth and Herold. He described, too,
the manner in which he led the Federals to Garrett's farm early in the

[27] *Official Records,* Series I, Vol. 46, Part 1, pp. 1320–21.

morning of April 26. But there was no mention of his escape from the funeral party that afternoon.

As for Doherty's report, the War Department put it in cold storage. Lieutenant Edward P. Doherty won official commendation for his part in the capture of the fugitives at Garrett's farm, and also a spot promotion to captain, but he was not called upon to testify at the trial of the conspirators.

Doherty resented being thus ignored. He had captured and interrogated David Herold, Booth's intimate accomplice. He felt, with what seems considerable justification, that he could offer valuable evidence concerning the expedition to Garrett's farm. Accordingly, after the trial opened he took pen in hand. Doherty's letter to Headquarters is quoted herewith. The italics are his.

> Camp 16th N.Y.V. Cavalry
> Lincoln Barracks D.C.
> May 19, 1865
>
> Col. N. B. Sweitzer
>   Comdg. 16th N.Y.V. Cavalry
>   Colonel,
>
> The Assistant Judge Advocate told me that my testimony would not be taken at the Military Commission, now in session at the "Arsenal" Washington D.C.
>
> I consider this strange, from the fact that *I commanded* the detachment that captured Booth and Harold, and was the *only* Commissioned Officer present at the capture. I took Harold out of the barn *myself*—conversed with him, and had immediate charge of him, until I delivered him on the Gunboat to Col. Baker.
>
> In justice to my command and myself I call your attention to the above *facts.*
>
> I am Colonel
>
>> Very Respectfully
>> Your Ob't Servant
>> Edward P. Doherty
>> Capt. 16th N.Y.V. Cavalry.[28]

Captain Doherty's letter also went into the cold storage file, but some weeks after he wrote it he was listed for $5,000—the second biggest share of the reward money.

After an all-day gallop overland, Colonel Conger reached Washington on a blown mount about 5:00 P.M.[29] For two nights he had been without sleep. Under other circumstances, the detective officer would have been all in, but under the circumstances of fame and fortune, he dashed into

---

[28] National Archives, War Dept. Records, File "C," E.B., JAO, p. 7.
[29] Oldroyd, *op. cit.,* p. 78.

Secret Service Headquarters as though he were Mercury and had just arrived on Pegasus. Or so his high-speed delivery of the intelligence from Garrett's farm would lead one to believe.

Colonel Lafayette Baker was given the word at once. Conger also delivered to the Secret Service Chief the items of evidence taken from the man who had died on Garrett's porch. Colonel Lafayette Baker's semi-autobiographical *History of the United States Secret Service* indicates that Baker was highly elated by news of Booth's capture: "It is not often that I am unbalanced by tidings of any sort; but I sprang to my feet and across the room, and felt like raising a shout of joy over the triumph of justice. . . ."

Stanton's reaction to the "triumph of justice" was, it would seem, not quite so jubilant as the Secret Service Chief's. Or so the latter ultimately reported in his book.

Joyously excited, Baker shouted for his orderly. A carriage was rushed to the curb for his use. Taking Conger along, the Secret Service Chief leapt into the vehicle. They were driven at top speed to the War Secretary's residence on K Street.

The chief and the detective officer roused Stanton from a siesta. Here is Lafayette Baker's account of the incident:

> When I entered the room, he was lying upon a sofa. . . . I rushed into the room and said, "We have got Booth." Secretary Stanton was distinguished during the whole war for his coolness, but I had never seen such an exhibition of it in my life as at that time. He put his hands over his eyes, and lay for nearly a moment without saying a word. Then he got up and put on his coat very coolly.[30]

Lafayette Baker wrote or dictated that passage in 1866 when he was no longer Chief of the National Detective Police, no longer employed by the Government, and no longer on the "ins" with Stanton. Either his tongue bulged his cheek when he composed it, or his gray-green eyes were fixed on an ulterior motive.

For "coolness" had never been a Stanton virtue. Every person who knew the War Secretary, everyone who had dealings with him in Washington, knew that Edwin M. Stanton was given to excited shouting and frenzied outbursts. His frantic performance during the *Merrimack* crisis was well remembered by his intimates. Everyone on Capitol Hill knew of his wild rampage against General Sherman. At Seward's house on the night of the assassination he had been close to hysteria.

Future readers would see mockery in Lafayette Baker's description of Stanton's reaction to the news of Booth's capture. Eisenschiml suggests that when Stanton lay silent for a moment with his hands over his eyes "he exhibited all the symptoms of a person who dreaded a deadly blow."[31]

---

[30] *Op. cit.*, p. 540.
[31] *Op. cit.*, p. 150.

What (Eisenschiml asks) did Stanton expect to hear next? The historian wonders if Lafayette Baker intended to imply that Stanton was stricken with fright—the fear that Booth had been taken alive. Then, hearing that Booth was dead, he arose and coolly donned his coat.

Perhaps the analyst reads too much into Lafayette Baker's lines. Baker's pseudo-history cannot be taken too literally. If Baker desired to throw suspicion on Stanton, there was no need (by the time he published his book) to approach the subject with such devious subtlety. To give Stanton the benefit of doubt, he may have merely rubbed weak eyes after being suddenly roused from a nap.

Conger and Baker handed Stanton the items taken from the dead captive, including the little red book—Booth's diary.

The Secretary promptly directed the Secret Service Chief to requisition a tugboat, proceed to Alexandria, and meet the steamer coming up the Potomac with the assassin's corpse. The remains were to be transferred to monitor *Montauk*, lying off the Navy Yard. Lafayette Baker was to have charge of the body.

Conger and Baker departed at top speed. Conger doubtless repaired to a couch of dreams that featured an elegant mansion with a gilded gazebo and a stable of Arabian stallions. Hastening to the water rendezvous at Alexandria, Lafayette C. Baker probably entertained similar dreams, but with the mansion on a larger scale.

Entertaining his own dreams, War Secretary Stanton sat down to read the assassin's diary.

Up the Potomac chugged the Government tug, *John S. Ide*. Somber-sounding name, "Ide." Another one of those strange coincidences—that the body of an assassin who had been obsessed with the "Ides of March" should be lugged to Washington in a tugboat named *Ide*.

"I delivered over the body of Booth, Herold, and the two Garretts to Col. L. C. Baker, at 3 A.M. the 27th day of April, 1865."[32] So reported Lieutenant Edward P. Doherty upon arriving in Washington with his cavalry troop. But even this specified time proved discrepant.

According to Oldroyd's research: "The steamer *Ide* reached Alexandria at 10:40 on the 26th, and Herold and the body of Booth were transferred to the tug on which Baker [the Secret Service Chief] went. . . ."[33] Possibly Doherty was a stickler for form, and did not sign some sort of delivery manifest until three o'clock the following morning. In any event the two tugs must have rendezvoused around midnight. To continue with Oldroyd:

> The officer of the monitor *Montauk* stated that at 1:45 A.M., 27th, a tug came alongside, on board of which was Colonel Baker, the detective, with a dead body, said to be that of J. Wilkes Booth. . . . Said body was placed

---

[32] *Official Records*, Series I, Vol. 46, Part 1, p. 1322.
[33] *Op. cit.*, pp. 78–79.

on board for safekeeping. Herold was put in double irons and placed in the hold of the vessel. The body of Booth was taken out of the blanket in which it had been securely wrapped before leaving Garrett's farm, and placed on deck in charge of a guard.[34]

In the foregoing it is impossible to dissect Oldroyd's writing from the Navy's. Evidently the historian fell in with the Naval style in referring to "said body." The "securely wrapped before leaving Garrett's farm" sounds like the polite historian, if not like a horse blanket too short to cover the feet.

Not long after the corpse from Garrett's farm was placed on board monitor *Montauk*, a dispatch was sent by Commodore J. B. Montgomery, commandant of the Washington Navy Yard, to Gideon Welles, Secretary of the Navy:

> David E. Herold, prisoner, and the remains of Wilkes Booth were delivered here at 1:45 this morning. The body of Booth is changing rapidly. What disposition shall be made of it? It is now on board the iron-clad Montauk.[35]

By dawn the news was abroad in the capital. Workers abandoned their breakfasts and dashed for the horse cars. Gentlemen ordered their carriages. Congressmen requisitioned coaches. Ahorse and afoot, by every conceivable conveyance from wheel barrow to post chaise, the populace of Washington swarmed to the Navy Yard. To quote one account: ". . . thousands hurried down to the river, staring in grim fascination at the death-ship." Nobody was allowed close aboard the dark monitor. The body was not to be seen by the public. But word leaked ashore. Noon press wires hummed with descriptions of the assassin's corpse. By afternoon, typesetters in New York were preparing headline editions. The morrow's *Tribune* would say of Booth's remains: "His hair was badly matted, his clothing soiled, and the body looked more like that of some dirt-bearer than of the whilom fop."[36]

As noted by Commodore Montgomery, it had been subjected to "change." Manifestly he referred to the corruption of all flesh mortal after *rigor mortis* sets in. The journey from Garrett's farm to Washington had been hard on the passenger. Apparently there was no ice on the monitor. The corpse was laid out on an improvised bier on the iron deck. The horse blanket had been exchanged for a tarpaulin.

A canvas awning was stretched over the deck to shield the corpse and its inquisitors from the sun and from the inquisitive public eye. Under this airless tent rapid inquest was held in midmorning.

---

[34] *Ibid.*, p. 79.
[35] Dispatch quoted in Oldroyd, p. 79.
[36] New York *Daily Tribune*, April 28, 1865.

Surgeon General Barnes supervised the necropsy. Colonel Lafayette Baker was in subsidiary command. Other Government officials and military men at the inquest (as listed by Oldroyd) included Judge Advocate General Holt, Special Judge Advocate Bingham, Major Thomas T. Eckert, an unnamed officer (Barnes' assistant), William G. Moore (Clerk of the War Department), Lieutenant Luther Baker and Lieutenant Colonel Conger.

Before proceedings were begun, Stanton and Gideon Welles issued the following order to the Navy Yard commandant:

> Immediately after the Surgeon-General has made his autopsy, you will have the body placed in a strong box and deliver it to the charge of Colonel Baker, the box being carefully sealed.[37]

The order, of course, was dictated by Stanton who, as War Secretary, outranked the Secretary of the Navy. But Stanton's assumption of supreme command over this affair was odd in one respect. He was not the President of the United States. It seems strange that Andrew Johnson was not invited to inspect the body on the monitor. (At least, the War Department records make no mention of such an invitation.)

None of the officials on board the monitor had been personally acquainted with John Wilkes Booth. Perhaps they had studied his photograph, or glimpsed him at some time or another on stage—meaning in costume and make-up—but not one was qualified to identify the body.

Formal necropsy, however, was easy. The man was as dead as any who had been shot through the back of the neck.

Stanton would probably have liked the body buried before noon. But there was a peculiar difficulty: the corpse bore little or no resemblance to the photographic portraits of John Wilkes Booth.

Doubtless Stanton was satisfied that the matter resulted from "change," but someone in the party was troubled. This contorted corpse with matted hair, blotched forehead, wild eyes and snarling teeth—could it really have belonged to the matinee idol, once the Apollo of the footlights and the glass of fashion?

Identification was demanded. Stanton issued peremptory orders. Colonel Lafayette Baker must round up a number of witnesses.

Oldroyd states that the persons brought to monitor *Montauk* to view the body were these:

Charles Dawson, clerk at the National Hotel, well acquainted with Booth.

J. L. Smith (otherwise unidentified).

Alexander Gardner, well-known Washington photographer.

Timothy H. O'Sullivan, Gardner's assistant.

---

[37] Oldroyd, *op. cit.*, p. 79.

Dr. J. F. May, a Washington physician, "who had some two years before removed a tumor from Booth's neck."[38]

Oldroyd's list (like his standard account of the inquest) is incomplete. He leaves out a local dentist, Dr. Merrill, who seems to have been summoned to the *Montauk* that morning. And a local lawyer, Seaton Munroe, Esq., who was brought to the inquest by Judge Advocate General Holt. There may have been two or three others, whose observations, for reasons best known to Stanton, were stricken from the record. Lafayette Baker's history says a young woman was taken on board the vessel to look at the body.

> At the Government autopsy, April, 1865, one of General Baker's men took on board the monitor where Booth lay, a young woman who had known Booth. She cut a lock of hair from the dead man's head, but Baker, acting upon Stanton's order not to permit Booth tokens or souvenirs of any kind, took the lock of hair from the young woman.[39]

Baker's account would be more reliable if the woman brought on board to identify Booth were named. It could hardly have been Bessie Hale, for people would have recognized the Senator's daughter—the last thing Stanton would have risked. Laura Keene would have wanted no hair of the assassin's head. The sheared "lock" sounds like Ella Turner. So does the official censorship.

Stanton's reaction to the incident is substantiated by numerous accounts. Wilson states that Stanton was determined that no Southern sympathizer should have a chance to "gloat over the remains" or to "secure a trophy."[40] Soon after the body was buried, Government efforts were made to suppress the sale of all photographs of John Wilkes Booth.

If the effort was to "blot out" Booth, Stanton soon must have realized he had tried to censor the moon. Scores of Booth photographs were in circulation: little portraits known as *cartes des visites*, theatrical cards, Brady photos. The moment these were officially banned they became collectors' items. One month to the day after the body was buried, the War Department issued to various departmental commanders the following order:

> If you have prohibited the sale of photograph likenesses of J. Wilkes Booth, the Secretary of War directs that the prohibition be removed.[41]

Perhaps by that date Stanton had been made aware that a man could not be erased from existence even by a Government fiat, or perhaps he realized nobody would "rally around" Lincoln's assassin as a symbol. But the War Secretary's "no trophy" order may have stemmed from another,

---

38 *Ibid.*
39 Baker, *op. it.*, pp. 507–08.
40 *Op. cit.*, p. 241.
41 *Official Records*, Series I, Vol. 46, p. 1227.

deeper motive. It seems just possible he did not want that "lock of hair" to leave the monitor because that tangled and rusty strand did not resemble the curly, raven locks of the stage Adonis.

For similar reasons the War Department may have censored Booth's photograph—until such time, at least, as those who viewed the remains on the monitor forgot the grisly features of the corpse.

Newsmen heard that Alexander Gardner and Timothy O'Sullivan had boarded the *Montauk*. The *Tribune* reported:

> Yesterday a photographic view of the body was taken before it was removed from the monitor. It was then placed in an ordinary gray army blanket in which it was sewed up.[42]

The *Tribune* means the body was placed in the army blanket and sewed up, not the "photographic view." But that photograph might, indeed, have been sewed up with the shroud. Figuratively, if not literally, it was buried with the body from the *Montauk*. So far as is known, nobody ever saw that picture of the corpse which was taken on the monitor.

Undoubtedly Gardner gave the glass plate to Lafayette Baker or to Stanton. But the Secret Service Chief made no mention of it in his history. Stanton never mentioned it. War Department records are absolutely silent on the subject. The photograph never reached public domain. Perhaps it never reached the War Department files. The answer may lie undeveloped in the muds at the bottom of the Potomac.

The official inquest records on Booth's body are sketchy, to say the least. Stanton was too busy that morning to spend time on a coroner's board; news of Booth's capture had to go to the Army forces still out on the man-hunt. A thousand War Department details needed attention. About ten A.M. a messenger brought Stanton the following dispatch:

> Bryantown, April 27, 1865
>
> Hon. E. M. Stanton,
>   Secretary of War:
>
> I arrived here at 8:20. I think from all I can hear that Colonel Wells is on the right track, and that Booth and Herold are still on this side of the river.
>
> WINF'D S. HANCOCK,
> Major-General, &c.[43]

Stanton answered at once:

> Booth and Herold were traced by Baker to Garrett's barn, three miles from Port Royal, yesterday morning . . . Booth, in making his escape, was killed and Herold captured. . . . They crossed the Potomac Saturday night or Sunday night. Their horses were left in the swamp and should be secured; also all persons who aided their concealment.[44]

---

[42] New York *Daily Tribune*, April 29, 1865.
[43] *Official Records*, Series I, Vol. 46, Part 3, p. 987.
[44] *Ibid.*

This is the first news we have had that Booth was killed "in making his escape" from the burning barn. The War Secretary repeated it that morning in a number of messages to troops in the field. But, of course, one cannot look at official statements too literally.

Let us now view the corpse with the eye of some of the participants at the inquest. In particular, those who were credited by the authorities (and by many later historians) with positively identifying Booth's body.

From examination of Seaton Munroe taken by Brigadier General Joseph Holt, Judge Advocate General, United States Army, on board the monitor *Montauk*, Washington, D.C., April 27th 1865:

> Q. Have you examined carefully the dead body claimed to be that of J. Wilkes Booth, and now on board of this vessel?
> A. Only by close inspection of the features . . . I am confident that it is the dead body of J. Wilkes Booth.
> Q. Are there any special marks which enable you to recognize it?
> A. I recognize it only from its general appearance, in which I do not think I can be mistaken.[45]

Now it seems strange that this witness does not recognize any "special marks" on the body, but identifies it merely by "general appearance." Lawyer Munroe must have been professionally, if not otherwise, acquainted with Booth. Else why would the Judge Advocate General have bothered to bring him to the inquest? Yet the actor (as his friends could have declared) had been scarified by several stage battles, and by some fracases off stage. And Booth owned other "special marks."

Just two or three days before the capture at Garrett's farm, Secretary Stanton had received a letter from a Mr. H. C. Young of Cincinnati. The writer proclaimed himself a "loyal man" eager to aid the authorities in identifying the "villain Booth." This citizen wrote:

> I have known him well for several years, and have attended on him while sick at the Burnett House in this city about one year ago last month. If I remember right he has several scars on his arms & body and one either on the side of his head or on the forehead at the edge of the Hair, all of which he has told me, he received in stage fights, except one, which I believe is on his arm which I think he said a "lady" made. I also think and am pretty sure that he has the initials J.W.B. in india ink on one of his hands near the thumb. Although I have known him so well & would recognize him any where I never charged my memory with the above marks, for little did I ever think that a man who had been a friend of mine would commit the most outrageous crime on record.[46]

For one who had not "charged his memory," Citizen Young recalled booth's "marks" with considerable clarity. The youthful actor W. J. Ferguson could have detailed several of Booth's scars. It was Ferguson who saw Booth accidentally dagger himself on the stage at Ford's while

---

[45] National Archives, War Dept. Records, File "M," JAO.
[46] National Archives, War Dept. Records, File "Y," Doc. 18, JAO.

playing Romeo. Ferguson also knew that Booth had stabbed himself by mishap in Albany while playing Pescara in *The Apostate*. ". . . in falling, the actor's dagger fell first and he struck upon it, the point entering the right armpit, inflicting a muscular wound one or two inches deep."[47] Both injuries must have left scars. There was also the scar left on his face by Henrietta Irving.

It was odd that Judge Holt's witness missed these "special marks," but perhaps Mr. Munroe found the corpse too repugnant for close scrutiny. Too, scars have a way of fading. Probably many of Booth's intimates were unaware of his scarred armpit. He may have brushed his hair over the gash on his temple. None of these marks would have been quite so noticeable as initials tattooed on a man's hand.

In Booth's case, these initials are usually described as "pricked in india ink." A great deal was made of the "J.W.B." on the actor's hand. It would seem he showed those initials to Cox and Thomas Jones, to the Confederate soldiers on the road to Bowling Green, to the family at Garrett's farm. Apparently because of those initials he had assumed the name of "John W. Boyd." Willie Jett recalled them vividly in ultimate testimony after his recapture. (Jett recalled, too, that Herold was "tattooed," and had tried to rub the "H" off his forearm.)

One would think, then, that the "J.W.B." would have been an infallible identification mark. After researching the matter years later, Booth's biographer, Wilson, came to believe it so. He wrote that Booth possessed "one distinctive mark of identification of which too little had been noted, the initials 'J.W.B.' which were pricked in India ink on his right hand." Wilson avers that since the corpse did possess this distinctive initialling, that fact should have gone far to settle the matter of identity.

Why, then, was "too little" of that fact "noted"? Why, for instance, did witness Seaton Munroe fail to notice it? *Did* the corpse have the initials "J.W.B." on its right hand?

Evidently it did.

Charles Dawson, clerk at the National Hotel, "identified the body of Booth by the initials on the hand." In so doing, Dawson stated, plausibly enough, that he had "frequently observed" Booth's hand when the actor was signing the hotel register. And he had chided Booth, saying: "What a fool you were to disfigure that pretty hand in such a way." Yet Wilson notes Booth's hand was big, ". . . a large hand about which he often jested."[48]

Years later, the guard on deck, Sergeant Peddicord, recalled seeing the initials "J.W.B." on the corpse's hand.[49]

---

[47] Quoted in Sandburg, *op. cit.*, p. 313.
[48] Wilson, *op. cit.*, p. 275.
[49] Letter published in Roanoke (Va.) *Evening News*, June 6, 1903, as noted in Wilson, *op. cit.*

Wilson also tells us that historian Oldroyd told *him* (in 1927) that Henry Clay Ford, "one of Booth's most intimate friends," had viewed the body "which had just been brought up from the Garrett farm." Ford assured Oldroyd the body "was certainly John." For there were "the same old India ink initials on his hand."

But Colonel Oldroyd, relating this anecdote to Wilson, went on to state that he was "positive that all those who knew Booth intimately, all the actors who had last appeared in the same plays with him . . . went to the Navy Yard and identified the remains of Booth."[50]

What became of the records concerning this mass identification? The War Department files in the Archives contain no such bulky data on the *Montauk* inquest. Who were "all those actors" who went to the Navy Yard? Contemporary news accounts say nothing of a flock of theater people going out to the monitor.

Why did historian Oldroyd leave out this important detail when he published his history of the case in 1901? When Oldroyd published that Government-approved volume, he made no mention of the initials "J.W.B." on the dead man's hand.

Wilson says that Oldroyd *did* mention the initials "pricked into his [the body's] hand."[51] But Wilson slips up. Here is the statement made in Oldroyd's volume: "His body was fully identified by the initials on his arm in India ink. . . ."[52]

His hand? His arm? Where were those initials on John Wilkes Booth? Hotel clerk Dawson saw them on the right hand of the corpse. So, apparently, did Sergeant Peddicord. Years later Thomas A. Jones said he saw them on Booth's right arm. Willie Jett and others testified they saw them on Booth's hand.

However, secret intelligence had other information, missed by Wilson's research and by the research of latter-day historians. On the very day the fugitive was shot at Garrett's farm, official word from Baltimore—Booth's home town—was dispatched to War Secretary Stanton. The message follows:

Baltimore, April 26, 1865.

Hon. E. M. Stanton,
Secretary of War, Washington, D.C.

Sir: The following marks are upon the person of Booth by which he may be recognized: On his right arm are the initials of his name, and on his left hand, between the forefinger and thumb, a small cross, and across the same hand several spots, all in India ink.

J. L. McPhail,
Provost-Marshal-General, State of Maryland.[53]

---

[50] *Ibid.*, p. 275.
[51] *Ibid.*, p. 197.
[52] Oldroyd, *op. cit.*, p. 80.
[53] *Official Records*, Series I, Vol. 46, Part 3, p. 963.

No wonder the War Department made "little" of the "J.W.B." on the corpse's right hand!

Historian Wilson points to another means of positive identification: Booth's teeth. A dentist, Dr. Merrill, was brought to the *Montauk* to view the corpse. No subsequently published account seems to contain this practitioner's first name, but it was said he had recently filled (or "plugged," to use the contemporary term) two of Booth's teeth.

Wilson tells us the jaws of the corpse were forced open. The "well-known Washington dentist" peered in. The fillings were "fully identified."[54]

Parenthetical is the fact that in 1872 such a necropsy was employed to solve a famous Baltimore murder mystery, the Goss-Udderzook case.

Mr. Goss, an inventor, staged an explosion and fire in his laboratory. A charred corpse was found wearing Goss's jewelry. Widow Goss applied for the insurance. Mutual Life, Knickerbocker and Travelers insisted on careful autopsy. A dentist visited the morgue. The teeth in the charred skull bore "plugs" and a crown which were not the inventor's. Goss was later tracked to New Jersey.[55]

Criminologists at the time made much of the case as a pioneer in the science of dental identification, but perhaps the Balitmore authorities had never heard of Dr. Merrill's probe on board the *Montauk* seven years before, when the dental work of the corpse was "fully identified" as John Wilkes Booth's.

There was one marking borne by John Wilkes Booth which experts considered as indelibly his as the brand on a valuable horse. It was left upon Booth's person by a surgeon. It has come down to us through history as the "Mark of the Scalpel."

The surgeon who left this mark on Booth was a Washington practitioner, Dr. John F. May. We do not know how the inquest officials became informed on the actor's surgical scar, or May's operating. Perhaps Lafayette Baker's detectives heard about it. Perhaps the clue came from David Herold. While the inquest proceeded on the *Montauk's* deck, it seems that Herold was being grilled in the bowels of the monitor. At any rate, the testimony elicited that day from Herold contains the following:

Q. When, if at all, did you first become acquainted with J. Wilkes Booth?

A. I do not remember exactly. I think I was a clerk with Wm. S. Thompson, Druggist, corner of 15th St. and New York Avenue, two years ago this spring. It was the night Booth played the "Marble Heart"—about two years ago, the time when Booth had a ball taken from his neck by some Surgeon in Washington.[56]

---

[54] Wilson, *op. cit.*, p. 199. Dental identification also noted in Van Doren Stern, *op. cit.*, p. 399.

[55] Baltimore newspapers, February 6, 1872–October 1873.

[56] National Archives, War Dept. Records, File "H," R.B., JAO.

In 1887 Dr. May wrote a detailed account of the inquest episode, prefacing this with a description of the operation he performed on Booth. Because identification of the surgical scar was taken by the authorities as absolutely conclusive, May's essay has since been accepted as conclusive evidence.

The surgeon's story (briefed) goes as follows:

"Some time before the assassination," a handsome young man, accompanied by a friend, entered May's office. The handsome man introduced himself as Booth, and said he was playing an engagement with Charlotte Cushman. He wanted a "lump" removed from the back of his neck, provided the operation did not keep him off stage, and asked Dr. May to report the operation as "removal of a bullet."

Dr. May recognized the lump as nothing more than a "fibroid tumor" [evidently the type commonly called a wen]. Of course, it did not contain a bullet. The surgeon was puzzled by Booth's request, but decided to "humor" the patient. [Why did Booth invent the "bullet" tale? Probably typical braggadocio, indicative of Booth's puerile love of self-glorification.]

Dr. May removed the wen. He warned Booth that it would leave a noticeable scar if the wound were broken before it healed. The closure "united perfectly." But about a week afterward, Booth rushed into the office with the wound torn open. It seemed that in the play, Miss Cushman had embraced him so forcefully that the "wound opened under her grasp." The result was "a large and ugly scar."

On the morning of April 27, 1865, Dr. May was summoned to the *Montauk* inquest. "As I was very busily, and as I thought, more usefully engaged in rendering services to the living, than in examining the bodies of the dead . . . I did not respond. . . ." Then Dr. May received a second summons. ". . . I deemed it most prudent to obey. I therefore started for the Navy Yard. . . . On the way a third messenger was met on his way to my house, who was no less than the chief of the detective corps, the noted Colonel Baker." Colonel Baker conducted Dr. May to a cabin on the *Montauk*, "where the commissioners were in session."

May was led out on deck. There was the body "concealed by a tarpaulin cover." Surgeon General Barnes and an assistant stood by.

> By his [Barnes'] order the cover was removed, and to my great astonishment revealed a body in whose lineaments there was to me no resemblance to the man I had known in life! My surprise was so great that I at once said to General Barnes, *"There is no resemblance in that corpse to Booth, nor can I believe it to be that of him."* [Emphasis supplied.]

Then May asked if there was a scar on the body's neck. Barnes said there was. May described it. Barnes exclaimed: "You have described the scar as well as if you were looking at it. . . ."

May's reminiscent account concludes: "The body being turned, the back of the neck was examined and my *mark* was unmistakably found by me upon it." At Dr. May's request, the body was then placed in a sitting position. "Looking down on it, I was finally enabled to imperfectly recognize the features of Booth. But never in a human being had a greater change taken place, from the man whom I had seen in the vigor of life and health, than in that of the haggard corpse . . . its whole facial expression sunken and sharpened by the exposure and starvation it had undergone. The right lower limb was greatly contused, and perfectly black from a fracture. . . ."

Dr. May's essay, containing the foregoing account, was read to the Columbia Society of Washington, D.C., in February, 1909. Wilson quotes it at much length, calling it an "invaluable contribution."[57]

The surgeon's written account contains some small discrepancies. Before writing his memoir, Dr. May should perhaps have consulted the War Department Records. Therein he could have found his on-the-spot testimony as transcribed during the *Montauk* inquest.

On file, this interesting document was entitled: "Examination of John Frederick May, taken by Brigadier-General Joseph Holt, Judge Advocate General, United States Army, on board the Monitor *Montauk*. Washington D.C., April 27th 1865."

In this question-and-answer testimony, May described Booth's tumor operation and Miss Cushman's reopening of the wound. Then (to quote the testimony):

> . . . I told the Surgeon General these facts this morning before I looked at the cicatrix at all, and said that he would probably find a large ugly looking Scar, instead of a neat line. He said it corresponded exactly with my description. The scar looks more [crossed out] as much like [the effect of] a burn [as the cicatrix from] a Surgical operation.
>
> Q. Have you, since you came on board this vessel, examined the dead body which is alleged [note the wording] to be that of J. Wilkes Booth?
>
> A. I believe it to be Sir; I have no doubt that it is. I believe I have only seen Booth once since the time to which I have referred.
>
> Q. Do you recognize the body as that of J. Wilkes Booth from its general appearance, and also from the particular appearance of the Scar?
>
> A. I do recognize it, though it is very much altered since I saw Booth. It looks to me much older, and in appearance much more freckled than he was. I do not recollect that he was at all freckled. I have no doubt it is his body. I recognize the features. When he came to my office, he had no beard excepting a moustache.
>
> Q. From the nature of this wound, even apart from the general appearance, you could not be mistaken as to the identity of the body?
>
> A. From the wound [crossed out and written over] Scar, I think I could not be [crossed out and written over] but I also recognize [crossed out and re-written] in connection with the recognition of the features, which though much changed and altered, still have the same appearance,

57 *Op. cit.*, pp. 202–207.

(I think I cannot be mistaken). I recognize the likeness. I have no doubt that it is the person from whom I took the tumor, and that it is the body of J. Wilkes Booth.[58]

A strange document, considering. And here are some of the things one might consider.

(1) May says Booth's scar resembles the cicatrix *of a burn*. (2) The corpse is *freckled*. Dr. May does not recall (nor does anyone else) Booth as being freckled. (3) In his later essay May states he could not recognize the body when he first saw it. In original testimony he tells Judge Holt he had *no doubt* it was Booth, although "very much altered." (4) Testifying, May declares that *he could not fail to recognize the body by the Scar*. This is crossed out, carefully re-worded. So is his next statement. The result is a garbled paragraph, as though May is sputtering uncertainly. (Incidentally, such erasure and re-wording constitutes a "palimpsest." Today such alteration, unless initialed by the deponent, would automatically invalidate a document.)

Two more points raise question-marks over the statements of Dr. May.

Booth's "alleged" body was drilled through the neck, but Dr. May makes no mention of the bullet-holes and their relation to the "Scar." Neither in testimony nor in later account does he locate the scar on the corpse with professional exactitude. Could it be that the shot through the neck damaged or distorted the surgical cicatrix?

Finally, Dr. May's essay says the "right leg" of the corpse was broken. But Booth broke his *left leg* when he jumped to the stage at Ford's Theater!

Immediately after Dr. May's examination, Surgeon General Barnes performed an autopsy. Two "spinal spools" were removed from the neck of the corpse. These vertabrae showed that the man had been drilled through the spinal cord. The "spools" were delivered to the Army Medical Museum in Washington.[59] The body was delivered over to Colonel Lafayette Baker.

As Oldroyd relates the story:

> At 2:45 the same day [April 27th] Colonel Baker quietly took the body away, leaving the officers at the Navy Yard astonished by its sudden departure. The commandant called for an explanation by the marine officer. . . . He said: "This unusual transaction deprived me of the opportunity of inclosing the body in a box prepared for it by the Department. The box is now on board the *Montauk*. . . ." Colonel Baker, with the assistance of Lieutenant L. B. Baker, and sailors to row the boat, took the body down the Eastern Branch, and around to the landing . . . of the Arsenal grounds. . . .[60]

---

[58] National Archives, War Dept. Records, File "M," JAO.
[59] They are there to this day.
[60] *Op. cit.*, pp. 80–83.

This departure of Baker and cousin with the body created more than a stir among the Navy Yard officials. According to the Secret Service Chief, he ordered the corpse taken from the monitor in late afternoon. The body was lowered into a skiff in full view of the crowds ashore. Then they lowered an enormous ball and chain into the skiff, and pulled away. The ball and chain were intended to make the onlookers think Booth's corpse would be buried at sea.

The crowds acted as Colonel Baker had expected—pushed and mobbed along the riverbank in effort to trail the skiff. Baker boated on down through the twilight to Geeseborough Point, a dark, desolate and dismal marsh where the Army "cast its condemned horses and dead mules." In this reeking sludge of animal carcasses and skeletons, Baker and nephew waited until midnight. Then they rowed upstream to the channel leading to the landing of the Arsenal Penitentiary.[61]

Relishing the grisly, Baker adds dime-novel melodrama to the scene. The timing is controversial, but the continuity is roughly accurate. Some time that night the body was spirited through pitchy dark into the Arsenal. Wrapped in an Army blanket, it was placed in a gun box with the name "BOOTH" lettered on the underside of the lid.[62] Then it was buried in a shallow hole in the corner of a vault where ammunition was normally stored. The ground was smoothed over so it would look undisturbed.

But this body was not going to rest.

While Lafayette Baker and his cousin, Lieutenant Baker, were playing hide-and-seek with the body in the gruesome marshes of Geeseborough Point, the dictator in the War Office was issuing military dispatches.

Stanton's gorge must have risen at the confusion and delay at the inquest. From the War Office he dashed off a telegram which remains on record.

WAR DEPARTMENT
Washington City, April 27, 1865—9:50 P.M.

Major-General Halleck,
Richmond:

A rebel officer named Willie Jett conveyed Booth from the Potomac across the Rappahannock. He has gone to Richmond. Please have him looked up, arrested, ironed, and sent here.

Edwin M. Stanton[63]

How did Stanton know Jett had gone to Richmond?

---

61 Baker, *op. cit.*
62 Witness testimony quoted in Wilson, *op. cit.*, p. 296.
63 *Official Records*, Series I, Vol. 46, Part 3, p. 967.

Thomas B. Florence published the *Daily Constitutional Union* in Washington. Its editorials were considered "anti-Government." It had the reputation of being "sensational."

Pro-Administration factions tend to call any anti-Administration paper "sensational" as a matter of course. The paper's masthead proclaimed it to be "an Independent, Union, Democratic, Conservative Newspaper." But shortly after the *Montauk* inquest Florence's journal exploded a front-page bombshell.

The *Constitutional Union* screamed, "Hoax!" It said Booth's capture, death and burial amounted to fraud, and it contended Booth had escaped.[64] The Richmond *Examiner* copied. "We know Booth escaped." Press wires flashed the sensation across the country. Said the Louisville *Journal*, "Baker and his associates have wilfully conspired to swindle the United States Treasury."[65]

Touched off was a stormy controversy that would embarrass the Government from there on out. The issue has never been satisfactorily settled.

Was it Booth's body?

Lafayette C. Baker said yes.

War Secretary Stanton said yes.

The Government avowed an official yes.

Washington officials to this day say yes.

But a number of scholars, researchers and interested parties came to say no.

In consequence, some historians believe *The Constitutional Union* might have been right.

Others say maybe.

And those willing to accept the word of Stanton and Lafayette C. Baker and Dr. May state that the body was John Wilkes Booth's.

When the question first exploded, the War Department rushed the case into its top-secret files. Speedily furnished other sensations, the public (as was expected) forgot about Booth.

The Government wanted to let the sleeping dog lie. But (unexpectedly) men and events began kicking the sleeping dog. Eventually the War Department had to open its files, but by that date items of evidence were gone, key documents were missing.

The fact is that *all* the facts of the Booth case were not, and never will be, divulged. From Garrett's barn to secret grave in Washington Arsenal, the story is as devious and murky as a mystery serial which contains insoluble clues and has no final installment.

No one knows who shot the fugitive in the barn.

Or how long he lived after he was shot.

---

[64] Noted in Wilson, *op. cit.*, pp. 198–99.

[65] Contemporary newspapers, Library of Congress.

The body is spirited off through wilderness by Lieutenant Baker, who also takes with him Confederate Willie Jett.

The party with the body disappears for a time, during which Jett escapes to Richmond.

The corpse which eventually reaches Washington bears "no vestige of resemblance" to John Wilkes Booth. It "changes."

Identification must therefore rest on "special marks." One witness fails to note such marks. A second sees "J.W.B." on the corpse's hand. But a secret intelligence report says the initials are on Booth's arm.

A dentist presumably identifies the teeth. But the inquest officials are not satisfied. (And for good reason, since dental identification is in its infancy.)

So identification finally depends on a surgical scar—which resembles a burn. But the surgeon's original testimony concerning the scar is garbled. We are never told the exact location of the cicatrix. Afterwards the surgeon's memory proves erratic (or does it?). He says the *right leg* of the corpse was broken.

The secret inquest is rushed, the corpse suddenly removed from the war vessel. Finale: a burial episode which might have been devised by the Brothers Grimm, but was probably designed by that other storyteller, Lafayette Baker.

Why the super secrecy?

Why the frantic haste?

Why the high-speed inquest, especially after the body seemed "doubtful"? One may believe responsible officials, wanting to make doubly certain, would have called many witnesses—close friends of Booth— *members of his family!* Good citizen Edwin Booth would have come at once. So would his mother or Rosalie. *At time of inquest, Junius Brutus Booth was no farther away than the Old Capitol Prison!* He was not summoned to identify the body.

And why was it not shown to Dr. Mudd or the other conspiracy suspects, including Mrs. Surratt? Or perhaps to Ella Turner. And if their testimony was subject to mistrust, certainly two other witnesses could have been called upon to identify the remains. What of Miss Bessie Hale and (of course) Louis Wiechmann? None of these persons was summoned to the inquest.

The records are so confused that no historian knows with certainty who attended the inquest. Oldroyd stumbles on the detail. Wilson tells us that Colonel Clarence Cobb, intimate friend of Booth, was sent to the inquest by Paymaster Benjamin Price. Surgeon General Barnes informed Cobb that his visit was unnecessary since no more witnesses were needed. He told Cobb that "he [Barnes] and nine others had fully identified the body."[66] Meaning only ten people saw the cadaver? But Barnes himself

---

[66] Wilson, *op. cit.*, p. 199.

apparently did not "identify" the corpse. In a brief on the Lincoln Assassination issued by the Medical Museum of the Armed Forces Institute of Pathology (Washington, D.C., 1957) the statement is made that "Surgeon General Barnes and his assistant probably examined Booth's neck only, since that was the part showing cause of death." An odd qualification under the circumstances.

One final means could have been employed to certify identification. In possession of the War Department was the left boot taken from the injured fugitive by Dr. Mudd. At a moment's notice this boot could have been produced for comparison with the one on the corpse. But this simple measure was not applied.

So the record fogs and fades, as mysterious as that never-seen photograph taken by Alexander Gardner.

This we know: Identification of the body rested largely on the "Mark of the Scalpel"—the scar left on the back of Booth's neck by Dr. May's surgery.

This we know also: Immediately after Dr. May gave his testimony, Surgeon General Barnes performed an autopsy and removed two "spinal spools" from the neck of the corpse.

And when Barnes cut into the nape for those "spinal spools" what happened to that all-important identification mark on the back of the neck?

On the day Booth's capture was announced General Lafayette Baker received a lady visitor. The lady was Madam Loreta Velasquez, confederate espion given to masquerading as Lieutenant Harry Buford, complete with whiskers.

In a memoir published by Madam Velasquez in 1876 (*Women in the War*), she tells of calling on Baker in his Washington hotel. On this occasion she was clad in feminine finery, and Baker received her graciously. Another visitor, a gentleman, was there. In the course of conversation he remarked, "I'm glad they got Booth." According to Madam Velasquez, Baker replied, "So am I. I intended to have his body dead or alive, or a mighty good substitute for it."

One can only wonder what a Confederate spy was doing in Baker's headquarters in Washington. And, of course, Baker's mention of a "substitute" adds another question mark to the riddle.

PART

V

Conspiracy Is Tried

The quality of mercy is not strain'd;
It droppeth as the gentle rain from heaven.
Upon the place beneath; it is twice bless'd . . .
— *Merchant of Venice*

In as much as the military is a more arbitrary and despotic system than the civil, so is even-handed justice the more necessary in it. Mercy (which is one form of favoritism) should not be confounded with kindness. It implies wrong known both to the offender and the judge. Justice and mercy are totally incompatible. There can be no such compound as justice seasoned with mercy. The least particle of the latter destroys the former.
— BRIGADIER-GENERAL JAMES B. FRY
Army and Navy Journal, Sept. 22, 1883.

CHAPTER 22

"Court of Death"

THE TRIAL OF Booth's accomplices formally opened on May 9, 1865, but court proceedings did not fully get under way until the 10th.

On that day Jefferson Davis was captured as he fled through Irwinsville, Georgia.

On that day Lincoln had been five days entombed in his burial vault at Springfield.

And on that day a dreary file of eight prisoners clanked into the dock of the makeshift courtroom in Washington's Arsenal Penitentiary to face trial for murder and an assortment of other crimes on charges that have baffled inquiring judicial minds ever since.

The accused were tried by an extemporized Military Commission. Not one (not even Lewis Paine) could be charged with first-degree homicide. But charges included attempted homicide, accessory to assassination, subversive activities, and aiding and abetting Lincoln's assassin. All eight of the accused were charged with treason by the general indictment, and that charge alone could mean a death sentence.

It was held that Lincoln's assassination was a military crime. That the President was killed "while actually in command of the army, as Commander-in-Chief." For this reason "the conspirators were excluded from any right to a trial in the civil courts."[1]

Stanton, naturally, sponsored this view. On his own initiative, the War Secretary had decreed that all who had aided or abetted Booth should be subject to the death penalty. Throughout the war he had favored military trials under martial law whenever occasion furnished the pretext.

But Andrew Johnson, President of less than a month, was troubled. Evidently he suffered some doubt about the legality of a military trial under the present circumstances. At least, he was not prepared to issue a White House fiat without support from the Government judiciary. Before deciding the matter, President Johnson appealed for the legal opinion of Attorney General James Speed. Should the parties charged with conspir-

---

[1] Oldroyd, *op. cit.*, p. 115.

ing to assassinate President Lincoln be tried before a military tribunal or handed over to the civil courts?

The trial began in May, but Speed's opinion concerning its legality did not appear in print until July—after the trial was over! This led at least one critic, ex-Attorney General Edward Bates, to suspect that Speed's opinion had been "gotten up . . . to bolster a jurisdiction, *after the fact.* . . ."[2] Oldroyd, however, implies that Speed answered President Johnson's inquiry before the question of the military trial was decided.[3] Johnson's biographer, Lloyd Paul Stryker, does not discuss the matter in his volume. In fact, Stryker does not discuss the trial of Booth's accomplices. Presenting a favorable portrait of Andrew Johnson, the biographer may have considered the Military Commission a blemish for which the new and inexperienced President was not responsible.

At any rate, Attorney General Speed's opinion (whenever arrived at) read as follows:

> That if the persons who are charged with assassination of the President committed the deed as public enemies, as I believe they did, and whether they did or not is a question to be decided by the tribunal before which they are tried, they not only can, but ought to be, tried before a military tribunal. If the persons charged have offended against the laws of war, it would be palpably wrong for the military to hand them over to the civil courts, as it would be wrong in a civil court to convict a man of murder who had in time of war killed another in battle.[4]

And from the White House had come the following Presidential Order. One may note the date in support of the contention that Johnson had first conferred with his Attorney General before sponsoring the military trial.

Executive Chamber
Washington City, May 1, 1865

Whereas the Attorney General of the United States hath given his opinion:

That the persons implicated in the murder of the late President, Abraham Lincoln, and the attempted assassination of the Honorable William H. Seward, Secretary of State, and in an alleged conspiracy to assassinate other officers of the Federal Government at Washington City, and their aides and abettors are subject to the jurisdiction of, and lawfully triable before a Military Commission.

It is ordered. 1st. That the Assistant Adjutant General detail nine competent military officers to serve as a Commission for the trial of said parties, and that the Judge Advocate General proceed to prefer charges against said parties for their alleged offences, and bring them to trial before said Military Commission; that said trial, or trials, be conducted by the said Judge Advocate General, and as Recorder thereof, in person, aided by such Assistant, or Special Judge Advocates as he may designate, and

---

[2] Quoted in Eisenschiml, *op. cit.,* p. 230.
[3] *Op. cit.,* p. 115.
[4] Quoted, *Ibid.*

that said trials be conducted with all diligence consistent with the ends of justice, the said Commission to sit without regard to hours.

2d. That Brevet Major General Hartranft be assigned to duty as Special Provost Marshall General for the purposes of said trial, and attendance upon said Commission, and the execution of its mandates.

3d. That the said Commission establish such order, or rules of proceeding as may avoid unnecessary delay, and conduct to the ends of public justice.

Andrew Johnson[5]

The Assistant Adjutant General lost no time in appointing the "nine competent military officers to serve as a Commission." There seems to have been no delay over the question of "competence." In fact, the celerity with which the Assistant Adjutant General selected the nine would almost lead one to suspect that the nine had already been hand-picked by someone a little higher up than an Assistant Adjutant General. It seems apparent that the selective hand belonged to Edwin M. Stanton.

The officers appointed to sit as judges on the tribunal were:

Major General David Hunter, U.S.V.
Major General Lew Wallace, U.S.V.
Brevet Major General August V. Kautz, U.S.V.
Brigadier General Alvin P. Howe, U.S.V.
Brigadier General Robert S. Foster, U.S.V.
Brevet Brigadier General James A. Ekin, U.S.V.
Brigadier General T. M. Harris, U.S.V.
Brevet Colonel C. H. Tompkins, U.S.V.
Lieutenant Colonel David R. Clendenin, 8th Illinois Cavalry.

Big guns of the tribunal were the ranking generals: Major General David Hunter, who served as presiding officer, and Major General Lew Wallace.

Hunter was a stern soldier. No one could doubt his patriotic dedication to the Union Cause. Personal friend of Lincoln, he had accompanied the "Rail Splitter" on the President elect's uneasy journey from Springfield to Washington in '61. During the war he had commanded troops in action against Jubal Early. The Confederates hated him because he had burned V.M.I. and had organized Negro regiments. He was in War Secretary Stanton's confidence—which does not mean he toadied to Stanton, but suggests that Stanton saw in Hunter a general who might be used. Discipline and duty were shibboleths avowed by David Hunter. But neither by training nor predilection would he prove an impartial jurist.

Lew Wallace was another Hunter—a dedicated volunteer, a veteran combat leader with opinions forged in the crucible of Shiloh, a general who could call Secession suspects "scoundrels" and at drop of a hat order such "scoundrels" heavily ironed. Wallace would be best remembered as author of *Ben Hur,* a best-seller that made him a fortune in subsequent

---

[5] National Archives, War Dept. Records, "Adjutant General's Office."

years. It was said that he became a Christian while researching the Biblical background for the novel, but in 1865 he seems to have believed the sword mightier than the pen. On the Military Commission he displayed all the qualities of a "hanging judge."

The other members of this military tribunal—with the possible exception of Foster and T. M. Harris—were ranking non-entities on the pages of history. General Foster, at least, seems to have adhered to the early Anglo-Saxon concept that the accused must be held innocent until proven guilty by the evidence. In that, Foster served on the Commission as an officer of distinction.

General T. M. Harris distinguished himself in the other direction. Years after the drama (in 1892) Harris wrote a little volume on the assassination and the conspiracy trials. The book proved to be a depository of erroneous data, arbitrary opinion and flagrant bias. For example, the General states: "The Canadian conspirators are . . . shown to have been drinkers. All of their diabolical schemes are most probably the product of . . . alcoholic stimulants."[6] A fair-minded thinker would, of course, have wondered about alcohol's influence on General Grant. In addition to these failings, General Harris admitted to an abysmal belief in quackery. For he as much as stated that his judgments had been influenced by phrenology!

Writing of Dr. Mudd, General Harris declared:

> He [Dr. Mudd] might just as well have admitted his complicity in the conspiracy. Mudd's expression of countenanace was that of a hypocrit. *He had the bump of secretiveness largely developed* [emphasis supplied] and it would have taken months of acquaintanceship to have removed the unfavorable impression made by first scanning of the man. He had the appearance of a natural born liar and deceiver.

In Harris' behalf it may be noted that during the early Gaslight Era the pseudo-science of phrenology became something of a fad. Criminologists for a time tried hard to detect such qualities as cunning, deceit, avarice, rapacity and homicidal tendency in the "bumps" and configurations of the individual cranium. All men with low, bushy eyebrows were potential murderers (except those who weren't). Conical heads meant this; bulging temples meant that. But the whole fantasy was pretty much exploded in the mid 70's when a ferocious criminal presented the authorities with a head that owned almost exactly the same cranial measurements as Daniel Webster's.[7] That General Harris, as of the 90's, continued to believe in phrenological humbug says something for his judicial capacities.

As "conductors" of the trial before the military tribunal, Stanton appointed (or approved the appointment of) Judge Advocate General Joseph

---

[6] T. M. Harris, *op. cit.*, pp. 76, 77, 80.

[7] The criminal was a murderer named Edward (Dr. Lurio) Ruloff. After he was hanged in Binghamton, N.Y., for a series of vicious crimes, his head was kept for years in a glass jar at Cornell University.

Holt, Judge Advocate Henry L. Burnett, and Special Judge Advocate John A. Bingham.

Brevet Major General John F. Hartranft received the unpleasant assignment to a tour of duty as Special Provost Marshal in charge of the prisoners.

To accommodate the trial, a room on the third floor of the Arsenal Penitentiary was hastily converted into a court. Space must have been at a premium when the judges were sitting, the prisoners were in the dock, prosecution and defense counsel were on the floor, reporters and correspondents were at table, witnesses and military guards were present, and the audience flocked in. Oldroyd reports the improvised courtroom as being "thirty by forty-five feet square," (an exceedingly peculiar square); and adds that the ceiling was "about eleven feet high, supported by three wooden pillars." There were four windows with heavy iron gratings which "afforded tolerable ventilation." Two anterooms accommodated court and witnesses.[8]

"The room was whitewashed and painted for the occasion." Furnishings included "cocoa matting" for the floor, and new tables and chairs. "Gas was introduced in case the court should protract its sittings until after dark."

The members of the Military Commission were seated at a long table which ranged one side of the room. On the opposite side was a table for court reporters, correspondents and defense counsel. In center floor: the witness stand, facing the judges' table. The prisoners sat in line-up on a platform which extended across the far end of the room. According to Oldroyd this platform was "raised about one foot from the floor." It was "about four feet broad, with a strong railing in front of it."[9] But the historian who details all this trivia gives us next to nothing on the intellectual dimensions of the trial.

As has already been noted, the decision to try Booth's accomplices (or alleged accomplices) in a military court had, at the outset, raised serious doubts in the mind of one distinguished jurist. But the question of a military *vs.* civil trial remains, perhaps, debatable. On the military side it may be argued that the war *was* going on when Lincoln died by assassination, the President *was* Commander-in-Chief of the nation's armed forces. And some of the accused were suspected of enemy partisan or espionage activities.

The competence of the Military Commission was another matter, as was the validity of the trial procedure. Strangely enough, no contemporary or later critic forcefully summarized what seems a most patent flaw in this so-called trial of the conspirators.

For the trial opened on May 9—just twenty-two days after the arrest of Mrs. Mary Surratt.

---

[8] *Op. cit.*, p. 116.
[9] *Ibid.*, p. 119.

Paine, too, had been under arrest only a little over three weeks.

O'Laughlin and Arnold had been in prison only a little over three weeks.

Atzerodt had been less than three weeks under arrest.

Dr. Mudd had been less than three weeks under arrest.

David Herold had been just two weeks in prison.

What this meant to the accused can be imagined by the plight of the insignificant Spangler. Penniless, virtually friendless, the incoherent stage hand did not have counsel at court until three days after he went on trial![10]

Held incommunicado, in solitary confinement, none of the other defendants in the dock had been able to procure counsel until the last, desperate minute. And none of the defendants (with the possible exception of Paine) had a clear idea of the charges they were going to face.

On the 10th of May, all eight, including Mrs. Surratt, found themselves facing charges which could cost them their lives.

Enter the prisoners.

They file in through a door at the left-hand end of the dock. Arnold first. Then Dr. Mudd, Spangler, O'Laughlin, Atzerodt, Paine, Herold, and Mrs. Surratt. Each of the male prisoners is followed by a soldier in the horizon blue of the Veterans Reserve Corps. The guards sit with them—or, as noted by Oldroyd, "sandwiched between them."

As the prisoners moved to their places, "their fetters clanking at every step, they formed an impressive procession."[11]

The men were ironed with so-called "stiff shackles"—handcuffs fixed to a metal bar which held the wrists pinned about fourteen inches apart. These paralyzing manacles prevented any independent movement of the hand. To impede the prisoner's pedal extremeties, the ankles were shackled by iron cuffs connected by a short length of chain. Paine and Atzerodt were further burdened by ball and chain. Dragging their chains, the men hobbled and lurched to their seats.

Ben Perley Poore dashed off some journalistic sketches of the prisoners in the dock.

> Sam Arnold was of respectable appearance . . . with dark hair and beard and good countenance. Spangler, the stage-carpenter, was a chunky, light-haired, rather bloated and whisky-soaked looking man. Atzerott (sic) had a decided lager beer look. . . . O'Laughlin might have been taken for a native of Cuba, short and slender, with luxuriant black locks, a delicate moustache and whiskers. . . . Payne (sic) was . . . tall, muscular, defiant, with a low forehead, blue eyes, thin lips, and black, straight hair, with much of the animal and little of the intellectual. Dave Herold was what the ladies call a pretty little man, with cherry cheeks, pouting lips, an incipient beard, dark hazel eyes, and dark, long hair. . . . Dr. Mudd . . . was about sixty years of age, with a blond complexion, reddish face, and blue eyes.

[10] Eisenschiml, op. cit., p. 237.

[11] Oldroyd, op. cit., p. 120.

Concerning the unfortunate woman in the dock, Poore wrote:

> Mrs. Surratt naturally attracted the most attention as she entered the room where the Military Commission was held every morning, the irons which connected her ankles clanking as she walked. She was a rather buxom-looking woman dressed in deep black, with feline gray eyes, which watched the whole proceedings.[12]

Poore invalidates his sketches with such biased adjectives as "feline" for Mrs. Surratt's eyes. His and similar reports would raise a storm of controversy in regard to Mrs. Surratt's "chains." The day's pictorial press represented the unhappy widow as laden with irons. The subject created much angry debate after the trial.

Some observers insisted that Mary Surratt was neither manacled nor chained. Historian Oldroyd notes the exception in her behalf.

> General Hartranft was severely censured for placing manacles upon Mrs. Surratt, and he answers this charge by saying that he was marshal of the court . . . [and] during this period of over two months she never had a manacle or manacles on either hands or feet, and the thought of it was never entertained by anyone in authority. She was shown some favors while in prison. Being a woman, she was allowed to choose what she wished to eat, while the other conspirators were fed army rations.[13]

A critical eyewitness, Colonel Henry Kyd Douglas, C.S.A., ex-staff officer of the famous "Stonewall Brigade," substantiates General Hartranft's "official" statement. Needless to say, this young Confederate did not cherish any bias in favor of the conspiracy trials and the Federal authorities in charge. He was there himself as a prisoner, and he resented his involvement.

Douglas kept a journal. In it he recorded his impressions of that court as he saw it. He thought the male prisoners (Paine excepted) were "generally a sorry lot, low enough to be capable of any crime." He described Mrs. Surratt as "rather an attractive and amiable looking woman, a widow, 'fair, fat and forty.'" Douglas goes on: "Mrs. Surratt was not ironed during the trial." He notes that General Hartranft "would not permit it." And he adds that the General "sent her daily from his table not only the substantials but the delicacies. . . ."[14]

This humane and gentlemanly conduct on the part of General John Hartranft did not follow the official War Department attitude by any manner of means. If she was not burdened with chains, Mrs. Surratt was weighted in the dock by the invisible irons of a military justice determined to exact its pound of flesh. If the lady was at all perceptive, she must have suffered as painfully as any of her chained and manacled fellow prisoners.

[12] Poore, *op. cit.*, pp. 184–86.
[13] Oldroyd, *op. cit.*, p. 132.
[14] Henry Kyd Douglas, *op. cit.*, p. 344.

Court opened at the stroke of ten on a Wednesday morning. Proceedings began with a reading of the Presidential Order that convened the Commission. The prisoners were asked if they "had any objections to any member of the Commission." By way of answer "they all severally replied they had not."[15]

This formality briskly observed, the judges of the tribunal, the Judge Advocate General and his assistants, and the court reporters were sworn. Then the prisoners were arraigned.

The eight accused were jointly charged with "maliciously, unlawfully, and traitorously, and in aid of the existing armed rebellion against the United States of America . . . combining, confederating, and conspiring, together with . . . Jefferson Davis . . . and others unknown, to kill and murder, within the Military Department of Washington . . . Abraham Lincoln . . . and lying in wait with intent . . . to kill . . . Andrew Johnson . . . and . . . Ulysses S. Grant. . . ."[16]

Counsel for the defense would be quick to note that this blanket indictment was full of holes. Holes as big, say, as the one Atzerodt walked through when he departed for Rockville on the morning after the murder. Holes as obvious as the question of Mrs. Surratt's "lying in wait" with intent to kill anybody. Surely Dr. Mudd had "lain in wait" for nobody in his back-road domicile near Bryantown. And the thought of shabby Spangler "combining, confederating and conspiring together with . . . Jefferson Davis" should have provoked mirth in any court that retained a vestige of humor.

In turn, each prisoner stood up to plead, "Not guilty."

The accused had been informed of the right to engage counsel.

Right to procure counsel was all but negated by the inability of the prisoners to contact suitable lawyers. Shortly before the trial commenced, the Judge Advocate's Office forwarded bids from the defendants to various law agencies or attorneys in the locality. On the day court opened most of the prisoners were still desperately attempting to obtain defenders. Several attorneys had flatly refused to represent Mary Surratt. Typical was Mr. H. F. Zimmerman's rejection of her case. On May 11, this lawyer wrote to Assistant Judge Advocate Burnett:

> Yours of yesterday come to hand, informing me that Mrs. Surratt, desired to see me to consult about obtaining Counsel for her; I desire to say that my acquaintance with Mrs. Surratt is but a store acquaintance; our family never visited each other; and I therefore decline having anything to do in the matter.[17]

---

15 Oldroyd, *op. cit.*, p. 127.
16 Pitman, *op. cit.*, pp. 18–19.
17 National Archives, War Dept. Records, File "Z," Doc. 288, JAO.

Dr. Mudd was in similar straits, as is evinced by the following exchange.

May 9, 1865

Dr. Morgan
Maryland Ave., Washington
Sir

Samuel Mudd, now on trial before a Military Commission in this City has expressed a desire to see you in reference to the employment of counsel. Please attend to this matter at once. By reporting at this office you can procure a pass.

Very respectfully
H. L. Burnett

The reply came back:

Dear Sir,

About three or four months since I was cassually (*sic*) introduced to Dr. Mudd, but never having any intimacy, I decline the interview with him.

Your Obt. Servt
James E. Morgan[18]

The day after trial opened, Burnett wrote in Dr. Mudd's behalf to an attorney named Henry A. Clark. Clark bluntly refused to serve.[19]

But a defense team eventually assembled.

The Hon. Reverdy Johnson, Mr. Frederick Aiken and Mr. John W. Clampitt for Mrs. Surratt.

General Thomas Ewing, Jr., for Samuel Arnold, Dr. Mudd and Spangler.

Mr. W. E. Doster for Paine and Atzerodt.

Mr. Walter Cox for Michael O'Laughlin.

Mr. Frederick Stone for David Herold.

The defense mustered some able pleaders in Reverdy Johnson, General Ewing, Walter Cox and William E. Doster. Facing anything like a conventional court of justice, these four would undoubtedly have reduced to a pulp the bill of indictments drawn up by the War Department lawyers.

Keystone of the defense team was Reverdy Johnson. When solicited to appear in behalf of Mrs. Surratt, he had accepted at once. His name must have sent a shudder through the Cromwellian soul of the Military Commission. A free-thinking individualist, Reverdy Johnson combined in his stout person and personality the staunch independence of a John Adams and the common-sensical courtroom wisdom of a Holmes.

The Baltimore lawyer was a devoted Marylander, but first, last, and in between an American, dedicated to the principles of Democracy and the Bill of Rights. It was said he had a vocabulary of "only six hundred words" —refreshing brevity in a day of torrential forensics. It was also said of him

---

[18] National Archives, War Dept. Records, File "M," Doc. 268, JAO.
[19] National Archives, War Dept. Records, File "C," Doc. 283, JAO.

(by a Judge Dennis) that he "was cursed by neither nerves nor liver, but [was] the robust embodiment of *mens sana in corpore sano*."[20] Reverdy Johnson was blind in one eye. But Reverdy Johnson could see more and farther with his good right eye than many a contemporary jurist equipped with austere, gold-rimmed glasses.

A citizen with the courage of his convictions, Reverdy Johnson had never been afraid to stand up alone and be counted. He had made a name for himself as a pleader of unpopular cases. When Maryland sent him to the Senate he frequently stood in solitude, voting against the impassioned majority.

In an era of religious prejudice, Reverdy Johnson had risked anathema by advocating Christian tolerance and liberalism. Should streetcars be allowed to run on Sunday? No, says the Hon. Waitman T. Willey of West Virginia. Allow horse cars to run on Sunday, and we "violate the laws of God." Senator Johnson smiles at this Sabbatarian with a twinkle in his good right eye. "We may make our conduct conform to their general spirit," he says of Scriptural injunctions, "but a literal construction would be inconsistent with the purpose which the Maker of the World intended."[21]

In an area containing a large pro-Slavery element, Reverdy Johnson had spoken out as a Freedom advocate. "I have thought slavery wrong since I was capable of thinking!" He denounced human bondage as an institution calculated to "shock the heart of every free man which beats true to the inspiration of the Goddess of Liberty."

The Civil War was not yet over before the segregation issue aroused acrimonious controversy in the District of Columbia. Willard Saulsbury of Delaware sponsored a "Jim Crow" law to prevent Negroes from riding on Washington streetcars. This, in the capital of the nation which had warred "to make men free!" Reverdy Johnson countered: "If a black man proposes to ride in a first class car upon any of the railroads . . . he has just as much right . . . as a white man. . . ."

In a State imbued with sectional provincialism, Reverdy Johnson had risked life and limb by supporting the Union. He called Secessionists "mad and wicked men." He was devoted to the Flag of Freedom. "The man who is dead to its influence is in mind a fool or in heart a traitor."[22]

Of course, the patriot who voiced these Union sentiments was cordially hated by the rabidly Secessionist factions in Maryland. Only one faction hated him more. Spokesman for this other rabid faction was Benjamin F. Butler of Massachusetts. A cartoon of Butler would show him as a grafter who had looted the South. He posed as a super patriot. Because

---

[20] Bernard C. Steiner, *The Life of Reverdy Johnson* (Norman Remington Co. Baltimore, 1914), p. 17.

[21] Quoted in Steiner, *op. cit.*, p. 95.

[22] *Ibid.*, p. 53.

Reverdy Johnson had, early in the war, defended persons accused of disloyalty, Butler called him a "rank and bitter secessionist and worse than the others because he conceals it."[23]

As though liberalism were not enough to offend the Butler clique, Reverdy Johnson objected to the Union loyalty oath. Perhaps he saw it as a tissue of words which might or might not attest the loyalty of the swearer. Half the subversives under arrest had at one time or another sworn the Oath of Allegiance.

"On the question of taking an oath," says Steiner, ". . . Senator Bayard of Delaware had refused to take it, and Johnson argued it was unnecessary for him to do so. . . . Johnson said that he [himself] had taken the oath under protest. . . . The oath was . . . bad . . . since it disqualified a man from office without conviction of a crime."[24]

When Reverdy Johnson made his appearance at the counsels' table in the courtroom of the Arsenal Penitentiary, a strong defense for Mrs. Surratt seemed assured.

The two junior counsels, Aiken and Clampitt were trying their first important cases. Both would deal some telling legal blows when given fair opportunity. So would Walter Cox, defending Michael O'Laughlin.

A surprise at the defense table was General Thomas Ewing, Jr., a war veteran who enjoyed prestige as General Sherman's brother-in-law. The judges of the Military Commission must have regarded this Union officer with some dismay when he arrived on the scene to plead for Dr. Mudd.

As for the other defense attorneys, both Stone and Doster were experienced enough. But Doster entered the courtroom to face tall obstacles. We recall him as the Washington Provost Marshal who, early in the war, incurred the vengeful displeasure of influential Lafayette Baker. Now, pleading for Paine and Atzerodt, he assumed a burden which would have baffled the biggest of law firms. He could do little more than offer a token defense for the Seward assassin. Involved with Paine, he lacked adequate time for Atzerodt's case, and it would have taken concentrated legal genius to defend the unprepossessing roustabout from Port Tobacco.

Stone was at equal disadvantage in the case of David Herold. Herold's sisters had made a heartbreaking attempt to provide him with the best counsel available. But what, after all, could be said for Booth's bosom chum and getaway associate?

At best, all of the attorneys on the defense team faced an exceedingly vexatious problem in pleading for Booth's accomplices. At worst, they were up against virtually impossible odds. And trial conditions from the outset were decidedly "worst."

In civil courts and in normal courts-martial proceedings it was customary for the accused to be given a pre-trial copy of the indictment or the charges

---

23 *Butler's Book* (Boston: A. M. Thayer & Co., 1892), p. 234.
24 *Ibid.*, p. 66.

to be faced. The accused was normally presented with a list of the witnesses who would appear against him. He was offered adequate opportunity to procure counsel. His counsel was given adequate opportunity to prepare a defense.

The Military Commission in Washington dispensed with these time-old elements of justice. The defendants in the dock had no inkling of the charges until they were read in court. They were compelled to procure counsel after the trial commenced.

The defense lawyers were compelled to prepare their briefs while the trial was going on. They had no chance to confer with the accused before the proceedings commenced; no chance to consult law libraries, to conduct investigations, to spadework the legal research necessary in complex cases.

The defenders were also compelled to round up friendly witnesses while the trial was under way—an almost impossible task. Many witnesses had to be traced hither and yon, then offered expense money or subpoenaed and provided with transportation. Of course, the majority were reluctant to appear. Who wanted to speak friendly testimony for a "Secesh" conspirator like Arnold, or stand as character witness for grubby Atzerodt?

Another immense disadvantage for the defense lay in the court's handling of prosecution witnesses. Time and again some new "surprise witness" was produced by the Judge Advocate's Office. Time and again the Bureau of Military Justice introduced some new and unexpected angle. The defense attorneys were given no opportunity to procure counter witnesses or obtain counter evidence.

The defense lawyers protested that they were not provided with official copies of the court record in time for adequate study. Prosecution witnesses were sometimes dismissed before the defense had opportunity to digest the testimony and prepare suitable cross-examinations. General Hunter conceded the point. He proposed that the Government's witnesses should be detained for at least a day. But Judge Advocate General Holt offered immediate objection. Hunter promptly backed down.[25]

Even the courtroom setup militated against counsel for the accused. Defense witnesses were compelled to face the military tribunal while being cross-examined. They were not permitted so much as an inquiring glance at the defense attorneys who sat at the table behind them.[26]

One may readily imagine the unhappy incoherence of some timid witness facing a battery of grim-jawed generals and flinty-eyed advocates—Lew Wallace aiming a finger like a pistol; Judge Advocate General Holt booming an objection. The backwoods farmer, the stablehand or the hotel clerk would swallow his Adam's apple before he dared speak up to that tribunal. And the defense witness who might have screwed up an ounce of courage

---

[25] Noted in Eisenschiml, *op. cit.*, p. 237.
[26] DeWitt, *op. cit.*, p. 39. Also noted in Eisenschiml, *op. cit.*, p. 236.

had only to glance at the charade of misery in the prisoners' dock, which was enough to drain any citizen's spunk.

Some months after the trial the House Judiciary Committee conducted a Congressional probe into the generalized conspiracy allegations. One of the minority members was A. J. Rogers of New Jersey, who commented:

> The prisoners, said to have been incited to murder by . . . Jefferson Davis, were brought to hear these charges and specifications with irons upon them, with irons, too, of an unusual construction, irritating and painful, well calculated to distract their attention from the sayings of the military prosecutor. . . . Since the trial of Cranbourne in 1696 . . . no prisoner has ever been tried in irons before a legitimate court anywhere that English is spoken.

Rogers went on to remark that "the parties alleged to have been incited by Mr. Davis" had been held "in constrainment and in pain, with their heads buried in a sort of sack, devised to prevent their seeing! In this plight, from dark cells, they were brought to be charged with having been incited by Mr. Davis, and to it they pleaded not guilty."[27]

It seems doubtful if the history of American jurisprudence contains a trial wherein defendants and their counsel entered court under similar handicaps.

Most of the Government leaders and Army heads preferred secrecy. There were skeletons in the War Department's closets. There were ghosts behind the Government's doors. But as usual the authorities wanted to carry water on both shoulders. On the one hand, they feared adverse publicity. On the other, they coveted public acclaim. To attain the latter, they must publicize. But once they publicized, they invariably risked the former.

Coveting public acclaim, War Secretary Stanton apparently wanted to take the chance. The involved generals were for the most part against it. Judge Advocate General Joseph Holt favored holding the trial *in camera*.

On the night of May 10, Holt's assistant, Colonel Burnett, requested Stanton's firm decision. Burnett's message follows:

> Sir
> This evening you expressed the opinion that the charges and specifications should go to the *Associated Press* with the synopsis of today's proceedings, but at the same time directed me to consult with Judge Holt in reference to the matter. His opinion is decidedly against any publication of the charges, and in favor only of a very brief synopsis. How shall it be?
> I have the honor [etc.]
> H. L. Burnett

Playing it safe, Stanton passed the buck. He endorsed Burnett's inquiry:

---

[27] House of Representatives, Report No. 104, p. 32.

I directed that you should be governed by the opinion of Judge Holt.
You will [consider?] yourself under his instructions and to be governed by
his opinion.[28]

This left Holt balancing the buckets. Poised between the devil of Stanton's opinion and the deep blue sea of public relations, Holt decided to
risk the ocean. The press was informed of the charges. A detailed synopsis
went to the newsmen. And on the second day of the trial the courtroom
doors were thrown open to the public.[29]

Had the military dreaded the public eye, they must have been highly
encouraged by the deportment of the spectators. Appealing for admission,
crowds crushed crowds at the penitentiary gate. Tickets were at a premium.
The Colosseum on Roman Holiday could scarcely have drawn a more avid
audience.

Stanton had doubtless foreseen a public approval of military justice. He
could have based his opinion on the reaction to the announcements of
Booth's death. Every groan, every drop of blood had been reported with
relish in the press. At a mass meeting in Dayton, angry citizens had resolved "that the body of Booth be taken to mid-ocean and there buried."[30]
This was only one of hundreds of suggestions for punishing the assassin's
corpse.

Writing in a Philadelphia journal, "Medicus" expressed the popular
mood by exulting over "Booth's agonizing death throes." This commentator
(a doctor) told his readers that he had seen similar cases on the battlefield.
Men who had been shot through the spinal cord in the neck suffered
paralysis of the body. But the mind remained clear, and the slowly dying
victim endured the most exquisite agony. It was God's will (said "Medicus") that Booth should have "writhed through the tortures of the damned"
even as "he saw before his eyes the sheeting flames of hell."[31]

In an atmosphere saturated with sadism of the "Medicus" brand, no
forecaster had reason to predict that the quality of mercy would drop like
the gentle rain from heaven on the courtroom in the Arsenal Penitentiary.
Sympathy for Booth's accomplices was not to be found among the
spectators.

To Colonel Henry Kyd Douglas, the trial was reminiscent of the French
Revolution. The young ex-Confederate from the "Stonewall Brigade" was
lodged in a room next to Mrs. Surratt's. His door opened into the courtroom,
affording him a ringside view. His first glimpse of the court in session
imprinted itself on his memory as "a strange scene."

---

28 National Archives, War Dept. Records, File "B," Doc. 490, JAO.
29 Oldroyd, *op. cit.*, p. 127.
30 New York *Daily Tribune*, April 29, 1865.
31 Philadelphia newspaper, April 27, 1865. Copied in New York *Tribune*, April 28,
1865.

Douglas described it as "the most severely solemn tribunal [he had] ever faced." He "never saw a smile upon the face of judge, counsel or spectator." "Ladies of position, culture and influence . . . sat about the Court, near the judges [and] talked to the prosecutor." Their "scowls and scorn, white teeth and scorching eyes, augmented the general horror."

When Douglas took the stand as an unwilling Government witness, the lady spectators glared at him wrathfully. "Still fuller of vengeance were the glances they cast at poor Annie Surratt, when on the stand as witness for her mother."

The young Colonel believed that Paine and the men in the conspiracy with Booth "merited death." But he felt that Mrs. Surratt "was offered up as a burnt sacrifice to the wrath of her sex." He did manage to add: "I confess I do not judge these women harshly nor think they were without excuses, for everything about them cried out for vengeance. . . ."

In the eyes of Henry Kyd Douglas the trial of the conspirators was "a shameless farce." The "Court was organized to convict." Totally lacking were "judicial decorum, fairness, calmness . . . passion decided everything." As Douglas viewed it, Justice sat on this occasion "with unbandaged, bloodshot eyes." General David Hunter presided over "a Court of Death."[32]

It is only fair to recall that Colonel Douglas saw the trial through the eyes of a Confederate veteran. The war was hot in his blood in the spring of '65. And his years of soldiering under the zealous Stonewall Jackson probably had biased his thinking for life.

But there were Northerners—Union patriots—whose views came close to coinciding with those expressed by young Douglas.

In respect to Speed's conclusion that the military trial was in order, ex-Attorney General Edward Bates wrote in his diary: "I am pained to be led to believe that my successor, Atty. Gen. Speed, has been wheedled out of an *opinion* to the effect that the trial is lawful. If he be, in the lowest degree, qualified for his office, he must know better."[33]

Speed had rested his opinion on what he called "the laws of war." The retired Attorney General made hash of that dictum. Where, Bates demanded, were the *laws of war* to be found? "There is no such thing as the *Laws of War*," wrote Bates. "War is the very reverse of Law—and its existence always implies . . . the absence or disregard of all law."[34]

True, the distinguished Union jurist, Francis Lieber, had made an effort to codify rules of warfare during the Civil War. But the Confederacy had never formally acknowledged or accepted the Lieber Code. Nor had the Union war leaders made any particular effort to abide by Lieber's rules.

---

[32] Henry Kyd Douglas, *op. cit.*, pp. 341-343.
[33] Edward Bates, "Diary," *Annual Report of American Historical Society*, 1930, IV, p. 483. Also quoted in Eisenschiml, *op. cit.*, p. 230.
[34] Bates "Diary," p. 501. Also quoted in Eisenschiml, *op. cit.*, p. 244.

Speaking for the defense, General Thomas Ewing would strike this target in his closing argument. Were the accused charged with violating the "common law of war."? Ewing shook his head. "This is a term unknown to our language—a *quiddity*—wholly undefined and incapable of definition. It is . . . just what the Judge Advocate chooses to make of it."[35]

But the entire trial proceeding would turn out to be just what the Army Judge Advocate, or the War Department (in effect, Stanton) chose to make of it. From the outset the Commission's rulings militated against the defense. At the very beginning the prosecution struck a foul. The blow fell on the leading pleader, Reverdy Johnson.

Johnson had hardly entered the courtroom to plead for Mrs. Surratt when General T. M. Harris objected to the Marylander's presence at the bar. Reverdy Johnson was suspect; he had never taken the Union loyalty oath. Or so it was said!

Countering hotly, Reverdy Johnson produced the certificate of allegiance required of United States Senators. General Lew Wallace observed that this should certainly suffice—one of the few lenient opinions offered by Wallace while he sat on that military tribunal. Outranked, General Harris withdrew his objection. The distinguished Marylander was then permitted to serve as Mrs. Surratt's counsel.[36]

Johnson opened his plea with a matter-of-fact statement concerning his acceptance of the case.

> I am here at the instance of that lady [pointing to Mrs. Surratt], whom I never saw until yesterday, and never heard of . . . thinking that I could be of service to her, protesting, as she has done, her innocence to me . . . I deemed it right . . . that she should not go undefended. I knew I was to do it voluntarily, without compensation; the law prohibits me from receiving compensation; but if it did not, understanding her condition, I should never have dreamed of refusing. . . .
>
> I am here to do whatever the evidence will justify me in doing in protecting this lady from the charge upon which she is now being tried for her life. I am here detesting from the very bottom of my heart everyone concerned in this nefarious plot . . . and I am not here to protect anyone whom, when the evidence is offered, I shall deem to have been guilty—even her.[37]

Johnson's opening address drew immediate objections from the prosecution. Again his loyality came under attack. Epithet and detraction answered his plea for logic and reason. His motives were questioned, his character traduced.

---

[35] Pitman, *op. cit.*, p. 318. Also quoted in Eisenschiml, *op. cit.*, p. 243.
[36] Oldroyd, *op. cit.*, p. 127.
[37] *Ibid.*, pp. 127–28.

It was too much for the honest Marylander. Realizing the case was compromised, he folded his portfolio with dignity and withdrew.

With Reverdy Johnson thus disposed of, the Judge Advocate's Office and War Secretary Stanton were practically assured of the desired verdict.

During the third week in May the Union legions assembled in Washington for a Victory parade. The entire Army of the Potomac; the entire Division of the Mississippi; two hundred thousand Boys in Blue!

Early in the morning of the 23rd packed throngs walled the canyon of Pennsylvania Avenue. At 9:00 A.M. General George Gordon Meade barked the order. "Forward march!" Drums began the beat out beyond Capitol Hill.

Wave after wave of cheering greeted the riders at head of column: generals on prancing horses, like animated equestrian statuary. Then the color guards, massed battle flags like floating gardens of bunting. Then bands—blazing bonfires of sound. Then the men—a river of blue.

The city roared and shook to the tramp, tramp, tramp! of companies, regiments, brigades. Unit after unit paraded in mechanical precision. The caissons rolled along. The cavalry evoked storms of cheering for "Little Phil!" But the city saved its loudest roar for the troops led by the wiry soldier on the horse caparisoned with flower garlands. "Sherman! Sherman! Sherman!"

All Wednesday Sherman's men came down the Avenue. Mile after mile of gleaming muskets. Mile after mile of legs going in unison. Mile after mile of forage caps and bearded faces and rump-swung canteens.

The wiry soldier at column's head sat tiredly erect, his eyes fixed forward. Behind him tramped the blue Juggernaut. Echoing from Capitol Hill to White House, pulsing through the city's blood.

The bands blazed up where the Avenue turned toward the White House.

"The Union forever! Hurrah, boys, hurrah!

"Down with the Traitor! Up with the Star!"

Down with the Traitor!

Did it echo through the airless windows of the distant Arsenal Penitentiary? If so, there must have been those in the dock of that improvised courtroom who felt a numbing chill down the spine. And there must have been others in Washington who experienced a chill. Someone on the White House reviewing stand?

"The reviewing stand," noted Ben Perley Poore, "erected on the sidewalk in front of the White House, was a long pavilion decorated with flags and bearing the names of principle victories won. . . . President Johnson occupied the central chair . . . with Lieutenant General Grant . . . and members of the Cabinet at his right and left hand. . . . As each brigade commander saluted, President Johnson would rise and lift his hat. General Grant sat for the whole time immovable, except that he would occasionally make some commendatory comment as a gallant officer or brave regiment passed. . . ."[38]

When Sherman cantered into view, "the multitude . . . sent up shouts that must have made the heart leap, and the enthusiasm increased as he approached the Presidential stand . . .

"After passing the President, General Sherman wheeled to the left, dismounted and joined the reviewing party. . . . He shook hands cordially with President Johnson and General Grant, but when Secretary Stanton advanced with outstretched hand he remarked, 'I do not care to shake hands with clerks,' and turned away. Never was there a more complete 'cut direct' . . ."[39]

Stanton's thoughts? Nobody knows.

Sherman's thoughts? Not long after that extraordinary incident he wrote his sister: "Washington is as corrupt as Hell, made so by the looseness and extravagance of war. I will avoid it as a pest house."[40]

So the general who had defined war as "hell" did not stay in the capital to witness the trial of eight nonentities accused of violating the "common laws of war." One wonders what those eight nonentities would have thought had they witnessed the little scene between General Sherman and War Secretary Stanton at the climax of that victory parade.

But all they heard of it in the distant courtroom was the thudding of the drums, beating in muffled echo against the windows.

The prisoners in the dock, who had dared to defy this military giant, must have known they were doomed.

CHAPTER 23

Verdict and Execution

THAT three would die was a foregone conclusion. Nothing on earth could have saved Lewis Paine—his defense was a mere formality. Although David Herold claimed he accompanied Booth under duress, his sworn statement contained obvious mendacities that served to tighten the rope around his neck. George A. Atzerodt might have had a case. He had walked out on the killing, refusing to slay Andrew Johnson. Yet his splut-

---

[38] *Op. cit.*, p. 189.
[39] *Ibid.*, p. 191.
[40] Sherman's Home Letters, pp. 349–50.

tered protestations of innocence (probably exaggerated as to virtue on his part) were so worded as to assure him a place on the scaffold.

Mrs. Surratt's fate was another matter. So were the chances of Arnold, O'Laughlin, Spangler and Dr. Mudd. But all eight prisoners at the bar faced the blanket indictment which charged them with, among other things, treasonably conspiring with Jefferson Davis and "others unknown." If direct complicity with Booth could not be proven, there remained this deadly charge of treasonous conspiracy with Davis. And if conspiracy with Jefferson Davis proved unprovable, there were still those ghostly "others unknown"—the deadliest of all conspirators to conspire with. Altogether the indictment was so inclusive that its only loophole seemed to be a hangman's noose.

On the morning of May 10th the formal indictment was read in court by President of the Commission, Major General David Hunter. None of the accused had as yet been provided with counsel. When the volunteer defense attorneys finally had a chance to study the indictment, it must have struck them with the impact of an avalanche.

It was charged that all eight defendants had "maliciously, unlawfully, and traitorously, and in aid of the existing armed rebellion against the United States of America, on or before the sixth day of March, and on divers other days between that day and the fifteenth of April, 1865, combined, confederated and conspired with John H. Surratt, John Wilkes Booth, Jefferson Davis, George N. Sanders, Beverly Tucker, Jacob Thompson, William C. Cleary, Clement C. Clay, George Harper, George Young, and others unknown, to kill and murder President Abraham Lincoln, Vice-President Andrew Johnson, Secretary of State William H. Seward, and Lieutenant General of the United States Army Ulysses S. Grant." The indictment concluded that, "in pursuance of that conspiracy, on April 14, 1865, [the defendants] in association with John H. Surratt and John Wilkes Booth, murdered President Lincoln, assaulted with intent to murder . . . Seward, and lay in wait with intent to kill and murder Vice-President Johnson and General Grant."[1]

If the lawyers at the defense table were stunned by the multiplicity of charges, what of the defendants? Perhaps Paine and Arnold glimpsed some of the meaning behind the verbal barrage. Possibly Mrs. Surratt recognized the names of Jacob Thompson, Beverly Tucker and Clement C. Clay. Perhaps they meant something to Dr. Mudd. But the other prisoners—especially Atzerodt and the illiterate Spangler—must have been utterly bewildered by the indictment. George N. Sanders, William Cleary, George Harper, George Young—who were *they*?

Thompson, Tucker, Clay and Sanders were, of course, leaders of the

---

[1] Pitman, *op. cit.*, pp. 18–19.

Confederacy's so-called "Canadian Cabinet"—the Rebel group head-quartered in Montreal behind a pseudo-diplomatic front. Cleary, Harper and Young were agents working with the Canada group. The operations of this Montreal outpost of the Stars and Bars were cloaked in super secrecy. But the United States Government had indisputable evidence linking the Confederate camarilla in Canada with Tom Hines' army of saboteurs in the "Copperhead" movement, with the Lake Erie raiders under Captain Beall, with the Rebel raiders who struck in Vermont, with Confederate financial manipulators on Wall Street, and with the saboteurs who touched off the New York fire raid.

The U.S. Government had yet to establish proof that the Confederate camarilla in Canada (and Jefferson Davis) sponsored the assassination conspiracy. Formal accusation on the basis of sheer assumption was the typical police-state method. And it was exemplary of War Department procedure under Secretary Stanton. But the charges could not hold water in a court of law—or even in a military court-martial—unless something more than mere assumption were produced. If the indictment against the eight on trial was to hold together, the Government must now prove the connection between the Confederacy's Canadian underground and the assassination strike in Washington.

Faced with this immediate imperative, the Army Judge Advocate's Office and everyone concerned in the Bureau of Military Justice were (it would seem) up against it. Here was a whale of a cart far out in front of a nebulous horse. But Stanton had dictated the rig. Somehow the indictment had to be harnessed up with some sort of evidence. Judge Advocate General Joseph Holt and his confreres did their best in the brief time available.

On May 12 the Judges Advocate (for the Prosecution) put on the stand their chief witnesses to establish the linkage between Booth, John Surratt, the Canadian camarilla, Jefferson Davis and the assassination plot.

The first Government witness was Mr. Richard Montgomery. Montgomery testified that he had visited Canada during the summer of 1864, "remaining there the greater part of the time until the 1st of April, 1865." According to Oldroyd: "During Montgomery's stay in Canada he was in the service of the United States Government, seeking to acquire information in regard to the plans and purposes of the rebels who were assembled there."[2] Colonel Oldroyd's description is exemplary of the official historian's aversion for the word "spy." (As will be seen, the treatment of Montgomery in Oldroyd's text may be taken as indicative of the Government's sensitivity in respect to the employment of such spies as Mr. Montgomery.)

Historian Eisenschiml is more openhanded in his treatment of Montgomery. He was (says Eisenschiml) a "professional spy who was in the

---

[2] Oldroyd, *op. cit.*, p. 221.

habit of taking money from both the Confederate and the Federal governments."[3]

But Eisenschiml, too, blurs the point. For he impeaches Montgomery's integrity with this description of the man's spy activities. In operating as a "dual spy," Montgomery played a role common enough in the tricky game of secret intelligence. More than one Union spy insinuated himself into the Confederate underground by posing as a Rebel spy. Classic examples: Timothy Webster of McClellan's espionage service, and "Colonel Phil" Henson, Union spy who pretended to serve as a secret agent for Longstreet. Like Webster and Henson, Montgomery had fed false information to Rebel Headquarters, and had spirited secret Confederate dispatches to United States intelligence officers to be steamed open and read before ultimate delivery. All this is legitimate enough in the field of military espionage. One may question a spy's individual integrity, but his integrity can hardly be judged by his operational moves in an essentially tricky game.

Aware of Montgomery's espionage background, the Army officers of the Military Commission did not question his personal integrity. Nor did it occur to them to question his story. It was just the kind of story they expected to hear.

Montgomery stated that he had made the acquaintance of the Confederate leaders in Montreal. He said Jacob Thompson took him into his confidence in the summer of '64 and told him they could have Lincoln "put out of the way." Montgomery declared that he talked again with Jacob Thompson in Montreal in January '65. At which time the Rebel envoy confided "that a proposition had been made to him to rid the world of the tyrants Lincoln, Stanton, Grant and some others. The men who made the proposition . . . were bold, daring men, and able to execute anything they would undertake without regard to cost." Montgomery recalled that Jacob Thompson "said he was in favor of the proposition, but had determined to defer his answer until he consulted with his Government at Richmond, and was only then awaiting its approval."[4]

Montgomery testified to encountering Paine several times in Niagara Falls and in Canada. He said Paine posed on these occasions as a Canadian, and that Clement Clay had identified Paine as a Canadian.

Montgomery asserted that Booth had twice visited Confederate headquarters in Montreal during the latter part of 1864. Apparently the actor's last visit had been made in December. Montgomery stated that he learned of Booth's visits from William Cleary.

Montgomery further testified to being with the Rebels in Montreal when the New York fire raids were plotted. He stated that he immediately left Canada and carried the word to Washington, and that he also advised

[3] *Op. cit.*, pp. 212–213.
[4] Quoted in Oldroyd, *op. cit.*, p. 219.

the Federal Government of impending Confederate raids on Buffalo and Rochester, New York. Witness disclosed that in his role as Confederate agent he had used the alias "James Thompson." In conclusion he stated that he did not know whether Jefferson Davis had advised Jacob Thompson on the assassination plan or not. He gave it as his impression that Davis had done so.[5]

Having voiced this testimony, Mr. Montgomery stepped down. It was surprising testimony, all things considered. Although it failed to prove that Jefferson Davis was personally involved in the assassination conspiracy, it definitely linked Booth and Paine, the two chief assassins, with the Confederacy's leaders in Canada. But that was the least surprising of Mr. Mongomery's assertions.

Consider the matter. Here is the Government's own witness—a Federal agent—testifying that he had warned the authorities in Washington about the Confederate plot to burn New York City. Surely the Army officers of the Military Commission must have pricked up their ears. What had the War Department, forewarned, done to prevent that fire raid? The answer lay in blocks of charred ruin in Manhattan.

Nor was that all. If this Federal agent were to be believed, the War Department had word of the assassination plot four months before Lincoln was slain. There it was in Montgomery's testimony. *The United States Secret Service had a line on the assassination conspiracy as early as January, 1865!*

Here was news that should have brought the generals and colonels of the Military Commission to their feet. It would seem, however, that not one of them saw the point. Still more surprising is the fact that contemporary and later historians missed this point. By word of its own witness, the Government disclosed gross negligence in respect to protecting the President.

But the United States War Department was not on trial for the murder of Abraham Lincoln. So the Army officers of the military tribunal fixed a steely attention on the eight defendants in the dock. Judge Advocate General Joseph Holt produced another witness to prove that the assassination conspiracy was sponsored by Richmond agents in Canada.

The second witness was Dr. James B. Merritt, American, physician, long-time resident of Windsor, Ontario. Six days after Lincoln's murder, General James B. Fry, Provost Marshal General of the United States, had dispatched to Dr. Merritt the following message:

> The Secretary of War authorizes me to pledge your protection and security, and to pay all expenses connected with your journey both ways, and in addition to promise a suitable reward if reliable and useful information is furnished.[6]

---

[5] Pitman, *op. cit.*, p. 26.
[6] *Ibid.*, p. 36.

It would be interesting to know just how Secretary Stanton became acquainted with the name of this over-the-border physician, and just why he appealed for Dr. Merritt's testimony. War Department records are shy on the subject of Merritt's antecedents. But Canadian records are not. In Windsor, Ontario, Merritt had the reputation of an unscrupulous quack. Within the week of his arrival in Washington, the War Department received word from Canadian sources on the doctor's unsavory medical practice. The Department was also advised that Merritt had acquired the repute of a noisy Secession sympathizer.[7]

Nevertheless, the Judge Advocate's Office put Dr. Merritt on the witness stand. The gist of his testimony was that he had heard various Rebel agents in Canada damn Lincoln as a tyrant and declare that "Old Abe" would never serve another term if elected. Merritt went on to state that on April 10, 1865, he had advised a Justice of Peace in Galt, Canada, that Lincoln was to be assassinated.[8]

For this valueless information the Government paid Dr. Merritt an award of $6,000. Historians would wonder why. The dubious physician's testimony contributed little to the Government's case. And it aroused a storm of protest from the Canadian authorities, who did not like it advertised that one of Canada's officials (even so minor an official as a small-town Justice of Peace!) had been advised four days ahead of time that President Lincoln was to be assassinated. In which respect the Government of Canada seems to have been far more sensitive than the Government of the United States.

Continuing their efforts to implicate Jefferson Davis in the assassination plot, the managers of the conspiracy trial produced other surprised witnesses. A Mr. Sandford Conover took the stand. In February '65 this interesting character had appeared as a witness in Montreal against the Rebel raiders who had looted a bank in St Albans, Vermont. At that time Conover declared himself to be a native Virginian, said he had evaded Confederate Army service and had "gone North" in October 1864. Now, facing the military tribunal in Washington, he said he'd been born in New York, had been drafted into the Rebel Army while living in North Carolina, had served as a clerk in the Richmond War Office, and had deserted to the North in December '63. These discrepancies did not seem to trouble the Judge Advocate's Office.

Conover described himself as a newspaper man. He had been (he said) a roving correspondent for the New York *Tribune*. His work had brought him into contact with Confederate secret agents and saboteurs. He had learned that they were plotting to burn Northern cities, to poison municipal water supplies, to sabotage Croton Reservoir at New York, and to spread yellow fever in the North by means of "infected clothing." Conover testi-

---

[7] Noted in Eisenschiml, *op. cit.*, p. 214.
[8] Pitman, *op. cit.*, p. 35.

fied that he had heard of the assassination plot in February, 1865, and had sent word of it to the *Tribune*.[9]

Here was another Government witness testifying to advance information on the assassination conspiracy! True, Conover's word would be impeached, and doubt would arise that he actually flashed the story to Greeley's journal as stated. But if Conover *had* submitted such a story, who could believe the *Tribune* editors would not have immediately informed the Washington authorities? Once more a Government witness had testified to War Department negligence.

From other witnesses put on the stand by Judge Holt, the officers of the Military Commission heard more of the same. Here was a blind peddler, Samuel Jones. He said that he had sold his wares around Confederate Army camps, and while so doing had heard Confederate officers discussing the assassination conspiracy. Still other witnesses supported Conover's testimony concerning Rebel plans to sabotage Northern cities by fire and poison.

As a clincher Judge Holt produced Henry Von Steineker. Under oath this witness told a remarkable story. He said that in the spring of 1863 he had "gone South" to join a regiment in the famous Stonewall Brigade. Von Steineker testified that after enlisting in Jackson's élite corps, he served as an engineer officer in the topographical section under General Edward ("Old Allegheny") Johnson. He said that in the summer of 1863, while the troops were bivouacked in Virginia, John Wilkes Booth visited Jackson's camp. According to the witness, Booth discussed assassination plans with a group of Jackson's officers. Details were largely left to the Court's imagination. But Von Steineker mentioned names, including those of General Johnson and Colonel Henry Kyd Douglas. One name he did not mention was his own. For it evolved that Von Steineker's true name was Hans Von Winklestein. The Judge Advocate's Office was aware of his alias. And aware of other interesting facts about the witness. But for reasons best known to Judge Holt and his associates, these facts were not introduced with Von Steineker. They would come out later.

A number of letters were placed in evidence to substantiate the Government's claim that Richmond (hence Jefferson Davis) had sponsored a wide-spread murder plot. Perhaps the most convincing of these was Sam Arnold's letter to Booth, containing the line: "Do not act rashly or in haste . . . go and see how it will be taken at R———d. . . ." No one could doubt that Arnold thus advised Booth to consult with the Richmond Government before unleashing an assassination strike. Still, this letter failed to implicate Davis. Rather, it tended to show that Booth (in late March, at least) had not consulted with the Richmond Government.

The "Leon" letter was also introduced as evidence. Although it hinted at conspiracy, it was written in obvious code—spy jargon which the

[9] *Ibid.*, p. 29.

Bureau of Military Justice had been unable to decipher. Again, it proved nothing in respect to Jefferson Davis.

Neither did the mysterious "Selby and Leenea" letters placed in evidence along with the testimony of Mrs. Mary Hudspeth. Summoned from New York City to testify, Mrs. Hudspeth told the Military Commission that she had found the two letters on a horse car. Date: November 1864. Two strangers had occupied the seat ahead of her—two men who rode with their heads together, whispering. One of the gentlemen was dark and handsome with a scar on his right cheek. In leaving the car, they dropped these letters.

The "Selby" letter contained the line, "*Abe must die, and now. . . . The cup failed us once and might again . . . strike for your home, strike for your country. . . .*"[10] The other letter, postmarked St. Louis, was addressed to "Dearest Husband" from "Leenea." It, too, was couched in conspiratorial terms. Mrs. Hudspeth had turned these missives over to General Dix who had forwarded them to Stanton's office. But what did they mean? What did they prove? General Dix himself took the first letter to be a hoax.[11]

Perhaps the weirdest item of correspondence introduced as evidence was a code letter which had supposedly been fished from a river at Morehead City, North Carolina. The find was made early in May by a wharf builder, Charles Deuel, and one of his workmen. Somehow (just how remained unexplained) Deuel and his companion were able to decipher the letter's mysterious code. Original and decoded version were forwarded to the War Department just in time for the Conspiracy Trial.[12]

In an envelope addressed to a "John Wise," the letter reads as follows:

Washington April the 15 . 65
Dear John.
   I am happy to inform you that Pet has done his work well, He is safe, and old Abe is in hell. Now sir all eyes are on you. You must bring Sherman.
   Grant is in the hands of old Gray ere this. Red Shoes showd a lack of nerve in Sewards case, but he fell back in good order. Johnson must come, old Crook has him in charge. mind well that brothers oath and you will have no difficulty, all will be safe and enjoy the fruits of our labour. We had a large meeting last night. all were bent on carrying out the program to the letter—the rails are laid for our safe exit—old————allways behind lost the pop at City Point. Now I say again the lives of our brave officers and the life of the South depends upon the carrying the program into effect. No. two will give you this, its ordered no more letters shall be sent by mail, when you write sign no real name, and send by some of our friends who are coming home. We want you to write us how the news was

---

10 *Ibid.*, p. 40. Quoted in Eisenschiml, *op. cit.*, p. 247.

11 Dix letter to Ass't. War Secretary Dana, reproduced in Eisenschiml, *op. cit.*, p. 249.

12 National Archives, War Dept. Records, File "D," Statement of Charles Deuel, JAO.

received there. We receive great encouragement from all quarters. I hope
there will be no getting weak in the Knees. I was in Baltimore yesterday,
Pet had not got there yet. Your folks are well and have heard from you.
dont loose (sic) your nerve.

O'B   no. five.[13]

Not the least remarkable feature of this sinister letter was its flotation
in a North Carolina river. Although presumably plucked from the water,
it bore no signs of immersion.

Defense Attorney Walter Cox questioned the item's validity. He observed that the ink was "no more blurred, I think, than any paper on this
table. It looks as if it had been written and dropped in the water immediately before it was found, for the very purpose of being picked up by the
Government agents, to be used as evidence."[14]

So it would seem this letter bore the elongated earmarks of a hoax. Yet
it may have been a deliberate deception to confuse the Federals. Too, the
letter's puzzle contains one curious jigsaw overlooked by contemporary
and later analysts. Booth's mother often called him "Pet." Did the writer
have that in mind? Was "O'B no. five" someone intimately acquainted
with the assassin?

Fake or genuine, the "John Wise" letter proved nothing specific. Yet the
officers of the tribunal appear to have regarded it, along with much else
that was vaporous, as direct evidence in support of the general indictment.

The presentation of the case against Jefferson Davis, the Canadian
camarilla, and the eight defendants in the dock ranks high as a classic of
confusion. With evidence that had neither context nor continuity, the
incompetent, irrelevant and immaterial were mixed in an absolutely
indigestible potpourri. The desperate defense lawyers must have had
extreme difficulty in following the prosecution's argument. The military
judges, too, must have been dazed. Not to mention the eight on trial.

For example, during one day's proceedings, the Court agenda embraced
the following:

Charles Bulger and John Gunther testified that Edward Spangler
stayed at his (Spangler's) boardinghouse for several days after the assassination.

Thomas Raybold, ticket seller, testified that on or about March 7 he
broke the lock to Box 8 at Ford's Theater. Reason: some customers arrived
late, the box contained the only seats then available and he, Raybold, had
to force the door. Witness stated: "I do not know that the lock was
ever repaired. I never thought of having it fixed."

H. E. Merrick took the stand to corroborate the theater man's story.

William R. Smith testified to seeing Booth pursued off stage by Major
Stewart.

---

13 National Archives, War Dept. Records, File "A," JAO.
14 Pitman, *op. cit.*, p. 68.

Jacob Ritterspaugh stated that Spangler struck him in the mouth on the night of the assassination. Ritterspaugh had exclaimed, "That was Booth who ran out!" Spangler had snarled: "Shut up; keep quiet; what do you know about it?"

G. W. Bunker, clerk at the National Hotel, testified to finding a large gimlet in Booth's trunk after the assassination.

Charles B. Hall swore that Sam Arnold had assisted him at bookkeeping in Mr. Wharton's store at Fortress Monroe.

James Lusby testified to seeing John Lloyd drunk in Marlboro on Good Friday. On cross-examination, the witness stated he "was not quite as tight as Lloyd."

Matthew J. Pope stated that a gentleman called at his stable to sell a large bay horse, blind in one eye. "The features of the man were like those of Atzerodt. . . . I have found an umbrella left by the man."

Miss Margaret Branson testified that she first met Paine at Gettysburg on the morning after the battle.

Dr. Nichols, Superintendent of the Government Insane Asylum, took the stand to say that "if a man attempted to murder a sick man in bed, and assault four others in the same house, witness would suspect him to be insane." But, "Madmen seldom say they are mad."

Margaret Raigham, servant to Mrs. Branson, said that Paine had attacked a Negro servant girl. "She refused to clean his room; he threw her down, stamped on her, and said he would kill her."

The "Leon" letter was placed in evidence.

Mr. Raybold, recalled, explained again about forcing the door to Box 8—the Presidential Box.

Ephraim Smoot testified that "Zad" Jenkins, Mrs. Surratt's brother, was looked upon the first year of the war as a Union man, afterward as a "Secesh" sympathizer. Smoot stated that he had talked with Thomas Nott (or Knott), bartender at the Surrattsville tavern, the Saturday after the murder. Nott blurted, "My God, John Surratt knows all about this."

A Mr. Roby stated that after the elections of 1863 he heard "Zad" Jenkins declare that he'd been "offered office under the damned Government, but he would not hold office under such a God damned Government as the Government of the United States."

The Court adjourned.

What could General Hunter and his colleagues have made of that one day's melange, that *olla-podrida* involving Spangler's Easter whereabouts, Atzerodt's umbrella, the broken lock on the door to the Presidential Box at Ford's, Paine's barbarous temper, Booth's gimlet, Lloyd's inebriacy, Arnold's bookkeeping job, hearsay evidence concerning John Surratt, and the alleged opinions of Mrs. Surratt's splenetic brother? Tossed into the miscellany is the "Leon" letter with its jargon. It is exhibited as tangible proof of conspiracy. But the writer remains unidentified, the substance unintelligible. As well place in evidence the original Abracadabra or an indecipherable anagram in Bantu.

Remarking the mass of irrelevant evidence, the *World* correspondent caustically observed that "the wideness of the subjects discussed makes one imagine that the object of the Commission is to write a cyclopedia. . . ."[15] But it would seem the object of the trial managers was obfuscation. In this they were assisted by the soporific Washington climate, the somnolent weather of May, the steaming days of June.

A lethargic dullness entered the courtroom. Stagnant, overwarm, the imprisoned air imposed literal fog on figurative. Weighted with the soups, the roasts, the gravied dumplings, wines and puddings of the customary noonday meal, the military gentlemen of the tribunal must have been beset by heavy torpor during the endless, fly-buzz afternoons. With papers adhering to damp fingers, collars glued to perspiring throats, and flannel tunics pasted to shoulderblades, mentalities too must have become sticky. Yet these officers, playing both judge and jury, were duty bound to weigh and consider the evidence, to doubt this argument or accredit that, to study opinions and to ponder legalities. For comparison: chess problems in a Turkish bath.

In consequence lost in the tons of testimony were such odd little items as Witness Raybold's statement concerning the broken lock on the door to the President's box. Mr. Raybold, ticket seller at Ford's, recalled that he himself broke that important lock on the night of March 7, just three days after Lincoln's inaugural. Why? Well, he'd sold four orchestra tickets in advance to a man named Merrick. During Act One, Merrick's party failed to arrive, so the seats were obligingly given to other customers. When Merrick and party came late, Raybold showed them to Box 8, which happened to be unoccupied. But he could not find the doorkey. So he broke the lock with an obliging kick. And "never thought of having it fixed."

A queer story, surely. Queerer still, because the Merrick in mention happened to be day clerk at the National Hotel, and in the same theater party was a Mrs. Bunker, who bore the name of the night clerk at Booth's hotel. Was it coincidence that people who knew Booth were involved in the lock-breaking episode? Nobody pursued that point.

Recalled to the stand, Raybold added that the lock on Box 7 had also been broken. When? He did not know. Vaguely he remembered that Booth had occupied Box 7 about two weeks before the assassination. At any rate, all locks to the Presidential box at Ford's were useless as of April 14. More coincidence? The tribunal judges merely stared. Raybold's testimony seemed to exonerate the suspected Spangler. But nobody pried

---

[15] George A. Townsend, *The Life, Crime and Capture of J. W. Booth* (New York: Dick & Fitzgerald, 1865), p. 69. Quoted in Eisenschiml, *op. cit.*, p. 238.

further into the ticket seller's extraordinary tale. Nobody concentrated on Raybold himself, or on the odd involvement of hotel clerk Merrick.

Similarly the officer-judges accepted much of the evidence, their cerebrations as alert as those of gourmands surfeited. Dully they read meaning into such riddles as the "Selby and Leenea" letters and the "John Wise" letter, gravely crediting Joseph Holt's solution of the admittedly insoluble. The logic followed a simple syllogism. Conspirators write cryptic letters; here is a letter cryptically worded; ergo, this missive is conspiratorial. Just how the tribunal deduced from the proffered evidence that Jefferson Davis was responsible for the assassination conspiracy remains a riddle beyond any solution.

Tried *in absentia,* Davis was found guilty. So were the other Confederate leaders named in the general indictment. So were "others unknown."

But the Court was not trying the "others unknown." Those spectres would never be sentenced. Neither would ex-President Davis and the subordinate Confederate leaders who were indicted.

Only the eight wretched prisoners in the dock would be subject to official verdicts and summary sentences. Little people. Minor pawns. Dummies as mute and helpless as waxworks figures in a chamber of horrors.

On them would fall the deadliest of all penalties—the penalty of serving as an "example."

The Government *vs.* Lewis Paine. Or, to give him his right name, Lewis Thornton Powell.

What could be said for this fierce young giant from the Florida frontier? Obviously very little.

With malice aforethought and intent to kill, he had savagely assaulted the United States Secretary of State. Only a freak of chance—the incredible armor of Mr. Seward's neck-brace—had saved the Secretary's life. Only another freak of chance—the misfire of a pistol—had prevented the slaying of Frederick Seward. Paine had slashed and battered other members of the helpless household with brutality untrammeled. He had given no quarter, and it could hardly be contended that he deserved any.

Paine asked no quarter. In a detailed (if not wholly reliable) confession, he had admitted himself Booth's accomplice. He admitted the attack on Seward with intention to assassinate. He made no appeal for mercy, offered no excuses. Throughout the trial and to the last moment of his life he posed as a statue of defiance, unyielding, unrepentent.

So the Prosecution had one of those rarities, an open-and-shut case. A procession of witnesses testified as to Paine's comings and goings. He was indentified as Private Lewis Powell, C.S.A., captured at Gettysburg. Identified as an inmate of Mrs. Branson's boardinghouse in Baltimore. Identified as an escapee who had signed an Oath of Allegiance in Fauquier Country, Virginia. He was trailed by evidence to the Surratt house on H

Street, Washington. Identified as the man who had called himself "Mr. Wood," "the Reverend Wood," "the Reverend Paine." As the man who had finally lodged at the Herndon House as "Mr. Paine."

He was a parole violator (admitted). A conspirator (admitted). An enemy of the State (admitted). An accomplice of the killer who assassinated Lincoln (admitted). An assassin who had butchered five victims, leaving two of them at death's door (admitted). Under the circumstances it seems doubtful that Lewis Paine, in any court, any where, in any period of the nation's history, could have been successfully defended.

Paine's defense counsel, Mr. W. E. Doster, tried. With considerable logic he argued that Paine was a victim of environment and upbringing—a product of his time. False gods, false standards, a deadly diet of hate propaganda and war propaganda had turned young Paine into a potential murderer. Then the war, the shock of battle, the death of his two brothers at Murfreesboro—all this had unseated his reason. The rampage at the Seward house resulted from homicidal mania, argued Doster. Lewis Paine had lost his mind.

Doster's insanity plea did not quite follow the argument that Paine's character had been fashioned at Vulcan's Forge. Nor did defense counsel's medical evidence hold up. For Doster offered as proof of Paine's insanity the fact that Paine suffered from constipation!

We have no way of knowing whether retarded peristalsis constituted standard evidence of mental derangement in those days. Actually, in the realm of abnormal psychology, and in the diagnosis and treatment of the insane, it appears that the average doctor groped in the dark with few standards to go by. But Mr. Doster must have come by the concept somewhere. If, indeed, it were a medical postulate, a great many citizens must have spent a great many hours closeted with private anxieties about their mental faculties.

Medical postulate or no, the insanity plea was rejected by the Military Commission. Perhaps some of the generals had their own private reasons for rejecting it on the grounds presented.

As for Paine's courtroom deportment, sitting in the dock with shoulders erect, chin up, eyes front, he appeared to be the most levelheaded and self-willed of the prisoners. In talking with his prison guards and with General Hartranft, he seems to have been fully self-possessed and rational. He may have been hallucinated. But he was not the only young stalwart of his time who thought himself a Spartan hero.

Yet he may have been temporarily deranged when he rampaged through the Seward home. He may have been brandy-crazed, or even drugged. But one fact seems certain. Paine could have been a foaming maniac, and the nation's pioneer defender of the criminally insane would have urged no brief in his behalf. Paine himself had seen to that.

So far as is known, William H. Seward never uttered a public word then or later in regard to the Paine insanity plea.

The Government *vs.* David E. Herold.

Whereas Paine's defense rested on a feeble (if wholly unsubstantiated) insanity plea, Herold's tottered on the far flimsier claim that he was a semi-irresponsible imbecile. Of the eight defendants in the dock, Herold is the most elusive as a character. His own statements reveal a talent for evasion. He wears the personality of a chameleon. Had he not become enmeshed with Booth, it seems likely that his aptitudes would have led him to racetrack, gambling hall, or narcotics den.

Friendly witnesses took the stand to describe the ex-drug clerk as "trifling." Druggist Francis S. Walsh called him "unstable." Neighbors testified that he had seemed to them harmless and likable. The family physician characterized him as "very light, trivial, unreliable . . . with . . . the mind of an eleven-year-old child."[16]

To this depiction the judges of the Military Commission listened with decided skepticism. In reviewing the evidence against David Herold, one is compelled to share the tribunal's mistrust. Herold's original testimony, recorded by the authorities soon after his capture, did much to condemn him as a foxy liar.

His claim that he had not been in Washington on the evening of the assassination strike was dubious to say the least. Still, it was an artful line for Herold to take. Only two witnesses who believed they saw him in the capital on that fatal evening could be produced. Stableman Fletcher and Sergeant Cobb. Conceivably Fletcher, on the dim-lit avenue, could have been mistaken. There was an old saying to the effect that "It'll never be noticed on a galloping horse." As for Sergeant Cobb, he could not positively identify Herold in court. "He is very near the size of the second horseman," Cobb squinted at the prisoner. "But, I should think, taller, although I can't be sure." Cobb thought that the horseman who followed Booth across the bridge "had a lighter complexion than this man."[17]

Here was an opening for the defense. Mr. Frederick Stone did not make the most of it. Probably Prosecution would have nailed it shut by asserting that it did not signify much one way or the other. Whether Herold was or was not in Washington at the hour of the killing did not alter the fact that he had aided and abetted the assassin's escape through Maryland and had accompanied Booth to Garrett's farm.

Herold had joined Booth on the highway to Surrattsville (admitted). He had ridden with Booth to the vicinity of Bryantown (admitted). These admissions, patently undeniable, were about the only ones Herold had been willing to make. He said he went on to Bryantown by himself. That

---

16 Pitman, *op. cit.*, p. 97.
17 *Ibid.*, p. 85.

when he next met Booth, the actor's injured leg was bandaged. In his statement, Herold skipped Dr. Mudd's entirely. Then he nimbly side-stepped the journey to the home of Colonel Cox.

Herold claimed that Booth had forced him to hide in the swamps. Under compulsion he had accompanied Booth to the farm of a man named "Thomas." This, of course, bore reference to Thomas A. Jones, Cox's half brother. Herold must have known Jones' full name, but again he covered for this benefactor.

"We went to Thomas' at one or two o'clock Saturday night," Herold's testimony reads. "Asked him if we could get a boat to cross the Potomac. I said, 'John, I don't think I want to go with you.' Said he, 'You have got to go with me. My leg is broken. If you run away I will shoot you, and parties in Washington will implicate you.'"

According to Herold's statement, he continued to plead with Booth. "I begged Booth to let me leave him. I told him I must go home, mother didn't know where I was. He said I must stay with him; that if I would go to Mexico with him we would make a fortune as soon as we became acquainted with the Spanish language. I told him it didn't make any difference about making an independent fortune, I preferred to go home."[18]

Then (continues the statement) Herold found "an old bateau" on the riverbank. Booth compelled him to go on, swore to implicate him otherwise, or (to quote the sinister vernacular then in usage) to "put him through." Herold had "tried again to get away, but could not." Just why a nimble young quail hunter could not escape from a cripple on crutches was a question Herold failed to answer. He admits spending a number of nights "in the pines." What prevented him from dashing into the under-brush, or sneaking off while Booth slept?

Paragraph by paragraph, the drug clerk's statement is so much subter-fuge and camouflage. Carefully he blurs the account of the Potomac cross-ing. With equal care he avoids naming Mrs. Quesenberry, the lady on the Virginia side of the river. He says a "Confederate soldier" told them where Dr. Steward lived.

Concerning the meeting with the Confederate troopers at Port Conway, Herold's story is as hazy as amnesia. Although he names Jett as the volunteer guide to Garrett's farm, he consistently refers to Brainbridge as "Bennington." Ruggles is merely anonymous, "one of Mosby's men."

Again, Herold is vague about the Garrett family. Describing his journey to Bowling Green, he wanders into deeper vapor. In his entire account he makes no mention of dining at Dr. Mudd's and at the Garrett's. Yet he can remember such trivial detail as " . . . wanting something to eat, I gave a man a dollar for about fourteen or fifteen biscuits and three slices of bacon." With his memory brightening and dimming like a light, it seems apparent that an agile intellect controlled the recollective gasjet.

---

[18] National Archives, War Dept. Records, File "H," R.B.P. 38, JAO.

When shown a photograph of Michael O'Laughlin, Herold declares: "I have seen that man in Baltimore. His name is Locklin, Laughlin or Mc-Laughlin."

Experts acquainted with modern techniques of evasion in prisoner-of-war interrogation would recognize the craft in these tricks of half truth, vagueness and clarity, this skipping from meaningless generalities to inconsequential specifics. His skill becomes even the more apparent when one recalls that Herold voiced this statement on the night after his capture. He must have been close to exhaustion after his journey to Washington. His captors had not been gentle. Then, sitting in the hold of monitor *Montauk*, with irons forged on his ankles and wrists, he was given no time to think it over. At once the Federal interrogators were on top of him. In the light of that trying situation, his tricky testimony appears remarkable.

Of course, the Federals knew he was fibbing here and fabricating there. But where? That was *their* problem.

Deftly Herold inserted a number of leading declarations that should have given the Bureau of Military Justice something to think about. For example, he stated that while he and Booth were "in the pines" they heard about the assault on Secretary Seward. "I was told so by a negro, who said that Secretary Seward and two of his sons had been killed. Booth made the remark that he was very sorry for the sons, but he only wished to God that Seward was killed; and that if a man he called Ed Henson, or Hanson, I believe, belonging to Mosby's command, and a man with him, had done their duty, they would have put Johnson through."

Herold also quoted Booth as saying: " 'There are 35 others in Washington, and four that ought to have joined me, and you [Herold] could have gone to the Devil.' "

Here was a bone for the Federals to chew on. As Herold doubtless expected, his interrogator returned to the point before the grilling was concluded.

> Q. Did he [Booth] tell you who these 35 men in Washington, or any of them, were?
> A. He did not. He mentioned one or two names. I recollect the name of Ed Henson or Hanson. He said five men ought to have met him. He also mentioned the name of (pause)—I don't know. He said that there was a letter he wrote and they all signed their names to it—I mean the five—giving their reasons for doing such and such things.
> Q. What was the letter about?
> A. I don't know. . . . He said it would be published. He must have sent it through the post office. . . . He said it would be in the "Intelligence."
> Q. Can you remember the names of any other parties?
> A. No, sir.[19]

---

[19] *Ibid.*

So there was this alleged letter. And a man named Henson or Hanson from Mosby's command had been expected to kill Andrew Johnson. And "35 others in Washington" were in on the plot. True or false? Very possibly false. Yet the Bureau of Military Justice should have made a determined effort to check these assertions.

At least, the Judge Advocate's Office should have subjected Herold to an intensive grilling. Probably he looked forward to a prolonged interrogation, never thinking that his captors would throw him into solitary, gag him, bury him alive for two weeks, then rush him to a trial wherein he was not permitted to open his talkative mouth.

But David Herold evidently misunderstood the game. If he did not overestimate the intelligence of his captors, he certainly underestimated the danger of his position. All his smart finesse was wasted. His interrogators were not interested in pursuing possible leads. They wanted an immediate specimen for the gallows, and they had precisely what they wanted in the person of David E. Herold.

Apparently defense counsel despaired of representing this sharp errand boy as a simpleton. Standing for Herold, Mr. Frederick Stone addressed the tribunal in a tone of apology. "May it please the court: at the earnest request of the widowed mother and estimable sisters of the accused, I have consented to act as his counsel in the case now before the Court."[20]

Having exonerated himself as Herold's pleader, Mr. Stone was in a poor position to exonerate Herold. At one point in his address, Stone conceded: "Of the fact that this boy, Herold, was an aider and abettor in the escape of Booth, there is no rational or reasonable doubt. He was clearly guilty of that crime, and must abide by its consequences."[21]

Perhaps that speech, more than anything contrived by the prosecution, put Herold on the path to the gallows.

The Government *vs.* George Andrew Atzerodt.

Little could be argued for Atzerodt. Prosecution had him dead to rights as a Potomac blockade-runner, a contraband smuggler, a confidant of Port Tobacco subversives, a member of the Booth gang who had been in on the original plot to abduct Lincoln. In addition to these several criminal activities, he had been party to the assassination conspiracy, had been in Washington on the fatal day and night, and had (it was contended) "lain in wait" for Vice President Andrew Johnson.

To all but the last, the prisoner had made admission. Perhaps not entirely frank admission. But he had uttered at least two so-called "confessions"—one made to the Marine captain on board monitor *Saugus*,[22] and

---

[20] Pitman, *op. cit.*, p. 268.
[21] *Ibid.*, p. 272.
[22] Quoted in Chapter 14.

one made two days later (April 25) to Colonel H. H. Wells. In digest: Atzerodt admitted that he'd been willing to participate in a plot to abduct Lincoln, but had drawn the line at murder.

In his formal statement to the authorities, Atzerodt declared that he met Booth and Paine at the Herndon House on the evening of April 14, and at that time Booth had unexpectedly saddled him with the assignment to slay the Vice President.[23] Atzerodt claimed he immediately refused. Booth had then menaced him, told him he had to go through with it. Atzerodt protested. He went that night to the Kimmel House, and early next day departed for Montgomery County to stay with his Cousin Richter.

For the defense, the overburdened Doster produced numerous witnesses to Atzerodt's Washington wanderings and to his flight to Rockville, Maryland. Other friendly witnesses testified that Atzerodt was an amiable fellow, had never made any particular trouble, and was known in Port Tobacco as a notorious coward. The cowardice theme was emphasized to convince the military tribunal that Atzerodt would never have entertained the thought of killing tough Andy Johnson. Finally, there remained the fact that Johnson had not been assassinated. This last was perhaps the strongest argument in Atzerodt's favor.

Unhappily for the oaf from Port Tobacco, the prosecution had a stronger argument. Against Atzerodt's protest that he had refused to enter the assassination plot stood the fact that he had taken a room at the Kirkwood House. Why, on that fatal Good Friday, had he moved into the Vice President's hotel?

His room at the Kirkwood House had secreted an arsenal. How could the carriage painter, if innocent of murderous intent, explain the weapons and other evidences of skullduggery? Why had he hung around the Kirkwood bar asking questions about Andrew Johnson? Why had he asked the location of Johnson's room?

One thing certainly was beyond defense explanation. By his own statement Atzerodt knew of the planned assassination strike. And he knew of it well in advance. For, according to the "confession" he made to Marine Captain Monroe on board the *Saugus,* he was visited in Port Tobacco by John Surratt three weeks before the fatal day. To quote Atzerodt's statement (as reported by Captain Monroe): "Atzerodt came to Washington with Surratt and was told by Booth that he must assassinate Mr. Johnson. This he refused to do and Booth threatened to blow his brains out unless he complied. He still refused and returned to Port Tobacco. A second time Surratt came for him, and he came again to Washington and took a room at Kirkwood's. He was again asked to murder Mr. Johnson, and again refused."

After two invitations to murder, one could hardly credit Atzerodt's lame

---

[23] J. E. Buckingham, *op. cit.,* p. 35.

assertion that he "knew that the President's assassination was spoken of, but did not believe it would be carried into effect."[24]

Atzerodt's initial statement to Marine Captain Frank Monroe did not receive the attention it merited. For it names John Surratt as the go-between who twice fetched Atzerodt to Washington for an assassination conference with Booth. Could one then believe the contention (later popularized) that John Surratt knew nothing of Booth's assassination plans? Surratt was Booth's trusted ally. Surely he was in on the plot.

And of course George Atzerodt was in on it. Active participant or no, he knew what was coming on the evening of April 14. That he declined to kill Johnson was beside the point. The point, patently fatal, was his failure to expose Booth's deadly plan to slay Lincoln. He could have gone to the police with a warning. Instead, George Atzerodt got drunk.

The Government vs. Edward Spangler.

The case against Edward Spangler was as tenuous as an 80-foot rope. And, when it comes to evidence of felony, 80 feet of rope can be as tenuous as 80 inches of spiderweb unless the authorities can prove the rope is somehow connected with the crime.

The rope found in Spangler's carpetbag was never conclusively tied to anything. Neither was Edward Spangler. Yet both were specimens inviting suspicion. A man who kept 80 feet of rope in his bag must have been up to something.

What had Spangler been up to?

Aside from the rope, there was the fact that Spangler had served John Wilkes Booth as a handy-man, had fixed up a stable for Booth in "Baptist Alley" behind Ford's Theater, had been at Taltavul's bar with Booth on the afternoon of April 14th, and had helped the stage crew set up the Presidential Box for that evening's performance. Everyone knew that Spangler was a friend of the arch assassin, half servant to Booth, half crony. Booth had only to whistle, and Spangler would do his bidding.

Then, while working on the fatal box Good Friday afternoon, Spangler had damned Lincoln. Witness Joseph Burroughs testified to that. When "Peanut John" remonstrated, Spangler snarled that Lincoln deserved to be shot because of all the men who'd died in the war.

It was assumed the sleazy stagehand would not have hesitated to rig the President's box for a deathtrap. He could have angled Lincoln's chair and otherwise meddled with the seating arrangements. Detectives had supposed him responsible for the broken lock on the box door.

Another supposition: Spangler procured for Booth the length of wood (part of a music stand) which the assassin used in fastening the outer door of the box. Apparently Booth found the article on stage and ready to hand when wanted.

---

[24] National Archives, War Dept. Records, File "M," Doc. 26, JAO.

Spangler, himself, had admitted in a statement to the police that Booth summoned him to the stage door on the night of the murder. "He asked me to hold his horse." (But Spangler had hurried back into the theater where he stood by with the stage crew, waiting to dismantle the "Dairy Scene." It was "Peanut John" who did the horse-holding.)

Then there was Ritterspaugh's testimony. At the moment of the assassin's backstage flight the assistant stage carpenter had exclaimed, "That was Booth!" Whereupon Spangler had whirled on Ritterspaugh and belted him in the face.

Someone in the backstage dark had slammed the stage door in the face of Booth's nearest pursuer. Perhaps the door was slammed by spry Ed Spangler. Making his own exit, he had "looked guilty" to witnesses in "Baptist Alley." Mary Jane Anderson testified that Spangler had "slunk away."

Finally there was that anaconda rope found in Spangler's bag—a singularly evil item for the imagination to play with.

Spangler, himself, was an unprepossessing specimen. Untidy, scratchy, shifty-eyed, he was a difficult character for Thomas Ewing to defend.

But what did the Government's case amount to?

The defendant was one of Booth's friends? But Booth had dozens of Washington friends, including most of the people around Ford's Theater. Spangler broke the lock on the door of Box 8? No, that was disproved. Spangler helped Booth rig the President's box? Not a witness could be found to prove it. Spangler struck the assistant carpenter? What did that actually prove? Spangler slammed the door in the face of Booth's pursuer? Nobody saw the act (and it would seem Spangler was involved with Ritterspaugh at the moment of Booth's escape). He had a bad reputation? So did some Army generals. He made ugly remarks about Lincoln? So had some of the members of Lincoln's Cabinet.

Not one iota of evidence proved Spangler an accessory to Lincoln's assassination. The case against the bleary stage carpenter was as tenuous as an eighty-foot rope. And what did rope have to do with Lincoln's murder? Lincoln did not die by a rope.

But Edward Spangler almost did.

The Government *vs.* Samuel Bland Arnold.

Samuel Arnold stood convicted by his own handwriting. The "Sam" letter. Defense could not deny Arnold's authorship of this missive addressed to John Wilkes Booth. The handwriting was undeniably identified as Arnold's. And the letter undeniably identified Arnold as a Confederate partisan, a subversive conspirator and a member of the Booth gang.

But Arnold's counsel, the able General Thomas Ewing, Jr., contended that the letter, if nothing else, proved that Arnold had refused to enter the assassination conspiracy. Admittedly the young man from Baltimore had joined the conspiracy to abduct President Lincoln. Admittedly he had come to Washington on several occasions to participate in the kidnap enterprise. But as soon as murder was proposed, Arnold had backed out. Here it was in this letter posted to Booth three weeks before the assassination strike. Arnold had quit the enterprise, dropped out of the gang.

How, then, could this young man be accused of the charges in the indictment, namely of "combining, confederating and conspiring together with . . . Jefferson Davis . . . and others unknown, to kill and murder, within the Military Department of Washington and entrenched lines thereof, Abraham Lincoln . . . and lying in wait with intent . . . to kill . . . Andrew Johnson . . . and . . . Ulysses S. Grant." Not only had Arnold quit the enterprise; he had quit the area. At the time of Lincoln's murder, the accused was nowhere near "the Military Department of Washington and the entrenched lines thereof." He was in distant Fortress Monroe, where he had gone to take a job.

The palpable absurdity of the indictment in Arnold's case must have embarrassed the Judge Advocate General. The Army lawyers in the Bureau of Military Justice had tried to fashion a bill of particulars broad enough to cover all possible escape angles. The product was a Joseph's Coat of patchwork charges that, in effect, fitted none of the accused. And here was this awkward specification limiting the conspiratorial design to the military boundaries of Washington. (What of the possibility that a conspirator had followed Grant on the train to New Jersey?)

General Ewing lost no time in attacking the patchwork indictment. Speaking for the defense, he asked the Judge Advocate General for definitions. Were the accused on trial for conspiracy? Were they on trial for murder? Or were they on trial for "lying in wait?" Were they singly or severally charged with these various crimes? Ewing observed: "The offenses enumerated . . . are separate and distinct." He asked the Judge Advocate to specify which of the said offenses were charged against the individual accused.[25]

Replying for the Court, Assistant Judge Advocate Bingham declared that "it was all one transaction."[26]

General Ewing then requested a clarification of the laws involved. Where and in what legal code could one find prescribed the crime of "*traitorously* murdering?" What was the Judge Advocate's definition for "*traitorously* lying in wait?"

The astute Ewing had caught the Judge Advocate General out on a long limb of adverb blunders. The unhappy Assistant Judge Advocate did not know what to say. So he said it, anyhow. The crimes in reference (declared Bingham) came under "the common law of war."[27]

---

25 Pitman, *op. cit.*, p. 19.
26 *Ibid.*, quoted in Eisenschiml, *op. cit.*, p. 243.
27 Pitman, *op. cit.*, p. 247.

General Ewing pointed out in his summary for the defense, that nowhere had "the common law of war" been codified. Did the Court intend "to make and declare the past acts of the accused to be crimes, which acts the law never heretofore declared criminal . . . ?"[28]

Throwing verbs and adverbs helter-skelter, the Army lawyers compounded a silly grammatical blunder, violating the laws of zeugma. Then Bingham's argument concerning "the common law of war" constituted what some judicial critics called a fantastic flounder. Two obvious bumbles presaged a third, and it was not long in coming from Assistant Judge Advocate Bingham.

Evidence was introduced to show that the defendant, Samuel Arnold, had served for a time in the Confederate Army. Prosecution contended that his enlistment in the Rebel forces constituted a criminal act. Ewing objected. Did the prosecutor mean to imply that Arnold had entered the army to assassinate the President of the United States?

Bingham: "Yes, he entered into it to assassinate the President; and everybody else that entered into the rebellion, entered it to assassinate everybody that represented this Government. . . ."[29]

Here was a blanket indictment half the size of the American continent! For if Arnold could be thus charged, so could every Confederate soldier from top general to smallest drummer boy! In which case, the conspiracy trial surpassed anything in the history of kangaroo courts. Only three ex-Confederate servicemen sat in the dock. There should have been three hundred thousand!

For the rest of his days Samuel Bland Arnold would rail against the injustice of his indictment and subsequent conviction as an assassination conspirator. But perhaps the conviction made better sense than the indictment.

True, Arnold was not in Washington from March 21 to April 17, 1865. He had refused to answer Booth's final summons to the city. And on March 27 he had written to Booth from Hookstown, Maryland, the letter introduced as evidence of his intent. But what, exactly, had been his intent?

"I told my parents I had ceased with you," he advised Booth. "Can I, then, under existing circumstances, come as you request? You know full well that the G———t suspicions something is going on there; therefore, the undertaking is becoming more complicated. Why not, for the present, desist. . . . Time more propitious will arrive yet . . . ere long I shall be better prepared to again be with you."

Although Arnold's defenders construed the "Sam" letter as proof of the writer's intention to quit the Booth gang, the fact is that his words imply a temporary separation. He says, "Why not, *for the present,* desist?"

---

[28] *Ibid.,* p. 318.
[29] *Ibid.,* p. 239.

And: *"Time more propitious will arrive."* He tells Booth he may be with him *"ere long."*

With those lines Samuel Arnold came close to writing his own death warrant.

The Government *vs.* Michael O'Laughlin.

The charge levelled at O'Laughlin was that he had "traitorously lain in wait" with intent to "kill and murder" General U.S. Grant during the nights of April 13 and 14, 1865. The Judge Advocate's Office had considerable difficulty in supplying the prosecution with evidence to support this charge.

On the evening of April 13 Grant had been a guest at a soiree at the Stanton home on K Street. A band had serenaded the "Hero of Appomattox" and a festive crowd had jammed the curb to peer and crane at the lighted windows of the Stanton mansion. About half past ten a stranger pushed up to the front door and asked to see Secretary Stanton. Stanton's son, David, and Major Kilburn Knox barred the intruder's way. The man said he was an attorney and an old friend of Stanton's. Young Stanton and Knox caught a whiff of brandy and refused to admit the inebriated caller. Some time later the man reappeared, and said that he wanted to see General Grant. This time he was turned away by an Army Sergeant named Hatter.

David Stanton, Major Knox and Sergeant Hatter were put on the stand to tell this story—the only evidence which could be mustered in support of the "lying in wait" charge against O'Laughlin. Young Stanton had been asked to identify O'Laughlin when the latter was imprisoned on board a monitor. It had to be conceded that the identification made at that time was not positive. Testifying in court, Major Knox said he was "pretty certain" that O'Laughlin was the man he had seen at Stanton's door, but again there was a shadow of doubt. Sergeant Hatter confused the issue by stating that he had glimpsed O'Laughlin at nine o'clock instead of half past ten. He admitted that the accused had made no attempt to enter the house; had merely said he wanted to see General Grant.

O'Laughlin's defense attorney, Mr. Walter Cox, had little trouble in demolishing the prosecution's case. Suppose O'Laughlin *had* been there in the crowd? Suppose he had asked to see Secretary Stanton and General Grant? Stanton and Grant were celebrities. The fact that an out-of-towner might try to see a celebrity hardly composed evidence of "lying in wait" with an intention to "kill and murder."

Moreover, the inebriate at the door had not been positively identified. Sergeant Hatter's identification seemed dubious, and the time element was discrepant. The charge, Cox noted, did not make sense. Since the caller had first inquired for Stanton, just how did the Government deduce that Grant was the intended target of that visit?

The entire charge against O'Laughlin fell apart when Cox placed on the stand the little Irishman's drinking companions—the two Baltimore sports and the naval officer who had roistered in his company throughout the afternoon and entire evening of April 13. General Grant, of course, had not been in Washington on the fatal evening of April 14. Where did that leave the Government's charge against Michael O'Laughlin?

It left O'Laughlin facing the same general indictment which had trapped Sam Arnold. O'Laughlin, too, had served a short-term enlistment in the Confederate Army. It would appear that he also had enlisted for the express purpose of assassinating President Lincoln and all the other representatives of the Federal Government.

Perhaps a strong case could have been built against O'Laughlin had the Bureau of Military Justice acted less like a vigilante crew and more like an investigatory body bent on procuring facts. O'Laughlin had disappeared for a time on the evening of April 14. He might have carried out some detail which abetted Booth's getaway, touched off a disturbance somewhere to distract the police, or flashed an important message to the underground. It is even possible that he was with the hoodlums on Lafayette Square when the light went out in front of Gideon Welles.

O'Laughlin claimed he had visited Booth that morning to collect a debt. But the fact was that he had come to Washington in answer to Booth's telegraphic summons. Booth undoubtedly used him for something.

The Government *vs.* Dr. Samuel A. Mudd.

The specific charge against Dr. Mudd was that he had conspired with Booth, Herold, Paine and John Surratt as party to the assassination plot. And that he had harbored Booth and Herold after the assassination, thereby abetting their escape.

Louis Wiechmann took the stand as one of the principal witnesses against Dr. Mudd. The Government clerk told how he and John Surratt had encountered Dr. Mudd and Booth on the street in Washington the previous January. How the four had repaired at Booth's invitation to the National Hotel. How he, Wiechmann, had departed on an errand, leaving Booth, Surratt and the Doctor engaged in private conversation in Booth's room.

The Government endeavored to prove that Dr. Mudd had remained in touch with Booth right up to the eve of April. To that end, the Judge Advocate's Office produced as witness a lawyer from Troy, New York. This gentleman, Mr. Marcus P. Norton, testified to staying at the National Hotel on March 3. He said that he was in his room when the door suddenly opened, a stranger walked in, looked around, apologized, and backed out, declaring he had mistaken the room for Mr. Booth's. Norton identified the defendant, Dr. Mudd, as this intruder.

Other Government witnesses took the stand to swear they had seen the

Bryantown physician in Booth's company during the winter of 1864–1865. Four of Mudd's prewar slaves testified that he had frequently uttered "Secesh" sentiments, had cheered for the Confederacy, and had entertained Rebel partisans at his farmhouse. Two of these former slaves stated that Mudd had denounced President Lincoln in their hearing.

A white farmer, Daniel Thomas, stated that Dr. Mudd had told him in March that the South was invincible, and that Lincoln and his Cabinet would be killed before another month was out.

Surprise witness for the prosecution was the Reverend William A. Evans, a Negro minister. Evans testified that early in March he saw the accused go into Mrs. Surratt's house at 541 H Street. Just as Dr. Mudd entered the house, a man recognized as James Jarboe came out. The witness saw Jarboe shake hands with a young woman in the doorway. The witness believed this young woman was Mrs. Surratt's daughter.

For the defense, General Ewing called numerous witnesses who flatly negated the testimony of Messrs. Norton and Thomas, the Reverend Evans and the former slaves. A number of Mudd's neighbors declared they'd never heard him utter Secessionist sentiments. Several swore the doctor had been at his home in Bryantown from December 24, 1864, to March 22, 1865 —thereby seeming to refute the contrary evidence. It was admitted that Dr. Mudd visited Washington on December 23 and on March 23. But friendly witnesses claimed they were with him throughout the days in question. If their word could be taken for it, at no time during those visits did Dr. Mudd meet Booth, Surratt and Wiechmann. Nor did he go to the National Hotel.

Prosecution made the mistake of putting Anna Surratt and Honora Fitzpatrick on the stand to support the evidence of minister-detective Evans. The maidens made adverse witnesses. Anna Surratt swore she had never seen Dr. Mudd at her mother's house, and had never set eye on him or on James Jarboe until they appeared in court. Miss Fitzpatrick offered similar testimony. Defense put James Jarboe on the stand. Jarboe told the military judges that he had not visited the Surratt house in March 1865, and had not, in fact, been in Washington City at the time of the alleged visit. This rebuttal did much to weaken the damaging statements made by the Reverend Evans.

Defense could not as easily counter the charge that Dr. Mudd had knowingly harbored Booth and Herold on the dark morning of April 15. Perhaps he did not know (and had no reason to suspect) David Herold. But the contention that he was fooled by Booth's false whiskers was (and would remain) unconvincing.

A stronger point in Mudd's defense was that of accidental involvement. Obviously, if Booth had not snapped a leg-bone, he might never have called at Mudd's farmhouse. As originally planned, Booth's escape route wound from Surrattsville to Teebee, then veered over to Piscataway and

followed the main pike to Port Tobacco, on a wide swing west of Bryantown. Or so Atzerodt detailed it in his "confession" to Colonel Wells. It
would seem, then, that Booth's deviation to Mudd's came by accident of
unexpected injury.

Prosecution countered with Wiechmann's testimony that he had seen
Dr. Mudd draw some lines on the back of an old envelope and hand the
envelope to Booth. Assumption: it must have been a map showing the
various back roads to Mudd's farm. Proof? Again the Judge Advocate's
Office dealt in vapor. The lines could have represented the battle lines of
Bull Run, the boundaries of land for sale, or the drainage streams of a cow
pasture.

Mudd's case was sorely compromised by the testimony of the Federal
troopers who visited his home on the Tuesday following the assassination.
One of Lieutenant Lovett's detective teams recalled that Mudd immediately replied, "No!" when asked if two men had come to his house the
previous Saturday. Pressed on the matter, the doctor had finally admittted
two strangers visited him on the day in question, and he had treated one
for a leg injury.

For the prosecution, Bingham now bore down on the point that Mudd
must have recognized Booth and thus withheld information from the
authorities. Argument: had he been a loyal citizen he would have reported
the fugitives at once.

With this contention, the Government advocates walked into a snare
of their own making. General Ewing called Dr. George Mudd to the
stand. And George Mudd, loyal Unionist, was able to swear that his
cousin, Dr. Samuel Mudd, had come to him in Bryantown on Easter
Sunday morning, April 16. Dr. Sam had told him of the visit by the two
horsemen, and had asked George Mudd to relay the word to the Federals.
On Monday, April 17, George Mudd had conveyed the information to
Lieutenant Dana in Bryantown. But Dana had let the matter—and the
fugitives—ride until Tuesday, April 18. Not until that late date had the
soldiers gone to Dr. Samuel Mudd's house to investigate.

Here the Prosecution's argument broke down. Why would Samuel Mudd
ask his cousin to inform the authorities, and then, when the Federals
finally did get around to his house, promptly deny the very visit he had
reported? General Ewing quickly pointed out this incongruity. Lieutenant
Lovett's testimony settled the matter. On the stand Lovett stated: "We first
asked whether there'd been any strangers at his house, and he said there
were."[30]

As for Mudd's claim that he did not know he was harboring an assassin
on April 15, his defenders pointed out that the War Department did not
immediately identify Booth as Lincoln's killer. On arriving in Bryantown,
Lieutenant Dana had created the impression that his troops were hunting

---

[30] Poore, *op. cit.*, Vol. I, p. 258.

the outlaw, Boyle. Since the Federals did not announce a search for Booth, how could Mudd have been expected to know the crippled actor was wanted?

By way of countering this defense, the prosecution called John F. Hardy, one of Mudd's neighbors. Hardy said he remembered chatting with Dr. Mudd on the evening of Saturday, April 15. News of the assassination had been discussed. While Boyle was erroneously supposed to have been Seward's assailant, Booth was mentioned as the man suspected of killing Lincoln. Hardy recalled that Dr. Mudd said nothing about the horsemen who had visited him.

Bingham finally called Colonel H. H. Wells to the stand. Wells told of interrograting Dr. Mudd soon after the defendant's arrest. Witness stated that he showed the prisoner Booth's photograph, and that Mudd had said it did not resemble the man with the injured leg. Bingham offered this as evidence that Mudd had shielded the fugitive.

General Thomas Ewing labored mightily to save the life of the unhappy doctor. More than 70 witnesses appeared for the defense—a remarkable showing, considering the brief time allotted for their procurement. But Ewing's argument met objection after objection. Time and again, these objections were sustained while his own objections were overruled. Holt and Bingham had the final say. The Court rammed through the case against Dr. Mudd in an arbitrary fashion which caused George Townsend of the New York *World* to report that, "Dr. Mudd, if he be innocent, is in only less danger than if he were guilty."[31]

Was Dr. Mudd innocent? The charge that he conspired in Lincoln's murder dissolved for want of proof. However, he may not have been the guiltless bystander eventually publicized. His denials of Secessionist sympathy were not entirely consistent with known facts. He had been a slaveholder. Many of his Bryantown friends favored the Southern Cause. His conduct hinted at association with the Confederate underground.

Apparently he did talk with Booth and Surratt in Washington. Probably he knew about the abduction plot. It would seem he was "accessory after the fact" in abetting the flight of Booth and Herold. Evidently he set them on their way to Cox's farm, and perhaps he gave them Dr. Stewart's address.

Because the Rebel underground would have covered for him, and Federal secret intelligence covered its own operations, the case of Dr. Mudd remains behind a screen of mystery. With the exception of Oldroyd, no contemporary or later historian would contend that Samuel Mudd received a "fair trial." Certainly he faced a grimly prejudiced court. But all the prejudice was not on the Government's side. When it came to chicanery the Confederate underground was as adept at falsification and deception as the Bureau of Military Justice.

---

[31] Townsend, *op. cit.*, p. 68.

In respect to deception, one item of evidence which might have told against Dr. Mudd seems to have been overlooked. In reference: David Herold's statement to the authorities. The fact that Herold never mentioned the name of the practitioner who set Booth's leg suggests a fraternal bond of some sort between the Bryantown physician and the fugitives.

And in a statement made at the time of his arrest, Mudd swore that he had not seen Booth in Washington after the actor's visit to Bryantown in November or December of 1864. (See statement in Appendix.)

The doctor who knew the answers sat in the dock staring blindly at the shadow of the gallows.

The Government *vs.* Mary Eugenia Jenkins Surratt.

Under the general indictment, Mrs. Surratt was explicitly charged with receiving, entertaining, harboring, concealing and otherwise aiding and abetting John Wilkes Booth and his co-conspirators, with being a party to the assassination conspiracy, and with aiding the assassins and abetting their escape. Prosecution rested these charges on four principal claims.

First, Mrs. Surratt was the mother of John Harrison Surratt, a known Confederate spy and Booth's right-hand man. She and her family had always been outspokenly "Secesh."

Second, the Booth gang had used her boardinghouse as headquarters. Both Atzerodt and Paine had resided there for a time. Herold and reportedly Dr. Mudd had called there. Known spies Augustus Howell and Mrs. Slater had been her guests.

Then (and particularly damaging) she had carried messages for Booth on two occasions to her tavern at Surrattsville—a key post on the Rebel underground. She had alerted innkeeper John Lloyd, telling him to get the "shooting irons" ready. And she had delivered Booth's binoculars to the tavern on the afternoon of the assassination strike.

Finally, Seward's assassin had dodged into her house on the Monday evening following Lincoln's murder. Mrs. Surratt had sworn that she did not recognize Lewis Paine, a statement that seemed to impeach her veracity.

In presenting the case against Mrs. Surratt, the prosecution placed nine major witnesses on the stand. Six of these soon dwindled in importance. Chief witnesses for the Government were Louis J. Wiechmann, John M. Lloyd and Major H. W. Smith the officer who had arrested the accused.

Led from statement to statement by Assistant Judge Advocate Bingham, Wiechmann told a tale most damaging to the lady in the dock. He recalled his classroom friendship with John Surratt at St. Charles College. His visits to the family at Surrattsville. How he came to lodge in the boardinghouse on H Street. How, strolling with John Surratt, he met Booth and Dr. Mudd one January afternoon. How Booth thereafter became a frequent caller at the boardinghouse.

The back-room conversations between Booth and Mrs. Surratt and John —Atzerodt's arrival at the door—the entry of "Mr. Wood" who turned out to be the "Reverend Paine"—the strange doings in the household—the mysterious guests, Gus Howell and Mrs. Slater—the discovery of guns and daggers on Paine's bed—the frenzied scene in March when Booth, John Surratt and Paine raged into the house—Wiechmann recounted these incidents and episodes with seeming candor.

He told of seeing David Herold "with a band of musicians" at Mrs. Surratt's tavern in 1863 and at a later date (unspecified) at 541 H Street. Of conversations with the spy, Gus Howell. Of the shadowy conduct of Mrs. Slater. Wiechmann said that Mrs. Surratt informed him Mrs. Slater was a "dispatch bearer." He recalled that Mrs. Surratt and John Surratt drove off in a buggy with Mrs. Slater about three weeks before the assassination. And that afterwards Mrs. Surratt told him they were supposed to meet Howell, but the "blockade runner" had been arrested, and John Surratt had gone on to Richmond with Mrs. Slater.

Probably the decisive blow dealt Mrs. Surratt was Wiechmann's testimony concerning his two trips with her to Surrattsville—the first on April 11, when she conferred on the road with John Lloyd, and the second on that fatal Good Friday afternoon when she delivered a package from Booth into the hands of the tavern keeper. The prosecution argued powerfully that Mrs. Surratt had alerted Lloyd with messages from Booth. Bingham placed the innkeeper himself on the stand to corroborate this serious accusation.

Fat, sloppy Lloyd, snuffling and uneasy, made an exceptionally poor witness. Nevertheless, he testified to hiding escape gear in the tavern at John Surratt's insistence. He mumbled of the meeting with Mrs. Surratt on the road below Navy Yard Bridge, and vowed that she had told him to have the "shooting irons" ready. He said she repeated the instructions when he saw her at the tavern on the evening of April 14, and that she gave him a parcel containing Mr. Booth's field glasses.

Called to the stand, Lloyd's sister-in-law, Mrs. Emma Offutt, more or less reinforced the innkeeper's testimony. She admitted, however, that she did not hear the conversations between Mrs. Surratt and Lloyd.

Major Smith followed through with the story of Mrs. Surratt's arrest on the night of April 17. He detailed Paine's arrival at the house, the fugitive's improvised ditchdigger costume, Mrs. Surratt's cry of alarm at sight of the midnight caller, and her protest then and later that she did not recognize him.

Mrs. Surratt's defense counsel, Frederick Aiken and John Clampitt, fought valiantly to refute the Government's case. Twenty-five witnesses were placed on the stand for Mrs. Surratt. Neighbors characterized her as a woman of probity, a devout Christian, a regular churchgoer. They said they had never heard her utter disloyal sentiments. Among the character witnesses were five Catholic priests—Fathers Francis E. Boyle and Charles H. Stonestreet, who had known her for years, and Fathers Peter Lanahan, W. D. Young and J. A. Walter, her parish priest.

Aiken and Clampitt put Wiechmann through a severe cross-examination. They caught him on some small discrepancies, but on the whole he supported his testimony rather well. He did talk himself toward one pitfall. He said that he was sorry to take the stand against Mrs. Surratt—she was a good, kindly woman who had "treated him like a son." He added that he stood as a Government witness only because he felt it his duty as a loyal citizen to do so. Defense would check for future reference this assertion of dutiful loyalty.

Innkeeper John M. Lloyd did not hold up nearly so well under cross-questioning. Defense counsel caught him on several significant contradictions. Pressed on the point, Lloyd confessed he was not certain just when Mrs. Surratt spoke to him about the "shooting irons." Nor could he recall just what she'd said. Finally he admitted to being "in liquor" when he saw her late Good Friday afternoon at Surrattsville.

Lloyd was characterized as a chronic drunkard by half a dozen witnesses. Mrs. Offutt recalled that he was reeling when he returned to Surrattsville from Marlboro on Good Friday. Having drowned Lloyd's testimony with this evidence, defense counsel pointed out that the innkeeper had told the first party of police who called at the tavern that he knew nothing of the assassination and had never seen the fugitives. Special Officer Cottingham admitted that Lloyd had babbled in hysteria for two days after his arrest. Eventually Lloyd had sobered up and changed his story, confessing that he'd withheld information because he feared he might be killed. So said Officer Cottingham. Defense might have followed this angle further, but Clampitt and Aiken were doubtless satisfied they had impeached Lloyd's veracity.

Three witnesses were called to corroborate Mrs. Surratt's declaration that she had visited Surrattsville on legitimate business. John Nothey stated that she had come to see him on the afternoon of April 11 to collect a debt. A Mr. B. F. Gwynn, who lived near Surrattsville, said that he saw Mrs. Surratt at the tavern on Good Friday and that she gave him a letter for Nothey. Mrs. Surratt's brother, "Zad" Jenkins, swore that he had talked with her at the tavern on Good Friday, and that she mentioned the debt errand and showed him a pressing letter from Mr. Calvert.

Key witness for the defense was Anna Surratt. Brought in from the Old Capitol, she made an appealing figure in court. She testified that Atzerodt had stayed in her mother's boardinghouse as a lodger only one night. That afterward he called a number of times to see Wiechmann. That Paine boarded there for a brief time, calling himself "Wood." That a daguerrotype of Booth, found by the police behind a picture in her mother's parlor, had been hidden there because her brother, John, ordered it destroyed, and she, Anna, wanted to keep it. That she had not seen her brother since the 3rd of April. That she had liked Booth but her brother had advised her the actor was "crazy." That, Paine and Atzerodt excepted, she had never seen at her mother's house any of the men now on trial. That she had never heard anyone in the house "breathe a word" about an abduction or an assassination plot.

Colonel Henry Kyd Douglas, C.S.A., would recall the appearance of Miss Surratt in court as "pitiable." Afterward, this Confederate witness wrote: "She was tall, slender, fair, handsome; for her to stand the stare of the cruel, stony eyes riveted upon her was a trying ordeal. She must have known that her testimony made no impression on the tribunal, and toward the close of it she began to show signs of a collapse. The veins and muscles of her neck seemed swollen and she gave evidence of great suffering. General Hartranft was about to go to her, but knowing her horror of him as her mother's jailor, he, with delicate consideration, asked me to bring her from the stand. I brought her out, passing just in front of her mother, and as she reached my room she fell forward and fainted. The door was shut quickly, a doctor was called, and at his instance General Hartranft and I carried her below to his room. There she had a spasm and began to tear out her beautiful hair and to rend her dress. Women arriving, she was left with them. . . ."[32]

Mrs. Elizabeth Holohan (the tombstone-cutter's wife) corroborated much of Anna Surratt's testimony about boarding-house affairs. She did state that Booth, when he came to the door, usually inquired for John Surratt and asked to see Mrs. Surratt if John were not in.

One of the last witnesses for the defense was Augustus Howell, the "blockade-runner." Howell's testimony faltered with his statement that he had "no particular" occupation at the time of his arrest. In further stating that he had gone down to Richmond a number of times during the war, he confessed to being a spy. But he went on to testify that he had known the Surratt family for years. He declared that he had stopped at Mrs. Surratt's house on H Street because Washington hotels were too expensive for him and he had preferred the homey atmosphere of the boardinghouse. The witness remembered Wiechmann as especially cordial. He said that Wiechmann had sympathized with the Confederacy, saying he'd like to live down South.

Perhaps the weakest argument in Mrs. Surratt's defense was the contention that she failed to recognize Lewis Paine when he called at her house on the night of April 17. Defense tried hard to prove that Mrs. Surratt's vision was much impaired. Anna Surratt and Honora Fitzpatrick were among several witnesses called to testify that Mary Surratt could hardly see without her glasses. But boarder John Holohan told the Court that he had never heard mention of his landlady's nearsightedness, by her or any-

---

[32] *Op. cit.*, p. 346.

one in the household. Prosecution failed to point out the fact, but Anna and Nora were also in the vestibule when Paine arrived at the house that night. Certainly *they* were not nearsighted. Too, there was the matter of Paine's voice.

Nevertheless, the defense had scored. They had boiled down John Lloyd's evidence to a boozy mishmash and had introduced testimony which impugned Wiechmann's loyalty. The Judge Advocate General and his assistants could do little to salvage the soggy Lloyd. But they rushed reinforcements to the stand to bolster the embarrassed Wiechmann.

Several Government witnesses were called to testify that Wiechmann bore the reputation of a loyal pro-Unionist. As *prima facie* evidence, there was his report to Captain Gleason some time in March concerning suspicious activities in the house on H Street. And hadn't Wiechmann volunteered to go to Canada in search of John Surratt? Officer J. A. McDevitt testified to Wiechmann's zealous efforts in Montreal. McDevitt also noted that Wiechmann could have easily escaped in Canada had he been so minded.

To counter direct evidence in Mrs. Surratt's behalf, prosecution called a number of witnesses. "Zad" Jenkins' testimony was considerably devaluated by persons who described him as an outspoken Secessionist. Mr. Ephraim Smoot took the stand to testify that bartender Joe Nott at Mrs. Surratt's tavern knew all about the conspiracy and had named John Surratt as one of the leaders.

The last of the evidence was in by June 16th, and defense counsel faced the bar to deliver summations. John Clampitt began the closing argument for Mrs. Surratt by reading a brief which had been prepared by Reverdy Johnson. This brilliant legal exposition was made in behalf of all defendants, and it smote the Military Commission squarely on a most vulnerable point—the question of War Department jurisdiction and the legality of the military tribunal.

In effect, Reverdy Johnson contended that the present Court was unconstitutional. "Military tribunals can try none but military offenses," he argued, "and even those only when the persons committing them are members of the military forces." The jurist reminded the Court that "traitorous conspiracy" (the crime specified in the general indictment) was defined as treason. And, according to the Constitution, treason trials could only be held in civil courts. (This was a point driven home by General Thomas Ewing in summarizing for his clients. Ewing told the officers of the Military Commission: "Under the Constitution none but courts ordained and established by Congress can exercise judicial power [over civilians]. . . . Congress has not ordained nor established you a court. . . . You are, therefore, no court, and you have no jurisdiction in this case. . . ."[33]

---

[33] Pitman, *op. cit.*

It was reported that Judge Holt and his assistants paid little notice to the reading of Reverdy Johnson's argument. Nor were the officers of the tribunal attentive. General Hunter dozed. Lew Wallace drew idle sketches. The other officer-judges expressed boredom. The tribunal was not interested in hearing its own legality invalidated.

In respect to Mary Surratt, Johnson's brief noted: ". . . I have not remarked on the evidence in the case of Mrs. Surratt, nor is it my purpose." But the jurist added: "That a woman, well educated and, as far as we can judge from her past life as we have it in evidence, a devout Christian, ever kind, affectionate and charitable, with no motive disclosed to us that could have caused a total change in her very nature, could have participated in the crimes in question is almost impossible to believe." The jurist pointed out that Wiechmann and Lloyd were not "unsuspected" witnesses, and that the "particulars" would be discussed by associate defense counsel.

Frederick Aiken delivered the concluding argument in Mrs. Surratt's defense. Aiken reminded the Court that much of the evidence against the widow was circumstantial. Not one item of evidence (Aiken argued) proved that Mrs. Surratt had guilty knowledge of the assassination conspiracy. The pleader contended that Lloyd's testimony was manifestly worthless. And that Wiechmann, by his own statements, had revealed himself a disloyal character who had changed sides through opportunism and expediency.

Aiken declared in closing: "Even if the son of Mrs. Surratt . . . is to be classed with the conspirators . . . it is monstrous to suppose that the son would weave a net of circumstantial evidence around the dwelling of his widowed mother . . . and that they joined hands in such a dreadful pact is more monstrous still to be thought. . . ." It was a stirring, if not entirely logical summation.

The prosecution had the final say. Bingham did the orating. Much of his wordage went into answering Reverdy Johnson's contention that the Military Commission sat without jurisdiction. A generation of lawyers would debate the pro and con of Bingham's legalistic rhetoric. To the last he bombarded the Court with indefinables and abstractions. But in sum he presented the philosophy behind the Government's (or the War Department's) (or Stanton's) ukase. Argument: the rebellion itself was a gigantic conspiracy led by Jefferson Davis et al. The Army of the Republic had put down this vast conspiracy. The Commander-in-Chief had been murdered by assassins directly linked to Davis and the Confederacy by the fugitive John Surratt. The defendants at the bar were co-conspirators. And so on.

Bingham dealt only briefly with Mrs. Surratt's case. Briskly he reviewed the evidence. He conceded that Lloyd was a "weakling." But (declared Bingham) the innkeeper's testimony had not been controverted in any important particular. As for Louis Wiechmann, the man was a patriotic citizen who had done his best to support the Government and aid the forces of law and order.

Bingham concluded: "It is almost imposing upon the patience of the Court to consume time in demonstrating the fact . . . that John H. Surratt and Mary E. Surratt were as surely in a conspiracy to murder the President as was John Wilkes Booth himself." The Assistant Judge Advocate did not consume much time in that demonstration. His summation on Mrs. Surratt took something under half an hour. Whereupon he left with the Court "the decision of this dread issue."[34]

It was an issue that would be debated for the next nine decades. However, the officer-judges of the Military Commission were soldiers not given to prolonged ratiocination and judicial deliberation. Trial proceedings ended with Bingham's summation on June 28th. Court was immediately cleared. The prisoners were returned to their cells. The officers of the tribunal retired behind closed doors to find verdicts and devise sentences. Not only did these Army officers play both judge and jury, but (as was customary with courts-martial) the Judges Advocate of the prosecution sat with them to steer their deliberations. They arrived at their mass decision in less than 72 hours, although they did devote a goodly share of their high-speed deliberations to the case of Mrs. Surratt.

Was Mrs. Surratt guilty as charged? Was her involvement limited to Booth's abduction plot? Was she merely a passive onlooker who knew the conspirators were up to something, but remained ignorant of both abduction and assassination projects? Was she a wholly innocent bystander involved entirely without intent—a victim of circumstances?

While the officer-judges debate the enumerated possibilities, let us apprehend their judgment with a review of historical opinion. By and large, history's consensus is that Mrs. Surratt was not guilty as charged. Which is to say she knew nothing of the assassination plot and was in no way an active participant or intentional accessory. Did she carry messages from Booth to innkeeper Lloyd, and deliver to the Surrattsville tavern Booth's binoculars? Possibly—even probably. But she could have done so in all innocence, merely to oblige Mr. Booth. And even if one assumes she suspected some underground project were afoot, nothing in the trial evidence *proved* she knew the project involved an assassination strike.

A few historians concede she may have known about the abduction plot. On the surface of it, such knowledge seems likely. John Surratt may have tried to conceal purposes and intents from his mother, but Booth did a lot of talking. There were those back-room interviews with Booth and her son (Wiechmann was not the only witness to these episodes). Besides, mothers have a way of eliciting information from their sons. And Mary Surratt could not have been blind to some of the doings in her boarding-

---

[34] *Ibid.*

house. Especially the comings and goings of such characters as Paine and Atzerodt.

Writing in 1895, historian David M. DeWitt presented Mrs. Surratt as an innocent woman caught in a trap of circumstances and victimized by savage and prejudiced officialdom.[35] A number of modern writers, among them author Helen Jones Campbell[36] and playwright John Patrick,[37] present Mary Surratt as a lady entirely innocent of guile, a loyal American who was betrayed by a cheap-Jack informer and sacrificed on an altar of Yankee intolerance and (implied) religious prejudice.

By those who see Mrs. Surratt as entirely guiltless of collusion (or any subversion), Louis Wiechmann is usually beheld as the villain of the piece. The Government employee is described as an opportunist, a fabricator, a Secessionist turncoat who knew upon which side his bread was buttered.

Wiechmann may, indeed, have been a Secessionist turncoat. The files of the Bureau of Military Justice contain an undated report on the witness scribbled by Colonel John A. Foster. From the context with other reports on the subject, it appears to have been written early in May. It reads:

> Wiechmann was employed in the Commissary General's Office, and boarded with Mrs. Surratt. He had frequent conversations with fellow clerks about the blockade-running business and the money that could be made out of it. About time of Inauguration, spoke of a plot to assassinate all the Government officers.[38]

But suppose Wiechmann were a turncoat informer? A reformed subversive? A cat-jump opportunist who sought to save his own skin by running to the authorities? The unpleasant truth of the matter is that many felony convictions are thus obtained. American authorities have long catered to the man who turned "state's evidence"—the suspected or known offender who, through promise of amnesty or award, agrees to testify against former companions. We may suspect this man's "reform," mistrust his motives, despise him for knavery. Yet his testimony may prove uncontrovertable. In which case, personal motives or knavery fail to signify.

Wiechmann's character aside, his testimony concerning Mrs. Surratt and the doings in her H Street house remained largely uncontroverted by the defense. And much of that evidence indicated that Mrs. Surratt had knowingly entertained a subversive clientele. What of defense witnesses who described her as God-fearing, a devout churchgoer? The pastors and good neighbors apparently forgot that the great sin of 1865 was political heresy—a crime that had nothing to do with religious faith. What of those who characterized her as a lady of refinement, a devoted mother? Thou-

---

[35] Op. cit.
[36] Op. cit.
[37] Op. cit.
[38] National Archives, War Dept. Records, File "W," JAO.

sands of refined ladies and devoted mothers had been ardent Secession partisans. The Federal officers had only to remember such subversive ladies as Mrs. Rose Greenhow and Mrs. Philip Phillips.

But Wiechmann's was not the only testimony which imperiled Mrs. Surratt. The Bureau of Military Justice had in its possession a number of depositions which militated against her. There was her own statement made on the night of her arrest wherein she declared that her son had "never been away from home long enough to go South." There was her insistence that she did not recognize Paine when he came to her door that fateful night. Her daughter's statement regarding that episode put the matter in a dubious light. On April 28th, Anna Surratt had been interrogated at the Old Capitol by Colonel Foster. Questioned on Paine, she answered as follows:

Q. Was he a handsome fellow?
A. I would not know—I have not seen any remarkably handsome men since I have been in Washington. I didn't like him.
Q. When did you next see him?
A. I haven't seen him since.
Q. Didn't you see him the night he was arrested?
A. I didn't look at that man that came in at all.
Q. Not when we thought he was [John] Surratt?
A. Oh, I saw him then, but I didn't recognize him then because he had changed or something about him looked as if I had never seen him before.
Q. He had changed his dress, do you mean?
A. Well, he looked different, but there was something about him—about *somebody* that I had seen.
Q. Isn't there a conviction in your mind that he was the very man that you saw there who pretended to be a Baptist preacher?
[Illegible] I would not like to say. I have not thought of him since. I never shall forget my feelings that night.
Q. Would you ever forget that eye or the look that he had?
A. No, sir.
Q. Would you ever forget the eyes that he had at your house before?
A. They did not look like the eyes of the man that was at our house.
Q. How do you explain the fact of that man's coming there that night of your arrest?
A. I cannot say anything about it.
Q. Calling your mother by name?
A. I cannot explain anything about it.
Q. When he came, saying that he came to see her, calling her by name and saying that he had been sent there?
A. Indeed, I cannot explain about it. If I could, I would.[39]

In a statement made to the authorities on that same date (April 28th), Nora Fitzpatrick voiced the following declarations in regard to Paine:

Q. He wasn't a man that you would like to be alone with, was he?
A. No sir.

---

[39] National Archives, War Dept. Records, File "S," Doc. R.B.P. 79, JAO.

Q. How came it that you did not recognize him that night when you were all arrested, when he came in there?
A. Well, I was frightened that night.
Q. Was it because you were frightened, or because he was in disguise?
A. *No, I do not think he was disguised at all.*

Here, from a person most devoted to Mrs. Surratt and Anna, was testimony which must have settled all doubt as to whether Paine had been recognizable on the night in question. Colonel Foster pressed the point. "How different did he look this time from what he looked before?" And Nora answered: "He had a thing on his head."[40] But it is clear that she did not consider a pickaxe and this "thing" a disguise.

Honora Fitzpatrick made some other interesting statements to her interrogators. For example:

Q. Did you ever have any suspicions that all these men [Booth, Atzerodt, Paine, John Surratt] were contriving something? Did you never hear them talking as though they were?
A. No sir. Indeed, I never heard them say anything.
Q. Did they seem to act in a suspicious manner, having a great many things to say up in the corner and keeping away from the rest of the family?
A. *I know sometimes they were up at Mrs. Surratt's room.*
Q. How often did they do that?
A. Indeed, I don't know how often, but I know they went up there.
Q. Who would go up there?
A. Sometimes Booth would go up there, and sometimes Port Tobacco, and then Wood [Paine] sometimes.[41]

The Judge Advocate's files contained still other items of evidence which could have reinforced the Government's case against Mrs. Surratt. Some of this information came in during the trial. For instance, information concerning Mrs. Surratt's acknowledged friend, the "blockade-runner" Gus Howell. Here is a confidential memo filed by Colonel Foster:

In regard to Wiechmann's testimony of 18 May 1865, F. Evan Walker states that Howell is the [man named] Emack who stabbed him (Walker). States that he was a spy & subordinate of Genl Winder at Libby prison.

Foster jotted another memo on August Howell under date of May 28. "Wiechmann states that Howell was a notorious blockade-runner. Howell said that he could stomach any amount of Oaths. Threatened me [Wiechmann] if I said anything against him."[42]

With this sort of evidence in hand, it seems apparent that the Judge Advocate's Office was playing cat-and-mouse with Mrs. Surratt. But what was the object of the game? One would believe her dealings with secret agents Gus Howell and Mrs. Slater a powerful indication of subversive

---

[40] National Archives, War Dept. Records, File "F," JAO. (Emphasis supplied.)
[41] *Ibid.* Emphasis supplied.
[42] National Archives, War Dept. Records, File "W," JAO.

leanings and conspiratorial activity. Yet Judge Holt and his associates did not bear down on this point. Mystery still shrouds Mrs. Surratt's involvement with the two enemy spies—a matter overlooked by historians. But why did the Government glide over it?

Anyone attempting to analyze the case of Mary E. Surratt must inevitably come up against the curtain of secret intelligence. Confederate secret intelligence—as evidenced by John Surratt's underground activities and by the presence of spies Howell and Slater in Mrs. Surratt's house. And United States secret intelligence—as evidenced by the hidden hand of the U.S. Secret Service operating through the War Department. The analyst who tries to deal with these elements finds himself frustrated by War Department secrecy.

It is possible, then, that Mrs. Surratt was an active agent—one of that secret sorority which had included such Washington espions as the Widow Greenhow, Lilly A. Mackle and Miss E. M. Poole. Spy evidence against Mrs. Surratt could have been withheld to protect Union counter-intelligence agents in Maryland or Richmond, or to cover agents hunting for John Surratt in Canada. Satisfied the Court would convict her, anyway, Stanton and Holt could have preferred to have her sentenced as one of the assassination conspirators.

But if Mrs. Surratt did, indeed, operate as a Confederate agent, it would seem that offensive espionage was beyond her. More in keeping with her capacities would have been such subversive activity as seems to have engaged mysterious Nannie Lomax Green. Doster recalled that during the trial ordeal David Herold sourly remarked of Mrs. Surratt: "That old lady is as deep in as any of us."[43] But (according to Doster) Herold resented the strong defense erected in Mrs. Surratt's behalf. So his remark may have been no more than a nasty and vindictive effort to transfer guilt.

If true, the account published by Richard Smoot in 1904 would seem to cast a definite doubt on Mrs. Surratt's innocence, at least in respect to a knowledge of the abduction plot. This Smoot was the Maryland farmer who professed to working with the Charles County underground. After the war he moved to Fort Smith, Arkansas. He prefaces his memoir with: "So long as there was anyone likely to be injured by a revelation of the secrets I have kept hidden, I have kept my word inviolate."[44] Evidently he felt free to talk in 1904.

As Smoot tells it, he was visited at his farm near Port Tobacco by John Surratt early in 1865. Surratt wanted to purchase a boat that could carry fifteen men. Smoot had such a boat, and the price was agreed—$250. Surratt made down payment of $150, and Smoot turned the boat over to "Andrew Atzerott." Atzerodt placed the scow in charge of one George Bateman, who hid it up King's Creek.

---

[43] W. E. Doster, *op. cit.*, p. 277.
[44] R. M. Smoot, *op. cit.*, p. 1.

As time passed, Smoot became anxious about the balance ($100) due him on the boat. Atzerodt, evasive, told him to wait; spoke of a "desperate game." After further delay, Atzerodt advised Smoot to go to Surrattsville and ask tavernkeeper Lloyd about Surratt's whereabouts. Lloyd gave Smoot the address of the boardinghouse in Washington, and told him to see Mrs. Surratt.[45]

Smoot journeyed to the capital to call on the widow. She was at first suspicious. Then, when he explained his business, "her face brightened," and she became communicative. "She whispered to me that if I returned to the house on Friday, I would most likely see John and the boys."[46]

Smoot returned to Washington that Friday. He found Mrs. Surratt "in a state of feverish excitement." She said John had not yet returned. "She then informed me she was positive the boat would be used that night, and that I would get my money in a day or two. She most earnestly besought me to leave the city and not be seen at her house again."[47]

Alarmed by Mrs. Surratt's warning, Smoot promptly left the capital. Missing the last stagecoach to lower Maryland, he walked across the Long Bridge to Alexandria, Virginia, (eight miles) where he went to the City Hotel. Saturday morning, awakened by tumult, he learned Lincoln had been assassinated. Fearing implication, he hastened back to his remote farm. He was arrested late in April and confined in Carroll Prison. There he met the Fords and Dr. Stewart. He engaged Judge P. W. Crane as counsel. After ten days' confinement he was released.[48]

Printed in a small booklet (according to Library of Congress notation, only five copies of it remain extant), Richard Smoot's story is perhaps the only post-war testimonial from a Southern sympathizer bearing evidence against Mrs. Surratt. Smoot may or may not have manufactured this recollection. In detail his story seems to hold together. Against it stands the preponderant testimony of Mrs. Surratt's friends and neighbors. In any event, no evidence was produced which proved that Mary E. Surratt had guilty knowledge of the assassination plot.

Only the unfortunate woman in the dock—a stark figure in black— knew the whole truth. The answers would remain as though hidden by the midnight gauze of her funeral veil.

On June 30, 1865, the military tribunal returned the verdict. All eight defendants were found guilty of participation in the assassination conspiracy.

Dr. Samuel Mudd, Samuel Bland Arnold and Michael O'Laughlin were

---

[45] *Ibid.*, p. 4.
[46] *Ibid.*, pp. 4, 5.
[47] *Ibid.*
[48] *Ibid.*, pp. 6, 7.

sentenced to life imprisonment in the Federal Penitentiary at Albany, New York.

Edward Spangler was sentenced to serve six years in the Albany Penitentiary.

Lewis Paine, David E. Herold, George Atzerodt and Mary Eugenia Jenkins Surratt were sentenced to death by hanging.

But nobody believed that Mrs. Surratt would be hanged.

The sentence passed on Mrs. Surratt was contrived through deception. Long afterward the story leaked out. At first the military judges had stood five to four against, with only Generals Wallace, Harris, Howe, and Colonel Clendenin voting to hang the widow. Judge Holt argued and harangued in stormy session, then went to see Stanton. Details were never made public, but apparently at Stanton's instigation (certainly with his approval) the Judge-Advocate General came back with a compromise. If the tribunal would vote a unanimous death sentence for Mrs. Surratt, a petition of mercy would then be forwarded to President Andrew Johnson.

Generals Hunter, Foster, Kautz, Ekin, and Colonel Tompkins signed a petition recommending that the death sentence passed on Mrs. Surratt be commuted to life imprisonment. Holt promised to present the appeal to Johnson. According to Johnson, he never saw the petition. On the morning of July 6 he signed the four death warrants. *Date of execution was set for the following day!*

Desperate efforts were immediately launched in Mrs. Surratt's behalf. Anna Surratt, who had been released from the Old Capitol, rushed to the White House with Father Walter to beg for mercy. She was turned back at the White House entry by New York Senator Preston King. Mrs. Surratt's lawyers were similarly stopped at the entry by King and Senator James H. Lane of Kansas. Thomas Florence, editor of the *Constitutional Union*, was also turned away. So were Mrs. Stephen A. Douglas and other petitioners.

Reverdy Johnson telegraphed to Aiken and Clampitt, advising a last try with a writ of *habeas corpus*. Andrew Johnson negated the writ.

At ten o'clock in the morning of July 7, 1865, the scaffold stood ready in the Penitentiary yard. Ready, too, were the four newly excavated graves at the foot of the scaffold, the four pine boxes waiting to receive the bodies.

It was a molten morning. Sweat streamed down the faces of the spectators, the troops on duty, the newsmen waiting in the stifling sun. All could hear the outcry and lamentation occasioned by last farewells in the prison hall. Anna Surratt was there. So were Herold's sisters. Mrs. Wheeler had come to bid Atzerodt goodbye. Only Lewis Paine was left to walk the last mile unmourned.

A door opens in the prison wall. Mrs. Surratt comes out first, fainting, supported by two priests (Father Wigett and Walter) with soldier escort.

Next comes Atzerodt, shambling in chains, accompanied by a Lutheran clergyman and an armed squad. Then David Herold, tottering, weeping, prodded along the fatal walk by muttering troopers. Finally Paine, chin up, shoulders squared, striding barefoot, the personification of Spartan defiance. Someone has clapped a sailor straw on his head—a prank quite in keeping with the Guignol atmosphere of the proceedings.

Mrs. Surratt is half carried up the scaffold steps. The others are either boosted up or hauled up in her train. An umbrella is held over the woman's veiled head while her arms and ankles are bound. Quickly her companions are pinioned. General Hartranft reads the findings and the warrants. The spiritual advisers murmur words of solace. The nooses are lowered and adjusted. Death-caps are drawn over the four condemned heads. The victims are positioned over the traps.

Reporting for the *New York World,* George Alfred Townsend observed: "The two traps fell with a slam, the four bodies dropped like a single thing."[49]

The *Tribune* reporter noted that Paine's hardy physique prolonged his death struggle. Herold "died the next hardest. The deaths of Mrs. Surratt and Atzerodt were comparitively easy. . . . After the convulsions of all were over, Mrs. Surratt, Payne and Atzerodt hung with their heads bent forward, while that of Harrold (*sic*) inclined back, which latter was said by experts to be the only execution on correct principles."[50]

CHAPTER 24

War Department
Confidential

IN THE WAKE of the execution came storm. The gallows victims were hardly buried before adverse public reaction set in.

Throughout the conspiracy trial the Military Commission had been sharply criticized by opponents of the Administration and by liberal elements of the Northern press. It was said that Stanton ran the proceedings. That the Court had been "organized to convict."[1] That the defense lawyers

---

49 George Alfred Townsend, quoted in Oldroyd, *op. cit.,* pp. 198–206.
50 *New York Tribune,* July 8, 1865.
1 Poore, *op. cit.,* p. 203.

were incompetent. That the condemned (with Paine excepted) had been "sacrificed."

George Alfred Townsend left a picture of the tribunal etched in acid. "Excepting Judge Holt, the court has shown as little ability as could be expected from soldiers, placed in unenviable publicity, and upon a duty for which they are disqualified, both by education and acumen. Witness the lack of dignity in Hunter, who opened the court by a coarse allusion to 'humbug chivalry'; of Lew Wallace, whose heat and intolerance were appropriately urged in the most exceptional English; of Howe, whose tirade against the rebel General Johnson was feeble as it was ungenerous! This court was needed to show us at least the petty tyranny of martial law and the pettiness of martial jurists."[2]

Now that the trial was over, the public mind harbored a perceptive suspicion that the Army's Judge Advocate General, the Military Commission, the Bureau of Military Justice and the war lord behind the scene had been guilty of something worse than "petty tyranny." The frantic haste with which the defendants were placed on trial—the vaporus wording of the conspiracy indictment—the arbitrary rulings of the Court wherein every objection made by the prosecution was sustained whereas all objections made by defense counsel were overruled—these and other manifestations of a witchcraft proceeding began to bite into the national consciousness. Edward Bates, Orville Browning and other influential Northerners denounced the trial as a travesty and a judicial farce. On Capitol Hill a few Congressmen spoke warnings against military courts and bayonet rule. Editors described the mass executions as a barbarian festival, a Roman holiday.

Storm centered over the hanging of Mrs. Surratt—the first American woman to be executed by Federal order—the first to die for an alleged crime against the State. Were she guilty or innocent, her execution was bound to raise an emotional tide. Her family, her friends, the priests of her church were not alone in denouncing the militarists who had summarily condemned her. Many Northern liberals, who had expected her reprieve, protested her execution. Of course most Southerners denounced it as an outrage against all humanity.

The storm from the South—the accusation that the Yankee Government acted with unparalleled cruelty in condemning a woman to die—was not entirely justified by the code of Confederate military procedure. In a somewhat similar case, Confederate General Braxton Bragg had not hesitated to order the execution of Miss Pauline Cushman, caught behind Southern lines and condemned as a Union secret agent. In fact, General Bragg ordered this actress spy shot within twenty-four hours. Her death by firingsquad had been averted only when Federal troops swept into Bragg's camp and rescued her. And had they detected her in Richmond,

---

[2] Townsend, *op. cit.*, pp. 67–68.

the Confederate authorities would surely have hanged Grant's ace spy, Miss Elizabeth Van Lew—a lady who listened in on, and reported, some of the war plans discussed by Jefferson Davis.

Too, Northern critics were unrealistic in basing their protests on the fact of Mrs. Surratt's womanhood. As Judge Holt doubtless perceived, this emotional objection had nothing to do with justice. Hence, it could be set up as a straw dummy for easy demolishment. By directing the tribunal's attention to this simple target, he could divert the officer judges from the pressing and valid issue—the question of Mrs. Surratt's unproven guilt.

There, and there alone, lay the judicial infamy in the hanging of Mary Surratt. Concede it cruel to hang a woman—on the postulate that capital punishment is barbarous in many a case. But the homicide laws demanded the eye-for-eye penalty. The wartime espionage law demanded death for the captured espion. Government decree demanded death for treason. Yet Mrs. Surratt had been proven neither murderess nor spy. Was she executed for treason? If so, she was punished for a crime of which thousands of Southerners had been accused, and her execution was the very antithesis of equal justice under law.

Soon the story of Anna Surratt's visit to the White House, the frustation of her plea for mercy, was in circulation. Father Walter told her of being turned away by Senator King. Similar stories were told by other pleaders. Andrew Johnson was denounced as Mrs. Surratt's "executioner." It was said that Isaac Surratt was returning from San Antonio, Texas, armed with funds from his remnant regiment, in his mind the advice, "Go home and kill Andy Johnson."[3]

By the autumn of 1865 rumors of the Court's clemency recommendation were adrift. Now Johnson was labeled a monster, a Caligula who had ignored an official petition for mercy. There must have been some tempestuous wordage exchanged between Johnson and Judge Holt. By winter the President was at loggerheads with the Bureau of Military Justice. Eventually Johnson denounced the Judge Advocate General as "cruel and remorseless" and said that Holt exhibited the traits of Nero and of Draco.[4]

By that time people were saying Mrs. Surratt had been hanged "to keep her from talking." It was implied that she knew certain facts about the conspiracy which the Government preferred to cover up. This story did not conform with the tale that she was a guileless innocent. Nor with a cumulative rumor that her confessor, Father Walter, had (for some unspecified reason) prohibited her from making an eleventh-hour assertion of her innocence.[5]

However, a kind of substance was loaned to the suspicion that the gallows had been used as a gag. There were Herold's statement concerning

3 Related in H. J. Campbell, *op. cit.*, p. 270.
4 Welles, *op. cit.*, Vol. II, p. 423.
5 Rev. J. A. Walter, "The Surratt Case," *The Church News,* Aug. 16, 1891.

"thirty-five men"; the cloudy business of Booth's getaway from Washington; the fact, obvious and undeniable, that Lincoln had been unprotected at Ford's Theater; the persistent rumor that the arch assassin had never been captured. All convinced many people that influential parties in the capital had connived in the assassination conspiracy and that the four condemned were hanged to assure a silence.

This suspicion was supported by the muzzling of the prisoners before the trial, and by the Government's—or Stanton's—disposal of the four surviving conspirators. On July 15, 1865, the decree ordering Dr. Mudd, Arnold, O'Laughlin and Spangler confined in a prison in Albany, New York, was suddenly revoked. Arbitrarily, and for no reason ever divulged, the prisoners were ordered confined in Fort Jefferson on Dry Tortugas off Key West, Florida. From Gideon Welles we learn that this transfer was made at Stanton's insistence.[6]

An American version of Devil's Island, this military prison was complete with torture chambers, dungeons, and a moat patrolled by sharks. Not only was the prison considered escape-proof, but the convict marooned here was virtually insulated from all contact with the outer world. Moreover, he suffered a good chance of dying before his term expired. For the island was a festering plague spot located in the yellow fever belt. What better way to silence a prisoner than to isolate him on this American Elba and expose him to Yellow Jack?

It looked to many observers as though Stanton were determined to abolish the four who had escaped the gallows; or, at least, to banish these prisoners to a bourne beyond all means of grapevine communication with the mainland.

In retrospect it seems hardly possible that malice alone inspired the War Secretary's move. Or that the transfer was made in the interest of discipline or of maximum prison security. Numerous Northern prisons were disciplinary hells, and no one would reasonably have believed that Confederate or "Secesh" holdouts could, at that late date, have engineered a rescue break in Albany, New York. Eisenschiml discusses the supposition that the convicted conspirators were confined on Dry Tortugas as a silence measure, and offers much supporting evidence for speculation.[7]

Two of the prisoners believed the transfer to Dry Tortugas a death sentence. According to Oldroyd, Dr. Mudd cried out in despair when he heard of the reassignment. "Oh, there is now no hope for me! I cannot live in such a place!"[8] Years later, Samuel Arnold recalled that a prisoner dying of smallpox was placed in a cell close to the dungeon occupied by the conspiracy convicts. Arnold believed this "was done for the express purpose

---

6 Welles, *op. cit.*, Vol. II, p. 334.
7 Eisenschiml, *op. cit.*, pp. 180–183.
8 *Op. cit.*, p. 145.

of inoculating us with this fearful and loathsome malady."[9] Michael
O'Laughlin did succumb to yellow fever. He was silenced by death on
September 23, 1867. There is some evidence that Spangler contracted
tuberculosis while on the island.

From Captain George W. Dutton, Company C, 10th Regiment VRC,
came an interesting story concerning Dr. Mudd. Dutton commanded the
guard that took the prisoners to Dry Tortugas. "During a conversation with
Dr. Mudd on July 22, 1865, Mudd confessed that he knew Booth when he
came to his house with Herold . . . that he was afraid to tell . . . fearing
that his own and the lives of his family would be endangered thereby . . .
[and] that he was with Booth at the National Hotel on the evening referred
to by Wiechmann. . . ." Dutton declared that this confession was "volun-
tary and made without solicitation, threat, or promise."[10]

One may wonder why the doctor would have volunteered such a confession to a guard captain. The story smacks of invention somewhere in the
Bureau of Military Justice which seems to have become an industrious
fiction factory. Soon after the four conspiracy trial survivors were banished
to limbo, reports were leaked that all the hangees had "confessed" on the
eve of execution day. So far as in known, no one ever saw actual transcripts
of these last-minute confessions. General Lafayette C. Baker eventually
published the story of Mrs. Surratt's confession, identifying himself as her
confessor. He asserted:

> During my visits to the prisoners, before their execution, Mrs. Surratt
> confessed to me her complicity with the conspirators so far as the intended
> abduction was concerned, *but affirmed that she reluctantly yielded to the
> urging of Booth in aiding the plot of assassination. She insisted that her
> oath of fidelity bound her to see the fatal end of the conspiracy.*[11]

By Baker's own mouth we must doubt every word of the foregoing statement. Also by the obvious element of incongruity. During her stay in
Arsenal Penitentiary, Mrs. Surratt had been badgered time and again by
the Secret Service Chief, who made it a practice to call on her at the most
unexpected hours of day or night. After these interrogation ordeals, the
desperate woman must have come to regard Baker as an odious Bluebeard.
Under the circumstances, her "confession" to him seems the epitome of un-
likelihood. Baker probably spun the yarn out of no substance whatever.

Apparently Lewis Paine did voice some last-minute assertions. Facing
the gallows, he solemnly swore to General Hartranft, "Mrs. Surratt was
innocent of the murder of the President and any knowledge thereof."
Hartranft forwarded Paine's statement to War Secretary Stanton on the
morning of July 7, or so the story was subsequently told. Paine also

---

[9] Samuel Arnold, article in Baltimore *American,* December 1902.
[10] Quoted in Oldroyd, *op. cit.,* pp. 144-145.
[11] *Op. cit.,* p. 563. Emphasis supplied.

declared that had he not gone to Mrs. Surratt's house she would have been pardoned.[12]

To be sure, Paine's word remains as dubious as General Baker's. Evidently the young killer possessed some spark of chivalry which evoked a gratuitous effort to alibi the Widow. But the alibi may have been as groundless as Baker's report of a confessional. Paine was an expert in "cover stories." So was Lafayette Baker. So, too, was the Bureau of Military Justice. Mass lying from this official fount came to light not many months after the conspiracy trial.

Then the storm really broke.

The Judge Advocate's Office itself generated the tempest. So it seems peculiarly just that the whirlwind circled back to the doorstep of Holt and his associates.

The contretemps stemmed from the conspiracy indictment naming Jefferson Davis, Clement C. Clay and other Confederate leaders as the sponsors of Lincoln's assassination and the instigators of an underground effort to sabotage the North with fire, riot and poison. The public was beginning to wonder why these conspiracy leaders had not been hanged in company with Paine, Mrs. Surratt and the other gallows victims, who were manifest small fry by comparison. Throughout the conspiracy trial, Jefferson Davis had sat in a prison cell in Fortress Monroe. Clement Clay had also been captured and incarcerated. The Military Commission had found Davis and Clay guilty. How was it they were cheating the scaffold?

Six months after the execution of the lesser conspirators, the House Judiciary Committee demanded a review of the evidence against Davis and Clay. Radical Republican members of this Committee were in a hanging mood, for many of their constituents were clamoring for the realization of a promised "sour apple tree". But the radicals entertained a twofold motive. Determined to punish Jefferson Davis, they were equally bent on an effort to destroy Andrew Johnson. Booth's calling card had pinned on President Johnson a suspicion which his political foes were finding very useful. If evidence against Jeff Davis could lead to evidence implicating Andy Johnson in the assassination conspiracy, the Committee might literally kill two birds with one stone.

The investigating committeemen were in for an unpleasant surprise. At their behest Judge Holt summoned for examination the stellar anti-Davis witnesses of the conspiracy trial. Questioned by Congressman A. J. Rogers of New Jersey (minority committeeman) the stars began to fall. When Rogers was through, most of the galaxy was down.

In the end, the accounting looked like this:

Richard Montgomery, alias James Thompson: identified as former New York burglar and recidivist with long police record; exposed as unscrupulous perjurer.

---

[12] Oldroyd, *op. cit.*, p. 138.

Dr. James B. Merritt, Ontario physician: pronounced a fraud and quack after investigation ordered by Canadian Governor General Lord Monck; confessed perjurer.

Witnesses Snevel and Campbell (who had testified to being with John Surratt in Richmond and to overhearing Jefferson Davis and Judah P. Benjamin approve assassination plan): admitted to fabrication of evidence, subornation and perjury.[13]

Henry Von Steineker (right name, Hans Vonwinklestein): U. S. Army deserter (from Blenker's Division); Confederate Army deserter (from Stonewall Brigade); convicted horse-thief and dual turncoat rating court-martial (by both armies) at time of conspiracy trial.[14]

Sandford Conover alias James Watson Wallace (right name, Charles A. Dunham): confessed liar and impostor; admitted suborner of witnesses Campbell, Snevel and others; exposed as arch perjurer.[15]

There was so much more that it began to look as if nine-tenths of the conspiracy trial evidence against the Confederate leaders had been faked. Conover had been a star witness of the first magnitude, and with his fall the whole conspiracy case began to crack. It seemed that the man had run a "School for Perjury" at the National Hotel where recruits were secretly coached in fictitious testimony and promised lucrative fees for perjuring themselves (for example, Snevel received $475 and Campbell $625 for fraudulently testifying). The money came from the Judge Advocate's Office.[16]

The horrified House Committee recoiled from the mare's-nest it had uncovered, and Committee Chairman George S. Boutwell of Massachusetts did his best to smother the stench. Determined to expose the perjuries, honest Congressman Rogers found his efforts suddenly blocked. "The papers were put away from me," he reported, "locked in boxes, hidden; and when I asked to see them, I was told . . . that I could not." Chairman Boutwell reserved the documents for his own private inspection. Evidently he followed Stanton's directions, for in February, 1866, the War Secretary had advised President Johnson that publication of these records would be "incompatible with the public interest."[17] Years later, in an attempt to justify this tricky secrecy, Boutwell repeated Stanton's line.[18]

Nevertheless, the public became informed. Ignoring the perjury evidence, the majority members of the House Judiciary Committee found Jefferson Davis guilty of treason, as originally indicted, and also guilty of

[13] De Witt, *Impeachment and Trial of Andrew Johnson*, p. 138.
[14] Douglas, *op. cit.*, pp. 340–341.
[15] De Witt, *op. cit.*, p. 139.
[16] *Ibid.*
[17] House of Representatives Report No. 104, p. 30.
[18] Boutwell, *Reminiscences of Sixty Years in Public Affairs* (New York: McClure, Phillips & Co., 1902), Vol. II, p. 62.

complicity in Lincoln's murder. Plans were being pushed for a massive war crimes trial when star-witness Conover suddenly fled to Canada. One of the strangest developments of the affair was the Government's handling of Conover. The embarrassed authorities might have let him escape and disappear (as Henry Von Steineker Winklestein had already disappeared). Instead, Conover was trailed, captured, returned to the States, tried for perjury, convicted, and sentenced to ten years in Albany Prison.[19]

One can only conjecture concerning the motives behind Conover's arrest and incarceration. Perhaps the Judge Advocate General thought this gesture would serve to launder the reputation of his office. Perhaps various War Department leaders thought imprisonment the best way to shut a noisy mouth. We know the radical Republicans wanted to use Conover as a witness to implicate Andrew Johnson in Lincoln's murder (a scheme eventually foiled when the prisoner blurted out the whole machination). But the immediate motives in respect to Conover were again concealed by censorship. Yet the Government could not censor the fact of his capture, conviction and confinement. Out came the messy story of the "School for Perjury." Down came the storm on the Bureau of Military Justice.

The entire conspiracy trial was now compromised. Why, people asked, did the Bureau of Military Justice resort to the employment of known criminals, felons and crooks?

What the American public (South as well as North) did not realize was that underworld denizens may be most adept at secret intelligence operations. It remains an unpleasant truth that practiced thieves, forgers and other crime artists are often employed by the forces of secret intelligence, especially when wartime emergency dictates need. Naturally, governments are reluctant to admit this employment of felons, but "all's fair" in secret warfare.

Still, the testimony of felons is perforce dubious, and their presentation as courtroom witnesses seems the height of folly. To this day nobody knows why Judge Holt (with Stanton's approval) put such characters on the stand, nor why the Judge Advocate's Office resorted to faked testimony. By such resort the entire anti-conspiracy proceeding was jeopardized.

War Department files were crammed with evidence of Southern agents working hand in glove with "Copperhead" organizations in Ohio, Indiana, Missouri and elsewhere. This evidence continued to accumulate during the conspiracy trial. In fact, an active underground war, under obvious Rebel direction, continued for several months after Lincoln's assassination. Although analagous to the spasms of a body after death, the activity persisted and the dangers were present and real.

Immediately after Lincoln's assassination, President Andrew Johnson began to receive sinister warnings and threats by mail.

---

[19] De Witt, *op. cit.*, p. 173.

After Lincoln's murder the authorities could ill afford to disregard any threat on the grounds that it seemed implausible or contrary to so-called military chivalry. The files of the Bureau of Military Justice contained documentary evidence of numerous assassination schemes which would have horrified the punctilious Southern soldier, who would surely have rejected any thought of the poisoned needle as a weapon.

Yet the discovery of such a Rebel device was reported by the United States Provost Marshal General in St. Louis. The story of this secret weapon is interesting.

On April 26, 1865, Robert Smith, "barkeeper, colored," wrote President Johnson from St. Louis. A free Negro, well educated, Smith composed a remarkable letter. It was legible, intelligently phrased ("I deem it my duty to inform you of what is going on here. . . .") and unlike the bulk of informant letters, the writer volunteered his address (114 South Fourth St., St. Louis, Mo.).

Robert Smith stated that on the night of April 24, "between 12 and one o'clock," he overheard three men talking on the doorstep of his saloon. He had gone to the porch to close up for the night. The entry, there, was screened by latticework, and these men were shadowy figures against the lattice. The low-pitched voices mentioned Booth and someone named "Doc." Barkeeper Smith paused to listen.

One man said, "Booth is a damned fool."

Another growled, "It will cost as much to keep him [Booth] out of the way as it would to carry out the whole business. But it must be done. The chain is made, and the only way it can be done is by the knife. Doc ought to be in Washington now. If nothing happens we ought to hear from him by Tuesday."

The first man then said, "Now Doc is there, Old Andy Johnson, damn him, is the next one to be attended to. It won't do, by God, to let him stay."

Reporting this conversation, Smith warned the President to be on guard. He guaranteed the truth of his statement upon his oath, and added: "I am a colored man and you would be the last I would offend and the first to defend."[20]

Smith's letter was at once referred to Stanton's office. Assistant War Secretary Dana got in touch with the Provost Marshal, Department of Missouri. On May 5, the War Department received from this Provost Marshal an official affidavit sworn by Robert Smith.[21] In substance, Smith's formal deposition followed the statements made in his letter.

The Missouri Provost Marshal assured Dana that efforts were being made to track the men reported by Smith. In further corroboration of Smith's story, he advised that his agency had uncovered a certain "Doc."

---

[20] National Archives, War Dept. Records, File "S," Doc. 115, JAO.
[21] *Ibid.*, Doc. 115-A.

In January last one of my detectives reported that Dr. Jermaine and Thomas Parks of this city were industriously and secretly at work on a new style of pistol, the object being to get up one that could be discharged silently, to be used for assassinating army officers, detectives and prominent citizens obnoxious to Southern sympathizers. It was to be charged with a poisoned needle.

The Federal secret agent saw this lethal pistol, and the inventor let him fire it. The needle traveled about 20 feet and "lodged firmly in a pine plank." Dr. Jermaine told the agent that "it would not inflict a wound sufficient to kill unless the needle were poisoned." The agent was able to make a detailed sketch of this needle-gun.[22]

Late in February, the Provost Marshal had ordered the arrest of Jermaine and Parks. Parks was incarcerated in Gratiol Street Prison. But Dr. Jermaine "was absent from the city." His house was searched for the pistol, but it could not be found.

Then: "On the afternoon . . . of the assassination . . . my Chief of Police reported that Dr. Jermaine had returned from the East. He was accordingly arrested, but indignantly denied all knowledge of the pistol." Jermaine alibied his trip East by claiming it had to do with a "cotton transaction." He said he was in partnership with a Colonel Hillyard of Grant's staff. "In proof of this he produced a telegram containing certain instructions about 'cotton transportation,' signed C. L. Hillyard, dated either at New York or Washington." The Provost Marshal concluded lamely, "Under the circumstances, as no clue whatever could be obtained about the pistol, Dr. Jermaine was paroled and Parks was released."[23]

Of what significance is this story? No more, perhaps, than another indication of widespread assassination conspiracy. But several details are most intriguing. Here are subversive partisans in St. Louis talking about secret means for Booth's escape. Here is mysterious mention of a "Colonel Hillyard" on Grant's staff. Army records do not contain the name of such a staff officer, but the name seems to echo from somewhere. Didn't a Hillard or Hillyard work with Captain Fernandina in the Baltimore plot to kill Lincoln?

Odd, too, that this Dr. Jermaine went East in February 1865 (apparently to Washington) on a cotton transaction. We are reminded of another party who visited the capital about that time on a "cotton deal." Could Jermaine's interest in cotton have had any connection with the deal involving Mr. B. F. Ficklin? Was cotton a code term for something else?

The Federals may have missed an important ringleader in Dr. Jermaine. One thing seems certain: they uncovered a remarkable invention. In his report to Assistant Secretary Dana, the Missouri Provost Marshal enclosed his detective's drawing of the poison-needle pistol.

---

[22] National Archives, War Dept. Records, File "S," R.B.P. 71, JAO.
[23] *Ibid.*

Lurid as may seem this depiction of the St. Louis underground, the needle-gun lends the story a definite authenticity. Like minicam photography, it bears evidence to the fact that Confederate secret agents were far ahead of their time.

After the fall of France in World War II, the British (for reasons still undivulged) contrived a red-letter week end for Nazi officers in occupied Paris. On that chosen week end, the British underground wanted as many German officers incapacitated as Anglo-French cunning could incapacitate. To the *Maquis* went a shipment of noiseless little pistols which fired needles—phonograph needles! From the pistols the needles went into the fleshy posteriors of German *Leutnants, Kapitans* and *Stabsoffiziers* on the boulevard. The poison was just enough to keep the victims face down in bed for a few days. Or so the story was told.

Of course, the World War II authorities marked the needle-gun "top secret." They might have been surprised to learn that their secret weapon had been invented during the Civil War.

Far deadlier than Dr. Jermaine's needle-gun were some of the secret weapons developed by the Rains Bureau in Richmond: electrical mines, booby-traps, infernal machines—Rains pioneered in the development of such devices. One that took a toll of Union lives was the coal-bomb, an innocent-looking chunk of bitumen that could blast the bowels out of a steamship.

The War Department in Washington received official warning. From the Provost Marshal General of Missouri came a dispatch dated April 24, 1865. Enclosed was a statement sworn by one Edward Frazer. The covering docket read:

> Refers to Rebel plot for burning steamers on Mississippi river. States that a person named Minor Majors, purporting to be an authorized agent of the Confederate Government, purposed to pay him liberally, and actually advanced several sums of money . . . to secure his services [for] burning certain steamers in St. Louis and elsewhere. The money was furnished by Jeff Davis and the Confederate Gov't . . . Davis and Benjamin agreed to pay $400,000 for the burning of Long Bridge at Nashville. Large sums were paid by Confederate Gov't to other parties for similar services.[24]

Who was "Minor Majors" with his obvious pseudonym? What became of the deponent Edward Frazer? Apparently the War Department failed to follow the lead. But a few days after Frazer volunteered his deposition in St. Louis, the telegraph from Memphis reported the worst steamship blast in American history.

The story broke in the nation's news on May 1, 1865. Here are the headlines from the New York *World:*

---

[24] National Archives, War Dept. Records, File "F," R.B.P. 55, JAO.

THE EXPLOSION
FRIGHTFUL DISASTER ON THE MISSISSIPPI
THE MOST TERRIBLE STEAMBOAT ACCIDENT ON RECORD
1,500 LIVES LOST
RETURNING SOLDIERS MEETING A HORRIBLE DEATH IN
SIGHT OF THEIR HOMES
CURIOUS RUMORS OF THE CAUSE OF THE APPALLING
CATASTROPHE
A Torpedo Said To Have Been Concealed in the Coal
Seven hundred and eighty-six of those on board the SULTANA have been
found alive. . . .
The Memphis hospitals are full of wounded . . . many being badly scalded
and burned. The investigation ordered by General Washburne is proceed-
ing.[25]

This thunderclap from the Mississippi Valley echoed through the national capital on the eve of the conspiracy trial. That the *Sultana* was blown up by a Confederate bomb remained unprovable. (Bombings were extremely hard to track down, for the evidence was usually obliterated by the blast.) The big steamer may have struck a forgotten channel-mine. Or her boilers may have blown.

However, there was Frazer's deposition, and the United States Government had abundant evidence of coal-bombs and other devices from the workshop of G. J. Rains. In their blundering hurry, Judge Holt and his associates failed to develop the case. But there can be little doubt that the judgment of the military tribunal was in part influenced by the *Sultana* disaster.

Presentation of the "Selby and Leenea" letters as conspiracy evidence made the Government look ridiculous. Had the Judge Advocate's Office pursued this line (as was apparently the original intention) the comedy would have degenerated to farce. Who was going to believe that Confederate underground agents, cunning and ghostly, were accidentally dropping important missives in streetcars?

Yet Major Eckert of Stanton's office reported the finding of another such missive in still another horse car on November 26, 1864. According to Eckert, this letter bore reference to an abduction scheme and contained a sketch of Lincoln haltered by a rope. By marvelous coincidence, this correspondence was "afterward discovered to belong to Payne."[26]

Wonderfully enough, still another conspiracy letter was picked up in Washington by a Federal officer on the evening of April 28, 1865. According to the military police, the missive disclosed a plot involving 800 Rebel conspirators who planned to burn Philadelphia and other Northern cities.

[25] New York *World*, May 1, 1865.
[26] David Homer Bates, *op. cit.*, p. 298.

As reported by the office of Provost Marshal Ingraham, the finder of the letter, Sergeant A. P. McKenny, suffered an amazing experience. On the evening in mention, McKenny had stopped two "mysterious men" on the street to question them. He was about to arrest the pair when one of them whipped out a pistol and shot him, "the ball taking effect in his right breast near the nipple." Sergeant McKenny staggered back. Dying? No, the bullet had lodged in a packet of papers in the breast pocket over his heart. The two men "escaped across a vacant lot." Stunned, McKenny "discovered a letter upon the ground which the man . . . had pulled from his pocket with the weapon."[27]

Possibly Judge Holt refrained from courtroom presentation of the Eckert and McKenny finds because of the skepticism aroused by Mrs. Hudspeth and her letters and the adverse reaction to the code letter fished from a river in North Carolina. Certainly such indiscriminate strewing of underground mail bore the earmarks of hoodwink. The McKenny story (released for press publication) read like a fairy tale. So the Bureau of Military Justice was accused of flimflam. Another finger of suspicion pointed at Lafayette Baker. Before the conspiracy trial ended, some observers believed the U.S. Secret Service had manufactured much of the spy-letter evidence.

Having compromised the Government's case with this silly business of lost-and-found "conspiracy correspondence," the War Department could be challenged on any of its paper evidence. Loud and bitter was the controversy raised by Judge Holt's effort to prove the Richmond leaders guilty of sanctioning a campaign to introduce contagious disease in the North.

"Germ warfare." No subject can arouse more public feeling, can create angrier accusations, can invite hotter denials. In the lexicon of military chivalry such a mode of massacre had long been ruled an unthinkable abomination.

Unfortunately, like so much in the rulebook of warrior chivalry, this nicety too had been honored in breach as well as observance. As in the days of knighthood poison became a royal weapon, so did the secret introduction of plague come into practice by the military. For example, during the French and Indian War, General Lord Jeffrey Amherst tried to wipe out various North American tribes by giving the redmen blankets infected with smallpox germs. Amherst wrote to the commander of Fort Pitt: "You will do well to try to inoculate the Indians by means of blankets. . . ."[28]

Perhaps Dr. Luke Blackburn of New Orleans came across some early history containing Amherst's military dispatches. Or perhaps the Louisiana

---

[27] New York *Daily Tribune*, May 3, 1865.
[28] Quoted in William E. Woodward, A *New American History* (New York: Farrar & Rinehart, Inc., 1936).

physician read the line in Clausewitz: "To introduce into a philosophy of war a principle of moderation would be an absurdity." (The German military philosopher was widely read at that time, and he preached a concept of "absolute war" which excluded what he called "philanthropic principles.")

But little is known of Dr. Blackburn's background. He came into the Civil War foreground by landing in Bermuda in the fall of 1864. The island was suffering a yellow fever epidemic. Blackburn announced that he was there to call "a meeting of Medical Officers and Practitioners . . . for the purpose of discussing the nature, treatment, etcetera, of the prevailing fever." The conference was publicly announced on September 26 by James Tucker, Acting Colonial Secretary in Bermuda. Local physicians were requested to meet with Blackburn in the Hamilton Hotel.[29]

The announcement of this Blackburn conference was duly reported to the State Department in Washington by the U.S. Consulate in Bermuda. Blackburn lingered in Bermuda for a time, then departed. His departure led to U.S. Consular Dispatch No. 166, dated April 14, 1865 (the very day of Lincoln's assassination).

In this remarkable communique, C. H. Allen, the United States consul in Bermuda, reported that the New Orleans doctor had visited the island during a yellow fever epidemic "for the ostensible purpose of aiding the physicians here." It seemed that Blackburn had come from Canada. After a month's stay he returned to Halifax. Subsequently an informer in the office of N. S. Walker, Confederate Agent in Bermuda, had told Consul Allen that Blackburn's expenses were paid by the Confederacy, that "the sole object of his visit was to collect clothing from the dead of yellow fever, to be sent to New York and other Northern cities, and that . . . Blackburn collected three large trunks of such clothing." He had left these trunks with a certain party who was "to take charge of them until the following June."

For a price the informer agreed to show Consul Allen the trunks. Allen informed the local health officer, and the informer guided them to the house where the trunks were stored. The baggage was seized, taken to a Quarantine Station, and opened. The trunks were found packed with "wearing apparel and bedding . . . evidently taken from a sick bed . . . some poultices, and many other things which could have been placed there for no legitimate purpose."

"From the evidence before me," Consul Allen reported, "I believe the facts in relation to these trunks were understood by Confederate officers here, and . . . they have paid money to carry out the diabolical scheme."[30]

Just why the United States consul delayed this report on Blackburn

---

[29] National Archives, War Dept. Records, File "H," R.B.P. 96, JAO.

[30] National Archives, War Dept. Records, Transcript U.S. Consular Dispatch No. 166, JAO.

until April 1865 constitutes an unexplained mystery. But there it is in the official records. On April 26, Acting Secretary of State Hunter forwarded the Bermuda dispatch to Judge Holt with the comment: "Understanding that you are investigating cases of this character, I hand this to you for your consideration. . . ."[31]

Judge Holt was soon furnished with "corroborative" evidence as deponed by one Godfrey Hyams. It seemed that Lincoln was target for some of the evil luggage. And Croton Reservoir in New York was to be somehow poisoned.

Here was something for the Bureau of Military Justice to work on. Locating Dr. Blackburn should not have been too difficult for the minions of Lafayette Baker. Indeed, the secret police produced prompt results. But (typically) those results proved questionable. For the upshot was the arrest in St. Louis on May 6 of the mountebank Dr. Tumblety. It remained for the Canadian Government to track down the insidious Dr. Blackburn. On May 18, 1865, the Montreal telegraph reported Blackburn's arrest "on a warrant from Toronto, for a breach of the neutrality laws."[32]

Northern newspapers headlined the story. "THE YELLOW FEVER PLOT!" proclaimed the Detroit *Advertiser*. "Attempt to infect the White House!"[33]

On May 30, Mr. Cordial Crane of the Customs House, Boston, addressed an interesting letter on the subject to War Secretary Stanton. According to local news accounts, on August 3, 1864, a Mr. Harris had imported into Boston "trunks containing infected clothing." Crane wrote that the story led him "to examine the Register at the Parker House" where Harris was said to have stayed. The customs official had been unable to find Harris' name on the ledger. But:

"I found registered on the 26 of July [1864] the following names: Charles R. Hinter, Toronto, Canada West; J. Wilkes Booth; A. J. Bursted of Baltimore; H. V. Clinton, Hamilton, Canada West; and R. A. Leech, Montreal."

Crane concluded that he thought it "a remarkable circumstance that representatives from the above named places should arrive and meet at the Parker House at about the time Harris was on his way from Halifax with his clothing."[34]

Here, in sum, was the Federal Government's evidence concerning the Confederate effort in the field of "germ warfare." Long after the conspiracy trial Southern spokesmen would protest the charge, and critics would point to it as another example of fabrication by the War Department. However, the impartial historian must note that the case did not originate in Stanton's War Department. Evidence came through the State Depart-

---

[31] National Archives, War Dept. Records, File "H," JAO.
[32] New York *Daily Tribune*, May 19, 1865.
[33] Detroit *Advertiser*, May, 19, 1865.
[34] National Archives, War Dept. Records, File "C," Doc. 415, JAO.

ment and from Bermuda, and Blackburn was arrested by the Canadian authorities. The circumstantial linkage with Booth came from the Boston Customs Office.

Then, for reasons never clarified, the whole case dissolved into thin air. Dr. Blackburn mysteriously evaporated from the records. The "germ warfare" charge was shelved. Why? One has a choice of guesses.

Although the yellow-fever mosquito was then unknown, perhaps medical authorities quietly advised the War Department that the disease could not be transmitted by "infected clothing." Perhaps Dr. Blackburn was able to prove that his noxious trunks were merely dirty laundry.

One more surmise: perhaps the Federal lawyers were hoist on their own petard. Push a charge that the Confederates had violated the "laws of war," and defense lawyers might counter that the Federals had done the same. What about Sherman burning Columbia, Georgia? What about Ben Butler stealing a fortune from a bank in New Orleans? What about various Federal methods of interrogating prisoners of war?

The United States War Department had some dirty laundry of its own.

Moderns would call it "brainwashing." During the Civil War it was called something else. The torture of prisoners to elicit information was expressly forbidden by the Lieber Code. But the rules apparently were meant for the enemy's observance. When Confederates broke the rules, the Federals shouted, "Atrocity!" When they themselves broke the rules, the violations were marked "top secret." In any case, when Army officers want information, they want information.

Wanting information, the Federals pioneered a technique that the War Department kept secret for years. In the files of the Bureau of Military Justice, one finds a recommendation, dated April 22, 1865, that this technique be used on the assassination prisoners who were confined at the time on board Navy monitors.

This recommendation was addressed to General Augur. It came from Charles E. Cady, Surgeon, Headquarters 138th Pennsylvania Volunteers, 3rd Division, VI Army Corps. The surgeon remarks on the recent capture of "the suspects in the assassination tragedy." He goes on:

"During an experience of 3 years in the Army, I have upon numerous occasions procured from Rebel officers and soldiers much important information *while they were partially under the influence of chloroform.*" This treatment (writes Cady) might be used on the "supposed implicated parties now in custody." In closing, the surgeon offers specific instructions.

"Pure unadulterated chloroform should be used—such as in use in the Army—it should be carefully but rapidly administered; & while the patient is semi-anaesthetized he should be questioned bluntly and pointedly."[35]

---

[35] National Archives, War Dept. Records, File "C," Doc. 45, JAO.

The Confederates, then, were not the only innovators of devices which future historians would mistakenly associate with World War II. Nor were they the only violators of the Lieber Code. Stirring the imagination, Surgeon Cady's letter to General Augur evokes a melodramatic picture of Army doctors spirited on board monitors *Saugus* and *Montauk*, and weird operations below decks. So far as is known, the experiment was never tried on the assassination conspirators. But the recommendation was made, and it was tried on others, as Cady's letter discloses.

The United States Government was in no position to utter a wholesale condemnation of the Confederacy for violating the "laws of war."

What of the charge that individual Richmond leaders sponsored the assassination conspiracy? Did the Government have a case against Jefferson Davis and Judah P. Benjamin?

Not as the Judge Advocate's Office presented it, certainly. But (unless all of it were faked) the Bureau of Military Justice had in its possession a considerable body of evidence to show Davis' sanction, if not direct sponsorship, of the assassination plot.

Many witnesses volunteered pertinent information. For example, on April 16 Army authorities in Detroit sent to Washington a Charles Cowlam, who offered inside knowledge of the Rains Bureau.[36] One Joseph Powell, a former prisoner in Castle Thunder, offered testimony linking Richmond with the assassination.[37] Peleg Clarke, of Westerly, Rhode Island, advised the War Department that he had "heard John A. Seddon, brother of the late Rebel Secretary of War, tell J. W. Slaughter in 1861 that Lincoln and Seward would both be killed . . . that plans were matured and funds subscribed . . . and placed in the hands of President Davis."[38] Multiply such testimony many times over, subtract a large margin for error, and the figure remains impressive.

Filed by Judge Advocate General Holt was a document labeled, "May 1865; Evidence; Hann, Susannah." Purportedly sworn in Richmond by a Susannah Hann, this testimony is docketed as follows:

> States that she lived in Richmond 3 years with Mr. James L. Walker Murray. Booth and Surratt were at Murrays about three weeks before the fall of Richmond. Heard Murray tell his wife that they were fixing to kill Mr. Lincoln. Murray gave Booth when he left a small bag of money. Men & women both gave towards it. The women said they would give their last cent to have Mr. Lincoln killed. Robert Murray would have nothing to do with it. The plan of inviting Mr. Lincoln to the Theater was fixed upon in Richmond. Gives names of different persons that contributed towards death of Mr. Lincoln. . . .[39]

---

[36] National Archives, War Dept. Records, File "H," Doc. 632, JAO.
[37] National Archives, War Dept. Records, File "P," Doc. 586, JAO.
[38] National Archives, War Dept. Records, File "C," Doc. 341, JAO.
[39] National Archives, War Dept. Records, File "H," R.B.P. 88, JAO.

The attached deposition offers specific names and addresses.

John Tabb who lives on Franklin Street opposite Robinson's Apothecary also contributed money to Murray for Booth. Mrs. Tabb also gave money. The servants of Bowlin Haxall who lived next door to Jas Murray's say that Booth was also there and got money from Haxall. . . . Dr. Haxall on Grace Street also gave money. . . . Mrs. James Murray said Jeff Davis had given money to Booth to have him kill the President. John Tabb also said so—little Tommy Tabb carried money from Mrs. Tabb to James Murray. Mrs. Tabb asked her husband if Gen'l Lee and his wife had given any money to have the President killed. He said Yes. Mrs. Gen'l Lee sent a note to Mrs. Tabb saying that she, her son Fitzhugh, and Gen'l Lee had all given money for Booth to kill the President. . . .[40]

Could anything be more incredible than the foregoing document? Yes, something could: the way this evidence was handled by the Federal Bureau of Military Justice. Either the recorded statements were true, or they were false. If true, the parties named were guilty of sponsoring Lincoln's murder. If false, either deponent Susannah Hann was guilty of an outrageous perjury, or Federal agents were guilty of manufacturing a monstrous criminal libel. Judge Holt, then, should have gotten to the bottom of it. Susannah Hann should have been summoned to Washington. The Tabbs, the Haxalls, the Murrays, the Lees should have been closely interrogated. Jefferson Davis should have been ordered to testify. None of these actions was taken.

Instead, the Hann document went into a Bureau file. The Tabbs, the Haxalls and the other Richmond citizens in mention went unquestioned. The assassination conspiracy charge was never pressed against Jefferson Davis.

The Hann document may have been a fraud. Many of the letters exhibited in court as evidence of conspiracy may have been bogus. But the War Department had in its possession one written testimonial which could have been produced as unquestionably genuine. This article—perhaps the most important single item of evidence concerning the assassination conspiracy—was the diary of John Wilkes Booth.

Here was a virtual deposition in the assassin's own handwriting. Taken from the captive's body at Garrett's Farm, it was rushed to Washington by Lieutenant Colonel Everton Conger. Conger delivered the diary to Lafayette Baker, who carried the little red book in person to War Secretary Stanton. According to his own subsequent admission, Stanton received the book from Baker. "I examined it . . . with great care," Stanton recalled, "[and] read over all the entries in it. . . ."[41]

So far as is known, Stanton, Baker and Conger were the only Federal

[40] *Ibid.*
[41] *Johnson Impeachment Investigation,* p. 281.

leaders who ever saw "all the entries" in Booth's diary. In spite of its manifest importance, the little book was not produced as evidence, nor even mentioned, during the 1865 conspiracy trial.

Did the book contain a key to Confederate codes? Did it list conspiracy leaders? Did it mention certain accomplices, or exonerate persons held under suspicion? Nobody knows. The diary was given to Stanton. Nobody saw it for the next two years.

In 1867 Lafayette Baker published his *History of the U.S. Secret Service.* Therein Baker mentioned delivering Booth's diary to Stanton. Storm in House and Senate! What had become of the assassin's diary? Wherewith the little book was "re-discovered" in a forgotten War Department file— one of those files too secret for convenient remembrance. And now, when the diary was ultimately produced, eighteen pages of it were missing, cut from the section leading up to the night of Lincoln's murder. The residue— containing just two pages of Booth's diarizing—proved immaterial.

Baker claimed the little red book was intact when he gave it to Stanton. Stanton declared the excised pages were already missing. Conger's statements on the matter went unrecorded. If nothing else, then, the mutilated diary bore evidence to War Department or Secret Service skullduggery.

Bearing that evidence, Booth's diary may be seen today on exhibit in the Lincoln Museum in Washington.

Testimony manufactured. Witnesses suborned. Evidence tampered with, forgotten or destroyed. Weighted by these malfeasances, the conspiracy trial of 1865 sank into history's slough.

Eventually all conspiracy charges against Jefferson Davis, Clement C. Clay and other captured Confederate leaders were dropped. Named in the original indictment as chief conspirators, these prisoners were released by Presidential order in 1867.

Jacob Thompson was never brought to trial; neither was Beverly Tucker; neither was the notorious "Copperhead" leader, Clement Vallandingham.

So the names of these top Secessionists must be added to that long list of suspected accomplices and underground subversives who escaped indictment as assassination conspirators or Booth's abettors. To wit:

John F. Parker; Sergeant Cobb; the Officer of the Guard who permitted Atzerodt to escape; Colonel Samuel Cox; Thomas A. Jones; Colonel Hughes; Mrs. Quesenberry; Jett, Bainbridge and Ruggles; the Garretts. Not to mention such other suspects as Thomas and Nannie Green; Paine's landlady Mrs. Branson; Preston Parr; Joao Celestino; Benjamin Ficklin; and Booth's numerous lady intimates.

It would seem that after four of the condemned were hanged and four others sent to a living death on Dry Tortugas, the War Department wished only to prosecute "others unknown."

There remained one Booth accomplice who was too well known to be overlooked. Something had to be done about John H. Surratt.

Stanton deliberately permitted Surratt to escape. Of that, there is not the slightest shadow of a doubt. The War Secretary was informed that Surratt had fled into Canada, but not a single military agent was put on the fugitive's trail. Instead, in the summer of '65 General Baker sent some sleuths on a wild-goose-chase after a mythical Surratt in the mountains of Pennsylvania.[42]

Meanwhile, in Montreal a Confederate agent named Porterfield took Surratt under his wing. Presently furnished with money and a disguise, Surratt journeyed to St. Liboire, a village dozing in the woods of French Canada. There Surratt lived for a time in the home of a priest, Father Charles Boucher. Later in July, 1865, he was spirited to the home of another priest, Father Lapiere. In September he was on his way to Liverpool on the steamer *Peruvian*.[43]

On the crossing Surratt posed as a "Mr. McCarty." He sat at table with the ship's surgeon, Dr. McMillan. One night (talkative as ever) he told McMillan: "I have done such things that, if you should know them, it would make you stare."[44] McMillan did stare when the young man went on to confess that he was the fugitive John Surratt.

When the ship reached Liverpool, McMillan reported the matter to the American consul. The consul immediately sent word to the State Department in Washington, and followed the message with a dispatch (October 1, 1865) stating that Surratt could be found in Liverpool at the Oratory of the Church of the Holy Cross.[45] In response to the second message, the American consul in Liverpool received a dispatch from Acting Secretary of State W. Hunter, reading:

> I have to inform you that upon consultation with the Secretary of War and Judge Advocate General it is thought advisable that no action be taken in regard to the supposed John Surratt at present.[46]

If the negative dispatch surprised the American consul, it stunned the ship's doctor of the *Peruvian*, who saw a $25,000 reward slip from his grasp. Upon his return to Montreal, Dr. McMillan at once contacted the American consul in that city, who immediately reported the matter to the State Department. The State Department advised the War Department. Whereupon Stanton (November 24, 1865) issued a decree stating that the reward offered for the arrest of John H. Surratt had been revoked!

When queried on the revocation by a House Committee, Stanton's ex-

---

[42] National Archives, War Dept. Records, File "S," JAO.
[43] Oldroyd, *op. cit.*, p. 224 *et seq.*
[44] *Ibid.*
[45] Exec. Doc. No. 9, House of Representatives, 39th Cong. 2nd Session.
[46] *Ibid.*

planation was that he "thought it best." In justification he pointed out that seven months had elapsed since the reward was first offered, and the fugitive had not yet been arrested.[47] The House Committee had some difficulty in following this rationale. It was easier to follow the trail of John H. Surratt.

In the spring of 1866 John Surratt traveled from England to Italy. In Rome he joined the Papal Zouaves, enlisting under the name of John Watson. He was assigned to Company No. 3, stationed at Sezze. Soon after his induction, he visited the guard post at Velletri. There—the wheel of chance!—he encountered in the Papal Guard an old schoolmate from Maryland, a Canadian named Henri Sainte-Marie, who recognized him at once.

The two exchanged confidences. It would seem that Sainte-Marie got the better of the exchange. Surratt told his former classmate: "We have killed Lincoln, the nigger's friend." And: "Had it not been for me and Wiechmann, my mother would be living yet." Sainte-Marie asked him if he personally knew Jefferson Davis. Surratt declared, "No but I acted under the instructions of persons under Davis' immediate orders." Surratt added that the conspirators "acted under orders of men not yet known."[48]

With this startling information Sainte-Marie went straight to the Hon. Rufus King, American Minister in residence at Rome. In a special dispatch dated April 23, 1866, King relayed the story to Washington. For the third time in a year John Surratt had been "found."

Seward passed the business to Stanton. Stanton passed it to Judge Holt. Holt stalled it by demanding a sworn affidavit from Sainte-Marie. Seward suggested sending a special agent to Rome to expedite Surratt's arrest, but Stanton made no reply to Seward's note.[49]

Late in July, 1866, St. Marie's sworn statement was handed to Stanton. The War Secretary made no move. Prodding letters from State Department to War Department went unanswered.[50] Finally, in November, Rufus King called on the Pope's chancellor, Cardinal Antonelli, to ask if the Vatican State would release John Surratt for trial in America. Cardinal Antonelli replied in the affirmative, and took steps to have "Zouave Watson" detained under arrest while Washington decided what it wanted to do.

On November 6 Cardinal Antonelli ordered Surratt arrested at Veroli and brought to Rome. On November 8 the Zouave commander sent the following telegram to the Papal Chancellor:

> At the moment of leaving the prison [at Veroli] surrounded by six men as guards, Watson plunged into the ravine, more than one hundred feet deep, which defends the prison. Fifty Zouaves are in pursuit.[51]

---

[47] *Ibid.*, Report No. 33.
[48] Oldroyd, *op. cit.*, p. 229.
[49] Eisenschiml, *op. cit.*, p. 203.
[50] *Ibid.*, p. 204.
[51] Oldroyd, *op. cit.*, p. 231.

The fifty Zouaves never caught up with the amazing "Watson." Surratt made his way from Velletri to Sora, and from there to Naples where he was allowed to board the steamer *Tripoli* bound for Egypt. Surratt signed the passenger registry as "John Agostina."

The *Tripoli* put in at Malta. William Winthrop, U. S. consul at Malta, had been informed of Surratt's passage by the consul at Naples. But Winthrop "was hampered by legal quibbles and the slowness of the authorities to act."[52] Surratt was permitted to sail on.

On November 23 the steamer docked at Alexandria, Egypt. Four days later, U.S. Consul-General Charles Hale boarded the ship and apprehended Surratt who (still clad in his Zouave costume) insisted his name was Walters. Hale promptly advised the State Department: "Have arrested John Surratt, one of President Lincoln's assassins. No doubt of identity."[53]

On December 4, Naval Secretary Welles, at Seward's behest, dispatched the U.S. corvette *Swatara* to Egypt to pick up the prisoner. Early in January 1867 the *Swatara* delivered John Surratt to the authorities in Washington. He was lodged in the Old Capitol.

In 1865 the accused conspirators had been given no opportunity to procure lawyers, no time to prepare a defense. Prisoner John H. Surratt was now given better than five months to get one ready. On June 10, 1867, he was brought to trial before the Criminal Court of the District of Columbia. Although this was not a Military Tribunal, the War Department's hand showed in the proceedings. The District Prosecutor, E. C. Carrington, chose as associate counsels Edwards Pierrepont and Albert Gallatin Riddle. Pierrepont was a Stanton favorite. Riddle had been attorney for Lafayette C. Baker.

Over the Court sat Judge Fisher. Naval Secretary Welles shuddered at the appointment. Fisher (Welles noted) was Judge Cartter's tool, and Cartter was "a coarse and vulgar Radical [Republican] in the hands of Stanton."[54] The Radical faction took a singular interest in John Surratt. Shortly before he went on trial he was visited in his Old Capitol cell by Stanton's close friend, Congressman J. M. Ashley of Ohio, one of the prime movers in the effort to impeach President Andrew Johnson for treason. Apparently Ashley hoped to procure from Surratt evidence against Johnson.

The defense was conducted by attorneys Joseph H. Bradley, R. T. Merrick and Joseph Bradley, Jr. Prosecution seemingly endeavored to prove that John Surratt was in the nation's capital on the night of the assassination, acting as Booth's accomplice. No less than eight persons took the stand to swear they saw Surratt in Washington on April 14, 1865. Witnesses included Dr. William E. Cleaver, a friend of the Surratt family; David C.

---

52 *Ibid.*, p. 232.
53 *Ibid.*, p. 234.
54 *Diary of Gideon Welles*, Vol. III, p. 160.

Reed, a tailor who had known Surratt since childhood; Charles H. Wood, barber at Booker & Stewart's shop near Grover's Theater; Cipriano Grillo, an acquaintance of David Herold; and John Lee, the ace detective on O'Beirne's force. Susan Jackson told of serving tea to John Surratt in the house on H Street on the night of April 14. And Sergeant Joseph Dye stated that he saw Surratt dart in and out of Ford's Theater to call the time to someone at the curb shortly before the assassination. In sum, this testimony seemed most damaging. Defense counsel reduced the sum to zero.

Defense called John Cass, clothing merchant of Elmira, New York. Calmly, collectedly and with no apparent axe to grind, Cass swore that he saw John Surratt in Elmira on the morning of April 15. Several other Elmira citizens offered the same testimony. That fixed it. For Surratt could not possibly have been in Washington on the evening of the 14th and in Elmira, New York, on the 15th. Reference to available railroad trains and time tables settled—or seemed to settle—the question.

Altogether some 200 witnesses were called, among them actor John Matthews with his *ex capite* recital of Booth's letter to the *Intelligencer* (wherein only Paine, Herold and Atzerodt were disclosed as the assassin's signatory accomplices). The existence of Booth's mutilated diary also came to light at this time. Trial closed on August 11, with the jury deadlocked and John H. Surratt confident he could stay alive.

Early in the autumn of 1867 Surratt was released on $25,000 bail—the exact amount previously offered by the War Department (and subsequently canceled by Stanton) as a reward for Surratt's capture. (Sainte-Marie eventually received a Governmental reward of $10,000 for the "capture" in Rome.)

Then, with all the gravity of pseudo dignity, Surratt was again brought to trial. This time, as noted by Oldroyd, "the prosecution declined to proceed upon the charge of murder of Mr. Lincoln and proposed to try him upon the charges of treason and conspiracy."[55]

At this second trial Surratt's counsel, General Merrick and John G. Carlisle, Esq., made hash of the indictment. Counsel noted that the law in such cases required the indictment should be found within two years of the alleged offense, unless the respondent were a "fugitive from justice." The specified two years had elapsed, and the indictment did not state that Surratt was a fugitive![56] That settled that. Case *nolle prossed*. Surratt was freed.

Naval Secretary Welles saw through the sham with his needle eye. The Surratt Trial had been a farce. Welles jabbed sharply: "The judge was disgracefully partial and unjust . . . And his charge highly improper."[57]

But the public had its little show, and the spotlight now turned on a

---

[55] *Op. cit.*, p. 238.
[56] *Ibid.*
[57] Welles, *op. cit.*, Vol. III, p. 167.

three-ring circus—the impeachment of the President of the United States. In the turmoil and fantasy of that mudslinging match (Andrew Johnson vs. the Radical Republicans) John Surratt was forgotten.

In December 1870 Surratt reappeared for a moment on the lecture platform in Rockville, Maryland. His lecture, evasively worded, was not a success. Surratt made public admission of serving as a Confederate spy, but he did not go into detail on his wartime activities and devoted most of his address to the Lincoln abduction conspiracy. Publicly he denounced Louis Wiechmann as a subversive, a conspiratorial turncoat and a perjurer responsible for the "murder" of Mary Surratt.

John Surratt's audience was not interested. His trial had been an anticlimax, and well-meaning citizens were inclined to mistrust this young man who had remained in hiding while his mother went to the gallows. Nor could the loyal Unionist, the veteran Boy in Blue, understand the technical acquittal of this self-confessed spy who had been advertised by the War Department as Booth's chief accomplice.

What, indeed, could one make of the Trial of John Surratt—eight witnesses, including astute Detective John Lee, swearing they saw the defendant in Washington on April 14; citizens from Elmira swearing they saw him in that city on the morning of the 15th? Someone must have lied on the stand. Who? Why?

What could be made of the War Department's reluctance to bring Surratt to trial in the first place? Of Stanton's efforts to impede his arrest and return to the States? Of the five months' delay before the captured fugitive was finally brought to court? Surely Stanton and Judge Holt were aware of the statute of limitations. One can only conclude that Surratt's apprehension and trial were deliberately delayed. Why?

Did the dictator in the War Department fear an exposure by John Surratt of "others unknown"? Did he fear a disclosure of evidence that might have cleared Mary Surratt? Did he dread a revival of interest in the body that lay buried in a secret grave in Arsenal Penitentiary? Whatever Stanton's motives, they were never divulged.

The case against "others unknown" would evaporate. The case against Mary Surratt would never be reopened. But the body buried in a gunbox labeled "Booth" refused to remain at rest.

CHAPTER 25

Curtain Call

To a society reared on the Puritan concept of sin and atonement (with its legalistic corollary of crime and punishment) certain eventualities which followed in the train of Lincoln's assassination and the conspiracy trials seemed a manifestation of the Law and the Book. "The wages of sin. . . ."

Ella Starr Turner's attempted suicide was in keeping with the tradition. She recovered, and, according to press reports, made a scene in a Washington streetcar shortly after Booth's death was announced, throwing herself in the aisle and kissing Booth's picture. But her subsequent disappearance from the city and from history's record satisfied the Cromwellian moralists that the way of the transgressor was hard.

Then there was the suicide of one George B. Love. Picked up as a suspect during the general man-hunt, Love cut his throat with a penknife in the guardhouse at Fort Stephens. On his body was discovered a baggage check made out to Miss Starr. Love's self-destruction satisfied the credo.

So did the suicide of one Joseph Thomas, an inmate of Mrs. Branson's boardinghouse in Baltimore. Thomas was reported as having been a friend of Lewis Paine's. Stanton ordered the body disinterred and shipped to Washington for official examination. Department files contain no record of the inquest, but the suicide is noted with appropriate satisfaction.

In the wake of the mass conspiracy trial came other suicides.

In New York on the morning of November 12, 1865, ex-Senator Preston King tied a bag of bullets around his neck and jumped from the Christopher Street ferry. King was remembered as the politico who had prevented Anna Surratt and Father Walter from presenting President Johnson with a mercy petition in Mrs. Surratt's behalf.

In frustrating poor Anna Surratt, Senator King had been seconded by James H. Lane of Kansas. A freakish character in a Senate composed of showmen, this Lane was the last extrovert one would suspect of harboring any remorse. At Leavenworth, Kansas, on July 11, 1866, Senator Lane shot himself.

Mrs. Surratt's parish priest, Father Walter, saw the workings of guilty conscience behind these two suicides. The "conscience" legend continued to grow. Supposedly the Military Commission officers were wracked by remorse. According to Henry Kyd Douglas, "General Foster, the gentlest man of all that Court, committed suicide." (Douglas erred. Robert S. Foster did not kill himself.)

It was said that Louis Wiechmann endured agonies of remorse. Elaborating on the theme, Helen Jones Campbell states that Wiechmann retired to a small midwestern town, lived out his days in mortal fear for his life, and died confessing his guilt, but unshriven. We are told by the same writer that John M. Lloyd was also wracked by a guilty conscience and, dying, "screamed in terror" as he faced the Judgment Seat.

The legend was extended to include Willie Jett. Ostracized, he finally left Bowling Green, became a wanderer. Remorse unseated his mind. An account in the *Maryland Journal* of April 20, 1895, relates that he spent his last days in an asylum muttering, "Oh, Mr. Garrett, forgive me."

Although relished by a Victorian society, these repentance stories lacked foundations in historicity. Researching the Wiechmann tale, historian Lloyd Lewis uncovered an entirely different denouement. As Lewis tells it (*Myths After Lincoln*), just before Wiechmann died (June 2, 1902) he signed a declaration stating: "This is to certify that every word I gave in evidence at the assassination trial was absolutely true." It must be conceded as odd that the doctor ascribed Wiechmann's death to "extreme nervousness." But that, in the medical lexicon of the period, could have meant almost anything.

John M. Lloyd seems to have died of plain, unvarnished alcoholism. As for Jett, a relative (J. L. Marye) confided to an inquiring writer that Willie became a traveling salesman and eventually died of nothing worse, nor better, than paresis.

Genuine mystery did enshroud the fate of John F. Parker, the delinquent constable who failed to guard Lincoln's box. Soon after the assassination, this wretched policeman was returned to duty with the White House Guard! Mrs. Lincoln's maid, Elizabeth Keckley, would recall that Mary Lincoln upraided Parker in a stormy scene. But that was all. Incredibly, he was allowed to remain on the police force. Then, in 1868, he was suddenly dismissed. Why? For sleeping in a streetcar while on duty! Thereafter he simply disappeared. No one knew, or knows, what became of John F. Parker.

Stanton's death in December, 1869, added another suicide story to the list. Legend has it that he had confessed, "The Surratt woman haunts me." Journalist Ben Perley Poore wrote in his *Reminiscences:* "There are many at Washington who believe that Mr. Stanton committed suicide by cutting his throat with a razor. Caleb Cushing was positive that he did . . . but Hon. E. D. McPherson, of Pennsylvania . . . clerk of the House of

Representatives, procured from the attendant physician a statement that Mr. Stanton died a natural death."

The attendant undertaker, R. F. Harvey, seems to have been less ready to voice a statement. According to an account published in Baltimore in 1903, the mortician's son recalled that Harvey refused to discuss the Stanton case and "no human being ever succeeded in getting him to deny or affirm anything on the subject." But the funeral was held in close privacy. And it is perhaps significant that the attendant physician who issued the official word on the case was Stanton's old friend, Surgeon General Barnes.

Seemingly in line with the Stanton story was the sudden death of General Lafayette C. Baker, who had expired in Philadelphia on July 3, 1868, at the robust age of forty-four. Baker had applied for the lion's share of the reward for Booth and Herold. His first bid, insinuating an entitlement to the $75,000 offered by the War Department, had been pruned to a modest $3,750. In anticipation of more, Baker had plunged into a hotel enterprise in Michigan. The reduction must have been a blow. Eisenschiml notes that press reports attributed Baker's death to typhoid fever. The official death certificate gave the cause as meningitis. One can draw ones own conclusions concerning the discrepancy.

Then there was the strange case of Boston Corbett. For years he enjoyed the fruits of fame, traveling the country as a celebrity. In 1887 he was awarded a job as doorman to the Kansas State Legislature. One day while the house was in session he drew a pistol and opened fire at the legislators. Overpowered, he was committed to an asylum at Topeka. He escaped, headed for Enid, Oklahoma. Then he vanished as though dissolved in thin air.

Tragedy descended on Major Henry Rathbone and Clara Harris, the couple who sat in the fatal box with the Lincolns at Ford's Theater. The Major and Clara eventually married and took up residence in Germany. In Hanover, two nights before Christmas, 1883, something snapped in Rathbone's mind. He tried to kill his children, and when a nurse intervened, he shot his wife to death and stabbed himself. Doctors saved his life, but he spent the rest of his days in an insane asylum at Hildesheim.

It was not generally known that Mrs. Lincoln attempted suicide—an effort frustrated by her attendants. This was in Chicago in 1875. The public learned that Mrs. Lincoln was committed, briefly, to an insane asylum. For years her conduct had been most irrational. Soon after Lincoln's funeral she placed his monogrammed shirts on public sale. Then she tried to sell her wardrobe in New York City. She was obsessed with a desire for money.

Although Lincoln had left an estate worth well over one hundred thousand dollars (her widow's share was one-third), Mary Lincoln constantly pleaded financial distress. Sums were raised in her behalf. Friends

made generous donations. Robert Lincoln sent funds. Yet her importuning
was continuous; time and again she declared herself as being in dire want.
In 1869 she took Tad to Europe to put him in school. In her fine biography
of Mary Lincoln, Ruth Painter Randall tells how Mrs. Lincoln's friend,
Mrs. James H. Orne, found her living in Frankfurt in "a small, cheerless,
desolate looking room with but . . . two chairs and a wooden table with
a solitary candle." Mrs. Lincoln wept about her poverty. She said that
people were persecuting her.

After her release from the asylum in 1876 Mary Lincoln took up residence in France. In 1879 she suffered an accidental fall and returned to the
States as an invalid. She retired to Springfield to live with Mr. and Mrs.
Ninian Edwards. There she shut herself into the seclusion of a darkened
room. Thus self-entombed, Mrs. Lincoln died in 1882. Surely Lincoln's
widow was the victim of cruel tragedy. But was she twice victimized? No
historian has quite been able to explain her obsession with money. Could
her continual impoverishment suggest blackmail?

Booth's pistol shot ricochetted to wound the destinies of many persons.
Naturally it affected his own family.

"God help us, what a curse is on the Booths!" wrote Edwin Booth
despairingly after one setback. Johnny's ghost haunted the family. As
when snide remarks were made to little Edwina Booth, or when Mary
Holmes Booth, staring at nothing, would begin to weep.

Junius Brutus Booth seldom mentioned John Wilkes. Joseph (Doc)
Booth refused to speak his name. Rosalie Booth suffered melancholia.
Asia and her husband, John Sleeper Clarke, quarreled savagely after the
assassination, and went to England to live in semi-exile. Edwin Booth
Clarke, Asia's first-born, had gone to Annapolis and become a naval
officer. He was lost at sea. Nobody saw him go overside—he just disappeared. Did he go deliberately?

Every now and then one of the Booths would receive a menacing letter.
From vicious cranks. Or blackmailers. A number of women badgered the
family, posing as the married or unmarried widows of John Wilkes Booth.

Indeed, he may have married one of these trulls. Or a couple of them.
He may have fathered a child or two. Apparently one of the "widows"
fastened herself on Rosalie. It was said that poor Rosalie was unmercifully
swindled.

Rosalie Booth died in January, 1880. Rumor spoke of a mysterious
assailant. She had been living with her brother, Dr. Joseph Booth, in
Long Branch, New Jersey. One evening when the doctor was out, a
knock came at the door. Rosalie answered. A heavy missile, thrown from
the dark, struck her in the temple. The blow caused her death. Or so the
story is related in a book by Izola Forrester. More of which presently.

To his dying day Edwin Booth kept a picture of John Wilkes by his bedside. It was there at his home on Gramercy Park in New York City (the Players' Club) when he died. It is there today.

Eleanor Ruggles tells us that the melancholy tragedian—perhaps America's greatest Shakespearian interpreter—had written: "I cannot grieve at death. It seems to me the greatest boon the Almighty has granted us." He referred to it as "that dear old Doctor, Death."

Doctor Death called for Edwin Booth on June 7, 1893.

Edwin Booth's funeral was held on the morning of the 9th. And on that day and hour when his casket was being carried from the Little Church Around the Corner in New York City, Ford's Theater in Washington, D.C., collapsed with a seismic roar.

Headlines in the *Washington Evening News* shouted:

HORRIBLE CALAMITY AT 10:00 A.M.

ABOUT 50 CLERKS KILLED, 400 IN THE RUINS.

THIRD FLOOR OF THE EDIFICE GAVE WAY . . .

The theater, taken over by the War Department, had been converted into a storehouse for Army records. The inside structure, jerrybuilt, was not stout enough to stand tons of filing boxes, tons of carbon copies. Engineers had been digging to enlarge the basement. Suddenly sand had caved, bringing the structure's three floors crashing down.

Actually 22 clerks were killed in the disaster, 68 injured. By eerie coincidence, among the records stored in the theater were those of the Army Medical Corps, including the Surgeon General's reports of the inquest held over the body on the monitor *Montauk*. Were some of the records lost in this avalanche of fire and mortar?

The rumor that John Wilkes Booth had made a get-away from Garrett's farm persisted.

Did Booth die at Garrett's farm? Or did he make good an escape? Pro and con, informed historians and other interested parties have argued the question for nearly a century. Early in 1903 the question was treated to headlines in the national press.

On the morning of January 13, 1903, a barfly who called himself David E. George committed suicide in the town of Enid, Territory of Oklahoma. The man, an elderly and lonely drifter, had been making his living as a house-painter.

He was an alcoholic and a drug addict. He expired gloomily from a dose of strychnine, self-administered in Enid's dusty Grand Avenue Hotel. One wonders why the story made the local paper. There were many solitary nobodies drifting around the Cherokee Strip. Causes of death were usually more interesting—gunfire or perhaps a lynching. Nevertheless, this shabby suicide was reported in that evening's edition of the Enid *Daily Wave*.[1]

The suicide was discovered by another inmate of the hotel. This man testified that he heard groaning and moaning, rushed into George's room and found the old codger in convulsions. A physician was summoned. Dr. A. R. Field arrived "within five minutes." Before the doctor "could prepare a hypodermic, Mr. George was dead."[2] The remains were dispatched to Penniman's Undertaking Parlor, destined for Potter's Field.

But the body of the lonely suicide did not go to a pauper's grave on the outskirts of Enid, Oklahoma. It was destined to go into the barn of a lawyer who lived in Memphis, Tennessee. There it would remain above ground for the next twelve years, while the cobwebs gathered on its pine box, while the affidavits gathered on its history, so to speak—while the barn became a garage.

The body found no rest. Early in the 1920's it went on the road, traveling from town to town through the American hinterland. It was traveling in 1930. Still traveling, apparently, in 1940. So far as is known, it is still above ground.

We are told that all strange phenomena are explicable. The answer to this particular one lies in an affidavit sworn in Enid, Oklahoma, ten days after the passing of David E. George. The affidavit reads:

> Enid, Oklahoma Territory
> (January, 23, 1903)
> On the evening of January 13th I was startled and surprised by reading in the *Enid Daily News* of the suicide of David E. George, of El Reno. . . . I went to the morgue with Mr. Harper on the 15th and identified the corpse of David E. George as the man who had confessed to me at El Reno [in 1900] that he was John Wilkes Booth, etc.
> (Signed)   Mrs. E. C. Harper[3]

At this point enter Finis L. Bates, a Memphis lawyer. Bates must have read about George's suicide, for Mrs. Harper's surprising statements made national news. Bates immediately took the steam cars for Oklahoma Territory. He wanted to see the corpse of this wanderer who had confessed he was John Wilkes Booth.

Back in the late 1870's, Bates had been adventuring down in Granbury, Texas. There he had made the acquaintance of a frontier saloonkeeper, one John St. Helen. Believing himself about to die of asthma, this bar-owner had called upon the young lawyer to listen to a confession. St. Helen panted out an astounding story.

"I am dying. My name is John Wilkes Booth and I am the assassin of Abraham Lincoln. Get a picture of myself from under the pillow. I leave

---

[1] Enid *Daily Wave*, January 13, 1903.

[2] Wilson, *op. cit.*, p. 246.

[3] In article by F. L. Black, *The Dearborn Independent*, April 25, 1925.

it with you for future identification. Notify my brother Edwin of New York City."[4]

St. Helen recovered. Some days later, Bates walked on the prairie with the revived bartender. St. Helen poured out a wonderful narrative. He said (according to Bates) that Andrew Johnson had instigated the President's murder. That he had conferred with Johnson at the Kirkwood House for over an hour on the afternoon of April 14, 1865. That Andrew Johnson told him it had been arranged for General Grant to leave the capital. And that he (the assassin) would be permitted to escape from Washington.

Bates admitted he had not believed St. Helen's story at the time, and had neglected to take notes while it was uttered. However, he purported to recall every word of that gratuitous "confession" years later in 1900. In that year, he addressed an inquiry to the Government, asking "if it would be of any importance to develop the fact to the War Department of the United States that John Wilkes Booth, the assassin of President Lincoln, had not been captured and shot by the Federal troops, as was supposed." He claimed that he had discovered conclusive evidence which proved Booth had escaped.

The official answer was an immediate "no." The lawyer's letter, returned to him, bore a blunt notation from Judge Advocate General G. Norma Lieber. "It is recommended that he [Finis L. Bates, Esq.] be informed that the matter is of no importance to the War Department."

Bates then began to assail the Government with petitions. Although he proclaimed an interest in historical accuracy and in setting the record straight, Finis L. Bates also expressed a mercenary motive. He reminded the Government that War Secretary Stanton had offered $50,000 for the capture of Lincoln's assassin. Lawyer-like, he claimed that offer "to be yet valid and subsisting."[5]

Bates had, it seemed, spent years investigating John St. Helen. At the outset the investigation had been hampered because St. Helen had disappeared from West Texas. Bates had eventually traced him to Fresno, California, but there had lost the trail. Bates had not given up. He had written letters to people who might be interested. Had traveled here and there to show persons acquainted with Booth the St. Helen tintype. Had amassed a wealth of testimony which convinced him, at least, that St. Helen was, indeed, J. Wilkes Booth. Typical testimony: that General Albert Pike, C.S.A. (another Memphis lawyer) had glimpsed St. Helen in Fort Worth, Texas, and exclaimed, "My God, Booth!" In 1900 Bates attempted to cash in on the wealth of testimony. But official Washington had remained distinterested.

And what had all this to do with a derelict who committed suicide in Oklahoma Territory in 1903? Bates said it had everything to do. Gazing

---

[4] Bates, *op. cit.*, p. 30.
[5] Quoted in Wilson, *op. cit.*, p. 227.

upon the stray cadaver in Enid, he immediately pronounced David E. George to be none other than his old Texas acquaintance, John St. Helen!

At Penniman's Parlor, where he viewed the remains, Bates had the undertaker comb the corpse's hair in the style worn by Booth. He sat the body in various postures. He compared it with photographs of Booth and with what he claimed was the St. Helen tintype. Thereupon Lawyer Bates announced to the world that David E. George, John St. Helen and John Wilkes Booth were one and the same.[6]

Manifestly Bates had burdened himself with a three-dimensional problem. In addition to proving that St. Helen was Booth, he now endeavored to prove that George was St. Helen. As might be expected, he botched this triple play. But he tried. He had the unclaimed body of David E. George embalmed and shipped to Memphis. For the next five years he badgered the authorities with his award claim. The Government was as cold to the embalmed evidence of David E. George as it had been to the tintype of John St. Helen.

In 1907 the frustrated lawyer published a book entitled: *The Escape and Suicide of John Wilkes Booth, or the First True Account of Lincoln's Assassination, Containing a Complete Confession by Booth, Many Years after His Crime.*

The book created a mild sensation, if the term may be applied to a sale of some 70,000 copies. It could hardly be considered a documentary work, however, for too much of the text proved palpable fiction. The author (from long-range memory) transcribes the original St. Helen "confession" in great detail. In that alleged divulgence, St. Helen had declared that another man was trapped in the barn in his (Booth's) stead. According to St. Helen, while he (Booth) was proceeding toward Garrett's farm in company with Jett, Ruggles and Bainbridge, he lost "some papers and a diary" in a wagon. A man named "Ruddy or Robey" was sent back to retrieve these items. When he reached Garrett's farm that evening, this messenger was met by David Herold. Booth (St. Helen) had meanwhile taken cover in the woods. Robey went with Herold into the barn. And it was Robey who was shot dead that night by the Federals.

Booth (St. Helen) escaped to Mexico. There he lived for a time disguised as a priest. Then he made his way to California where he met Junius Brutus and his mother in San Francisco. This was in "1866 or 1867."[7] From there he drifted to Texas and assumed the role of John St. Helen. The escape to Mexico, allegedly abetted by friends in the deep-South Confederate underground, sounded far more plausible than the get-away described in the "confession" attributed to David E. George. In that version, George (Booth) was hidden in a steamer trunk and smuggled on board an ocean vessel. Escaping overseas, the fugitive spent several years

---

[6] Bates, *op. cit.*
[7] *Ibid.,* p. 228.

wandering incognito around Europe before he went to Texas as John St. Helen.

The David E. George "confession" story contained another odd feature. As George tells it (or Bates tells it for him), he—presumably J. Wilkes Booth—was "much struck" by the performance of a young actress he saw in Enid in 1900. Calling on the soubrette, he informed her that he was writing a play and asked her if she would consider the feminine lead. This play was to be called *A Life Within the Shadow of Sin*. The subject was John Wilkes Booth. George proposed to be in the cast and manage the company.[8]

Altogether Bates' book expounds a case too fabulous for credence. Booth becomes John St. Helen. St. Helen becomes David E. George. This ramified interchange of characters, "confessions" and aliases left many readers highly skeptical.

Critics discovered in Bates' text a host of inaccuracies and glaring discrepancies. For example, he (or someone) had doctored some of the affidavits presented as proofs. The St. Helen tintype was crudely re-touched. A tintype of David E. George had obviously been faked by superimposing the St. Helen head on the sitter's body.

All this convinced the critics that the George-St. Helen story amounted to flimflam. Bates found himself with a body on his hands. Encouraged by the public response to his book, he offered the "Booth mummy" to Henry Ford for $100,000. Ford's interest in Americana did not include mummified derelicts. But the publicity was worth it to the enterprising Bates. He began to exhibit the mummy at county fairs. Soon it was featured as a sideshow attraction.

The mummy was finally sold to a carnival. By the early 1920's it had "played" all over the Southwest. Later it traveled the carnival circuit from Chicago to Venice, California. Finis L. Bates must have reaped a tidy fortune in book and theatrical royalties for the "capture" of John Wilkes Booth.

In 1925 *The Dearborn Independent* launched a searching investigation into the Bates-St. Helen-George-Booth tale. The inquiring journalist, F. L. Black, tore much of the alleged confessions to tatters. The mummy was pronounced a rank impostor.[9]

In 1929 Booth's biographer, Francis Wilson, tore most of the remnant tatters into presumable shreds. Wilson found evidence that Franklin Robey, the overseer at Cox's farm—the Robey presumably shot in Booth's stead—was still alive in the year 1889.[10] The author exposed the spurious St. Helen-David E. George tintypes. Wilson tracked down a multiplicity of errors in Bates' garbled book. One that seemed most flagrant to Wilson:

---

[8] *Ibid.*, p. 299.

[9] F. L. Black, articles in *The Dearborn Independent*, April–May 1925.

[10] *Op. cit.*, pp. 270–271.

Bates had his alleged Booth breaking a *right* instead of *left* leg. But the Tennessee lawyer must have seen, or heard of, the account by Dr. May.

Bates' book had long been under fire when Wilson pitched in. But the riddling of Bates' story could not refute all contentions concerning the possibility of Booth's escape. The exposure of a Memphis lawyer as something of a fraud does nothing to establish the integrity of, say, General Lafayette C. Baker.

Which leads to the point that Finis L. Bates may have been an out-and-out swindler, but even a swindler may do some clever guessing. And most swindles are based on a certain amount of plausibility.

To begin with there *was* this John St. Helen, frontier saloonkeeper in Granbury, Texas, who claimed to be John Wilkes Booth.

There was later a *bona fide* David E. George, who, before he committed suicide in Enid, Oklahoma, told a woman in neighboring El Reno that *he* was John Wilkes Booth.

The asthmatic St. Helen of Texas undoubtedly did pour out a windy "confession" to young Lawyer Bates.

The "confession" made by David E. George was originally attested not by Bates but by the hearer, Mrs. E. C. Harper.

Apparently St. Helen did wander off around the turn of the century. A Texas saloonkeeper might, after a number of months, turn up under another name in the wilds of Oklahoma.

Bates fell down in his rush to prove the two were one, in attempting to meld them both into Booth, and in endeavoring to sell the mummy of David E. George to the United States Government. No question that in his effort to exploit the mystery he manufactured evidence, falsified various documents, and embellished the two "confessions" with fiction of his own invention.

Yet elements of Bates' original story were worthy of official investigation. There is something hasty and peremptory in the way the authorities in Washington rejected the lawyer's initial inquiry. Even before Bates entered a reward claim, the War Department refused to concede the possibility of Booth's escape.

In summarily rejecting the alleged Booth body (the corpse of David E. George) the War Department made no effort to examine that specimen. An official inquest before the body became mummified might have settled the matter at the outset. Indeed, if Bates had been exposed in 1903, he might have been prosecuted for attempting to defraud the Government.

Examiners in 1903 could have determined that the body was not Booth's. A number of witnesses well acquainted with John Wilkes Booth were alive in 1903. Actors who had played with Booth were still living. John Matthews was still alive (he died in New York City in 1905). Sam Arnold was still alive (he died in Johns Hopkins Hospital in Baltimore in 1906). John H. Surratt was living in Baltimore (he did not die until 1916).

Friends of the Booth family could have gone to an inquest. Apparently these persons were not called upon to view the body on display in Memphis.

The Government left the investigation up to magazine writers and journalists such as F. L. Black of *The Dearborn Independent* (who did not get around to the case until 1925, and was not provided with pertinent secret intelligence data in the War Department files).

Certainly there were strange elements to the St. Helen-George case. Although sheer coincidence may have been involved, one peculiar angle went entirely unremarked. Even Finis L. Bates failed to notice this oddity. St. Helen gives his first name as John. George's first name is David. But if the juxtaposition of those names seems easily coincidental, the man who discovered George's suicide in the Grand Avenue Hotel in Enid signed his affidavit "Lee Boyd." *Boyd*—the name assumed by John Wilkes Booth in his flight through Maryland and Virginia.

But the George-St. Helen story has still another peculiar linkage with Booth and the Lincoln murder case. This has to do with Boston Corbett. After Corbett went berserk while serving as doorman for the Kansas State Legislature in 1887, he was committed to an asylum in Topeka. Escaping from the asylum, Corbett made for the great open spaces. In the early 90's he was (according to Oldroyd) traveling as a patent medicine salesman in Oklahoma and Texas. He made his home in Enid, Oklahoma![11]

And there the story of Boston Corbett—indeed, that strange man himself—dissolves in vapor. In 1913 the writer Byron Berkeley Johnson made an effort to trace Corbett after his flight from the Kansas asylum. The writer consulted a report on Corbett prepared by Judge Huron for the Kansas Historical Society. Huron had been appointed Corbett's guardian after the latter was sent to the Topeka Asylum. According to Huron's account, Corbett fled to Neodesha, Kansas, after his asylum escape. "In Neodesha [he] met a man who [had] served with him as a prisoner in Andersonville. Told him he had been so shamefully treated he was going to leave the country and go to Mexico."[12]

Kansas State Secretary C. H. Sessions advised Byron Berkeley Johnson: "Judge Huron has done everything in his power to locate his ward . . . but has learned nothing from him since he bade farewell to his old comrade in Neodesha."

Some time after Corbett disappeared from Neodesha, a patent medicine vendor calling himself Corbett put in a claim for pension money. Judge Huron discovered this man was a swindler, and sent him to prison. But the fact that one patent medicine salesman went to prison for impersonating Corbett in 1903 does not verify the conclusion (drawn by some historians)

---

[11] *Op. cit.*, pp. 100–101.

[12] Bryon Berkeley Johnson, *Abraham Lincoln and Boston Corbett* (Boston: The Lincoln and Smith Press, 1914).

that Corbett never showed up in Enid, Oklahoma, as a medicine vendor.

In the late 1920's, historian Lloyd Lewis made an effort to learn what had become of Boston Corbett. Lewis concluded that Oldroyd's story on Corbett contained inaccuracies, but "evidence of Corbett's residence in Enid, Oklahoma, may have been more accurate. . . ."[13]

Some accounts tell us simply that Corbett disappeared. It has been supposed that he was killed or committed suicide somewhere in the Southwest. But there remains something manifestly strange in the vanishment of this Civil War veteran who was a national celebrity even in 1900. Stranger still that he should appear, however briefly, in Enid, Oklahoma—where David E. George (or was he John St. Helen?) currently posed as John Wilkes Booth.

So Boston Corbett disappears.

John St. Helen disappears.

Only David E. George remains, in the form of a mummy touring the carnival circuit as "John Wilkes Booth."

Could this Enid derelict by any stretch of the imagination have been Booth? Most of the investigators have said no. But journalists are not professional detectives. Most of the skeptics concentrated on the dubious Finis L. Bates and on the aging mummy. George himself was not interrogated.

Even Black, of *The Dearborn Independent,* concedes one or two inexplicables in the case. This George, a shabby house painter, entered Oklahoma as an odd peregrine. He was a man of some education. He put a "house painting" ad in the local paper—a curious gesture for a simple workman. At El Reno, where he lived for a time, he engaged in amateur theatricals, entertaining the townsfolk with what were remembered as surprisingly good performances. When he first attempted suicide in 1900, he was close to death, and he signed a deathbed confession that he was Booth—admittedly a strange act if he were an impostor, for what would it profit him after death?

F. L. Black and Francis Wilson made much of the fact that George's deathbed signature did not closely resemble the "J. Wilkes Booth" of the actor who killed Lincoln. Yet there was some resemblance, and it seems rather remarkable that there was any similarity. Moreover, the dying George, a morphine addict, was in dire distress when he signed the alleged confession.

Finally F. L. Black presents the following as decisive: "William J. Ryan embalmed the body of George at the Penniman undertaking establishment. . . . Mr. Ryan says he never believed that it was the body of John Wilkes Booth for the eyes were blue *or blue-gray* and John Wilkes Booth *had black eyes.*"[14]

---

13 *Op. cit.,* pp. 295–296.
14 *The Dearborn Independent,* April 25, 1925. Emphasis supplied.

Wilson follows the foregoing line concerning the eyes of the dead man at Enid, and states: "The eyes of the fanatic Booth . . . were as black as night."[15]

But what of Asia Booth Clarke's statement that John Wilkes' eyes were hazel?

In the mid-1920's, Dr. Clarence True Wilson, a prominent churchman and lecturer, produced a study entitled, *The Trail of John Wilkes Booth, or Did Lincoln's Murderer Escape?* The author declares: "I soon learned that . . . Booth escaped." And asserts: "Everyone in his family knew about it."[16]

On Lincoln's Birthday, February 12, 1925, the Minneapolis *Daily Star* published an arresting headline.

LINCOLN'S ASSASSIN ESCAPED? NIECE OF JOHN WILKES BOOTH SAYS
HE LIVED 38 YEARS AFTER CRIME

The story was copyrighted by the International News Service—a reputable American syndicate. The *Daily Star* had interviewed Blanche De Bar Booth, at that time a resident of Minneapolis. Gist of the story was that a man had called on her in the late 80's and "had convinced her that he was her uncle John Wilkes Booth."[17]

One might call the publication of this startling story sensational journalism, but the source of the story was Miss Blanche De Bar Booth.

Later, she diluted the sensationalism to some extent. In a letter to Francis Wilson she stated that a man had knocked at her hotel door, and called, "Blanche, or Blanchie, don't you want to see Johnnie?" Thinking the fellow a prankster—some member of her theatrical troupe—she had told the caller to go away. The unseen visitor shoved a card under her door, said he would call again. The name on the card: John Wilkes Booth.

The mysterious caller never returned. Wilson quotes Miss Booth as declaring in her letter: "I wish he had. I would have put such questions to him as would soon have determined whether or not he was a fraud."[18]

It would seem Blanche De Bar Booth admitted a margin of possibility, a chance at least, that "Johnnie" might have been genuine.

Researching the Lincoln murder case, the modern writer, Alva Johnson, uncovered a bizarre item in the Beloit (Wis.) *Daily News* of April 20, 1898. The item quoted a soldier named Kenzie as stating that the man who died at Garrett's farm was red-haired. Kenzie claimed that he inspected the body on the porch of Garrett's farmhouse. Lifting the

---

[15] *Op. cit.*, p. 274.
[16] Reported in Minneapolis *Daily Star*, Feb. 21, 1925.
[17] Wilson, *op. cit.*, p. 259.
[18] *Ibid.*, pp. 259–260.

blanket, he discovered that the corpse had reddish hair and ruddy features.

Historian Lloyd Lewis, quoted in letter to the Washington *Star* (May 18, 1929):

> In hunting new material about John Wilkes Booth and the assassination of Abraham Lincoln, I was referred to [John P.] Simonton by Major Willis Crittenberger of the War Department. Simonton had shortly before retired after 40 years of service. His researches into the mystery surrounding the death of John Wilkes Booth, assassin of Lincoln, exceed those of any other man of his time. During his service in the Judge Advocate's Office he was regarded as an expert on evidence, and his search into the papers and facts concerning Booth was microscopic. *At the end of 40 years study of the question from all angles he still believes that Booth avoided justice and that the War Department in 1865 killed an innocent man for the assassin.* However, in recent years, he told me he had become doubtful, due to new evidence, and admitted that the Government probably had buried the right man.

The italics are supplied in the foregoing to emphasize a most peculiar inconsistency. An authority on the Booth case, an "expert on evidence," a War Department insider with access to the files—this specialist states that after forty years study he *still believes* that Booth "avoided justice" and an innocent man was killed in the assassin's stead. Then (in a puzzling qualification) he refers to doubt in "recent years" and "new evidence." He concludes rather lamely that the Government "probably buried the right man," after all.

What new evidence did John P. Simonton refer to? The letter in the *Star* (Lloyd Lewis) does not say. One may assume from the date of this letter that "recent years" meant sometime around the early 20's. If "new evidence" was produced during the period in question, it must have eluded such meticulous researchers as Otto Eisenschiml.

But Simonton's statement to Lewis was oddly worded, to say the least. For in spite of a contrary probability he "still believes."

From the *Des Moines Register* (Des Moines, Iowa, June 24, 1931):

> H. L. Frost, who led the New Hampshire Cavalry in the search for John Wilkes Booth after the assassination of President Lincoln, was buried here yesterday. . . . He [always] maintained Booth was not burned to death in a barn (*sic*) while trying to elude his pursuers, but escaped and died later in Enid, Oklahoma.

One of the queerest modern accounts of Booth's demise comes from the pen of Richard Wilmer Rowan, author of a documentary history of secret intelligence. In this book, *The Story of Secret Service* (published in 1937), we find the following:

"Lieutenant Colonel Green of the Thirteenth New York Cavalry had detailed Lieutenant Edward A. Dougherty and fifty men to pursue Booth. *They located him with Harriot and other conspirators in a log cabin,* and in forcing the assassin's surrender, one of the detail, Sergeant Boston Corbett, shot him. Booth died as a result of the wound."[19]

Did Rowan's pen slip? Or did he see a military report faultily describing Garrett's tobacco barn as a log cabin? Aside from that (and more important), who were the "other conspirators" in mention?

In the autumn of 1937, Izola Laura Forrester published a volume arrestingly entitled *This One Mad Act.* Readers would recognize Miss Forrester as a popular magazine writer and the author of innocuous light fiction of World War vintage (*The Girls of Bonnie Castle, The Door in the Mountain, Kit of Greenacre Farm*). Now Miss Forrester surprised the public by announcing herself as the orphan daughter of the actress Rita (Ogarita Wilkes) Booth. Pridefully Miss Forrester laid claim to John Wilkes Booth as her grandfather.

Concerning this relationship to Booth, Izola Forrester's story is fairly convincing. According to Miss Forrester, old records disclosed that J. Wilkes Booth and Izola Mills D'Arcy (her grandmother) had been united in holy matrimony by the Rev. Peleg Weaver at North Cos Cob, Connecticut, on January 9, 1859.[20]

In Miss Forrester's account, it is not clear why this marriage was kept secret from the very outset. We are told that the couple met in Richmond, and the marriage resulted from a "whirlwind courtship." We are left to imagine that Booth abandoned his wife soon after the honeymoon. Later, meetings occurred. But secrecy persisted throughout the Civil War. Why? Booth's underground activities, naturally. And it seemed that his bride (Miss Forrester's grandmother) mysteriously operated in the Shenandoah region as a member of the Confederate Secret Service.

Issue of the marriage were two children—a boy, Harry Jerome, and the girl who eventually went on the stage as Ogarita Wilkes, later Rita Booth. After Lincoln's assassination, Booth's secret wife posed as a widow, of course, and took an assumed name. She lived in dread that her two children would be ostracized. She did, however, retain contact with the Booth family. Rosalie Booth contributed to their welfare.

Miss Forrester tells of her own gypsy, backstage childhood—a sense of mystery in the background—letters to her grandmother and mother from "Aunt Rosalie"—a sealed Saratoga trunk—and so on. Highly romanticized, the story reads like a serial in a polite magazine for housewives. There are gaps in the continuity and much that goes unexplained; the writer admits to bafflement concerning some of her grandmother's past and her mother's attitudes. Apparently Edwin Booth remained inaccessible as a relative.

---

[19] R. W. Rowan, *op. cit.,* p. 694. Emphasis supplied.
[20] *Op. cit.,* p. 181.

Yet Augustin Daly, well-known theatrical producer, befriended Rita Booth. Another family friend was the actor John Matthews.

Miss Forrester declares that John Wilkes Booth survived long after the Civil War. She claims that Booth's wife (her grandmother) met him in California in 1869. She professes a belief that Booth finally took refuge in India. Here she becomes vague. The account wanders into an Erewhon of misty premise and speculation. She does refer to Booth's membership in the Knights of the Golden Circle, with a reminder that the activities of this underground brotherhood were never fully disclosed.

However, two statements by Miss Forrester are most intriguing. She asserts that her uncle, Harry Jerome, a Broadway drifter who died in Bellevue in 1918, established "by the mere fact of his own existence" proof that Booth escaped.[21] For this man who was Booth's son (Miss Forrester speaking) had been born in the year 1870.

She also states that in 1908, while gathering material for a magazine article, she interviewed General James R. O'Beirne, then a judge on the New York bench. They discussed O'Beirne's part in the manhunt for Booth and the drama at Garrett's farm. In concluding his recollection of the chase, the older soldier smiled grimly. "I am telling you something that you will never find on any record," he confided. "We were all pledged to secrecy in those days. You can't use it now, but follow it up. There were three men in that warehouse, and one got away."[22] He left Miss Forrester to guess the name of the escapee.

The question of Booth's escape derives from the fog which shrouded the body delivered by the U.S. soldiers and Baker's secret agents to the authorities in Washington. If it *was* Booth's corpse, the matter, of course, is settled.

If it *wasn't* Booth's corpse, we are left with a thousand questions. Whose was it? How did Booth escape? Who covered the getaway? Why?

Those very questions were plaguing the Government in 1869 when President Andrew Johnson ordered the body disinterred and delivered unto the keeping of the Booth family. Then, at long last, the Booths and a few intimate friends were permitted to view the remains. And it is the family's acceptance of the remains at this time which, according to Washington officials and such historians as Oldroyd and Wilson, once and for all decided the issue.

But the details of that final and private inquest are interesting.

For four years Edwin Booth had been endeavoring to obtain from the War Department permission to have his brother buried in Baltimore. In 1867 he wrote an appeal to General Grant, noting that he had "once received a promise from Mr. Stanton that the family . . . should be per-

---

21 *Ibid.*, p. 110.
22 *Ibid.*, pp. 304, 305.

mitted to obtain the body when sufficient time had elapsed. . . ."[23]

When sufficient time had elapsed—a significant condition. One may assume that Secretary Stanton meant the body might be obtained when public excitement subsided, or the South was fully subdued—something like that. He may have had other reasons.

In February, 1869, with Stanton no longer in office, President Johnson released the body with the following order:

> Executive Mansion
> February 15, 1869
> The Honorable Secretary of War will cause to be delivered to Mr. John Weaver, Sexton of Christ Church, Baltimore, the remains of John Wilkes Booth. . . .
>
> Andrew Johnson[24]

Edwin Booth went with Sexton Weaver to Washington to "receive the remains." The disinterment was performed by Harvey & Marr, Washington undertakers, who went out to the Arsenal grounds to exhume the body.

The Harvey & Marr parlor was located on F Street, just around the corner from Ford's Theater. According to Oldroyd, a lad named Speare "drove the furniture wagon that brought the remains of Booth to the alley in the rear of Ford's Theater, almost to the very door from which he started on the night of April 14, 1865."

Brief inquest was held at Harvey & Marr's. Oldroyd continues:

> The box was somewhat decayed, but the lettering on it was legible. When the box was opened and the body taken from the blanket which was wrapped around it, it was found that four years' burial had brought it to decay. The skull was detached, and, when lifted out, a dentist who had filled Booth's teeth, identified his work, *thus proving the identity of the body beyond a doubt.* The hair was in its natural state and hung in long ringlets.[25]

Note that at this inquest at Harvey & Marr's, identification rested on the dental work. Of course the body, which had not been embalmed, bore few recognizable lineaments after four years' burial. Anything else could hardly have been expected when it defied ready recognition at the time it was delivered to monitor *Montauk.*

Edwin Booth did not look at the body. We learn from Oldroyd: "A report was made to Edwin Booth, who was in the front office, and who, when informed of the examination, expressed his satisfaction and then directed Mr. Weaver to take the body to Baltimore."[26]

The body was taken to Weaver's undertaking establishment in Baltimore. There it was viewed, at request, by John T. Ford, by the comedian Charles Bishop, by actress Blanche Chapman and her sister Ella, by Henry Clay

---

[23] Quoted in Wilson, *op. cit.*, p. 286.
[24] Wilson, *op. cit.*, p. 288.
[25] *Op. cit.*, p. 209. Emphasis supplied.
[26] *Ibid.*, pp. 209–210.

Ford, Colonel W. M. Pegram, Mr. Henry C. Wagner—all close friends of the family.

Miss Chapman would recall that John Ford unexpectedly beckoned her out of rehearsal. He told her he wanted her to "keep her eyes and ears open and her mouth shut." With Ella and Bishop they left the Holliday Street Theater and hurried to Weaver's, near by. They entered a back room. Joseph (Doc) Booth, elderly Mrs. Booth and Rosalie were there. So was what "seemed" to Miss Chapman to be "a mummy wrapped in a brown-colored sort of blanket."[27]

As Miss Chapman recalled it (in a letter written to Francis Wilson in 1927) the corpse's eyes and nose "though shrunken a little, had not receded as is usual. The skin was brown and shriveled, the lips gone, and wonderful teeth were exposed."

Joseph Booth spoke first. He said that if the body was John Wilkes Booth's (Miss Chapman recalled that he never once referred to him as "brother") it would have "but one plugged tooth in its head."

Mr. Weaver produced a dentist's chart. Joseph Booth handed it to Charles Bishop. Bishop went to the corpse, drew down the lower jaw, "inserted his fingers and took out the plugged tooth." It was shown to the witnesses present.

Weaver then cut the blanket. Miss Chapman saw a slit shoe. Bishop unwrapped "what seemed to be a bandage." Witnesses "saw the broken bone."

Weaver asked Ella Chapman to cut a lock of hair, "but Ella turned away." Blanche Chapman performed this detail. Weaver gave the lock to Mrs. Booth. The old mother began to weep "as she separated the strands of hair." She gave strands to Blanche and Ella Chapman.

As they left the undertaker's parlor, Henry Clay Ford said to Blanche Chapman, "I could see every feature in that face of John Wilkes Booth."

This reference to facial features is far from consistent with the report from Harvey & Marr, emphasizing dental identification. Evidently John Wilkes Booth's own brother, Joseph, immediately saw the need for this resort. Miss Chapman remembers that as Joseph Booth's first remark. If the body is John's "it has but one plugged [filled] tooth in its head."

Here is a confusing bit of testimony. It does not seem to agree with the records of the Washington dentist who had worked on Booth's teeth. Dismayed by the discrepancy, historian Wilson inserts a quick footnote. "There was another tooth filled, so recently that 'Doc' Booth could not have known of it."[28]

Yet Weaver, who had just brought the body from Washington, was on hand with a dental chart. Did he correct Joseph Booth's assertion? Miss Chapman does not report it as corrected.

[27] Quoted in Wilson, *op. cit.*, p. 294.
[28] *Ibid.*, p. 294.

Of course, Miss Chapman's memory could have been faulty. For her word-for-word account of that Baltimore inquest was written fifty-eight years after the event! An amazing mnemonic feat, all things considered. Few elderly persons can recall with exactitude what someone said fifty years ago.

However, Wilson offers the statement of another witness—a deposition filed with the Maryland Historical Society about the time Bates aroused the St. Helen-Booth controversy. The deponent is Colonel William M. Pegram.

Pegram notes that on the right leg of the body he viewed at Weaver's "was a long cavalry boot, coming up to the knee. The left leg was disjointed both at knee and ankle, the latter having been broken. . . ."

Then Pegram's account reads: "It will be remembered that Dr. Mudd . . . cut the boot from the left leg and manufactured a shoe from the boot's foot, in which we saw the remains of the actual foot lying in the casket."[29]

And here is another mistake. Another explanatory footnote is called for. Wilson writes: "This is a slight error. The left boot . . . is still intact and in possession of the Government, at Washington."

Conceivably the witness in Baltimore could have mistaken an old shoe for a truncated cavalry boot. But here is an important line in Colonel Pegram's account—and one entirely overlooked by historian Wilson. Describing the corpse, Pegram states: "The skin was drawn over the grinning skull, which showed the splendid teeth for which Booth was noted, *there being only a single filling*, which was identified by the dentist who did the work."

Now here are two witness accounts which say that the body brought to Baltimore had but one filled tooth. Yet Booth's Washington dentist testified that two of Booth's teeth had been filled. And Wilson tells us that "under oath" Henry C. Wagner, another witness, supported Colonel Pegram's statement with an affidavit declaring "I hereby certify that the said statement is absolutely correct in every particular."

So a third witness testifies that this body had but one filled tooth! Yet Booth's Washington dentist testified to two fillings.

Pegram's sworn statement closes with the assertion: "The family fully identified the body."[30]

The family? Edwin Booth waiting "in an outer office" at Harvey & Marr's? Joseph Booth, who is mistaken about the dental work? The distracted women?

The Baltimore inquest took place on February 17. The body remained in the undertaker's vault until June while Edwin Booth acquired a suitable

---

[29] *Ibid.*, p. 297.
[30] *Ibid.*

family plot in Greenmount Cemetery. There, on June 26, a quiet funeral service was held with family and intimate friends in attendance.

President Johnson's order: no monument should be erected over the remains.[31] So the body lies in an unmarked grave. Almost symbolic that no headstone was to label it "John Wilkes Booth."

Thirty-four years later, one of the pallbearers, a Mr. Basil Moxley, talked. Describing the obsequies as a "mock funeral," Moxley said the burial had been arranged to console Booth's mother, that family and friends were party to a "well-intended deception," and that the body interred at Greenmount was not Booth's. A former doorman at Ford's Opera House, Baltimore, Moxley said he had known John Wilkes Booth intimately. He had examined the remains at Weaver's closely, and, contrary to report, the body in question had red or reddish brown hair.

Headlines in the Baltimore *American* (June 6, 1903):

NOT BURIED HERE!
REMARKABLE DISCOVERY BY MR. BASIL MOXLEY!
He says another body was interred in
Greenmount for that of the assassin![32]

The news account noted that Moxley's story came as an echo to the clamor raised by the contentions of Finis L. Bates. And it quoted an angry disclaimer by the son of R. F. Harvey, the Washington undertaker who had exhumed the remains at Washington Arsenal. "I cannot assert that my father knew John Wilkes Booth personally, or that he identified the body after it was taken from the arsenal; but I will wager my last dollar that the body he shipped to Baltimore was that of John Wilkes Booth. It was positively identified both at the arsenal and after it was in my father's undertaking place."[33]

We are not told who identified it "at the arsenal."

On March 31, 1922, two Civil War veterans swore out an affidavit stating that the body sent north from Garrett's farm was not Booth's. The old soldiers gave their names as Joseph Ziegen and Wilson D. Kenzie. They said they had served with the cavalry troop which surrounded Garrett's barn. They said the man dragged from the barn wore the uniform of a Confederate soldier, and that on his feet were mud-caked yellow brogans— the service footgear of Johnny Reb. Deponents stated that the commanding officers on hand had sworn them to secrecy.[34]

Headline in New York *Herald Tribune* (February 22, 1925):

[31] Ruggles, *op. cit.*, p. 223.
[32] Quoted in Forrester, *op. cit.*, p. 335.
[33] *Ibid.*, p. 341.
[34] *Ibid.*, p. 299.

"GRAVE OF LINCOLN'S ASSASSIN"
MADE KNOWN AFTER SIXTY YEARS!

Reported is the statement of Colonel James Hamilton Davidson, U.S.A., Commander 122nd Infantry at Portsmouth, Virginia, during the Civil War. According to venerable Colonel Davidson, Booth's body was buried in the basement of a warehouse in Portsmouth. Or so he was informed by Colonel Lafayette Baker, Chief of the Federal Secret Service, who appeared in Portsmouth soon after the announcement of Booth's capture at Garrett's farm.

Baker told Colonel Davidson the corpse was "buried in a deep grave and covered with acid. The grave was then filled in with limestone and earth. . . . 'Every man of us is pledged to secrecy'. . . ."

Colonel Davidson, breaking long silence, observed: "That was sixty years ago. There can't be any harm in telling it now. The country ought to know."[35]

Slain at Garrett's and buried in Baltimore? Shot elsewhere and buried in a secret grave? Or an escapee to Mexico, Texas, California? The ending of Lincoln's assassin remains unproven.

But there were plenty of corpses available at the end of the Civil War. Unknown soldiers left here and there in shallow graves. And many with black hair. Many with scars. Corpses of infantrymen shot through the neck. Corpses of cavalrymen with broken legs (or legs that could be appropriately broken).

When dealing with powerful and unscrupulous men who would connive at the murder of a President—with secret agents and hidden operators—with military opportunism and governmental secrecy—who can say an escape was not rigged, a substitution was impossible? Also, we know that evidence exists linking dissident elements in the North to an assassination conspiracy. We know that Northern subversives had sworn to kill the President. We know there were unscrupulous leaders in Washington making a tremendous underground drive for power.

It is the informed consensus that a camarilla of Lincoln-haters in Washington—Northerners with big axes to grind—hoped to profit by Lincoln's death. To the extent that they withdrew the President's protection, exposed him as a target for the suspected enemy, and facilitated the escape of known conspirators, they were *particeps criminis*—accomplices to the greatest crime in American History.

One thing is certain—the whole history of the Lincoln murder case was veiled by official and unofficial censorship.

Robert Todd Lincoln died in 1926. Some time before he died, he burned a great collection of his father's letters and private papers.

---

[35] New York *Herald Tribune*, February 22, 1925.

A friend, Mr. Young, stopping in on a visit to Mr. Lincoln's home in Manchester, Vermont, was appalled to see these documents going up in flames.

"Mr. Young at once remonstrated. . . . Mr. Lincoln replied he did not intend to continue his destruction—but the papers he was destroying *contained the documentary evidence of the treason of a member of Lincoln's Cabinet,* and he thought it was best for all that such evidence be destroyed."[36]

At the instigation of Dr. Nicholas Murray Butler of Columbia University, the residual papers were placed in the Library of Congress with the restriction that they remain sealed until 1947.

When made public in 1947, these documents failed to divulge any dramatic historical disclosures. If Mr. Young's story were true, it would seem the evidence of a traitor in Lincoln's Cabinet had been consigned to the oblivion of flames.

Says the pamphlet issued by the Medical Museum of the Armed Forces Institute of Pathology in Washington, D.C.: "Confusion and mystery still surround the shooting of Abraham Lincoln, and we probably will never know all the facts. One thing is sure . . . his murder was part of a larger conspiracy."

But the facts of the murder conspiracy are lost to history. Probably they will never be unearthed. All participants in the great conspiracy are now dead. The last surviving witness to Lincoln's assassination—Mr. Samuel J. Seymour of Arlington, Virginia—died in 1956. (He was five years old when his godmother took him to see the President at Ford's Theater. Throughout his childhood he believed that the man who "fell" from the box and staggered across the stage—Booth—was the one who was shot.)

All the players are gone. The audience is gone. The whole American scene has changed. Of the 32,000,000 Americans who lived in that day and time, nearly all, all, are long since gone. To put it in the stanzas of a poem Lincoln loved:

> *The saint who enjoyed the communion of Heaven,*
> *The sinner who dared to remain unforgiven,*
> *The wise and the foolish, the guilty and just,*
> *Have quietly mingled their bones in the dust. . . .*

Not only that generation, but the succeeding generation . . . dust.

Yet Abraham Lincoln, the man they tried to kill, did not die. Embodying the mind, heart and conscience of Democracy, America's greatest American, Abraham Lincoln lives on.

---

[36] Emanuel Hertz, *The Hidden Lincoln* (New York: The Viking Press, 1938), Preface. Emphasis supplied. Also quoted in Van Doren Stern, *op. cit.,* p. 406.

Appendix

A. TRANSCRIPT OF BOOTH'S LETTER "TO WHOM IT MAY CONCERN"[1]

——, ——, 1864.

My Dear Sir:

You may use this as you think best. But as some may wish to know *when, who* and *why,* and as I do not know *how* to direct it, I give it (in the words of your master):—

"To whom it may concern."

Right or wrong, God judge me, not man. For be my motive good or bad, of one thing I am sure, the lasting condemnation of the North.

I love peace more than life. Have loved the Union beyond expression. For four years have I waited, hoped, and prayed for the dark clouds to break, and for a restoration of our former sunshine. To wait longer would be a crime. All hope for peace is dead. My prayers have proved as idle as my hopes. God's will be done. I go to see and share the bitter end.

I have ever held that the South were right. The very nomination of Abraham Lincoln, four years ago, spoke plainly war—war upon Southern rights and institutions. His election proved it. "Await an overt act." Yes; till you are bound and plundered. What folly! The South were wise. Who thinks of argument or patience when the finger of his enemy presses on the trigger? In a *foreign war,* I, too, could say, "Country, right or wrong." But in a struggle *such as ours* (where the brother tries to pierce the brother's heart), for God's sake choose the right. When a country like this spurns *justice* from her side, she forfeits the allegiance of every honest freeman, and should leave him, untrammelled by any fealty soever, to act as his conscience may approve.

People of the North, to hate tyranny, to love liberty and justice, to strike at wrong and oppression, was the teaching of our fathers. The study of our early history will not let me forget it, and may it never.

This country was formed for the *white,* not for the black man. And, looking upon *African slavery* from the same stand-point held by the noble framers of our Constitution, I, for one, have ever considered *it* one of the greatest blessings (both for themselves and us) that God ever bestowed upon a favored nation. Witness heretofore our wealth and power; witness their elevation and enlightenment above their race elsewhere. I have lived among it most of my life, and have seen *less* harsh treatment from master to man than I have beheld in the North from father to son. Yet Heaven knows, *no one* would be more willing to do *more* for the negro race than I, could I but see a way to *still better their* condition.

---

[1] From Wilson, *op. cit.*

But Lincoln's policy is only preparing the way for their total annihilation. The South *are not, nor have they been, fighting* for the continuance of slavery. The first battle of Bull Run did away with that idea. Their causes *since* for *war* have been as *noble* and *greater far than those that urged our fathers on.* Even should we allow they were wrong at the beginning of this contest, *cruelty and injustice* have made the wrong become the *right,* and they stand *now* (before the wonder and admiration of the world) as a noble band of patriotic heroes. Hereafter, reading of *their deeds,* Thermopylae will be forgotten.

When I aided in the capture and execution of John Brown (who was a murderer on our western border, and who was fairly *tried* and *convicted,* before an impartial judge and jury, of treason, and who, by-the-way, has since been made a god), I was proud of my little share in the transaction, for I deemed it my duty, and that I was helping our common country to perform an act of justice. But what was a crime in poor John Brown is now considered (by themselves) as the greatest and only virtue of the whole Republican party. Strange transmigration! *Vice* to become a *virtue* simply because *more* indulge in it!

I thought then, *as now,* that the abolitionists *were the only traitors* in the land, and that the entire party deserved the same fate as poor old Brown; not because they wish to abolish slavery, but on account of the means they have ever endeavored to use to effect that abolition. If Brown were living, I doubt whether he *himself* would set slavery against the Union. Most, or many of the North do, and openly, curse the Union if the South are to return and retain a *single right* guaranteed to them by every tie which we once *revered as sacred.* The South can make no choice. It is either extermination or slavery for *themselves* (worse than death) to draw from. I know *my* choice.

I have also studied hard to discover upon what grounds the right of a State to secede has been denied, when our very name, United States, and the Declaration of Independence, *both* provide for secession. But there is no time for words. I write in haste. I know how foolish I shall be deemed for undertaking such a step as this, where, on the one side, I have many friends and every thing to make me happy, where my profession *alone* has gained me an income of *more than* twenty thousand dollars a year, and where my great personal ambition in my profession has such a great field for labor. On the other hand, the South has never bestowed upon me one kind word; a place now where I have no friends, except beneath the sod; a place where I must either become a private soldier or a beggar. To give up all of the *former* for the *latter,* besides my mother and sisters, whom I love so dearly (although they so widely differ with me in opinion), seems insane; but God is my judge. I love *justice* more than I do a country that disowns it; more than fame and wealth; more (Heaven pardon me if wrong), more than a happy home. I have never been upon a battle-field; but oh! my countrymen, could you all but see the *reality* or effects of this horrid war as I have seen them (in *every State,* save *Virginia*), I know you would think like me, and would pray the Almighty to create in the Northern mind a sense of *right* and *justice* (even should it possess no seasoning of mercy), and that he would dry up this sea of blood between us, which is daily growing wider. Alas! poor country, is she to meet her threatened doom? Four years ago I would have given a thousand lives to see her remain (as I had always known her) powerful and unbroken. And even now I would hold my life as naught to see her what she was. Oh! my friends, if the fearful scenes of the past four years had never been enacted, or if what has been had been but a frightful dream, from which we could now awake, with what overflowing hearts could we bless our God and pray for his continued favor! How I have loved the *old flag* can never now be known. A few years since, and the entire world could boast of *none* so pure and spotless. But I have of late been seeing and hearing of the *bloody deeds* of which she has *been made the emblem,* and would shudder to think how changed she had grown. Oh! how I have longed to see her break from the mist of blood and death that circles round her folds, spoiling her beauty and tarnishing her honor. But no, day by day has she been dragged deeper and deeper into cruelty and oppression, till now (in my eyes) her once bright red stripes look like *bloody gashes* on the face of heaven. I look now upon my early admiration of her glories as a dream. My love (as things stand to-day) is for the South alone. Nor do I deem it a dishonor in attempting to make for her a prisoner of this man, to whom she owes so much of misery. If success attend me, I go penniless to her side. They say she has found *that* "last ditch" which the North have so long derided and been endeavoring to force her in, forgetting they are our brothers, and that it is impolitic to goad an enemy to madness. Should I reach her in safety, and find it true, I will proudly beg permission to triumph or die in that same "ditch" by her side.

A Confederate doing duty upon his own responsibility.

J. Wilkes Booth

B. OFFICIAL STATEMENT MAJOR H. R. RATHBONE[2]

District of Columbia

County of Washington vs. Henry R. Rathbone, Major Brevet Major in the Army of the United States being duly sworn says, that on the 14th day of April Instant, at about 20 minutes past eight o'clock in the evening he, with Miss Clara H. Harris left his residence at the corner of 15th and H. Streets and joined the President and Mrs. Lincoln and went with them in their carriage to Fords Theatre in Tenth Street. The box assigned to the President is in the second tier, on the right hand side of the audience and was occupied by the President and Mrs. Lincoln, Miss Harris and this deponent and by no other person. The box is entered by passing from the front of the building in the rear of the dress circle to a small entry or passageway about eight feet in length and four feet in width. This passageway is entered by a door which opens on the inner side. The door is so placed as to make an acute angle between it and the wall behind it on the inner side. At the inner end of this passageway is another door standing squarely across and opening into the box. On the left hand side of the passageway and very near the inner end is a third door which also opens into the box. This latter door was closed. The party entered the box through the door at the end of the passageway. The box is so constructed that it may be divided into two by a moveable partition, one of the doors described opening into each. The front of the box is about ten or twelve feet in length and in the centre of the railing is a small pillar overhung with a curtain. The depth of the box from front to rear is about nine feet. The elevation of the box above the stage including the railing is about ten or twelve feet.

When the party entered the box a cushioned arm chair was standing at the end of the box furthest from the stage and nearest the audience. This was also the nearest point to the door by which the box is entered. The President seated himself in this chair and, except that he once left the chair for the purpose of

[2] National Archives, War Dept. Records, File "R," R.B., JAO, p. 74.

putting on his overcoat, remained so seated until he was shot. Mrs. Lincoln was seated in a chair between the President and the pillar in the centre, above described. At the opposite end of the box—that nearest the stage—were two chairs. In one of these, standing in the corner, Miss Harris was seated. At her left hand and along the wall running from that end of the box to the rear stood a small sofa. At the end of this sofa next to Miss Harris this deponent was seated, and the President, as they were sitting, was about seven or eight feet and the distance between this deponent and the door was about the same. The distance between the President as he sat and the door was about four or five feet. The door, according to the recollection of this deponent, was not closed during the evening.

When the second scene of the third act was being performed and while this deponent was intently observing the proceedings upon the stage with his back towards the door he heard the discharge of a pistol behind him and looking round saw through the smoke, a man between the door and the President. At the same time deponent heard him shout some word which deponent thinks was "Freedom." This deponent instantly sprang towards him and seised (*sic*) him. He wrested himself from the grasp and made a violent thrust at the breast of this deponent with a large knife. Deponent parried the blow by striking it up and received a wound several inches deep in his left arm between the elbow and the shoulder. The orifice of the wound is about an inch and a half in length and extends upwards towards the shoulder several inches. The man rushed to the front of the box and deponent endeavored to seise him again but only caught his clothes as he was leaping over the railing of the box. The clothes, as this deponent believes, were torn in this attempt to seise him. As he went over upon the stage, deponent cried out with a loud voice "Stop that man." Deponent then turned to the President. His position was not changed. His head was slightly bent forward and his eyes were closed. Deponent saw that he was unconscious and, supposing him mortally wounded, rushed to the door for the purpose of calling medical aid. On reaching the outer door of the passage way as above described, deponent found it barred by a heavy piece of plank, one end of which secured in the wall and the other resting against the door. It had been so securely fastened that it required considerable force to remove it. This wedge or bar was about four feet from the floor. Persons upon the outside were beating against the door for the purpose of entering. Deponent removed the bar and the door was opened. Several persons who represented themselves to be surgeons were allowed to enter. Deponent saw there Colonel Crawford and requested him to prevent other persons from entering the box. Deponent then returned to the box and found the surgeon examining the Presidents person. They had not yet discovered the wound. As soon as it was discovered, it was determined to remove him from the Theatre. He was carried out and this deponent then proceeded to assist Mrs. Lincoln, who was intensely excited, to leave the Theatre. On reaching the head of the stairs, deponent requested Major Potter to aid him in assisting Mrs. Lincoln across the street to the house to which the President was being conveyed. The wound which deponent had received had been bleeding very profusely and on reaching the house, feeling very faint from the loss of blood, he seated himself in the hall and soon after fainted away and was laid upon the floor. Upon the return of consciousness deponent was taken in the carriage to his residence.

In the review of the transaction it is the confident belief of this deponent that the time which elapsed between the discharge of the pistol and the time when the assassin leaped from the box did not exceed thirty seconds. Neither Mrs. Lincoln nor Miss Harris had left their seats.

H. R. Rathbone

Subscribed and sworn before me this
17th day of April, 1856 (*sic*)
A B Ollie
    Justice (indecipherable) D.C.

C. WIECHMANN'S INITIAL POLICE STATEMENT[3]

Statement of Louis J. Weichman
Met Herold three times in his life. First time at Mrs. Surratt's in '63. Last time eight or ten weeks ago.

Surrat (*sic*) studied divinity. Was in Express Office in this city in January. It was on Good Friday that I went with Mrs. Surratt to the county—Surratsville. She gave me ten dollars with which to hire horse. Nothe was the man who owed her money. Gwinn was her agent. Noff was present. Started from here about half-past two; got there about four; remained until half-past six. Did not eat; drank port wine sangaree. Left there at 6½; got back here at half-past nine; retired about ten o'clock. Hired the horse from Brooks on G Street. Surrat left the house with a woman by name of Slater, March 27th. Came back on the 3 of April. Had nine or eleven pieces of gold. Hollohan boarded there. I had been there, at Surrattsville, with Mrs. Surratt, on the Tuesday previous to Good Friday—same week Mrs. Surrat told me to go and get Booth's buggy. Booth had sold the buggy, but gave me ten dollars to hire one with.

Left at 9; arrived at 12. Roads muddy. Stayed 15 minutes. She went on to Gwinn's house; took dinner; drove up to Surrattsville with Gwinn. Saw Nothe there. Got back here about 8 o'clock. Nothe, Gwinn and Mrs. Surratt in the parlor. Drove there once in March 1864. First time Mrs. Surratt took a basket with food in it—cakes. Next time a package which she said contained china dishes—a round package—6 or 8 inches in diameter.

I made Booth's acquaintance on same day that Surratt did—on the 15th of Jan. last. Dr. Mudd introduced Booth to us both. Booth called Mudd and Surratt out and had private conversation with them. Drew something on back of envelope—did not seem to be writing. Met Booth frequently at Mrs. Surratt's. Surratt and Booth used to have private interviews. Met Booth at Mrs. S.'s at the hotel; walked down 7th Street; over and at restaurant near Ford's theatre. Atzerodt, Harold and Surratt were all there; also Hollohan. Went from there to Hollohan's. Time Booth played his last piece, he played for the benefit of McCulloch. After 4th of March wrote to Bishop McGill, at Richmond, Oct. 27th, 1864, and March 15th, 1864. Received reply from him. Shows Sec'y. Booth was at Mrs. Surratt's house at half-past two o'clock on day of the assassination.

Surratt came to me once to have me write something flowery about Booth's having withdrawn from the stage and become speculator. Surratt said he had taken twenty shares in oil himself; that Booth had made $10,000. I have had discussions on politics. Lady hit me over the head with brush—Mrs. Surratt. It was about slavery and our soldiers. Mad because I went down stairs with blue pants on. Paine has been at the house twice; first time ten weeks ago. Enquired

[3] National Archives, War Dept. Records, File "W," R.B., JAO, p. 99.

for Mr. Surratt—out. I invited him in. He said his name was Wood. He came again, and second time gave his name as Paine. Said he had been in the South, but had come North and taken the oath. Stayed there three days. Found false mustache in my room. Went upstairs in third story and found Surratt and Paine playing with bowie knives. Also saw two revolves (*sic*) and five setts & pins.

Miss Anna Ward; had no doubt spoken to her. Miss Mary Murray: Keeps Herndon House. Met Atzerodt. He said, "Have you seen Paine?" I said "No; is he at the Herndon House?" He said "Yes." On night of April 18th left Porterfield's house in ————. Have seen two letters from Surratt. One to his mother, and the other to Miss Ward. The one to his mother was dated April 12th; that to Miss Ward, ———— Anna Ward is teacher at convent on corner of 10th and G. Streets. Saw telegram from Booth. It read: "Telegraph John number and street at once."

Mrs. Slater is a blockade runner. Learned from Mrs. Surratt that she and Surratt had gone to Richmond on March 27, 1865. Hollohan has seen her at the house twice. I saw her but once; always had her veil down. A man by the name of Howell was there in the beginning of February. Think him a blockade runner. Mrs. Surratt said he was. His movements about the house were suspicious; would not go out nights. Saw Surratt last on April 3d. Took oysters with him. Said he saw Benjamin and Davis, and they said Richmond would not be evacuated. Had been bad and dissipated for some time; had been in house of ill-fame.

Mrs. Surratt made the remark,—"a funny looking preacher," as to Paine. J. H. Surratt is 21 years of age. Think he went once to Richmond in March, '64. Told me by route of Baltimore. Joseph Surratt, living in Steubenville, is a cousin to Anna Surratt. Told Capt. Gleason my suspicions several weeks ago.

D. DR. MUDD'S STATEMENT[4]

Statement of Dr. Samuel A. Mudd, Bryantown, Maryland, (April 21st 1865):
Dr. S. A. Mudd, residing four miles North of Bryantown, Md. being duly sworn deposes and says.

Last Saturday morning April 15th, about four o'clock, two men called at my house and knocked very loudly. I was aroused by the noise, and as it was such an unusual thing for persons to knock loudly, I took the precaution of asking who were there before opening the door. After they had knocked twice more I opened the door, but before doing so they told me they were two strangers on their way to Washington; that one of their horses had fallen by which one of the men had broken his leg. On opening the door I found two men. One on a horse led by the other man who had tied his horse to a tree nearby. I aided the man in getting off his horse & into the house, and laid him on a sofa in my parlor. After getting a light I assisted him in getting up stairs where there were two beds, one of which he took. He seemed to be very much injured in the back, & complained very much of it. I did not see his face at all. He seemed to be tremulous and not inclined to talk, and had his cloak thrown around his head & seemed inclined to sleep, as I thought, in order to ease himself; & every now & then he would groan pretty heavily. I had no proper pasteboard for making splints, and went & got an old bandbox & made one of it, and as he wanted it done hastily I hurried more than I otherwise would. He wanted me to fix it up anyway, as he said he wanted to get back, or get home and have it done by a regular Physician. I then took a piece of the bandbox & split it in half, doubled

---

[4] National Archives, War Dept. Records, File "E," 315, JAO.

it at right angles, took some paste and pasted it into a splint. On examination I found there was a straight fracture of the tibia about two inches above the ankle. My examination was quite short and I did not find the adjoining bone fractured in anyway. I do not regard it a peculiarly painful or dangerous wound. There was nothing resembling a compound fracture. I do not suppose I was more than three quarters of an hour in making the examination of the wound & applying the splint. He continued still to suffer and complained of severe pain in the back especially when being moved. In my opinion pain in the back may arise from riding. I judge that in this case it originated from his fall and also from riding, as he seemed to be prostrated. He sometimes breathed very shortly & as if exhausted. He was a man I should suppose about five feet ten inches high and appeared to be pretty well made; but he had a heavy shawl on all the time. I suppose he would weigh 150 or 160 pounds. His hair was black and seemed to be somewhat inclined to curl. It was worn long. He had a pretty full forehead & his skin was fair. He was very pale when I saw him and appeared as if accustomed to in-door rather than out-door life. I do not know how to describe his skin exactly, but I should think he might be classed as dark, & his paleness might be attributed to receiving this injury. I did not observe his hand, to see whether it was small or large. I have been shown the photograph of J. Wilkes Booth and I should not think this was the man from any resemblance to the photograph; but from other causes I have every reason to believe he is the man whose leg I dressed as above stated.

In order to examine and operate upon his leg, I had occasion to cut his boot longitudinally, in front of the instep. It seems that when he left my house this boot was left behind. Yesterday morning my attention was called to this boot—which is a long top-boot. On making an examination of it I find written on the inside, in apparently a German hand, what I take to be "Henry Luz, Maker, 445 Broadway, J. Wilkes." I did not notice the writing in this boot until my attention was called to it by Lieut Lovett. [Boot produced and identified by deponent as the one taken from the leg of the wounded man]. I have seen J. Wilkes Booth. I was introduced to him by Mr. J. C. Thompson, a son-in-law of Dr. William Quinn, in November or December last. Mr. Thompson resides with his father-in-law, and his place is about five miles Southwesterly from Bryantown, near the lower edge of what is known as Zechiah Swamp. Mr. Thompson told me at the time that Booth was looking for lands in the neighborhood or in this county; he said he was not very particular where, if he could get such a lot as he wanted, whether it was in Charles, Prince George or St. Mary's Co; and Booth inquired if I knew any parties in the neighborhood who had any fine horses for sale. I told him there was a neighbor of mine who had some very fine traveling horses, and he said if he thought he could purchase one reasonable, he would do so and ride up to Washington on him instead of riding in the stage. The next morning he purchased a rather old horse, but a very fine mover, of Mr. George Gardner Sr. who resides but a short distance from my house. I would know the horse if I should see him again. He is a darkish bay horse, not light bay, with tolerably large head and had a defect in one eye. Booth gave eighty dollars for the horse. I have never seen Booth since that time to my knowledge until last Saturday morning. When I assisted the wounded man into my house on Saturday morning last, the other party with him, who appeared to be very youthful, took charge of the horse & said he would keep it and the other one until they could be put in the stable; & the young man came into the house. After setting the wounded man's leg the best I could for the time, I think I walked around to my farm-yard & gave some directions, and when I returned breakfast was ready, and as this young man was up & knocking about, I asked him to come to breakfast. He did so, but the other man remained up stairs in bed. I did not know who this young man was, but he remarked that he had seen me. He appeared to be a very fast young man and was very talkative. He was about five feet two or three inches high, I would not be positive as to his height. He had a smooth face and appeared as if he had never been shaved; his hair was black, & I would consider his complexion dark. I did not notice his eyes very particularly. He wore a dark-colored business coat. I have seen the photograph of Harold but I do not recognize it as that of this young man. He seemed to be well acquainted throughout the whole country and I asked his name. He gave it as Henston, and that of the wounded man as Tyser or Tyson. I did not hear either of them address the other by the first name. The only thing that excited my suspicions, upon reflecting upon these circumstances was, that after breakfast, when I was about leaving for my farm-work, this young man asked me if I had a razor about the house, that his friend desired to take a shave, as perhaps he would feel better. I had noticed that the wounded man had whiskers and a moustache when he came into the house. After dinner I went to see the patient and although he kept his face partly turned away from me, I noticed that he had lost his moustaches but still retained his whiskers. I did not pay sufficient attention to his beard to determine whether it was false or natural. This young man asked me if I could fix up, clumsily, some crutches for his friend to hobble along with, and I went down to the old Englishman I had there, who had a saw and augur, & he and I made a rude pair of crutches out of a piece of plank & sent them to him. This young man mentioned the names of several parties in this neighborhood whom he knew; among others several here in Bryantown. He mentioned being in the store of William Moore. He did not say when. I think he said he knew Bean who kept store here; & he knew very well Len Roby, Rufus Roby & Major James Thomas Sr. He inquired the way from my house to Bryantown, although he represented in the morning that they had come from Bryantown. He said he knew Parson Wilmer who lives at a place called Piney Church. He said also that they had met two persons, a lady & gentleman walking somewhere near Bryantown that morning, & enquired of them the way to my house, & that they also met a negro but did not state where; & that they also inquired of him the way to my place. I saw only one of the horses which these men rode to my house. She was a bay mare, moderately long tail, dark mane & tail. I won't be certain whether she had a star in the forehead or not; she appeared to be a mettlesome, high-spirited animal. I saw her after dinner between twelve & one o'clock, when this young man & I rode over to my father's place in order to see if we could get a carriage for the wounded man; but I found that the carriages were all out of repair except one, and we could not get that one. He then concluded to go to Bryantown to get a conveyance to get his friend over as far as his friends, Mr. Wilmer. I then went down to Mr. Hardy's and was in conversation with him fully an hour, when I returned home leisurely and found the two men were just in the act of leaving. The young man inquired of me the nearest way to Mr. Wilmer's. I told them there were two ways; one was by the public road leading by Beantown; the other led across the Swamp directly across from me; by which they could save a mile; both are easterly. This road from my house is directly across in a strait (*sic*) line. It is not a public way, but by taking down a fence you can get through. They concluded to take this latter route, and I gave them the necessary directions. I did not see them leave my house. The man on crutches had left the house when I got back, and he was some fifty to seventy yards from me when this young man came to me and began to inquire of me the directions. I do not know how or where Booth got a conveyance away from my house. He did not go in a carriage ut he undoubtedly went on horseback. When they came there in the morning this young man said that one of the horses would not stand without tying I asked that both of them should be put in the stable. He held one of the horses until I returned into the house with the wounded man, when I called a colored boy named Frank Washington, and sent him round to take the horses to the stable. I have also a white man named Thomas Davis who has charge of my horses, and I judge that he saw the horses which were in the stable during Saturday. I judge that between four & five o'clock on Saturday afternoon they left my house. I do not know where they went. I have not been spoken to by any one for professional advice in their behalf since that time, and have not seen either of them since. It is about four miles across from my house to Parson Wilmers; and by the public road it is about five miles. I suppose they could go in about an hour or an hour and a half by walking their horses. I suppose in a day or two swelling would take place in the wounded man's leg; there was very little tumefaction in the wound, and I could discover crepitation very distinctly. It would be necessary to dress it again in two or three days if it were left in a recumbent posture, but if moved at a moderate rate, I do not know as it would aggravate it very much unless it was struck by something. I do not know much about wounds of that sort; a military surgeon would know more about those things.

Samuel A. Mudd.

E. DR. STEWART'S STATEMENT[5]

Statement of Dr. R. H. Stewart, Washington, (May 6, 1865).
Being first duly sworn says:

I reside in King George County, Va. I have resided there all my life. On Sunday, April 23rd, I had been at tea with my family & had just concluded when some one was announced at the door. I went to the door and found two men brought up by Mr. Bryant, & a Mr. Chrisman came with them. They were on horseback. I think the smallest one was on the ground when I saw them. It was after dark. I asked "Who are you?" Said he, "We are Marylanders in want of accommodations for the night." I said, "It is impossible; I have no accommodations for anybody." He then said his brother had broken his leg, & had been recommended to come to me to do something for his leg & to aid them in their journey. I told them I was no surgeon; I was only a physician. I think he said that Dr. Mudd had recommended him to me. I do not know Dr. Mudd. I have heard of Mudds in Md. but do not know them. I said that nobody was authorized to recommend anybody to me. Then he remarked that they were very weary & hungry, & wished I would accommodate them if possible. I told him no, I could not, but I could give them something to eat. The man with the broken leg said very little; he did not say who he was; they kept urging me so that at last I said, "I don't want to know anything about you." I did not wish them there, because my family was large, my house was full, & I did not like their appearance. He pressed me saying, "If you will listen to the circumstances of the case, you will be able to do it." I told him it was impossible.

I did not like the manner in which they urged the thing on me. I asked them who they were & where they were going. They said "We are Marylanders & want to go to Mosby." I said "Mosby has surrendered, I understand; you will

5 National Archives, War Dept. Records, File "S," JAO.

have to get your paroles." They inquired who could send them up to Fredericks-burg. I said I could not possibly do it. I was asked if I knew who could do it. I told them I had a neighbor near there, a colored man, who sometimes hired his wagons, & probably he would do it if he was not very busy; & it would be no harm to try. . . .

I agreed to give them something to eat & they walked into the house to get it. I then went out to Mr. Bryant who brought them there & asked him if he knew anything about these men. He said no; they had come to him out of the marsh & asked him if he could send them to my house. I said, "It is very strange; I know nothing about the men; I cannot accomodate them; you will have to take them somewhere else." . . . I went into the house, and the men had finished their meal, & I remarked, "The old man is waiting for you; he is anxious to be off; it is cold; he is not well & wants to get home." They got up immediately & went out. They were in my house not more than a quarter of an hour. . . .

F. BOSTON CORBETT'S OFFICIAL STATEMENT[6]

Statement of Sergeant Boston Corbett, Washington, May 1st, 1865:

I saw [Booth] in the act of stooping or springing, and concluded he was going to use his weapons. I immediately took steady aim upon him with my revolver and fired—shooting him through the neck and head. He was then carried out of the barn before the fire reached him; was taken to the Piazza of the house. . . . Lieut. Doherty, and the detective officers who were in front of the barn, did not seem to know that I had shot him, but supposed he had shot himself, until I informed Lieut. Doherty of the fact—showing him my pistol which bore evidence of the truth of my statement, which was also confirmed by the man placed at my right-hand who saw it. . . .

G. REWARDS[7]

BOOTH PURSUIT AND CAPTURE

E. J. Conger, detective	$15,000.00
Lafayette C. Baker, detective	3,750.00
Luther B. Baker, detective	3,000.00
Lieutenant Edward P. Doherty, in command of the cavalry . . .	5,250.00
James R. O'Beirne, detective, ...	2,000.00
H. H. Wells, George Cottingham, Alexander Lovett, each $1,000 .	3,000.00
Sergeant Boston Corbett, Sergeant Andrew Wendell, Corporal Charles Zimmer, Corporal Michael Uniac, Corporal John Winter, Corporal Herman Newgarten, Corporal John Walz, Corporal Oliver Lonpay, Corporal Michael Hormsbey, Privates John Myers, John Ryan, William Byrne, Philip Hoyt, Martin Kelly, Henry Putnam, Frank McDaniel, Lewis Savage, Abraham Genay, Emery Parady, David Baker, William McQuade, John Millington, Frederick Dietz, John H. Singer, Carl Steinbrugge, and Joseph Zisgen, each $1,653.85	43,000.00
	$75,000.00

[6] National Archives, War Dept. Records, Trunk 10, File "C," R.B.P. 10.
[7] Oldroyd, *op. cit.,* pp. 87, 88.

ATZERODT CAPTURE

Major E. R. Artman, 213th Pennsylvania Infantry	$1,250.00
Sergeant Z. W. Gemmill, 1st Delaware Cavalry	3,598.54
Christopher Ross, David H. Baker, Albert Bender, Samuel J. Williams, George W. Young, James Longacre, privates 1st Delaware Cavalry, and James W. Purdman [Burton?], citizen, each $2,878.78	20,151.46
	$25,000.00

PAINE CAPTURE

Major H. W. Smith	$1,000.00
Richard C. Morgan, Eli Devore, Charles H. Rosch, Thomas Sampson, W. M. Wermerskirch, detective, each $500.00	2,500.00
J. H. Kimball, citizen	500.00
P. M. Clark, citizen	250.00
Susan Jackson, colored	250.00
Mary Ann Griffin	250.00
	$5,000.00

Bibliography

Abbott, John C., and R. H. Conwell, *Lives of the Presidents*, H. Hollett & Co., Portland, Me., 1896.

Baker, Gen. Lafayette C., *History of the United States Secret Service*, privately published, Philadelphia, 1867. Revised edition, *The United States Secret Service in the Late War—Perilous Adventures, Hairbreadth Escapes and Valuable Services of the Detective Police—by General Lafayette C. Baker, Organizer and First Chief of the National Secret Service Bureau of the United States*, John E. Potter & Co., Philadelphia, 1889.

Bates, David Homer, *Lincoln in the Telegraph Office*, D. Appleton-Century Co., New York, 1907.

Bates, Edward, *The Diary of Edward Bates*, GPO, Washington, D.C., 1933.

Bates, Finis L., *The Escape and Suicide of John Wilkes Booth, or the First True Account of Lincoln's Assassination, Containing a Complete Confession by Booth Many Years After His Crime*, Pilcher Printing Co., Memphis, 1907.

Beyer, William Gilmore, *On Hazardous Service*, Harper & Brothers, New York, 1912.

Bishop, Jim, *The Day Lincoln Was Shot*, Harper & Brothers, New York, 1955.

Blaine, James G., *Twenty Years of Congress from Lincoln to Garfield*, Henry Bill Pub. Co., Norwich, Conn., 1884.

Boutwell, George S., *Reminiscences of Sixty Years in Public Affairs*, McClure, Phillips, & Co., New York, 1902.

Bradford, Gamaliel, *Union Portraits*, Houghton Mifflin Co., New York, 1916.

Browning, Orville, *The Diary of Orville Hickman Browning*, Illinois State Historical Library, Springfield, 1933.

Buckingham, J. E., Sr., *Reminiscences and Souvenirs of the Assassination of Abraham Lincoln*, Rufus H. Darby, Washington, D.C., 1894.

Burnett, H. L., *Some Incidents in the Trial of President Lincoln's Assassins*, D. Appleton, New York, 1891.

Busch, Francis X., *Enemies of the State*, Bobbs-Merrill, New York, 1954.

Campbell, Helen Jones, *The Case for Mrs. Surratt*, G. P. Putnam's Sons, New York, 1943.

Campbell, W. P., *The Escape and Wanderings of John Wilkes Booth Until Final Ending of the Trial by Suicide in Enid, Oklahoma, January 12, 1903*, privately published, Oklahoma City, 1922.

Chittenden, Lucius E., *Recollections of President Lincoln and his Administration,* Harper & Brothers, New York, 1901.

Clarke, Asia Booth, *The Unlocked Book,* G. P. Putnam's Sons, New York, 1938.

Coulter, Ellis M., *A History of the South,* Louisiana State University Press, Baton Rouge, 1950.

Crook, Wm., *Through Five Administrations,* Harper & Brothers, New York, 1907.

Cuthbert, Norma B. (Ed.), *Lincoln and the Baltimore Plot,* The Huntington Library, San Marino, Cal., 1949.

Dearing, Mary R., *Veterans in Politics; the Story of the G.A.R.,* Louisiana State University Press, Baton Rouge, 1952.

DeWitt, David M., *The Assassination of Lincoln and its Expiation,* The Macmillan Company, New York, 1909; *The Impeachment and Trial of Andrew Johnson,* The Macmillan Company, New York, London, 1903; *The Judicial Murder of Mary E. Surratt,* Baltimore, J. Murphy & Co., 1895.

Douglas, Henry Kyd, *I Rode With Stonewall,* University of North Carolina, Chapel Hill, N.C., 1940.

Doster, William E., *Lincoln and Episodes of the Civil War,* G. P. Putnam's Sons, New York, 1915.

Dye, John Smith, *A History of the Plots and Crimes of the Great Conspiracy,* privately published, New York, 1866.

Edmonds, S. Emma E., *Nurse and Spy in the Union Army,* W. S. Williams & Co., Hartford, 1865.

Eisenschiml, Otto, *Why Was Lincoln Murdered?,* Little, Brown, Boston, 1937; Halcyon House, New York, 1939; Grosset & Dunlap, Inc., New York, 1957; *In The Shadow of Lincoln's Death,* Wilfred Funk, New York, 1940.

Ellis, Dr. John B., *The Sights and Secrets of the National Capital,* United States Pub. Co., New York, 1869.

Flower, Frank A., *Edwin McMasters Stanton,* Saafield Pub. Co., Akron, Ohio, 1905.

Fry, James B., *Military Miscellanies,* Brentano's, New York, 1889.

Forrester, Izola, *This One Mad Act; the Unknown Story of John Wilkes Booth and his Family,* Hale, Cushman & Flint, Boston, 1937.

Gobright, Lawrence A., *Recollections of Men and Things at Washington During the Third of a Century,* Claxton, Ramsen & Haffelfinger, Philadelphia, 1869.

Grant, Hamil, *Spies and Secret Service,* Frederick A. Stokes Co., New York, 1915.

Grant, Jesse, *In The Days of My Father, General Grant,* Harper & Brothers, New York and London, 1925.

Grant, Ulysses S., *Personal Memoirs,* The Century Co., New York, 1895.

Hamlin, Charles E., *The Life and Times of Hannibal Hamlin,* Cambridge, Printed at the Riverside Press, 1899.

Harris, General T. M., *Assassination of Lincoln; a History of the Great Conspiracy,* American Citizen Co., Boston, 1892.

Hertz, Emmanuel (Ed.), *The Hidden Lincoln,* The Viking Press, New York, 1938.

Horan, James D., *Confederate Agent*, Crown Publishers, New York, 1954.

Howard, Hamilton G., *Civil War Echoes—Character Sketches and State Secrets*, Howard Publishing Co., Washington, D.C., 1907.

Hurd, Charles, *Washington Cavalcade*, E. P. Dutton, New York, 1948.

Johnson, Byron B., *Abraham Lincoln and Boston Corbett*, The Lincoln and Smith Press, Boston, 1914.

Jones, Thomas A., *John Wilkes Booth*, Laird and Lee, Chicago, 1897.

Julian, George W., *Political Recollections*, Jansen, McClurg & Co., Chicago, 1884.

Keckley, Elizabeth, *Behind the Scenes; or Thirty Years a Slave, and Four Years in the White House*, G. W. Carleton & Co., New York, 1868.

Kimmel, Stanley, *The Mad Booths of Maryland*, Bobbs-Merrill Co., New York, 1940.

Laughlin, Clara E., *The Death of Lincoln; the Story of Booth's Plot, his Deed and the Penalty*, Doubleday, Page & Co., New York, 1909.

Lewis, Lloyd, *Myths After Lincoln*, Harcourt, Brace and Company, New York, 1929.

Lomax, Elizabeth L., *Leaves From an Old Washington Diary*, Dutton, New York, 1943.

Marshall, John A., *American Bastille*, T. W. Hartley & Co., Philadephia, 1883.

McClellan, Gen. George B., *McClellan's Own Story*, Chas. L. Webster, New York, 1887.

Mearns, David C., *The Lincoln Papers*, Doubleday, Garden City, N.Y., 1948.

Morris, Clara, *Life on the Stage*, McClure, Phillips and Company, New York, 1901.

Morse, John T. Jr., *Abraham Lincoln*, Houghton Mifflin Company, Boston, 1921.

Mudd, Nettie (Ed.), *The Life of Dr. Samuel A. Mudd*, Neale Publishing Co., New York, 1906; Continental Book Co., Marietta, Ga., 1955.

Oldroyd, Osborn H., *The Assassination of Abraham Lincoln*, privately published, Washington, D.C., 1901.

Perkins, Jacob R., *Trails, Rails and War; the Life of General Grenville M. Dodge*, Bobbs-Merrill Co., Indianapolis, 1929.

Piatt, Donn, *Memories of the Men Who Saved the Union*, Belford, Clarke & Co., Chicago, 1887.

Pinkerton, Allan, *History and Evidence of the Passage of Abraham Lincoln from Harrisburg, Pa., to Washington, D.C., on the Twenty Third of February, Eighteen Hundred and Sixty-one*, New York, 1906; *Professional Thieves and Detectives*, G. W. Carleton & Co., New York, 1880; *Spy of the Rebellion*, G. W. Carleton & Co., New York, 1883.

Pitman, Benn, *The Assassination of President Lincoln and Trial of the Conspirators*, Moore, Wilstach and Baldwin, Cincinnati, 1865.

Poore, Ben Perley, *Perley's Reminiscences*, Hubbard Brothers, Philadelphia, 1886.

Pratt, Fletcher, *Stanton, Lincoln's Secretary of War*, W. W. Norton & Co., New York, 1953.

Randall, Ruth Painter, *Mary Lincoln, Biography of a Marriage,* Little, Brown and Co., Boston, 1953.

Richardson, Albert D., *The Secret Service: The Field, The Dungeon, and Escape,* American Publishing Co., Hartford, 1865.

Riddle, Albert Gallatin, *Recollections of War Times, Reminiscences of Men and Events in Washington; 1860–1865,* G. P. Putnam's Sons, New York, 1895.

Robinson, Stuart, *Infamous Perjuries of the Bureau of Military Justice,* privately published, Louisville, 1865.

Rowan, Richard Wilmer, *The Story of Secret Service,* Garden City Publishing Co., New York, 1939.

Ruggles, Eleanor, *Prince of Players: Edwin Booth,* W. W. Norton & Co., Inc., New York, 1953.

Sandburg, Carl, *Abraham Lincoln: The War Years, Vol. IV,* Harcourt, Brace & Co., New York, 1939.

Seward, Frederick W., *Seward at Washington,* Derby and Miller, New York, 1891.

———— *Reminiscenses of a War-Time Statesman and Diplomat,* G. P. Putnam's Sons, New York, 1916.

Sherman, W. T., *Home Letters of General Sherman,* Charles Scribner's Sons, New York, 1909.

Skinner, Otis, *The Mad Folk of the Theater,* Bobbs-Merrill Co., New York, 1928.

Smith, Don, *Peculiarities of the Presidents: Strange Facts Not Usually Found in History,* Wilkinson Press, Van Wert, Ohio, 1938.

Starr, John W. Jr., *Lincoln's Last Day,* Frederick A. Stokes Company, New York, 1922.

Steiner, Bernard, *Life of Reverdy Johnson,* Norman Remington Co., Baltimore, 1914.

Stern, Philip Van Doren, *The Man Who Killed Lincoln,* The Literary Guild of America, New York, 1939; *An End to Valor,* Houghton Mifflin Company, Boston, 1958.

Stewart, Sen. Wm. M., *Reminiscences,* Neale Publishing Co., New York, 1908.

Smoot, R. M., *The Unwritten History of the Assassination of Abraham Lincoln,* John Murphy Co., Baltimore, 1904.

Stryker, Lloyd Paul, *Andrew Johnson,* The Macmillan Company, New York, 1929.

Tarbell, Ida M., *The Life of Abraham Lincoln,* The Macmillan Company, New York, 1928.

Townsend, George Alfred, *The Life, Crime, and Capture of J. W. Booth,* Dick & Fitzgerald, New York, 1865.

Tiffany, Francis, *Life of Dorothea Lynde Dix,* Houghton Mifflin Company, New York, 1890.

Todd, Charles Burr, *Story of the City of Washington,* G. P. Putnam's Sons, New York, 1889.

Vallandigham, Rev. James L., *A Life of Clement L. Vallandigham,* Turnbull Brothers, Baltimore, 1872.

Velasquez, Loreta Janeta, *The Woman in Battle,* T. Belknap, Hartford, 1876.

Warden, Robert B., *Private Life & Public Services of Salmon P. Chase,* Wilsatch, Baldwin and Co., Cincinnati, 1874.

Welles, Gideon, *Diary,* Houghton Mifflin Company, Boston & New York, 1911.

Williamson, James J., *Prison Life in the Old Capitol,* privately published, West Orange, N.J., 1911.

Wilson, Francis, *John Wilkes Booth,* Houghton Mifflin Company, New York.

Winter, William, *Vagrant Memories,* George H. Doran Co., New York, 1915.

Woodward, W. E., *A New American History,* Farrar and Rinehart, New York, 1936.

Index